1950

LONDON BOARD OF EDUCATION

ORGANIZE OR STARVE!

Brenda Wall, an Australian, and Ken Luckhardt, a Canadian, have been involved in anti-Apartheid work since 1976. Their involvement in the Free Southern Africa Committee (Edmonton, Alberta, Canada) led them to leave the academic environment to work full-time for the South African Congress of Trade Unions (SACTU) on this history project.

Organize or Starve!

The History of the South African Congress
of Trade Unions

by

Ken Luckhardt and Brenda Wall

INTERNATIONAL PUBLISHERS
NEW YORK

First published by Lawrence and Wishart Ltd London 1980
Published in the U.S.A. by International Publishers, 1980
© The South African Congress of Trade Unions, 1980

This book is sold subject to the condition that it shall not, by way of trade or otherwise, be lent, re-sold, hired out, or otherwise circulated without the publisher's prior consent in any form of binding or cover other than that in which it is published and without a similar condition including this condition being imposed on the subsequent purchaser

Library of Congress Cataloging in Publication Data

Luckhardt, Ken.
   Organize or starve.

    1. South African Congress of Trade Unions.
I. Wall, Brenda, joint author.   II. Title.
HD8801.A5S6314   331.88'0968   80-13201
ISBN 0-7178-0575-1

Printed in Great Britain

CONTENTS

	List of Illustrations	6
	Acknowledgements	9
	Statement by the President of SACTU	11
	Statement by the General Secretary of SACTU	15
	Message of support from General Secretaries of British Trade Unions	17
	Dedication	20
	Preface	25
	Chronology	28
	Map of South Africa	30
	Abbreviations	31
1.	Apartheid and the Black Working Class – the Problem Defined	35
2.	The Heritage of Struggle	39
3.	SACTU Appears Upon The Scene	90
4.	Ruling Class Response	100
5.	'Asinamali' (We Have No Money)	151
6.	Organize or Starve!	169
7.	... But Not for Bread Alone	259
8.	Strikes and Industrial Actions	273
9.	Women Play a Leading Role	297
10.	SACTU and the Congress Alliance	332
11.	SACTU on the International Front	371
12.	State Repression	403
13.	Looking Back	440
14.	The History Updated	443
15.	International Links are Forged	471
16.	'An Injury to One is an Injury to All'	493
	Appendix I: Declaration of Principles Adopted at the Foundation Conference of the South African Congress of Trade Unions, on 5 March 1955, and included as a Preamble to its Constitution	497
	Appendix II: The Freedom Charter	499
	Indexes	500

LIST OF ILLUSTRATIONS

	page
Stephen Dlamini (President	11
John Gaetsewe (General Secretary)	15
SACTU Martyrs	22/23
Natal Trade Unionists, 1930s; Indian sugar workers	56
J. B. Marks; James Phillips	71
Early Trade Union victims of the Suppression of Communism Act	81
Witwatersrand Workers' Council of Action; Dissolution of SAT & LC	85
SACTU Foundation Conference	93
Industrial Conciliation Act (1956) cartoon	115
Clydesdale Mine Disaster	139
Alexandra Bus Boycott, 1957	153
£1-a-Day (headline); SACTU £1-a-Day demonstration	160
Railway Workers Union, Transvaal	173
Metal workers; Mine workers' compound	188
Gert Sibande; Three farm workers	198
Farm Labour Scandal (headlines)	199
FCWU mass trial; Transvaal Trade Union leaders	220
Mark Shope	221
SACTU Activists in the Eastern Cape	231
SACTU Trade Unionists in the Western Cape	238/239
Billy Nair; Curnick Ndlovu	247
Moses Mabhida	248
Durban municipal workers; Memory Vakalisa	251
Johannesburg dustman	269
Milling workers; African Milling Workers Union	278
Amato textile strike; Port Elizabeth bus strike	292
Durban nurses' strike; Three victimized workers	314
Ray Alexander; Elizabeth Mafekeng	319
Frances Baard; Liz Abrahams; Phyllis Altman	329
Archie Sibeko gathers workers' demands; Congress of the People delegation	336

1958 Stay-at-Home	353
Chief Lutuli	359
ICFTU visit to South Africa, 1959 (headlines)	387
Treason Trial protest	409
SACTU calls for international boycott	419

ACKNOWLEDGEMENTS

This SACTU history project has reflected a sense of internationalism throughout its many stages. The primary researchers and co-authors, Brenda Wall and Ken Luckhardt, are Australian and Canadian respectively. Prior to this work, they were involved in the Free Southern Africa Committee, an anti-Apartheid support group based in Edmonton, Alberta, Canada. In September 1978, the researchers began a four-month period of identification and retrieval of original SACTU documents and related materials which had been scattered throughout Europe, Africa and North America. Following this initial work, the next five months were spent in conducting life-history interviews with SACTU comrades in exile in Tanzania, Zambia, Swaziland, England and Canada. Another six months were devoted to writing and preparing the manuscript for publication.

The three chapters dealing with the post-1964 SACTU history were drafted under the guidance of a SACTU Editorial Board. This Board was composed of SACTU National Executive Committee members Phyllis Altman, John Gaetsewe, Moses Mabhida and Eli Weinberg. The authors wish to express their sincere appreciation to all SACTU comrades and particularly the Editorial Board for their collective encouragement and assistance throughout every stage of the project.

Such a project requires the assistance of many organizations and individuals. Primary and secondary materials were obtained from the following sources: the British Library; Colindale Newspaper Library; DEFA Research, a department of International Defence and Aid Fund; Rhodes House Library, Oxford University; Marx Memorial Library; South Africa Research Project, Warwick University; the School of Oriental and African Studies; and Gwendolyn Carter, University of Indiana. Individuals deserving special mention for assistance with documentary materials include Shula Marks, Brian Bunting, Saru Naicker and David Hemson.

Historical photographs included in the text are taken largely from the personal collection of Eli Weinberg. Other photographs were taken from progressive South African papers of the day – e.g. *The Guardian* and *New Age*. Several people in the Publications Department of the

International Defence and Aid Fund provided advice and expertise in the preparation of photographs, a map and cover design.

Funding for the project most clearly demonstrates the international solidarity that SACTU receives for its educational work. In Canada, the Canadian University Service Overseas (CUSO), Canadians Concerned about Southern Africa (CCSA), Ryerson Sociology Department (Toronto, Ontario), the Free Southern Africa Committee (FSAC) (Edmonton, Alberta), the Woodsworth Irvine Socialist Fellowship (Edmonton) and Alyce and Dennis Bartels, all donated funds for various stages of the project. A special note of appreciation is extended to Nellie and Doug Miller and David Beer who have assisted the project from the CUSO office in Lusaka, Zambia. In Europe, the International University Exchange Fund (Geneva), Norwegian Council for Southern Africa and the Amalgamated Union of Engineering Workers (Technical, Administrative and Supervisory Section, TASS), Britain contributed substantially. In New Zealand, the New Zealand Seamen's Union and the Wellington Amalgamated Watersiders' Industrial Union of Workers expressed their internationalism with financial support.

All these forms of assistance made possible the most important contribution – the recounting of the workers' struggles by the SACTU workers and leaders themselves.

STATEMENT BY THE PRESIDENT OF SACTU

Stephen Dlamini, President

The publication of this history coincides with the twenty-fifth anniversary of the South African Congress of Trade Unions. SACTU history does not start with SACTU's birthday, nor does it end with its silver anniversary. It is an ongoing process, because the South African Congress of Trade Unions represents the movement of the South African working class and that, as we know, will never stop until the workers have achieved their rightful place in society, namely not only as producers of all wealth, but also as owners of all wealth.

It is the custom of some governments to publish some of their hidden activities and documents after the expiry of a certain period. Some of these governments would not dare to publish all their machinations, since it would probably substantially influence their chances of survival. SACTU has never had hidden documents and never carried out secret diplomacy. The documentation in this book is from resolutions and decisions which were always published and were always open to public inspection and debate. Why, then, write it all over again? We found it necessary to reiterate the events of the past twenty-five years precisely because we invite public inspection of our record and, particularly, such a book is needed for the new generation of trade unionists which has grown up in South Africa. We ourselves are training new ranks of trade union leaders and it is important that they should examine our past and draw conclusions from it for the future. Perhaps we can thus equip them to be better trade union fighters.

This history is not a mere record of meetings, campaigns, resolutions and policy decisions. Behind this record there stand thousands, nay tens of thousands, of South African workers who took the decisions, attended the meetings, participated in the campaigns. Invariably, they suffered and made sacrifices in the pursuit of their ideals. Sleepless nights, anxieties, disruption of personal comforts and lives are a visible part of this record. Many paid the supreme penalty, many still languish in jails. In judging this record one must not forget these deep fountains of human courage, dedication and perseverance. This history is not just a memorial to a great organization, but a tribute to all the brave, selfless men and women who were part of it. This is *their* history. They *made* it.

A word of thanks is due to those who *wrote* it and it is an expression of SACTU's international links of solidarity that the research, compilation and the writing have been done by an Australian and a Canadian, Brenda Wall and Ken Luckhardt. They have performed a meritorious service for the South African workers and we are grateful to them. Theirs was a labour of love and no one involved in the writing and preparation of this book derived any financial gain from it. Although they prepared the material, the book was edited by a SACTU Editorial Board appointed by the National Executive Committee. The final responsibility is therefore ours alone.

Our history continues. Perhaps this book should end with an incomplete sentence, a kind of unfinished symphony. The trade union movement in our country is on the move — new sections of workers are joining the unions, new unions are being formed, new leaders are arising. There are new tasks, and new pages of history are being written. The South African Congress of Trade Unions is there and it is playing its part in making decisions, in rendering help and advising, in leading and planning the onward march of the workers of South Africa. Out of their rich experience and tradition the workers founded SACTU which will go on to advance further to greater heights of organization and unity. Repression and terror by the racist oppressors have not been able to stem the trade union movement. Their plans to 'bleed the African trade unions to death' have failed in the past and will fail in the future.

The task before us at present is to equip and lead the workers in vital struggles against the attempts of the exploiting classes and their government to place upon the shoulders of the working people the burden of the immense costs of Apartheid and military expenditures. We will organize the workers to resist increases in rent and fares. We will lead the workers in determined struggles for higher wages to meet the costs of capitalist-created inflation. We will vigorously oppose the government's plans to turn every African into a foreigner in his own land; we will resist wholesale removals and we will fight with everything at our command against this regime whose objective it is to enslave our people forever and to deprive them forever of all rights of citizenship. Our struggle will not stop until the workers of South Africa have achieved *their* objective – total liberation of all who live in our country, irrespective of race and colour, total liquidation of all forms of domination and exploitation, and the establishment of a just and democratic society in South Africa.

AMANDLA NGAWETHU!
POWER TO THE PEOPLE

Stephen Dlamini
President
South African Congress of Trade Unions

November 1979

STATEMENT BY THE GENERAL SECRETARY OF SACTU

John Gaetsewe,
General Secretary

Dear Friends,

The story that appears in these pages has never been fully told before. Many people have written about South African workers, but up to this day we have never heard from the oppressed workers themselves; they have struggled and sacrificed in silence. Now, for the first time, the workers' history, the history of the South African Congress of Trade Unions (SACTU) has been written. The most striking aspect of this history is the fact that African workers have never ceased to organize, to resist, to commit their lives in struggle against exploitation and oppression under Apartheid.

Over the years, our people have confronted the fascist and racist regime in South Africa. It was not one man, nor one woman, not two people, but thousands. Many of those who participated in the struggle have died and some of them are serving long terms of imprisonment. I would like to commend the authors of this book for writing the story of all our gallant comrades.

I have often been asked questions such as why SACTU was formed; what has it achieved; what did it stand for and what does it stand for today? This book provides invaluable information which answers all these questions. I therefore wish to recommend that you read this book and, more importantly, use it effectively in your support of the struggle of the workers and people of South Africa.

Fraternally,

John Gaetsewe
General Secretary

November 1979

MESSAGE OF SUPPORT FROM GENERAL SECRETARIES OF BRITISH TRADE UNIONS

British complicity in Apartheid makes it essential that British workers understand the plight of the South African workers and with that understanding express solidarity through all possible means with the workers' struggle there. Our workers commonly labour for the same British corporations that exploit the Black working class, and particularly African workers, under the profitable conditions of Apartheid. The struggle is one, and we stand side by side with our brothers and sisters in South Africa.

We recognize SACTU as the workers' organization and the workers' voice, the trade union movement that for twenty-five years has supported and continues to promote the principle of non-racial workers' unity. In this twenty-fifth year of SACTU's creation, we call upon British workers, indeed workers throughout the world, to mobilize around the SACTU banner and programme. The publication of this SACTU history receives our fraternal support and we pledge to do all in our power to ensure its use in the education of trade union members about the necessity of decisive action against Apartheid. The SACTU motto is our motto — 'AN INJURY TO ONE IS AN INJURY TO ALL'.

Fraternally

Jack Brown
Amalgamated Textile Workers' Union

John Boyd
Amalgamated Union of Engineering Workers
(Engineering Section)

Ken Gill
Amalgamated Union of Engineering Workers
(Technical Administrative and Supervisory
Section)

Ray Buckton
Associated Society of Locomotive
Engineers & Firemen

Alan Sapper
Association of Cinematograph Television
& Allied Technicians

Ken Thomas
The Civil & Public Services Association

Albert Spanswick
Confederation of Health Service Employees

Bill Sirs
The Iron and Steel Trades Confederation

SUPPORT FROM GENERAL SECRETARIES OF BRITISH TRADE UNIONS 19

Geoffrey Drain
National & Local Government Officers' Association

Owen O'Brien
National Society of Operative Printers Graphical and Media Personnel

Lawrence Daly
National Union of Mineworkers

Sydney Weighell
National Union of Railwaymen

W. H. Keys
Society of Graphical and Allied Trades

Charles D. Grieve
Tobacco Workers' Union

Moss Evans
Transport & General Workers' Union

DEDICATION

SACTU dedicates this book to the following comrades who gave their lives in the workers' struggle:

Viola Hashe (Vice-President, SACTU; Secretary General of the South African Clothing Workers Union). One of the militant leaders of SACTU and the ANC, Hashe was banned from trade union activities in 1963. She died after a short illness in 1977.

Wilson Khayinga and **Zinakile Mkaba** (Port Elizabeth Local Committee members). These two men, along with V. Mini, were executed in November 1964 for alleged sabotage and complicity in the death of a police informer. Their execution set a precedent in South African legal history as three other men were hanged for the *actual* murder.

Elijah Loza (Chairman, Cape Western Province Local Committee). Loza died in detention on 2 August 1977 after sustaining injuries at the hands of the security police.

Leslie Massina (General Secretary of SACTU; Secretary, African Laundry, Cleaning and Dyeing Workers Union). Massina died in 1976 of natural causes in Swaziland, where he had lived in exile following his release from the Treason Trial in 1961.

Caleb Mayekiso (Secretary, Port Elizabeth Branch of the South African Railway & Harbour Workers Union). Mayekiso died in jail in 1969 of 'natural causes' (according to the police), although he was in good health when detained.

Vuyisile Mini (Executive Member and Organizer, Port Elizabeth Local Committee). Mini is remembered as one of SACTU's most militant leaders. He was hanged, along with Khayinga and Mkaba, in November 1964.

Mary Moodley (Organizer, Food and Canning Workers Union). Moodley was active in both trade union and political struggles throughout the 1950s and 1960s. She was banned in 1963 and spent the next sixteen years restricted to the area of Benoni. She died of natural causes in October 1979.

Joe Morolong (Commercial and Distributive Workers Union, Cape

Town). Morolong was a trade union organizer who spent almost one third of his life and half of his adult life in jail or under restrictions. Residents of Detshipeng Reserve, the remote area to which he had been banished, reported that he was murdered in November 1977.

Lawrence Ndzanga (SACTU National Executive Committee; Organizer, South African Railway and Harbour Workers Union). Ndzanga died in the police cells on 9 January 1976 while detained without trial under the Terrorism Act. His wife, Rita, also a SACTU trade unionist, was in detention at the time of the murder of her husband; she was refused permission to attend the funeral, although she was later released with no charges laid.

'Looksmart' S. Ngudle (Commercial and Distributive Workers Union, Cape Town). Ngudle was a SACTU leader in the Western Cape. His death on 5 September 1963 was officially recorded by the Apartheid régime as 'suicide by hanging'. An inquest was called for when a cellmate insisted on reporting details of Ngudle's treatment in jail. To prevent this, the state banned Ngudle (as a banned person cannot be quoted) and he became the first South African to be banned after death!

Our dedication pays tribute not only to these courageous leaders but also to countless other workers who have been killed in the course of the struggle for trade union rights in South Africa. To all of these fallen comrades, SACTU says: 'HAMBANI KAHLE' (Go Well)! To SACTU leaders presently incarcerated in the prisons of Apartheid and to the militant workers carrying forward the programme of SACTU, we say 'BASEBENZI MANYANANI' (Workers Unite)!

Viola Hashe

Elijah Loza

Leslie Massina

Caleb Mayekiso

Vuyisile Mini

Mary Moodley

Joe Morolong

SACTU salutes these men and women
who lived and died in struggle

Lawrence Ndzanga

'Looksmart' S. Ngudle

Preface

Twenty-five years ago, in March 1955, the South African Congress of Trade Unions (SACTU) was founded at an Inaugural Conference in Johannesburg. For a quarter of a century, SACTU has distinguished itself as the first non-racial trade union coordinating body, promoting the common class interests of *all* workers, regardless of race or colour. SACTU has also been in the forefront of the political struggle against the national oppression of all Black people in South Africa – Africans, Indians and Coloureds. The purpose of this book is to commemorate SACTU's twenty-fifth anniversary and in so doing call upon all progressive forces, in South Africa and throughout the world, to redouble their efforts to bring an end to the Apartheid system.

The history presented in these pages is necessarily incomplete. Hundreds of SACTU documents have through the years been confiscated in raids carried out by the South African state; they are stored in government buildings, unavailable to the millions of Black South Africans who are deprived of the opportunity to study and learn from the struggles of the recent past. Far more important than the loss of recorded history are the many comrades, veteran trade union leaders, who are forced to waste their lives rotting in the prisons of Apartheid. Their crime? That of struggling for a free and democratic South Africa, devoid of all forms of racial oppression and class exploitation.

For these reasons, the complete history of the workers' struggle against Apartheid, led by SACTU, can only be told after liberation. The prison gates will be flung open wide and the state archives will become a people's library accessible to all friends of the Revolution. Only under those conditions will all aspects of this long struggle – the gains, the setbacks and the sacrifices – be available for critical analysis and investigation.

These realities should not cause despair, but instead should inspire everyone to work that much harder for the day of liberation when not only the rich history of the South African struggle can be fully recorded but the new society of the future created. This book, based on all existing SACTU documents and materials available outside South Africa, is meant to be another step forward in this process. The primary purpose is to pay tribute to the dedication of SACTU workers through a documentation of the role that SACTU has played in the liberation struggle for the past twenty-five years.

For those readers not familiar with the Apartheid system, it is important at the outset to explain certain terminology. As Hilda Bernstein has stated:

The language of apartheid is a totally necessary part of its ideology. Without the special words and phrases that have been created, the ideology would disappear, because it is not a theory constructed on the basis of reason, but an expedient developed to disguise the truth and erected on the basis of a special language.

The opponents of apartheid are forced into a semantic trap: once you begin to use the language of apartheid, you have already accepted something of the premise. Yet it is impossible to write about South Africa today without using some of this special, and totally misleading, language.[1]*

This book avoids the 'language of apartheid' to the extent possible. Africans, Indians and Coloureds (people of mixed parentage) when referred to collectively are spoken of as 'Blacks'. Blacks are *not* described as 'non-Whites,' except where that paternalistic terminology has been used in historical quotations. To use the term 'non-White' or 'non-European' (which is only slightly less obnoxious in the South African context) is to define the majority of the population in terms of the minority, the oppressed in terms of the oppressor. Similarly, the term 'Bantu', Apartheid's term for African people, is completely avoided except where discussing government legislation or quoting government officials.

In addition, 'pass laws' refer to Apartheid legislation which requires all Africans over the age of sixteen to carry a pass (reference) book at all times and produce it on demand. It is the 'pass laws' which constitute the greatest burden for the African people in that they restrict the freedom of movement and choice of occupation. 'Pass-bearing' Africans are further oppressed by a mass of regulations and legislation, generally referred to as 'Influx Control,' which controls the number of Africans entering, residing or working in the urban areas. Finally, Africans may be forced to leave a prescribed area (that is, one considered 'White', but where in fact a large number of Africans live and work); this forced removal is commonly known as being 'endorsed out'. Other expressions which are peculiar to South Africa are defined in the text itself.

* See notes at end of each chapter.

NOTE

1. H. Bernstein, *For Their Triumphs and Their Tears: Women in Apartheid South Africa*, International Defence and Aid Fund, London, 1978 (rev. ed.), p. 5.

CHRONOLOGY

1919	Formation of the Industrial and Commercial Workers Union of Africa (ICU)
1924	Introduction of Industrial Conciliation Act
1941	Formation of the Council of Non-European Trade Unions (Transvaal) (CNETU)
1941	Formation of the African Mine Workers Union
August 1946	African Mine Workers strike
1948	Rise of the Nationalist Party to state power
1950	Introduction of the Suppression of Communism Act
1952	Defiance Campaign Against Unjust Laws
1953	Introduction of the Native Labour (Settlement of Disputes) Act
October 1954	Dissolution of the South African Trades & Labour Council (SAT & LC)
5–6 March 1955	Formation of the South African Congress of Trade Unions
June 1955	Congress of the People (Kliptown)
9 August 1956	Women's march to Pretoria to protest against the Pass Laws
1956	Introduction of Industrial Conciliation Act 1956
7 January 1957	Beginning of Alexandra Bus Boycott
26 June 1957	Congress Stay-At-Home
1957	£1-a-Day Campaign initiated by SACTU
14–16 April 1958	National Stay-At-Home
31 May 1959	Beginning of Potato Boycott
October 1959	Formation of the Federation of Free African Trade Unions of South Africa (FOFATUSA)
November 1959	Formation of the All-African Trade Union Federation (AATUF)
21 March 1960	Sharpeville massacre
30 March 1960	Unlawful Organizations Act used to ban the African National Congress (ANC) and Pan-Africanist Congress (PAC)

March–April 1960	Nation-wide strikes in response to banning of the ANC
1961	Port Elizabeth Bus Boycott
29–31 May 1961	National Stay-At-Home
7 February 1962	Beginning of International Solidarity Campaign
1962	Introduction of the Sabotage Act
1963	International Labour Organization (ILO) voted to expel South Africa
1963–4	Repression under the 90- and 180-day detentions

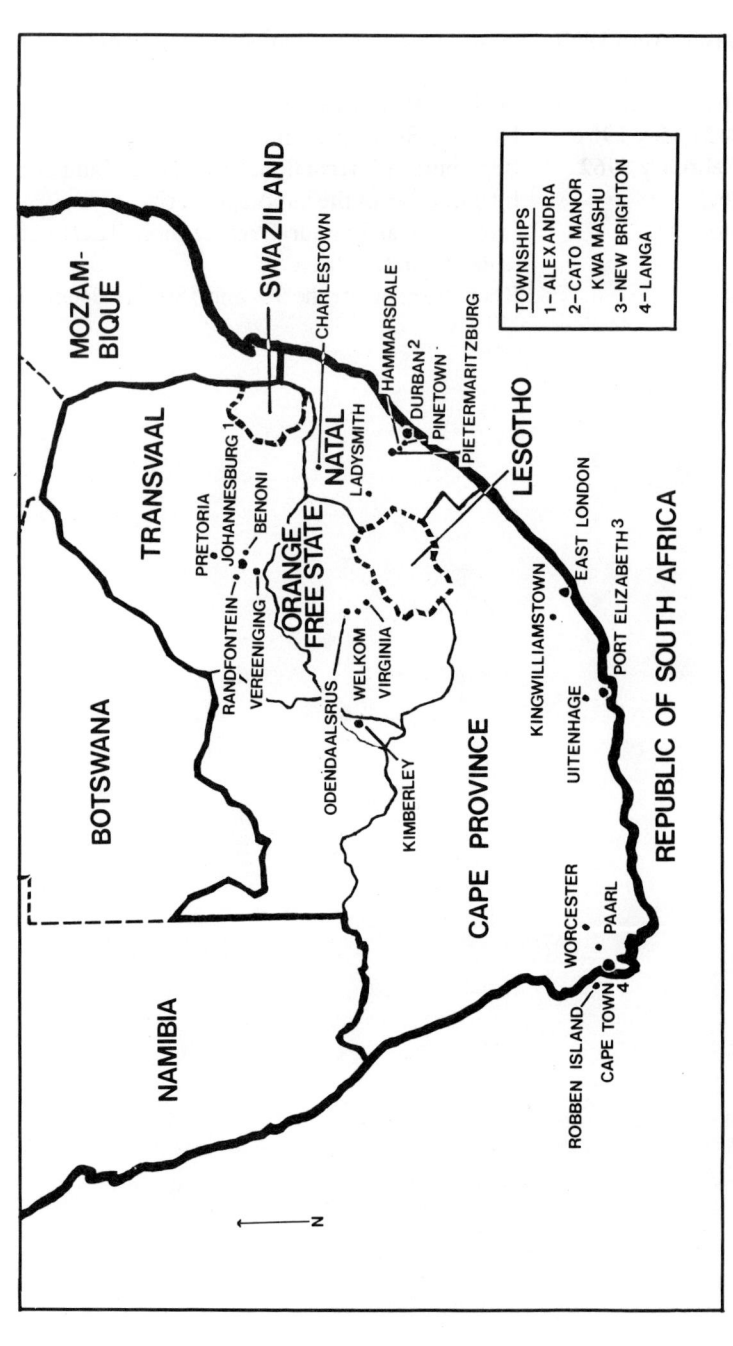

ABBREVIATIONS COMMONLY USED IN THE TEXT

AALC	African-American Labour Centre
A-FCWU	African Food and Canning Workers Union
A-FMBWU	African Furniture, Mattress and Bedding Workers Union
AFTU	African Federation of Trade Unions
AMWU	African Mine Workers Union
ANC	African National Congress (South Africa)
A-TWIU	African Textile Workers Industrial Union
AATUF	All-African Trade Union Federation
AFL-CIO	American Federation of Labour-Congress of Industrial Organizations
BLAA	Bantu Laws Amendment Acts
CWP-LC	Cape Western Province-Local Committee (SACTU)
CNLB	Central Native Labour Board
CPSA	Communist Party of South Africa
CA	Congress Alliance
COP	Congress of the People
CCSATU	Coordinating Council of South African Trade Unions
COLA	Cost of Living Allowance
CNETU	Council of Non-European Trade Unions (Transvaal)
FPAWU	Farm, Plantation and Allied Workers Union
FOFATUSA	Federation of Free African Trade Unions of South Africa
FSAW	Federation of South African Women
FCWU	Food and Canning Workers Union
GWU-AW	Garment Workers Union of African Women
GWU	Garment Workers Union
ICU/ICWU	Industrial and Commercial Workers Union of Africa
IC Act	Industrial Conciliation Act

ICFTU	International Confederation of Free Trade Unions
IDAF	International Defence and Aid Fund
ILO	International Labour Organization
IMF	International Metalworkers Federation
ISCOR	Iron and Steel Corporation of South Africa
LC	Local Committee (SACTU)
LKB	Langeberg Ko-Operasie Besperk
MC	Management Committee (SACTU)
MWU	Metal Workers Union
NIC	Natal Indian Congress
NSIEU	Natal Sugar Industrial Employees Union
NCC	National Consultative Committee (Congress Alliance)
NEC	National Executive Committee (SACTU)
NOC	National Organizing Committee (SACTU)
NUCW	National Union of Clothing Workers
NUCT	National Union of Commercial Travellers
NUDW	National Union of Distributive Workers
NL (SD) Act	Native Labour (Settlement of Disputes) Act (1953)
OFS	Orange Free State
PAC	Pan-Africanist Congress
PE	Port Elizabeth
PDL	Poverty Datum Line
PUTCO	Public Utilities Transport Corporation
SOWU	Shop and Office Workers Union
SACWU	South African Clothing Workers Union
SACPO/ SACPC/CPC	South African Coloured People's Organization/ Congress
SACOL	South African Confederation of Labour
SACOD/COD	South African Congress of Democrats
SACTU	South African Congress of Trade Unions
SAFCI	South African Federated Chamber of Industries
SAFTU	South African Federation of Trade Unions
SARHWU/ SARH (N-E) WU	South African Railway and Harbour (Non-European) Workers Union
SAIC	South African Indian Congress

SAIRR	South African Institute of Race Relations
SAT & LC/T & LC	South African Trades and Labour Council
SATUC/TUCSA	South African Trade Union Council/Trade Union Council of South Africa
SC Act	Suppression of Communism Act (1950)
TUC (UK)	British Trades Union Congress
Tvl	Transvaal
Tvl IS & MWU	Transvaal Iron, Steel and Metal Workers Union
TWIU	Textile Workers Industrial Union
WFTU	World Federation of Trade Unions

1 APARTHEID AND THE BLACK WORKING CLASS – THE PROBLEM DEFINED

... it must never be forgotten that Apartheid and racial discrimination in South Africa, like everywhere else, has an aim far more important than discrimination itself: *the aim is economic exploitation*. The root and fruit of apartheid and racial discrimination is profit.[1]

Migrant labour. Pass laws. Poverty wages. Victimization at the workplace. Unemployment. Repression. Imprisonment. Banning orders. Death. These are the ingredients of exploitation that shape the lives of millions of African workers from the cradle to the grave under Apartheid.

Understandably, the United Nations, church and humanitarian organizations have described Apartheid as a 'crime against humanity'. Although subjectively correct in the abstract, this formulation masks the real nature of the system of class exploitation that forms the basis of Apartheid. As such, the crucial issue of by whom and through what means Apartheid will be destroyed is left unaddressed. In order to address these crucial issues, we begin by adding the concrete qualification that Apartheid is a 'crime' against *working class humanity*. Only through the realization that Apartheid society is but one specific example of capitalist social formations can we begin to come to terms with the reality of and dialectical interrelationship between race, class and the liberation struggle in South Africa.

The complex interaction of racial and class dynamics is easily concealed by the appearance of social realities under Apartheid. Race and racial discrimination *appear* to be the single, dominant consideration determining and affecting all aspects of social life. Black people, regardless of class position, are systematically denied equality of opportunity in the political, economic, educational, cultural and sporting spheres. Africans, the overwhelming majority of the population, cannot vote, cannot own land, and cannot move freely; they are, instead, instructed by the White minority through custom, legislation and state-administered violence as to where to stay, to live, to work, to walk and even to sit. Voteless and voiceless, Africans, Coloureds and Indians are without doubt oppressed as a nation. Unless and until Black South Africans seize state power, there can be no freedom or liberation from this national oppression which has spanned the past three hundred years of colonialism, capitalist development and Western imperialism.

Notwithstanding this primacy of race in the definition and implementation of Apartheid, we must search beyond the appearance of things to discover the social realities. It is in the economic relations of production that we discover *why* Apartheid structures are so vitally necessary to the maintenance of the South African ruling class. Like all human societies, South Africa must ultimately be understood in regard to the production process wherein human labour power produces the material requirements for the maintenance and progressive development of social life itself. And, as in all capitalist societies, this human labour power is exploited by a non-productive, ruling (capitalist) class which owns and controls the means of production in the interest of capital accumulation and resultant political power. South Africa's uniqueness rests with the fact that class exploitation follows so closely along racial lines, with the Black, and predominantly African, working class bearing the burden of this exploitation endemic to capitalism. In discussing the dynamics of race and class in South Africa, Joe Slovo states,

... for all the overt signs of race as the mechanism of domination, the legal and institutional domination of the white minority over the black majority *has its origins in, and is perpetuated by, economic exploitation.*[2] (emphasis added)

Thus, just as national liberation is a requisite to freedom from racial domination under Apartheid, so too is class emancipation a requisite to freedom from economic exploitation, the *raison d'être* of production under Apartheid capitalism.

The realities of Apartheid render Black workers and their dependants exploited *both* as workers (i.e. sellers of labour power) and as disenfranchised citizens of South Africa. In the struggle for a democratic society free from all forms of exploitation and oppression, the Black working class must obviously be the driving force of the revolution. They must be organized industrially into disciplined and militant trade unions, and they, as a class, must be mobilized to wage mass resistance and struggle against the ruling class and its imperialist partners at all possible levels. Their participation, spirit of militancy and leadership will not only shape the parameters of struggle but also the contours of a liberated South Africa. As we have seen, insofar as Black workers suffer the double yolk of national oppression and class oppression, their emancipation from both is a necessary condition for the freedom of not only their class but of all South Africans.

This book outlines and pays tribute to the South African Congress of Trade Unions (SACTU), which was formed in 1955 with these principles and objectives as the basis of its existence. To organize the unorganized Black, especially African, workers into mass-based, national unions that would challenge the power of the bosses was its primary task on the trade union front. Yet it was not a trade union movement based on racial divisions. As the first non-racial trade union coordinating body, SACTU defended the rights and promoted the aspirations of *all* workers, regardless of race or colour. For this reason, its membership always included a number of White workers who refused to succumb to the pressures to accept a racially-divided workforce and White domination in society generally. SACTU was the only trade union coordinating body in post-war South African history to promote working class unity, in theory and *in practice*.

SACTU, from its inception, committed itself to the political struggle against national oppression with equal dedication. Rejecting the reformist *cum* reactionary call for 'no politics in the trade union movement', SACTU became a member of the Congress Alliance in 1955. Led by the liberation movement of South Africa, the African National Congress (ANC), the Congress Alliance consisted of organizations representing nationally oppressed Africans (ANC), Indians (South African Indian Congress, SAIC), Coloureds (South African Coloured People's Congress, SACPC) and progressive Whites (South African Congress of Democrats, SACOD).

Despite Nationalist Party legislation and repression, SACTU gained strength on both the trade union and political fronts. Organizing drives, closely coordinated with Congress Alliance campaigns, struck a chord with the mass of exploited workers. From an initial membership of 20,000 in 1956, SACTU ranks grew to 55,000 workers in 1962, immediately prior to the massive state repression directed against all progressive organizations in the early to mid-1960s. From 1964 onwards, SACTU was forced to convert its activities to the conditions of underground work, and has continued to spearhead the workers' struggle.

NOTES

1. Mark Shope, SACTU Report to Solidarity Conference, Accra, Ghana, 1964.
2. Joe Slovo, 'South Africa – No Middle Road', *Southern Africa: The New Politics of Revolution*, Penguin, Harmondsworth, 1976, p. 118.

2 THE HERITAGE OF STRUGGLE

SACTU owes its existence to the decades of struggle and sacrifice that preceded it. History always points the way forward. Two generations of progressive trade unionists before SACTU had grappled with the basic dilemma in South African trade unionism – the racial division of the working class within the context of a rapidly developing industrial capitalism.

Beginning in the 1920s, each decade and in certain periods different geographical areas, conceived various strategies to advance the workers' struggle according to the principles of working class unity. In the course of the struggle, many victories were won but many mistakes were made. In the earlier years especially, it was not uncommon for progressive White trade unionists to think and act within the confines of a European model of trade unionism transplanted onto South African conditions. Such an approach could only lead to White paternalism and failure. Yet these struggles were themselves part of a dialectical process that on the one hand gave impetus to African workers to forge their own structures and class consciousness, and on the other hand forced progressive Whites to rethink and reformulate trade union strategies based on the concrete conditions of racial capitalism. The result, many years later, was the emergence of SACTU as the first non-racial trade union coordinating body.

We have only a short space in which to document these early struggles and pay tribute to the individuals who led them. The emphasis in this chapter will be on the organization of the most exploited – the African workers. In terms of time, the concentration will be on the 1940s and early 1950s, the years that formed the immediate background to the emergence of SACTU.[1]

The Industrial and Commercial Workers Union of Africa (ICU)

Whereas the interest of the workers and those of the employers are opposed to each other, the former living by selling their labour, receiving for it only part of the wealth they produce; and the latter living by exploiting the labour of the workers; depriving the workers of a part of the product of their labour in the form of profit, no peace can be between the two classes, a struggle must always obtain about the division of the products of human labour, until the workers through their industrial organizations take from the capitalist class the means of production, to be owned and controlled by the workers for the benefit of all, instead of for the profit of a few. Under such a system he who does not work, neither shall he eat. The basis of remuneration shall be the principle from every man according to his abilities, to every man according to his needs. This is the goal for which the ICU strives along with all other organized workers throughout the world. Further, this Organization does not foster or encourage antagonism towards other established bodies, political or otherwise, of African peoples, or of organized European labour.

Preamble to 1925 revised Constitution of the ICU[2]

The decade of the 1920s witnessed the rise and the fall of the ICU, the first nationally-based African workers' organization and political movement in South African history. From its initial base amongst Cape Town dock workers, the ICU extended its influence to all provinces by the mid-1920s; in the late 1920s the base shifted to Natal and by 1929–30, for a number of reasons, it had virtually collapsed into localized and weak factions that formed the basis for the more serious trade union organizing work in the 1930s. Membership figures are difficult to verify, but there is good reason to believe ICU claims of 100,000 workers during the peak year of 1927. For all of its contradictions – and they existed at every possible level – the ICU was instrumental in founding a tradition of Black workers' militancy. Yet, ironically, the structure and leadership weaknesses of the ICU rendered the movement incapable of directing that very same rank-and-file militancy.

The ICU was formed in January 1919 in Cape Town, when A. F. Batty, founder of the unsuccessful Labour Democratic Party, asked Clements Kadalie to assist in organizing a permanent organization of Black workers to give him greater electoral strength. Kadalie, an immigrant from Nyasaland (Malawi) became Secretary of the Union, which had its base primarily among Coloured dock workers and railway workers. The intitial strength of the ICU came through successful strike action on the Cape Town docks in 1919; over 2,000 workers came out and despite police harassment and White workers' strike-breaking, wage increases of nearly 100 per cent were secured by 1920. This was to be one of the very few strike actions ever endorsed by the ICU throughout the next decade.

Organizing efforts in Bloemfontein (Orange Free State), were being conducted simultaneously by Selby Msimang, with the primary struggle there being around general wage increases for African workers facing cost of living increases after the First World War. Msimang's union, the Industrial and Commercial Workers Union (ICWU) invited Kadalie's union to merge in 1920, but Kadalie resisted until it was agreed that he would be allowed to be the principal figure. In the interests of workers' unity and the necessity of forming a national organization, Msimang conceded the leadership position to Kadalie. Thus, in Bloemfontein, the ICWU of Africa was born on a platform of trade unionism designed to organize 'One Big Union' of Black workers throughout the country. Although explicit political activity was eliminated from the initial charter, perhaps in deference to the South African Native National Congress (to become the African National Congress in the 1920s), the ICU passed resolutions that attacked the pass laws and system of contract labour. The prohibition against involvement in political activity soon became an impossible and undesirable mandate for the ICU to follow.

Until 1923, the ICU, reflecting Kadalie's dominance, had its strength primarily in the Western Cape Province. The 1923 Conference, for example, consisted almost exclusively of delegates from the Cape; this also meant that the Coloured working class community was represented in higher proportions than would be the case when the ICU expanded to establish branches throughout the country. In 1925, although the Conference was convened in Johannesburg, the Cape accounted for ten of the fifteen branches represented. By 1927, however, each province had approximately equal representation, although the Natal branches – under the leadership of A. W. G. Champion – accounted for over 61 per cent of the ICU's revenues (as compared with the Cape's 3·6 per cent).

The temptation to explain the strengths and weaknesses of the ICU in terms of individual leaders must be guarded against. Rather, the main reason for the meteoric rise of the ICU and its popularity with the African and Coloured workers must be located in trends in the political economy following the First World War. Kadalie's description of the ICU as a '. . . beacon of light on the horizon' means essentially that it was the first mass-based movement to emerge following the consolidation of White colonialism via the formation of the Union of South Africa in 1910. The last 'native' rebellion had been forcefully put down in 1906, and since then the conquered Africans had been searching for an organizational structure within which they could resist incorporation into the dominant capitalist economy. Despite White

(English) missionary rhetoric about 'integration' and 'eventual equality', the real role of Blacks as cheap labour and oppressed citizens was firmly established by the end of the war. The war 'fought to end all wars' had only made their working and living conditions more precarious.

Wartime industrialization accelerated the growth of the Black proletariat. In the process, the pre-capitalist reserves were disrupted through labour migration to the cities and were increasingly incapable of providing subsistence for their inhabitants. In the cities, African labour faced a rising cost of living with poverty wages and ruling class authoritarianism with no effective counter-organization. To express their discontent, African workers carried out numerous spontaneous strikes on the mines and in the cities between 1918 and 1920. It was this working class militancy which formed the basis of the ICU rise to national prominence in the early 1920s.

The heavy-handed leadership of Kadalie and Champion, however, placed narrow parameters on the programme of the ICU. The Union became highly bureaucratic and too concerned with constitutionalism at the top, yet amongst its membership the disciplined organization of workers was almost completely non-existent. Organized along the syndicalist lines of a general workers' union, the ICU included in its ranks teachers, domestic servants, dock workers, rural agricultural workers and even small traders. In short, the ICU brought together the extremes within the oppressed community – from the rural migrants to the urban petty-bourgeois aspirants, the latter in many respects reflecting the class background of their leaders. Teachers, for example, often entered the ICU as bureaucrats with no trade union experience or interest but only in order to gain higher wages than their profession would pay. This was especially the case in Natal, where at one time the ICU was reported to have no less than 58 *paid* staff members.

The most glaring contradictions within the ICU came at the level of trade union politics, and particularly the leadership's inability to decide on a consistent policy towards White workers and their trade unions. This was admittedly a problem made more difficult by the fact that the majority in the Communist Party of South Africa (CPSA) held firmly to the belief that the White working class would lead the revolution against capitalism in South Africa. Kadalie, in his more radical moments, spoke of the necessity to struggle on both economic and political fronts and also of the desirability of working with White Communists who disagreed with the prevailing line of the party. But Kadalie's lack of political clarity extended far beyond the question of the CPSA. In the space of these short years, Kadalie worked with such diverse groups as the pro-Apartheid Nationalist Party, the SA Labour Party, the SA Trade Union Congress, the British TUC and even the Communists when all other options had been closed to him.

The major conflict between Kadalie and the CPSA was only superficially the question of race, as Coloured and African members James La Guma, Johnny Gomas and Edward Khaile, among others, were very capable CP members holding key positions in the ICU until 1926. The Communists' criticisms of the ICU leadership concerned (a) its unwillingness to organize disciplined, industrial unions (rather than the amorphous general workers' union), to introduce rank-and-file democratic control of Union funds and elections, or to pursue an active policy of strike action, and (b) 'inefficiency, dishonesty and unconstitutionalism'. The latter charge was made by La Guma following a national tour of ICU branches in 1926, whereupon he concluded that Kadalie was the 'arch pilferer' of them all and a 'dictator in embryo'.

The ultimate result of this conflict was the purge of all Communists from the ICU at an Executive Committee meeting in Cape Town and then confirmed at the 1926 Conference in Port Elizabeth. Although local branches objected to this action, the decision was upheld at the 1927 Conference held in Champion's stronghold of Natal. The CPSA could offer no serious opposition to the purge as most White Communist trade union leaders were still caught up in the 'White workers first' policy. The simple fact was that at this time the ICU, for all its weaknesses, had been the only trade union to emphasize the organization of the most exploited workers in South Africa.

Kadalie's purge of the Communists, however, was not done with any principle in mind. Instead, it was part of his larger strategy of building ICU strength through foreign support. Having given up on the White unions in South Africa, and having been predictably betrayed by the Nationalist-Labour Pact Government following the elections of 1924,[3] Kadalie then turned his attention to White, liberal organizations with 'mother-country connections' back in Britain for assistance. Connections with British Labour Party persons, who warned Kadalie against any involvement with the CPSA, were pursued and greatly strengthened with the purge of the Communist members in 1926. In Kadalie's words, it 'brought immeasureable support from the liberal European public opinion'.

In April 1927, Kadalie extended his European contacts by attending the International Labour Organization (ILO) meetings as an unofficial delegate from South Africa. This made Kadalie the first African trade unionist to attend an ILO Convention. After a five-month tour of Europe and lengthy discussions with trade union centres, especially in Britain, he returned to South Africa with not only a Europeanized conception of trade union structures (which had little to do with South African realities) but also a new European-drafted Constitution for the ICU.

With these new friends in Europe, Kadalie was intent on proving that the ICU was not anti-White. The National Council was persuaded to endorse his motion that the ICU apply for direct affiliation to the South African Trade Union Congress (SATUC). The thinking behind this move was that such an affiliation would strengthen and further legitimate the ICU as a trade union organization while simultaneously forcing White trade union leaders to recognize Kadalie's close ties with British trade union and political centres. To its discredit, the SATUC again responded with a racist reflex and turned down the application, suggesting instead that periodic consultations should be held between the two bodies. Kadalie responded, 'We have no intention of allowing the TUC to patronize us as inferiors. We will have full status or nothing.'

This rejection by the SATUC also showed it to be a 'narrow racialist body, devoid of any true working class spirit'. Most disheartening for many Communists in the labour movement was the fact that veteran trade union leader, William ('Bill') Andrews, helped to draft the rejection memorandum. As Simons and Simons conclude:

In yielding to white power without a protest, Andrews and Stuart isolated the ICU at a time when it desperately needed the backing of organized labour. . . . They admitted that the white labour policy was unjust, yet recommended in effect that it should be maintained. They claimed to lead the white workers, yet succumbed to their anti-Native prejudice. They professed faith in democratic rule, yet feared that the ICU might outvote the minority. They paid lip service to the idea of working class solidarity, but relied on racial antagonism to keep their own ranks united. The ICU had offered friendship in all sincerity and suffered a rebuff.[4]

Kadalie was not only to be rejected by the TUC but by his own ICU as well. During the time he was away in Europe, the ICU centre of strength had dramatically shifted to Natal. By 1927 it was under the leadership of A. W. G. Champion, whom Kadalie had recruited from his position as President of the Transvaal Mine Clerks Association in 1925. Champion, after moving to Natal in late 1925, built an ICU empire around himself in much the same fashion as Kadalie had done elsewhere.

Conditions for rural African migrants in Natal were deplorable. For instance, the ICU won an important legal case in the Supreme Court that outlawed a Durban city by-law ordering all Africans to be dipped in disinfectant tanks along with their belongings before entering the city. From this initial victory, the Natal ICU focused attention on African squatters being removed from European-owned land. Rural Natal labourers flocked to the ICU in great numbers, and at times chiefs would deliver their entire tribes to ICU membership.

With a revolutionary political leadership and discipline, the ICU might have been capable of forging a truly mass workers' movement to challenge the ruling class. But instead, the ICU soon began to disintegrate over leadership rivalries between Kadalie and Champion. The 'cult of personality' approach characteristic of both reflected the fact that they had not developed organically out of the working class but rather came in 'from the outside'. They lacked any clear analysis of the society in which they lived, and consequently their conception of change was piecemeal, reformist and most commonly bourgeois in direction.

When Champion returned to his native Natal in 1925, he utilized his connections to bring in a large Zulu membership and then imposed a heavy financial obligation on members in the form of dues. With the large revenues that came in, Champion developed a personal network of organizations – businesses, a newspaper, social clubs – through which he provided a variety of services for members. With those monies investments were made in real estate ventures, cooperatives, purchases of grain (presumably to be resold to members) and similar operations. In other words, instead of organizing the exploited and dispossessed to fight against the bosses and the state, the ICU leaders cautioned against strike activity and tried to compensate the victims of capitalism through these petty-bourgeois schemes. Champion even tried to pass a motion at the 1927 Conference which would have levied each member £1 to subsidize land purchases, but this was defeated by the delegates. Aside from a betrayal of working class struggle, these priorities understandably led to financial corruption. The sick, old age, unemployment and death benefits offered workers upon joining the ICU were seldom, if ever, realized.

There were also many occasions where the ICU failed to support militant workers who spontaneously struck against their employers. A coal workers' strike in Natal in 1927 led the ICU officials to side with the mining company and declare the strike illegal; Durban dockers also on strike were left unassisted on two occasions. Other strike-breaking incidents were part of the ICU leadership's attempt to divert the workers' militancy away from class struggle. The ICU *Workers' Herald* of November 1928 proudly editorialized that the ICU was 'glad to say that owing to the broad outlook of the ICU administrators the strike weapon has only been used on three occasions . . .'

By 1928 an internal crisis concerning the misuse of ICU funds became public knowledge and disintegration proceeded rapidly. Two years later, the ICU consisted of nothing more than local structures with no hope of rebuilding the national organization of 100,000 members that had existed in 1927.

Despite the many weaknesses and contradictions that characterized the ICU in the 1920s, one cannot overestimate its importance in establishing a tradition of African working-class resistance to exploitation. For the first time in modern South African history, the ICU provided African and Coloured workers with the opportunity to experience trade union organization and collectivization of working-class protest. Although hindered by opportunistic leadership at the national level, many ICU local branches became the source of Black trade union leaders of the next two decades. In fact, the sons and daughters of many ICU veterans became SACTU militants in the 1950s. In this respect, Kadalie's personal assessment of the effect of the ICU is not far off the mark:

The many trade unions of the African workers which have sprung up in all big cities of the Union of South Africa owe their existence to the pioneering work of the 'mother ICU' which blazed the trail in the industrial field.

Ironically, the disintegration of the ICU into more local and regional organizations created the very conditions which allowed for the elimination of the three major weaknesses of the ICU – i.e. the absence of working-class leadership, the lack of clarity in the political struggle and the failure to organize trade unions along industrial lines. The new emphasis would be on class struggle at the point of production and it is in the decade of the 1930s that we see great advances in African trade unionism throughout the country.

The 1930s: The Rise of African Industrial Unionism and Afrikaner Nationalism

The rapid disintegration of the ICU created the conditions for a reassessment of strategy and tactics in building a trade union movement amongst the African proletariat. Aside from the continuity of individual organizers, there was a qualitative break between the ICU structures of the 1920s and the new unions that were to emerge in the 1930s. The major distinguishing feature of the emerging African unions was their organization along industrial lines. Only in this way could workers directly challenge the employers as the cause of their exploitation, and only in this way could their organization reflect the overall changes in the political economy associated with industrialization.

The other significant development worthy of attention is the rise of 'Christian-Nationalist' trade unions in the latter half of the decade. As we shall see, these 'unions' were part of the political assault on the working class led by the Afrikaner proto-fascist organizations.

These two related developments on the trade union front can be understood only in relation to major changes occurring in the overall structure of South African capitalism.

Firstly, the rapid process of industrialization resulted in the manufacturing sector contributing a greater proportion to the National Income than the agricultural sector for the first time in 1930. By 1943 manufacturing had outstripped mining. This industrial expansion brought with it a dramatic growth of the urban proletariat, both White and Black. 'Poor White' Afrikaners rushed from the farms to the cities in record numbers – an estimated 11,000 per year between 1921 and 1936 were reduced to unskilled wage earners in the unfamiliar urban setting.

The African proletariat increased by even greater proportions. The urban African population trebled between 1921 and 1946; between 1933 and 1939, approximately 400,000 Africans were added to the industrial labour force, doubling previous levels. The majority of this newly 'freed' labour force, i.e. those stripped of all means of production in the reserves and hence obliged to sell their labour-power to White capital in the cities, settled in the Transvaal. Thus, by the late 1930s, the overall proletariat had greatly stabilized in comparison with the previous decade.

Secondly, the traditional categories of skilled and unskilled labour rapidly gave way to a new category of worker – the semi-skilled operative, a human appendage to the machine. Both Africans and Afrikaners (especially women) assumed these positions as they entered the urban work force. Former artisans were either displaced, or, more frequently, reduced to overseers of African workers. The state acted wherever possible to protect the racial division of labour and White supremacy, but there was no doubt that the cheaper labour of African operatives was incorporated to meet the demands of industrial capitalist production. White industrial employees accounted for 35·9 per cent of all production workers in 1933; by 1950, they represented only 24·4 per cent.

Thirdly, and closely related to this change in the racial and technical composition of labour, craft unions were losing strength to new industrial unions which, in contrast, tended to be multi-racial in membership. Registered union membership (this excluded Africans) increased by 100,000 between 1933 and 1937, and by 1942 accounted for a quarter of a million workers. Craft unions failed to organize this new proletariat which instead was mobilized by 'left' trade unionists, in particular individual Communist Party members. A large proportion of these industrial unions consisted of Afrikaans-speaking Whites.[5]

This shift created tensions within the South African Trades & Labour Council (SAT & LC), which had replaced the SATUC in 1930 as the recognized body of organized labour. In the Cape, the Cape Federation of Labour Unions, under the leadership of Bob Stuart, refused to merge with the T & LC. Many progressive trade unionists in the T & LC fought the reactionary craft unions for over two decades and generally speaking were able to hold the Council to progressive positions. For example, T & LC affiliation was open to all *bona fide* unions, including African trade unions. In practice, however, the T & LC as a federation did little to further the development of African workers and consequently gained little respect from the most exploited section of the work force.

The rise of unregistered African unions in the 1930s took place within the context of these important shifts in the political economy. By 1945, an estimated 40 per cent of the African industrial labour force was 'unionized' in one form or another – in some cases as parallel unions of registered unions or more often as independent militant unions that received little assistance from organized labour. The rich history of individual dedication and sacrifice, in the face of tremendous obstacles, to build African unions is a story that can only be sketched here. It is important to realize that some of these unions and many of the organizers had direct continuity with the SACTU struggles of the 1950s.

Having chosen the path of industrial unionism, and lacking a national coordinating body, the African trade union movement of the 1930s and early 1940s defies gross generalizations. Organizers in each geographical area grappled with local conditions and developed specific strategies accordingly. What follows is a brief outline of these struggles by area.

In the Transvaal, the industrial centre of South Africa, Communists like Jimmy La Guma, purged by Kadalie from the ICU, had begun the difficult task of organizing Black workers in 1927. By the late 1920s, Willie Kalk, Solly Sachs, Fanny Klenerman and Ben Weinbren, among others, had organized registered unions among furniture, garment, sweet, laundry, catering and distributive trade workers. The organization of African workers was occurring simultaneously in the laundry, tailoring, engineering and baking industries. These efforts coincided with political education classes run by the CPSA in its drive to bring Africans into the party and reverse the old pattern of White domination (and often White prejudice as well). Among the recruits were Africans who later played leading roles in the trade union and liberation movements – for example, Johannes Nkosi, Gana Makabeni and Moses Kotane. Some of the trade unions formed by members of the Communist Party in the late 1920s, such as the Laundry Workers Union and the Clothing Workers Union, have remained in existence to this day (although under different names). They testify to the rich experience of over half a century of Black trade unionism.

In 1928, a South African Federation of Non-European Trade Unions (SAFNETU), consisting of five African unions representing about 10,000 workers, formed on the Rand. The Federation affiliated to the Red International of Labour Unions in 1929. Also in that year, five new African unions in dairy, meat, canvas, transport and engineering became affiliates to the coordinating body. Although the Party line had called for non-racial trade unions as the ideal, the reality was that Black workers first needed to solidify their collective strength against not only capital but also White workers firmly committed to the industrial colour-bar. Despite attempts to cooperate with White unions in the same industries, and regardless of Black solidarity with White workers' struggles, the latter invariably failed to support African workers in strike situations. The Federation did, however, claim to have sponsored the first joint strike of Africans and Whites against victimization of garment workers in Germiston. A joint committee of all trade unions in the laundry industry was also heralded as a breakthrough. Demands from the Federation were not particularly radical, avoiding the colour-bar issue and campaigning for a 48-hour working week and 'equal pay for equal work'.

Rising unemployment during the Depression years led to a brief but significant decline in the employment of Black, particularly African workers; the latter were in many cases forced back onto the reserves as the few jobs available went to 'poor Afrikaner Whites'. Police actions against African workers, unassisted by their White counterparts, also contributed to instability for these newly formed African unions. Finally, internal Communist Party conflicts over the acceptance of the 'Native Republic' thesis, led to purges of the very organizers who had made such a valuable beginning in the organizing of these unions.[6] These divergent factors combined to weaken the Federation and led to its disappearance by the turn of the decade.

Another Communist-initiated body – the African Federation of Trade Unions (AFTU) – emerged on the Rand during the Depression years. The current thinking was to raise African unions to a 'higher political level' by focusing on broader issues such as unemployment and anti-pass campaigns. A successful Johannesburg May Day demonstration in 1931, which brought together Africans and Whites, shouting 'We Want Bread' and 'Work or Wages', encouraged the leaders to believe that White workers were beginning to show signs of enlightened thinking. Such was not the case, however, and the state intervened by imposing tighter curfews on Africans and arresting Communist leaders throughout the country.

Another purge within the CPSA led to the expulsion of more trade unionists in September 1931. These included Bill Andrews, Solly Sachs and Ben Weinbren. Unemployment was the main issue of the day, and despite occasional unity of poor Afrikaners and Africans, the state succeeded in driving the racial wedge between these workers. The Europeans were called the 'unemployed' and given the dole; Africans were 'loafers' and endorsed out of the urban areas.[7]

The AFTU had been reduced to only two African unions in early 1932. Internal disputes between the African Clothing Workers Union and African Laundry Workers Union on the one hand and the AFTU on the other added to the problems on the Rand. The eventual strategy that dominated organizing work was that of registering unions of White, Coloured and Indian workers, and then forming parallel, unregistered unions of Africans. On one point all agreed: only with strong African unions *might* the White and privileged labour aristocracy be forced to concede common interests were shared by all workers.

As pointed out previously, the mid- to late-1930s witnessed another period of industrial expansion. With this came a renewed effort to organize African workers. In this period Wage Board investigations were called for more frequently on behalf of the grossly underpaid African workers. With new wage determinations achieved, African trade unionists had to fight for their enforcement as employers unscrupulously evaded the law. Over £25,000 was regained from employers underpaying their African labour in 1938 alone. These tangible rewards of trade union membership gave African workers more encouragement to join together in common struggle.

In addition to the continuing work of CPSA organizers, two new forces emerged on the African trade union front. Firstly, Gana Makabeni, ex-CPSA and ICU member, led the African Clothing Workers Union and a nucleus of other unions entirely under African leadership in the broom and brush, sweet, tobacco, rope and canvas, tin, metal and iron and numerous other secondary manufacturing industries. By 1940, these unions formed a Coordinating Committee of African Trade Unions.

The second grouping centred around the work of Max Gordon, a Trotskyist who re-organized the African Laundry Workers Union in 1935. In the next few years, Gordon, with financial assistance from the SA Institute of Race Relations (SAIRR) rebuilt other defunct unions, created new unions in commercial and distributive trades, baking and a General Workers Union; he also trained many Africans in the basics of trade union work. By 1939, between 15 and 20,000 African workers under Gordon's direction merged into the Joint Committee for African Trade Unions. Gordon served as General Secretary of the Joint Committee and Africans acted as secretaries of affiliated unions. In 1940, Gordon was interned as a 'safety measure', and David Gosani replaced him as General Secretary as the African workers preferred not to have Whites in leadership positions any longer.

The Joint and Coordinating Committees attempted a merger in 1938 but nothing came of this as Makabeni and others insisted that Whites should not fill offices in any affiliated unions. Gordon at that time was secretary of four African unions and refused to relinquish these positions. As Makabeni pointed out in 1939, 'Must we have European leaders even in our association?'[8] None the less, many of the unions of both bodies came together to form the Council of Non-European Trade Unions (CNETU) in 1941, the progressive Council that led the African workers' struggle throughout the 1940s.

Conditions in the Western Cape, with its large proportion of Coloured workers, differed greatly from the heavily industrial Transvaal. Also, the day-to-day organizing work of Cape Town Communists was not directly affected by the internal battles and purges in the north. The dominant trade union groupings in this area in the 1930s were the aristocratic, craft unions and the Cape Federation of Labour Unions, which although it had a large proportion of Coloured workers, was still dominated by White leaders and White supremacist ideas. In the mid-1930s, however, militant trade unionists such as Ray Alexander, Johnny Gomas, Jimmy La Guma, Eli Weinberg, J. Ngedlane and J. Shuba, to name only a few, began to make their presence and that of African workers felt throughout the Western Cape.

One of the most important struggles in the early 1930s centred on the garment/clothing industry, where the aim was to organize the industry on a non-racial basis and simultaneously to establish a base against the CFLU's reformist policies. Solly Sachs, leader of the Transvaal Garment Workers Union (GWU), had asked Eli Weinberg to help organize in the Cape Town area in 1932. Weinberg, along with La Guma, Gomas and Ray Alexander had formed the African GWU by 1935. With success in this key industry, other workers in the leather, rope, milling and chemical industries soon became the focal point of Black union organization.

Ray Alexander deserves special mention for the pioneering work done in Cape Town in this decade. Trained in trade union work by Bill Andrews and J. Shuba, Alexander was distinguished by her methodical organizing around the real concrete demands of the workers in each industry. Once, while working for the Commercial Workers Union, certain reactionary elements in the Union called for her resignation because she had been seen walking with a 'kaffir' (J. Shuba) down the streets of Cape Town. Unwilling to give in to White chauvinism, Alexander insisted that the workers must decide if such behaviour was grounds for dismissal. The workers responded by re-electing her as Secretary.

As Afrikaner nationalism in the trade union movement raised its ugly head in the mid- to late-1930s (see below), the struggle in the Western Cape focused on the transport workers. Africans, Coloureds and

Indians were being removed from the Spoorbond, an Afrikaner 'Christian-Nationalist' Union that by 1936 had 16,000 members. Through the efforts of H. October, W. Driver, Alexander and others, a conference was held in October of that year in the same hall where the ICU had been founded back in 1919. The conference called for a minimum wage of 1s. an hour to make up for the wages lost by Black workers during the Depression, equal opportunity for skilled work and an increase in the number of Black railway workers. The SA Railways and Harbour Workers Union (SARHWU) emerged from that historic meeting, and by 1943 the union had expanded to all provinces with a membership of over 20,000 workers.

These Western Cape initiatives were boosted on the political front by the removal of CPSA headquarters from Johannesburg to Cape Town in 1936. The progressive weekly, *The Guardian*, also added to the political and trade union work when it began publication in Cape Town in 1937; although this paper would be forced to change its name many times in the next twenty-five years, it continued to provide an invaluable source of analysis and discussion on the political and trade union struggle in all areas of the country.

Natal was distinguished from all other areas in South Africa by its large Indian community. In fact, despite stereotypes that picture all Indians as petty-bourgeois merchants, no less than 80 per cent of the Indian community in Natal were exploited as workers in the sugar and secondary manufacturing industries and also by the municipalities. This reality led to the emergence of militant Indian trade unionists and political activists in the 1930s.

Previously, the Indian trade union movement had begun in earnest in 1917–18, with unions organized in printing, furniture, garment, leather, tobacco, liquor and catering trades. These ethnically-based unions for Indians, coupled with the anti-Communist inclinations of A. W. G. Champion's ICU legacy, made for a racially divided and conservative trade union movement in Natal throughout the 1920s. In 1930, however, the national anti-pass campaign organized by the CPSA put Durban at the centre of progressive political activity – and state repression. While other cities drew only a few hundred demonstrators, 3,000 came out in response to the call of the Durban Branch. After four hours of speeches, a protest march through the city was prevented by police who proceeded to viciously attack and stab to death the dynamic leader, Johannes Nkosi. The government then banned Party members, including trade unionist Gana Makabeni, from the province for a period of two years. Nkosi became a martyr and a symbol of the African militancy against state repression and class exploitation. SACTU activists in the 1950s frequently visited Nkosi's grave as an inspiration in their struggles.

The emergence of a radical political trade union movement amongst Indian workers is a story not yet fully appreciated in South African history. In Natal, two people – George Ponnen and H. A. Naidoo – deserve special mention for the role they played in promoting non-racial trade unionism and class consciousness amongst Indian workers. Both from working class families, they became 'inseparable comrades' at work in the clothing factories of Durban, at night school and at political meetings during the rise of the 'Grey Shirts' fascists in 1933. From attendance at Anti-Fascist League rallies in their twenties, George and H.A. (as they were known locally) were influenced by Labour Party member and trade unionist A. T. Wanless, Eddie Roux, CPSA organizer in Natal, and Errol Shanley, trade union leader in Durban. They became the first South Africans of Indian origin to join the CPSA.

Rebuilding the Party after the 1930 repression was the major priority, and the strategy was to create strong unions for African and Indian workers. Their first major struggle was, as in other centres, in the garment industry, where the majority Black workers were controlled by a White executive led by J. C. Bolton. Ponnen and Naidoo resisted the temptation to form a separate union for Black workers and instead mobilized Black workers to take control of their union by challenging Bolton and his cronies; an attempt by Bolton to purge the two from the union leadership was defeated by the Black workers' unity.

Ponnen recalls his first involvement in a strike in November 1934. An Indian worker had been caught stealing some unmade pants material. The employer responded by drilling five three-quarter inch peep-holes in the Black workers' toilet walls and set up a system of constant surveillance. Humiliation and resentment of the workers led Ponnen and Naidoo to call all workers together and organize strike action the following morning. Whites, Africans, Indians and Coloureds stood together, forcing the boss to plug up the holes and grant further concessions to demands submitted by a non-racial workers' delegation. In Ponnen's words, 'This was the first time that White women workers and Black workers struck together one-hundred per cent united.' The following day, the police charged the two organizers with leading an illegal strike; Bolton refused Union support to the defendants and also persuaded two White women workers to testify against Ponnen and

Naidoo. A light fine of £2 each was assessed and workers came forward to pay the fine.

This example typifies the approach taken on the Natal trade union front. The attempt was at all times to work for non-racial workers' unity, whether in strikes or in negotiations through the industrial relations machinery of the Industrial Conciliation Act. The most important struggle in Natal in the 1930s was the strike at Falkirk Iron & Steel, where again Ponnen and Naidoo were instrumental in leading the workers to a victorious settlement.

Their involvement in this dispute began one evening when iron and steel workers came to ask for assistance in forming a union of Indian, African and Coloured workers. After many secret meetings and the drafting of a Constitution, the Iron & Steel Workers Union (Natal) was formed with H. A. Naidoo as Secretary and P. M. Harry, a factory worker, as Chairman. Harry was fired when the employer heard about the Union and Black workers downed tools and came out on strike. The young Union had to fight not only the boss but also the White unions, the police and even A. W. G. Champion, former ICU leader and by then Native Commissioner. At one mass meeting during the strike, Champion attempted to divide the unity of the workers by telling Africans to go back to work and not to join the Indians who, in Champion's words, were nothing but 'shop keepers and exploiters'. Ponnen instantly stood up and spoke to the African workers:

You know why you are on strike. You know why the African, Indian and Coloured workers who work together in the factory are united. You know why you formed the Union . . . Champion tells you that Indian workers are . . . shop keepers. As far as we know none of us here own shops. The only one who owns a shop is Champion himself. He is the shop keeper and he is the exploiter.

Ponnen told African workers to make a choice, either follow Champion or stand united with their fellow Indian and Coloured workers. As Ponnen recalls, 'The African workers with some war cry started marching towards Champion and his cronies. Champion saw there was trouble and made quickly to the gate with his henchmen – half running.'[9]

The workers stood firm in the prolonged Falkirk strike that lasted 13 weeks. Whenever 'Bantu Affairs' authorities came to seek a compromise, they were met with the workers' militant singing of freedom songs. Throughout the strike, food rations and strike funds were provided by the otherwise reactionary Natal Indian Congress

Natal Trade Unionists, 1930s.
Left to right: Errol Shanley, D. Naidoo (H.A.'s sister), H. A. Naidoo, P. M. Harry, George Ponnen

Indian sugar workers and families, Natal, 1930s

(which largely represented the merchant class). A united stand proved successful as the strike ended with a reduction in working hours and wage increases.

The effect of the strike was dramatic. Between 1936 and 1945, at least twenty-seven unions for Black workers were organized in Natal. The majority of these unions covered African and Indian workers. The sugar industry was also organized during the late 1930s, and will be reviewed in the next section. These union-building campaigns not only radicalized Indians as workers but also as oppressed citizens. The Natal Indian Congress would eventually be transformed into a radical grouping within the Congress Alliance of the 1950s. Indian trade unionists like Ponnen, Naidoo and M. P. Naicker would prove to be equally involved in these struggles to weld the Indian community to the liberation movement.

All of these regional campaigns to form non-racial and/or African unions in the 1930s shared the common political perspective, that is, the necessity to bring workers into the political and trade union struggle. Consequently, newly organized Black workers became involved in the Anti-Fascist campaigns and later in the decade in the Non-European United Front which challenged all forms of political oppression against the Black community. In 1935, when the Mussolini fascists invaded Abyssinia, dock workers in Port Elizabeth, Durban and Cape Town refused to service Italian ships. Such internationalism clearly demonstrated the workers' awareness that the struggle was not for economic gains alone.

Progressive trade unionists were not the only ones to organize workers in the 1930s. Beginning in 1938, the 'Christian-Nationalist' assault on White Afrikaner workers began in earnest; a decade later the Nationalist Party was able to come to power on the basis of a class alliance that included the new generation of White Afrikaner workers. Although this movement began with the formation of the Broederbond (Bond of Brothers) secret society back in 1918, only in the late 1930s did the Nationalists place priority on weaning the Afrikaner workers away from their working class organizations.

Although the appeal was put in ideological terms, the rise of Afrikaner nationalism on the trade union front resulted from the fact that Afrikaner workers had been greatly proletarianized in the cities during the Depression years. Most important, these workers had come increasingly to accept trade unionism along class, not racial lines. To arrest this process, a number of cultural-political-economic organizations emerged to counteract these effects of industrial capitalist development. In addition to the Broederbond, the Federasie van Afrikaanse Kultuurverenigings (Federation of Afrikaans Cultural Society), or FAK, the Reddingsdaadbond, and the Blankewerkersbeskermingsbond (White Workers Protection Society) focused their energies on the transport, garment, mining and other industries where Afrikaners worked in large numbers. These workers were reminded that they were the 'chosen people' of South Africa, destined by God to rule, and that their organization should bolster Afrikaner, not class solidarity. Communism, liberalism and especially working class solidarity in non-racial trade unions were 'foreign' and dangerous threats to the 'inherent right of the Whites to rule'.

The Christian-Nationalists' only major success on the trade union front was in the railways, where the Spoorbond claimed 16,000 members in the mid-1930s and forced the dissolution of the National Union of Railway and Harbour Servants. The railways were the single largest employer of Afrikaner labour. In 1939, one in every eleven adult male Afrikaners worked on the railways.[10] The attraction of Afrikaners to the Spoorbond had little to do with the sentiments for nationalism or protection of the *volk*, but rather concerned the protection, reservation and increase in jobs under the 'civilized labour policy' (see Chapter 4).

Elsewhere the strategy was to take over existing unions controlled by 'foreigners' rather than form competing unions. In mining, an alternative union (Die Afrikanerbond van Mynwerkers) created in 1937 failed as the Chamber of Mines concluded a closed shop agreement with the White Mine Workers Union in exchange for industrial docility. From then on the Afrikaner organizers bored from within through what was termed the Reform Movement and after assassination, sabotage, court cases and strikes, eventually took control of the White miners' union in 1948, the year the Nationalists came to power.

In the garment industry, Afrikaner employees were production workers and mainly women. But the Garment Workers Union, led by Solly Sachs, had established a sense of non-racial class solidarity that was not easy to break. Wage increases from £1 to £7 per week, a reduction in hours from 50 to 40 per week, and an increase in paid annual leave from 2 to 28 days were secured under Sachs' secretaryship of the Union. Although Sachs was continuously maligned as 'that communist Jew Sachs', he was able to win numerous libel cases in court and in some instances bankrupt these Afrikaner societies.

In other words, only where the material class interests of Afrikaner workers could be improved was Afrikaner nationalism successful. These limited gains were also made possible by a White trade union leadership in the SAT & LC that had failed to promote a serious campaign for non-racial working class unity.

Another important factor in explaining this partial success was the class composition of the Nationalist front organizations. Very few Afrikaner workers were leaders of these groups. The organizers were for the most part petty-bourgeois in class background and ambition. The interest in mobilizing Afrikaner workers was based on the desire to *control* a mass base '... with the strongest emphasis upon the effective disciplining of "the people"'.[11] Of more strategic interest was the accumulation of finance capital to promote an Afrikaner capitalism that could compete with English-speaking capitalists. The Spoorbond alone created its own savings banks in 1937 with a total capital of £170,000. In fact, many of the Nationalist industrial and financial groups to emerge in the 1940s and later were financed from the dues extracted from Afrikaner workers, a large proportion of whom were not engaged in productive labour but rather were salaried staff (as in the railways) or White overseers of Black labour (as in the mines).

On balance, the Afrikaner Nationalist attack on trade unions failed in its direct attempt to control the White labour force before 1948. But it did serve to manipulate the existing contradictions in the registered trade union movement and indirectly led to the breakup of the T & LC in the early 1950s. Once in power, the Nationalists used the Suppression of Communism Act to get rid of the 'foreign' agitators who had escaped the attacks of the previous two decades.

The War Years and the CNETU

During the war years, the geographical centre of African trade unionism returned to the industrial hub of the Transvaal province. Twenty-five years of struggle, through the various strategies discussed above, culminated in the formation of the Council of Non-European Trade Unions (CNETU, or Council hereafter) in November 1941. The Council, in turn, owed its existence to the renewed militancy of rank-and-file Black workers, faced with increased demands on their labour to satisfy the war effort and increased attacks on their standard of living. Alex Hepple describes these years: 'The new factory workers, the emerging African proletariat, suffered all the evils of urban poverty ... but brought new vigour to African labour and political organizations.'[12]

Again, these currents make sense only in terms of changes occurring in the society at large. Between 1940 and 1946, another 115,000 Africans entered the industrial labour force. The employment was increasingly in the manufacturing sector; the ratio of those working in mining to manufacturing, construction and electricity had dramatically shifted from 316:87 in 1932 to 328:321 in 1946. During these years, the unity and strength of African workers succeeded in forcing increased wages due to the state's and the employers' priority of maintaining uninterrupted production. African wages in manufacturing increased to a wartime high of 26·6 per cent of White workers' wages as compared with 19·8 per cent in the late 1930s; this ratio was to decline to 18·5 per cent again by 1957. These increases are largely explained by Wage Board investigations forced through by the initiatives of the growing African trade union movement. African workers covered by resultant minimum wage determinations increased from 1,084 to 67,632 by 1943. Real earnings also rose significantly from an average of 9·8 per cent (1931–40) to 51·8 per cent (1941–46). These aggregate indices suggest, firstly, the tremendous rate of pre-war exploitation and, secondly, the fact that gains were made only when African workers were well organized along class lines and willing to act against the system of capitalist exploitation.

In November 1941, the CNETU brought together the various strands of Transvaal African trade unions that had emerged in the previous decade. The inaugural meeting was presided over by Moses Kotane (ANC, CPSA). Discussions resolved that although the SAT & LC Constitution admitted African unions on an equal basis, the T & LC had done little to foster meaningful non-racial workers' unity. If the African and Black workers' conditions were to be properly addressed, the emphasis had to be on creating even stronger Black unions and this had to be led by a coordinating body with this as its priority. Hence, the CNETU became the new force in the Transvaal and the major industry within which to organize would be mining. At the 1941 Conference, Gana Makabeni was elected President; Dan Tloome, Vice-President; David Gosani, Secretary; and James Phillips, Trustee.

Unions large and small, strong and weak affiliated to the CNETU in the first few months. In 1944, a smaller council in Pretoria merged with the Johannesburg centre to form the Transvaal CNETU. Although there were plans to expand the CNETU on a national basis, the bulk of the affiliated membership remained on the Rand. By 1945 the Council claimed a membership of 158,000 in 119 unions; this equalled about

40 per cent of the 390,000 African workers in commerce and manufacturing.

Geographically, the CNETU affiliation broke down as follows: Johannesburg (50 unions; 80,000 members); Pretoria (15; 15,000); Bloemfontein (10; 5,000); Kimberley (5; 3,000); East London (10; 15,000); Port Elizabeth (19; 30,000) and Cape Town (10; 10,000). The following industries were represented by these workers: iron, steel and engineering; mining; commercial and distributive trades; municipal services; transport; building; laundry; timber; cement and brick and tile; food; chemicals; explosives; and tobacco.

The accuracy of these figures has often been questioned, but as always with unregistered unions in South Africa there is seldom reliable data to substantiate numerical claims. It would be fair to assume that the difficulties associated with maintaining African unions – inability to collect dues at the workplace, little finances to pay full-time organizers and officials,, and the migrant labour system, among others – would render this claim inflated if only paid-up members in good standing were considered. African unions, however, cannot be measured by such quantitative standards. The important index is the fact that at least this many African workers were at one time members of CNETU affiliates and, what is more, subjectively considered themselves a part of the working class struggle.

The CNETU had reasonably cordial relations with the T & LC during the war years. Working with T & LC progressives, the Council campaigned for government recognition of African trade unions under the IC Act. Although focusing its efforts on organizing African workers, the Council's leaders saw the body not as an end in itself but as a necessary step toward the creation of a new, truly non-racial coordinating body. James Phillips, CNETU Executive member, recalls discussions to this effect as early as 1943, but the Council on its own had no resources to initiate such an endeavour. Too many progressive trade unionists in registered unions were still committed to the belief that the T & LC could be used to realize the goal of working class unity. Another twelve years would pass before this illusion was finally shattered and SACTU could emerge to fulfil this task.

A strike wave by militant African workers between September and December 1942 brought the CNETU's attention to the immediate realities of wartime labour conditions. Often without sanction from union leaders, African workers struck for immediate wage increases after having been promised such raises in 1941. Government tactics of delaying implementation of increases, fixing minimums considered too low by workers, or actually cancelling increases led to no less than nineteen strikes in this four-month period.

State repression was not uncommon in many of these situations, although wage concessions were frequently given in the early 1940s so as not to create even greater unrest during the war effort. In September 1942, 400 Natal coal miners set fire to the company's buildings after their protests against conditions went unheeded. These included assaults by White overseers and mine policemen, overcharging in company stores, inadequate rations, concrete slabs for beds, and twelve-hour periods underground without food. Although the courts agreed that the complaints were valid, thirty-five miners were imprisoned for from one to five years for public violence.

In December, the Johannesburg City Council agreed to pay its municipal workers the largest increase recommended by Wage Boards (24s. per week, a 60 per cent increase) only after 2,000 African workers staged a one-day strike. Three weeks later, Pretoria city employees demonstrated against the city's refusal to follow suit; police were called in and killed fourteen Africans and wounded over one hundred more. A Commission of Inquiry blamed the Minister of Labour for having first exempted Johannesburg from paying the increase (thus prompting the first strike), but also added that disputes would be settled more peacefully if African trade unions were recognized under the law. Strike action occurred in the sweet, dairy, brick and railway industries as well during this period in 1942.[13]

Even the Minister of Labour Madeley had hinted that such a solution might be in the works when he broke with racist traditions and spoke at the CNETU Conference in November 1942. Begging for confidence in the government, the Minister stated, 'Recognition of your unions will come about; but you must rely on me.' Three weeks later, Madeley introduced War Measures Act No. 145 of 1942, outlawing strikes by Africans and continuing government policy of non-recognition of African unions. The WM Act introduced the 'carrot' of more Wage Board investigations and limited wage increases rather than the 'stick' of direct repression. The latter was limited to heavy penalties against union leaders who 'incited' workers to strike action.

The CNETU urged a national minimum wage of 40s. (£2) a week for all unskilled workers, but the increases allowed were in almost all cases held to 25s. to 27s. per week for workers in some thirty industries in the Transvaal. Although illegal strikes continued, the CNETU did not actively promote strike action, particularly as it tried to promote the twin policies of improving African workers' conditions at home and supporting the war effort against fascism abroad. It seems, however, that African workers in South Africa chose the former as the more crucial struggle. Whereas in the entire decade of the 1930s, 26,254 Black workers struck, accounting for a loss of 71,078 man-days (or 2·7 per striker), between 1940–45, 52,394 strikers accounted for the loss of 220,205 man-days (or 4·2 per striker).[14]

Tending towards reformist policies, which included working with the Department of Labour Officials, Gana Makabeni lost favour with the more progressive elements in the Council by 1945. In that year he was replaced as CNETU President by J. B. Marks, Chairman of the African Mine Workers Union (AMWU). Makabeni attempted to form a splinter organization – the Council of African Trade Unions – in the late 1940s, but with little lasting success. With a more politically solidified leadership, the CNETU became more directly involved in militant action as evidenced by its role in the famous Mine Workers' Strike of 1946.

Before discussing that strike, brief mention should be made of two important trade union victories elsewhere in the country. In Cape Town (and the Western Cape region), Ray Alexander and other comrades were successful in forming the Food and Canning Workers Union (FCWU) in February 1941. For the next three decades this union would serve as a model of militant trade unionism throughout South Africa as well as provide experience and leadership within SACTU in the 1950s.

In 1941, also, a long struggle in the Natal sugar industry ended successfully. In that year the first wage improvement for mill workers was granted as a result of a dispute initiated by the Natal Sugar Industry Employees Union (NSIEU). A ten shilling per month increase in that year was followed by a Wage Board determination in 1942 which with a cost of living adjustment brought the total weekly wage to 35s. (£1 15s. 0d.). These wages were still deplorable but nevertheless marked the first victory for the Union since its formation in 1937.

Sugar milling companies were scattered throughout the Natal countryside, making organization of the mixed African and Indian workers exceedingly difficult for the Union based in Durban. Even tougher was the organization of the field workers, mostly Africans, who laboured under slave conditions imposed by the sugar barons. These workers were covered by the Masters and Servants Act as agricultural workers and were not included under any trade union legislation. The

NSIEU was a registered union for Indian workers with a separate African section that worked in harmony with the registered branch. The Natal Sugar Field Workers Union covered the agricultural labourers.

Early accounts of organizing vividly portray the conditions of exploitation in this industry:

> When the organisers first went to Illovo they found the sugar workers living in conditions that could only be described as 'barbarous'. The workers were living in the most primitive corrugated iron shanties. In one section they were living in sheds that had previously been used as stables for the company's mules. Toilet facilities consisted of pit latrines and one communal tap per 150 people, often situated a quarter mile from the workers' homes.
>
> Wages for mill workers averaged £3 per month plus rations of mealie rice, mealie meal and salt; usually only sufficient to last two people a fortnight, although the family receiving these rations often consisted of from five to eight people. The working day was from nine to ten hours with no annual leave. During the 'off-season', that is, after the cane had been cut and the mills were being repaired and put in order for the next crushing season, workers regularly worked over the week-ends without overtime (*Workers Unity*, November 1961–January 1962).

In addition, child labour was prevalent and companies were notorious for planting spies in the Union and victimizing workers who dared to struggle for union representation. Even though the mills were covered by the Factories Act, employers in the rural areas disregarded the law, especially in terms of hours of work.

Again, Indian leaders such as George Ponnen, H. A. Naidoo, M. P. Naicker, R. R. Pillay and L. Ramsunder were instrumental in forming the Union back in 1937. They were assisted by P. M. Harry, Mike Diamond, P. T. Cooper and Wilson Cele, who was responsible for organizing the African section of the industry. Only total dedication led to these initial successes: meetings could not be held on company property and so workers gathered on river banks or along the seashore. Ponnen recalls, 'Many a time we risked our necks because the thugs hired by the employers waited for us with cane knives in various cane fields.'[15] For many years, these organizers spent every weekend travelling up and down the Natal coast meeting the workers; trips were even made on weekday nights in emergency situations. In 1943, when Naidoo left Durban for Cape Town, he was replaced by veteran trade unionist Errol Shanley. Shanley was on the Executive of the CPSA District Committee, Secretary of the Durban T & LC branch from 1940–47, and later a member of the South African Congress of

Democrats, in addition to holding executive positions in many unions during the 1930s and 1940s.

The African Mine Workers Strike of 1946

200,000 subterranean heroes who, by day and by night, for a mere pittance lay down their lives to the familiar 'fall of rock' and who, at deep levels, ranging 1,000 to 3,000 feet in the bowels of the earth, sacrifice their lungs to the rock dust which develops miners' phthisis and pneumonia.[16]

Occasionally . . . one event seems to crystallise the contradictions and conflicts of an entire stage of social development and the reactions to it point the way to the future development of a particular social formation. Despite its apparent failure, the 1946 African Miners' strike was such a milestone in South Africa's social and political development.[17]

The 1946 African Mine Workers' Strike was a watershed in the struggle of the people against class exploitation and oppression. The largest strike in South African history (in terms of participants), and led by *migrant* workers, those who are at the base of the cheap labour system, signalled the end of one era and the beginning of another. Our account must begin by giving the background to the 1946 strike and conclude by discussing implications for future trade union struggles.

Although the CPSA had tried throughout the early 1930s to organize these most oppressed workers, the migrant labour system and state-employer combined resistance to any union organization rendered these efforts ineffectual. At best, leaflets were issued calling on workers to form compound committees to voice complaints against an inhuman wage structure unchanged for thirty years and intolerable working conditions. Demands for a wage increase from 1s. 8d. per shift to 4s. for an eight-hour day were ignored by the mining companies through their Chamber of Mines. Police regularly arrested anyone trying to organize the 250,000 African miners during the 1930s, thereby adding to the difficulties. The SA Mine Workers Union (SAMWU), the registered body for White workers, could have assisted greatly were it not for the fact that these privileged workers regarded Africans as 'boys' or 'kaffirs' rather than fellow workers. Wage increases for Whites gave them 19s. per shift in 1933, and their strikes usually resulted from White overseers refusing to supervise additional African workers.

African migrants from the reserves received virtually no assistance from the African National Congress during the 1930s. The ANC was at that time still concentrating its energies on liberal strategies of reform and for that reason had failed to establish strong roots in the African proletariat. By the late 1930s, however, the ANC began to realize that its strength and its future depended on overcoming this alienation from the workers' struggle.

The mining companies argued that wages were sufficient because the reserve economy adequately supplemented the total subsistence of the migrant and his family. This self-serving assertion was exploded in the early 1940s. The Lansdowne Commission Report (discussed below) on the mining industry showed that the reserves suffered from declining productivity and impoverishment. Landlessness had become acute: for example, on the Ciskei Reserve, 30 per cent of the people owned no land, 60 per cent owned five cattle or less, and another 20 per cent owned nothing at all. Other reserves followed this pattern. The Fagan Commission of 1948 concluded that, 'Reserve production is but a myth.'

This rural poverty forced vast numbers of African males to become labour recruits in the mines. Between 1933 and 1939, an estimated 135,000 peasants became proletarians in the mining industry alone – representing an increase of 50 per cent of African mine labour. Another index of this incorporation of rural Africans into the dominant capitalist relations of production is reflected by the ratio of peasants to the total economically active African population over 15 years of age: in 1921, this ratio was 50 per cent and by 1946, only 17 per cent. The reserve economy by the late 1930s simply could not support the cheap labour system under capitalism. Yet, with total unconcern for the fate of its African workforce, the mining bosses continued to argue that wage increases for Africans would destroy the industry and create unrest among the White working class. The Smuts United Party government, the political front for the Chamber of Mines, continued to implement and refine the influx control measures that ensured the sale of labour power in its migrant form.

In August 1941, the Transvaal ANC, encouraged by Gaur Redebe and Edwin Mofutsanyana, convened a conference to discuss the formation of a mine workers' union. Eighty delegates from forty-one organizations, including the CNETU, the CPSA and the SAIRR resolved to organize mine workers in the mines and also on the reserves before recruitment. At this meeting, the African Mine Workers Union (AMWU) was born out of a committee of 15 members, with J. B. Marks and James Majoro as President and General Secretary respectively. The CPSA played a leading role in this initial effort as it had made the organizing of mine workers a major priority at its 1940 Party Conference.

The Union, prevented by the mining companies from organizing on mine property, proceeded cautiously but with determination. Night meetings in mining compounds were convened by organizers who took jobs at the mines; leaflets were distributed to mobilize workers around basic economic demands. Uriah Maleka, later a SACTU activist in the 1950s, first became involved in trade union work through the influence of J. B. Marks and he was one of the many young organizers to work in the mines during these years. CNETU leaders from other unions also assisted the AMWU campaigns. A few days prior to the 1946 strike, John Motsabi (African Building Workers Union) recalls climbing chains and ropes to throw leaflets into the mine compounds in the middle of the night. He also tells the story of how women food vendors would be allowed into the compound area and would wrap food in political leaflets before handing them to the workers. Through such persistent and creative methods the Union gained strength and members. By 1944, the AMWU claimed to represent 25,000 workers, each paying 1s. enrolment fee and a monthly subscription of 6d.

Among these members were approximately 2,000 African mine clerks who decided to join the Union after the Chamber of Mines ruled that clerks, like mine labourers, would be excluded from the statutory cost-of-living allowance of 1942. Majoro was a leading member of the Native Mine Clerks Association and his AMWU secretaryship enhanced contacts with potential members.

The strike wave of late 1942 discussed in the last section also indirectly influenced the development of the Union. In January 1943, the African Gas and Power Workers Union, representing men who supplied electricity to the mines, struck against Victoria Falls Power Company. The Company refused wage increases for fear of sparking off similar demands by African mine workers. In response to the imminent crisis, the Smuts Government appointed the Witwatersrand Mine Natives' Wage Commission under Justice Lansdowne to investigate wages and working conditions of African mine workers on the Rand.

The AMWU, under J. B. Marks's able leadership, presented evidence before the Commission documenting intimidation by mining company officials against union organizers and workers and in effect demanded an end to the cheap labour system. Wages in 1942 were 2s. per shift, whereas back in 1890, they had been 2s. 6d. The Union demanded regular wage increases; a statutory minimum wage and a Wage Board investigation; COLA payments; total abolition of the compound system, the racial division of the labour force and restrictions on the freedom of movement; and recognition of the AMWU.

The Lansdowne Commission reported in December 1943, and as mentioned previously, exposed the hold that the Chamber of Mines had on the Smuts government.[18] The Chamber set an 'average daily maximum wage' which no company could exceed without penalty. In 1943 over three-quarters of the 308,374 African workers received less than this daily average. Out of these starvation wages, mine workers had to subtract costs for boots, mattresses and other bare subsistence items, totalling 15 per cent of their total cash earnings. The Commission also reported an increase in first-time recruits as compared with returning recruits, again 'due to the deterioration of the Reserves'. In 1943, 64 per cent of the re-recruits returned to the mines after only five months, in contrast to the '12 months of idleness' claimed by the Chamber. Most startling was evidence showing that even *if* a worker were permanently employed in the mines, and *if* his family in the reserve had access to land (remember, 40 per cent did not) and with a good year, the family would experience a shortfall between income and expenditure of £10 4s. 4d. for surface workers and £9 4s. 10d. for underground workers. In other words, assuming a stay in the reserves of only five months per year, 41·2 per cent of African workers earning 2s. per shift or less would have a shortfall over a two-year period greater than their annual cash wage.

Against these so-called 'perfectly adequate' wages as the Chamber of Mines put it, the Lansdowne Commission recommended wages and other benefits equalling an annual increase of £10 4s. 0d. for surface workers and £11 14s. 7d. for underground workers. This would amount to a £2·6 million increase in the wage bill for the mining capitalists, no great burden on the £43·6 million working profit of 1942. The Commission refused, however, to recommend the recognition of the AMWU, resorting to the old paternalistic argument that African miners '. . . have not yet reached the stage of development which would enable them *safely* and *usefully* to employ trade unionism as a means of promoting their advancement'.

The recommendations were rejected by the state and the mining capitalists, with the result that surface wages increased by only 4d. per shift and underground workers' wages by 5d. The costs of these small increments were furthermore borne by the tax-payers, not the companies. The AMWU Conference of 1944 brought together 700 delegates from every mine, 1,300 rank-and-file workers, the ANC President-General, Dr Xuma, and many African CNETU trade unionists to discuss the Lansdowne Commission Report. Even the Paramount Chief of Pondoland, V. Porto, telegrammed his support. The AMWU termed the recommendations 'hopelessly inadequate and unsatisfactory', demanded a Wage Board inquiry and called on the labour movement to protest victimization of AMWU members.

Chamber of Mines' policy was to get rid of anyone trying to organize African workers. Spies were planted in the Union and the government added to War Measures Acts (which already prevented Africans from striking) Proclamation 1425, prohibiting gatherings of more than twenty persons on mine property. This made the holding of meetings virtually impossible, and also meant a great reduction in the finances of the Union as dues could not be easily collected and new members could not be recruited.

In short, the crisis was intensifying rapidly as the war came to an end. Food shortages in South Africa in 1945 made matters worse as compound rations were reduced and canned beef substituted for fresh meat. With their families starving on the reserves, a group of miners protested outside the compound kitchen at the Mooderfontein East Mine in March 1946; police attacked them, resulting in the death of one worker and forty were injured. Food protests were common at other mines as well.

The April 1946 AMWU Conference of 2,000 delegates drew up a new set of demands: a minimum wage of 10*s*. per day; two weeks paid annual leave; a £100 gratuity after fifteen years' service; payment of repatriation fares; and the repeal of War Measure 1425. The demands were ignored and one-day protests occurred. The CNETU Annual Conference in July resolved to give support should there be an AMWU strike, and Prime Minister Smuts decided to 'let things develop'. On 4 August 1946, at a public meeting held at Newtown Market Square, Johannesburg, over 1,000 delegates resolved to take strike action on 12 August. The Chamber prepared for the strike by discussing emergency procedures with White workers rather than negotiating with African workers.

Between 12 and 17 August, an estimated 70,000 to 100,000 African mine workers shut down totally or partially twenty-one mines. Reports vary considerably on the actual mines affected, but monthly production fell to its lowest level since 1937. Smuts declared himself 'not unduly concerned' because the strike was the result of agitators against whom 'appropriate action' was being taken. 1,600 police were placed on special duty and compounds were sealed off under armed guard.

On 13 August, the CNETU, with support from the ANC and the Transvaal and Natal branches of the Indian Passive Resistance Council, agreed to call a general strike within forty-eight hours. Police broke up the meeting, arrested J. B. Marks and proceeded to raid the Union office.[19] The same day witnessed the shooting of six strikers by police at the Sub Nigel mine, while six more were trampled to death in the panic. The following day workers at the same mine staged an underground sitdown strike and were driven up 'stope by stope, level by level' to the surface by baton-wielding police who stampeded the workers back into the compounds. Another large group of strikers marched towards the Chief Native Commissioner's Office to recover their passes in order to return to the reserves. They were surrounded and attacked by the police and then forced to return to the compounds.

The conservative Native Representative Council refused to function in protest against police violence. A CNETU mass rally in Johannesburg was banned, and James Phillips (Chairman of the Strike Committee) and Gana Makabeni were given five minutes in which to disperse a crowd of 600 supporters. By the time the strike had ended (17 August), Phillips and 87 other trade unionists had been arrested. At least 12 Africans had been killed and over 1,200 injured, yet the Chamber of Mines gave the strike only six lines in its 1946 Annual Report and the government refused to appoint a commission of inquiry. The arrested were tried under the Riotous Assemblies Act and Native Labour Regulations Acts; most were given suspended sentences of nine months. In 1946, also, the entire Executive of the CPSA was charged with sedition, but the case was quashed in 1948 for lack of evidence. The newly elected Nationalist Party would soon resort to legislation instead of the courts to silence its opponents.

The strike was without doubt defeated by the combined force of the State and the employers. In 1949, another small increase of 3d. per shift was conceded, still leaving wages lower than the Lansdowne Commission had recommended. For the AMWU, the next few years brought the collapse of the Union as organizing workers was made virtually impossible by the companies and the state. This was paralleled by the decline of African trade unionism on the Rand in the second half of the decade. By 1949, an estimated 66 African unions had become defunct and the CNETU was weakened accordingly.

The overall effect of the strike, however, went far beyond the failure

J. B. Marks, President, Council of Non-European Trade Unions; Chairman, African Mine Workers Union

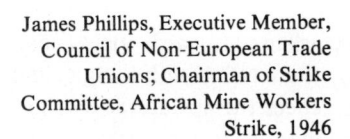

James Phillips, Executive Member, Council of Non-European Trade Unions; Chairman of Strike Committee, African Mine Workers Strike, 1946

of the Union to obtain the original demands. State-endorsed violence indicated the extent to which the miners' actions had shaken the system. When one realizes that these were *migrant* workers, the immensity of this achievement is clear. These workers held out for a week before they were overwhelmed by the superior force of a government which used machine guns and batons to drive the workers back to work.

Caught between different fractions of the bourgeoisie (the mining companies demanding a continuation of the migrant labour system and the industrial capitalists wanting a stabilized urban proletariat), the Smuts Government tried to satisfy both sections but ended up pleasing neither. This was one of the factors that led to the pro-Apartheid Nationalist Party's ascension to power in 1948 through a coalition of White Afrikaner workers, agricultural capital and the urban petty-bourgeoisie.

The strike also forged a new alliance in progressive circles with greater emphasis on mass mobilization and mass action. Previous tensions between the CPSA and the ANC were largely overcome with the emergence in the latter of a Youth League committed to a more radical theory and practice. The effect was crucial: for the first time in many years African trade unionists came in touch with ANC leaders. With the repression against and decline of African trade unions following the strike, many African trade unionists moved into key positions in the ANC. Also, following the lead set by Moses Kotane and others, CPSA members became more prominent in the ANC leadership than had been the case in the early 1930s. Finally, the post-strike period saw new relationships established between the different organizations of nationally oppressed groups. The maturity of this inter-racial solidarity would be christened with the formation of the Congress Alliance in 1955.

These significant shifts were inevitably oriented towards the African working class. Mass action demanded by the ANC Youth League had to be rooted in the urban proletariat to reflect the structural changes that had characterized the political economy. It was, indeed, the African trade union movement, with its unmistakable class consciousness, that radicalized the ANC and put it at the centre of the non-racial liberation movement that has led the struggle since the early 1950s. Just as the 1922 White mine workers strike had precipitated a reactionary alliance between White capital and White labour, the 1946 strike created the conditions for a progressive alliance between all those segments of South African society that suffer both class exploitation and national oppression. For these reasons, it would not be an exaggeration to say that the African Mine Workers' Strike radically altered the course of South African history.

The Suppression of Communism Act

What the Nationalists had failed to do by means of slander, intrigue and subversion, they accomplished by an act of parliament. Although the explicit aim of the Suppression of Communism Act (SC Act) was the banning of the Communist Party of South Africa, the scope and implementation of the Act reveals the unmistakable goal of attacking the progressive trade union movement which was determined to create non-racial working class unity.

The SC Act was only one of a whole barrage of draconian legislation enacted by the Nationalists in 1949–50. The Unemployment Insurance Act (1949) excluded the majority of Africans from benefits; the Railways and Harbours Amendment Act (1949) enforced racial segregation on the trains; the Prohibition of Mixed Marriages Act (1949) and Immorality Act (1950) outlawed sexual relations in any manner between persons of different 'racial' groups; and the Group Areas Act (1950) imposed compulsory residential segregation on Whites, Coloureds, Malays, Asians and Africans. Amidst the suffering and repression resulting from these and subsequent Acts, the solidarity of all oppressed national groupings was also enhanced as an unintended consequence.

The SC Act, and as amended, had little to do with communism *per se*. A loosely-defined 'communism' in the Act allowed the government to ban organizations and individuals deemed to be furthering the aims of communism. In effect, one was (and still is) a 'Communist' if the government said so, and through a 1951 Amendment all ex-Communists were made subject to the Act, i.e. 'once a Communist, always a Communist'. Individuals so designated could be forced to resign from holding public office, from belonging to specified organizations, from attending gatherings, or from leaving defined areas. In 1966 the Act was extended to cover Namibia (South West Africa), and in 1976 the terms of the Act became a part of the Internal Security Amendment Act.

Let us now discover what exactly constitutes 'communism' in South Africa. According to the 1950 Act:

'Communism' means the doctrine of Marxian socialism as expounded by Lenin and Trotsky, the Third Communist International (the Comintern) or the Communist Information Bureau (Cominform) or any related form of that doctrine expounded or advocated in the Union for the promotion of the fundamental principles of that doctrine and includes, in particular, any doctrines or scheme

(a) which aims at the establishment of a despotic system of government based on the dictatorship of the proletariat under which one political organization only is recognized and all other political organizations are suppressed or eliminated; or
(b) which aims at bringing about any political, industrial, social or economic change within the Union by the promotion of disturbance or disorder, by unlawful acts or omissions or by means which include the promotion of disturbance or disorder, or such acts or omissions or threat; or
(c) which aims at bringing about any political, industrial, social or economic change within the Union in accordance with the directions or under the guidance of or in co-operation with any foreign government or any foreign or international institution whose purpose or one of whose purposes (professed or otherwise) is to promote the establishment within the Union of any political, industrial, social or economic system identical with or similar to any system in operation in any country which has adopted a system of government such as is described in paragraph (a); or
(d) which aims at the encouragement of feelings of hostility between the European and the Non-European races of the Union the consequences of which are calculated to further the achievement of any object referred to in paragraph (a) or (b).[20]

Those 'listed' as Communists had virtually no recourse to the courts, especially with the passage of amendments designed to cover 'loopholes' in the principal Acts. Organizations declared unlawful had to cease all their activities and property would be liquidated. Other organizations suspected of furthering the aims of communism as defined could be investigated – i.e. their premises could be searched, members interrogated and documents seized.

Attendance at gatherings was increasingly circumscribed for individuals falling under the application of the Act. An Appellate Court decided that a person must be notified in advance and given the right to show cause why such an order should not be issued, but this was overruled by the Amendment of 1954 which abolished the necessity of advance warning. The 1954 changes also prohibited the playing of recorded messages of banned persons at meetings. It also specified that a 'listed' or convicted person was prohibited from standing for election to Parliament or Provincial Councils.

The latter Amendment represented an emergency action made necessary by banned trade unionist Ray Alexander's decision to run for the elected position of Native Representative in 1954. Sam Kahn and Brian Bunting, both CPSA members, had been forced to vacate this position and despite a slander campaign against Alexander, she was elected by a large majority. She was physically prevented from taking her seat in Parliament by police who then issued notice to her prohibiting her candidacy.

The Minister of Justice was empowered to further extend prohibition on gatherings by preventing any or all gatherings in given locations for specified periods of time. In 1962, during the height of repression, the Johannesburg City Hall steps and the Grand Parade in Cape Town were so designated. In effect, many banned persons were prevented from attending social gatherings, defined in such a way as to include bioscopes (cinemas), sporting events and even funerals. Further amendments in subsequent years made it an offence to communicate with a 'listed' or banned person, and such persons were further prevented from practising as advocates, attorneys or notaries, or even from assisting other professionals in these fields.

Although the scope of the SC Act allowed the government to victimize anyone, the application of the Act in the early 1950s was primarily directed against progressive trade unionists. The original draft of the Bill had in fact included provisions for the banning of trade unions, but opposition from registered unions led the government to exempt all unions covered by the IC Act. In other words, African trade unions and all progressive unionists holding leadership positions in registered unions were outside the scope of these exemptions. With little or no recourse to the courts, these trade unionists bore the brunt of the legislation between 1951 and 1954, as the government attempted to convert the South African trade union movement into a docile preserve of 'Christian-Nationalist' ideology and control.

The first union victims of the SC Act were J. B. Marks (President, AMWU), Issy Wolfson (Tailoring) and Solly Sachs (Garment); the latter two, as Executive members of the T & LC, were removed from their elected positions. The T & LC reluctantly called a conference of registered trade unions to discuss the effects of the Act on the trade union movement. African leaders were prevented from attending the discussions, and the T & LC as an organization in the final analysis did nothing to oppose these fascist measures. Progressive unions – garment, food and canning and laundry – staged short protest strikes, but effective action was obviously limited with the lack of T & LC support.

Solly Sachs, who had thwarted efforts by the Afrikaner nationalists to take control of the union, was unable to resist this legislative attack. Ordered to resign from his position in the Garment Workers Union on 8 May 1952, Sachs defied the legislation and spoke to a large GWU protest meeting whereupon he and many workers were arrested after a baton charge by the police. A six month sentence was suspended and Sachs left South Africa a dejected man. His valiant contribution to the workers' struggle was recognized by the rank-and-file however, as they elected his understudy Johanna Cornelius by a 4-to-1 margin over the Nationalist opposition. James Phillips, Chairman of the Coloured Branch of the GWU and CNETU Executive member was also banned in June 1953.

Similar victimization against Piet Huyser, National Organizer of the Amalgamated Union of Building Trade Workers of South Africa, led Alex Hepple to speak for all such banned persons:

The convenient Supression of Communism Act has provided the Government with the means to clear the path for the disrupters. In the process the Union suffers. It loses [men and women] with a fine record of service. [Their] achievements on behalf of [their] fellow workers are contemptuously ignored ... the [Act] will hold the workers in chains. Without their trusted and experienced leaders and cowed by the fear of persecution and tyranny, workers of all races will be completely at the mercy of those who wish to exploit them.[21]

Hepple goes on to point out that contrary to the government propaganda regarding the 'threat' these banned persons represented, each one of them had been democratically elected by rank-and-file workers. Union leaders in and of themselves could not possibly threaten the society as they, unlike the ruling class, are directly responsible to the masses and effective only if supported by that proletarian base.

Even the Minister of Labour admitted that the banned leaders 'were probably among the most competent trade union organizers in the country', and had done 'a great deal for their members', but he added that the purpose of the legislation was to preclude those persons from controlling the unions.[22] The Afrikaner newspaper, *Die Bouwerker*, was even more explicit when it declared that trade unionists faced with banning orders could absolve themselves by stating that 'they are opposed to the full legal recognition of trade unions for Natives'.[23]

By the end of 1955, *fifty-six* trade unionists had been driven out of their positions under the SC Act. These included twenty-eight Whites, seventeen Africans, seven Coloureds, and four Asians. From registered unions, nine of the twenty-six Executive members of the T & LC had been among this group. Through decades of struggle many of these persons had laid the basis for the formation of SACTU as the first non-racial trade union coordinating body, yet they were prevented, except for underground activity, from openly contributing after 1955.

Among these banned leaders, certain persons deserve special mention for the role they played in unions that became the strength of SACTU and/or their individual behind-the-scenes contribution to SACTU strategy and tactics.

Ray Alexander (see Chapter 9).

H. T. (Harry) Gwala began trade union organizing work amongst Africans in the distributive trade, chemical building and brick and tile industries in the mid-1940s. Throughout the years, whenever he was not banned, he led the SACTU Local Committee in the Pietermaritzburg area and was also very active in the ANC. Gwala served eight years on Robben Island and after his release took up trade union work again. In 1977, he was re-arrested and imprisoned for life and remains one of the most respected militants in South African trade union history.

Becky Lan replaced Ray Alexander as General Secretary of the Food and Canning Workers Union, when the latter was banned in 1953. Although not 'listed' as a Communist under the Act, Lan received a two-year ban on attending gatherings in 1954. She was banned from all trade union activity in 1956, making her the sixth FCWU leader to be removed from office since 1950.

J. B. Marks was President of the AMWU and Chairman of the CNETU. Of the many African leaders, Marks was perhaps the most influential in bringing younger persons into the trade union and political struggle. Active in the CPSA and the ANC, Marks acted as adviser to SACTU following 1955, and frequently contributed analysis and editorial comment in *Workers Unity*, the SACTU paper.

A. P. Mati was one of the veteran leaders in Port Elizabeth. He served as organizer of the Laundry Workers Union, the African Commercial and Distributive Workers Union, Secretary of the SA Railway and Harbour WU. At the time of his banning in October, 1953, he was ex-Chairman of the ANC in Port Elizabeth. Mati provided political and trade union training for the militant corps of ANC-SACTU comrades who led the Congress campaigns in the 1950s.

John Motsabi joined the union movement in 1942, as a member of the Furniture, Bedding and Mattress WU. He soon became actively involved in the Building and Allied WU in the mid-1940s until his banning orders were issued in 1953. Once an Executive member of the CNETU, Motsabi worked closely with Elias Motsoaledi, Isaac Moumakoe and George Maeka, also CNETU Executive members banned in the early 1950s. As Transvaal ANC Provincial Secretary, Motsabi often brought the workers' struggles into the national liberation movement and continued to assist SACTU following his banning.

Mike Muller served as General Secretary of the Textile Workers Industrial Union from 1950 until banned in 1953. He had previously held the same position in the Pretoria CNETU. From an Afrikaner background, Mike rejected White supremacy and assisted in organizing African workers on both trade union and political fronts. He acted as adviser to SACTU following 1955, but later deserted the movement.

George Ponnen was the first Natal trade unionist to be banned under the Act. Following his organizing work in the 1930s, Ponnen became secretary of unions in rope and mat, tea, coffee and chicory, twine and bag, brewing and mineral water industries. He was also full-time honorary secretary to the Tobacco WU and honorary adviser to Natal unions in tin, food and canning, broom and brush, hospital, railways and harbours, chemical, distributive and municipal industries and undertakings. On the political front, Ponnen and his militant wife, Vera, defied the custom of South African society and married across 'racial' lines. Both were actively involved in SACTU campaigns in the 1950s and 1960s, bringing many younger persons into the movement and providing their apartment in Durban for secret SACTU meetings.

Arnold Selby came from a White working-class background. He worked in many industries, including mining, until the early 1940s, when he joined the CPSA and subsequently devoted his energies to trade union organizing. Between 1945 and 1950, Selby was National Organizer for the Sweet, Distributive and Textile workers. An outspoken critic of Apartheid, Selby fled South Africa shortly after the State of Emergency in 1960 and continued to assist SACTU in international solidarity work.

Dan Tloome became active in trade union work in the 1930s. A CPSA member, he served as Vice-President and later as Secretary of the CNETU until he was banned in September 1953. In 1949, Tloome was elected to the ANC National Executive and was very much involved in the planning of the Defiance Campaign of 1952. Following his banning, Tloome became printer and publisher of *Liberation*, a theoretical journal that guided Congress Alliance, including trade union, policy in the mid-1950s. Tloome has continued to assist in SACTU work throughout the years.

Gladstone Tshume was another of the veterans of the Port Elizabeth area as organizer of the African Textile workers. Bettie du Toit has said of Tshume that he '. . . always considered the workers to be the vanguard of the democratic movement and showed towards them a spirit of humility'.[24] Banned in October 1953, Tshume then used his lay preacher position to benefit as his church became the venue for numerous political speeches and organizing efforts. He died of a heart attack in 1957, and was given an ANC funeral. He remained a legend to the Port Elizabeth comrades due to his consistent challenging of the Special Branch police, whom he referred to as 'hired spies' and 'rapists of human thought'.

Bettie du Toit was an Afrikaner trade unionist who became a CPSA member and progressive NEC member of the T & LC. Du Toit was involved in textile, food and canning and laundry unions, and was one of the few Whites to participate as a volunteer in the Defiance Campaign in 1952. She was banned in 1952, and in exile has recently written *Ukubamba Amadolo: Workers' Struggles in the South African Textile Industry* (1978).

Eli Weinberg came to South Africa in the late 1920s as a political exile from Latvia. In Cape Town and Port Elizabeth, Weinberg organized and represented garment and sweet workers. From 1943 until his banning ten years later, Weinberg served as General Secretary of the National Union of Commercial Travellers; he also sat on the T & LC Executive during this time. Following his removal from trade union office, he played an invaluable role as a political photographer; his photos provide a visual record of the workers' and people's struggle against Apartheid and class exploitation. Weinberg also contributed his trade union experience to SACTU work in the 1950s and 1960s.

The banning of these and many other principled trade union leaders between 1951 and 1954 greatly facilitated the move to the right within the Trades and Labour Council leadership, the final episode that preceded the formation of SACTU.

The Betrayal of Principle

The registered trade union movement became a microcosm of the two contending political currents that characterized South African life between 1947 and 1954. The gap between White labour aristocrats and the African proletariat widened during these eight years, and the progressive T & LC leaders that had bridged this gap since 1930 were by 1954 forced to concede the T & LC to the right-wing. The fact that it took that many years for the White supremacists to assert their control is itself testimony to the role this progressive minority played within the T & LC and out of proportion to the rank-and-file base among registered workers. On the other hand, some would suggest that it was unrealistic to believe that the T & LC could be the united home for all workers, and that African trade unionists were anxious to create a new, non-racial coordinating body long before SACTU emerged.

Early signs of a T & LC shift from its long-standing principle of trade union unity and call for full recognition of African trade unions can be traced to September 1945. An NEC resolution calling for greater participation for African unions on Industrial Councils was opposed by White union leaders in mining, iron and steel and certain sections of the transport industry. In 1946 the NEC itself, and with no prior consultation with its affiliates, expressed its hostility and distance from African workers when it cabled the World Federation of Trade Unions to report on the Mine Workers' strike. The cable read:

Appears natives were misled by irresponsible people. Police methods controlling strike drastic but warranted. Such action was necessary to maintain law and order and prevent chaos.

A. P. Mati

Dan Tloome

Early trade union victims of the 1950 Suppression of Communism Act

Gladstone Tshume

Eli Weinberg

Although affiliates subsequently forced a retraction, this attitude of the T & LC leadership was a signal of things to come.

Until the Nationalists came to power in 1948, the T & LC principles withstood growing internal opposition from pro-Nationalist unions. At the 1947 T & LC Annual Conference, L. J. van den Berg (Secretary, Iron and Steel Trades Association) and George McCormick (Secretary, Engine Drivers and Firemens Union) were defeated in their attempt to amend the Constitution in order to bar affiliation of African unions by a vote of 115 to 30. This prompted the first 'break-away' as six Pretoria unions left the T & LC and formed the Coordinating Council of South African Trade Unions (CCSATU) in 1948. The new body denied affiliation to any union allowing full rights of membership to African, Coloured or Indian workers. By 1954 the CCSATU represented 13,000 workers in 7 affiliated unions. Thus, on the eve of the Nationalists' rise to power, Afrikaner nationalism had scored its first, although numerically limited, success against a united trade union movement.

Following the election, the imminence of new Apartheid trade union legislation (see Chapter 4) led the T & LC Executive to embark on a campaign of self-imposed betrayals that would culminate in the dissolution of the T & LC six years later. Contrary to T & LC resolutions, President Calder opened the September 1948 CNETU conference by proposing parallelism between African and registered unions. Each segment, rather than being united in one body, would have its own coordinating body with the paternalistic proviso that European trade unions '. . . will assist you in the improvement of your conditions and see to it that you get a square deal'. J. B. Marks, President of the CNETU, was quick to respond:

We emphatically say that the right to organize into trade unions is the birthright of all workers, irrespective of their race or colour . . . It is the desire of the Council to see one powerful coordinating body that will embrace all workers . . . and it is to this end that our Council is working.[25]

One year later, the T & LC Executive formed a Sub-Committee to 'examine its relations with African trade unions'. In order to assess the views of affiliated unions, the 'Unity Committee' (as it was erroneously called) sent out a questionnaire to registered and African unions: only three of thirty-seven African unions bothered to respond, the rest expressing their contempt of parallelism through silence. At the April 1950 T & LC Conference, a card vote yielded a vote of 61,716 to

55,580 in favour of a resolution calling for a separate consultative committee for African trade unions under T & LC guidance. Yet, hypocritically, delegates voted unanimously in favour of inclusion of African unions under the IC Act.

The T & LC 'Unity Committee' was not really concerned with African trade unions at all. Rather, the emphasis focused on the declining T & LC membership and what could be done to reverse that trend. From a base of 111 unions representing 184,000 workers in 1947, the numbers were reduced to 52 unions representing 82,600 by 1952. In 1949 and 1950 alone, at least twenty unions representing 25,884 workers left the fold. Led by the boilermakers, ironmoulders, woodworkers and electricians, many unions in this second massive defection formed yet another coordinating body – the S.A. Federation of Trade Unions (SAFTU) in 1951. SAFTU claimed sixteen unions and 80,000 workers in that year. Most of these unions disaffiliated because of the T & LC's 'African policy' and also because of their fear of being implicated with progressive trade unionists being purged under the SC Act. At the T & LC-sponsored conference of registered unions called to discuss the SC Act, fifty delegates from the CCSATU walked out in protest when a motion calling for support of the Nationalists was defeated; another group followed soon after when cooperation with the government was similarly rejected.

Progressives on the 'Unity Committee' could no longer participate in a body that concerned itself only with unity of registered unions and pandered to White prejudice. In September 1950 the NEC decided that it would support the call for exclusion of African trade unions at the 1951 conference. Seven NEC members voted against the motion, including Bettie du Toit and Eli Weinberg. Du Toit charged the T & LC with introducing Apartheid in the trade union movement at a time when the entire international community was condemning it. Weinberg resigned from the 'Unity Committee' in January 1951, stating:

It is obvious to me that if I remain a member of the Unity Committee, I shall be accepting full responsibility for the proposals and recommendations which are contrary to my own judgment and which, in my opinion, strike at the very roots of trade union unity.[26]

Nor were African leaders in the CNETU taken in by the T & LC's lack of principles. In response to the proposal for a parallel body, the CNETU rightly pointed out that 'dividing the T & LC on racial lines is a strange way of uniting it'. With political foresight, the CNETU called instead for the creation of a new trade union centre that would be open to registered and unregistered unions. An amendment by Jacob Nyaose (African Bakers and Confectioners Union) calling for exclusion of White workers in such a body was soundly defeated, showing once again the advanced class consciousness of the African proletariat. Unity had also become a necessity as well as an ideal as the Urban Areas Act of 1950 was being used to remove African union offices from the Transvaal cities.

Thus, by 1954, the registered trade union movement had disintegrated into five coordinating bodies (the SAT & LC, SAFTU, CCSATU, the Western Province Federation of Trade Unions, and the Federal Consultative Committee of Railway Unions). The CNETU had maintained its strength at 22 unions representing approximately 10,000 workers.

1954 was a year of conferences that changed the course of South African trade union history. The CNETU held its annual conference in April, with the two-fold task of fighting the Native Labour Act (1953) and the retrograde actions of the T & LC. On the latter question, George Maeka (President, CNETU) outlined the Council's position:

It is high time that our Council should take the initiative to bring about a joint struggle by all unions who stand by the principle of workers' unity . . . We must tell the T & LC and other trade unions quite bluntly that (creating a body for registered unions only) is an illusion. Racialism is poison to the trade union movement. It is the very weapon that the government is using to destroy the unions. You agree to exclude Africans in order to get the racialists and nationalists to come to your conference.[27]

The conference referred to in Maeka's statement was that called by the T & LC 'Unity Committee' for early May in which all registered unions and coordinating bodies would search for a common base (of White supremacy) in order to re-unite the many coordinating bodies in existence. Only the CNETU was refused an invitation to these May meetings in Cape Town. At this conference, progressives were defeated in their attempt to pass resolutions against Nationalist legislation and, what is more despicable, they were prevented from bringing Africans into the conference deliberations. The FCWU had refused to attend because the African FCWU had not been extended an invitation.

At another CNETU meeting in August, the Council again emphatically rejected parallelism and instead called for a mass campaign to organize the unorganized. 'Workers' Councils of Action'

Witwatersrand Workers' Council of Action Conference, 1954

Front row, left to right: J. Ndamoyi, (unidentified), G. Kika, C. Sibande.
Back row: P. Beyleveld, B. Lan, L. Massina, (unidentified), L. Levy, W. Mkwayi, A. Mphahlele, (unidentified), O. Mpetha (*lower picture*)

THEY FOUGHT DISSOLUTION OF T.L.C.

were to be established throughout South Africa to realize this goal. As had been said throughout the decades of struggle, White workers would agree to unity only in the face of well-organized and strong African unions.

The Second T & LC 'Unity Conference' was held in Durban on 5 October 1954 where it was agreed to form the SA Trade Union Council (SATUC) with a colour-bar Constitution that would exclude African trade unions from affiliation. Speaker after speaker claimed that it was necessary to forsake principles in the short run for the sake of White workers' unity. Ruling out of order an amendment by the National Union of Distributive Workers that would have allowed African union affiliation, the Conference voted 184,814 to 31,977 to form the SATUC. Of the 19 unions voting against the motion, 14 issued the following statement after the vote:

> We deeply regret the decision to exclude African unions from the proposed Trade Union Council. . . . The interests of the African workers are in the long run no different from the interests of the Coloured, European and Indian workers. It is to the advantage of the employers and their Government to divide the workers. Division is a policy directed by the bosses and not the workers' interests. . . . We the undersigned delegates are determined to carry on a struggle against the policy of racial discrimination and work for the achievement of a single trade union organization embracing all sections of the working class.[28]

The fourteen unions were as follows: FCWU and African FCWU; TWIU and African TWIU; the Food, Canning and Allied WU; Chemical WU and African CWU; Twine and Bag WU; SA Canvas and Rope WU (Cape Town); NUDW; Jewellers and Goldsmiths (Jhb); and the National Baking Industrial Union. All but the last three became SACTU affiliates after 1955.

Not only were African trade unions excluded from the new TUC, but the two African representatives of T & LC affiliated unions in attendance at the October conference were prevented from addressing the delegates. B. J. Caddy, Chairman, asked any African delegates to leave the hall, but then added, 'I don't think there will be any objection to them taking seats at the back of the hall and remaining as observers.' Such was the degree of racist contempt that the White aristocracy of labour held for the exploited African workers.

Among the progressives, many of whom had fought for decades for principled working class unity in the T & LC, the responses ranged as follows:

Nancy Dick (Banned Secretary, TWIU, Cape Town)
Those who voted for these measures have done so with their eyes open. Their resolution, were it not so tragic, would be laughable Whilst accepting that unity of all workers is the true principle of trade unionism, they did not have the guts to stand by this principle. Having seen the light, they prefer the dark.

Arnold Selby (Banned TWIU leader)
It is a cowardly capitulation to the Nationalists who are out to break the trade union movement . . . Posterity will judge those who have betrayed this principle (of unity).

Joey Fourie (Banned Secretary, Hairdresser Employees Union, Cape Town)
To me the formation of the new TUC is one of the most colossal sell-outs of the working class in this country. The remarkable part of it is that our trade union leaders have not learned that appeasement of fascism and fascists has never yet paid dividends.

Eli Weinberg (Banned NUCT leader; ex-T & LC Executive)
The dissolution of the T & LC is an achievement of the reactionary section who have endeavoured during the past few years to appease the Malanite race theorists. It was only possible through government aid in removing many of the devoted and experienced leaders. New brave determined leaders are arising in the trade union movement. In the long run the Nationalists and their lackeys, the splitters, will be defeated.

Ray Alexander (Banned Secretary, FCWU)
There is obviously a strong section of organized workers which has not succumbed to the pressure of the Government and the racialists. To this section I say: 'Do not be afraid, have courage, the future lies with you. Go forward.'

African trade unions leaders in the CNETU also condemned the dissolution but placed greater emphasis on the future:

Isaac Moumakoe (Banned Secretary, African Milling WU; Vice-President, CNETU).
It is a step towards the transformation of the present trade unions into government-controlled bodies under police supervision. It is urgent that workers establish a trade union movement reaffirming the basic trade union principle which fundamentally conflicts with Apartheid.

John Motsabi (Ex-Executive Member, CNETU)
Parallelism is basically equivalent to apartheid . . . It is imperative that the Non-European Trade Unions come together with the democratic progressive White trade unions to form a militant workers' federation, free from the opportunism which has hitherto crippled the struggle.[29]

The banning of the T & LC progressives under the SC Act had eliminated the largest obstacle to introducing the colour bar within the registered coordinating bodies. But for the reactionaries this victory only hastened the advancement of workers' unity. In a word, the dissolution of the T & LC created the last of the necessary conditions for the emergence of the South African Congress of Trade Unions.

NOTES

1. Many books have been written detailing early South African trade unionism, although most focus undue attention on White unions and workers – e.g. B. Weinbren and I. Walker, *2,000 Casualties*, Natal Witness, 1961. More comprehensive treatments can be found in E. Roux, *Time Longer than Rope*, University of Wisconsin, Madison, 1964, and E. S. Sachs, *The Anatomy of Apartheid*, Collet's (Publishers) Ltd, London, 1965. The one book that incorporates trade union and political history and is essential reading is H. J. and R. E. Simons (Ray Alexander), *Class and Colour in South Africa, 1850–1950*, Penguin, Harmondsworth, 1969.
2. Quoted in *South African Labour Bulletin*, vol. 1, no. 6 (September–October 1974), p. 21. The following discussion on the ICU draws heavily from this issue of *SALB* and Sheridan W. Johns III, 'Trade Union, Political Pressure Group or Mass Movement? The Industrial and Commercial Workers' Union of Africa', *Protest and Power in Black Africa*, Ed., R. I. Rotberg and A. A. Mazrui, Oxford University Press, New York, 1970. An autobiographical account of the ICU is provided by Clements Kadalie in his *My Life and the ICU*, Frank Cass & Co. Ltd, London, 1970.
3. Kadalie assisted the Pact Government to come to power in 1924 by working against the re-election of the Smuts United Party. When the new Government quickly put into effect the Industrial Conciliation Act of 1924, which excluded African workers from the definition of 'employees' under the Act, Kadalie realized that he had been duped by the Hertzog Government. His support for the Labour Party component of the Pact Government, with its slogan 'Workers of the World Unite for a White South Africa' reflects Kadalie's political confusion.
4. Simons and Simons, op. cit., p. 371.
5. This information draws heavily on Dan O'Meara, 'Analysing Afrikaner Nationalism: The "Christian-National" Assault on White Trade Unionism in South Africa, 1934–1948', *African Affairs*, vol. 77, no. 306 (January 1978) and O'Meara, 'The African Mine Workers' Strike and the Political Economy of South

Africa', *Journal of Commonwealth and Comparative Politics*, vol. XIII, no. 2 (July 1975).
6. The 'Native Republic' thesis refers to the change in the CPSA political programme for South Africa, wherein the goal was shifted from that of an immediate transformation to socialism led by the White working class to the creation of a democratic, independent Native Republic led by the African majority. In this context, the struggle was to be directed against the imperialism of the Boers and the British.
7. Simons and Simons, op. cit., p. 456.
8. ibid., p. 511.
9. Interview, George Ponnen.
10. O'Meara, 1978, p. 65.
11. Quoted in A. Hepple, *Trade Unions in Travail*, Unity Publications (Pty.) Ltd, Johannesburg, 1954.
12. A. Hepple, *South Africa: A Political and Economic History*, Pall Mall Press, London, 1966.
13. A detailed analysis of the 1942 strike wave is found in M. Stein, 'Black Trade Unionism During the Second World War', unpublished article. Warwick University.
14. O'Meara, 1975, p. 153.
15. Interview, George Ponnen.
16. Statement by Sol Plaatjes, first General-Secretary of the ANC, 1914.
17. O'Meara, 1975, p. 146.
18. For example, revenues from the gold mining companies paid for approximately 50 per cent of raw materials imported for South African industry. Hence, the Chamber of Mines argued that the migrant, cheap labour system was essential for the maintenance of economic stability and growth.
19. Eli Weinberg, an adviser to the AMWU, says that the 'nerve centre' of the Union was in a secret location during the strike. Interview, Eli Weinberg.
20. *Laws Affecting Race Relations in South Africa, 1948-1976*, compiled by M. Horrell, SAIRR, Natal Witness, Pietermaritzburg, 1978.
21. Hepple, 1954, pp. 53, 62.
22. Simons and Simons, op. cit., p. 598.
23. Hepple, 1954, p. 60.
24. Bettie du Toit, *Ukubamba Amadolo: Workers' Struggles in the South African Textile Industry*, Onyx Press, London, 1978, p. 133.
25. Both quotations are from the *Guardian* (Cape Town), 9 September 1948.
26. ibid., 25 January 1951.
27. ibid., 1 April 1954.
28. *Saamtrek*, 8 October 1954.
29. *Advance*, 21 October 1954.

3 SACTU APPEARS UPON THE SCENE

The Building of a Non-Racial Trade Union Movement

For African workers in particular, the emergence of SACTU in March 1955 represented a new thrust in the history of workers' struggles in South Africa. As one African trade unionist described it, 'In the factory, the birth of SACTU was like rays of sunshine piercing through the dark.'[1] The 'dark' referred to here is the period during which the Trades and Labour Council (T & LC) dominated the trade union movement in South Africa. Although the T & LC Constitution had always stated that membership was open to all 'bona fide' trade unions, the needs of the majority of workers, the African workers, had never been properly served by this body.

Apart from the efforts of the Communist Party of South Africa (CPSA) in the 1930s and 1940s, and the activities of the Council of Non-European Trade Unions (CNETU) in the Transvaal, there had not been any systematic attempt to organize African workers into trade unions. For all progressive-thinking workers and trade unionists, the dissolution of the T & LC therefore opened up new possibilities to determine the kind of trade unionism necessary for South Africa – that based on the principles of equality and unity of *all* workers in the struggle against class exploitation and national oppression.

From October 1954 until March 1955 a small group of progressive trade unionists threw all of their efforts into building this kind of trade unionism. The fourteen unions which had opposed the dissolution of the T & LC, representing workers in shops, chemicals, food, canning, textiles, jewellers, goldsmiths, baking, canvas and rope, tin, twine and bag industries, set up an interim committee immediately following the dissolution. At its first meeting, the committee passed the following resolution:

In pursuance of our desire to retain the principles embodied in the Constitution of the T & LC (1949) we delegates who attended the recent conference and voted against the resolution to dissolve the SAT & LC, agree on the establishment of a committee whose object shall be (a) to co-ordinate the future plans of the dissenting unions; and (b) to seek to organize a conference with the object of establishing a Trade Union centre as soon as possible, but not later than April, 1955, based upon the principle of non-discrimination on the grounds of race, colour or creed.[2]

The committee was renamed the Trade Union Coordinating Committee (TUCC). Among its members were many who later became SACTU activists – Don Mateman (TWIU), Aaron Mphahlele (A-TWIU), Cleopas Sibande (A-TWIU), Leon Levy (NULCDW) and Leslie Massina (A-LCDWU). From the beginning, the principles on which the committee was established were stated clearly:

Only a strong trade union movement can fulfil its task of defending and advancing the workers' interests. Only a united trade union movement can be strong. The interests of the African workers are in the long run no different from the interests of the Coloured, European and Indian workers.

It is to the advantage of the employers and their government to divide the workers in this country. Workers' salvation lies in unity and it is our duty to bring the knowledge home to our fellow workers.

We are determined to carry on a struggle against the policy of racial discrimination and to work for the achievement of a single Trade Union organization embracing all sections of the working class.

An extremely significant step was taken when the TUCC invited representatives of the CNETU to one of its earliest meetings. At that meeting, a resolution was passed proposing that the planned conference be called jointly by the two bodies. For, although the CNETU had concentrated on organizing Black workers exclusively, many of its leaders had since the mid-1940s seen the necessity for a united trade union movement. Both groups were firm in their commitment to this principle of unity; they refused to submit to the government and employers' attempts to divide the working class along racial lines. In South Africa, to defend this principle requires relentless struggle against a ruling class which has continued, by means of specific racist legislation, to smash any such attempts at unity. However, this principle has remained throughout as one of the fundamental policies of what is now known as SACTU.

The SA Trade Union Council (later TUCSA), on the other hand, accepted the government's Apartheid divisions and consciously embarked on a programme of excluding African trade unions from its ranks. In spite of this, the TUCC demonstrated an attitude that also became the basis of SACTU's policy towards TUCSA in later years.

The desire of the Committee is complete unity in the Trade Union movement, and it will endeavour to cooperate with any other body, which though differing on constitutional principles, is pledged to the same end. There is a great measure of common interest between the trade unions associated with this movement and those participating in the work of the Trade Union Council and it is sincerely hoped that close cooperation will be achieved on matters which affect all sections.[3]

For the moment though, the Committee was concentrating all its energies on preparations for the birth of the new trade union centre. Events moved quickly from October to March. Regular meetings of the TUCC were held and there was concern on the part of every member to maintain continuity, especially in the fight against the proposed legislation, the IC Bill. African trade unionists in particular wanted no delay in calling a conference to establish a new body which would represent their interests and fight for their rights as workers. The activities of the Committee during these five months centred on three areas: the planning of the conference; the revising of the Constitution of the T & LC (1949) to fit the objectives of the proposed new body, and discussion of how best to organize opposition against the IC Bill. The Committee also concentrated its efforts on popularizing the idea of a new trade union coordinating body; they drew up pamphlets to acquaint workers with the issues at stake and arranged meetings with non-affiliated African trade unions. The necessity to take the issues directly to workers at the factory level was expressed continually.

SACTU's Inaugural Conference – A Watershed in the Struggle Against Apartheid

The aspirations of progressive trade unionists from all parts of South Africa were finally realized on 5 and 6 March 1955 in Johannesburg at the Inaugural Conference of SACTU. Here, a handful of workers announced their intention of organizing the enslaved workers in the mines, docks, railways and on the farms, as well as in every factory and workshop. They announced, in fact, their intention to attack and bring down the bastion of White supremacy. Some 66 delegates from 33 Unions were present, representing a total of 41,253 workers of *all* races. As well, three Unions representing 11,350 had observer status and a further 51 representatives attended as either observer delegates or fraternal delegates from other organizations.

By far the largest group of workers represented came from the textile, laundry and food and canning industries.[4] Other delegates spoke on

SACTU Foundation Conference, Trades Hall, Johannesburg, 5–6 March 1955

behalf of thousands of workers from a wide variety of industries and concerns throughout South Africa – e.g. iron and steel workers, chemical workers, stevedoring and dockworkers, tin workers, rubber workers, tobacco workers, milling workers, those in the cardboard and paper industry, railway workers, mine workers and many more. The Conference itself was an exciting and historic event. One of the most significant documents to come out of the deliberations was the 'Declaration of Principles Adopted at the Foundation Conference of SACTU' which lays down firmly the basic principles on which SACTU was built. Part of this document reads as follows:

The future of the people of South Africa is in the hands of its workers. Only the working class, in alliance with progressive minded sections of the community, can build a happy life for all South Africans, a life free from unemployment, insecurity and poverty, free from racial hatred and oppression, a life of vast opportunities for all people.

But the working class can only succeed in this great and noble endeavour if it itself is united and strong, if it is conscious of its inspiring responsibility. The workers of South Africa need a united trade union movement in which all sections of the working class can play their part, unhindered by prejudice or racial discrimination. Only such a truly united movement can serve effectively the interests of the workers, both the immediate interests of higher wages and better conditions of life and work as well as the ultimate objective of complete emancipation for which our forefathers have fought.

We firmly declare that the interests of all workers are alike, whether they be European or non-European, African, Coloured, Indian, English, Afrikaans or Jewish. We resolve that this co-ordinating body of trade unions shall strive to unite all workers in its ranks, without discrimination, and without prejudice. We resolve that this body shall determinedly seek to further and protect the interests of all workers, and that its guiding motto shall be the universal slogan of working class solidarity: 'AN INJURY TO ONE IS AN INJURY TO ALL.'

These principles remain today as a foundation on which the working class movement in South Africa must be built and SACTU alone has remained true to these principles throughout its existence.

The Constitution presented to the Conference delegates was based on the old T & LC (1949) Constitution which had been revised and redrafted by a sub-committee of the TUCC.[5] Further amendments were made to the Constitution at the Inaugural Conference and the Declaration of Principles adopted became the Preamble to the new SACTU Constitution (see Appendix I).

What was the significance of the new name which was adopted –

'SACTU'? During the Conference there was a lively debate over whether to keep the name of the T & LC or whether to change it completely. Those in favour of retaining the name argued that they wanted the new body to 'not only adopt the old T & LC policy but this time to carry it out'.[6] Those against felt that there would be too many suspicions on the part of workers of the name 'SAT & LC (1955)'. Pious Mei, of the African Tobacco Workers Union, expressed their fears:

> It is quite obvious today that we are being asked to go to the cemetery and dig up the ghost of the dead body which was killed in Durban. . . . We have come here to save the soul and the spirit of the workers, not to pacify those who have deserted us.[7]

Mark Shope, of the African Laundry, Cleaning, and Dyeing Workers Union, said that the old SAT & LC 'did not cater to African trade unions and therefore there should be no association with that body'. He moved and Stella Damons (NULCDW) seconded, that the new organization be called the South African Congress of Trade Unions.[8] The vote was taken and the results were thirty-three in favour and twenty-six against, indicating that there was still a lot of sentimental attachment to, or pride in the legacy of the defunct SAT & LC. Some trade unionists obviously perceived this new body as merely a continuation of the old body, but comments made at the time by African trade unionists indicate that they regarded it as a much more revolutionary trade union body than the SAT & LC had been.

Among the various resolutions passed at this Conference, the one dealing with Organizing the Unorganized is particularly significant. If implemented, it too would signify a distinct break from the past practices of the T & LC. The resolution read:

> This Conference affirms that its main task in the coming period is to initiate, stimulate and to undertake the organization of trade unions where none exist amongst South African workers and to strengthen trade unions which are in existence but require support.
> The Conference recognizes that only by drawing into the ranks of organized labour the thousands of workers now unorganized, can the Trade Union movement make its maximum contribution to the working class struggle, for its liberation from exploitation and race discrimination.
> Conference therefore instructs the NEC to take in hand without delay, a practical and determined programme for the recruiting and training of trade union organizers.[9]

In his Chairman's address to the Conference, Piet Beyleveld also stressed the importance of organizing the unorganized workers, specifically African workers:

It must further be the task (of this Federation) to organize the vast masses of exploited and unorganized African workers and to educate the workers who misguidedly believe that they can safeguard their own rights while they exclude their fellow-African workers from the struggle.[10]

The tasks facing the newly-created SACTU were numerous and formidable, but the spirit in which the delegates left the Conference ensured that the challenge would not be taken lightly. The elected officials entrusted with the responsibility of seeing these tasks carried out were drawn from the ranks of both Black and White trade unionists, men and women. An Executive Committee of nineteen was elected, which included Pieter Beyleveld (TWIU) as President, Cleopas Sibande (A-TWIU) and Lucy Mvubelo (GWU-AW) as Vice-Presidents, Leon Levy as Treasurer and Leslie Massina as General Secretary. Others serving on the first NEC were J. Nkadimeng, M. Shope, J. Fillies, P. M. Mei, I. Topley, C. Jasson, O. A. Olsson, W. H. Ross, A. Mahlangu, B. January, B. Nair, C. Mayekiso, V. M. Pillay and S. Damons.

Soon after the Inaugural Conference, in May 1955, the formation of SACTU was strengthened by the principled decision of the CNETU to dissolve and in turn merge with the new non-racial trade union centre. The resolution passed at the CNETU Conference on 5 May 1955 is of historical significance to the progressive trade union movement in South Africa.

This Conference of the Transvaal CNETU warmly welcomes the establishment of SACTU.

We consider that the workers of South Africa, both black and white, have reached the stage where the existence of a national, non-racial trade union co-ordinating body has become a prime necessity of the workers' movement. It is for this reason that the Transvaal CNETU has taken a leading part in convening and forming the South African Congress of Trade Unions.

Having achieved the establishment of SACTU, this conference now considers that the historic task of the CNETU has been accomplished and that its proud tradition of leading the struggle of the African workers will now be best carried on by the new national body.

It is, therefore, hereby resolved that all steps shall be taken without delay to merge the Transvaal Council of Non-European Trade Unions with the South African Congress of Trade Unions and the Executive Committee is hereby instructed to complete the merger in a spirit of brotherhood and solidarity.

SACTU and the Political Struggle

By clearly recognizing the link between the struggle for economic gains and the general political struggle, the founders of SACTU were calling upon the workers of South Africa to fulfil their historic role – to become the spearhead in the struggle for national liberation. Rejecting the slogan of 'no politics in the trade union movement', SACTU leaders refused to divorce the struggle for political rights and power from the day-to-day struggle for higher wages and improved working conditions.

In his address to the Inaugural Conference, the Chairman explained this clearly:

> You cannot separate politics and the way in which people are governed from their bread and butter, or their freedom to move to and from places where they can find the best employment, or the houses they live in, or the type of education their children get. These things are of vital concern to the workers. The Trade Unions would therefore be neglecting the interests of their members if they failed to struggle for their members on all matters which affect them. The Trade Unions must be as active in the political field as they are in the economic sphere because the two hang together and cannot be isolated from each other.[11]

The same principle was later enshrined as one of the main points in the Statement of Policy submitted to the First Annual Conference of SACTU held in Cape Town in March 1956:

> SACTU is conscious of the fact that the organizing of the mass of workers for higher wages, better conditions of life and labour is inextricably bound up with a determined struggle for political rights and liberation from all oppressive laws and practices. It follows that a mere struggle for the economic rights of all the workers without participation in the general struggle for political emancipation would condemn the Trade Union movement to uselessness and to a betrayal of the interests of the workers.

Resolutions passed at the Inaugural Conference dealing with opposition to Bantu Education and the forced removal of Africans from their townships near Johannesburg (the Western Areas Removal Scheme), demonstrated that even at this early stage SACTU was fully committed to the wider issues of national oppression and lack of political rights among the Black (African, Indian and Coloured) community. Also, from the outset, SACTU allied itself with those groups involved in the struggle for national liberation in South Africa, led by the African National Congress (ANC), representing the most exploited group. SACTU realized that Black workers were exploited both as workers and as citizens, and that it was crucial to unite with the ANC, the South African Indian Congress (SAIC), the Coloured People's Congress (CPC) and the Congress of Democrats (COD) to overthrow the entire Apartheid system.

Hence, a major reason for adopting 'SACTU' as the name of the new organization was to ensure consistency with the other four Congresses. All five bodies were united together in late 1955 into the Congress Alliance. From this beginning, SACTU recognized that the ultimate aim of the workers' struggle was total liberation, freedom for all people from every kind of oppression and exploitation and the opportunity to build a free and democratic South Africa in which all could participate equally.

In 1955, Dan Tloome, though himself banned from trade union activity by this time, expressed the views of SACTU members:

There are two types of African trade union leaders. On the one hand, there is the Union leader who confines himself to trying to obtain the economic demands of his members; on the other hand, there is the trade unionist who sees in the worker a person who is both exploited and oppressed, and realizes that in order to improve the position of the workers it is necessary to struggle for both political and economic ends. The latter are active members of the liberatory movement and share their valuable experiences with the political leaders.[12]

In a later chapter we examine in detail SACTU's role in the Congress Alliance during the 1950s and 1960s. Even in its first year of existence though, SACTU firmly allied itself with the other Congresses and participated in the Congress of the People held in Kliptown, in June 1955, where the Freedom Charter (see Appendix II) was adopted. This marked the beginning of a close relationship between SACTU and the liberation movement which continues to this day.

A trade union movement, however, has specific tasks in the struggle. It is a class-based organization, not representing any one national grouping. SACTU, although an equal partner in the Congress Alliance, saw its major task as that of organizing the unorganized workers of South Africa. Only by organizing and uniting to defend their common interests against employers and the state, could they gain the strength necessary to win their demands and contribute to the struggle for eventual emancipation from the system of capitalism and Apartheid. The major force to be organized to advance this struggle was the African working class, those with nothing to lose but their chains, and everything to gain.

In 1955, SACTU, operating on a shoestring budget, with an affiliation fee of only 10s. per union, plus 1d. per member per month, began to organize. From a body which represented an actual affiliated membership of 20,000 workers in 19 unions in 1956, SACTU through its organizing campaigns built up the membership strength to 46,000 in 35 unions by 1959. By 1961, 53,000 workers (including 38,791 African workers) affiliated through 51 unions to SACTU. After years of struggle and sacrifice, South African workers of all races, but especially African workers, had a coordinating body to represent their interests and fight for their rights *as workers*.

NOTES

1. Interview, Eric Mtshali.
2. Minutes of meeting of the Interim Committee of Dissenting Unions, Durban, 7 October 1954.
3. Quoted in Linda Ensor, 'TUCSA's Relationship with African Trade Unions – An Attempt at Control, 1954–1962', *Southern African Labour History*, Raven Press, Johannesburg, 1978.
4. The three largest unions (by branches) were represented as follows: FCWU (9,000); A-FCWU (3,600); TWIU (4,000); A-TWIU (3,100); NULCDW (2,626); A-LCDWU (2,000).
5. Those involved in this important work included banned trade unionists (e.g. Eli Weinberg and Ray Alexander), Leon Levy and others whose names cannot be mentioned here.
6. O. A. Olsson, Minutes of the Inaugural Conference of SACTU, Trades Hall, Johannesburg, 5–6 March 1955.
7. Minutes, Inaugural Conference, SACTU.
8. ibid.
9. ibid.
10. Chairman's Address, Inaugural Conference.
11. ibid.
12. M. Horrell, *South African Trade Unionism: A Study of a Divided Working Class*, South African Institute of Race Relations (SAIRR), 1961, p. 79.

4 RULING CLASS RESPONSE

The South African ruling class response to SACTU can be summarized in one word: hostility. Like the Transvaal CNETU before, and even more so because of its non-racial theory and practice, SACTU directly challenged the economic base of Apartheid – the cheap labour system. The entire political superstructure that rests upon that base of exploitation was similarly threatened as a result.

It is crucial at the outset to define the ruling class. Far too often, and especially in the case of Apartheid, the ruling class is reduced to the political party in power, in this case the Nationalist Party since 1948. As we will show, such a conception is far too narrow. It is also dangerous in that it creates confused analysis and can easily lead to incorrect practice in the course of struggle. Such thinking also reinforces the liberal theories of social reform that never come close to touching the structural relations of exploitation that are the fundamental basis of Apartheid. Apartheid cannot 'put on a human face' – it can only destroy or be destroyed.

The ruling class encompasses far more than the government in power. It is comprised of two social groupings: firstly, the *capitalist* class as owners of the means of production and whose members live off the profit derived from exploiting human labour power; and secondly, the entire *state apparatus* (government, legislature, judiciary, administrative bureaucracy, police and the military). Together, both social forces generally share the same overall interests in maintaining the *status quo*, and, more specifically, the dominant relations of production under capitalism.

This does not mean that the interests of the state and the capitalist class are identical. Indeed, on many specific issues it is not uncommon to find differences of opinion, even conflict, between and within both sectors. This is true of all capitalist societies and South Africa is no exception.

These intra-ruling class conflicts, interesting and important as they may be in given circumstances, must not divert our attention from the larger identity of interests that all rulers share in relation to the ruled. In regard to SACTU, both segments of the South African ruling class share the common assumption that the organization of African workers into economically and politically effective trade unions is a threat to the state's structure of Apartheid institutions and the capitalist's source of profit.

As a trade union body, SACTU was the only group in the Congress Alliance to directly confront the capitalist class in South Africa, that is, a class 'in and for itself'. The following statement leaves no doubt that SACTU understood the relationship between the state and the capitalist class within the ruling sector:

> SACTU is a working class organization representing the interests of working people, more especially that of the homeless, voteless and landless masses of the working class of our land, whose daily lives are at the mercy of the dominating white minority. SACTU conducts a fierce struggle against exploitation.
>
> Capitalism thrives on profits derived from the workers, on the exploitation of workers and the deprivation of human rights. Such is the nature of capitalism and it holds no brief for the aspirations of the producers of its wealth. It rejects everything that stands in the way of profits and uses its power mercilessly to crush its opposition. . . . It is the nature of capitalism to use many devices to camouflage its naked exploitation of the workers. In South Africa, the device used to create super profits is racial discrimination. . . . They (white people) perpetuate myths of superiority and encourage workers to remain divided through racial hatred.[1]

Here, then, is a precise statement that identifies the ruling class and explains how class exploitation under capitalism is promoted by the Apartheid state through its political structures and ideology of racism. Although the final sentence of this passage generalizes about all 'white people', it obviously refers to White power-holders as they are the only sub-minority of the White population with the means of institutionalizing a given ideology of White supremacy. SACTU has thus given a concrete example of what is meant by the statement, '. . . the ruling ideas of any epoch are the ideas of the ruling class'.

Ruling class hostility towards SACTU, its affiliated unions and leaders can now be fully understood. The identification of the profit motive at the root of Apartheid, as the driving force of the system that creates misery, poverty and death for the Black masses, signals to those who rule that SACTU is not a trade union movement willing to accept concessions or compromise. Only the total liberation of the people from the double chains of class exploitation and national oppression will complete SACTU's historic task. The formulation also warns all reformist elements, both inside and outside South Africa, that even without Apartheid South African capitalism remains a fundamentally exploitive system to be struggled against.

Because the state and the capitalist class interact with workers in different areas of social life, each has responded to SACTU initiatives according to its respective domain and interests.

The state response to SACTU was, understandably, in the political sphere, notwithstanding those specific industries where it directly employs Black labour. Legislation and the administrative machinery and physical force to implement it became the dominant method of state intervention against working class unity and progress. This legislation falls into two categories: (a) anti-working class laws affecting Black workers in general; and (b) specific political laws designed to crush SACTU and other Congress Alliance organizations and victimize their leaders and followers. This chapter will outline the former, while Chapter 12 will describe the latter – used primarily in the early 1960s. Together, this 'law and order' strategy constitutes the thrust of the state's response to SACTU.

The capitalist class interacts with workers (and SACTU) within the capital-labour relationship, spatially restricted to the point of production. By and large, employers in South Africa, increasingly multi-national in origin, have *always* accepted the racist structure of Apartheid society and agreed to work within it. The rush of foreign capital into South (and Southern) Africa, eager to accumulate super-profits by taking advantage of legislated or customary racial inequalities, could be explained in no other way. This gross exploitation of Black labour long predates the existence of specific Apartheid structures as we know them since 1948. As the history of capitalism the world over shows, capital *creates* these conditions of privilege and poverty rather than only passively accepting them, as though they were natural.

More to the point, there are no laws in South Africa that oblige employers to pay Black Workers starvation wages or force them to labour under slave conditions on the farms, in the mines and in the factories. They choose to do so. No law has ever prevented an employer from negotiating with a democratically-elected trade union representative or a factory committee formed by Black workers, with or without official sanction from the government. Yet, in most cases, they refuse to do so. No law forces employers to break strikes, import scab labour from the reserves or invite the Special Branch police to victimize workers. Yet this is done regularly. These choices are freely made by the employing class who are circumscribed in their individual and collective actions only by the unwritten laws of capital accumulation.

Despite rhetoric to the contrary, the capitalist class benefits from Apartheid. Even in those given situations where Apartheid laws appear to conflict with the imperatives of capital, new avenues of exploitation (e.g. Border Industries and Bantustan investments) are quickly found. Capitalism and Apartheid, rather than being antithetical to one another, act as harmonious partners in the exploitation and oppression of the Black people of South Africa.

Finally, TUCSA's response to SACTU is included in this chapter to illustrate the role that the White trade union leadership played in assisting the interests of the ruling class. Despite their relatively privileged position within the whole working class, White workers are *not* part of the ruling class. None the less, it is important to show how the dynamics of racial politics led this segment of the producing class to betray its class interests and identify opportunistically with the forces of oppression. This also allows everyone to better appreciate the entire range of historical opposition to the principled non-racial trade unionism of SACTU.

The Capitalist Apartheid State and Labour Legislation

A strong body of responsible opinion stressed the serious danger which faced the country if Native trade unions were allowed to continue uncontrolled or unguided as at present.
> Paragraph 1634, Industrial Legislation Commission, 1951

... the principal function of the trade unions will disappear.... These organizations will not so much be entrusted with the function of obtaining better wages and working conditions; ... they will be mainly entrusted with the task of regulating domestic affairs, as between the employers and employees. And for the rest, of looking after the spiritual welfare of the workers.
> B. J. Schoeman, Nationalist Party, House of Assembly Debates, 19 March 1942

A study of labour legislation in South Africa supports the view that a fundamental role of the state is to intervene in the class struggle whenever necessary to maintain the capital-labour relations of exploitation. Successive amendments to legislation passed early in the century, and, in certain cases, entirely new legislation, has been a direct response to two forms of struggle: that between different fractions of capital (e.g. agricultural versus industrial) and that more decisive struggle between capital and labour. The result is a complicated morass of anti-worker legislation which purposefully divides the working class along racial lines and hence creates the conditions for coopting the minority White workers away from working class solidarity. A divided proletariat also enhances the profits extracted from the production process in general.

This labour legislation is distinguished by (a) those Acts covering 'registered' trade unions consisting of non-African workers (i.e., Whites and Coloureds)[2] and (b) those Acts of repressive legislation applicable to only African workers and their 'unregistered' unions. The former is largely covered by the Industrial Conciliation Act (hereafter IC Act) of 1924, as amended in 1937 and 1956; the latter consists of many separate Acts which limit the rights of African workers at and beyond the workplace. Such a dichotomy defies a simplistic division of the workforce along lines of racial oppression alone. That is, it is not merely a Black versus White division. For example, there are many cases where Coloured workers in registered unions act in ways contrary to the interests of their fellow African workers in unregistered unions. The point to stress, however, is that these legislated divisions have been consciously created by the state sector to stabilize the labour process and promote the class interests of employers who control production.

SACTU's struggles against the IC Act of 1956 and the Native Labour (Settlement of Disputes) Act of 1953 cannot be properly understood without first outlining the 'logic' and parameters of legislation enacted earlier in this century.

Decades before the Nationalists came to power, the IC Act of 1924 provided the legislative cornerstone of a divided working class. It emerged out of a crisis of interrupted production in the mining industry, whereby White miners conducted strikes in 1907, 1913 and again in 1922 against the companies' practice of incorporating cheaper, unskilled African labour into jobs customarily reserved for Whites. The famous White miners' strike of 1922, the Rand Revolt, was the most crucial factor leading to the new industrial relations machinery. For the South African Mine Workers Union (SAMWU), representing White workers, the issue at stake was nothing less than that of 'preserving a White South Africa'. In what became a virtual civil war during the month of March, the Smuts Government came to the defence of the mining industry by calling in the troops. When the strike officially ended on 16 March, at least 214 had been killed and four more were subsequently hanged after being convicted of murder in the courts. Although the Rand Revolt and the White miners' strikes of the previous decade were crushed by force, their reoccurrence was inevitable unless the state acted quickly to devise industrial relations legislation that would satisfy White mining capital and would emasculate the militancy of White labour.

No less important was the expressed fear that African workers, the most exploited, would perceive the value of strong working class organization. Such a threat to 'industrial peace' might well go beyond manageable limits. A Government Inspector voiced these fears before a Commission in 1914:

Some natives are realising that it is in their interests to form a combination. In answer to the question of whether he thought the natives had learnt lessons in combination from the events (of the 1913 strike by White miners), the Inspector replied, 'I am sure of it. . . . What they learnt in a week last July might in the ordinary way have taken them 15 years to learn.'[3]

Notwithstanding the White Inspector's underestimation of the 'learning speed' of African workers, the Smuts Government of the day intervened in the class struggle to enact the IC Act of 1924. The essentials of this Act remain in force today.

The goal was to create institutionalized structures that would remove class conflict from the point of production and install it in the safety of polite discussions convened around government-supervised tables. The 1914 Commission had recommended the advantages of such a system:

Recognition creates responsibility . . . experience proves that organization in the open, made sober by recognition, is a very different thing from organization which has to fight against contempt or antagonism. . . . (Further) the organization of labour is an aid to the authority of a conciliation board, because much labour can then be dealt with as a whole. Moreover, the (trade union) official is *more likely to take the business point of view* and examine the situation (more) calmly than the workman who has some personal grievance rankling in his mind. (emphasis added)[4]

Thus, statutory bodies – known as Industrial Councils – representing employers and employees came into being. In full accord with the wishes of mining and other capitalist quarters, the right to strike was essentially lost through a cumbersome procedure which if not followed made the withdrawal of labour power illegal.

Most important, the overwhelming majority of the workforce – the African proletariat – was specifically excluded from the terms of reference of the IC Act. This was done by declaring that all pass-bearing natives' would *not* be considered 'employees' under the Act. African women workers were, however, covered by legislation until the mid-1950s when they were legally required to carry passes.[5]

White workers demanded and received many benefits as the *quid pro quo* for forsaking hard fought for rights gained through previous struggles. In the context of South Africa, these benefits came inevitably at the expense of the Black, particularly African, workers. The most important gains, however, were reaped by the capitalist class and the state, those who increase profits and power by having a weak and divided working class. Militant actions and strikes by registered unions (those covered by the IC Act) declined from an average of 37 involving over 42,000 workers annually between 1919 and 1922, to an average of 6 involving only 393 White and Coloured workers between 1923 and 1929. Workers in registered unions lost control of and interest in their organizations as bureaucrats who accepted class collaboration and racial discrimination came to the fore as leaders of the majority of such unions.

Within ten years, another Government Commission reported that employers found the IC Act to their liking. Cases were cited where employers' organizations actively encouraged the formation of unions in their factories. The IC Act was a classic case of 'historical compromise', and like all subsequent labour legislation in South Africa, strengthened the power and privilege of the propertied segment of society. It also proved that when direct physical repression is not a viable strategy, the state can also discover 'peaceful' means of maximizing exploitation.

Legislation alone, however, has never curtailed efforts to organize African workers. Throughout the 1930s and 1940s, progressive trade unionists campaigned for the inclusion of Africans as 'employees' under the Act. They also used loopholes in the Act to struggle for extension of benefits to the most exploited workers. Not everyone who opposed the legislation, however, did so for principled reasons. Many White-dominated or led trade unions called for changes solely out of sectional self-interest; if Africans were to be a permanent part of the urban working class, the White workers agreed that their organization would eventually be necessary to prevent the bosses' desire to employ cheaper, Black labour as a meaning of lowering production costs. Others agreed that African unions should be registered in order to place greater restrictions on their political activities.

The Second World War, representing another crisis of capitalism but on a world-wide scale, brought with it additional legislative attacks on African workers. In order to ensure continuous production to meet wartime schedules, and to quell the dramatic rise of militant African trade unions, the Smuts Government enacted War Measures Acts No. 9 and No. 145 in 1942. The Minister of Labour assumed the right to intervene in any industrial dispute designated harmful to the war effort. War Measures Act No. 9, allowing for the appointment of an arbitrator and a ban on strikes and lockouts in disputed industries, was withdrawn at the end of the war. Act No. 145, however, remained in effect until 1953, when it was incorporated into the Native Labour Act.

The reason is straightforward: under this extension the provisions covered all industrial undertakings in which Africans were involved. In this way, an ostensibly wartime measure became in fact an outright attack on all African workers and their organizations. A supplementary War Measure No. 1425 further prohibited gatherings of more than twenty Africans on mine company property, an obvious reflection of the government's fear of the African Mine Workers Union that later carried out the famous strike of 1946. Yet during the war years, African workers were never intimidated by these 'emergency' measures; nor were they willing to succumb to ideological pressures to place an intercapitalist world war above that of their own crisis of exploitation within the borders of South Africa. Between 1942 and 1945, no less than sixty 'illegal' strikes of African workers took place.

The large increase in the absolute size of the permanent urban African proletariat, coupled with the unmistakable signs of their incorporation into militant and well-organized trade unions under progressive (often Communist) leadership prompted the state and capitalist class to put their heads together and come up with new legislation to stave off a potentially revolutionary situation. The Smuts Government tabled the Industrial Conciliation (Natives) Bill in 1947, and as the name implies, the goal was to somehow bring together the two separate types of labour legislation that had prevailed since the 1920s. The 'Smuts Bill' envisaged some form of limited or qualified recognition of African trade unions. As in the early 1920s, the main argument for recognition was voiced in a negative manner, i.e. without it, there could be no effective regulation and control.

The 1948 election victory of the Nationalist Party brought all of these gentile discussions of how best to deal with African unions to an abrupt halt. The Nationalists held no brief for such liberal deliberations

– their philosophy towards African workers, indeed the whole working class, was spawned in Nazi Germany and had been clearly outlined by the new Minister of Labour, B. Schoeman, while speaking in Parliament back in 1942:

> Firstly, (my party) contends that wage control and wage fixation should be entirely in the hands of the state. Secondly, and this is the most important principle – self-government in industry must be eliminated. . . . (They) are things of the past . . . (and) should be eliminated from our economic life.
>
> In regard to the Non-Europeans, the unhealthy economic position which is gradually arising and which will become more and more intense, should be entirely eliminated. My party maintains that this can only be done by fixing a definite quota for Europeans and Non-Europeans in unskilled, semi-skilled and skilled occupations. . . . I want to assure the people of South Africa that when my Party soon takes over the government of this country we intend giving the people the new economic order.[6]

Shortly after coming to power, the Nationalists appointed an Industrial Legislation Commission of Enquiry to investigate all areas relevant to industrial relations in South Africa. The Enquiry received submissions from all concerned parties and published its findings and recommendations in 1951. Following the lead taken by the 'Smuts Bill', the Enquiry favoured qualified recognition of African trade unions. By 1953, the Nationalists rejected this approach and instead introduced the Native Labour Act.

Before discussing that legislation, it is instructive to summarize the position taken by different fractions of capital in submissions to the Enquiry. Employers' organizations in secondary industry supported recognition of African unions in order to 'bring them under control'; no one favoured granting full equality of rights to African workers under the IC Act. The Motor Industry Employers Association spoke for industrial capital when it said, '. . . the European is the custodian of this country and whatever legislation is introduced must be introduced for European supremacy'.[7]

Mining and agricultural capital, on the other hand, totally opposed any such recognition, limited or otherwise. Mining capitalists feared the strength of the AMWU, and rural White employers envisaged an exodus of cheap, African labour to the cities with the higher wages and improved working conditions that registered status would bring. Recognition would also be tantamount to admitting that African labour had become urbanized and had certain rights as workers, propositions that were never conceded by Apartheid philosophers or slave-driving White farmers.

African trade unionists, progressive Whites, and liberal organizations such as the South African Institute for Race Relations (SAIRR), all supported unqualified recognition of African unions. Gana Makabeni, representing the CNETU, repeated the long-standing demand: 'Our fight here is for the recognition of African Trade Unions, that is the Amendment of the Industrial Conciliation Act to include Africans as "employees".'

The Enquiry recommendations were, on the whole, gradualist in that they called for a very slow, evolutionary process that *might* eventually lead to full status for African trade unions that were no threat to the system. Yet the entire Report read as if motivated by a deep fear of the consequences if these liberal reforms were not implemented. The Nationalists, eager to put into practice their Nazi-like dogma of racial separation, preferred 'control through repression' as an indication that the 'new economic order' had arrived on South African soil. The decline of African trade unionism following the 1946 Mine Workers' Strike, the move to the right by White trade union leaders in the SAT & LC, the concern of the Nationalists to promote the interests of Afrikaner agricultural capital, the banning of progressive trade unionists under the Suppression of Communism Act – all of these factors taken together led the Nationalist Party to believe in 1953 that they could 'bleed the African trade unions to death'.

Native Labour (Settlement of Disputes) Act No. 48 (1953)

Continuing in the tradition of passing separate legislation for African workers, the Nationalists introduced the Native Labour Act in 1953 to permanently extend provisions allowed in the War Measures Acts of the 1940s. All strikes and lockouts of African workers were illegal, as were actions that might instigate strikes or lockouts. Sympathy strikes were also outlawed. In 1959, the Act was amended to make violators of the Act subject to maximum fines of R1,000 (£500) or three years imprisonment, or both. These penalties for Africans were far more severe than those allowed for White or Coloured workers under the IC Act.

A further Amendment prohibited an African from representing workers at Industrial Council or Conciliation Board meetings. Also forbidden was the collection of trade union dues or contributions to sick benefit funds from African workers by means of 'stop orders', unless authorized by the Minister of Labour.

Most importantly, the Native Labour Act established a separate industrial conciliation machinery for Africans. This amounted to an unwieldy, White-dominated bureaucracy consisting of Bantu Labour Officers, Regional Bantu Labour Committees, Works Committees (if desired by workers in establishments with not less than twenty African employees) and a Bantu Central Labour Board. This complicated and highly paternalistic procedure for settling disputes and fixing wages incorporated in the Act was doomed from the outset. Yet, it is clear that the purpose of the Act was not only to deny recognition of African trade unions but to threaten their very existence. As Minister of Labour Schoeman had said in Parliament during the debate on the Enquiry recommendations:

... if we give them that incentive to organize and they should become well organized – and again bearing in mind that there are almost 1,000,000 native workers in industry and commerce today – they can use their trade unions as a political weapon and they can create chaos in South Africa at any time. I think that we would probably be committing race suicide if we gave them that incentive.[8]

Between 1953 and 1963, African workers, their unions and their coordinating bodies successfully resisted the Native Labour Act. Organized and unorganized workers alike effectively boycotted the machinery of Labour Officers, Works Committees and the Central Labour Board. In so far as all basic freedoms of association, collective bargaining and the right to strike were taken away, the legislation soon became known as the Slave Labour Act – to be opposed at all costs.

As early as 1952, the CNETU accused the government of attempting to replace legitimate trade unions with dummy surrogates 'run from the pass office'. This made reference to the system of labour bureaux introduced in 1949 to facilitate the distribution of African labour, i.e. the removal of urban Africans to the countryside for employment as cheap farm labour. The Native Laws Amendment Act of 1952 gave legitimacy to these removals by proclaiming all urban areas subject to influx controls. For example, an African could remain in an urban area for no longer than 72 hours unless he/she carried a work or work-seeker's permit. The purpose was clearly to allocate 'surplus' African 'labour units' to agricultural capital, the close ally of the Nationalists.

Industrial capital, however, was not disadvantaged by these

measures. Shifting the reserve army of labour to the countryside created no shortage of labour, and it also lessened the potential political threat posed by large numbers of urban, unemployed Africans. Moreover, the constant threat faced by African workers of being 'endorsed out' of the cities allowed the further cheapening of labour-power by the industrialists.

Returning to the Native Labour Act, CNETU National and Regional conferences in 1952, 1953 and 1954 urged African workers to refuse to operate the machinery created and thus prove the unworkability of the Act. To all registered unions, the Council warned that the Act was only the first instance of the Nationalists' plan to attack the entire working class. White trade union leaders were too preoccupied at the time with setting up their new Apartheid trade union structures – e.g. the SATUC (or TUCSA as it it was known later) – to heed the Council's advice.[9]

SACTU carried on the tradition of the CNETU and continued to lead the attack on the Act. A pamphlet was prepared and distributed to African workers that explained the Act and advised workers in great detail what to do if harassed by Native Labour Officials. Of particular concern was the close collaboration between these Officials, the employers and the Special Branch police the moment a dispute arose. But it was the workers themselves who soon realized that the Labour Officers could offer nothing more than the *status quo* on the wage front, and, more commonly, charges of 'incitement to strike' or 'participation in illegal strikes'. The mere presence of the Special Branch also convinced workers that the Act was designed to guarantee their continued exploitation.

African workers were encouraged by SACTU to demand direct negotiations with the employers, either through existing trade unions or factory committees. Whenever possible, SACTU assisted unorganized workers in fighting court cases under the Act. The state collected thousands of Rand in fines from poverty-stricken Africans, and countless man-days of labour were lost to production through the imprisonment of workers. But resistance continued. By 1958, SACTU was able to claim that not a single *bona fide* African trade union had agreed to work within the machinery of the Act. On the wage front, the £1-a-Day campaign, not the Labour Officers, had brought about wage increases for African workers.

Given these realities, it is easy to understand that the most consistent response of African workers was the strike weapon. By the late 1950s, even the government seemed to realize that the Slave Labour Act had failed to crush the African unions. The result was greater victimization. In April 1958, the Director of Non-European Affairs in Benoni circulated a letter to all employers of 'native' labour, reminding them that any African discharged as a result of participation in strikes, demonstrations or absenteeism, was not to be re-hired without official approval. Employers were also instructed to keep separate files on these individuals and send the files to the local Labour Bureau on a regular basis.

Throughout these years, SACTU used the press to counter public statements such as those uttered by S. D. Mentz, Chairman of the Central Native Labour Board (CNLB). In 1956, in Cape Town, Mentz told employers that Africans were 'too childish' to master trade unionism, using as 'evidence' the 150 years it had taken Europeans to do the same. SACTU correctly responded that it had taken that long to win certain struggles, not to 'master' trade union ideas. Furthermore, since the government had attacked *all* workers, 'it must be concluded that in government circles, no worker is considered ready for trade unionism. . . . Once workers organize they are ready.'[10] The fact that African workers had organized almost total opposition to the Native Labour Act proved beyond any doubt that Mr Mentz and his many stooges (which included a few African businessmen on Regional Committees) had no conception of the issues at stake.

In 1960, seven years after the Act was introduced, the CNLB held its first annual conference. In all this time, only ten Works Committees had been formed amongst the one million African workers covered by the Act.[11] Instead, the strength of African trade unionism through SACTU had increased dramatically. Although successful in victimizing thousands of African workers, the Slave Labour Act had not 'bled' their unions 'to death' as promised, nor had it accomplished its overall objective of consolidating the cheap labour system that is the basis of capitalist production under Apartheid. The explanation was given by George Maeka (President, CNETU) in 1954: 'the Native Labour Act cannot kill unions which are based in factories rather than offices'.

Industrial Conciliation Amendment Act, No. 28 (1956)
The Nationalists' 'new economic order' on the industrial relations front was made complete with the IC Act of 1956, first tabled in 1954 and finally published in November two years later. Amending the IC Act of 1924, the new Act significantly changed the machinery of industrial

relations to conform with the general policies of Apartheid being imposed on the society at large. Whereas the Native Labour Act had ensured an inferior status for African workers, the new IC Act attacked the remaining 30 per cent of the workforce in two major areas: (a) the internal structure and scope of registered trade unions; and (b) the racial composition of the workforce by job category.

This two-pronged attack had been predicted and was subsequently examined in an excellent series prepared for *The Guardian* by Ray Alexander and other progressive journalists. The series ran in late 1951 and early 1952, before either of the Acts under consideration were officially introduced, but the accuracy of the articles was uncanny in its precision. One article quoted E. S. (Solly) Sachs, veteran leader of the Garment Workers' Union (Transvaal), and gives a good sense of the thinking that prevailed in progressive circles in May 1952:

It is a common tactic of all fascist governments to launch an attack first upon the weakest and most defenceless section of the people (e.g., the Native Labour Act), and having achieved their ignoble aim, then to proceed to deal with the stronger sections. One may state with certainty that if the Native workers are deprived of their freedom today, the European, Coloured and Indian workers will be deprived of theirs tomorrow.

The 'tomorrow' in this case applied to the IC Act and its enforcement of further racial divisions within registered unions with 'mixed' memberships, i.e. combinations of White and Coloured workers.

The principal provisions of the Act that entrenched trade union Apartheid were:

(1) no further 'mixed' unions would be registered under the Act;
(2) any existing 'mixed' union may separate into uniracial unions if more than half of either the White or Coloured members choose to break away. The funds and property of the original union could be divided by mutual agreement, or by the Industrial Registrar if necessary;
(3) any existing 'mixed' union that does not voluntarily divide into separate racial unions must have separate racial branches of Europeans and Coloureds; meetings must be separate and only Whites can serve on the Executives of different branches; mixed meetings of shop stewards and mixed congresses are also prohibited. (Exemptions may be granted by the Minister in cases where such separation would render one of the two branches inoperable due to too few members);
(4) the Minister may declare any industry or occupation an essential service and prohibit workers therein from striking; and

(5) no union will be allowed to affiliate to a political party or to take any part whatsoever in elections.

Difficulties of implementation led to further amendments to the Act in 1959. 'Mixed' unions were required to state in their Constitution whether in new areas they would cater for White *or* Coloured workers; in other words, 'mixed' unions could no longer recruit new members on a non-racial basis even if they had complied with internal racial separation. Also, companies involved in 'processing, canning or preserving of any perishable foodstuffs' (the food and canning industry) were listed as essential services, and thus all workers in the industry lost the right to strike. This clause clearly was an attack on the Food and Canning Workers' Union (FCWU), one of SACTU's strongest affiliates, as well as an assurance to rural Afrikaner capital that its profits were being cared for by the Nationalists.

Finally, a further amendment prevented employers from deducting subscriptions from African workers where Industrial Council agreements had been extended to cover them. Exemptions would require Ministerial approval. The overall goal of these many amendments in 1956 and 1959 is obvious: to create an even more racially-divided working class and even stronger employers' organizations in the ongoing class struggle.

Not content with amending old legislation, the 1956 Act introduced Clause 77, which legislated statutory Job Reservation (JR). This legal brainchild of the Nationalists reads as follows:

Reservation of work in the undertaking, industry, trade or occupation concerned in the specified area and any portion thereof or in any specified type or class of premises in the specified area for persons of a specified race or for persons belonging to a specified class and the prohibition of the performance of such work by any other person.

In plain English, Clause 77 authorized the Minister of Labour to reserve any job for members of a given racial group. It was explained in Parliament by the new Minister de Klerk as '... a precautionary measure to safeguard the standards of living of the White workers of South Africa and to ensure that they will not be exploited [sic] by the lower standards of living of any other race'.[12]

Again, practical difficulties of implementation led to further amendments in 1959. Earlier rhetoric about 'safeguarding the economic welfare of any race in any undertaking . . .' was replaced by wording giving the Minister autocratic power to instruct the Industrial Tribunal

Industrial Conciliation Act (1956): Job Reservation

to investigate any industry for the purpose of issuing a JR determination. Furthermore, the Tribunal was empowered to use 'any method of differentiation or discrimination it may deem expedient' in its recommendations. And, Industrial Council agreements in any industry could now be overruled by the Minister's JR determinations. All of these provisions might now be extended to the mining industry which had been previously excluded.

Introduction of statutory JR for any industry thus made legal what had been customary practice since the earliest days of South African capitalist development. The 'industrial colour bar', ensuring that jobs should be reserved for Whites wherever they are able and willing to work, had its origins in the mining industry. The Mines and Works Act of 1911 restricted certificates of competency in skilled occupations to Whites in the Transvaal and the Orange Free State; Africans were not allowed to hold such certificates until 1956, yet this was nullified in practice.

This in no way meant, however, that Africans did not perform skilled work — in fact, quite the contrary! It only meant that wages and conditions did not reflect their actual work. Similarly, the Apprenticeship Act of 1922 (as amended in 1944), although it did not formally discriminate against Black workers, in practice prevented advancement because of their impossibility of attaining the educational levels demanded. Opposition from White trade unionists who held controlling positions on Apprenticeship Boards further blocked technical training education for Black workers. In any case, White employers in most trades simply refused to allow Black apprenticeships.

These early Acts and customary discrimination were reinforced by the 'civilized labour' policy originating with the Pact Government of 1924. Applied primarily in the public sector, the purpose was to employ as many Whites as possible, paying them 'civilized' wages commensurate with a 'European standard of living' even if they performed unskilled work. As the SAIRR says, 'White workers were employed in various lower-skilled posts, and were paid at higher rates than those received by Black employees doing similar work in private sectors of the economy.'[13] For 'uncivilized' labour, i.e. all 'non-Whites', poverty wages were the order of the day.

More recently, the Native Building Workers Act of 1951 was the first Nationalist Party attempt to deal with the fact that thousands of Africans were performing skilled work in the construction industry on the Rand. Under the Act, Africans were prevented from doing such work except in African townships where they were paid one-third less than workers of a different race doing equivalent work elsewhere. At a time when the government was promoting township development as a means of racially segregating the population, this Act also lowered the state's overall labour costs in housing construction.

In addition to these specific pieces of legislation, many Industrial Council agreements included similar colour bars, eliminating the need for statutory Job Reservation.

The 1956 JR legislation and subsequent determinations, although in fact covering a small percentage of the total labour force,[14] served notice to all concerned that the 'civilized labour' policy was in South Africa to stay. Profits for White capital, privilege for White workers, poverty for the majority – the crucial ingredients of Apartheid capitalism were firmly entrenched.

Although JR appears to be an absurd proposition to outsiders, like all South African legislation it is understandable within the imperatives of the Apartheid political economy. Behind the racist ideological rhetoric was the inescapable fact that industrialization had qualitatively transformed the production process. Skilled work previously performed exclusively by White artisans was now increasingly done by semi-skilled Black 'operatives'. For example, in the metal engineering industry, Wolpe reports that 'new technology ... e.g. automatic lathes and drilling machines are turning out work previously done by skilled operatives paid at the rate of 86·5 cents per hour. The non-White operatives are getting the same job done for 22 cents an hour.' The same applied to the building industry, where a new 'operator' category for the 'non-White' worker was created between that of labourer and artisan. Wages for these workers averaged 60 per cent of artisan wages.[15] This process is known in South Africa as 'job dilution'. The data clearly shows that Apartheid is not contrary to the interests of capital accumulation.

The IC Act became effective on 1 January 1957. By mid-1959, the Industrial Tribunal had investigated twelve industries and published determinations for five of these. Almost without exception the request for investigations came from pro-Apartheid White trade unions and their members.

The first and most notorious case was that of the garment industry, when in 1957 the jobs of Coloured and African (mostly women) workers were threatened by JR for Whites. Coloureds and Africans staged walk-outs to show that the industry could not function without them, while the Transvaal Garment Workers Union took the issue to the courts. The Cape Provincial Division of the Supreme Court sided with the Union; it was this setback that prompted the 1959 Amendment that gave the Minister the power to introduce JR on any basis.[16] In South Africa it has become common practice to diminish the role of the courts by increasing executive powers.

Aside from the intimidation value to employers considering the promotion of Black workers through job dilution, the simple fact was that JR or not, White workers were not being squeezed out of employment by Black workers. On the contrary, White (especially Afrikaner) workers had voluntarily left their traditional occupations to assume better paying, more prestigious and in many cases overseer positions. The irreversible integration of Black workers into the permanent, urban proletariat was a product of industrial capitalism; contrary to Nationalist propaganda, it had nothing to do with interracial competition between racial groups within the total working class.

Therefore, the JR Clause 77 and the trade union Apartheid clauses of the IC Act complemented one another. On the trade union side, many White members of 'mixed' unions broke away to form their own uniracial unions. Yet the legislation hardly eliminated 'mixed' unions. By 1960, 56 'mixed' unions remained registered under the Act.[17] Although this points to the unworkability of the legislation, most of these unions were exempted for practical reasons rather than for their political opposition. The majority were affiliated to coordinating bodies, like TUCSA, that had no fundamental disagreement with White supremacy.

In sum, history had repeated itself. The original IC Act of 1924 had responded to a crisis of capitalism by buying off the militancy of the White workers and their leaders in return for the privileges of racism and colour-bars. Strikes by registered unions declined accordingly. The major revision of the Act in 1956 tried to solve another crisis, except now the threat came from the Black workers and their political organizations, making the crisis all the more severe to overall structural stability in South Africa. White workers, their unions and federations again opted for White supremacy, and as before strikes by registered unions declined from 39 in 1954 to 10 in 1958. Only SACTU and its affiliated unions remained to fight the IC Act of 1956, legislation designed to disorganize the organized.

SACTU Versus Trade Union Apartheid and Job Reservation
SACTU's attempts to mobilize a united trade union front against the IC

Act met with little success. Despite the occasional verbal utterance against the Act, TUCSA and other coordinating bodies further to the right politically, preferred to oppose SACTU rather than the government. Left to its own devices, SACTU was forced to deal with the deepened contradictions and divisions in the trade union movement resulting from the Nationalist legislation. The majority of SACTU affiliates, being unregistered African unions, were unaffected by the Act, yet paradoxically SACTU's strongest and best-organized affiliates were registered unions in food and canning, textiles and laundry and would be forced to decide how to deal politically with the Act.

The SACTU Management Committee (MC) initially organized an educational campaign against the Act, calling on local committees to hold local conferences and gather signatures on a petition to be submitted to the government in Cape Town during SACTU's first Annual National Conference in March 1956.[18] A strongly worded Conference resolution called on trade unionists in South Africa and throughout the world to protest against this 'fascist measure aimed at the destruction of free trade unionism that deprived workers of (a) the right to organize unions of workers irrespective of race, (b) free democratic elections of leaders without state interference, (c) freedom of occupation without race and sex restrictions, (d) freedom to withhold their labour power, and (e) the freedom of trade unions to achieve their aims through political action.'

National and provincial conferences of the FCWU and the NULCDW held following SACTU's conference called upon their members to join the campaign against the IC Act. By mid-1956, it had become obvious that the Bill would become law in early 1957 and also that a joint conference of trade union coordinating bodies against the legislation was not going to materialize. Only one question remained: what were the correct tactics to be followed by SACTU's registered unions?

Apartheid rules create divisions and conflicts among even the most progressive of trade unionists. For almost two years SACTU was to experience such division and conflict through a prolonged and often heated debate concerning how its registered affiliates should respond to the IC Act.

The debate began at a SACTU–NEC meeting in June 1956, six months before implementation of the Act. Piet Beyleveld outlined the options for registered unions: form separate uniracial unions, divide into racial branches, or in defiance of the law, deregister. All NEC members agreed that the most unsatisfactory solution would be the imposition of all-White executives on separate Coloured branches of SACTU unions with predominantly Coloured memberships. The ensuing discussions set the parameters of the debate that continued for eighteen months.

Leon Levy (SACTU President) reviewed the advantages many African workers obtained by working closely with progressive registered unions in their respective industries – e.g. laundry, food and canning and textiles. These SACTU unions had, in many cases, persuaded employers to extend benefits to African workers in Industrial Council agreements. Leslie Massina (General Secretary) went so far as to say that the only solid African unions were those which worked closely with registered unions, and this point was generally accepted. Don Mateman (TWIU) argued against deregistration: 'What we have we must keep. What we do not have we must fight for.'

Archie Sibeko (SAR & HWU, CT) agreed that trade unions must first bring concrete benefits to African workers before '... you could carry them further. If you were too much in advance of the workers you became apart from them.' But unlike other speakers, Sibeko stressed that the issue could be settled satisfactorily only if the workers *themselves* reached a decision through a 'process of struggle'. This point was accepted and the NEC called for discussions at all levels leading to a special conference to formulate policy.

The first clearly argued case for deregistration was made by Eli Weinberg in the March 1957 issue of *Truth*, the laundry workers' paper. He maintained that the IC Act, like its predecessor in 1924, would exact a toll too heavy for the progressive trade union movement to pay. Could the benefits of registration still help workers once they had been divided into racial branches? As registration was not compulsory, Weinberg recommended voluntary deregistration in order that: (a) Africans could be equal members of presently 'mixed' unions; (b) union funds, the Constitution and elections could be democratically controlled by the membership; and (c) strike action and political activities would not be so restricted. Admitting that many trade unionists were still enamoured with the 'benefits' of the IC Act, Weinberg concluded this article as follows:

... The African workers are on the move again, and they, no doubt, will again prove to the members of registered trade unions that the most effective way to secure benefits is workers' unity and not some kind of nebulous 'recognition' which is bound up precisely with the sacrifice of working class unity.

In response, Ray Alexander, writing under the pen-name of E. R. Braverman, wrote in the April issue of *Workers' Unity* that Weinberg had erred by focusing on the registration issue. Rather, in her opinion, the major threat was the Job Reservation clause and trade unionists should be discussing 'how to defend the workers' right to work'. Alexander agreed in principle that working class unity could be best served by deregistration, but in practice such a strategy required support from workers of all racial groups to be effective.

Can Eli Weinberg quote one union in which the White workers are likely to follow their 'non-White' fellow workers in rejecting the Act? And if White workers refuse to adopt this course of action must the non-White workers act on their own account, leave the White Executive registered union, to negotiate industrial council agreements, submit memoranda to the industrial tribunal, sit on apprenticeship committees . . . I should like to know what guidance E. Weinberg has for the Indian, Coloured and African garment, bus men, leather and building workers?

Whether one agrees that JR was the largest threat in the Act or not, this exchange between veteran trade unionists reflects the differences of analysis and opinions that emerged early in the SACTU debate.

The NEC meeting held on 11 April 1957, one day before the Second Annual Conference records a significant shift from the discussion of the previous June meeting. Two specific proposals prepared by the MC read: '(a) (We appeal) . . . to all registered Trade Unions to resist all efforts to split their organization on racial grounds and if necessary to forgo registration under the IC Act;' and (b) '(we call) upon newly formed Trade Unions not to register under the IC Act, but to form broad multi-racial Trade Unions.' When asked whether the consequences of deregistration had been considered, Massina is minuted as saying, '. . . we must not fall into the trap of being super Trade Unionists. We must go to the workers and let them decide.' Uriah Maleka (A-FMBWU) added that failure to support deregistration would reduce SACTU's criticism of the Act to the reformist position of the SATUC.[19]

The Second Annual National Conference was opened by Ben January (NULCDW) with warnings that great sacrifices would have to be made by SACTU unions as all other coordinating bodies essentially supported the Nationalist legislation. The first full delegate debate on the IC Act and MC proposals was then initiated by Oscar Mpetha (A-FCWU, CT) who boldly stated that unless trade unions mounted a counter-offensive they would soon be nothing more than 'cogs in a Nazi-like Labour Front'. In opposition to the proposals for deregistration, Don Mateman (TWIU) offered a vaguely-worded amendment that argued against such open defiance.

Militant African leaders, by and large, strongly opposed Mateman's amendment. Mpetha put the case this way: 'Must we beg that a piece of paper will negotiate for us? Let us have the confidence in our workers and let us not underestimate our strength. I ask Conference not to accept the amendment.' John Gaetsewe (A-LCDWU) reminded delegates that when African workers were first confronted with the Native Labour Act they had boycotted the legislation and still managed to gain victories through struggle and collective strength. Although Mateman and other TWIU delegates argued that the amendment was not a compromise to the Nationalists, the tone of the discussion continued to support the original motions.

Examples were given of how Coloured workers in the Cape had won wage increases only after unregistered African workers had joined them in unity. Other delegates pointed out that for many years the old SAT & LC and registered unions had campaigned for inclusion of Africans as 'employees' under the Act; the campaign not only failed but African women lost their 'employee' status and were instead given passes. Maleka and Mpetha captured the sense of the discussion in their closing comments: 'A trade union exists because it has members, not because it is registered,' and 'We must reject the Act in toto for it is our doom to accept it.'

Despite the heated discussion, delegates realized that no alternative wording to either the original motion or the Mateman amendment would resolve the basic disagreement. Thus, as a temporary compromise, it was agreed that the incoming NEC would study both proposals and re-convene a special conference to be held in December 1957. In September, the FCWU held its 16th Annual Conference and called upon SACTU to publish a pamphlet to the workers, explaining the provisions, application and effects of the IC Act. Reiterating its total opposition to the Act, the FCWU agreed that until such time as greater unity within the whole trade union movement had been achieved, it would comply with the Act and alter its constitution to confine membership to Coloured workers. Within the context of the Act itself, this decision made sense in that it reflected the racial composition of the union members.

With all registered unions required by law to implement the IC Act by 1 January 1958, and with only the unaffiliated National Union of Distributive Workers (NUDW) in support of SACTU's Conference to discuss the IC Act, SACTU could not wait for the Conference to issue advice to registered unions. The October–November issue of *Workers' Unity* carried a lengthy but ambiguous statement by President Levy. While recognizing that circumstances varied greatly in each industry, Levy advised unions to refuse to comply with the Act in those situations where the unity of the workers would otherwise be smashed. He added that fears of losing sick funds and other benefits should not be an obstacle as these benefits had come from struggle, not government benevolence. Even if Industrial Councils were lost, private agreements between capital and labour could still be negotiated outside the Act. The strength of the deregistration argument had, however, lost a great deal of practical importance by this time. Following the FCWU, the TWIU also agreed to form separate uniracial unions, with the TWIU amending its constitution to cater for only Coloured workers, the vast majority of its membership.[20]

Therefore, the SACTU Special Conference held in December 1957, was predictably anti-climactic. With the three strongest SACTU registered unions complying with the trade union Apartheid clauses of the Act, the previous debate dissolved into a general resolution calling on new unions consisting of 'employees' under the Act to refuse to register and instead incorporate African workers into their ranks. Presently registered unions were advised to follow the path most appropriate to their respective situations. Separate uniracial unions were considered preferable to separate branches with all-White Executives (as TUCSA advised). Finally, in working for eventual deregistration, registered unions should establish multi-racial federations of uniracial unions in a given industry, conclude private agreements outside the Act whenever possible and campaign for repeal of the Act.

In sum, this debate reveals the divisions created even within the progressive trade union movement by Apartheid legislation. While there were exceptions, African leaders clearly favoured the deregistration strategy and thought the registered unions should defy the Act to correspond with the African trade unions' resistance to the Native Labour Act. Even African leaders of unions in food and canning and laundry, where the registered unions had been crucial in advancing the organization and interests of African workers, spoke out in favour of deregistration. African textile union leaders constitute the exception.

(Recent interviews with SACTU African leaders in exile suggests that this position regarding the IC Act is still strongly held.)

Patterns are more difficult to find among the registered union leaders. Factors that came into play were numerous. Regional variation may have made JR more important than the registration issue in certain areas – e.g. the Western Cape. There is also the legacy of experience of working within registered unions and the associated industrial conciliation machinery that certain leaders appeared unwilling to forgo. To others, compliance may have seemed a practical necessity because their memberships would simply not accept the short-term sacrifices associated with the loss of registered status. Yet there is no evidence to show that these registered unions seriously attempted to educate their Coloured members on the long-term political advantages of deregistration. The exception was the FCWU which under the influence of Ray Alexander carried out a full discussion. On the other hand, the TWIU Executive, it seems, never really discussed deregistration as a serious possibility. And to some, the unwillingness of registered unions to follow the lead proposed by their African brothers and sisters was reflective of the structural or political limitations on trade unions as revolutionary organizations. That is, trade unions are regarded as essentially defensive capitalist institutions organized to protect workers and are thus inherently reformist.

These larger theoretical questions cannot be resolved in abstract discussions but only in the course of the class struggle itself. In South Africa, the issue rested squarely on the progressive trade unionists' perception of the IC Act. Was it beneficial to the workers' struggle (if only extended to include *all* workers) or was it a restriction? John Gaetsewe, General Secretary of SACTU, sees the Act as a definite obstacle when he says,

Unity is the only way to push forward. Those that have some benefits from the registration should throw that away and come back to those who are not registered and be unified and fight together for the benefits of all workers. . . . Registration has got strings . . . the set up in South Africa means that registered workers continue to benefit from the suffering of African workers.[21]

SACTU opposition to Job Reservation was far less controversial. The garment industry determination prompted *Workers' Unity* to run feature articles exposing the threat that JR posed to Black workers in all industries. As on many issues, TUCSA and FOFATUSA unions, whose members were also threatened by JR in many cases, refused to cooperate with SACTU's efforts to build a united labour front against Nationalist legislation. Lucy Mvubelo's Garment Workers Union of African Women (GWU-AW) was a case in point. Yet when garment workers staged walk-outs to protest against JR, SACTU-FCWU workers who had been recently retrenched and encouraged by the authorities to fill the garment vacancies, refused to scab on their fellow workers.

Without a united labour opposition, most actions were rearguard and defensive in nature. A 1961 JR investigation of the textile industry brought a quick response from the TWIU, which represented 3,453 Coloured workers. The TWIU memorandum pointed out that the most important jobs − spinning and weaving, for example − were performed by members of all racial groups. The decline of White workers in the industry (from 28 per cent in 1939−40 to 13·3 per cent in the late 1950s) resulted from a voluntary departure and not inter-racial job competition. The TWIU warned, however, that imposition of JR quotas would lead to inter-racial conflict; it would also lead employers to relocate in border industrial areas thus jeopardizing the very jobs of White workers that legislation was designed to protect. No JR determination was ever scheduled for the industry.

In addition to the Nationalists' obsession with keeping Black workers 'in their inferior place', JR was also devised to protect and provide employment for White workers in a period of capitalist recession. In practice, Coloured workers in the Western Cape − workers who were skilled tradesmen largely responsible for the development of secondary industry in that area − were the most affected by JR. This explains the importance accorded this aspect of the IC Act by Ray Alexander in Cape Town. The SACTU Local Committee attempted to educate and mobilize the relatively conservative Coloured workers through a pamphlet entitled, 'Has Your Union Pulled Its Weight?' The TUC leadership of Coloured unions was attacked for conceding to the principle of White supremacy, and Coloured rank-and-file workers were encouraged to make a stand for trade union independence and unity. Many Coloured unions did become disenchanted with TUCSA during these years but, for the most part, were unwilling to join the ranks of SACTU.

Although the SACTU NEC promised to issue a pamphlet on JR, the urgency of explaining the implementation and effects of Clause 77 led Ray Alexander and her husband Jack Simons to publish at their own expense a forty-page booklet, entitled 'Job Reservation and the Trade

Unions'. The booklet covered the history of the colour-bar, reviewed the current IC Act in its entirety and carefully assessed the position taken by various trade union coordinating bodies. Coloured workers were encouraged to break from their White-executive controlled TUCSA unions and form new, independent unions that would represent their interests and those of African workers. Although Ray had been banned for six years, her 1959 pamphlet provides an excellent example of the invaluable leadership role she continued to play in the Western Cape.

SACTU as a coordinating body continually attacked the silence of other federations on the JR issue. Failing to achieve bilateral cooperation with other bodies, SACTU's 1960 Conference resolved that new initiatives be undertaken to organize an All-In Conference in Cape Town. The Sharpeville–Langa massacres of 1960, and the removals under the Group Areas Act had politicized a certain portion of the Coloured community and brought them closer to the Congress Alliance. The SACTU MC and the Cape Town Local Committee were thus able to obtain assistance from some unaffiliated Coloured unions in organizing the JR Conference which was held on 2–3 June 1962. Cardiff Marney and Norman Daniels served as Secretary and Chairman respectively.

Alex Hepple, former Parliamentary leader of the Labour Party, opened the Conference by reviewing the history of the colour-bar in South Africa, reminding delegates that JR was an outgrowth of the mining capitalists' treatment of Black labour. Specific instances of JR determinations under the 1956 Act were discussed and delegates rallied around the slogan: 'We do not want borrowed jobs.'

Seven of the unions sponsoring the JR Conference were SACTU affiliates. Ninety delegates, representing forty-six unions with nearly 60,000 workers, attended the proceedings; thirty-four of these were SACTU unions. Among the nineteen observers was a representative from Mvubelo's GWU-AW (FOFATUSA). TUCSA, however, refused to send any official delegates or observers, again betraying the interests of working class unity against Nationalist legislation. A Continuation Committee consisting of SACTU, TUCSA and independent unions was struck to organize post-Conference activities, and subsequent SACTU MC meetings suggested forming a Johannesburg JR Committee. Further initiatives against JR failed to materialize in the wake of heightened state repression in the early 1960s.

The Wage Boards

Another vital component of the state's legislative stranglehold on African workers is the Wage Act. Originally passed in 1918, the Act was changed in 1925 and became a supplement to the IC Act of 1924; further amendments in 1937 and 1957 increased the power of capital over labour.

The Wage Act, theoretically, is designed to protect African workers against exploitation by unscrupulous employers and serve as the principal means of increasing their wages. It operates in industries or areas where employers and employees are unorganized, although farm workers, domestic servants and government employees are excluded from the Act. The Act authorized the establishment of a Wage Board, whose members are appointed by the Minister of Labour and whose purpose is to recommend minimum wage rates and working conditions for undertakings not covered by Industrial Council agreements under the IC Act. *If* the Minister approves the Board's recommendations, a Wage Determination is then published. African workers, again in theory, are protected under the Act against retrenchment, demotion or punishment for membership of a trade union or active involvement in trade union work outside the workplace.

In practice the Wage Boards have acted to maintain starvation wages and assure industrial capitalists high profit margins. Employers commonly use low minimum wages set by Wage Boards as arguments against wage increases demanded by African workers. Agricultural capital simultaneously benefits as low urban wages keep exploited slave labour in the rural areas.

Wage Board policy was to recommend wages which would not endanger the supply of labour to the farmers, that is, to keep wage levels as close as possible to the abominably low standards of the rural areas. The Board also exploited a provision of the Act which made it compulsory for it to take 'payability' of an industry into consideration when fixing minimum wages. Hence, employers consistently attempted to present the image that they were on the brink of bankruptcy, and here it was SACTU's efficient research work that exposed these deceptions.

Wage Board investigations often dragged on for lengthy periods, at times taking three to four years before wage determinations were set in place. The effect of such delays was to make increases, even if scheduled, hopelessly out of date in relation to the rising cost of living.

Moreover, there were intervals of ten to fifteen years between investigations in some industries.

Over the years, it was common for registered trade unionists to make submissions to Wage Boards in support of African wage demands and also to sit as additional members when specific expertise could be provided. In 1957, trade unionists were denied the right to automatically sit on the Boards or have their memoranda considered. Also, unions lost the right to request Wage Board investigations, now the exclusive preserve of the Minister.

These restrictions complemented the grand design of the Nationalists to crush legitimate working class action and organization. The Amendments must also be regarded as a response to the momentum developing around SACTU's national minimum wage (£1-a-Day) campaign. During the 1957 Alexandra Bus Boycott, the Minister promised to investigate forty-five industries, the majority of which lacked any minimum wage limits. By 1959, SACTU reported that only twelve, or about 25 per cent, had been undertaken.

More importantly, many of these wage determinations had not recommended wage increases, and in the case of the food and canning industry had actually called for wage cuts on the basis of alleged difficulties for the industry during the recessionary years of the late 1950s. This attack on already below subsistence wages coincided with the 1959 Amendment to the IC Act which made food and canning an 'essential industry' and thus prohibited strikes.

Early indications of the government assault on FCWU came in 1957 when Liz Abrahams (Acting General Secretary) was prevented from sitting on the Wage Board investigation for the industry. The Union was described as 'unrepresentative', an absurd statement as it represented more than 51 per cent of the workers (as required by law) and had participated in wage determination and Industrial Council agreements already in effect. The reason for this decision was made clear in 1958, when Wage Determination No. 179 and No. 180 signalled wage cuts of up to £1 6s. 6d. per week for certain categories of workers. Only the strength of the FCWU and support from the Congress Alliance prevented the Afrikaner monopolies from imposing these wage reductions (see Chapter 8).

In 1959, SACTU called for an end to these state-controlled Wage Boards and their replacement by a national, legislated minimum wage for *all* workers of £1-a-Day. The Ninth Annual Conference in 1963 passed a resolution that was subsequently submitted to the government, stating:

(SACTU) is convinced that the Wage Board is used by employers and the government as a smoke-screen to prevent direct negotiations with workers and their trade unions and also as a means to create the false impression that something is being done about poverty wages. . . . Having noted the Chairman of the Wage Board's statement that non-White workers will have to wait another 15 years before they can get a living wage, Conference calls upon the government to dissolve the Wage Board and forthwith replace it with legislation providing for a national minimum wage and the protection of working standards.

Bantu (Native) Laws Amendment Acts

It was stated at the outset that repressive legislation against African workers was cumulative. This is so in two respects: firstly, in the straightforward sense of laws piled on top of previous laws, each a greater restriction on the freedom of the people. Secondly, the laws were cumulative in the sense that laws directed against Africans as workers affected their lives as citizens beyond the workplace, and laws increasing national oppression also could be used to counter their collective struggles to improve working conditions and increase wages. The Bantu Laws Amendment Acts, passed successively since 1937, qualify as cumulative in both meanings of the term. In general, these Laws consisted of blanket legislation which blocked loopholes and/or created tighter controls over and above specific Acts passed through the decades. In specific cases, the Laws attempted to refine the system of migrant labour and influx control that rules the day-to-day life of every African in South Africa.

Insofar as the migrant labour system guarantees a cheap, dependable supply of sweated Black labour for capitalist production, many of these Amendment Laws affected Africans as workers. It is only those aspects of the Laws which will concern us here.

Nationalist Party Amendments in 1952 and 1957 sped up the process of removing Africans from urban areas unless they were employed there. As we have seen, in 1952, all urban areas became 'proclaimed areas' subject to influx controls; previous to that, the 1937 legislation merely allowed local authorities to apply for 'proclaimed' status voluntarily. Along with the mandatory restrictions on the rights of Africans in urban areas came the establishment of labour bureaux where African workers and work-seekers were forced to register. These bureaux ensured that Africans remained 'temporary sojourners' when they were not serving the needs of the White man; they also provided an administrative means of removing 'undesirables' as defined, for example, by the Native Labour Act discussed above. This included the African unemployed. Between 1953 and 1963, there were 334 local and 353 district labour bureaux established, with over one million African workers registered.

Tighter controls were implemented in 1957 as a response to the popular momentum of Congress Alliance mass campaigns. There is little doubt that the Amendment Laws were directed against the ANC and SACTU. Meetings attended by Africans in urban areas could be prohibited. Africans could be prevented from entering places of entertainment in 'White areas' if their presence might be a 'nuisance'. The definition of 'undesirable' persons was further broadened to allow for more forced removals, and new reference books were issued, incorporating all of the separate documents Africans were required to carry at all times. Dr H. F. Verwoerd, Minister of Native Affairs, explained the government policy regarding these changes as follows:

Our attitude is that when the Native is employed in the White area (i.e. the urban area) – even if he has been there for one or two generations – then he is here in the service of the White man whose territory it is. . . . They cannot have permanent rights in Johannesburg or Cape Town or in any other White city. They are there as long as they are employed there and as long as the White community continues to accept them there . . .[22]

SACTU campaigned against these 1957 Amendments for the obvious reason that the right of freedom of association for African workers was virtually destroyed. Factory committee meetings, employer–African employee meetings, protest meetings – every possible type of contact between racial groups in the urban areas could be outlawed by the legislation. It was under the constant threat of legal intimidation that SACTU organizers were forced to work in their daily struggles to communicate with African workers and respond to their economic and political aspirations.

The Amendment Act of 1963 was passed during the period of heavy repression and victimization of SACTU and the Congress Alliance activists. Extensions of earlier restrictions and the deletion of old clauses that gave Africans some form of minimal protection reflected the strength of the government *vis-à-vis* the liberation forces in the early 1960s. The 1963 Amendment Laws:

(a) *interfered with the previous right of Africans to live in their place of origin.* A Labour Officer might deprive an African of the right to work or live in an area if such employment is in excess of a maximum quota determined by the Minister of Bantu Affairs;

(b) *further directed and controlled African labour.* An African might not be allowed to perform his work if a Labour Officer did not consider that work *bona fide*, i.e. in the interests of employers, employees, or 'in the public interest'. This was applicable to continued employment as well as new employment. Furthermore, the Minister of Bantu Affairs might arbitrarily set Job Reservation quotas for given areas, thus transferring control of African work-seekers from the Department of Labour to the Department of Bantu Administration and Development. An African domestic might be prevented from living on his/her employer's premises (previously unlegislated) and the definition of an 'idle' person subject to removal from an urban area was changed to include all those convicted of offences related to any of the repressive political legislation passed in the early 1960s – e.g. the Unlawful Organizations Act, Sabotage Act, etc. (see Chapter 12);

(c) *disrupted African family life.* The 1963 legislation deleted old clauses of the 1945 Urban Areas Act that had guaranteed the right of African women to reside with their husbands in urban areas where the latter had been employed continuously for two or more years. New clauses were added to restrict African families living together in rural areas, unless all family members/dependants directly laboured in farming operations.

(d) *authorized the removal of unhealthy African workers from urban areas.* Workers suffering from diseases could be sent to rural areas where few facilities were available. Treatment was not compulsory. (The effect would obviously be an increase in mortality amongst Africans and a greater threat to the general public health);

(e) *established labour depots for Africans seeking work and/or not having approved accommodation.* These were nothing short of detention camps where African workers were kept until directed to jobs selected by the authorities;

(f) *further diminished the rights of African women.* In addition to all the restrictions placed on African male labourers, African women seeking work in urban areas had to have a reference from either the rural chief, headman, or Bantu Authority. The purpose was to keep the African women in the permanent status of a 'child' *vis-à-vis* the law (and subordinate *vis-à-vis* the male population).

These are merely the main provisions of the Act which, 'seeks

absolute power over the lives of all African people in South Africa'...
(and) 'seeks to ensure that the lives of Africans, from birth to death, will
be controlled by officialdom'.[23]

SACTU was in virtually no position to fight the 1963 Act as much of
its leadership was being held in prison under the 90-day detentions. One
large SACTU-NIC protest meeting was convened in Durban in mid-
March 1963, where over 1,200 persons signed a petition against the
enactment of the legislation. Of all the clauses contained in the draft Bill,
SACTU focused its attack on (b) above. The total power of decision
given to the Labour Officer meant that trade union organizers and
officials might be endorsed out of the urban areas if their work was not
considered *bona fide* employment. In actual fact, the state chose
detention without trial, torture and long-term imprisonment rather than
endorsement out of urban areas as the main weapon against SACTU
activists.

This lengthy review of state-introduced and enforced anti-working
class legislation – both before and after the ascension of the Nationalists
to power in 1948 – clearly illustrates the role of the state in guaranteeing
and maintaining the availability of a cheap, unorganized Black labour
force. Far too often the critique of Apartheid ends with an analysis of
the state alone, but as pointed out above, the state never acts in a
vacuum. It acts to promote the general order and structure of the basic
relationships that define social life – the most decisive being the capital-
labour relationship in the process of social production. Although the
Apartheid state bears the brunt of domestic and international criticism,
the capitalist class is that sector in South African society whose
interests in capital accumulation are best served by Apartheid. In the
following section and subsequent chapters we will demonstrate the
bosses' response to the official Apartheid policies established after
1948.

The Capitalist Profit Motive and Apartheid

Those who arbitrarily separate the state from the capitalist class also
argue that if capitalism were only allowed to develop 'freely' in South
Africa, Apartheid would be gradually undermined. The suggestion that
Black workers stand to gain from a capitalism unfettered by racial
legislation, makes a mockery of serious social analysis and is an affront
to the oppressed peoples who, long before the Nationalists came to
power, suffered exploitation at the hands of mining, agricultural and
later industrial capital. All fractions of the propertied class have

survived through profits reaped from the expropriation of wealth produced by the Black working class. SACTU expressed its understanding of this fundamental fact when it said that capitalism '... holds no brief for the aspirations of the producers of its wealth . . . in South Africa, the device used to create super profits is racial discrimination' (quoted above).

Having examined the legislative 'devices' of racial discrimination above, this section will begin to unfold the other half of the equation: capitalism plus Apartheid ensures exploitation of the Black working class. Whereas Chapter 6 will document capitalist exploitation by industry, the purpose here is to look at one specific area where there would appear to be a conflict between the profit motive and racial segregation. Also, we will briefly illustrate a case where capitalist 'concern' for the fate of its African workforce is shown to be a mere illusion.

Border Industries

As SACTU has already stated, the economic reality of class exploitation in South Africa is camouflaged by the racial legislation of Apartheid. For example, Job Reservation, would appear to interfere with the continuous flow of labour power into capitalist production insofar as jobs are allocated by racial quotas. The ability of capital and labour to exchange their commodities in the marketplace, according to the ideal model of capitalism, is thus directly affected by state intervention. Indeed, there were many concrete examples of employers' organizations objecting to JR following introduction of the 1956 legislation for precisely this reason.

In order to explain this paradox it is necessary to think of all capitalists as a whole and not simply a single company or even industry. While it is definitely the case that JR interfered with the momentary imperatives of given companies in given industries, this does not necessarily mean that the class interests of capital in relation to those of labour were negatively affected. This would be so only if the value of labour power increased. In fact, we shall see that JR allowed the value of labour-power to be further reduced and hence served the interests of the employing class.

With JR determinations being introduced in the mid-1950s, an outlet for capital to realize its goal of uninterrupted accumulation was simultaneously required. This came in the form of Border Industrial

Areas. Similarly the Nationalists' preoccupation with removing 'unproductive' African labour from the urban areas necessitated the creation of alternative or supplementary productive areas for Africans so affected. Border industries thus satisfied both profit and racial motives.

In 1956. the Tomlinson Commission recommended the establishment of industrial production centres adjacent to and/or within the African reserves. Four years later, a government memorandum on decentralization of industry defined border industries as

... those localities or regions near the Bantu areas, in which industrial development takes place through European initiative and control but which are so situated that the Bantu workers can maintain their residences and family lives in the Bantu areas and move readily to the places of their employment.

A Permanent Committee for Location of Industry, consisting of senior bureaucrats and officials of agencies concerned, was formed to implement this decentralization scheme. Renamed the Decentralization Board in 1971, this body assumed many of the functions previously performed by the Industrial Development Corporation created during the Second World War.

Prime Minister Verwoerd spoke of these White-owned industries on the perimeters of reserves as a means of utilizing (exploiting) African labour without causing social problems in the White cities. The production process would be labour intensive, with African workers ideally returning to the reserves nightly or on weekends. Trade union organization would also be easier to control, so the argument went.

But how did the Border Industries scheme satisfy the interests of capital? Companies were enticed by a long and impressive list of concessions to locate or re-locate their factories in border areas. These concessions included: cash grants towards the cost of removal; low-interest loans to cover land costs, factory buildings, plant and equipment, operating capital and erection of housing for White personnel; tax concessions in relation to wages paid to Africans and the book value of the plant; price preferences on state-purchased goods produced in the border areas; and transportation rebates – both rail and harbour. Furthermore, the government would undertake to provide infrastructural developments such as water and power, road transport and industrial townships.

As if this were not enough to lure capitalists to border areas, the government promised to intervene in current and future Industrial

Council agreements and Wage Determinations to ensure that lower wages could be paid to the Black (predominantly African) workers. Where necessary and desirable, the state would provide technical and vocational training for African labour. Exemptions from other racially-based statutory differentiations would be made on a case by case basis, on condition that Black and White workers would not be employed at the same level of work, that facilities were racially segregated, and that no White would be under the authority of or be replaced by a Black worker.

Before outlining the implementation of border industries, let us pause to consider the capitalist logic of what first appeared to be an 'economically irrational, Apartheid' measure. By forcing Africans to labour in 'White areas' and to reside in 'Black areas', the latter could be expected to provide a portion of the means of subsistence for the African worker and family. Thus, the overall cost of labour power (the wage) could be proportionately reduced. Whether or not the reserves could actually provide that portion of subsistence was irrelevant (at least to the capitalist) – it was sufficient to assume this to be the case. In fact, they couldn't. But for the employer class as a whole, any lowering of the value of labour power allows a maximization of surplus value extracted from the process of production. Border industries, in theory, could not have been more to the liking of the South African capitalist class.

In practice, the same was true. Between 1960 and 1970, border industries were encouraged in Rosslyn, Brits, Rustenburg, Mafekeng and Zeerust (near the Tswana homelands), Pietersburg and other towns in the Northern and Eastern Transvaal; in Harrismith in the Orange Free State; in Hammarsdale, Pietermaritzburg, Newcastle, Ladysmith/Colenso and Richards Bay in Natal; and East London/Berlin, Kingwilliamstown, and Queenstown in the Eastern Cape.[24] As Hepple points out, however, the original image of factories erected on the borders of large reserves proved incorrect. Instead, many factories sprang up near the 236 'Black spots' or separate areas scattered within 'White areas', i.e. Black areas not incorporated into the larger homeland-reserves.

The effect was to merely extend existing metropolitan areas and thus reproduce the prevalent conditions of exploitation, albeit at a higher rate. Writing in 1969, Hepple contends that only 189,541 jobs had been created for Africans, perhaps even an overestimate in that increased unemployment resulted in the urban areas where existing companies closed down their operations. Also, large numbers of Whites and Coloureds were drawn closer to African areas in the process. In other words, the government propaganda about job creation for Africans was largely a myth after only the first decade.

Where Nationalist promises were kept was in the area of greater exploitation of African labour power. Again to quote Hepple, 'Employers are usually left to pay their African employees whatever they please.'[25] The clothing industry was the most obvious example, where a machinist in the Hammarsdale border area received R10.50 a week, compared with the legal minimum of R15.00 in Durban, twenty-seven miles away, or R17.73 in Port Elizabeth and East London. General labourers in the same clothing factory had their wages reduced to R6.75 a week, as compared with R10.50 in Port Elizabeth. The irony of the clothing industry example is that the reactionary White workers who had called for a Job Reservation determination found their employers resettling in cheap labour border areas. (See Chapter 8 on strikes at Hammarsdale.)

Lower wages were also the rule in the textile, motor, engineering and canvas goods factories located in border areas. By 1969, the Minister of Labour had arbitrarily intervened to lower statutory wages in six Industrial Council agreements. The exploitation of African workers in border areas was furthered with Proclamation No. 74 of March 1968, which limited employment to annual contracts subject to renewal through tribal labour bureaux administered by government-appointed chiefs and headmen. Thus, the border areas scheme falls within the general policy stated by Mr Froneman, Deputy Chairman of the Bantu Affairs Commission in 1968:

We are trying to introduce the migratory labour pattern as far as possible in every sphere. That is in fact the entire basis of our policy as far as the White economy is concerned, namely a system of migrant labour:[26]

While the government Minister thinks in terms of 'Black' and 'White' economies, the capitalist class does not need to enter into such banalities. Notwithstanding specific cases whereby a given company or industry might be adversely affected by Apartheid labour legislation, the overall schema of Apartheid not only maintains capitalist interests but it promotes them to higher levels of profit. Subsequent capital investment inside the homelands themselves – especially by foreign (imperialist) capital – would only serve to strengthen the general point that Apartheid is good for capitalism.

The Clydesdale Disaster

These workers have built the wealth they have never earned. They have made South Africa glitter with gold but they have not a rag to cover their body in. How does that happen?[27]

Some facts to consider:

An estimated 32,000 African mine workers died between 1900–1960. This was an average of three deaths per shift.

On 28 December 1959 African mine workers complained of rumblings in the Clydesdale Colliery. One day in early January 1960 at 4.20 p.m. miners on the day shift smelled gas and rushed to the pithead, only to be ordered to return to work below. Twenty African miners going to work on the late shift smelled gas as they went underground. When they refused to go to the coalface, mine officials gave them the choice of returning to work, or being arrested by mine police. Two were arrested and eighteen went down under. At 7.20 p.m., three hours after the warning by the workers, the Clydesdale cave-in occurred, killing 429 Africans and 6 Whites.

On 16 August 1960 another cave-in at the Village Main Reef Mine claimed the lives of another 11 Africans and one White.

These mining disasters can only in part be attributed to natural forces. The underlying cause of the deaths of these 447 miners and countless others in similar disasters was the profit motive in an industry notorious for the leading role it has played in exploiting migrant African labour in South Africa.

An underground African mine worker, in most cases a foreigner to South Africa imported on contract, received 3s. per shift in 1959–60. His White counterpart, usually working in a supervisory position, earned £3 per shift, or twenty times more. But the lion's share of the value of production went to the mining companies. In 1959, profits for that year alone were as follows: Anglo-American (£7·7 million); De Beers (£21·4m); Consolidated Gold Fields (£2·3m); and Rand Mines (£3m).

Compensation paid to the dependants of the Clydesdale victims was equally deplorable (see Chapter 9). Payment of the pitiful sums further depended on the companies being able to trace the families of the migrant workers from Mozambique, Malawi and Tanzania and elsewhere. One of the most shocking aspects of the Clydesdale disaster was the fact that the mining company took weeks to provide a list of the full names of its African labourers. They had been known only by their

Christian names and clock number – e.g. Jim, Clock No. 3. As SACTU said in a press release: 'Only in South Africa, where Africans are regarded as numbers and not men, could such a state of affairs arise.'

When pressed for a list of the slain workers, the company spokesman stated, 'There's not a hope of getting a list today. It's a lot of checking. We're too busy.' This failure to maintain above-ground an accurate record of workers was in contravention of the Mines and Works Act of 1911. In contrast, the White miners' names were released immediately following the disaster. Two months later, some of the Africans listed by the company as among the dead were discovered living in Basutoland (Lesotho).

Finally, in such a clear case of culpable homicide – where workers' warnings went unheeded and they were ordered to return to obviously unsafe conditions and eventually their death – the state decided to lessen the charge to simple negligence under the Mines and Works Act. The charges and fines eventually levied were astounding:

- for failing to report the subsidence on 28 December (nearly a month before the fatal accident)

    Company £50
    Officials £50 (or 14 days)

- for committing acts or omissions likely to endanger the safety of the men working underground (e.g. cutting pillars and top-coaling in Section 10 of the mine)

    Company £100
    Two Officials £22 10s. 0d. (or 47 days)

- for undermining the house of a Mr Muller

    Company £10
    Official £5 (or 7 days)

- for undermining the Vereeniging–Heilbron Road

    Company £10
    Official £5 (or 7 days)

- for undermining the Wolwehoek–Oranjeville Road

    Company £5
    Official £2 10s. 0d. (or 7 days)[28]

In total, only £260 in fines were issued against the company and its officials for the death of 435 miners at the Clydesdale mine, *an average of twelve shillings per worker*. The Magistrate in passing sentence said that he had taken into account that the company had suffered the 'loss

COULD 440 MINERS HAVE BEEN SAVED?

NEW AGE

Vol. 6, No. 15. Registered at the G.P.O. as a Newspaper 6d.
NORTHERN EDITION   Thursday, January 28, 1960

Crowds of Africans wait at the shafthead of the Clydesdale mine where 434 African miners and six Europeans were trapped underground last week in the worst mining disaster ever to hit South Africa.

From Ruth First

JOHANNESBURG.

FIVE full days after the shocking tragedy at the Clydesdale coal mine—the most horrible accident in the history of all South African mining—not only have the names of the missing African miners not yet been released but there are a number of other questions that the public wants to ask:

Why are the names of the African miners entombed underground still not listed?
Are reports that in the old mine underground rumblings were heard three weeks ago correct?
Was the old shaft too near the surface and a danger to life, but kept working nevertheless?
Why was no notice taken of the first underground falls three hours before the full tragedy occurred?

(Continued on page 2)

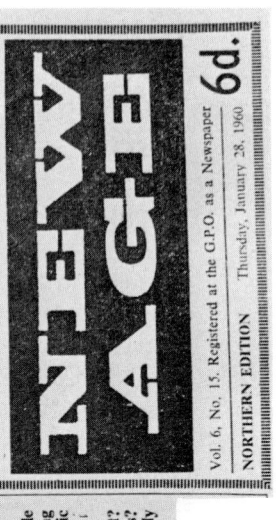

of a valuable mine and many thousands of pounds'. The murder of 435 men was incidental. It is upon this bedrock of exploitation of African labour *for capitalist profit* that Apartheid squarely rests.

TUCSA Accepts Trade Union Apartheid

African workers could always see who were their friends and who were their enemies.[29]

TUCSA[30] hostility to SACTU came from two sources, one passive and the other active. Firstly, the average White rank-and-file workers belonging to TUCSA unions chose to cling to the relative privilege they received under Apartheid rather than promote the solidarity of labour. Secondly, the TUCSA leadership, which had emerged from the dissolution of the Trades & Labour Council in 1954 as clearly on the right-wing of trade union politics, strongly objected to the political trade unionism that SACTU promoted. This section will review some of the major strains in the TUCSA–SACTU relationship, while Chapter 11 exposes TUCSA's attempt to destroy SACTU through the creation of FOFATUSA.

All trade union coordinating bodies in South Africa must ultimately be judged according to their position on African workers and their trade unions. Only in this way it is possible to determine their respective attitudes towards Apartheid trade unionism. TUCSA, to its credit, is not one of the ultra-reactionary bodies but rather stands more in the 'middle' of the political spectrum. Yet such a statement should not be misinterpreted. TUCSA owes its creation in 1954 to the fact that it betrayed the cause of working class unity. From that historic decision, its concern for African workers was always circumscribed by its more fundamental concern that White workers needed protection from unorganized Africans who were easy prey for the employers. But instead of promoting working class unity, TUCSA chose the path of paternalism and opportunism in its relations with the African workforce. TUCSA was fully complicit in the Nationalist Party's attempt to crush legitimate trade unionism in South Africa.

Although excluding African unions from affiliated status, TUCSA still could not openly support the IC Act of 1956 and all of its ramifications. As Alexander and Simons pointed out,

> The TUC can claim with justice that it made strenuous efforts to stop the passage of the Bill. At no point in the campaign, however, did the Council argue that workers of all colour groups should be allowed free access to any

trade or calling. Its whole case rested on the contention that the Bill would be less effective than existing arrangements in safeguarding the standards of White workers. It disagreed with the Government on a question of method, not principle.[31]

As already mentioned, the SACTU Management Committee sent a letter to the TUC Executive in June, 1955, urging maximum cooperation and unity in opposing the legislation. The TUC response was indicative of the position it would take towards SACTU over the months and years to come: the General Secretary told SACTU that it (TUCSA) '. . . would determine its own policy and prepare its own campaign'. The letter also mentioned that the TUC would be meeting with the Minister of Labour soon.

This rejection of unity was a highly calculated move by the TUC Executive as Mr T. C. Rutherford, President, offered the government one of its many historic compromises. If the government would introduce Job Reservation as a special piece of legislation to be put into effect prior to Apartheid trade unionism (i.e. the splitting of 'mixed' unions), and if it was shown to be practicable, then the TUC would 'discuss . . . its (the government's) further proposals under the IC Bill.[32] In short, the TUC accepted White supremacy on the one hand, and paternalistically attempted to protect the position of its White executive in 'mixed' unions on the other. The government was obviously pleased to see that registered unions were thinking and willing to act along racial lines. The compromise was rejected, however, and the Nationalists pushed ahead with their legislation.

TUC credibility was further reduced by statements made by Rutherford and the TUC's so-called opposition to the Bill. For example, 'We appealed to the Minister to allow us to keep our organization intact so that we could co-operate with the Government *in devising ways and means of preventing the ever-increasing Native labour force from continuing to menace the European standard of living*' (emphasis added).[33] And, in his opening address to the 1956 TUC Conference, Rutherford promised that '. . . the TUC will not do anything contrary to the laws of the land'.[34] Delegates then resolved that there would be no strikes against the IC Act, and that White workers should be protected against African competition. Thus, despite the occasional liberal rhetoric against Job Reservation, the TUC in the space of two short years had clearly shown itself to be one more enemy of the African workers.

The TUC also began its programme of undermining SACTU at

about this time. While on the one hand rejecting SACTU initiatives for workers' unity, the TUC on the other hand attempted to 'liaise' with the very same African workers it would not accept as constitutional equals. This was clearly a rearguard action necessitated by SACTU's increased popularity.

The TUC approached African unions and paternalistically offered to use its resources and energies to assist those unions to gain strength and efficiency. This programme was assisted by Lucy Mvubelo, the renegade African unionist who broke with SACTU in 1957. The eventual outcome of this attempt to woo African workers into the reformist camp was the formation of the Federation of Free African Trade Unions of South Africa (FOFATUSA) in 1959. Because the underlying TUC motive in this action was to improve its international image by being able to claim African 'membership', we therefore discuss FOFATUSA and its failure in Chapter 11.

At one of the TUC-sponsored 'liaison committee' meetings held in late 1956, Dulcie Hartwell (General Secretary) had the audacity to tell African workers that the TUC had only temporarily sacrificed its principles, and that the 'liaison committee' would hopefully evolve into a coordinating body of African trade unions. Leslie Massina, SACTU's General Secretary, countered Hartwell on every point from the audience. He told Hartwell that African workers firstly did not need the TUC's self-serving help as it would only lead to an acceptance of Nationalist legislation; secondly, SACTU already existed as a coordinating body for African workers and if the TUC seriously wanted to 'liaise' why had it rejected all of SACTU's offers for unity?

SACTU's Special All-In Conference on the IC Act was, as reported previously, rejected by the TUC. Meanwhile, at the TUC's 1957 Conference, Rutherford was still warning delegates, '... we must not be provoked into disobeying the law, however distasteful [sic]'.

For SACTU, unity of *all* workers was more than a rhetorical slogan, but the prospects for such unity in the 1950s were another matter entirely. *Workers' Unity* of October–November 1957 carried a lengthy editorial written by Ray Alexander in which she argued,

... the White workers are joining hands with the Nationalists as though the real enemies are not the bosses but their Non-White fellow workers. The tragedy in our country is that with very few exceptions White workers have put racial solidarity before working class solidarity ... (F)or them the sole purpose of Trade Union organisation and industrial legislation is to preserve the White man's privileges and standard of living.

Alexander gave additional evidence showing that White unions had objected to the IC Bill only because they believed that 'non-White' workers were becoming more competitive and threatened to oust White workers from privileged positions. Her conclusions reflected the thinking of the majority of SACTU leaders, particularly the African trade unionists:

> Therefore to base a policy on the assumption that in the present set up of trade unions there is a possibility of real working class unity – does not correspond to reality . . . (and) does not reflect our own present situation. . . . We must win him (the White worker) over. We must explain to him again and again that his identifying with the bosses on a racial basis will lead him to disaster. An important factor to bring about workers' unity will be the strength of organisation amongst the African, Coloured and Indian workers.[35]

This position was reinforced by the fact that early investigations into JR had been requested by the White workers themselves. Also, by March 1958 the TUC had joined the South African Confederation of Labour (SACOL), a central organization formed to facilitate interaction between White coordinating bodies and the government. SACOL represented the pinnacle of the White labour aristocracy.

Despite these many examples of TUC hostility, certain SACTU leaders, seemingly those with more involvement in the registered trade unions, continued to call for the impossible. Leon Levy's Presidential speech to the 1958 Conference stated this position as follows:

> Our efforts in the past have been rebuffed. The SATUC has refused to join with us in any action. . . . As a result, many of our affiliated unions have hardened in their attitude toward having any dealing with this body, but we cannot agree with them. The struggles of the workers requires unity of all workers. . . . No matter how often our overtures are rejected, we must look for ways of establishing our ideal – unity.

In principle, of course, all SACTU activists supported workers' unity, but in practice the question was one of emphasis, especially given the limited resources available.

The National Union of Distributive Workers (NUDW) often played a broker role between the TUC and SACTU. The NUDW had remained unaffiliated to any co-ordinating body, yet its leadership always supported the principles advanced by SACTU. In 1958, J. R. Altman brought NUDW greetings to the TUC Conference in this way:

> A genuine desire to further the interests of the trade union movement must lead your Council to seek closer collaboration with those unions and organizations

which have steadfastly upheld the principles of the old SATLC (i.e. SACTU), rather than those who rejoiced at the untimely demise of that Council.[36]

The contradiction was, of course, that Altman was addressing many delegates actively responsible for that 'demise' and that the reiteration of principles *ad nauseam* had little to do with the struggle in practice. By the late 1950s, only the naïve could fail to see that TUC policy, in consultation with the ICFTU, was to crush SACTU through whatever means were necessary and available.

The TUC's disregard for African workers reached an all-time low in 1960 when it refused to assist SACTU in its campaign for adequate compensation for the victims of the Clydesdale mining disaster. The TUC refused to send a representative to the SACTU-convened memorial meeting held in Johannesburg, attended by church officials, political organizations and even the White mine workers' unions, the bastion of 'White Baaskap' in South Africa.

But the winds of change were in the air. Nationally and internationally, SACTU had become the organization recognized as representing the aspirations of South Africa's Black workers. At ILO Conferences, the TUC was increasingly humiliated by the international community for its colour-bar that prevented affiliation of African trade unions. Something obviously had to be done to salvage TUC credibility abroad.

The Eighth TUC Conference, held in East London, in March 1962 agreed to: (a) change the name of the organization to TUCSA; (b) to open its membership to 'all *bona fide* trade unions'; and (c) to call for a national minimum wage of R40.00 per month for all workers. Thus, for the first time since its creation in 1954, the new TUCSA dropped its official colour-bar and offered equality in affiliation status to African trade unions. No one could deny the progressive nature of this move, although again the motivation behind it was questioned by observers at the time. In addition to the international pressure, the TUC President L. C. Scheepers hinted at another reason when he told delegates that it was necessary to persuade African trade unions '. . . to adopt a moderate policy . . .' Sectional self-interest and paternalism are obviously difficult qualities for liberal White trade unionists to shed. Statements attributed to Johanna Cornelius (TUC Executive member) that these changes would 'put SACTU out of business' added to the suspicions concerning TUC motives.[37]

Although African trade unions failed to rush to TUCSA's 'open door', the non-racial constitution once again forced SACTU to come to terms with TUCSA's role in the trade union movement. The SACTU NEC had anticipated this reversal of policy and discussed its implications for SACTU work. Most agreed that it was nothing more than a face-saving move and any temptation to believe that TUCSA had changed its fundamental politics should be carefully guarded against. Speakers recounted the 'imperialist connections' of TUCSA (referring to its ICFTU ties) and strongly argued against unity at any cost: 'We wanted the unity of workers on realistic terms — not on terms which would reduce the workers to impotency as had been done with workers in unions affiliated to the TUC.' There was also no evidence to suggest that TUCSA had modified its anti-SACTU stance. Because SACTU-NEC representatives from the Western Cape and Natal were absent from this meeting, it was resolved that informal discussions must take place before an official position was recorded.

TUCSA's policy changes brought to the fore the entire range of ambiguities and contradictions regarding practical unity in South Africa. SACTU discussions between February and October 1962 reflected these problems. Prior to the SACTU National Conference in April, two MC meetings grappled with the formulation of a correct political position to be taken to delegates for debate. Was this the time for unity with TUCSA and on what basis? What did the TUCSA amendments really mean?

A tentative agreement was reached by the MC on the following points: (a) previous objections to TUCSA were not primarily associated with its colour-bar constitution but rather its support for the colour-bar in the economy generally; thus, unity could be achieved if and only if TUCSA extended its opposition to colour-bars at the point of production; (b) TUCSA must end its 'no politics' position and agree with SACTU that the African workers' struggle is fundamentally a political struggle (as had been the White workers' struggle earlier in the century); and (c) no meeting of joint executives could occur unless approved by the Conference delegates.

Mark Shope, Acting General Secretary, addressed Conference delegates on the TUCSA issue, stating:

We know that whilst there are some White workers who genuinely believe in working class unity, we are forced to state that the majority of White workers treat the non-White workers with disdain. To them, the non-White worker is a 'boy' or a 'girl'. The capitalist class has deliberately fostered these attitudes among the White workers by making them the aristocrats of the labour force.

The non-White workers and trade union leaders will no longer accept an inferior position. In SACTU they have found a home where true equality is practised. *Non-White trade unionists are no longer prepared to have the official titles of trade union secretaries while they are, in fact, glorified messengers.*

The policy statement prepared by the SACTU–MC was then read to the delegates. Congratulating TUCSA for dropping its constitutional colour-bar, and repeating SACTU's pledge to strive for the unity of all workers, the document hastened to point out that a common policy between the two bodies had not yet been attained. SACTU would only unite on the basis of the strength it had developed amongst African workers, and if TUCSA agreed to:

(a) fight for full and equal workmen's compensation, unemployment insurance, guaranteed annual leave on full pay for all workers, including those on the farms, in domestic service and on the mines and also for the *right of every worker, African, Indian and Coloured, as well as White, to engage in skilled occupations and to advancement in industry* (emphasis in original);

(b) campaign for the right of African workers to take strike action to protect their living standards (i.e. campaign for the repeal of the Native Labour (Settlement of Disputes) Act and the Masters and Servants Act); without this the admission of African trade unions is of no practical value; and

(c) to campaign for full political equality of all South Africans and to end all racial discrimination – e.g. pass laws, influx controls, etc.

If and only if TUCSA met these conditions would SACTU agree to unity. The document concluded on the ambiguous note that SACTU 'will at all times stretch out the hand of friendship to the TUC to co-operate on specific issues'.

Leon Levy's Presidential Address, read in his absence as a banned person by George Monare, repeated the essential position and posed the problem this way: 'The question is which policy is right for the trade union movement: colour bar, job reservation, *baaskap*, Apartheid OR equality of rights and status for all workers regardless of colour and a united fight against capitalist exploitation. . . . SACTU believes the latter is the right policy for the trade union movement.'

Don Mateman (TWIU) led the discussion amongst delegates, who by and large were more outspoken in their criticism of TUCSA and more suspicious of any interaction with that body than the executive. Stephen Dlamini (TWIU, Durban) reminded everyone that no trade union movement could be considered progressive unless it was totally supported by African workers. The luxuries accorded the TUCSA unions had been gained by the sweat of African workers, and the TUC was a

> white mamba which had thrown out the African workers . . . (and) though the mamba was toothless it still had poisonous fangs. . . . If the TUC was sincere . . . why didn't it dissolve itself and join SACTU? They didn't do this because they are still white mambas.

Although many speakers opposed any talks between SACTU and TUCSA, Uriah Maleka (A-FMBWU) proposed that the best way to expose the latter would be to publicly challenge it to carry out specific actions as outlined in the policy statement. This position and the policy statement were then accepted by the delegates.

Following the Conference, however, minutes of SACTU meetings record confusion over the practical application of the policy statement. A meeting was convened with Mr O'Donoghue, TUC General Secretary, but TUCSA expressed no greater interest in cooperation with SACTU than before.

None the less, certain SACTU executive member(s) proceeded with the drafting and distribution of an 'Open Letter to White Workers'. The Letter, contrary to the spirit of the Conference discussion, went unnecessarily out of its way to appease the fears of White workers. For example, phrases like, 'We do not hate you', 'We do not want to take your jobs as some of you fear', and 'Our demands are the same' were reflections of a strained desire for unity that had little or no basis in reality. Although subsequent Management Committee minutes suggest that relations between African and registered unions in a few industries may have improved slightly, the overall reaction by SACTU comrades was one of severe censure of this 'Open Letter'. As Uriah Maleka said, 'it is hard to work with someone who is trying to get rid of you'.

As for TUCSA, it continued its anti-SACTU activities as before. In June 1962 TUCSA refused to send an official delegate to the All-In Conference against Job Reservation held in Cape Town and discussed above. More importantly, at a time when the entire international community was condemning the Sabotage Act and repression being carried out against SACTU leaders, TUCSA distinguished itself with silence.

In 1964, the TUCSA Conference called for the recognition of African trade unions under the IC Act because, in the President's words, lack of such status would render African workers 'tools of the politically unscrupulous'. As evidence, T. P. Murray referred to the Sabotage Trials that were part of the state's repression against SACTU and the Congress Alliance. Two years later, after SACTU had been virtually forced to go underground, President Scheepers callously reminded everyone that South Africa was still a 'free democracy'. As for African workers, TUCSA's paternalism sounded like a voice shouting from the debates of the 1920s:

> Unless responsible leadership is provided now, the African workers will eventually create their own organizations . . . if these organizations fall into the wrong hands the consequences could be disastrous for the whole nation. . . . It is because TUCSA sees these immediate and long-term dangers that it favours the organization of all workers under responsible [sic] leadership.

And speaking of the past, the 1966 TUCSA Conference recorded what must be one of the most incredulous comments in the history of South African trade unionism: 'South Africa has had industrial peace for the past forty years, *due in large measure to our sensible legislation*' (emphasis added).[38]

Such statements speak for themselves. Can there be any doubt as to why Black workers in South Africa turned to SACTU as the only trade union body to lead their struggle against class exploitation and oppression? Working class unity under Apartheid, although in principle correct, is indeed a difficult objective to achieve in practice!

The purpose of this chapter has been to outline the breadth and depth of hostility to SACTU between the years 1955 to 1964. The ruling class – consisting of the state and the capitalist class – and the co-opted White trade union bodies, each in its respective sphere, combined to place obstacles in SACTU's path in every conceivable manner. The fact that SACTU survived these attacks and went on to build the first powerful non-racial trade union coordinating body in South African history is testimony to the tremendous dedication of SACTU activists. Even more to the point, SACTU successes in the final analysis can only be explained by the fact that its campaigns and objectives were fully supported by the exploited masses themselves. With this necessary background, we can now turn our attention to the real work of SACTU – organizing the unorganized African workers.

NOTES

1. Mark Shope, Acting General Secretary, Report to Seventh Annual Conference, 1962, p. 2.

2. In the legislation, and hereafter in the text, 'Coloureds' refers to Coloured and Indian persons.
3. Quoted in R. Davies, 'The Class Character of South Africa's Industrial Conciliation Legislation', *South African Labour Bulletin*, vol. 2, no. 6 (January 1976), p. 6.
4. ibid., p. 11.
5. Prior to the Second World War, the most important legislation affecting African workers was as follows: various Masters and Servants Acts passed in the four territories (Transvaal, Orange Free State, Natal and the Cape) between 1856 and 1904; the Native Labour Regulation Act, No. 15 of 1911; the Mines and Works Act of 1911; the Mines and Works Amendment Act of 1926; and the Apprenticeship Act of 1922 (re-enacted in amended form as Act No. 37, 1944). These Acts deal almost exclusively with the conditions of employment, yet they are only a small proportion of the laws affecting Africans, Indians and Coloureds as citizens of South Africa. See *Laws Affecting Race Relations in South Africa, 1948–1976*, op. cit., for greater detail.
6. Quoted in SACTU, First Annual National Conference, 1956.
7. L. Welcher, 'The Relationship between the State and African Trade Unions in South Africa, 1948–1953', *South African Labour Bulletin*, vol. 4, no. 5 (September 1978), p. 18.
8. Quoted in Brian Bunting, *Rise of the South African Reich*, Penguin, Harmondsworth, 1964 (rev. ed.), p. 35.
9. P. Beyleveld, A. Gelb and B. Lan, three progressive trade unionists, were defeated in attempts to get a resolution against the Native Labour Act passed at the 'Unity Conference' of White coordinating bodies in May 1954.
10. *New Age*, 17 May 1956.
11. In 1978, only 24 Works Committees could be traced, according to *Laws Affecting ...*, op. cit., p. 241.
12. Quoted in *Cape Times*, 7 February 1956.
13. *Laws Affecting ...*, op. cit., p. 248.
14. Between 1956 and 1976, twenty-eight Job Reservation determinations were gazetted; only thirteen were still in effect in 1976. Exemptions to these determinations further reduced the actual numbers of workers affected. Ibid.
15. Harold Wolpe, 'Class, Race and the Occupation Structure', *Societies of Southern Africa in the 19th and 20th Centuries*, vol. 2, 1970–1971, pp. 98–118.
16. Minister of Labour de Klerk had once served as Secretary of the White Afrikaner union – Die Blankewerkersberskermingsbond – which had led the attack on Black garment workers and the Transvaal Garment Workers Union for many years. Another JR determination imposed on the industry in 1960 was qualified by many exemptions granted due to a growing scarcity of White workers.
17. Thirty-one unions had complied with the Act by forming separate racial branches; six were exempted for not having enough members of one racial group to form separate unions/branches; twelve were exempted from having all-White executives; seventeen were exempted from holding separate meetings; and eighteen were not required to form separate branches.
18. One month prior to the SACTU Conference, the Cape Town Local Committee staged protest demonstrations outside the House of Assembly during night sessions debating the Bill. Police took away placards, recorded the names of participants

and inspected the pass books of Africans participating. A SACTU leaflet condemning the Bill was distributed at the demonstrations.
19. The Minutes also record that Natal SACTU unions were not concerned with registration, but rather more concerned with fighting the capitalists than the government.
20. An exemption had been requested and rejected. White workers joined the Afrikaner union – Blanke Tekstielwerkers Nywerheidsunie van Suid Afrika. B. du Toit, op. cit. The NULCDW also divided into separate uniracial unions, with the larger Coloured union retaining the name and the new White union being known as the LCDWU of South Africa. Both remained SACTU affiliates (the former until 1963), but eventually joined TUCSA following repression against SACTU.
21. Interview, John Gaetsewe.
22. Quoted in A. Hepple, *A Trade Union Guide for South African Workers*, SACTU Publication, Johannesburg, 1957.
23. SACTU Memorandum on the Bantu Laws Amendment Acts, 1963, submitted to the Bantu Administration and Development. 7 March 1963.
24. *South Africa: Basic Facts and Figures*, SAIRR, Johannesburg, 1973, p. 29.
25. A. Hepple, *South Africa: Workers Under Apartheid*, International Defence and Aid Fund, London, 1969, pp. 59ff.
26. ibid., p. 24.
27. Moses Mabhida, quoted in *New Age*, 11 February 1960.
28. SACTU, Seventh Annual National Conference, General Secretary Report, 1962.
29. Interview, Stephen Dlamini.
30. The SATUC changed its name to TUCSA at its Eighth Annual National Conference in 1962. Hepple says this decision was made to distinguish the SATUC from SACTU. Hepple, 1966, op. cit., pp. 244–5.
31. Alexander and Simons, *Job Reservation and the Trade Unions*, Woodstock, Cape, 1959, pp. 28–9.
32. Quoted in *Morning Star*, March 1956, and A. Hepple, 1966, op. cit., p. 243.
33. Quoted in *Morning Star*, November 1955.
34. SATUC, Second Annual Conference Report, 1956.
35. E. R. Braverman (Ray Alexander), *Morning Star*, vol. 3, no. 25 (October/November), 1957.
36. SATUC, Fourth Annual National Conference, East London, 10–13 March 1958.
37. Quoted in *New Age*, 15 February and 29 March 1962.
38. Hepple reports that only seven African unions were affiliated to TUCSA by 1966. Of those, the National Union of Clothing Workers (NUCW) accounted for 75 per cent of the total 4,000 African members in TUCSA. The NUCW had resulted from a merger of the GW-UAW (FOFATUSA) and the South African Clothing Workers Union (SACWU), and there had been considerable controversy regarding the appropriateness of the ballot that led to the pro-TUCSA affiliation vote. Hepple, 1966, op. cit., pp. 244–5.

5 'ASINAMALI' (WE HAVE NO MONEY)

One pound a day for the factory worker who today cannot buy what he makes. One pound a day for the miner who earns his pthisis and goes home broken and to die. One pound a day for the farm labourer who today ploughs the bitter furrow of misery. One pound a day for the builder of mansions who lives in a shack. . . . A minimum wage of one pound a day for all the workers in the land. One pound a day. Five pounds a week. More food to eat, clothes, warmth. A little light in the deep night of poverty. Freedom from pass laws, freedom from the midnight police terror. Freedom from the 'ghost squads' haunting the street corners. Freedom from prisons and forced farm labour – the horned fingers and welts ploughed into sorry flesh. Freedom to walk without fear as the companion of the heart . . .[1]

The £1-a-Day Campaign is regarded as SACTU's most successful achievement in the 1950s and 1960s. Demanding a legislated, national minimum wage of £1-a-Day for all workers, the campaign touched a central nerve and pinponted the cause of the misery suffered by the majority of the people: the perpetuation of the cheap labour policy fostered by the South African ruling class. The event which provided the impetus for the prolonged campaign was the Alexandra Bus Boycott of 1957, a spontaneous demonstration of mass resistance to increased exploitation in the form of higher bus fares. This action by the masses reflected a seething undercurrent of working class hostility and highlighted the need for significantly higher wages for African workers.

'Azikwelwa' (We Will Not Ride!): The 1957 Transvaal Bus Boycott

On 7 January 1957, workers from Johannesburg and Pretoria townships refused to ride to work in buses owned by PUTCO (the Public Utility Transport Corporation) following a one penny (25 per cent) increase in fares effective that day. This spontaneous act of defiance marked the start of a three-month period during which an estimated 70,000 workers boycotted the buses; amongst them, more than 20,000 African workers *each* walked a total of 2,000 miles.

They walked in the heat and torrential rains of a South African summer, harassed, arrested and beaten up by the police. Women walked, with babies on their backs and bundles of washing on their heads. On one occasion, two young boys were found exhausted by the roadside after having collected a large load of washing from a home in one of the White suburbs several miles away. Police had apparently stopped them, accused them of stealing the washing and drove them back to the White woman's home to prove that they were telling the truth. After their story was confirmed, the police officers dropped them there, forcing them to walk the same distance back to Alexandra again – a total of 18 miles!

Cyclists' tyres were punctured by arrogant policemen, reactionary Whites drove through puddles splashing the workers as they walked, and boycotters were constantly stopped and searched for no reason. Yet, despite all of this harassment, the people continued to walk.

The bus company, PUTCO, was established in 1945 when the state intervened in the transport system for African workers. Previous boycott actions had forced retractions of fare increases by private transport firms with the result that a single public company with direct government participation was formed.[2] This allowed the government to create conditions favourable to a low wage structure, a necessity for the rapid development of the manufacturing sector in the postwar era. Yet it was the very existence of Apartheid – which caused African townships to be located far from city centres and places of work – that created a continuous financial crisis for the Company. By 1957, £311,000 was required for PUTCO services. Rather than increasing employers' subsidies for African transport in a year of economic decline, the government allowed PUTCO to increase fares and thus shift the burden onto the African proletariat.

The workers demonstrated, however, that they were not a passive African labour force to be exploited at will by the state in the interests of capital accumulation. This historic Bus Boycott showed that whatever improvements the African people have won have been the result of their own bitter and determined efforts in the face of overwhelming odds. With the announcement of the fare increase an Alexandra People's Transport Committee (PTC) was organized, including the ANC and other local township organizations. Activists began distributing protest leaflets and calling street-corner gatherings, culminating in a mass meeting of residents on 6 January. The boycott decision was taken and residents demanded:

(1) the immediate restoration of the old fares;

'Azikwelwa': We Will Not Ride
Alexandra Bus Boycott, 1957

(2) an increase in the number of buses on the routes to eliminate the endless queues; and
(3) shelters at bus stops to protect people from bad weather.

On Monday, 7 January, 50,000 Africans from Johannesburg townships refused to board PUTCO buses. An estimated 15,000 workers walked to work in Johannesburg. 'Azikwelwa' ('We will not ride') became the catchword and reflected the solidarity of workers throughout the next three months. Seven days after the start of the boycott the buses were running empty, causing PUTCO a loss of £7,000 in the first week. A further 20,000 people from Moroka and Jabavu townships added strength to the campaign.

Later in January, African workers and their families began boycotting the municipal beer-halls, attacking another very visible institution of oppression. Profits from beer-halls made up an important part of the Native Revenue Account responsible for township amenities and this action was regarded as a threat to municipal finance. The Non-European Affairs Department toured the townships in loudspeaker vans appealing to residents not to associate beer-halls with the Bus Boycott. Their efforts failed.

In early February, workers in other areas of the country, particularly the Eastern Cape, called sympathy boycotts and refused to ride local buses. 'We have to stand with our brothers in Johannesburg,' replied a worker as he walked from New Brighton on the morning of 11 February. A well-organized working class in Port Elizabeth and Uitenhage carried out a 90 per cent effective boycott for two weeks. In another Witwatersrand township, an estimated 4,000 residents not only boycotted the local bus service but also generated fresh demands against their local fare of sixpence. Similar acts of solidarity followed in Bloemfontein and Brakpan township.

Two months passed and the solidarity of the people remained strong. Both the capitalist class and the government were forced to deal with the crisis by combining forces to protect their common interests against those of the workers. The employers, represented by the Chambers of Commerce and Industry, reversed earlier expressions of sympathy with the boycotters once production and efficiency in the workplace began to suffer. The Chambers realized that to grant basic wage increases, as demanded by SACTU, would only set a dangerous precedent that would jeopardize their position as exploiters of human labour-power.

The state, as protector of profits in general, took the lead in victimizing boycotters and their supporters. Sympathetic White drivers offering rides to workers were fined under the Motor Carrier Transportation Act. Pass raids and imprisonment of boycotters increased with each passing week, including the arrest of 2,000 workers sleeping 'illegally' at Wemmer Mens' Hostel, Johannesburg. Police violence was demonstrated at a Lady Selbourne meeting outside Pretoria on 31 January, when Joel Ramothebe was killed. The workers' solidarity increased in the face of these tactics and by the end of February the government had failed completely in dividing the workers or co-opting the moderate leaders of the PTC.

PUTCO's financial situation was by now desperate and, as threatened, the Company closed down all services on 1 March. It was clear that the economic burden of Apartheid transport could no longer be strapped to the backs of an already super-exploited African working class. But on that day, boycott leaders, PUTCO representatives and members of the Chamber of Commerce met and discussed a proposal whereby the five-penny bus tickets could be cashed in for one penny apiece and the services would be temporarily subsidized by the Chamber through a special £25,000 fund. The suggestion was apparently acceptable to these boycott leaders but the final decision rested with the boycotters themselves. Even before the meetings had been convened, however, statements had been given to the press which indicated that a 'settlement' had been reached.

The people stood strong in their commitment to 'Azikwelwa', not satisfied with the conditions of the 'settlement'. A deadlock lasted another four weeks as dissensions within the PTC between the Africanist faction and the ANC leadership were played out.[3] In early April, the boycott began to break and decisions were taken by township residents, often with reluctance, to end the boycott. By 15 April, full services were running in all centres. Two months later the government passed the Native Services Levy Act, which required employers to make a monthly transport subsidy payment for each African employed in commerce and industry. The government also contributed to the fund. It had been a long and arduous struggle but the determination of the people had ensured an ultimate victory over attempts by the combined ruling class to impose additional financial burdens on the African workers.

Starvation Wages
The workers' militant response directly reflected their economic

conditions and the boycott action signalled to the ruling class a heightened consciousness among workers of the nature of their exploitation. At the time the Bus Boycott was initiated, the average minimum wage for African workers amounted to £11 0s. 0d. per month. SAIRR surveys in 1953 and 1954 revealed that the *essential* minimum expenditure for an African family of five in Johannesburg was £23 10s. 4d., but that the total income of an urban African family of five averaged no more than £15 18s. 11d. By 1957, the situation had deteriorated.

In its memorandum presented to the employers, SACTU demonstrated how the real wages of African workers had declined in the previous decade. In a comparison of wage rates paid to the lowest category of workers, they focused attention on the desperate and urgent plight of the African workers. Some examples of wages (including COLA) for 'unskilled' work in 1948 and 1957 were as follows:

Industry	1948	1957	
Building	£2 3s. 4d.	£3 4s. 2d.	
Chemical	£2 7s. 0d.	£2 18s. 3d.	in certain areas
	£1 13s. 0d.	£2 11s. 9d.	1950–51 Wage Determination
		£1 16s. 4d.	juniors, under 18
Distributive/	£2 8s. 0d.	£1 19s. 9d.	Jhb; under 18
Commercial		£3 0s. 9d.	Jhb; over 20
		£1 17s. 6d.	Germiston; under 18
		£2 15s. 9d.	Germiston; over 18
Meat	£1 16s. 3d.	£2 11s. 9d.	
Engineering	£1 18s. 0d.	£2 11s. 3d.	Iron and Steel
Motor	£2 7s. 0d.	£2 16s. 7d.	
Sweet Manu-			
facturing	£2 6s. 3d.	£3 12s. 6d.	
Textile	£2 3s. 9d.	£3 8s. 9d.	weaving
		£2 14s. 0d.	canvas
		£2 1s. 3d.	flock
Garment	£2 3s. 9d.	£3 17s. 0d.	
Furniture	£2 9s. 6d.	£3 6s. 9d.	
Laundry	£2 1s. 3d.	£3 0s. 0d.	
		£2 5s. 0d.	juniors; under 18

Even if one considered the Retail Price Index calculated by the SA Bureau of Census and Statistics, it is obvious that living standards for African workers had declined steeply. This Index was based on a study of middle-income European family budgets. However, while the Index reflects an increase of 44 per cent (on all items) and 56 per cent (food) between 1948 and 1957, 'the actual increase as it affected the average "non-European" family is far steeper. It would not be an exaggeration to place it between 65 and 70 per cent.'[4]

SACTU examined the wages of workers in four fairly representative industries — chemicals, commercial and distributive, engineering and motor. They found that the average wage of the African workers in 1948 was £2 4s. 0d. per week; by 1957, this had only increased to £2 15s. 1d. The increase in money wage amounted to 25 per cent. However, the increase in the cost of living, according to the Index, was 44 per cent and the calculated real increase in cost of living for African workers in the Rand–Pretoria–Vereeniging area was 65 per cent. The conclusion drawn for these workers was that wages had failed miserably to keep pace with increased prices and expenses by between 20 and 40 per cent.

Even some employers' organizations had recognized that there was a need to improve the deplorable rates of pay for 'unskilled' African workers. The March 1957 issue of *Commercial Opinion*, an employers' journal, declared that there was an average shortfall of £7 11s. 5d. between the monthly income of unskilled workers and their minimum necessary expenditures. It commented:

These figures are stark and simple. There is no way of juggling them to belie the story they tell. . . . In general the consequences are misery, malnutrition and a dangerous state of mind.[5]

Early in 1957 also, the newspaper *Umteteli wa Bantu*, owned and published by the Chamber of Mines, conducted a survey of income and expenditure of African families. The conclusion was that an income of £31 per month was necssary for adequate and decent living for a family of five living in Johannesburg African townships.

In the course of the Bus Boycott, African workers succeeded in drawing attention to their poverty wages and employers and the government were compelled to take notice of their situation. Many promises were rhetorically made, including one by the Minister of Labour de Klerk, who announced that he had drawn up a list of 45 trades and industries for immediate investigation by the Wage Board. More than one year later, the Wage Board had reported on only one of the 45 undertakings, revealing the callous disregard government bodies held for African workers and their poverty-stricken families. The following statement is more indicative of the policy put into practice:

To plead that you must pay the Natives who are employees a 'civilized' wage means only one thing in this country — White wages. To want to pay Natives White wages fails in the first place to take account of their productivity; in the second place it does not take their living standard into account.[6]

Both the employers and the state continued to evade the real issue of class exploitation by crying out for increased productivity. SACTU clearly responded to this distraction in a 1961 memorandum:

Our rank and file members find it difficult to understand the numerous articles and discussions which the press reports on the need for increased productivity in South Africa and employers should clarify their concept of productivity as this is open to various interpretations. Workers, for instance, interpret the employers' demand for increased productivity to mean an indirect speeding up of productivity and of one worker doing the job of two or more to compensate the employer for the increased wage bill arising from general wage increases. This has caused the workers to be most suspicious of the call for increased productivity as they cannot interpret it in any other way.[7]

SACTU rejected these ruling class diversions and instead insisted that the central issue was the necessity of wage increases for the majority of South African workers. Only by demanding a greater share in the economic wealth that they had produced could the 'living standard' of the African workers improve.

'Azikwelwa' to 'Asinamali'

Workers! You know your wages are too little. Your children are hungry. Prices are too high. You have no money for food, for rent, for transport. Workers, only unity can help us. This is what we must learn from the boycott. When we stand together we can make our voices heard.

If we want more money we must have strong Trade Unions.

If all workers join with SACTU we can win these demands.

Not promises, but your own unity can get our demands . . . . Let's all stand together — for £1-a-Day — for an immediate increase in wages.

Trade Unions make us strong.[8]

In the midst of the Bus Boycott when the militancy of the masses reached its highest peak, SACTU, sensing that the workers were ready to be mobilized around broader issues, seized the moment to introduce the national working class demand of £1-a-Day.

On 10 February 1957, SACTU convened a Workers' Conference attracting some 300 trade union delegates and thousands of unorganized workers. Leaflets distributed beforehand drew the link between the fare increase and the general poverty of the African workers created by the profit system. Leslie Massina, General Secretary, emphasized this point at the conference:

> The Bus Boycotters have shown up, as never before, the terrible hardships of African families on their present wage scales . . . ASINAMALI (WE HAVE NO MONEY) exactly states the position of the workers today. They simply cannot live on the miserable wages they are getting.[9]

'Asinamali-Sifun'Imali' became the slogan of the campaign – 'We have no money – We want more money!' The Conference resolutions articulated clearly the workers' demands: (a) the average minimum wage of £11 0s. 0d. a month was totally inadequate; (b) the COLA, pegged since March 1953, bore no relation to the actual cost of living; (c) the government claim that £15 0s. 0d. per month represented a living wage was 'absolutely unrealistic'; and (d) the majority of workers earn wages which were below the Poverty Datum Line (PDL) and are ill and undernourished. The major resolution passed determined the direction of SACTU's major work throughout the rest of the 1950s and 1960s.

> (We) demand a minimum wage of £1 per day, including the cost of living allowance for all workers throughout the country, and (SACTU) pledges itself to struggle for the achievement of this aim.[10]

An intensive campaign began and was carried out on every possible level. Deputations and memoranda demanding £1-a-Day were served on employers; strikes, mass rallies and demonstrations, distribution of hundreds of thousands of leaflets and press coverage occurred in all corners of the country.

From the beginning, the £1-a-Day campaign converged with SACTU's plan for organizing the unorganized. The 'Plans for a Mass Enrolment into the Trade Unions' adopted by the SACTU MC after the Workers' Conference reflected the realization that workers need to be organized into trade unions or even some lesser form of organization (such as factory committees) in order to win their demands on the wage front. A definite sense of immediacy characterized the campaign. The Bus Boycott had aroused the militancy of the people and they were now searching for a way forward. SACTU saw it as the duty of the democratic movement to keep up the initiative and 'prevent the mass spirit from frittering itself away in disillusionment and false paths'. The proposal was to launch an immediate drive for 20,000 new members and the emphasis was placed on recruiting all workers into SACTU

FORWARD TO A MINIMUM WAGE OF £1 A DAY

SACTU's May Day Message To The Workers

SACTU women, Rita Ndzanga (*left*) and Mabel Balfour at £1-a-Day Demonstration, early 1960s

first, and then allocating them to industrial unions as soon as possible. SACTU recruitment forms – in all languages – were printed as well as 15,000 badges and stickers. Speakers notes were issued to all local committees, which were given the responsibility of organizing mass meetings and local recruitment programmes. At the national level, John Gaetsewe became the principal spokesperson for the overall campaign and at each NEC and Annual Conference meeting emphasized the necessity for organizing workers at the point of production:

> If we do nothing when the (recruitment) forms are completed we will make a laughing stock of ourselves and will disillusion the workers. We must help workers frame their demands and take up all complaints at the factories. Factory committees should be formed wherever possible. Existing unions are asked to be as generous as possible with office space for newly formed unions and officials must also give advice and assistance to new organizers.[11]

Throughout the first year of the campaign, £1-a-Day Committees were formed in all major centres and industrial areas were zoned to facilitate organizational work. Educational work assumed a priority and local committees began to print their own leaflets and to hold mass rallies to mobilize workers around the £1-a-Day demand. The July 1957, Asinamali Rally held in Johannesburg, the fifth of its kind throughout the country, drew 500 workers from Klerksdorp, Pretoria, Johannesburg, the East and West Rand, representing some 60,000 workers in total. At this meeting, a worker from Benoni spoke for all African workers when he told the crowd:

> It is not because we are stupid that our children fall ill, but because we have no money. It is not because we do not know how to look after our money that we cannot pay our rent or transport fares but because our wages are so low that they do not cover the cost of our most urgent needs.[12]

At this rally, Gaetsewe pointed out that it was not only Black workers who earned less than £1-a-Day but that many White women workers in the tobacco, distributive, sweet, laundry and textile industries as well were often paid below SACTU's minimum wage demand. He stressed the need for unity of *all* workers in the struggle for higher wages.

SACTU's consistent attempts to achieve this unity with other trade union coordinating bodies met with the same response on the £1-a-Day campaign as with all other issues. However, there were some individual unions not affiliated to SACTU which expressed support for the campaign. The National Union of Distributive Workers (NUDW) and Garment Workers Union (No. 2 Branch) in particular voiced their approval of SACTU's initiative. 'Whatever differences there are among us, none can fail to support the demand for £1 a day,' said Mrs B. Flusk, GWU No. 2 Branch.[13]

SACTU affiliated unions threw their whole-hearted support behind the wage campaign. By the end of 1957 workers in the metal, milling, garment, textile, laundry and food and canning industries, led by their SACTU unions, were advancing demands for £1-a-Day. Their enthusiasm for the campaign reflected the urgency and correctness of these demands:

Our workers have come to look to the £1 a day campaign to end their sufferings and hardships of their low wages. But they feel that work for the campaign is far too slow. There should be a conference for delegates from all factories in order to study and discuss reports on the campaign and make plans to push it.[14]

Everywhere the call went out for a National Conference which would add momentum to the campaign.

A National Conference on the £1-a-Day demand will help the campaign considerably. Action is better than words. The campaign will create a higher degree of unity in the Trade Union movement than we have yet seen.

The campaign to organize 20,000 workers is our most urgent task. It has been proved that when the organized give the unorganized a lead, the latter will fight with the same courage and unity in demanding higher wages.[15]

Subsequent to these calls, Workers' Conferences were convened in the Western and Eastern Cape areas, the Transvaal, Natal, Klerksdorp, and Kimberley in February 1958. In turn, they prompted a National Workers' Conference in March of that year.

At this stage of the campaign there had been little response from the ruling class. In June 1957, the MC had approved a memorandum prepared for circulation entitled: 'The Urgent Need for a General Increase in Wages Particularly for the Lower Paid Categories of Workers, and a National Minimum Wage of £1-a-Day.' After its approval by SACTU affiliated unions and meetings of rank-and-file workers, it was circulated to the SA Federated Chamber of Industries (SAFCI), the Johannesburg Chamber of Commerce and the Transvaal and OFS Chamber of Mines. The SAFCI assured SACTU that they would send SACTU proposals to its member organizations for comment from different geographical areas and that they would take SACTU's suggestion for a joint meeting to their Non-European Affairs Committee in November. Nothing more was ever heard from the SAFCI. The Johannesburg Chamber responded as follows: 'While interested in the matter of Non-European earnings, it (the Chamber) is not a registered employers' organization, nor does it deal with specific requests or demands related to conditions of employment.'[16] As long as profits were not threatened and the cheap labour system was intact, the bosses ignored the SACTU demands and the interests of Black workers.

From the beginning of the campaign, however, SACTU activists were extremely clear on the role of the bosses and stressed that they should not be believed when they claim an inability to pay a minimum wage of £1-a-Day. Moses Mabhida, for instance, pointed out that these employers had paid White European labour to come to South Africa with the assurance of receiving much higher wages than their Black counterparts. 'The African worker has been crucified on the cross of gold in the Transvaal and on the mealie stalk in the Orange Free State,' said Mabhida, focusing on the wage discrepancy in various industries and pointing to the £36,000,000 profits realized in the gold mines – all of this made possible only by the availability and exploitation of cheap Black labour.[17]

In 1959, the campaign was strengthened by the exciting events of that year, the year in which the militancy of the masses once again reached a high point. Women's demonstrations against passes, beerhalls and dipping tanks (all described in Chapter 9) highlighted the need for stronger organization amongst the masses. After the 1959 SACTU Annual Conference, a much closer working relationship was forged between SACTU and the ANC, with both recognizing the urgent necessity of organizing workers and peasants into their respective organizations. Out of the SACTU Conference came renewed emphasis on forming new unions in the basic industries. The £1-a-Day campaign was to be conducted in the following manner: (a) by building powerful unions in the transport and metal industries, (b) by creating workers' factory committees as a step towards the formation of trade unions, and (c) by demanding a minimum wage of £1-a-Day and higher wages for all workers.

Some members of the SACTU-MC felt that by 1959 the demand for £1-a-Day was outdated as it was well below the subsistence level. Suggestions were advanced, for example, that the call be for '30 bob a day', but it was finally agreed that the demand for £1-a-Day for every day of the week (as compared with every working day) be advanced. An updated memorandum was prepared for distribution and a set of £1-a-Day lectures written for educational use.

In 1960, the fruits of the previous year's organizing work were realized:

> We announce with the greatest possible pride that the period April 1959 to October 1960 has been the period of our greatest achievement. We have grown in stature both nationally and internationally. Through our consistent £1-a-Day campaign, we have forced the entire country to recognize the need for increased wages and we have scored notable victories in the metal, distributive, textile, laundering, furniture and other industries. In some industries, the minimum wage has leapt in the past year from £2 18s. 3d. per week to £4 0s. 0d. per week. Our membership figure (52,583) is the highest it has been in the five years of our existence.[18]

In Natal especially, SACTU's organizing campaign had borne results; over 5,000 new members had been recruited since the political upsurge of 1959. The victories on the wage front, though significant, still left the workers' wages below the subsistence level as the PDL had increased to approximately £27 0s. 0d. per month. In contrast, the majority of workers still earned less than £15 per month. The £1-a-Day slogan remained relevant and the organizing of workers into the trade union movement a necessity for strengthening the collective struggle against poverty wages.

As a result of SACTU's persistent efforts to approach employers, some breakthroughs occurred in 1959. After the circulation of updated memoranda to all employers' organizations, the SAFCI asked for 274 copies for distribution to all its affiliated members and members of ASSCOM (Associated Chambers of Commerce) agreed to meet with SACTU at a round-table conference (though they stressed that they would be acting in their private capacities and not as ASSCOM members). At the meeting the employers asked SACTU 'not to go too fast', 'not to undo all the good which was being done [sic]', and tried to prove that the £1-a-Day demand was 'frivolous and unrealistic'. SACTU refused to accept their contention and continued to demand that the workers who produced the wealth of South Africa be paid a living wage.

Successful Workers' Conferences were organized once again in February 1960 and held simultaneously throughout the country. Even during the five-month declared State of Emergency following the tragic Sharpeville massacre, SACTU Head Office again served demands on all national employer organizations for increased wages. Local committees too, continued to present workers' demands to the bosses: Durban LC submitted a memorandum to all provincial employers' groups in November 1961, focusing attention on unemployment, low wages, poverty and the problems facing the rural people; in Port Elizabeth, the LC circulated a memorandum directed towards the City Council in November 1961, concentrating on rents, police raids, Labour Bureaux, passes, unemployment and the need for a national minimum wage. In all areas the demand for a living wage had been linked with the related issues of class exploitation and national oppression.[19]

In addition, the demand for a legislated, national minimum wage was put forward in memoranda submitted or in oral evidence to Wage Boards by the Witwatersrand (Wits), Durban, Cape Western Province Local Committees and the FCWU and TWIU affiliated unions. The demand had also been the subject of negotiations by individual unions and their employers when discussing wage increases. In Durban, this was done by the Tin, Twine & Bag, Municipal and Match Workers Unions; in the Transvaal, by the Farm, Plantation and Allied Workers Union and the Printing and Tobacco Factory Committees. In Port Elizabeth, the Transport Workers Union demanded £1-a-Day for all workers in the industry.

SACTU's insistence on the need for legislation had been in their own words 'like a yeast fermenting in the industrial life of South Africa'.[20] In January 1962, SACTU prepared a Draft Bill and presented it to the Minister of Labour. Copies were also sent to Members of Parliament and the Bill was given national press publicity. So great was the pressure that the all-White Parliament was forced for the first time to debate the issue. The demand was rejected largely on the advice of Professor Steenkamp, Chairman of the Wage Board, who had been consulted by the Cabinet. This merely confirmed SACTU's position that the Wage Board served the class interests of the bosses, not the workers.

Despite the increasing repression against SACTU activists in 1962 and 1963, SACTU continued to place great emphasis on the £1-a-Day campaign. In 1963, 'with a tremendous blast of press publicity', the Rembrandt Tobacco Company announced that it was paying a minimum wage of R2 (£1) a day to all its employees.[21] No credit was given to SACTU for its relentless campaign, but SACTU correctly claimed this as their victory, even though limited. In the same year TUCSA stated that it had always supported the demand for a national minimum wage. SACTU responded:

We ask them how? Did they take the struggle to the factories and workshops? Did they expose their officials to jail and other penalties, or did they simply pass pious resolutions at conferences and submit demands to that slow, ponderous body, the Wage Board?

We do not regard R2 a day as a living wage, but as a minimum wage only, and we resolve to continue to fight, with whatever resources remain to us, for all workers of all races.[22]

These resources were dwindling, however, with the increasing attacks by the ruling class against SACTU leaders and rank-and-file workers. This led many to pose the question: 'Are we being smashed because we *dared* to demand living wages for the workers who have built South Africa into this great industrial state?'[23] Certainly the £1-a-Day campaign would have been part of the reason for the extent of state retribution against the progressive movement as it was this campaign above all others that directly challenged the basis of exploitation and Apartheid in South Africa. At its 1963 Conference, SACTU defiantly resolved that it would 'continue to fight the system of cheap labour and call upon all affiliated unions to continue their active struggle for immediate increases for all workers and a national minimum wage of R2 a day'.[24]

In summary, the £1-a-Day campaign is viewed as a tremendous success by those who were involved in its implementation. Perhaps the only differences of opinion concerned the emphasis of the campaign. Some have suggested that too much emphasis was placed on trying to influence the state rather than focusing on the capitalist class. 'Looking back I think we were flogging the wrong horse. We should have focused it against the employers, not the government that wouldn't change the wage structure.'[25] Others, however, believe that the emphasis was correctly placed because companies were waiting for a law to be passed before they would act.[26] John Gaetsewe, active leader of the campaign at the national level, felt that the emphasis was evenly balanced, that the demands were being placed on both the employers and the state, but that 'the pressure at the point of production was the key strategy as our only strength was in the factories'.[27] Even during the campaign there were those who were critical of unions that did not demand £1-a-Day in their negotiations with their employers, stressing the need to confront the problem at the point of production (and exploitation) instead of waiting for legislation to be enacted.[28]

The call for a legislated minimum wage awakened the state and the capitalist class to the realization that they could not continue to extract such super-profits from the workers without a further sharpening of the class struggle. Some important gains were achieved in this struggle and many workers were paid higher wages as a result. But the main victory in the campaign was in the education of workers about the nature of racial capitalism in South Africa and the organization of thousands of new trade unionists. The successes of the 1960 and 1961 Stay-At-Homes pointed to the fact that the most militant response to the strike call came from those industries where SACTU's organizing campaign had made the most inroads. This was undoubtedly one of the reasons why the state stepped in to crush the workers' movement in the next few years.

NOTES

1. A. Hutchinson, 'June 26', *Fighting Talk*, July 1957.
2. In August 1943, 15,000 men and women walked 9 or more miles from Alexandra township to their places of work for 9 days until the bus company gave in and reduced the fare from the proposed 5*d*. to 4*d*. Again in 1944, the people resisted another attempt to increase fares. This time they walked for seven weeks and the final victory came in 1945 when PUTCO took over and reverted to the original fare.
3. During the bus boycott, the Africanist element constantly encouraged the people to extend the boycott into a national strike. The Africanists were dissenters from ANC policy, preferring a more racialist, Black nationalist line. Many were expelled or broke away from the ANC to form the Pan Africanist Congress in 1959.
4. The Urgent Need for a General Increase in Wages Particularly for the Lower Paid Categories of Workers, and a National Minimum Wage of £1-a-Day', SACTU memorandum.
5. Quoted in ibid.
6. M. M. Viljoen, Deputy Minister of Labour, 21 May 1959, quoted in A. Hepple, *Poverty Wages – The Shame of Low Wages in South Africa*, Johannesburg, June 1959.
7. Quoted in the Report of the Acting General Secretary to the SACTU Seventh Annual National Conference, 1962.
8. Excerpt from a SACTU leaflet, published in *New Age*, 21 March 1957.
9. *New Age*, 7 February 1957.
10. *Workers Unity*, March 1957.
11. Minutes, SACTU–NEC meeting, 11 April 1957.
12. *Workers Unity*, July 1957.
13. *Workers Unity*, August–September 1957.
14. Aaron Mahlangu, Sec. African Milling Workers Union, ibid.

15. Ronnie Press, General Secretary, TWIU, ibid.
16. *New Age*, 15 August 1957.
17. Discussion on £1-a-Day at the Second Annual National Conference. 14–16 April 1957.
18. Fifth Annual National Conference Report, 1960.
19. Report, Acting General Secretary, Seventh Annual National Conference, 1962.
20. ibid.
21. Since South Africa became a Republic and changed to a decimal currency in 1961, the campaign changed the demand from £1-a-Day to 2 Rand-a-day (R2).
22. Report to the Ninth Annual National Conference, 28–29 March 1964.
23. ibid.
24. *Spark*, 28 March 1963.
25. Interview, Moses Mabhida.
26. Interview, Uriah Maleka.
27. Interview, John Gaetsewe.
28. Minutes SACTU–MC Meeting, 20 October 1960.

6 ORGANIZE OR STARVE!

A Worker's Lament

From five in the morning,
My lean body is crushed against the jostling crowd.
For Pittance, I make my way among the passengers,
Swaying coaches make my heart to jerk in fear,
That I may not my little ones see any more
Yet for food and rent I must work.

'SEBENZA' (work) The whole day long;
The foremen and the Induna scream
They shout because the boss explained: 'productivity.'
Pale lips; hunger exposes my empty stomach,
Starch water only my stomach has breakfasted.
Hunger takes away pride from a man's self respect.
But the burning heart for revenge vows:
'KAHLE' (wait), a day will come; me boss, you boy.

The listless sun leaves to the night,
To blanket the light.
Thousands of pattering feet homeward drag
And leave the Shops to the watchman.
Again I join the jostling crowd,
Fifteen miles homeward journey to travel.
Crammed like Jeppe Station victims,
I stand on a bench to save myself
Being crushed to death.

M. Rammitloa
taken from *Spark*, 7 February 1963

In an early document entitled, 'SACTU and Organizing the Unorganized', the new non-racial trade union coordinating body committed itself to organizing workers in the metal and transport industries. This decision reflected a recognition of the necessity to bring the principles and structures of trade unionism to the vast majority of South Africa's workers, the exploited African working class.

The majority of the unorganized workers were labouring in the agricultural fields (700,000), the mines (500,000), the railways and docks (150,000) and the metal industry (150,000), as well as tens of thousands of workers in domestic service, commercial, distributive and service trades, building and construction and numerous other secondary manufacturing industries. At this early stage in SACTU's development (around 1955-56), mining and agriculture were considered of such great magnitude and complexity that organizing in those areas would be beyond the resources of the organization at the time. It was therefore proposed and resolved that the main effort be directed towards the organizing of metal, transport and dock workers. However, it was not until 1958 that special National Organizing Committees (NOCs) were established for these industries; prior to that time Local Committees were directed to focus attention on these sectors.

The 1959 SACTU Conference extended the NOC structures to include the mining and agricultural workers. One year later the principle of forming General Workers Unions as a transitional form of organization leading to new industrial unions was endorsed by SACTU delegates. The purpose of the first section of this chapter is to review the difficulties encountered and progress achieved by the four NOCs and the GWUs in different geographical regions.

NOC: Transport

Under the general category of transport there were three areas of concentration – the railways, the docks and public transport (buses in particular). Of these, SACTU considered the railways the most important sector to organize.

By 1962, Black workers made up almost 50 per cent of the 218,000 workers employed by the South African Railway and Harbour Administration. Of these 108,000 Black workers, 99,800 were Africans, 7,600 Coloureds and 600 Indians. As the railways and harbours administration was directly owned and controlled by the Apartheid regime, SACTU's efforts in organizing transport workers to improve working conditions and gain higher wages led to a direct confrontation with the architects of modern-day White supremacy. A special corps of railway police watched over the workers and one of their most important tasks was to track down trade union organizers. The fate of one of SACTU's key organizers is described as follows:

When they went to pay the fine for the organizer of the Railway Workers Union, to get him out of gaol, they did not recognize him as he had been so badly assaulted. The assault had taken place when two Railway policemen had arrested him for 'trespassing on mine property'. His face had been beaten to a pulp.[1]

The average wage for African workers in 1962 was approximately £8 0s. 0d. per month, including all allowances. At that time, too, almost half of the African labour force – 43,467 – were listed as casuals. These casual workers would be engaged for a specific construction job but were often kept on afterwards, sometimes remaining 'casuals' for years. In this way they were daily paid and subject to dismissal on only 24 hours notice. They also had no leave or pension privileges, nor were they granted marriage allowances. Labourers other than those engaged for construction jobs were hired on a temporary basis and could become permanent after five years.

Temporary and permanent employees did receive fifteen days paid leave a year, but if they left before the current year was completed they did not receive any pro-rata leave pay. A worker with interrupted service did not receive any leave pay. Permanent employees were given marriage allowances and could qualify for a pension at the age of 60. However, all of these benefits were awarded as privileges and many workers found that on dismissal they could not make claims for benefits to which they regarded themselves entitled.

Railway workers in most areas of the country suffered under the additional burden of the compound system. Housed in dirty, ill-lit, cold and crowded rooms, the workers had no freedom of movement and numerous restrictions were placed on their ability to hold meetings and carry on discussions. Food was provided but was of poor quality. As soon as a railway worker lost his job, for whatever reason, he was evicted from the compound and no alternative accommodation was provided for him.

Another source of resentment was the Administration's policy of transferring workers from one department to another and from city to city, making it impossible for the maintenance of any semblance of family life. If a worker had a house in one city, upon transfer there was little chance of getting another in the new location; the worker would be forced into the compounds and the family left to fend for itself.

The treatment of African railway workers by White foremen was particularly degrading. Archie Sibeko recalls many of these racist overseers lining up African workers and ordering them to go to the former's White homes in the plush suburbs to perform domestic labour.

Equally deplorable were some of the jobs given to Africans while working for SAR & H. Louis Mkize, later involved in the formation of the African Chemical Workers Union in Durban, once worked as a 'spanner boy'. This job entailed holding the tools for the White workers for the slave wage of only £6 12s. 6d. per month.

More than any other group of workers in the major sectors of the South African economy, railway workers were subject to constant harassment and victimization if they were involved in trade union activity. In an article on the railwaymen in *Workers Unity*, 1962, Lawrence Ndzanga elaborated:

> As soon as a worker is known as a shop steward or active member of the SAR & HWU (in all centres) he is immediately transferred to a remote area. His wages are reduced and in this way attempts are made to punish him for his trade union activity and immobilize him for future activity. But the majority of workers so transferred bring the message of trade unionism with them.[2]

Despite these obstacles, the African workers had been organized in their union, the SAR & H (Non-European) WU since its formation back in 1944. Throughout the SACTU years further attempts were made to improve the lot of these workers and bring more into the union. The well-established SAR & HWU in the Transvaal, under the able leadership of Lawrence Ndzanga, affiliated to SACTU in 1955. By 1960, there were four branches of the union with a total affiliated membership of 4,677 workers from Durban, Port Elizabeth, Cape Town, and Johannesburg.

Initial struggles in the SACTU years centred around efforts to end the senseless suspensions of workers from their jobs. There were many cases of workers against whom the Administration had complaints being suspended, sometimes for several months. Often their passes had not been signed off and they could not take other work. With SACTU assistance, legal action reduced the frequency of suspensions and victimization of railway workers.

Each area of the country posed different problems of organizing, making it one of the most difficult industries to penetrate. Nevertheless, with strong leadership, many important struggles were waged and won through the SACTU years. Among the many activists who dedicated themselves to workers on the railways, the following deserve special mention: Lawrence Ndzanga in the Transvaal, assisted by his wife Rita (More), Caleb Mayekiso and Alven Bennie in Port Elizabeth, and Greenwood Ngotyana and later Archie Sibeko in Cape Town. In

South African Railway and Harbour Workers Union, Transvaal. Lawrence Ndzanga, Organizer *(top left corner)*

Durban, popular leader Philemon Tsele organized railway workers in the 1940s. Under the guidance of Natal SACTU LC Chairman, Moses Mabhida, these workers combined into a powerful union between 1956 and 1960; after Mabhida fled South Africa in 1960, Curnick Ndlovu carried on this valuable work.

Archie Sibeko has talked of some of the ways in which organizers were able to contact workers and assist them clandestinely. Sibeko had himself worked on the railways in the early 1950s before becoming a full-time functionary for SACTU.

> When I left the railways I still had my uniform which continued to do a lot of good work for me! . . . Outsiders are not allowed in, so to organize the workers was very difficult. We had to trespass all the time. Because of my overalls, I could go straight through the guard box without any problem, straight to the workers . . . then we'd lie down, eat, talk. . . . Because of my uniform, I could also go inside the Head Office and fetch railway forms for complaints . . . I would take about a hundred (they would give them to me easily) and then I would sit down with workers and later draw up a list of demands to submit. . . . Many complaints were solved this way. The system was discovered by Lawrence Ndzanga, who informed us that you can do a lot of good work using the Railways itself.[3]

Sibeko was also greatly assisted in his work by fellow-Congressite Ben Turok. As a member of the Provincial Council, he could take up pass cases and other matters with the Langa location township officials and so Sibeko continuously brought Turok many of the workers' complaints. In this way, other problems such as family dislocations, hostel accommodation and acquiring permits to seek work were taken up and the needs of the workers properly served.

Ndzanga is remembered as a very shrewd organizer and became a legend amongst railway workers in the Transvaal. Armed with the same tactics he later passed on to others, Ndzanga penetrated the formidable barrier put in place by the R & H Administration against SACTU activists. Leon Levy, SACTU President, recalls that he was 'an all-rounded individual who tried desperately hard to organize railway workers and as a result there were always railway workers coming to the office to register complaints. He put his whole life into it and achieved some modicum of success.'[4] As veteran organizer in the industry, Ndzanga became coordinator of the NOC (Railways) for SACTU nationally.

The Transport NOC was established in May 1958, in an attempt to build a solid national union and coordinate the campaign throughout the country. By 1959, several thousand leaflets, incorporating the £1-a-Day demand, had been issued and funds collected to engage organizers in the Transvaal, the Western and Eastern Cape areas. The NOC prepared a memorandum on railway wage rates and working conditions and this was submitted to the Minister of Transport and other MPs; on occasion such memos led to questions being raised in Parliament about the workers' plight.

The Railways Administration stepped up its anti-union activities, trying every possible means to prevent African workers from joining their union. Hundreds of workers were dismissed and some who found work outside the railways were victimized as the Special Branch forced the new employers to dismiss them. The refusal of the Administration to reinstate workers who had successfully won appeals at the appeal board was another source of irritation. In other cases, workers were transferred from urban to remote rural depots, sometimes merely for carrying leaflets in their pockets. Officials of the union were commonly arrested for trespassing on Railway property.

Abusive practices by the Administration against the workers intensified. One of these included the demotion of employees from their normal work to 'punishment' work at lower rates of pay. This occurred when workers quarrelled with Superintendents and were reported to Inspectors who then assigned them lower-paying jobs. Workers in turn demanded representation to eliminate the discretionary powers given to the individual Superintendents.

During the 1961 Stay-At-Home, compound workers in mines, docks and railways were taken to work under armed escort, with military units standing by. With the exception of Port Elizabeth, docks, railways and mines functioned normally. On 6 December 1961, the office of the SAR & H (N-E) WU was raided and individual membership cards were confiscated. After that, workers whose cards were taken were threatened with dismissal by railway officials if they did not immediately resign from the Union, and more workers were again assigned jobs at lower rates of pay. Subsequently, SACTU sent a letter of protest to the Minister of Transport asking whether this intimidation was sanctioned by his office. The ILO was also informed and international trade union bodies responded in great numbers.

Despite these attempts to crush the unity of workers, the Transport NOC continued to function and voice the demands of the unorganized workers. A joint meeting of railway organizers from all areas convened in late 1962 and decided to publicize the demands of the Black workers at the same time as the reactionary White union was doing the same on behalf of the minority White workers. The latter had already rejected all suggestions by the progressive union for a joint campaign. The essential demands of the Black workers as put forward by the committee were: (a) R2.00 a day; (b) permanent, not casual labour after three months; (c) unemployment insurance, sick leave, improved Workmen's Compensation and treatment; (d) full trade union rights and (e) three weeks annual leave. In compliance with the overall attempt to create national unions, the SAR & H (N-E) WU became a national body in September 1962.

During 1963 and 1964, every railway union official was either detained or banned. Union offices were under constant surveillance and workers were threatened upon entry, leading SACTU to state:

This is surely a measure of the strength of these unions that this intimidating action is used against the workers, who still join and support their unions. Hundreds of cases of railway workers illegally dismissed or victimized have been taken up with success by our Unions and workers have been reinstated.

Yet the victimization continued to intensify and the losses to the trade union movement were great indeed:

Caleb Mayekiso, Secretary of the P.E. branch of the Union, was banned in 1963, detained under the 90-day law, sentenced to 18 months in prison in 1964 and for a further 3 years upon completion of the first term. He was again detained in 1969, but before being charged this very healthy person died in jail of 'natural causes'.

Curnick Ndlovu, Secretary of the Durban branch, received a 20-year sentence in 1964 for 'sabotage'.

Lawrence Ndzanga, National Secretary of the Union and SACTU-NEC member was banned in 1963 and forced to resign from trade union activities, then detained again in 1968. During the recent 1976 Soweto uprisings, Ndzanga was taken into detention once more, but this time he was brutally murdered by the Apartheid regime.

The repression, incarceration and murder of these SACTU working class leaders testifies to the progress being made in organizing the unorganized workers as part of the larger struggle against class exploitation and national oppression.

Dockworkers were also included in the terms of reference of the Transport NOC. Previous to 1955, unions of dockworkers existed in various port cities, particularly in the Cape. Though dockworkers were predominantly migrant workers and were also housed in compounds, their employers were private stevedoring companies and not the state as in the case of railway workers. For this reason, SACTU decided to organize separate unions for dockworkers.

J. Ngulube represented 500 workers from the Cape Town Stevedoring and Dockworkers Union at the Inaugural Conference of SACTU in March 1955. SACTU's original document on organizing the unorganized made reference to the 'stable organization' and 'fine tradition' of unions in the Cape Town docks. Ngulube and Simon Makheta became the main organizers amongst dockworkers during the SACTU years. In 1956, after an intensive organizing campaign amongst Port Elizabeth dockworkers by Alven Bennie and Vuyisile Mini, the PE Stevedoring and Dock Workers Union affiliated to SACTU. It was these workers who carried out a prolonged strike in 1957–58 which eventually required the combined forces of the bosses and the state to crush. This particular struggle and that of the Durban dockworkers are documented in Chapter 8 where we discuss conditions and strikes in the industry.

Although SACTU failed to organize a large, national union of dockworkers, local leaders were always actively assisting these workers to improve their conditions. The difficulty again involved penetrating the prison-like compounds to make contact with workers. Furthermore, whenever a work stoppage was threatened, the state quickly moved in to protect this strategic industry with whatever degree of force necessary. The absence of sustained union organization should in no way detract from the persistent and militant class consciousness that spontaneously erupted in pitched battle on the waterfront and provided an inspiration to other Black workers in secondary manufacturing industry.

The organizers were similarly victimized, particularly after the liberation movement turned to sabotage activities against government installations in the early 1960s. In 1963, while working in the Port Elizabeth SACTU LC, Vuyisile Mini was arrested along with two other ANC militants, Wilson Khayinga and Zinakile Mkaba. All three were charged with committing acts of sabotage and complicity in the death of a police informer in January of that year. Held in solitary confinement under the 90-day law, these three men were finally sentenced to death in March 1964; they were hanged in Pretoria Central Prison on 6 November 1964. The three liberation fighters walked defiantly to their death singing one of the many freedom songs composed by Mini, a musician and poet of exceptional quality.

In addition to railway and dockworkers, the Transport NOC concerned itself with employees who worked for local bus companies in the various industrial centres. These workers were organized in two areas as a result of SACTU initiatives, in Johannesburg and Port Elizabeth. Chapter 8 details the struggles of the Bay Transport Co. workers and the assistance given to these Port Elizabeth workers.

In Johannesburg, the first attempt to organize in this sector of the transport industry began in October 1955. John Parker recalls,

> It was in this magazine, *New Age*, that I saw a page making an appeal to join SACTU. I came across it and with a few friends, thought that this could be our weapon to form a union. We went to the Market Street (SACTU) office and requested advice, intending to organize workers to affiliate to SACTU.[5]

Armed with advice from SACTU, these men began to organize their fellow PUTCO workers on a clandestine basis, knowing they would be dismissed if discovered by the employers. By sending letters to other employees at their home addresses and also receiving replies in their residential locality, they succeeded in mobilizing a major section of the workers. When they felt strong enough, they sent a delegation of three to ask the bosses for wage increases. Although increases were promised, the three were promptly fired. The mass response by the remainder of the workers shocked the bosses who had to quickly retreat, reinstating the three leaders immediately. Other grievances of the workers regarding obligatory overtime work and the lack of benefits from the so-called 'Welfare Committee' set up to cater for the families of workers were then raised with the employers.

Although the Transport Workers Union (Transvaal) began on a firm footing, the Committee of the Union eventually succumbed to the persuasion of the employers in exchange for a few minor reforms. Those who stood strong for full trade union rights and refused to betray the real interests of the workers were singled out for persecution. McKenzie Mvubelo, husband of Lucy Mvubelo (Garment Workers Union of African Women) was one of these stalwarts; his 'reward' for standing by the workers was a vicious personal assault carried out by thugs while he was distributing leaflets. This obvious act of political vengeance left Mvubelo with severe injuries and paralysis.

The Union had managed to unite workers from all PUTCO departments — drivers, conductors, those in the workshops, maintenance, servicing and the yards. In March 1956, the Union affiliated to SACTU with a membership strength of 400 and before its collapse the Union had expanded to other depots and other bus companies. The original struggle began at the Wynberg depot and spread to the Kliptown depot and Van Zyl's bus service. From the SACTU Head Office, General Secretary Leslie Massina devoted much time to the organization of the bus workers in the Johannesburg area.

Workers at Van Zyl Bus Co. carried out a strike against the Company after they had refused to discuss the workers' grievances. Boycotting the Native Labour Act machinery, the workers stood firm in their actions. As a result, twenty-one workers were arrested and eventually sentenced to a fine of £25 each or five weeks (reduced to £15 or three weeks, suspended for three years); 45 additional workers were given the latter sentence as well.

The victimization against members of this Union had the effect of weakening its internal strength and crushing it eventually. Nevertheless, it remains as one of the many examples of a valiant attempt by industrial workers to form their own union with the assistance of SACTU.

This then is a record of attempts to organize transport workers in South Africa under the NOC formed by SACTU. On a national scale, SACTU efforts met with the greatest results in the railways sector, but in all sectors of the industry workers gained considerable improvements as a result of SACTU's campaign and their own determination to improve their lot as exploited workers. This work was all the more remarkable when one considers that the campaign lacked trained personnel, had limited financial resources with which to hire sufficient organizers and had to contend with the repression meted out by the employers and the state.

NOC: Metals

The NOC for metals was established in June 1958 to coordinate the organization of workers in this crucial South African industry. It was not the first Committee set up specifically for the purpose of organizing metal workers, however. In May 1953 a small Non-European Metal Workers Joint Committee, consisting of African and progressive White trade unionists, was formed for this task. The Joint Committee was formed by the Southern Transvaal LC of the old SAT & LC, the Transvaal CNETU and two small African engineering unions, the Transvaal Non-European Iron, Steel and Metal Workers Union (hereafter Tvl. IS & MWU) and the African Motor Industry Workers

Union with a combined membership of approximately 300 workers.

The potential membership of these unions would have been approximately 100,000 workers, the largest of whom had only recently come into this rapidly expanding industry and were for the most part ignorant of trade unionism. In spite of the banning orders imposed on Committee members during this period, the fact that the Native Labour Act was being implemented for the first time, the limited financial resources and personnel to tackle this industry, the Committee managed to increase its membership fivefold to 1,500 workers by 1954.

In that year one of the few progressive White trade unionists in the engineering industry and a person who was to a large extent responsible for the setting up of this new Committee, Vic Syvret, represented the interests of *all* metal workers at a WFTU conference in Europe. At this conference he exposed the conditions faced by these workers in South Africa. Wages were low, workers were forced to work long shifts, the work was heavy and exhausting and they often laboured in very hot temperatures. At that time, the majority of African workers were classed as labourers and basic wages were set at £2 2s. 6d. per week, including COLA. After two consecutive years with the same employer they would receive £2 6s. 4d. A small percentage of African workers were classified as Operatives and received wages ranging from £2 14s. 8d. to £4 5s. 0d.; however, most of the Operatives were Coloured and Indian workers.

White workers' wage rates varied from £10 0s. 0d. to £13 9s. 0d. per week for higher-rated operators, although the actual average wage amounted to nearly £15 0s. 0d. In comparison, very few Black workers were paid a higher rate than the prescribed minimum. The 46-hour week prevailed for all workers regardless of colour, but whereas White workers were granted three weeks paid holiday with a holiday bonus of £32 10s. 0d. (and four weeks after working 12 consecutive years with the same employer), Black workers were allowed only two weeks holiday and no bonus. While Sunday yielded double-time pay, general overtime rates differed for each racial category, with Whites receiving time and a half pay for the first six hours and thereafter double time until the usual starting time of the next shift; Black workers were paid time and a third until the next normal shift. As well, White workers were paid an extra 10 per cent for night shift work with no extra pay granted to Black workers. Various incentive bonuses existed for Whites only.

The Motor Industry Agreement in force was based on the same racist principles as the Engineering Agreement; the highest wages and the best conditions for White workers and correspondingly, the lowest wages and worst conditions for African labourers. For example, a juvenile labourer under 18 years of aged earned from £1 4s. 9d. to £1 10s. 9d. per week, including COLA. A labourer over the age of 18 received from £1 15s. 0d. to £2 16s. 7d., also including COLA. The basic earnings of White journeymen on the other hand were £12 3s. 5d. but the actual average pay was £14 to £15 per week. White workers had a Sick Benefit Fund from which they received numerous benefits including sickness and accident pay while off work. Africans were allowed six days sick leave with full pay during any period of 52 consecutive weeks, but were excluded from the Sick Fund.

At the time of SACTU's formation, the Tvl IS & MWU was the only viable trade union for African metal workers. However, by July 1956 new unions had been formed in both Port Elizabeth and Cape Town with SACTU LC assistance in each area. The Transvaal union supported a number of strikes throughout 1955; between April and September of that year workers at African Lamps, Thermo Welding, African Pressing and Diecasting, Wickmans and Phoenix Foundry engaged in strike action against their conditions of exploitation. At Prima Steel in Benoni also, improvements had been won as a result of the militant actions taken by these East Rand workers.

During the strike at African Lamps, Industria, the Union organizer Nimrod Sejake was arrested and charged with illegally striking along with another 78 workers. Sejake was fined £10 for inciting an illegal strike and the other workers later won an appeal against their fines of £3 each. The workers also won a 1d. per hour increase from their bosses.

Sejake himself had been recruited by the veteran J. B. Marks and given the gigantic task of organizing iron and steel workers prior to 1955. He became one of SACTU's most militant organizers, rousing the low-paid Black metal workers to take frequent strike action. Graham Morodi, a clothing worker at the time, assisted Sejake on the weekends. He recalls Sejake's style of work:

> We said to him that he shouldn't only use strikes because nearly every week there were strikes. We said you should have some negotiations first . . . the employers might agree to the demands. . . . But Sejake was more militant than us.[6]

Vic Syvret spent a great deal of time assisting Sejake in organizing Black metal workers for SACTU even though he was then employed in the office of the registered union for White artisans, the Amalgamated

Engineering Union (AEU). He had previously lost a leg in an accident when working as an engineer. Eventually he gave up his job with the AEU to organize African metal workers on a full-time basis. To the credit of the AEU officials, they agreed to continue to pay him a small allowance so that he could do this work. During his working years, Syvret consistently set aside between one-third and one-half of his monthly salary to distribute to SACTU and other progressive organizations, although both he and his wife were in poor health. When he left South Africa for a life in exile in the German Democratic Republic in 1960, Vic continued to perform international solidarity work for SACTU and the ANC until his recent death.

In October 1955, the Executive of the Transvaal IS & MWU requested that SACTU's first National Organizer, John Nkadimeng, be permitted to work full-time for their Union. Sejake was the only organizer left after the resignation of the Secretary and the Union Executive thought that Nkadimeng was the strong person needed to assist Sejake in this most difficult industry. As this was one of the strategic industries to be organized by SACTU, permission was granted. The Union continued to advance with the assistance of the Joint Metal Workers Committee, but it was still agreed that a nationwide attack on the entire industry was a requisite for improving the conditions of African metal workers as a whole. Much of Nkadimeng's time as an organizer was spent in trying to obtain compensation for workers who suffered severe burns and other injuries in their jobs.

In Port Elizabeth, the African Iron, Steel and Metal WU was formed by the Local Committee in September 1955. Wilton Mkwayi undertook the main responsibility for organizing metal workers in the Eastern Cape. As discussed elsewhere, the Port Elizabeth LC had a solid corps of organizers and thus Mkwayi received assistance from others in this task.

In Cape Town, a Metal Workers Union affiliated to SACTU in early 1956, with an initial membership of 370 workers. An early victory for workers at Lystra zip factory gave the MWU momentum in its recruitment of additional members. Workers at this factory went on strike after the Labour Department had neglected to call a Conciliation Board as promised.

Archie Sibeko, Secretary of the SACTU LC in the Western Cape, and Ben Turok, Secretary of the new MWU, approached the workers jointly at the factories, although by this time Turok had been banned and had to 'hide around the corner' while Sibeko contacted and discussed the local situation with the workers. At the zip factory, Sibeko addressed a large group of militant Coloured women and though the employers pleaded for the women to return to work, they were ignored. The police were summoned and were astonished to find that women workers were so intent on listening to an African man, a 'Kaffir' to them. Sibeko was arrested along with Turok who was discovered nearby and both were taken to the police station for about an hour. On their release at about 4.30 p.m., Sibeko was intending to return to his home not far away, but the police were adamant that he be driven back to the factory. They begrudgingly told him that 'those women are still there and won't go to work until they see your face'. Sibeko comments:

It was a great victory, not only for these Coloured workers but for the whole area (of Paarden Eiland). We were working in this area all the time and with something like this, the news spreads immediately that the workers have won.[7]

In fact, these workers had been influenced in their actions by the success of a previous strike at Boston Bag Co. in the same industrial area (described below). Skilful organizing was being systematically carried out by SACTU activists who saw the importance of organizing workers in the townships before attempting to do so at the factory where victimization was a threat. By visiting the workers in the evenings and on weekends, they could gradually win them over and in this way build up the strength of the Union away from the scrutiny of the bosses; sometimes over 50 per cent of the workforce was organized in this manner before approaching workers inside the factories.

The Metal Workers Union was subsequently able to penetrate the larger factories such as Stewart and Lloyds and proceeded to organize workers into a viable structure. Although frustrated by problems of discontinuity among organizing personnel, the membership strength of the MWU climbed to over one thousand members at one time. The Union had difficulty maintaining a constant membership, however, and was seldom recognized by the metal employers. Turok also says that it could not get a proper base amongst Coloured workers in the factories because of the largely unskilled and shifting labour force. There were exceptions regarding union recognition by the bosses, especially when Turok (a White) went to put forward the workers' case; conversely, the employers would not deal with 'his boy' (Sibeko) when he came by himself. Following the arrest of Ben Turok for High Treason in December 1956, his wife Mary replaced Ben as Secretary and in this way the Union maintained continuity.

As in the case of transport, the metal industry was considered vitally important to SACTU's overall aims and objectives. In the document entitled 'Organizing the Unorganized' (referred to above), the task was clearly set out. A programme of organization to be coordinated with the Joint Committee included the immediate establishment of contact with the main undertakings such as the Iron and Steel Corporation (ISCOR) and Vander Bijl, the rapid training of active workers, the establishment of shop-stewards or factory committees, and the drafting of national demands. Also to be included were demands concerning working conditions regarding accidents and safety, assaults, unsanitary workplaces, excessive overtime and the withholding of pay.

By 1957, the Unions existed in the Transvaal (with Sejake as Secretary), Western Cape (Turok), Eastern Cape (Mkwayi) and in Natal (Billy Nair). A first step was taken towards the formation of a national union with the creation of a 'Committee of United Metal Workers Unions'. It was, however, only after the NOC was created in 1958 that the national organizing of metal workers really got off the ground. Riddled with the usual problems of lack of personnel and finances, the campaign gained strength after the 1959 Conference when SACTU leaders re-pledged their active support.

Research carried out by MWU and published in the May 1959 issue of *Workers Unity* revealed the position of South Africa's exploited African metal workers in comparison with Australian workers doing the same work. The latter earned as much as four to five times more than their South African counterparts. In particular, figures showed that while the Australian labourer earned nearly 90 per cent of the wages received by the Australian journeyman, the South African labourer earned only 20 per cent.

Paying these wages, the Australian capitalists make large profits and keep their factories going. How much greater must be the profits of the South African bosses who pay so little to the unskilled workers?[8]

In fact the profits of those Apartheid bosses amounted to a total of just less than £50 million in 1954.

It is just because of their greed for more and more profits every year, that the bosses force down the conditions of the workers. So a small group of exploiters is able to oppress hundreds of thousands of workers.[9]

Who were these bosses? Fourteen of the largest engineering firms, including Union Steel Corporation, Thomas Barlow and Sons, Ltd, and

Dorman Long (Africa) Ltd, controlled between them enormous sums of capital and employed thousands of workers. They also worked closely with the state-controlled enterprises like ISCOR and Dunswart. The employers were, as usual, themselves well-organized in the Steel and Engineering Industries Federation (SEIFSA), making it imperative that the Black workers be organized in the class struggle.

The state monopoly ISCOR was established in 1928 with the express purpose of creating an iron and steel industry in South Africa to meet the needs of the mining magnates and of other industries, including the state-owned railways. The gross exploitation of the workers by ISCOR allowed the Corporation to sell its products to the other monopolies at a price which protected the profits of the latter, while simultaneously assuring maximum surplus value for itself. Highly dangerous working conditions existed at ISCOR and many workers suffered burns and other serious injuries often resulting in death. The workers were 'bound hand and foot' to ISCOR, but when disabled they were sacked and rejected. In 1961, according to a report given in *Workers Unity*, 85 per cent of the African workers at ISCOR were receiving £3 10s. 0d. (R7) per week and the highest wage an African worker could expect to earn was £4 7s. 0d. (R8.70).

These wages, although still far below the breadline, represented an increase over previous poverty wages and came as a direct result of SACTU pressure and the MWU demand for a minimum wage of £1-a-Day. In 1960, workers in the industry won an increase of 6d. per hour on the basic wage, bringing it up to £3 10s. 9d. per week.

MWUs in all provinces had been active at the local level organizing metal workers' rallies and publicizing conditions in the industry. The strongest union by 1961 was in the Transvaal, with branches in Johannesburg, Pretoria, Boksburg, Benoni, Germiston, Kempton Park, Krugersdorp and Vereeniging. Richard Takalo was the Union Secretary at this time, having replaced Gilbert Hlalukwana. Other SACTU activists such as George Monare were recruited to assist in the work whenever time was available. The Union's major efforts in the early 1960s were directed towards organizing the highly exploited workers at the ISCOR and Vander Bilj plants. The state operation was much more difficult to tackle than the private plants due to the restrictive compound life forced upon the employees. Meetings were impossible in the compounds as security guards patrolled these vast enclosures night and day. In the private operations, SACTU organizers found it much easier to meet the workers during lunch hour and after work and address them inside factory gates. The tactics used to penetrate ISCOR included mobilizing people from the townships to distribute leaflets and form factory committees from within.

The NOC appointed a full-time organizer to work amongst the 7,000 steel workers in Pretoria in March 1961. As well, the Committee planned to cooperate with the Transport NOC to open a joint office in Pretoria. Special assistance was given the Port Elizabeth branch to organize workers at General Motors, Ford and other assembly plants. All of these efforts bore fruit during the February 7th campaign in 1962 as workers in this industry responded in the greatest numbers. Over 350 new union members were recruited during this period.

After these successes, SACTU called upon all its members to embark upon a three months' intensive campaign in the iron and steel and metallurgical industries. The Chairman of SACTU's MC asked every affiliated Union and all volunteers to 'think, eat, sleep and dream of the Metal industry'. There were two issues in particular that were to be the focal point of the campaign – higher wages and skilled training for Black workers.

No Blacks were allowed to become apprentices even though thousands of these workers performed semi-skilled and skilled jobs without adequate training and guaranteed opportunities for advancement. Black workers in every part of the country were required to do skilled work at less than skilled rates of pay. Therefore a major demand in the ensuing campaign was for the right of all Black workers to undergo training and to be eligible for apprentice programmes.

By 1962, the NOC had prepared an excellent memorandum to be distributed to all LCs and MWUs and then upon approval submitted to the Industrial Council for the Industry. The demands were as follows: for a new Agreement in the industry which would lay down the minimum wage of 25 cents per hour (inclusive of COLA) in all divisions; for a Medical Benefit Fund, made up of contributions of both workers and employers on the basis of 1 cent per hour per employee; for a maximum working week of 40 hours throughout the industry; for two additional public holidays (May Day and Easter) on full pay for all employees; for annual leave of three consecutive weeks; for a special height allowance to be paid to workers involved in jobs at excessive heights; for a holiday bonus of £45; for equal pay for men and women and the removal of all discrimination in wages, that is, the rate for the job; and for the establishment of a Death Benefit Fund. This memorandum was jointly submitted by the Metal Workers Unions of the Transvaal, Natal and the Cape.

On 27 and 28 October, the MWU held their first National Conference in Johannesburg for the purpose of discussing these demands and how best to proceed with their organizing campaign on a national basis. During the following year, 927 new members were added to the Transvaal branch of the Union alone.

In March 1963, the Toy and Plastic Workers Union merged with the MWU (Transvaal) to form a broader base in the struggle for higher wages; the umbrella structure retained the name of the MWU. Throughout the SACTU years it had been the intention to form a National Union of Metal Workers and at each successive conference of the Transvaal branch this was proposed and endorsed. A final attempt was made during 1963 and 1964 following a decision taken at the November Annual Conference of the Transvaal branch.

However, state repression against the Union leaders was mounting. Richard Takalo had been banned by the time of the Conference. In the Report presented to SACTU's Ninth Annual National Conference in 1964, it was reported that every single organizer of metal workers from every province had been detained or banned and removed from trade union activity. In addition, the Transvaal branch had to contend with the union-busting tactics of the government and against the splitting tactics of TUCSA, which despite SACTU's protests, formed a splinter Sheet Metal Workers Union. Despite these setbacks, workers continued in their struggle, fighting for the demands set out in the SACTU-MWU memorandum even though they had been robbed of their militant working class leaders. As for the TUCSA Union, it never really got off the ground as workers recognized that it had been created only to cause confusion.

NOC: Mining

I am a mine worker, employed in one of the richest mines on the Rand. I earn 2/5d a shift (and board), and I have to live in this compound with 40 other workers. This concrete bunk has been my home for the last 5 'monthly tickets' (about 30 weeks). My family is in the Transkei, and my children are starving. I once had a few cattle and a very small piece of land, but the Government has taken most of this away from me. After one more 'ticket' I shall go back to my family. But soon I shall have to come back here or go to work on a farm, so that my family and I might live.[10]

African workers in the metal industry suffer a high rate of injuries

Mine workers' compound

The NOC for the mining industry was formed by SACTU in 1961, although organizing work on the mines had been carried on sporadically since 1955. If the criterion of judgment is the creation of a properly functioning trade union, then it should be said at the outset that such a goal was never achieved. On the other hand, the failure itself reflects the conditions of exploitation in the South African mining industry more so than SACTU's inability to effectively organize this crucial sector of the African labour force.

As we have mentioned in previous chapters, the entire South African labour policy towards African workers – consisting of migrant labour, the compound system and gross exploitation – has its historical base in the mining industry. South Africa's industrial capitalist development owes its very existence to the exploitation of the rich natural resources found beneath the soil of Apartheid. Most notably gold and coal, but also diamonds, asbestos, manganese and iron have been the major source of accumulated wealth through the decades; almost 50 per cent of the annual value of foreign exchange has been earned through the export of these minerals.

The foundation of the amazing accumulation of profits in this industry is the callous and inhuman treatment of African mine workers. Unlike the normal course of capitalist history, conditions have deteriorated rather than improved over the years. Whereas the ratio of White to Black wages on the gold mines was 11·7:1 in 1911, it had increased only slightly to 12·7:1 at the time of the African Mine Workers Strike in 1946. In successive five-year periods beginning in 1951, the ratio increased from 14·7:1 to 15·5:1 to 17·0:1 to 17·6:1 in 1966. By 1969, the White workers' annual cash earnings were 20·1 times more than those of Black wage earners. The dramatic escalation in the rate of exploitation is thus closely associated with the history of capitalist development under the Nationalist regime since 1948.

The 1946 strike led to more concerted efforts by the Chamber of Mines to prevent the organization of African miners. Despite, or more correctly, because of this strike, the Chamber was obliged to argue:

The Gold Mining Industry considers that trade unionism as practised by Europeans is still beyond the understanding of the tribal Native; nor can he know how to employ it as a means of promoting his advancement. He has no tradition in that respect and has no experience or proper appreciation of the responsibilities arising from collective representation. No proper conduct of a trade union is possible unless the workers have that tradition and such a sense of responsibility. . . . The introduction of trade unionism among tribal Natives at their present stage of development would lead to abuses and irresponsible actions. . . . A trade union is outside the comprehension of all but a few of the educated Natives of the urban type; it would not only be useless but detrimental to the ordinary mine Native in his present stage of development.[11]

A summary review of subsequent difficulties encountered in organizing these workers puts SACTU's efforts in perspective.

African miners were (and are) contract labourers, recruited from the entire sub-continent and from reserves within South Africa by the Chamber's recruiting agency, the Witwatersrand Native Labour Association (WNLA). Contracts varied in length from six to twelve to eighteen months, and while under the total social control of the bosses African workers were 'housed' in fenced-in concentration camp-like compounds. Recruitment propaganda of 'free accommodation' translated in reality to concrete bunks for forty to fifty men per compound, while costs for coal and firewood were deducted from the starvation wages. It was company policy that African workers as migrants were not allowed to live with their families, unlike the White miners who lived in decent, subsidized housing. The company lure of 'free food' became the daily rations of 'mealie pap' (maize porridge) with some gravy, a mug of tea, two to three pounds of neck meat per week, some vegetables and nuts, but no milk or butter. Again, this diet had to be supplemented by purchases from the Company stores. Weekend 'tshwala' rations (traditional African beer) kept the workers duped in an attempt to dampen political consciousness and collective action. The usual miners' diseases – phthisis, silicosis, tuberculosis, etc. – hit African workers the hardest and their compensation was pitiful when compared with that available to White miners suffering from similar occupational handicaps. In 1962, an estimated 200 Africans were sent home weekly to die in the reserves or their foreign homelands after having contracted these diseases. Details of compensation for African dependants are reported in Chapters 4 and 9.

Company policy has been to intentionally promote internal cleavages within this heterogeneous African workforce. By housing workers according to ethnic and national backgrounds, the seething discontent tends to be chanelled into inter-ethnic or national violence. Yet beneath this superficial explanation was the common working class protest of all Black miners, regardless of origin. Malawians, Mozambicans, Namibians as 'foreigners' and Sotho, Tswana, Xhosa and Zulu South Africans share one experience in common – they are all expected to call the White man 'baas' (boss). This cements their unity and common objectives. As the 'home of the industrial colour-bar', the South African mining industry has not only ensured that racial and class exploitation function compatibly, but also that these ground rules distinguish South African labour policy in other industries.

SACTU, like progressive trade unionists in previous decades, realized that success in organizing African workers in general ultimately depended on organizing successfully the mine and farm workers. Although capitalist supervision of workers has been the most efficient in these industries, the structure of mining, unlike agriculture, carries with it the contradiction that hundreds of thousands of workers are combined in social production on the mine property. Divide-and-rule has thus always been in dynamic tension with its opposite: class consciousness and class struggle. The latter expresses itself only when conditions allow for such unity of all workers.

In the immediate aftermath of the 1946 strike, the understandable despair following the defeat of the strike and the virtual collapse of the African Mine Workers Union made the conditions of organizing especially problematic. Without a trade union, or some form of workers' organization, wages and working conditions were not likely to improve in what J. B. Marks called, 'the immoral economic backbone of the country'.

SACTU focused its campaign to re-organize African mine workers around the poverty wages which had only slightly improved after 1946. In 1955, it was reported that the gold mines paid 35,000 White workers £50 million per year and 273,000 African miners only £22 million annually. Of the profits, £23 million (larger than the entire African wage bill) was paid out to shareholders who lived all over the world and thus benefited from the sweat and blood of the African proletariat; another £17 million went into the government revenues. The Transvaal and Orange Free State gold mines had increased their working profits from £26·3 million in 1946 to £44·3 million in 1955.

The 1959 minimum and average wages for African miners were as follows:

		Underground	*Surface*
Minimum		3s. per shift	2s. 3d.
Average	gold	4s. 8d.	3s. 5d.
	coal	4s. 3d.	3s. 6d.

Despite formal and conventional colour-bars, Africans were performing skilled work in various mining sectors. In the Natal coalfields, for example, Africans and Indians operating coal cutting machines earned only £7 0s. 0d. per *month*, whereas unskilled White workers because of their skin colour received £2 9s. 2d. per *shift*. As SACTU stressed in its propaganda materials: 'It is not the work but the pay that is unskilled. Colour, not competency explains the difference in the wage rates.'[12] Furthermore, the surplus pool of African labour recruited by the WNLA served as a further factor to depress Black wages. In 1959, of the 432,234 African workers recruited, only 182,561 were South African in nationality.

In the early SACTU years between 1955 and 1960, contact was intermittent with mine workers. Banned ex-Chairman of the AMWU, J. B. Marks, P. J. Simelane (who organized miners in the Eastern Rand), Segwale (West Rand) and Leon Levy (SACTU President) seem to have been at the forefront of SACTU initiatives, which consisted primarily of propaganda leaflets distributed clandestinely in the compounds. In 1961, to commemorate the fifteenth anniversary of the 1946 strike, SACTU renewed its emphasis on organizing mine workers. NEC minutes of February 1961, report that an NOC had been formed to coordinate the work. The 1960 Clydesdale disaster provided the immediate background against which the NOC planned its campaign.

Focusing on the low wages, which were far below the £1-a-Day demand, and concentrating geographically on the Transvaal gold mines, the NOC strategy consisted of recruiting volunteers and co-opting leaders of affiliated unions to distribute leaflets near the mining compounds on weekends. The ANC mobilized a considerable volunteer force to assist in this highly dangerous work. Leaders from affiliated unions who actively participated in the campaign included, among others, Uriah Maleka (furniture), John Gaetsewe (laundry), Graham Morodi (LC Organizer), George Monare (clothing), Richard Takalo (metals), Dlamini (Transvaal GWU),[13] J. B. Marks (banned) and Eli Weinberg (banned). By November 1961, one full-time official and one organizer, Brown Ndavemavota, had been assigned to the Mining NOC. During this campaign these organizers were frequently detained, and Phyllis Altman, Assistant General Secretary, had to sit by the telephone in the SACTU office taking details of which police stations were holding the various SACTU organizers.

These organizers and volunteers met constant harassment whenever they neared mine company property. Ndavemavota was imprisoned for three months and because he was not South African was eventually deported to Malawi. Despite these frequent detentions for trespassing the NOC managed to distribute hundreds of thousands of leaflets to African mine workers; this was accomplished in large part as a result of Congress supporters who worked in the mines and smuggled the leaflets into the compounds. The only reported attempt to hold a large mass meeting occurred on 19 August 1961, fifteen years after the 1946 strike, but the meeting met with mixed results. Although intimidation before the meeting prevented a large turnout, and although a police ring was placed around the hall during the meeting, SACTU documents reveal that individual memberships increased. These members were signed up whenever they were able to get out of the compounds and visit the SACTU office. Total paid up members amounted to only 100 workers by November 1961. Beyond this, however, letters from mine workers often kept Head Office aware of the specific grievances and demands emanating from the point of production; these demands were then taken up with the companies concerned.

Head Office encouraged Natal and OFS to launch similar campaigns amongst coal and diamond workers respectively. Although a minimum amount of contact was achieved by the Durban LC with coal miners in Northern Natal, the diamond mines of the OFS became the second most active area outside of the Transvaal. The Kimberley LC, although situated in the Northern Cape, took up the cause of the badly exploited diamond workers who worked for mining magnate Harry Oppenheimer and his DeBeers conglomerate. These miners were not allowed to leave their fenced-in areas from the beginning to the expiration of contracts. Following a mine disaster at Odendaalsrus in May 1962, it was decided that an organizer would be sent to the OFS to assess the entire situation in both gold and diamond mining. In addition to the usual complaints, deductions from wages for boots, bad food, excessively low wages and extremely poor working conditions were highlighted by scattered committees of workers contacted. These conditions had led to violence between workers and mine police at a Virginia, OFS mine and a mass trial of 12 workers was held in a Ventersberg prison in 1959.

The Kimberley GWU intervened on behalf of the diamond miners in 1962. African miners were receiving only £3 every two weeks, had no annual leave and no sick pay. Calling for wage increases and 14 days annual leave, the GWU memorandum of demands forced Oppenheimer to concede only minimal increments, and not before documents and leaflets were seized by police from the Union office. Miners who had joined the GWU were also given five minutes to quit the Union or otherwise lose their job. This is the same Oppenheimer who parades himself in international circles as a 'liberal', anti-Apartheid politician in South Africa. As for the White workers, when SACTU sent its paper *Workers Unity* to the registered SA Diamond Workers Union, it received the following reply: 'As we are not interested in your literary dregs, kindly remove us from your mailing list.'[14]

Head Office assisted in these regional efforts by sending all £1-a-Day memoranda to the Chamber of Mines, but no acknowledgement was ever received. Correspondence with the National Union of Mineworkers (UK) called for British workers to pressure the parent mining companies to allow trade unionism among African workers in South Africa. Finally, SACTU submitted regular reports to ILO Conferences highlighting the deplorable and repressive conditions resulting from the migrant labour system. Aside from their educational value, none of these initiatives led to material improvements for the workers themselves.

Leon Levy, SACTU President during the 1950s, described the main problem in organizing miners as the lack of full-time organizers and resources to commit to the task. There was an attempt to re-assess the strategy in late 1961, as many observers felt that effective organization of mine workers must begin prior to recruitment, that is, on the reserves. Although Levy concedes, 'perhaps we did not do as much as we should have ... and perhaps we even lacked imagination to some extent,' he goes on to say that to devote the time and energy necessary to organize the mining industry would have left nothing for all the other work.[15] However, these efforts were not to go unrewarded as within ten years African mine workers would once again raise the banner of militancy in the early 1970s.

NOC: Agriculture

Farm Labour. Those are the words which tell a tale of human misery. They have become words of scandal, words which express the worst features of capitalist exploitation in South Africa.[16]

The exploitation of African farm workers became a national scandal in the 1950s. Combining the worst features of capitalism and Apartheid, the profit motive of White agricultural capital led to barbarous conditions for Africans who were herded into the fields to produce cheap commodities for export – wines, fruit and sugar.[17] The Nationalists, more so than governments before them, established policies that assured the White farmers a guaranteed supply of forced cheap, Black labour. In 1959, the Director of Prisons proudly admitted:

> The Department of Prisons has become the focal point for the farmer, from the Limpopo (River) to the Cape. They all want labour from us, but we cannot supply it all, but we are doing everything in our power to meet the emergency.[18]

By 1961, farm labour accounted for over one-third of the economically active African population; 86 per cent of all farm workers were Africans. In actual numbers, 1,441,470 Africans laboured on White farms as registered/contracted employees (731,424), casual/seasonal employees (583,475), and domestic servants (126,570). When dependants of African farm workers are considered, almost 3·5 million lived on the White farms in 1960. Coloured and Asian workers accounted for another 14 per cent of the workforce (239,356).

Farm workers are in many ways even more grossly exploited than mine workers, as the following chart of average annual earnings by economic sector shows:

Average Annual Earnings (in Rand)

	Year	Whites	Africans
Agriculture	1958	1,895.0	36.7
	1964	1,293.8	60.0
Mining	1967	3,668.4	202.0
Manufacturing	1963–64	2,169.0	413.6

The 1962 agricultural census revealed that the average income in cash and kind for African farm workers – including the wages of women and children – ranged between £2 (R4) and £3 (R6) *per month*. These are the years during which SACTU was calling for a £1-a-Day minimum wage for all workers as necessary for survival.

Thousands of African farm workers were killed either through starvation or abuse. They had no recognized legal rights once employed on the farms. Covered only by the archaic Masters and Servants Acts, Africans were subject to the whims and whips of the White master, who assessed fines and inflicted physical punishment for desertion or 'disobedience'. This was most commonly done through a hierarchical system of 'boss-boys' (*indunas*) who themselves survived only by beating, maiming and killing the productive workers. It was not uncommon for workers to labour 14 hours a day, with the wives and children of male workers forced to work at lower rates of pay to assist the latter in meeting contractual obligations. Education and health facilities were, and still are, virtually non-existent in relation to demand.

A large percentage of the African workforce on the farms has always been convict or forced labour. Dating back to the 1880s, when prisoners were hired out to wine-farmers by the Cape Government, the system was expanded throughout this century. By 1957–58, nearly 200,000 convicts were hired to White farmers a year, at a slave wage of 9*d*. a day.

Since 1947, long term prisoners have also been integrated into the farm labour scheme. Selected farmers are permitted to build jails on their land, to Government specification, and the Department of Prisons supplies guards. By 1963, there were 25 farm jails, 10 in the Transvaal, one in the Orange Free State, 14 in the Cape, housing more than 9,000 long-term convicts.[19]

By the early 1950s, an even more comprehensive programme of forced labour recruitment was sanctioned by the Apartheid system. The millions of Africans detained or arrested for petty offences (pass laws) were given the 'option' of paying a fine (or serving a jail sentence) or 'volunteering' for work on the farms. Poverty often forced Africans to literally give their lives in lieu of an inability to pay £1 or £2 fines. In 1957 alone, one and a quarter million Africans were brought before the courts for violations of petty offences, giving one a good sense of the potential farm labour recruits obtainable from this system. By 1953, an estimated 32,582 workers had been captured in this manner.

Government complicity in this pattern of exploitation was total and unconcealed. White farmers would simply advise authorities regarding their labour needs and the bureaucracy administering the lives of Africans would respond accordingly. The farmer became the surrogate policeman, jailer, and often executioner. In addition to government recruiting schemes, private agents roamed the countryside purchasing for £5 or abducting children from peasant families unable to feed their families. Thus, although the farmers were not slave-owners in the legal sense, they reproduced the conditions of slavery for one-third of the African population in the mid-twentieth century. Changes since the 1950s have not lessened the suffering but only refined the system in order 'to regulate the supply of labour with a view to correlating it with the demand'. This has entailed reducing the number of non-contract squatters and replacing them with annual contract migrants.

Space prevents an exhaustive documentation of the human suffering endured by agricultural workers and their families. Chapter 10 describes this in part as background to the Congress Alliance potato boycott of 1959. At this point, only one typical case will be mentioned. In response to the 'volunteer' system, a Johannesburg attorney, Mr Joel Carlson, successfully brought *habeas corpus* actions to free many so-called 'volunteer' farm workers in the Transvaal and Orange Free State. Evidence proved beyond doubt that these offenders of petty Apartheid laws had in fact been given no option but were merely picked up off the streets and sold to White farmers through the Pass Office for six to twelve month contract periods. Some of the captives had been productively employed in urban jobs at the time of their abduction. The evidence in the court also vividly portrayed the conditions on the farms: toes being chopped off to make escape impossible; deliberate underfeeding of workers to force expenditure of meagre wages in farm stores; and the infamous 'tot' system whereby juvenile labourers in vineyards were paid a portion of their wages in wine – resulting in a high incidence of alcohol-related diseases among children. Many court cases, however, did not lead to verdicts favourable to the workers, as government bureaucrats provided testimony on behalf of the White farmers. In fact, the government indirectly admitted its lack of concern for the fate of African farm workers by the fact that in 1959 there was only one Inspector to oversee the 100,000 farms in South Africa.

Against these realities, the effective organization of farm workers has always been an almost impossible task. Unlike mine workers, the production of farm workers is not highly socialized; that is, workers are not concentrated at clearly defined points of production but are instead scattered on large and small farms throughout the Republic. Nevertheless, one of SACTU's most impressive achievements in the basic industries was the formation of the Farm, Plantation and Allied Workers Union (FPAWU) in 1961. Although organizing work was done in the Cape and Natal, the Union had its base in the Eastern and Northern Transvaal. The potential for building a national Union was severely affected by the period of repression in the early 1960s.

Until the late 1950s, organizing of Transvaal farm workers was performed largely by one person, Gert Sibande, Transvaal ANC President. Banned from residing in urban areas, Sibande utilized his rural base and spent his entire life assisting ANC units in the political

Gert Sibande, Organizer of farm labourers and Transvaal ANC leader

Pass offenders being sold to White farmers in the Eastern Transvaal

Farm Labourer Beaten, Loses Eye

From M. P. Naicker

DURBAN.

A FARM labourer—18-year-old Joseph Ngcobo—has alleged in a statement to New Age that he was so severely beaten on a farm at Bethal that he lost an eye.

Another Farm Assault On A 16-Year-Old African

A CHAIN TIED HIM TO A COW AT NIGHT

JOHANNESBURG.

New Age exposes farm labour scandal, 1959

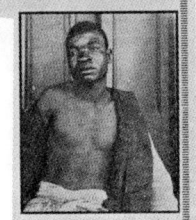

WHEN WILL IT STOP?

Farm Labour Agony Goes On

THERE ARE FOUR MORE INSTALMENTS OF THE FARM LABOUR SCANDAL THIS WEEK:

From Ruth First

"I CAN'T REMEMBER A DAY WITHOUT BEATINGS"
(Photo by Eli Weinberg)

mobilization of rural workers and peasants. Specific workers' complaints would be passed on to SACTU, who took these up as legal cases, demands for government reforms or memoranda sent to the ILO Conferences. Following the 1959 SACTU Conference decision to form NOCs in the basic industries, however, an agricultural NOC was formed in 1960 in the Transvaal. Working closely with Sibande, known in the movement as 'The Lion of the East', this particular NOC brought in SACTU leaders who themselves had been born and raised in peasant families in rural Transvaal. Thoroughly urbanized and proletarianized themselves, they were none the less able to return to the countryside of their youth and utilize the network of social relations to political and trade union advantage. Among those SACTU organizers were Uriah Maleka, Graham Morodi, John Nkadimeng and Elijah Mampuru.

The initial work involved education amongst farm workers about the purpose of trade unions, especially as many had no previous contact with anything but political organizations – e.g. the ANC. Fear and intimidation had to be overcome. White farmers told their workers that these organizers were 'Communists out to steal your money'. They also made it a practice of evicting African workers seen talking with known Congress leaders. Even the distribution of leaflets was a hazardous venture, although occasionally leaflets could be stuck in fence-holes to be picked up by workers when out of sight of the 'boss-boys'.

Prior to the formation of the Union, the agricultural NOC drafted a memorandum of demands that was submitted to the Transvaal Agricultural Union (TAU), a White farmers' society. The TAU Conference of March 1961 had included on its agenda a discussion item: 'The farm worker as a human being.' SACTU pointed out the increasing disparity between urban and rural wages and in turn demanded: hourly wage rates and a special additional allowance for food purchases; overtime pay beyond the 46-hour week; one month annual leave and the same holidays as given to urban workers; workmen's compensation and sick pay; the right to organize and negotiate wage and working conditions; more hospitals, dispensaries and doctors in the rural areas; improved housing; and the abolition of the Master and Servants Acts. 'These are the minimum and human demands of farm workers throughout South Africa today,' concluded the memorandum. The TAU Conference politely refused to seriously consider these demands, arguing that holidays and hours of work were the prerogative of individual farms and that all other issues raised were matters for government legislation.

On 8 October 1961 the Inaugural meeting of the FPAWU convened in Johannesburg, with representation from Morgenzon, Bethal, Kinross, Trichardt, Amersfoort, and Standerton in the Transvaal, and one delegate from the Cape. Prior to electing a Chairman, Secretary and working committee of eleven, the delegates discussed their common conditions of exploitation. Husbands were often the only paid workers of entire families forced to labour on the farms, and three cases of farmers deliberately running down workers on the roads were cited. Over 100 delegates (previously registered with the Agricultural Division, Transvaal General Workers Union) resolved to form the FPAWU and demanded, in addition to the above, £1-a-Day for workers receiving only a cash wage. For those receiving cash and land, the demand was for £5 0s. 0d. per month, plus five morgen of fertile land to plough with implements provided by the farmer. Other demands included a period of three months notice prior to eviction, no employment of juvenile labour and compulsory education for children of school age and an immediate Wage Board investigation.

These resolutions were submitted to the TAU, all relevant government ministries, the press and the international trade unions in agriculture. The National Union of Agricultural Workers (UK) responded with useful materials regarding rural organizing strategies and drafting of a constitution. By December 1961 district committees were established to collect research information regarding housing, transport, education and health facilities in the Eastern and Northern Transvaal.

The 1962 SACTU Conference welcomed the FPAWU as the first organized affiliate representing African farm workers. Only at the Durban 1959 Conference had rural people attended SACTU meetings in such large numbers. Delegate after delegate addressed the SACTU leaders and workers, describing in detail the conditions of subjugation they experienced on the farms. One worker spoke of wives and children being taken into custody for not having 'permits' in their possession, while another talked of the constant torture inflicted on workers who objected when forced to eat soil, dress in and sleep on potato sacks. Conference reiterated the FPAWU demands and called on all affiliated unions to contribute 50c per month to an organizing fund for farm workers.

Following the creation of the Union, Uriah Maleka handed over the organizer position to Elijah Mampuru. Mampuru was a veteran of rural struggles from earlier years. He had been one of the leaders of an organization known as 'Sebatakgomo', a political front for ANC work in the rural areas in the early 1950s. The word 'Sebatakgomo' has no direct translation into English, but its origin and meaning are derived from anti-colonialist wars fought by the African people. Whenever the people were about to be attacked, leaders would shout the battle cry: 'Sebatakgomo' as a warning and a call for mobilization. In the early 1950s, this organization raised the consciousness of the peasantry against Apartheid legislation, bureaucracy and complicity of the tribal chiefs in the exploitation of the people. Mampuru had since returned to work in the clothing industry from which he was co-opted to become FPAWU organizer in 1961.

Mampuru and Sibande, with a corps of assistants divided the Eastern, Northern and Southern Transvaal into regions. Mampuru soon gained the reputation as one of SACTU's best organizers; the tales spread by White farmers about him being a 'dangerous' person and a 'Communist' only enhanced his credibility with the people. Leon Levy recalls that Elijah would return from the rural areas with a long list of new members, £1-a-Day slips filled in and membership dues.[20] Mampuru himself tells many fascinating stories of his organizing exploits. For example, on one occasion he was held in detention for seven weeks, during which time the police tried to convince him that SACTU had been banned; he countered by telling the police that he read *New Age* regularly and knew that this was not the case. Despite many detentions of this length, Mampuru managed to sign up over 400 members during his first three weeks as an organizer. Another 886 members were added in a further six-week period. His success led Cape farm organizers to request that he work there for a short time, but he was banned before this could be arranged.[21]

By September 1962 the FPAWU's First Annual General Meeting recognized the limitations of the Union's resources. Most of the time had been spent defending individual farm workers against eviction and brutalization. The Union lacked enough full-time organizers and no one was available to continue the research necessary to effectively canvass the entire industry. All of these problems were made worse by limited finances and lack of transport. Nevertheless, the Union continued to bring the plight of farm workers to national and international attention. The 1962 Conference highlighted the contradiction between mass starvation and poverty-induced disease in the African community and the callous destruction of food – for example, the dumping of dairy surpluses into the sea — by the Apartheid regime. For all of these limitations, the FPAWU was regarded by many SACTU leaders as a well-organized Union with a dedicated cadre of activists and Executive members.

On one occasion, the Witwatersrand LC was informed through Mampuru that the FPAWU leaders wished to come to Johannesburg to meet with their fellow trade unionists in the city. Leaving the remote rural areas well before dawn, 110 persons walked over seventy miles to attend the meeting. Much to the amazement of SACTU leaders, who had expected perhaps ten delegates at the most, the farmworkers proceeded to give the most harrowing reports of their conditions of exploitation. In turn, the SACTU LC answered the many questions posed by the workers about how to form strong trade unions. One year later, the political situation had deteriorated to such an extent that the Johannesburg comrades feared that another visit from the FPAWU members would lead to their arrest. Consequently, the local Trades Hall was booked for a public meeting while simultaneously a small church hall on the outskirts of the city was to be the actual venue of the meeting. The police, realizing that they had been tricked, began to indiscriminately interrogate and beat up a number of workers and members of the Transvaal Indian Congress in an effort to discover the location of the meeting. The farm workers were never found, but this was the last year that FPAWU members were able to make contact with SACTU in Johannesburg.

Although the FPAWU never had organizational form in other provinces, similar efforts were sustained in the Cape and Natal. The Northern Cape LC kept the FPAWU informed of local conditions. At Smithsdrift, a special grazing camp had been built and if African workers' cattle grazed outside certain limits, the workers were arrested and fined £5. African widows were not allowed to keep cattle, yet they were required to pay a levy of 10s. per month. Also dairy workers whose job it was to milk cows were in the ambiguous position of not being covered by the Dairy Industrial Council but rather by the Masters and Servants Act. A loose organization of farm workers around Kimberley formed in the early 1960s, but there is no record of any sustained organization in the Northern Cape. In the Western Cape, the Food and Canning Workers Union assisted farm workers whenever possible; this was re-emphasized at the 1962 FCWU Conference. In the Eastern Cape, the ANC and SACTU Local Committee combined to assist workers on the orange and pineapple farms around Bathurst and Grahamstown. These efforts grew out of the successful potato boycott campaign in the Port Elizabeth area in 1959.

In Natal, most farm workers were associated with the sugar industry, which has been generally discussed in a previous chapter. The same conditions of work obtained in Natal as on the farms in other provinces. African workers' resistance on the cane fields was occasionally reflected by cane fires set just before the harvesting season, but of course such random acts of violence only increased the repression by the sugar barons.

Export earnings from sugar averaged above 15 million Rand in 1959 and 1960, with Huletts Corporation taking the largest share of profits which totalled R7·5 million for the seven largest companies in 1962. Despite the success in organizing the milling workers in the late 1930s, the field workers remained largely unorganized in the 1950s. The Durban LC began to place greater emphasis on the rural workers after the 1959 Conference, with SACTU leaders making trips up and down the Natal coast as Ponnen, Naidoo, Naicker and Shanley had done two decades before.

At a Durban Conference of Plantation workers in June 1962 the main SACTU speaker outlined the history of the sugar industry in Natal as a tale of pillage and enslavement of the Zulu people and merciless forced labour imposed on the indentured Indian labourers brought into South Africa in the second half of the nineteenth century. The speaker concluded,

the sugar industry, therefore, is built on slave labour – it is built on the sweat and blood of the Non-White peoples, particularly the Africans. . . .[22]

These conditions were expanded upon in more general terms at another Rural and Industrial Workers Conference held in Durban in December 1962:

The lives of the people are riddled with diseases: hunger and starvation are stock in trade for the African people. Children die before they are born; and our young people die before they reach the age of maturity – in fact childbirth has become a more bitter agony than death itself. Even where birth succeeds, children grow to be men – men who are sold like asses and livestock for the pleasure of the South African farmers. Let it be clear that those children we bear and bring forth are our children and not mere instruments of pleasure and convenience and it is for them that we shall ever struggle until freedom is achieved. The centuries old pass system still acts as a sluice which channels the labour of our people to where the masters want it.

Through these conferences, SACTU Natal worked to bring the urban proletariat and the rural workers and peasants into one united force. Working committees of rural labourers were organized throughout Natal by Stephen Dlamini, Memory Vakalisa and Eric Mtshali, among others. Although these committees were never as stable or as well organized as the FPAWU in the Transvaal, they were part of the militant tradition established by SACTU in Natal during these years.

General Workers Unions (GWU)

In 1960, the SACTU Fifth Annual Conference passed a resolution endorsing the formation of General Workers Unions. This decision appeared to be a clear departure from the policy of SACTU, and indeed progressive trade union coordinating bodies going back to the 1930s, which was to organize unions exclusively along industrial lines. In other words, for the first time since the ICU of the 1920s there was an encouragement to form GWUs that cut across different sectors of the economy. The explanation for this apparent reversal of policy, however, speaks to the strength and not the weakness of SACTU as a coordinating body. The resolution itself provides that explanation:

This Fifth Annual National Conference ... records with pride that the campaign to recruit 20,000 more trade unionists into the Trade Union movement has produced significant results, and takes pleasure in welcoming the new recruits into our ranks.

Conference appreciates the fact that the organizing of many thousands of workers in so short a space of time with the limited personnel available, rendered it impossible for Local Committees to form new trade unions for unorganized workers immediately and therefore fully endorses the establishment of General Workers' Unions, formed for the purpose of temporarily accommodating these workers.

With this aim in view Conference considers it undesirable to form Executive Committees of such unions and therefore instructs all Local Committees to maintain these general unions under their direct supervision and to allocate members of general unions to industrial unions as soon as practicable. Regular general meetings of the General Workers' Unions must be held, and there must be systematic contact with members of such Unions.[23]

None the less, many delegates questioned the wisdom of this resolution during the discussion preceding its adoption. The most commonly voiced reservation was that members of such amorphous unions might remain there indefinitely. If this were to happen, it would be next to impossible to fight for improvements in wages and working conditions, let alone conduct successful strike action against the particular capitalists in each industrial sector represented. No one, including those who supported GWUs, wanted to return to the unworkable structures of the ICU. Both Durban and Kimberley delegates from GWUs already in existence stressed that these were transitional structures, organizational nuclei for the creation of new, well-organized industrial unions. In Kimberley, for example, members had different symbols on their membership cards to identify their respective industrial sectors, whereas Durban cards specified the trade or occupation to which individual members belonged. Despite these assurances, an amendment calling for the provision that workers would be allocated to existing or new unions within one month was moved; it was defeated in that the original resolution stipulated that GWUs would only 'temporarily accommodate' workers.

Subsequent MC minutes reveal continued reluctance to endorse GWUs. In October 1960, the MC stressed that GWUs were to be administered by SACTU LCs and not by elected Executive Committees. A positive note was recorded, however, when it was suggested that LCs should form GWUs in association with the house-to-house campaigns being conducted in the African townships. The case of the Kimberley GWU, which had emerged independently in 1955, and thus had its own elected Executive would have to be dealt with separately as a special case. In December 1960, the MC asked the Wits LC to withdraw membership cards of certain unions not functioning effectively, implicitly suggesting their acceptance of GWUs as an interim step towards the creation of stable unions.

By April 1961, the MC had issued a special circular to the Cape Town, Port Elizabeth and Witwatersrand LCs – those areas without GWUs – instructing them to form GWUs and to collect a subscription fee of 4s. per member per month. Of this total, 3s. would go towards the union to be created, another 11d. would cover the LC's administrative costs and the remaining 1d. would go for SACTU affiliation fees. The circular emphasized that GWUs should be widely publicized among unorganized workers as a means of increasing SACTU's overall membership. One year later, the General Secretary reported to the 1962 Conference that all LCs had formed GWUs but re-emphasized the necessity of creating separate industrial unions as soon as possible.

The strength and importance of GWUs in the overall SACTU work varied considerably from area to area, and according to the assessment of this strategy by leaders in each area. In the Transvaal and the

Western Cape, GWUs emerged in the early 1960s although in both cases they were relatively weak. The heavily industrialized Transvaal with its tradition of industrial unionism mitigated against the GWU as a major priority; similarly, in the Western Cape, with a relatively small number of African workers as compared with the total Black working class population, the LC believed that it was preferable and manageable to continue organizing along industrial lines in secondary manufacturing industry.

Conversely, but for different reasons in each area, Kimberley, Port Elizabeth and Durban formed very effective GWUs during the decade 1955–64, and many victories were scored on behalf of unorganized workers as a result of this strategy. The purpose of this section is to review the scope and success of GWUs within the overall SACTU plan to organize the unorganized.

The *Kimberley GWU* was formed by J. Mampies independently of any SACTU LC in 1955. When it was first allowed to directly affiliate to SACTU in 1960, the Union had 700 members in railway, municipal, commercial and distributive, hospital, garage, domestic, engineering, building and meat industries and undertakings. Diamond miners and furniture workers were included in the 1963 membership listing. For nine years, the Kimberley GWU maintained close contact with SACTU Head Office, distributed SACTU propaganda materials, undertook SACTU campaigns and more or less functioned as a LC in the remote area of the Northern Cape Province.

The first contact between Kimberley organizers and Head Office came back in 1955, when Mampies wrote a letter requesting information about organizing the unorganized African workers in 'the City of Diamonds, the birthplace of (White) South African trade unionism'. Despite severe restrictions, which included being allowed by the local authorities to hold only one meeting per month, the GWU mobilized 700 workers for the SACTU National Workers' Conference which preceded the 1958 Stay-At-Home. The first visit from a SACTU national organizer did not occur until 1959, when a member of the Transport NOC travelled to Kimberley to respond to a threat of mass dismissals of railway workers. Shortly after that visit, J. Mampies, the Organizing Secretary, and other executive members of the GWU were detained for up to five months during the State of Emergency in 1960.

The Kimberley City Council maintained a 'permanent State of Emergency' directed against the GWU. The right of Union members to assemble was totally denied in the early 1960s, especially as the focal point of the Union's attack was the poverty wages paid by the Council to its African municipal employees. Whenever demands were presented to employers, the Special Branch and uniformed police were called in and Union officials arrested. In 1962, the entire seven-person Executive was arrested for holding an 'illegal' meeting on the Schmidtsdrift Reserve where an attempt was being made to organize farm workers. At the Second Kimberley GWU Annual Conference (after affiliation to SACTU), eighteen police cars and vans ringed the hall and police inside interrupted the proceedings with tape recorders and intimidation; the original venue had been closed to the unions at the last moment but the workers' determination won out as the Conference convened six hours later and continued throughout the night. Delegates representing towns and villages throughout the Northern Cape stressed the national struggle against low wages, high rents and pass laws. By 1963, most GWU leaders, including Aaron Mosata, President, had been banned and removed from positions in the trade union movement.

Although details of the Kimberley GWU struggles are lacking, it is clear from the records that do exist that this Union persevered through the dedication of workers in remote areas to be a part of the national campaigns led by SACTU and the Congress Alliance. The different industrial sectors within the GWU were never stable or strong enough to form separate unions affiliated to SACTU. Yet, none the less, the Kimberley case gives one example of how GWUs can unite unorganized workers around local and national issues.

In the industrial centres of Durban and Port Elizabeth, GWUs served a different purpose. Both Natal and particularly the Eastern Cape experienced rapid industrial development following the Second World War, with South African and increasingly foreign multinationals flocking to low wage areas to maximize profits. As workers experienced intolerable conditions in these circumstances, their organization into trade unions became an imperative. Yet stable, industrial unions to accommodate these African workers could not be built overnight, and in this context GWUs played the role of interim structures for thousands of unorganized workers.

In Durban, Billy Nair of the LC announced as early as September 1955, that a *Durban GWU* had been formed and was open to unorganized workers in all industries and undertakings. Although this was done without the official sanction of the SACTU NEC or MC, it should be pointed out that the LC regarded the GWU as a base from which new, industrial unions would subsequently emerge. The Natal

GWU actually developed out of crises being faced by workers drawn into new industrial low-wage areas like Pinetown and Hammarsdale, where wage determinations and Industrial Council agreements did not apply. These local and often desperate conditions led the LC to form a Pinetown GWU in late 1956. Stephen Dlamini was quoted in *New Age* articles stressing that the LC was being flooded with requests for organizers in these new industrial areas. Out of the funds collected from the GWU members the LC could partially subsidize the costs of sending organizers to Pinetown.

Between 1959 and 1960, as we discuss below, Durban SACTU membership increased by over 5,000 members. Most of these workers were initially enrolled by industrial sector in the GWU; by 1962, the GWU membership had declined to a more manageable, although still unwieldy, total of 2,000 workers still to be allocated to existing or new unions. This GWU catered for a wide range of workers from chemical, transport, stevedoring and garage industries in Durban itself, and in Pinetown, garment, road and power station workers were added to the rolls. Moses Mabhida recalls the GWU strategy of the late 1950s and considers it 'very appropriate'. He adds, 'In our minds we were organizing unorganized workers, and (this) was the only way to start.'[24]

The Durban GWU not only signed up these thousands of unorganized workers but, more importantly, took up their concrete demands with the local employers. In 1959, thirty-three workers in a skin and hides firm on the Durban wharf were dismissed for failing to report for work on a public holiday. As members of the GWU they turned to SACTU for advice, but at that moment the Department of Labour advised the employer to refuse to discuss the matter with all SACTU leaders. The employer, however, soon became dissatisfied with his newly-hired scab labour and agreed to open talks with SACTU that eventually led to all workers, including the so-called 'agitator,' getting their jobs back. Another spontaneous strike by 180 abattoir workers for £1-a-Day took place in July of that year. Fearful of a meat shortage in the city, the Durban municipality that employed these workers agreed to wage increases after being confronted by the SACTU LC. In these and other cases the Durban GWU served as the only organization to which an otherwise divided and badly exploited workforce could turn.

In the Durban area, veteran trade unionists like Stephen Dlamini, Memory Vakalisa and Moses Mabhida trained younger workers to recruit GWU members in their respective factories and places of employment. Among the latter were Soloman Mbanjwa, O. Chiya,

Elias Mbele, Louis Mkize, Eric Mtshali (Pinetown) and Mate Mfusi (Ladysmith). Through the determined work of these and other organizers, ten new industrial unions emerged out of the GWU in the early 1960s.

The Durban GWU, therefore, fulfilled its major function as an 'interim measure' on the road to industrial unionism. There were, however, undeniable problems associated with an amorphous structure catering for so many workers. At the 1960 SACTU Annual Conference, one Transvaal delegate congratulated the Durban comrades for their increase in overall membership but hastened to add that the failure to systematically collect affiliation fees would soon create problems for the LC. George Ponnen, banned adviser to SACTU in the 1950s, recalls some of these problems:

> Unless an appropriate machinery was created to administer the affairs of the General Workers' Union, the whole project might be a failure in the sense that thousands of workers would be enrolled as members for various industries and trades and effective attention would not be given to their complaints.[25]

In the Eastern Cape, the *Port Elizabeth GWU* symbolized the potential inherent in this strategy of organizing the unorganized African working masses; it was a significant factor in making the Eastern Cape the most militant SACTU-Congress Alliance area in South Africa. Led by Vuyisile Mini, Alven Bennie, Don Nangu, Paulos Temba and veteran trade unionists such as Caleb Mayekiso (TWIU) in the more established unions, the GWU responded to the immediate needs of African workers in large manufacturing plants that were part of multinational operations in the automobile and rubber industries.

Unlike Kimberley and Durban, the Port Elizabeth GWU did not emerge until after the 1960 Conference decision to support the formation of such unions. Previous to that, SACTU work in the area had been dominated by the established unions in food and canning and textile industries. Within two years, the GWU had a membership of 674 workers in the tobacco, leather, wine, domestic, baking, commercial and distributive, hospital, rubber, dairy and milling industries. The GWU also served as the base from which workers in SACTU's priority industries – transport and metals – were organized in the area. Although there were only a small number of separate industrial unions created from the GWU, the real importance of the Union's organizing work was in the mass mobilization of workers for the Congress campaigns of the early 1960s. The harmonious working relationship between the 'ex-ANC' members (the ANC had been banned in 1960) and SACTU strengthened a long-standing militant tradition in the Eastern Cape and thus made Port Elizabeth a major target of state repression.

Much of the organizing work was accomplished through house-to-house campaigns conducted after working hours. The Congress of the People (1955), numerous Congress Stay-At-Homes and the 1959 SACTU Conference added momentum to the GWU work that was financed by bazaars, concerts and the contributions of rank-and-file workers. At first the GWU and the LC itself used the offices of the TWIU as their base, but eventually each managed to support its own separate location. The Union was internally divided by industrial sector, with regular meetings of all groupings. Separate unions were temporarily created for leather, dairy and bus workers, but the five-month State of Emergency in 1960 interrupted the continuity and functioning of these new unions.

The full-time Organizing Secretary of the GWU was Alven Bennie, who organized workers in a wide range of industries and undertakings. Bennie had been asked by SACTU Executive members Leslie Massina and Mark Shope as early as 1956 to begin organizing the unorganized. As Alven put it, 'I was a paid organizer without any pay.'[26] While Bennie concentrated attention on dockworkers, Vuyisile Mini focused on metals and Paulos Temba (TWIU) organized domestic servants and distributive workers. Despite the difficulty of organizing domestics, the GWU had over 50 workers enrolled as members and with the assistance from comrades in other Congresses managed to organize a number of seafront hotels. Paulos Temba attributes much of the success of the GWU in this and other industries to the ability of the LC to call meetings of large numbers of workers and thus ensure that workers approached their bosses in unity and with strength instead of going to them as solitary individuals.[27] The majority of the work was conducted in the Port Elizabeth–New Brighton–Uitenhage area, but it was not uncommon for Bennie and others to travel to East London, Kingwilliamstown and Grahamstown as SACTU-Congress Alliance organizers.

As in Kimberley, the GWU in Port Elizabeth had to regularly contend with a hostile Department of Labour that encouraged employers to have nothing to do with SACTU. In late 1962, African GWU members at a local technical college were replaced by Coloured workers because they refused to accept the principal's insistence on having an African 'boss-boy' serve as an intermediary between himself and the African workers. Retrenched workers with up to 30 years service at the college were taken by SACTU leaders Mayekiso, Bennie and Nangu to the local Labour Inspector who refused to even meet the delegation. Following this defeat, the college made it a practice of hiring convict labour at even less cost.

In sum, the Port Elizabeth GWU's strength rests with its support amongst the masses. More than just a trade union to protect working class interests, it became an institution of and from the people. Along with the registered unions, the SACTU LC formed a cultural club which attracted even the local rugby enthusiasts. Inspired by Vuyisile Mini – singer, dancer, actor as well as liberation fighter – the GWU gained a committed membership that led the struggle during the subsequent years of victimization, life imprisonment and execution of some of the Eastern Cape's greatest leaders.

Although there was substantial reluctance by both Cape Town and Wits LCs to form GWUs, the 1962 SACTU list of affiliated unions records such unions in both areas, each having approximately 400 members. Lacking a complete historical record of the Cape Western Province LC activities, there is little indication of which industries were represented by these workers. However, new industrial unions were formed in Cape Town in the early 1960s, and they will be discussed in the following section. The only information available on the *Cape Town GWU* is found in an April 1962 edition of *New Age*, where it was reported that the Union demanded weekly minimum wage rates of R12 (£6) and R9 (£4 10s. 0d.) for urban and rural workers respectively, recognition of African workers as 'employees' under the IC Act, repeal of the Group Areas Act, and a call to employers not to co-operate with Apartheid authorities in removing Africans from the Western Cape.

In the Transvaal, on the other hand, the GWU strategy did lead to significant successes in organizing the unorganized amongst timber, plastic, paint, jewellery, stone crushing and quarrying, mineral water, transport and University of Witwatersrand workers. Wage increases and improvements in working conditions were won in a number of firms covered by the Union in 1961 and 1962. Two new unions – the FPAWU (discussed above) and the Printing Workers Union – emerged from the *Transvaal GWU* in these years.

Within a month of the decision to form the union, Graham Morodi became full-time organizer. Morodi had previously organized an active SACTU factory committee of tobacco workers at United Tobacco

Company (UTC) where he was employed. These workers became members of the Wits GWU and were assisted by SACTU in their struggle against the foreign-owned company and the FOFATUSA-controlled and TUCSA-affiliated African Tobacco Workers Union which did little to improve the lot of its members. The factory committee with SACTU support, however, forced the UTC to increase the wages of its African employees. Another active factory committee of biscuit workers employed by the Canadian George Weston conglomerate joined the GWU at approximately the same time. Morodi established harmonious relations with the local management of Weston's biscuit company in Springs, and the workers were even allowed to have union subscriptions deducted at the place of work — a rare occurrence for African workers. This changed abruptly after the Special Branch visited the local management advising them to ignore SACTU representatives. The Weston firm quickly agreed to forsake its workers and instead toed the line of Apartheid. By 1964, the leadership of the factory committee had been victimized and eliminated from the trade union movement.

The Wits GWU engaged itself in struggle against two cases of gross exploitation. In July 1961, 600 chemical workers at Klipfontein Organic Products were arrested for carrying out 'an illegal strike' against low wages (which ranged from £4 10s. 0d. to £7 1s. 6d. per week) and compound life characteristic of the mining and railway industries. SACTU and the GWU came to the defence of these workers by forcing the Department of Bantu Administration, through whom they were employed, to investigate this particular case of Apartheid tyranny. Bail and legal defence were also arranged by SACTU for the two leaders of the strike.

The most successful campaign was waged against the University of Witwatersrand, that 'civilizing institution' that paid its African workforce no more than £8 to £10 *per month*. In addition to low wages, these workers had been forced under the Group Areas Act to live in distant townships, the closest to the University being nine miles away. Low wages made transport costs difficult to pay, and many workers faced evictions from township housing for rent arrears as a result of their poverty wages. Through a highly-publicized campaign, the SACTU GWU exposed the University as an institution that sponsored cost-of-living studies that documented the below-subsistence wages for African workers, yet continued this trend itself by being amongst the lowest-paying employers. The GWU demanded a minimum wage of £1-a-Day for all workers, a 40-hour week, four weeks annual paid leave, better food, and the laundering of protective clothing as part of University services. Although not all these demands were met, wage increases of 15 per cent and a reduction in working hours resulted from this pressure.

These gains went a long way in showing that GWUs, if properly administered, could bring about the organization of unorganized workers and not necessarily reproduce the weaknesses of general unions of past decades. Leon Levy, SACTU President, says that while GWUs were not particularly liked, they were 'a quick way to form lasting unions'.[28] Graham Morodi, the GWU Organizer, speaks more positively of GWUs as a 'good strategy'. He stresses that workers were at all times registered by section and efficient records were kept of tobacco, milling, coal, municipal and transport workers brought under the GWU umbrella. In the Transvaal, this method of work was based on the division of labour whereby Morodi travelled in the field visiting workers wherever they worked and lived, while Shanti Naidoo performed the associated clerical work in the SACTU office.[29]

Thus, although GWUs developed unevenly in all SACTU areas, it seems fair to conclude that they did mobilize otherwise unorganized workers to participate in both economic and political struggles. The heavy repression of the early 1960s makes it impossible to judge these Unions on the basis of how many new and stable industrial unions were (or could have been) formed. On the other hand, in all cases, the GWUs brought about a much larger and more politicized mass base of support for SACTU and Congress campaigns. In the strict sense of trade unionism, Ronnie Press is probably most accurate when he says that the formation of GWUs should not be regarded as a separate SACTU strategy as the goal continued to be the formation of new industrial unions for Black workers.[30] The 1963 SACTU Annual Conference, held during the peak of repression, underscores the importance of GWUs as for the first time in SACTU history there was mention of organized workers in the OFS. The OFS GWU was catering for African workers in mining, commercial and distributive, furniture, municipal and domestic industries and undertakings.

Secondary Industry: The Base of SACTU Strength

Notwithstanding the work of the NOCs and the GWUs, SACTU's greatest achievement was the formation of new unions in secondary manufacturing industries in all four major centres of the country. This was due to the fact that the development of post-war industrial capitalism had ensured a very large, urbanized African proletariat that suffered under the double bind of the cheap labour system of racial capitalism and the entire range of Apartheid legislation directed against Blacks as citizens.

The backbone of SACTU LCs in all areas – Johannesburg, Port Elizabeth, Cape Town and Durban – consisted of branches of at least one, usually two, and in one case all three of the following unions: the Food and Canning WU, the Textile Workers Industrial Union and the Laundry, Cleaning and Dyeing Workers Union (LCDWU). Each of these unions had strong branches of African unregistered unions and in the registered unions (for Coloured, Indian and White workers) a history of progressive leadership. The leaders and members of these unions provided the experience and initiative that paved the way for organizing new, industrial unions after 1955.

The purpose of this section is to pay brief tribute to the organizing work of SACTU comrades in these four LCs. As it is impossible to document every effort in each industry, the goal is to provide the reader with a sense of the spirit and struggle that shaped SACTU unions in various parts of the country. For the newcomer to African trade unionism in South Africa, it is helpful to keep in mind that African trade unions are understandably unstable in the context of capitalist super-exploitation and White supremacy. Unions of African workers, lacking the protection offered unions in other capitalist countries, often rise and fall within a short space of time. Once formed, however, African unions never really die and are constantly being revived from the legacy of previous struggles. Just as SACTU revived unions dormant since the early 1940s, so too have unions in the 1970s re-emerged and re-organized around the banner of SACTU planted in the 1950s and 1960s.

Transvaal

As the Johannesburg complex was the centre of South African industry, so too was it the centre of SACTU. The Witwatersrand (Wits) LC, among the first to form after the creation of SACTU in March 1955, consistently accounted for the largest proportion of affiliated unions. At the 1956 Conference, the Wits LC represented ten of the twenty-nine affiliated unions and approximately 15,000 of the 29,514 SACTU members. In 1961, the Wits LC reported seventeen unions, but 1962 documents show that its membership had not increased substantially beyond the 15,000 member level, about 30 per cent of the total.[31]

With Head Office in Johannesburg, the SACTU structure in the Transvaal became more complicated than in other areas where LCs administered the entire range of SACTU activities. In Johannesburg, the membership of the LC and MC often overlapped, giving greater strength to SACTU work during periods of growth but also causing certain organizational problems during periods of heavy repression. Existing documents clearly reveal a decline in activity in the Wits LC during the first few months following the Treason Trial arrests of December 1956, and a similar lapse during the State of Emergency four years later. In the first instance, the arrests of SACTU officials and veteran leaders forced the co-optation of LC leaders into the MC, having the effect of lessening the organizing work amongst the unorganized as compared with the two previous years. In the second case, the mass arrests of 1960 created problems of continuity throughout all levels of SACTU and other groups of the Congress Alliance. Despite these momentary setbacks, however, the Transvaal unions set the pace for other areas of South Africa in the mid to late 1950s.

Among the more established SACTU unions, the laundry workers union distinguished itself as the vanguard on the Rand. Both the registered NULCDW and the unregistered African LCDWU provided a model of non-racial trade unionism. The African union, formed back in 1928, represented the majority of the labour force in the Transvaal laundry industry. Two large companies – Advance and Rand Steam – employed close to 6,000 workers and it was here that SACTU had its base. In addition to the vast network of depots and plants owned by these companies, a number of smaller laundry operations averaging 50–60 employees were also included amongst SACTU members. The union consistently demanded and won wage increases for its 4,000 workers, and on one occasion refused an increase for African workers until all workers received across-the-board pay hikes.

The Laundry Workers Union was instrumental in the development of SACTU both in the Transvaal and nationally. It should be stressed that White workers made up a significant portion of the total Union membership in the laundry industry. The White workers were employed in both the factories and the depots and along with Coloured and Indian workers provided an excellent example of non-racial trade unionism as advanced by SACTU. Because the registered Union had reasonably cordial relations with the managements of the two large firms, it was possible for Leon Levy, Secretary, to enter the factories and collect subscriptions on a weekly basis. Consequently, both branches were able to pay their dues to SACTU on a regular basis, and because of this the laundry union (and the FCWU) largely carried SACTU financially for the first two years. In 1957, when the state banned Levy and Leslie Massina (Secretary of the African union and SACTU General Secretary), the bosses took this opportunity to eliminate the stop-order system.

In addition to financial assistance, the laundry unions provided leadership to SACTU as a coordinating body. Every General Secretary since 1955 has come out of the African LCDWU. First, Leslie Massina served in that capacity from 1955 to 1960. He was followed by Mark Shope (Chairman, A-LCDWU), who in turn was replaced at a later date by John Gaetsewe (National Organizer of the Union). Shope's life history is a classic case of an African worker who overcame class and national obstacles to become a leader of his people in both trade union and political spheres. From a herd boy in the Northern Transvaal earning 3s. 6d. per month, he worked as a farm labourer watering orange trees for 5s. per month and next as a gold miner, where he was rescued from a cave-in but lost his hearing for three months. After going to Johannesburg in the early 1940s, his employment in the laundries quickly led Shope to become a dedicated trade unionist and leader of the ANC in the Jabavu township. Throughout this varied proletarian career, Mark put himself through a disciplined self-education which included matriculation and six university courses. Massina, the veteran, Shope and Gaetsewe were but three of the African trade union leaders to emerge following the heavy bannings of the early 1950s.

The African-FCWU and the African-TWIU also provided leadership and momentum to the Wits LC work. In textiles, the registered union was progressive but quite small in comparison with the African union of 1,600 members. The strength of the latter rested with the young, militant African workforce at Amato Textiles, a company in the hessian section of the industry. As discussed in Chapter 8, the Amato plant workers were heavily victimized under the Native Labour Act, as the bosses notoriously dismissed the entire workforce whenever there was a spontaneous walk-out by workers in protest against low wages and poor working conditions. Led by Edmund Cindi and Rufus Makuru, the African union became a symbol of working class militancy throughout the Rand. Although the union suffered greatly after the 1958 Amato strike, a solid corps of SACTU organizers emerged from the textile battles of the mid-1950s. Unlike the laundry union, however, the textile union was unable to maintain its SACTU subscription payments on a regular basis because so much of the financial resources went for court costs arising from prosecutions under the Native Labour Act. The leadership of the Union was also hit hard by bannings throughout the country; by the late 1950s, no less than 17 officers and organizers had been banned and removed from trade union activity.

The Transvaal branch of the FCWU was also led by the African segment of the Union, in particular African women who made up 60 or 70 per cent of the labour-intensive workforce. Two major companies – the Australian-owned H. Jones operation in Johannesburg and the Afrikaner farmer-controlled Langeberg Ko-operasie Besperk (LKB) plant in nearby Springs – equalled their other operations in the Eastern and Western Cape in exploiting seasonal labour and trying to crush SACTU initiatives. Led by SACTU and ANC militants – Christina Matthews and Mabel Balfour – the Transvaal FCWU won wage increases and arranged for three stop-order arrangements in 1955.

The Union's greatest victory came in 1959, when the entire African workforce of 200 women and 89 men at H. Jones forced management to pay holiday rates. When workers first realized that they had not been paid double time for working during the Christmas season, they walked out *en masse* and were promptly arrested and kept in jail for two and a half days. After the Union raised the £10 bail per person, the case went to the courts where defence counsel Joe Slovo pressured management to admit that workers had been paid even less than normal earnings by a company with an average annual profit of £120,000. The Magistrates ruled that the workers had not carried out an illegal strike but rather, as Slovo argued, had been locked out. The company initially refused to reinstate the 289 workers but relented within a month as the ANC and Congress Alliance threatened to boycott the company's products. As one worker concluded, 'This is not only our victory but the victory of all workers in South Africa who are not permitted to use the weapon of "tools down".'

In 1962, another dispute at National Food Storage developed when the company refused to give holiday pay for Easter work, and once again the FCWU lived up to its reputation of protecting its members by obtaining the extra earnings. In these and other FCWU struggles new leaders came to the fore. Harry Loots, whose first experience in a strike situation came with the 1959 lockout, went on to become Chairman of the Transvaal FCWU and SACTU MC member in 1962; he, along with Marie Mkwanazi and Miriam Monare continued to serve as worker-organizers in the industry.

Other older African unions reinforced the Wits LC in the Johannesburg area. The African Furniture, Mattress and Bedding WU (A-FMBWU), formed in 1934, claimed only 100 members when it first affiliated to SACTU in July 1955. As a result of the SACTU £1-a-Day campaign and heightened political consciousness during the turbulent period of the early 1960s, the membership increased to 850 in 1962. Unlike the African workers in laundry, textile and food and canning, those in the furniture industry had to work with a very hostile and reactionary registered union. The African union was not allowed to present its case before Industrial Council hearings and the registered union and bosses hid behind the law and refused to consider the plight of the African workers. In 1960, the Industrial Council for the industry dissolved following a dispute between employers and the registered union. African workers demanded a share of the thousands of pounds of assets of the IC, a portion of which consisted of their contributions. The demand was ignored and the money divided between the bosses and the non-African workers.

Despite small wage increases won through struggle, the majority of African furniture workers received less than £4 per week while White wages ranged from £8 to £12; Africans were prevented from doing skilled work, received no unemployment benefits and were discriminated against in sick pay and COLA benefits. In one case, the workers walked out for one day demanding higher wages. They were prosecuted for an illegal strike by the Department of Labour, although the employer privately admitted that African wages were far too low and that he would not have taken the workers to court unless pressured to do so by the Apartheid officials. Led by Uriah Maleka, Organizer and SACTU-NEC member, the Union gained a reputation for its militancy in the face of these obstacles.

The SA Clothing Workers Union (SACWU) dated back to 1928 and during its six years of SACTU affiliation maintained an average membership of 1,250 workers. SACWU represented African males, whereas the Garment Workers Union of African Women represented African women in the clothing industry. This sexual division had resulted from the fact that women workers were recognized as 'employees' under the IC Act until 1956, when they were forced to carry passes. At that time, both SACWU and the GWU-AW were affiliates of SACTU but pressure from TUCSA led Lucy Mvubelo to

H. Jones food and canning workers face mass trial, 1959

John Tsele, African Laundry Workers Union, Transvaal

Ronnie Press, Textile Workers Industrial Union, Transvaal

Mark Shope, SACTU General Secretary after Leslie Massina

break and join FOFATUSA (see Chapter 11). These conflicts left the African workers in the industry hopelessly divided. Despite their different conceptions of the objectives of African trade unionism, the two African unions agreed to merge into a new National Union of Clothing Workers, and by agreement each disaffiliated from its coordinating body for a period of one year. In 1963, members of the NUCW were called on to vote for either SACTU or FOFATUSA re-affiliation. The old conflicts re-emerged as the ballot gave workers the confusing choice of joining SACTU or 'FOFATUSA–TUCSA', the latter being a non-existent body. Although FOFATUSA received the greater number of votes, and despite press coverage that trumpeted this vote in favour of 'non-political trade unionism', pro-SACTU workers refused to accept the vote and continue, to this day, to constitute a solid SACTU faction within the Union. SACWU leaders who played an important role in SACTU included Viola Hashe (SACTU Vice-President) and George Monare, MC member and National Treasurer in the early 1960s.

The primary responsibilities of SACTU LCs in all areas concerned the promotion of SACTU policy and campaigns and the formation of new industrial unions. The combined experience and dedication of leaders from these established unions ensured that this task was successful in the Transvaal. Desperately short of a financial base, the Wits LC and Head Office itself could only maintain full-time organizers at the local and national levels if workers paid their subscriptions on time and in full. Under South African conditions, this was always a most difficult proposition. None the less, the Wits LC did manage to hire two organizers during these years – John Nkadimeng and later Graham Morodi. Through their efforts and those of other SACTU leaders, the following new unions joined the Wits LC between 1955 and 1963 (see table, p. 223).

In almost every case, these unions emerged as a result of SACTU's £1-a-Day campaign or through related LC assistance provided to workers during strikes, wage negotiations in either Industrial Council or Wage Board hearings or following dismissals. Many of these unions had a lifespan of no more than eighteen months to two years due to an inability of workers to pay dues regularly, victimization of leaders in factories who were then endorsed out of the urban areas and state repression during the early 1960s. In the case of certain unions, SACTU Head Office administered the finances of the unions through a trust account, and in nearly every case Leon Levy and Phyllis Altman

Union	Year	Membership (Maximum)
Tvl. Broom & Brush WU (R)	1955	600
Transport WU	1955	400
African Publisher, Newspaper & Distributor WU	1956	?
African Milling WU (R)	1956	700
Domestic WU	1957	500
Toy WU (later Toy & Plastic WU)	1957	235
African Building WU (R)	1957	100
Tvl. Municipal WU (later known as City and Town Council WU)	1959	100
Shop and Office WU	1959	750
Tvl. Hospital WU	1959	131
Tvl. Brewery & Distillery WU	1959	200
Tvl. Dairy WU	1959	400
SA Tin WU, Tvl. (R)	1960	170
SA Glass WU	1960	150
Farm, Plantation and Allied WU	1962	300
Printing and Allied WU	1962	250
General Workers Union	1962	400

(R) = represents old unions revived.

and others prepared detailed memoranda to wage hearings on behalf of these African workers. SACTU and *only* SACTU among coordinating bodies fought for wage increases and improved working conditions for African workers.

Each union listed reflects a specific struggle to organize Africans against their given conditions of exploitation. African milling workers, with assistance from LC member Aaron Mahlangu, were reorganized in the mid-1950s to protest against low wages of £2 18s. 0d. per week. In November 1957, over 1,500 workers walked out of six Johannesburg flour mills demanding the publishing of a Wage Board investigation that had dragged on for over sixteen months. When the workers dropped their tools, they marched directly to a SACTU meeting already in progress shouting 'Asinamali'. The strike led to 12·5 per cent increases, no prosecutions and no victimization as the bosses sensed the potential danger of the sympathy strikes that were occurring in related industries. *New Age* considered this 'the most successful African strike for a long time'.[32] Within a few months, SACTU received a hand-written letter stating that Union officials had been arrested and shop stewards were being prevented from collecting subs from workers; a third attempt to organize milling workers was promised.

Equally difficult was the organization of African building workers, forced by Job Reservation legislation to practice their skills in townships at very low rates of pay. The City Council housing division employers required two workers to build one and a half houses per day in the Southwestern townships for a weekly wage of £5 0s. 9d. The union was formed in March 1957, and Joe Qgabi and Brian Somana were elected as Chairman and Organizing Secretary respectively. They led the workers in their demands for £1-a-Day, thirty days annual leave, sick pay, a 40-hour week, protective clothing and union recognition. The Meadowland Housing Scheme was singled out for special attention by the Union. Labourers received only £2 2s. 5d. per week, corporal punishment was common, and 'task work' meant that weekend labour without pay was necessary in order to finish the excessive work load assigned during the week. Although the Union won small concessions during its existence, the harassment of its leaders and members resulted in deterioration of the Union in the late 1950s. Also to fight the City Council was the Municipal Workers Union which took up the issues of low pay and inhuman working conditions for sanitary workers and female toilet attendants.

Domestic servants, whose employment is based on the unwillingness of White South Africans to perform even the most elementary domestic labour, have always proven to be most difficult to organize. Scattered throughout the White suburbs, these workers are often forced to reside in shacks behind their master's home; they are in most cases also obliged to work a seven-day week. Domestics prepare the food that they and their starving families are never allowed to eat, and when they work in the hotels they watch 'surplus' food being discarded but are not allowed to satisfy their own starving stomachs. Wage rates are randomly determined according to the racist benevolence of the White employer.

With assistance and encouragement from the Wits LC, a small Domestic Workers Union emerged in the Pretoria and Johannesburg areas in the late 1950s. Gabriel Rapolai, a Union member, recalls the greatest obstacle being that of intimidation as domestics employed at private residences faced instant dismissal for even leaving to attend meetings: 'it was hard to live outside (the work location) because who would make tea for the master when he demanded it?'[33] Nevertheless, domestics in the hotels and to a lesser extent in private homes demanded a living wage, sick pay, and unemployment insurance benefits in 1961. In Pretoria, the Union was organized by John Mosupyi, a waiter, and in Johannesburg, Morris Masomela and Tibe Ntlatlane were, along with Rapolai, among the activists. SACTU Head Office greatly assisted these workers on an individual by individual basis. As it was illegal for an employer to deduct any money from wages unless specified in an agreement, Phyllis Altman (Assistant General Secretary) arranged legal assistance for domestics who were docked in pay for breakage or damage. Employers were irate when SACTU officials called them threatening legal action, but in most cases they were forced to stop this practice of wage gouging.[34]

The most stable of the new Transvaal unions was the Shop and Office WU. Assisted by Uriah Maleka and also by the registered unaffiliated National Union of Distributive Workers (NUDW), African workers in the commercial and distributive trades won pay increases and improvements in working conditions. The minimum wages in chain stores increased from £2 8s. 0d. to £4 0s. 0d. per week in 1960 as a result of workers' unity. The Union continued, however, to press for a living wage of R6 per week and an end to dismissals of older workers who had no pension coverage. Under the strong leadership of Marks Rammitloa, Secretary of the Union, poet and novelist, the Union also demanded recreational areas for Black workers who were prevented by law from entering 'Whites only' parks during lunch hours. The major campaign launched by the SOWU, and greatly helped by Head Office, was an attempt to prevent the extension of shop hours in the commercial centres. African workers, already facing very long working days when one considers the time necessary to commute to and from the townships, would only be more heavily burdened with such a change in hours and resultant shift work. African family life would be completely destroyed, and the late night travel would be unsafe for African women. As part of the campaign, the Union distributed leaflets to shoppers on the Johannesburg streets in order to gain greater mass support. By 1961, the SOWU reported that it was expanding to the West Rand, Kimberley, Cape Town and Pietermaritzburg areas in hopes of creating a national union to effectively fight the large South African chain stores. Repression against SACTU organizers in the following years interrupted this expansion, and Marks Rammitloa was banned and forced to take work as a night watchman.

In all of these examples, the creation of industrial unions was directed by SACTU activists in the Johannesburg area. The major drawback was the lack of adequate personnel and transport to respond to the numerous calls for assistance. In order to deal with these problems, efforts were made in the mid-1950s and again after the State of Emergency in 1960 to establish additional LCs in the industrial areas of the East and West Rand and Pretoria. In June, July and August 1956, LCs were established in these three areas. The East Rand LC in Benoni seemed the most stable of the three but all became defunct during the five-month Emergency in 1960. Efforts were made to revive these LCs, and in 1961 the Pretoria LC was able to mobilize a good response for the Congress Alliance Stay-at-Home; this walk-out included a large number of domestic workers who refused to go to work in the White kitchens and bedrooms for three consecutive days.

The problems of organizing at the local level were endemic to the structure and restrictions of Apartheid society itself. Organizers needed permits to enter the premises of employers to talk with workers. Such permits were not granted, leaving the factory gate or its equivalent as the only point of contact between organizers and large groups of workers. And at the factory gate, police did their best to ensure that SACTU personnel were harassed and arrested. In this situation, the only alternative was to train workers to do the organizing work from within the factories. This, in turn, required proper trade union and political education. SACTU developed a series of ten lectures covering a broad range of issues – from sweeping analyses of capitalism to concrete methods of organizing factory committees and articulating demands to employers. These lectures proved to be a most effective manner of offsetting some of the difficulties of organizing.

A National SACTU school was convened in May 1956, where Unions sent younger workers and potential organizers to study this series of lectures and listen to the experiences of veteran trade unionists, some of whom had been banned in the early 1950s. Among the lecturers were Eli Weinberg, Ray Alexander, L. Friedman, John Nkadimeng and Leon Levy. Plans to continue these schools never fully materialized, but LCs made frequent use of the lectures throughout the years. New lectures were added and old scripts modified to fit the changing conditions of trade union and political activity.

The major vehicle of trade union education was SACTU's newspaper, *Workers Unity*. The paper was produced continuously between 1955 and 1962, except during the periods of heavy repression such as the State of Emergency. Carrying stories on specific SACTU unions and their struggles, the Congress Alliance campaigns, Nationalist legislation, and international trade union activities, *Workers Unity* (and *New Age*) became the major source of trade union news to workers throughout South Africa. Its effectiveness was enhanced by the fact that it was printed in three African languages as well as English. From a four-page format in the early years, the paper became a 30-page quarterly magazine by 1962. The lion's share of the work for the paper was performed by Leon Levy, with assistance from Cleopas Sibande and Bob Hepple. Journalistic contributions were submitted from Melville Fletcher (PE), Ray Alexander (Cape Town), Billy Nair (Durban) and numerous Transvaal writers. SACTU activists outside the Transvaal province often felt that the coverage gave undue attention to Johannesburg struggles; while a quick review of the issues confirms this criticism, the responsibility for other LCs to contribute more stories to the paper also cannot be denied. Always on the verge of debt, the paper was financed by jumble sales and fund-raising socials. A sympathetic printer remained the paper's greatest financial asset; however, government pressure eventually led to the loss of this source of support.

Port Elizabeth

SACTU activity in the Eastern Cape was always distinguished by its disciplined and militant trade unionism and close relationship with the ANC and the Coloured People's Congress (formerly SACPO). The authorities were also quick to recognize these strengths, as the Port Elizabeth area experienced the greatest degree of repression throughout the 1950s and 1960s. In progressive circles, the PE–LC came to be regarded as a SACTU stronghold because of its ability to mobilize the masses around SACTU and Congress Alliance campaigns. As many of the specific struggles of this area are discussed in other sections, the purpose here will be to generally portray the dynamics of SACTU work in the Eastern Cape.

The combination of well-established, progressive unions in food and canning and textile and the determination to organize the unorganized workers in the post-war expansion industries (auto, rubber and iron and steel) led the First SACTU Annual Conference to describe the PE–LC as one which, 'works well, is most active, meets regularly and is closely associated with progressive organizations'.[35] In fact, had it not been for the fact that Parliament was debating the IC Act in Cape Town at the time, the NEC had earlier agreed to hold SACTU's 1956 Conference in

Port Elizabeth. One of the secrets to this early success in the Eastern Cape seems to rest with the political education instilled in younger SACTU activists by veteran trade union and political leaders, many of whom had been banned by 1955.

Among the veterans conducting regular political study classes and training young trade unionists were Gladstone Tshume (textiles), Raymond Mhlaba (laundries), A. P. Mati (railways and laundries), Gus Coe (food and canning), Arnold Lati, Sampson Ntunja (ANC), Tollie Bennum and Govan Mbeki (ANC). Learning from the experiences and sacrifices of these older leaders, a new corp of SACTU-Congress Alliance militants emerged: Vuyisile Mini, Wilton Mkwayi, Caleb Mayekiso, Alven Bennie, Stella Damons, Dolores Telling, Frances Baard, Stephen Tobias, Paulos Temba, Sophie Williams, Chris Ketani and Don Nangu and even younger comrades who entered the movement in the early 1960s. The veterans, although often associated with registered unions in earlier years, distinguished themselves in their commitment to organize the African masses outside of recognized structures and institutions; this tradition was maintained and advanced by the SACTU activists throughout the Eastern Cape.

Of the three established unions, food and canning and textile were solid unions in Port Elizabeth and nearby Uitenhage, while laundry was relatively weak in comparison with other areas. Both registered and African branches of the FCWU set the pace in struggling for wage increases, improved working conditions and an end to all forms of racial injustice. Prior to the major victory against wage cuts in 1959 (see Chapter 8), the PE branch won wage increases in 1955 and 1957; these increases resulted from direct talks between workers and employers as the strength of the Union completely paralysed the Native Labour Act machinery meant to neutralize the African workers. The mood of the workers is captured by the following comment made by the FCWU national negotiators in 1955:

In Port Elizabeth, we had a turnout of 600 workers at our emergency general meeting. They were in a fighting mood. They sang their union songs, which they had made up themselves, both at general meetings and meetings held at various factories. Their spirit was wonderful.[36]

During Wage Board investigations in East London in 1957, FCWU workers organized large demonstrations outside the bosses' offices, shouting demands for a minimum wage of £1-a-Day. Police followed

Union officials wherever they went, including accompanying them to the Wage Board hearings during the presentation of evidence.

From 1958 onwards, the state focused its attack on the FCWU in all areas of the country. In Port Elizabeth, the Union was forced to move from its city office under the Group Areas Act. Union officials were regularly harassed: Dolores Telling (Branch Secretary and Secretary, PE-LC) was prohibited from entering factories to meet with workers, and John Dladla, a loyal Union member, was deported to the Transkei. In May 1958, employers from one factory attempted to break the Union by sacking workers who served on the Executive Committee. A new committee was hastily 'elected' with management complicity and given access to Special Branch data on the Union on condition that the bogus leaders would have nothing to do with either SACTU or SACPO. The bosses and police were clearly trying to pry the Union from SACTU and also to create racial divisions between African and Coloured workers. The takeover was thwarted, however, and the FCWU regrouped to defeat the wage cuts of 1959. Frances Baard (Secretary, A-FCWU) was another target of the authorities, as she was prevented from entering her offices in the Korsten area, defined under the Group Areas Act as a 'Coloured area'. Also banned from entering the factories, she would only have to walk near the factory gate and workers would drop their tools and rush to discuss union matters. Other women leaders of the PE FCWU that deserve special mention are Lily Diedrichs and Florence Matomela.[37]

The two branches of the TWIU established an equally militant tradition in the Eastern Cape. Led by veteran trade unionist and SACTU–NEC member, Caleb Mayekiso, and worker-member Wilton Mkwayi, the Union represented 200 African and 600 registered workers in 1960, approximately 30 per cent of the local industry workforce.

As in other industries in the Eastern Cape, textile employers often chose to locate near reservoirs of cheap labour close to the reserves. The Belgian-owned Good Hope Textile Mills, in Kingwilliamstown, and Fine Wool Products, in Uitenhage, were part of the Nationalists' scheme to promote 'separate development' through the subsidization of corporations eager to exploit African labour power. At Good Hope, African workers received £2 per week, and only those deemed 'efficient' were given this paltry sum. At the Fine Wool factory in Uitenhage, a major producer of wool for jerseys and worsted material, Paulos Temba (Uitenhage A-TWIU organizer) recalls the difficulties faced in organizing these textile workers. For example, the only possible place to meet workers was at luncheon canteens outside the factory gates. Despite all the obstacles, Temba, Mayekiso, Mkwayi, Frances Tobias, 'Liz' Walton (Secretary) and Sophie Williams moulded a solid union membership in the area. They were greatly assisted by Melville Fletcher, National Organizer, who spent much of his time in Port Elizabeth.

A major victory was scored by the PE textile union in 1956 when 131 Fine Wool Products' workers struck against forced overtime. Initially convicted of conducting an illegal strike, the Supreme Court overruled this decision and thus established a very important legal precedent for many industries that practiced obligatory overtime. Six months later, however, three women textile workers were fired for again agitating against overtime work at the Uitenhage factory. The Department of Labour stalled in taking action after SACTU intervened, and correspondence produced at the time revealed that the Department had advised the company of earlier decisions defending the employers' right to get away with arbitrary changes in working conditions. Against all the odds, the TWIU branches managed to attain wages increases, shorter hours and protective clothing for PE textile workers the following year.

Organizing the unorganized became the hallmark of the SACTU LC during these years. In the face of the constant repression against the Congress Alliance in the Eastern Cape, the explanation for this success rests with the totally complementary relationship between the ANC and SACTU. ANC leaders were, for the most part, trade unionists and political activists who believed that working class interests should define the nature of the struggle. ANC and SACTU campaigns were never regarded as separate from one another, and members of both organizations committed equal energies to all Congress work. The ANC cell structure created under the M-Plan (Mandela-Plan) was at all times open to SACTU leaders, and through this underground operation many ANC cadre were readily available to provide support for SACTU petitions, rallies, strikes and other campaigns. Above ground, a permanent Liaison Committee of ANC and SACTU leaders from Port Elizabeth and Uitenhage met almost daily to discuss strategy and tactics.[38]

Herein lies the explanation for the PE–LC's ability to organize new unions in the first months of SACTU's existence. Frances Baard, NEC member, reported to the 1956 SACTU Conference that the following

SACTU activists in the Eastern Cape

Alven Bennie

Lily Diedrichs

Sophie Williams and Wilton Mkwayi

workers had been organized into new unions: sweet (100); milling (198); stevedoring (113); biscuit (75); cement (271); and leather (278). The affiliated unions roster provided by the General Secretary also included the SAR & HWU (300), Commercial and Distributive WU (231) and the African Iron & Steel WU (377), and of course the established unions in textile, leather, laundry and food and canning. Unions to be formed in later years included the Municipal WU (156), the Bay Transport WU (197) and the Mineral Water WU (33). These unions in many cases overlapped with the GWU discussed above, depending upon the time period under consideration. Like new unions in other areas, financial instability, transient labour under Apartheid and victimization resulted in the rise and fall of these unions.

In presenting the LC report to the 1956 SACTU Conference, D. Telling stressed that each of the new unions had close ties with the liberation movement. In fact, as Bennie explains, many of the newly organized unions emerged from SACTU efforts to mobilize workers according to the demands they had submitted to the 1955 Congress of the People in Kliptown. Here again, then, the ANC–SACTU relationship dictated the method of SACTU work. Furthermore, this organizing drive was conducted under the hostile eyes of the Apartheid authorities who refused SACTU applications for holding public meetings and banned all meetings of more than ten Africans for many months in 1957. The fact that organizing work was so closely associated with workers' concrete demands meant that the SACTU £1-a-Day campaign received great mass support in the Port Elizabeth area. In fact, Bennie suggests that the PE–LC had advanced the £1-a-Day demand for dockworkers during the 1957 strike, and it was partially as a result of the PE initiative that the SACTU NEC agreed to call for the national minimum wage campaign.

Another major campaign was launched by the LC to organize building workers, the majority of whom were Coloureds and initially reluctant to leave the registered Amalgamated Building WU and join with their fellow African workers. Stephen Tobias, a Coloured worker, strongly believed that SACTU offered the first opportunity for Africans and Coloureds in the building trade to unite against class and racial exploitation. Under constant threat of dismissal if discovered as an organizer, Tobias and others succeeded in forming an African Painting and Building WU in Port Elizabeth. V. Mini, who like Bennie, could often 'pass' for a Coloured, assisted Tobias by addressing workers in Coloured residential areas. On one such occasion, the police, heavily armed, raided a meeting and began arresting SACTU leaders; Mini turned the anxiety of the people into solidarity when with his magnificent baritone voice he led the entire audience in spirited song and thus prevented what might have turned into a violent confrontation. Although Coloured building workers were frightened to join the AP & BWU, they did become a vital component of the Congress campaigns in the Port Elizabeth area in the early 1960s.

Repression against SACTU and the ANC only angered the working class of the Eastern Cape. Treason Trial arrests hit the Congress movement very hard in late 1956 and even harder during the Emergency in 1960. The post-Emergency SACTU Conference expressed amazement that the PE–LC had been able to even maintain a functioning office during the five-month reign of terror. The Eastern Cape SACTU membership had climbed to 2,670 just prior to the Emergency, and the two newest unions in clothing and engineering were rendered inoperative during the disruptive months. Head Office considered the special problems faced by the LC and agreed to offer more financial assistance to pay rents and hire local organizers, who otherwise had to leave full-time union work and return to employment to survive.

The LC also launched campaigns against unemployment, high rents and convict labour. Municipal rent collectors made it a practice of double-stamping monthly rent payments to make it appear that tenants were in arrears and thus subject to prosecution; SACTU investigations protected many individuals vulnerable to this abuse. The use of convict labour was a particularly serious problem in the low-wage Eastern Cape, and SACTU fought this in not only the docks but also the rural areas where cases were reported of convicts inflicting serious injuries to their bodies in order to escape their penal servitude to the profit-seeking capitalist class. Campaigns against taxes imposed on Africans also generated popular support, especially as the revenues financed the regime's administrative control of the rural people. All of these efforts took on greater importance with the banning of the ANC in 1960, and SACTU's harmonious relationship with the liberation movement allowed it to continue the political work without any great disjuncture.

With the massive repression against the popular movements in the early 1960s, Port Elizabeth was hardest hit. Gross exploitation and oppression had created a model of unity, resistance and militancy among workers and the Black people as a whole. As we document in Chapter 12 SACTU comrades from the Eastern Cape – whether in prison or after their death – became the symbols and the martyrs of the workers' struggle. Mkwayi, Mayekiso and Mini are remembered not only for how many unions they organised, but more importantly for the spirit and dedication they brought to the struggle.

The Western Cape

Another thing that struck me (on my first visit to the FCWU office) and which affected me strongly while there, was in the making of tea. There was a queue of Whites and Blacks together and for the first time in my life I saw White women making tea for me! This impressed me; I saw that there was real equality there.[39]

Indeed, the contact with the FCWU and its militant leaders did have a profound effect on young Black workers like Archie Sibeko who later became SACTU leaders themselves. It was not only the non-racial office routines which influenced them, however; this powerful Union which SACTU once described as 'the bastion of the progressive trade union movement in South Africa' fought continuously for higher wages and better conditions for all workers and successfully organized thousands of previously unorganized African and Coloured workers into the Union. Many SACTU leaders emerged from the training given by the FCWU and the Union itself, along with the African-FCWU, provided the backbone of the Cape Western Province Local Committee (CWP–LC) throughout the 1950s and 1960s.

Many difficulties faced this particular SACTU LC during its existence, however. The majority of workers in the Cape Peninsula, Coloured workers, belonged to registered craft unions and although many of these unions remained unaffiliated to any coordinating body, they were relatively conservative. With a much smaller African labour force than existed elsewhere and with more restrictions placed on their entry into industry, it was an extremely difficult task to combine these workers, largely migrant workers, into strong trade unions of a lasting nature. Added to this was the fact that before SACTU came into existence, many exceptional trade union leaders had already been banned, leaving few experienced people to carry on the work. Despite all of these problems specific to the region, new leaders did come to the fore and were responsible for organizing a substantial number of workers into SACTU unions.

At SACTU's First Annual Conference in March 1956, delegates representing the Cape Western Province workers included the FCWU and A-FCWU (with their head offices in Cape Town), TWIU and A-

TWIU, NULCDW and A-LCDWU, SA Tin Workers Union, SA Canvas and Rope WU, Bag WU, Metal WU and the SAR & HWU. By the Eighth Conference in 1963, the SACTU LC had organized workers into new unions in garage and motor, brick, quarry and cement, and hospital industries and undertakings. In addition, an Amalgamated Workers Union represented soap, timber, mineral water, tea and coffee and glass workers.

From its formation in 1941, the FCWU grew from strength to strength, organizing branches all over the Western and Eastern Cape Province, the West Coast and the Transvaal. With Ray Alexander as General Secretary and Frank Marquard as President (until their respective bannings in 1953 and 1954), the Union worked in unison with the A-FCWU which was forced by racial legislation to separate from the FCWU in 1947. Both Unions continued to set an example of principled non-racial trade unionism, demonstrating the power of a united working class against exploitation by the employers. Precisely because of this, the government attacks on the Union leadership were more severe than in most other industries. Apart from Alexander and Marquard, the other officials to receive banning orders in the early 1950s were Gus Coe (PE branch), Sarah Wentzel (Secretary, Worcester branch) and in 1956 Becky Lan (Acting General Secretary after Alexander's banning) was forced to step down from this position.

Upon their affiliation to SACTU, the Union announced,

... It is not enough just to be affiliated. In every town where our Union is in existence we must help SACTU to organize the unorganized workers and build SACTU into a powerful all-in national trade union centre.[40]

Through the efforts of stalwarts like Oscar Mpetha, General Secretary of the A-FCWU, Elizabeth Mafekeng, President of the A-FCWU, and Liz Abrahams, General Secretary of the FCWU, SACTU was strengthened significantly in the Cape area. As well, the workers themselves provided a militant and disciplined lead for other workers to follow. In Paarl, Elizabeth Mafekeng and Liz Abrahams assisted in setting up an additional LC. During the SACTU years, national membership of both Unions increased substantially — from 1,500 in each in 1956 to 8,052 (FCWU) and 9,565 (A-FCWU) in 1962.

The Textile Unions provided a similar lead to the Cape Peninsular workers. As in the case of FCWU, several of its leaders had been banned well before SACTU's formation, most notably Nancy Dick and Alex Calmeyer. Those who were able to continue on in the same tradition in the SACTU period included Julius Busa, Ben (Kopie) Baartman, S. Mpoza and Joe Ndamoyi (Vice-Chairman of the National Union of A-TWIU and Chairman, Cape Branch until his death in 1956). All four worked at the Hex River Textile Mills in Worcester and took part in the historic strike which began in March 1956 (see Chapter 8). They typified the militant spirit of workers in the Worcester area where national Congress campaigns always took root amongst the working class. Though the Alexandra bus boycott had very few repercussions in Cape Town itself, Worcester textile workers (mostly Coloured women) demonstrated their solidarity in large numbers. By 1960, in the Western Cape, the Union membership was as follows: TWIU (1,300), A-TWIU (600), with the unity of African and Coloured workers being a unique characteristic of this area.

It was these textile leaders as well as some from FCWU who constituted the main force behind the establishment of the Worcester LC of SACTU, with Miss D. Africa as their Secretary. Suffering the same fate as committees in all centres – the bannings, banishment and imprisonment of leaders – this LC struggled to survive. Ben Baartman was banished from his home in Worcester soon after the 1956 strike and sent to a remote part of Zululand. From there he left South Africa in 1959. In 1960, Julius Busa was detained for five months during the State of Emergency and on his release was endorsed out of Worcester and sent to the poverty-stricken reserves.

Ben January, Secretary of the NULCDW in the Western Cape, was another strong leader and organizer of Coloured and African laundry workers; he served as SACTU–NEC member and Chairman of the CWP–LC as well. His Union, like the other established unions, took the lead in campaigns directed against not only the employers but all the Apartheid laws and restrictions oppressing the Black masses in South Africa. In the SACTU CWP–LC, the strong influence of these three unions was to be felt throughout the 1950s and 1960s.

This LC was the first to be set up immediately following the Inaugural Conference of SACTU in 1955. Ben January was elected Chairman; Archie Sibeko, Secretary; and Mrs Eaglehoff (TWIU), Treasurer. At a later date Louise Kellerman (FCWU) joined Sibeko as Joint Secretary. The foundation unions, in addition to the established unions discussed above, included the Cape Town Stevedoring and Dock Workers Union, organized by the Communist Party back in the 1930s, and the SA Canvas and Rope Workers Union, one of the 14 unions that opposed the dissolution of the SAT & LC in October 1954.

The first major campaign launched by the CWP–LC was that carried out against the IC Bill, in preparation for the March 1956 SACTU Conference in Cape Town. All local committees had been collecting signatures for a petition against the Bill beforehand, and the CWP–LC organized its own campaign culminating in a 9 February demonstration outside the Houses of Parliament. Ten minutes before the House of Assembly met in a night-session to discuss the Bill, workers gathered to express their indignation at this new anti-worker legislation. One of the SACTU leaflets read:

The mad dogs of racialists are out for blood. Not satisfied with having devoured the rights and ruined the life of the African, they now want the Coloured and Indian workers who will not be allowed to choose their own jobs or elect their own leaders. . . . This is not Trade Union democracy – but White baaskap![41]

The demonstrators were harassed and intimidated by the Cape Town police who took away placards, took down names and examined pass books of Africans. Archie Sibeko commented: 'This big display of force clearly shows how frightened the government is of the people. They know their policy is hated and opposed by the mass of South Africans.'[42]

This campaign and the convening of the SACTU Annual National Conference in Cape Town in March assisted the LC in its efforts to mobilize workers on all issues affecting their daily lives. At the Conference Ben January led the discussion on the IC Bill, declaring it a 'fascist anti-working class document dictated by capitalist and undemocratic interests and aimed at the destruction of free Trade Unionism'.

The £1-a-Day campaign took on great significance in the Western Cape where the majority of African and Coloured workers earned well below this amount. More than 300 workers attended the Regional Workers Conference in February 1958, representing 22 industries in the Cape Peninsula. Ben Turok and P. B. H. Curran, representing Africans on the Cape Provincial Council, tried to get a motion passed for a general wage increase for Black workers but the United Party teamed up with the Nationalists to defeat the motion resulting in a 50 to 2 defeat. Those representatives who attended the National Workers Conference in March 1958, returned to address meetings and report back to the workers in the African townships. 400 attended a meeting in a Nyanga Emergency Camp where Mase and Mlamla spoke, and a

Archie Sibeko

SACTU trade unionists in the Western Cape

Greenwood Ngotyana

Ben Baartman

Julius Busa

Ben January

similar meeting was addressed by J. Mosiane at Sakkiesdorp. At Langa, over 700 came out to hear J. Mphemba, Ndziba, Mamfanya and Kukulela, and the National Workers Conference resolutions were adopted at all these meetings.

Though not as strong as some of the other LCs for reasons explained above, the CWP–LC did have some unique advantages over other areas. For example, there always existed a very close relationship between the political movements and the progressive trade unions. ANC leaders almost exclusively had their origins in the working class. 'There was never an elite; we had no lawyers, doctors or even Reverends in the Western Cape ANC.'[43] This close relationship had a profound effect on the task of mobilizing African workers in the area. As soon as the SACTU LC had been formed, the ANC was called upon to give its total support and together the two organizations divided the Western Cape into zones, by industrial areas for SACTU work and by townships for ANC work. In each industrial area SACTU formed a committee of all trade unionists and interested workers. SACTU activists would assemble every day just before noon and would then divide up to address meetings in various areas. In this way they could best assist the unregistered African unions and take up whatever complaints they had. In essence, it was the forerunner of the General Workers Union concept and many new unions were formed out of these industrial area committees. Elijah Loza was responsible for the coordination of this organizing campaign in the Western Cape.

The strong links between SACTU and the ANC in the Western Cape were demonstrated in several ways. Effectively, the working class leadership of the trade union movement was at one and the same time providing the Cape ANC with its most militant leadership; Oscar Mpetha was President of the ANC in the Cape and Archie Sibeko was also on the Cape Provincial Executive. After the ANC was banned, the NEC set up new divisions for political work to be continued in each province. In the Western Cape, a committee of seven top ANC members was appointed, and of these seven, five were trade union leaders: Sibeko, Loza, Malindi, Huna and Ngudle. Lastly, it is an indication of the unity of political and working class struggle in the Western Cape that the majority of Treason Trial defendants were trade unionists.

Experienced trade unionists and Congressites assisted the LC with educational classes which were given frequently by people like Becky Lan, Ray Alexander, Reg September, Brian Bunting, Fred Carneson,

Oscar Mpetha and Ben January, many of them forced to elude personal bans to hold classes. Perhaps because of the solid training already received by the new SACTU activists locally, the CWP–LC seldom sent members to Head Office in Johannesburg for the National Training School held there. In fact, the Western Cape LC was in many ways a more autonomous body than other committees. Certainly when it came to its financial stability, LC members were somewhat bitter because of the lack of assistance from Head Office. As happened elsewhere, organizers went without wages for months, surviving only because of their strong commitment to the struggle. Sympathetic lawyers defended cases without charging for their services and as well as obtaining funds through the collection of subscriptions from workers, many movement supporters would assist SACTU from time to time.

The organizing of Black workers in their residential areas was recognized as a key strategy by the CWP–LC members. A successful strike which utilized this method extensively occurred in 1955. The Boston Bag Company of Cape Town employed over 90 young Coloured women workers and fourteen men. Wages ranged from £1 17s. 9d to £3 5s. 9d. per week (including COLA) for women and from £2 16s. 9d. to £4 5s. 0d. per week for men. In September 1955, a few women approached SACTU for assistance in organizing this factory and within a matter of weeks regular meetings were being held in one of the worker's homes. Every week forty to fifty young women could be seen tramping across the fields of Paarden Eiland and along the streets of Maitland on their way to meetings. The Union was growing fast when suddenly the Secretary, Ben Turok, was banned; SACTU LC Secretary, Archie Sibeko, took over the meetings and soon an application for registration was made and their demands were drawn up. On 17 October, the preliminary demands were handed to the employers whose reaction was as expected, hostile. The next day, a number of women workers were forced to sign a statement to the effect that they were satisfied with their working conditions. Word passed around the factory and many of these women refused to sign the statement. After the bosses sacked the workers' Chairman on the excuse that he had told others not to sign, 88 workers immediately got up and walked out behind their Chairman.

The initial walk-out lasted four hours, with workers returning to their jobs after being told that the strike was probably illegal. Reorganization of workers following the strike caused chaos in the factory and workers refused to work overtime. After two weeks, the bosses called the inspector in to threaten the workers who were not yet intimidated. Next came the Special Branch interference in cordoning off the factory at lunchtime, hoping to find the banned Secretary holding meetings nearby.

On 14 December, all 88 appeared in court on a charge of striking illegally and despite progressive lawyer Sam Kahn's excellent defence, five of the leaders were found guilty and fined £10 or a month in jail; the rest of the workers were remanded till 30 January. The workers' pressure had, however, forced the bosses to concede small increases. With the strike, troubles in the factory, and low production, they had endured enough and granted increases ranging from 4s. to £1 for various grades of workers. Sick leave was increased by four days and in future cleaning was to be done by specially employed workers instead of regular workers. These Boston Bag workers, young, militant Coloured women with no previous experience with the machinery of the police state, stood up against it and set an example for other unorganized workers in the Cape. The bosses had tried everything, including planting an informer in the Union's ranks. SACTU had approached this person with full knowledge of his activities but it was only after the ANC Branch in his township, Kensington, sent volunteers to his house to threaten him, that he retreated. Despite the bosses' attempts, the bannings and threats by inspectors, open police harassment and court cases, the workers remained united and strong and the Bag Workers Union gained sufficient strength to become an affiliate to SACTU.

Another new union was formed out of a strike by workers at General Box Co. in Retreat. The Department of Labour had granted a Conciliation Board and the 200 African and 100 Coloured workers appointed Archie Sibeko to represent them. Sibeko and Turok appeared at the meeting of the Board but the Chairman refused to let Sibeko speak because that was 'not allowed by law'. On hearing this all of the workers at General Box came out on strike. Employers were forced to grant concessions and a Timber Workers Union was formed as a result of this display of workers' solidarity.

However, the strike itself was not the success the SACTU LC had hoped for. This was due to the fact that the organizers were unaware that there was another large General Box plant in Stellenbosch carrying out exactly the same operations. When strike action was taken, the organizers thought that they had done the necessary groundwork; they had organized the ANC branch in the Retreat area to such an extent that there were no scabs amongst the unemployed in the townships.

However, as reports came in of large trucks coming every evening to the Retreat factory from Stellenbosch, they realized that an extra shift had been added to cover the work lost at Retreat. The police were ready for the SACTU activists when they arrived in Stellenbosch to organize the workforce. Through this experience an important lesson was learned – the necessity to organize *all* plants of the industry concerned and all sectors of the industry throughout the country.

Three weeks after the strike Sibeko was arrested under the Native Labour Act and was thrown into a cell with seven other prisoners jailed for pass offences. On hearing the reason for his arrest, his cell-mates offered him blankets and food and one older prisoner called upon the other prisoners 'to respect a workers' leader'.

The February 1960 edition of *Workers Unity* described the activities of the CWP–LC as progressing slowly but steadily, despite all the difficulties. Workers were being organized in the wine industry, docks, garages and railways; the SA Canvas and Rope WU had been affiliated to SACTU since 1955 and now the tin workers were being re-organized. The Committee was also active in attempting to dissuade Coloured workers disillusioned with TUCSA policies from forming their own purely racial Coloured federation, encouraging them to join with SACTU instead.

The early 1960s saw an upsurge in progressive trade unionism here as elsewhere in South Africa. Immediately following the massacres at Sharpeville (Transvaal) and Langa (Cape), workers in the Western Cape carried out strike action for sixteen days, and in 1961 the national Stay-At-Home was widely supported by Cape Town's Coloured workers. Liz Abrahams, Secretary of the FCWU, explained:

In particular, Coloured workers in the Western Cape showed they were no longer prepared to put up with the injustices and insults which they are forced to suffer as third grade citizens. Large numbers of them stayed at home and made it one of the most important demonstrations in the history of the Coloured people.[44]

In 1962, the LC actively campaigned against the removal of Africans from Cape Town, calling upon all workers to protest against these racist evictions.

SACTU, representing both Coloured and African trade unions rejects the Government's explanation that this removal is being carried out in the interests of the Coloured workers.

Africans and Coloureds have worked side by side in the Western Cape for nearly 100 years without friction or rivalry. They formed unions together and if it were not for the law they would have joint Trade Unions for the protection of their common interests today. . . . SACTU calls upon the Coloured workers in particular to reject this attempt to spread ill will and racialism between them and their fellow African workers.[45]

SACTU went on to state that the threat to Coloured workers did not come from the African workers but rather from the colour-bar. The fight against Job Reservation in the Western Cape was spearheaded by the CWP–LC and is detailed in Chapter 4.

By 1963, the LC had organized several new unions, including a General Workers Union (called the Amalgamated Workers Union) which catered for workers in various industries. Other new or revived unions affiliated to the CWP–LC and the people responsible for forming them were as follows:

Brick, Quarry and Cement WU (Mildred Lesier)
Garage and Motor Industry WU (Zollie Malindi and Bernard Huna)
Hospital WU (Christmas Tinto and L. Kukulela)
SAR & HWU (R) (Greenwood Ngotyana and Archie Sibeko)

There were also unions formed amongst African municipal workers, organized by Z. Nqose, and commercial and distributive workers, organized by Joe Morolong and 'Looksmart' Ngudle. As well, bakery workers were brought together by Elijah Loza and Simon Makheta was responsible for the dockworkers.

The established unions discussed above were of course strongly represented within SACTU but the growth of these new unions and especially the emergence of new African union leaders and organizers was encouraging. Just as in other areas, however, these achievements and successes were short-lived as Cape Town trade union leaders soon suffered bannings, torture, banishment, imprisonment and death. The militant spirit of Cape trade unionism could never be completely crushed, however, and recent struggles by workers in the FCWU testify to the legacy of SACTU struggles (see Chapter 14).

Natal

From a struggling LC dependent upon a few strong leaders from 1955 to 1959, the Natal SACTU unit blossomed into a massive organization catering to the needs of thousands of previously unorganized workers.

Credit must be extended to the militant and disciplined Natal trade union leadership but also to the masses of people, African workers and peasants in particular, who demonstrated to the Apartheid regime that they would no longer submit to the suffering and oppression imposed upon them. They stood up to declare their determination to fight back.

The tradition of non-racial trade unionism which had evolved in the 1930s in Natal and was revived again in the early 1950s provided the background for SACTU-Natal's growth and strength. Many of the unions which sent representatives to the Inaugural Conference of SACTU came out of this tradition. Those unions attending the 1955 Conference were:

Union	Delegate	Membership
African Domestic WU	Kuzwayo	200
African-TWIU (national)	J. Mkwanazi	4,000 (total)
African Tobacco WU	P. G. Mei	350
Chemical & Allied WU	B. Nair	400
Howick Rubber WU	M. Pillay	750
Natal Aluminium WU	V. S. M. Pillay	102
Natal Box, Broom & Brush WU	B. Nair	110
Natal Dairy WU	B. Nair	100
SA Tin WU (Durban)	M. Albai	600
Observers:		
Durban Rubber Industrial U	M. Taylor; Mr Stadler	200
African Milling WU	E. Mtshali	

In May 1955, the Durban LC was formed and the leaders elected to take responsibility were Billy Nair, fiery Indian trade unionist, as Secretary, and Stephen Dlamini, the militant African textile leader as Chairman. Moses Mabhida was also one of the main persons behind the establishment of the LC, and in later years Curnick Ndlovu strengthened the Committee Executive. Although these men provided a model for disciplined leadership in Natal, there was a shortage of additional comrades and as always, financial problems plagued the Committee in the early years of SACTU's existence. Apart from the national unions, other unions which remained strong SACTU affiliates during the first five years were the well-organized and militant Natal Dairy Workers Union (previously under the leadership of Kesval

Moonsamy, influential Natal Indian Congress leader, then handed over to Moses Mabhida in 1955), the Natal Aluminium Workers Union and the Natal Box, Broom and Brush WU; Billy Nair served as Secretary of the latter two unions. Moses Mabhida's task was also to organize railway workers, R. S. Balli led the FCWU and Stephen Dlamini continued to represent African textile workers. S. V. Reddy and M. P. Naicker, both actively involved in trade union organizing in Durban right up to 1954, continued to advise SACTU leaders, as did the other banned leaders from Natal discussed in Chapter 2.

Both Dlamini and Nair were among the 156 Treason Trialists arrested in December 1956, creating further problems for the LC in Durban. Nair alone had been organizing in some fourteen separate industries, building up unions for SACTU affiliation. Throughout his involvement in the Treason Trial, Dlamini went out to organize workers in Northern Natal whenever recesses in the proceedings allowed; among these workers were the grossly exploited coal miners of Newcastle and Dundee.

Within the booming textile industry in Natal, SACTU had some very militant organizers with a great deal of combined experience in their respective factories. Stephen Dlamini had worked in the textile industry since the mid-1930s, firstly in a factory which eventually relocated in a border area and then from 1952 at Hebox. Johannes Mkwanazi began working at Consolidated Textile Mills Ltd in Jacobs (this company was part of the Philip Frame conglomerate) in 1950 and worked there until he was dismissed along with other progressive unionists in 1957, on the pretext that the Company no longer needed them. They provided strong leadership to the African textile workers of Natal and also worked closely with progressive Indian and White trade unionists in the TWIU.

This Branch of the TWIU was seriously hampered by disruptive activities of certain right-wing elements within the Union headed by Alec Wanless. Under the guidance and determination of popular leader 'Mannie' Isaacs, however, the workers chose the progressive wing and soundly defeated the Wanless clique. Some important battles were won by textile workers in Durban, including a victory at CTM over the bosses' attempt to increase profits by laying off workers and depressing wages of those remaining. In 1957, 600 Indian workers came out on strike and with the assistance of Ronnie Press, National Secretary, and Leon Levy, SACTU President, they scored an important victory.

The Durban LC threw its weight behind the £1-a-Day campaign beginning in 1957. SACTU unions consistently called for the minimum

Natal SACTU leaders, Billy Nair (*left*) and Curnick Ndlova, serving 20-year sentences from 1964

Moses Mabhida, Chairman, Natal Local Committee;
SACTU Vice-President, 1957–

wage demand in their negotiations and successful rallies were held to popularize the campaign. However, it was not until after the 1959 Annual National Conference in Durban that mass mobilization of unorganized workers into SACTU Natal occurred. This impressive process has been described above and it will not be necessary to further detail the historic events of 1959 and following in Natal. It is our aim in this section to capture the spirit of this upsurge in progressive trade unionism and to document some of the struggles and emergence of two unions in particular – the African Municipal WU and the Chemical WU – as an illustration of this heightened activity.

By 1960, some 13 new Natal unions or unions which had been revived (R) affiliated to SACTU: the Clothing WU, Hammarsdale (500); Metal WU, Natal (600); SAR & H (N–E) WU, Durban (R) (3,500); Durban Indian Municipal Employees Society (1,600); Durban African Municipal Employees Union (650); the Twine and Bag WU, Durban (R) (250), Tea and Coffee Workers Union, Durban (R) (100); African Tea and Coffee WU, Durban (250); Baking Workers Union, Durban (450); Biscuit WU, Durban (150); Hospital Workers Union (500) and a General Workers Union (with 5,000 workers still to be allocated to existing or new unions).

SACTU's campaign on behalf of African municipal workers in their struggle against the Durban City Council provides an excellent example of the determination of these oppressed African workers to achieve their demands. A major figure to lead the workers in this campaign was SACTU activist Memory Vakalisa. Up until the early 1960s, he had been a worker in a biscuit manufacturing operation. As well as organizing the Baking WU, Vakalisa organized his fellow workers into the Biscuit WU, both new SACTU affiliates. After these accomplishments, Vakalisa was asked by the LC to focus attention on municipal workers.

Over 11,000 African workers were employed by the Durban Corporation (the Municipality). African workers were engaged in jobs ranging from sweeping streets to emptying lavatory buckets to building houses in the African townships. The wages averaged £2 15s. 0d. per week, well below the subsistence level, and it was on this basis of exploitation that SACTU began its organizing drive. Vakalisa recalls how the first strike initiated by the Union began:

A lot of (building) workers came into the SACTU office, standing up saying 'We belong to the Municipal Workers Union.' We asked them what they wanted and they first said they wanted to join the Union. Stephen Dlamini began writing out the tickets and as soon as he had finished writing they said, 'We've gone on strike!'[46]

Eighty-nine building workers at Kwa Mashu township came out in sympathy with two fellow workers who had been dismissed by the City Engineer's Department. These workers had been elected to voice the complaints of all the workers who had been forced to work in the rain on 8 November. As a result of their sympathy actions, all workers were retrenched. Progressive lawyer Rowley Arenstein came to the Union's assistance and with the strong leadership from Vakalisa as well, the majority of workers were reinstated; the Corporation refused to re-hire the original two workers who were dismissed but the Union found alternative work for them.

From these beginnings, the Union gained momentum and immediately drew up a list of demands to be submitted to the Municipality; the major issues were low pay and poor working conditions. The memorandum called for a minimum wage of £1-a-Day, a Medical Aid Fund, marriage allowances and trade union facilities, three weeks leave and all public holidays to be paid, as well as other improvements. The refusal on the part of the Mayor to meet with the Union delegates to discuss this memorandum unless the Department of Labour was also present, triggered off a militant response from the workers and had repercussions which continued for the next two years.

Determined to resist the machinery of the NL Act, the Union appealed to the Congress Alliance for help. The Natal Indian Congress and Congress of Democrats sent letters to the Mayor expressing their support for the workers' demands and the COD carried out a special campaign directed at Durban ratepayers. During lunch hour one Friday in late April 1961, COD volunteers dropped thousands of leaflets in the centre of the city's main thoroughfare, calling on ratepayers to insist that all municipal workers be paid £1-a-Day. On the following day municipal workers demonstrated outside City Hall demanding that the Mayor meet their deputation. Angry scenes took place after they were told the Mayor was away and workers would only disperse on the instructions of their Secretary, Memory Vakalisa, who assured them that further steps would be taken by the Union's Executive the following week.

In the next phase of the struggle, the City Council announced its decision to establish a company union-type 'works committee' thereby

Durban municipal workers challenge City Council, 1961

Memory Vakalisa, Secretary,
African Municipal Workers Union, Durban, 1961

sidestepping the African Municipal WU. An Advisory Committee was set up immediately with J. C. Bolton (City Councillor at this time) as Chairman, and their first recommendation was that the Corporation pay its unskilled workers an increase of R4.33 per month. A *New Age* report commented on the 'surprising speed' in announcing this pay hike. Though the Union welcomed any increases for their underpaid workers, the Executive pointed out that they still fell short of the Union's demands and also that the effect would be that more workers would now qualify for homes in Kwa Mashu where their incomes would be swallowed up by higher rents and transport expenses to and from work.

The Union continued to fight for recognition as well as improved wages and conditions. A new Committee was formed to assist the Union in pressing for its goals. The members included representatives from the Musgrave Ratepayers' Association, the Liberal Party, two lecturers at the University of Natal, Mr Arvind Desai (Natal Indian Youth Council), Amos Mgoma, former member of the banned ANC-Youth League, and Ronnie Kasrils, Secretary of the COD. Despite the pressure from this broad range of organizations and people, the Liaison Committee set up under the NL Act tried every method of circumventing the Union. They even went to the extent of trying to have Vakalisa removed by a small group of workers actively encouraged to organize a coup. J. C. Bolton (of the registered Garment WU in Natal) once again demonstrated his betrayal of genuine working class interests by his direct involvement in all of these devious machinations. All of these attempts were thwarted, however, as Vakalisa reported:

The stooges whom the Liaison Committee tried to use to subvert the Union failed miserably because they miscalculated the militancy of the workers. The Liaison Committee will continue to fail as the workers . . . are totally opposed to dummy institutions and will fight on until their Unions are recognized.[47]

Vakalisa, fondly referred to as 'the Mayor' by the workers, was unanimously re-elected Secretary and all loyal members of the Executive were returned to their positions by the rank and file. They continued to represent the interests of the African municipal workers throughout 1962 and 1963, although like other progressive unions the members and leaders were increasingly subjected to various forms of repression in those years. Vakalisa was forced to leave South Africa; he was replaced by Bruno Mtolo, who later viciously betrayed the workers and became a witness for the state against SACTU and Congress leaders, including Stephen Dlamini.

In 1962, another militant struggle was carried out by the African chemical workers from SA Titanium Products. This new company was British-owned and produced titanium oxide, a powder used in colouring and the production of metal and rubber. Louis Mkize, who had first heard about SACTU while working in the railways, was one of the workers responsible for setting up a factory committee at the titanium plant located at Umgobaba, some 26 miles south of Durban on the Natal coast. Approximately 1,000 African workers at SATP earned only £2–3 per week, factory conditions were extremely unsafe and living conditions in the nearby compounds intolerable.

Although management promised wage increases as soon as production reached full capacity, this was never realized. The factory committee contacted SACTU and with the latter's guidance the workers wrote to the Company headquarters in Britain outlining their complaints and even threatened to burn down the plant if their demands were not met. Simultaneously within the factory, the workers decided to march to management to demand the increases promised. By the following pay-day, workers had received significant increases in their pay packets, ranging from £1 to £3. As well, these men received huge sums in back pay covering the allowances they had not received for the previous three months.

This initial victory boosted the morale of African workers throughout the factory and they were ready to tackle other grievances, particularly those concerning working conditions. These included abuse by the foremen (many of them reactionary Afrikaners who treated Africans with total contempt), dangerous conditions of work and lack of protective clothing. Mkize was elected Chairman of the newly-formed Union, Raymond Makanya, Secretary and Shabane became Treasurer. As they were in the process of planning their strategy against these poor conditions, Makanya was singled out and abused by one of the foremen and when he retaliated was dismissed from work. The workers were united and walked out of the factory shouting 'Amandla' (power). The strike was 100 per cent strong on the first day.

That night workers decided to hold a meeting in the forest surrounding the compounds in order to avoid police harassment. All workers attended and Committees were elected: two were instructed to approach SACTU officials in Durban for assistance; four were to round up all those workers not living in the compounds; and four were to organize a deputation to visit management and present their demands. The workers called for the reinstatement of Makanya and the ending of all abusive practices by the foremen. Mkize was one of those chosen to consult SACTU and he returned with Stephen Dlamini who recalls being surprised to find the striking workers 'in the bush'. He addressed the workers and encouraged them to stand strong and united as the only way to win their struggle.

Police, armed with sten guns, were posted around the factory, making it impossible for the workers' delegation to enter the factory without being charged with trespass. After three days negotiations began and the management finally agreed to reinstate all workers and to refrain from prosecuting or victimizing any of the strikers. The jubilant workers returned to the plant after yet another victory over the bosses.

As time went by, however, victimization did occur and leaders of the strike, including Louis Mkize, were the first to be singled out. Police came in the middle of the night and forced him to pack up at gunpoint, took him to the compound manager who paid him, and he was then dropped off at a place close to Durban. Several other workers suffered a similar fate, corresponding with the treatment meted out to their fellow workers and SACTU leaders throughout the province.

The message of SACTU had spread much further afield than this factory on the South Coast by the early 1960s; additional local committees had been established in Pinetown, Ladysmith and Pietermaritzburg. SACTU activists were engaged in full-time organizing work in the Hammarsdale area as well.

Numerous efforts had been made over the years to maintain a functioning LC in Pietermaritzburg. In mid-1956, a Provisional Committee had been set up, and Moses Mabhida reported to the SACTU National Conference that bus and laundry workers were being organized. He also mentioned the difficulties of organizing in this area where migrant workers would return to the rural areas at the beginning of ploughing season. Although a functioning LC existed by 1960, the 1961 Conference Report explained that because of the arrest of Harry Gwala, SACTU leader in that region, the Committee's work was not progressing well. Other activists on the Committee included William Khanyile, Joel Kunene, Ngwenya, Shangase, and Anthony Xaba. By 1962, the LC had ceased to exist as a result of Gwala's banning and restriction of movement. Related problems included the lack of full-time officials to replace him and the inability of the Durban LC to provide financial assistance.

However, there are two aspects of the SACTU work in Pietermaritzburg which deserve attention. Firstly, the long tradition of struggle which existed among rubber workers at the Howick plant 14 miles out of the city, and secondly, an upsurge of militancy in the area in the early 1960s.

The Howick Rubber workers had been organized into different trade unions at various times since the war and in 1962 were part of the Rubber and Cable WU with a membership of 1,500 Black workers. Harry Gwala, outstanding trade union militant and ANC leader, had been organizing these workers before his first banning order in 1954. Respected leader Moses Mabhida also assisted these workers and worked alongside Fanyana Majozi who had previously been organizing dockworkers in Durban. Mabhida recalls an example of the militancy of these workers: on one occasion as they were preparing for a confrontation with management, they made up small stickers which simply said: 'Rubber burns!' The employers knew that this constituted a serious threat. The Union, despite its ups and downs, gradually increased to a maximum strength of 1,200 workers in 1960.

In 1961, the workers carried out their most determined and disciplined struggle for increased wages and in that same year brought the factory to a complete standstill during the national Stay-At-Home. In demonstrations, letters to management and at mass meetings, workers demanded increased wages and rejected management's proposals for 'works committees'. As a result nearly 1,500 workers gained increases of between 75c and R1.50 per week. It was reported that the bosses told workers that the pay hikes had nothing to do with the workers' strength and unity!

Other Pietermaritzburg SACTU affiliates in 1960 were the Cement, Quarry and Lime Workers Union, the Distributive and Allied Workers Union, the Laundry Workers Union and a General Workers Union. Records show that the 29–31 May Stay-At-Home was very successful throughout the industries in the Pietermaritzburg area, especially among rubber, garage, railway and municipal workers. A 60 to 70 per cent turnout was recorded overall. Difficulties mentioned above prevented the LC from capitalizing on this militancy after 1961.

In 1961, the Durban LC sent a young African trade unionist to Pinetown to establish another centre in this post-war industrial expansion area attractive to low-wage employers. Eric Mtshali, who had successfully organized an African Milling Workers Union for workers in the flour and sugar mills, became the full-time organizer in the Pinetown area. Totally dependent upon workers' financial support for his subsistence, Mtshali organized workers in the shoe, clothing, textile, transport (bus) and road-construction industries; in clothing, a counter union to J. C. Bolton's more effectively represented the interests of the workers. It was a measure of SACTU's success in this area that 75 per cent of the Pinetown workers supported the 1961 Stay-At-Home. Mtshali was forced to leave the country in 1962, and as always a shortage of personnel left Pinetown workers in a state of disorganization.

Another LC was established in Ladysmith in 1962, with Mate Mfusi and S. Mtambo as the leading organizers. After several house and factory meetings, 70 workers were enrolled into the General Workers Union under SACTU leadership and supervision. The main industries in this area were textile, chemical and coal mining. Before Mfusi could establish lasting roots among the workers of Ladysmith, she was charged with being illegally resident in the town and ordered to leave, but Mtambo carried on with the organizing work.

Hammarsdale, a border industry area, was another centre of SACTU activity in Natal. Esther Gwala worked as a full-time organizer for the SA Clothing WU and she was assisted by National Assistant General Secretary George Monare and also Johannes Modise. Local SACTU leaders too, including Dlamini, Mabhida and Queeneth Dladla, assisted these highly underpaid workers in Hammarsdale. Strike actions taken in this area are discussed in Chapter 8.

Some SACTU members in other regions were occasionally critical of SACTU-Natal's organizational tactics, especially in regard to the mass mobilization of thousands of workers into the GWU before establishing a base in individual industries. One can only view with great respect, however, the selfless work carried out by some of the most militant and dedicated trade unionists in the country. Billy Nair stands out as a 'true revolutionary' in the eyes of those who worked closely with him, and is remembered for his tremendous energy in organizing workers into SACTU unions despite continual police and Special Branch harassment. Although arrested in 1963 and imprisoned for 20 years in 1964, Billy Nair remains in the hearts and minds of workers throughout South Africa. Similarly remembered is Curnick Ndlovu, organizer of the railway workers and staunch defender of the rights of African township residents. Ndlovu, like Nair, remains cut off from his people for 20 years while he is incarcerated in the hell-hole of Robben Island. Dlamini too served eight years on Robben Island for championing the cause of the South African working class and the revolutionary struggle against capitalism and Apartheid; Stephen suffered the horrors of torture at the hands of the racist regime but managed to flee the country where, in exile, he remains the President of SACTU. The list is long: Mabhida, Vakalisa, Gwala . . . the SACTU Natal activists who were taught by the principled leaders of the 1930s and who in turn passed on their heritage and experience to the progressives of the present era.

In 1963, when most of the SACTU Natal leadership had been detained under the 90- and later 180-day laws, younger less experienced persons emerged to keep the LC functioning for a period of time. Johannes Mkwanazi, though underground himself, organized several people to carry on the work. Ignatia Mtalane, Dora Ngcobo and Mrs Kumalo ran the office with the assistance of R. G. Pillay. Mkwanazi was himself detained in 1963 but upon his release in 1964 found the SACTU office still functioning, a credit to the spirit that prevailed in the SACTU and Congress circles. After 1964, this task became increasingly difficult and dangerous, and the Durban LC, like other LCs, was forced to turn to the conditions of underground work.

NOTES

1. Phyllis Altman, *Workers and Trade Unions Against Apartheid*, WFTU, n.d., p. 3.
2. 'Lawrence Ndzanga Puts the Case for Railwaymen', *Workers Unity*, November 1961–January 1962.
3. Interview, Archie Sibeko.
4. Interview, Leon Levy.
5. Interview, 'John Parker'.
6. Interview, Graham Morodi.
7. Interview, Archie Sibeko.
8. 'Metal Workers Want More Than Idle Promises', *Workers Unity*, May 1959.
9. ibid.
10. *Workers Unity*, November 1959.
11. Quoted in M. Shope, General Secretary, Memorandum on the Conditions of African Miners in South African Gold Mines, submitted to the Miners International Federation, UK, 2 February 1974.
12. *Workers Unity*, November–December, 1958.
13. This Dlamini is not to be confused with Stephen Dlamini, Durban leader.
14. Minutes, MC, 20 October 1960.
15. Interview, Leon Levy.

16. *Workers Unity*, July 1959.
17. The export value (in Rand) of all agricultural products in the late 1950s and early 1960s was as follows: 1958–59 (290·2 million); 1959–60 (324·6 million); and 1960–61 (311·0 million).
18. Quoted in Rosalynde Ainslie, 'Farm Labour in South Africa', *Unit on Apartheid*, United Nations, no. 41/71. The data for this section is taken from this source, unless stated otherwise.
19. Ainslie, ibid.
20. Interview, Leon Levy.
21. Interview, Elijah Mampuru.
22. Report presented to Conference of Plantation Workers, Durban, 16 June 1962.
23. Minutes, SACTU Fifth Annual Conference, October 1960.
24. Interview, Moses Mabhida.
25. Interview, George Ponnen.
26. Interview, Alven Bennie.
27. Interview, Paulos Temba.
28. Interview, Leon Levy.
29. Interview, Graham Morodi.
30. Interview, Ronnie Press.
31. These numbers are somewhat misleading in the sense that certain national unions had their head offices in Johannesburg but also had branches with large memberships in other centres.
32. *New Age*, 28 November 1957.
33. Interview, Gabriel Rapolai.
34. Interview, Phyllis Altman.
35. Minutes, SACTU First Annual Conference, General Secretary Report, 1956.
36. *New Age*, 27 January 1955.
37. Interview, Stephen Tobias.
38. Interview, Alven Bennie.
39. Interview, Archie Sibeko.
40. *New Age*, 6 September 1955.
41. *New Age*, 9 February 1956.
42. ibid.
43. Interview, Archie Sibeko.
44. *Workers Unity*, November 1961–January 1962.
45. *New Age*, 9 August 1962.
46. Interview, Memory Vakalisa.
47. *New Age*, 5 April 1962.

7 ... BUT NOT FOR BREAD ALONE

The consequences of capitalism on the lives of working class people extend beyond the workplace *per se*. Although workers sell their labour power for only a specified period of time each day and each week, their proletarian status ensures that all aspects of social life are circumscribed by the realities of powerlessness. Under Apartheid in South Africa, Black workers and their families suffer these hardships to a degree unknown by their White working-class counterparts. In particular, workmen's compensation, unemployment and housing constitute three areas of Black proletarian life worthy of specific attention.

The purpose of this section is briefly to demonstrate that SACTU campaigns were not restricted to quantitative demands for higher wages. Rather, SACTU responded to the needs of workers created by the starvation wage system. In this way, SACTU was rooted in and moved with the consciousness of the people; the political effect was a merging of the economic with the political and a strengthening of the Congress Alliance in its struggle for total liberation from national oppression and class exploitation.

Workmen's Compensation
The April 1962 issue of the *Government Gazette* reported that £38,202 was owed to 4,800 'missing' workers who were eligible for but had not claimed workmen's compensation. The overwhelming majority were African workers. By 1966–67, 8,730 Africans, or 75 per cent of all those listed as eligible for benefits, were 'missing'. When asked to explain such a seemingly unusual situation, the Workmen's Compensation Commissioner stated, 'there is something about an African – call it superstition if you like – that makes him flee from the job or the place where he is injured on duty.'[1]

If he had been honest, the Commissioner, instead of resorting to racist mythology, might have admitted that the real reason that African workers injured on the job had not claimed their compensation was that they had in most cases been 'endorsed out' of the urban area as 'not serving the interests of the White economy'. Furthermore, the lack of proper record-keeping by employers and the WCC in most cases meant that 'Jim No. 5' or 'Tom No. 9' could not be traced. The companies, concerned only with exploiting the African's labour-power, failed to record his surname or address, or even if this were done, failed to pass on the relevant information to the WCC following the injury. In sum, when an African worker is injured in South Africa, physical suffering is accompanied by economic and social dislocation. Even if the injured worker manages to get a medical certificate, he/she would seldom be assigned to a lighter job until recovery; Africans physically unable to do the heaviest work are regarded by White capitalists as expendable and superfluous to the Apartheid economy.

Under the Workmen's Compensation Act of 1941, it is the responsibility of employers to notify the WCC of accidents and industrial diseases. In the case of African workers, this information is to be given to the Department of Bantu Affairs and Development. If this requirement is satisfied, the injured worker has a period of twelve months in which to claim the compensation owed; if this is not done, the *Government Gazette* then lists the names and claims and after one month all monies return to the state coffers.

As with all labour legislation in South Africa, 'race' is the major variable in the WC Act. Workers may be permanently or temporarily injured, totally or partially injured – both logical distinctions. But workers may also be injured 'as Africans', as distinct from Whites, Coloureds and Indians. Sections 83 and 88 of the Act enumerate special procedures and different (usually lower) rates for African claimants. For example, no compensation is payable to an African if disabled for less than seven days. In the case of death, African workers' dependants are eligible to receive 'one lump sum' payment, the amount of which is determined by the Commissioner; the amount, however, cannot exceed that given for permanent total disability.

In agriculture and mining, special provisions applied. In 1956, the WC Act included farm labourers for the first time, but claims could be made only on injuries resulting from the use of mechanically-driven machinery. In the mines, a new Pneumoconiosis Act in 1956 reduced the compensation available to Africans suffering from miners' diseases (silicosis, phthisis, TB, etc.) to a lump sum of £240. (Previous to that it had been possible to receive almost twice that amount in some cases.) For White workers suffering the same industrial diseases, four grades of compensation reflecting severity provided compensation to dependants, including children up to 18 years of age. In the case of death, African dependants must furthermore prove their eligibility to the Native Affairs Department before the pitiful lump sum payment is granted. In response to the 1956 law, *Workers Unity* spoke for all African mine workers when it said: 'Africans as a whole will gain nothing. We Africans who get this sickness are sacked at once. We go back to our homes with this little money, and die.'[2]

SACTU Head Office and affiliated unions – particularly the FCWU – responded to these appalling conditions by spending countless hours attempting to trace and contact injured Africans eligible for compensation. In addition, the WCC and employers' organizations were approached with the demand that an efficient system of record-keeping be instituted immediately. In general, SACTU inquiries were treated with contempt and hostility, particularly by certain mining, engineering and other companies in heavy industries where accidents were more frequent and managements least concerned about ensuring adequate compensation.

SACTU established an excellent series of lectures explaining the provisions of the WC Act and distributed these to all Local Committees and affiliated unions as a stopgap measure designed to inform African workers of their limited rights under the law. As for the law itself, SACTU's 1960 Conference demanded that compensation for all workers, irrespective of race and sex, be increased, and that disabled workers be given full pay during the time of their absence from employment and without long delays. These demands fell on deaf ears.

As for the so-called 'missing' claimants, a SACTU press release issued in 1962 exposed the hypocrisy of the Commissioner's statement quoted above:

It is remarkable how all trace of African workers is lost when money is due to them in spite of the fact that they are heavily tagged by passes, thumb-prints, identity numbers and all the other red-tape of Apartheid. If an African does not pay his poll tax, he is easily found.[3]

And for those who, according to the Commissioner, 'flee' from work following injuries, SACTU queried whether it was not strange that they 'kept fleeing' from certain companies more so than others.

The mention of the poll tax was not accidental, as this too had increased in 1960 to a minimum of £2 per year for each African male over the age of eighteen. No such tax applied to any other section of the population. This was but one of 160 compulsory and 681 voluntary levies imposed upon the African majority under Apartheid. These revenues, subtracted from already below-subsistence wages, financed the bureaucratic machinery that administered and controlled the movement of Africans from the cradle to the grave.

Unemployment: The Scourge of Capitalism
Unemployment is the disease of capitalism, it is one of the crimes for which the workers get punished.[4]

It is a well-established fact that capitalism cannot sustain conditions of full employment for its workforce. Insofar as production is geared towards the creation of profits and the accumulation of capital, rather than production for use to satisfy real human needs, it is in the interests of the ruling class to always have a 'reserve army' of unemployed labour that serves to depress the value of wages paid to those productively employed. When the wage demands of organized labour reach unacceptable levels, the capitalist class is then able to replace that labour with a portion of the reserve army. In other words, the crisis of unemployment is a structural feature of capitalist society and, as such, has little to do with the capabilities or inclinations of individual workers.

In South Africa, under the migrant, cheap labour system of Apartheid, it is no surprise that Africans suffer the most severe repercussions from unemployment — especially in periods of capitalist recession. In the late 1950s and early 1960s, this problem became particularly acute in the major industrial centres. Normal functioning of capitalist priorities, plus the Nationalists' policy of removing 'unproductive' African labour from urban centres, resulted in tremendous suffering for Black and especially African working class families.

Accurate and comprehensive data on the number of unemployed workers of all races is virtually impossible to find. The fact that even White unemployed workers, the most protected and privileged under Apartheid, were driven by circumstances to form a Johannesburg Council of Unemployed Workers in 1961 gives some indication of the seriousness of the situation. For Coloured and Indian workers, the problem was much worse. In Durban, an estimated 40 per cent of the entire workforce was out of work in 1962. Within the large Indian community, approximately 50 per cent, or 40 to 50 thousand workers, were jobless and destitute. Starvation was reported in the working class districts of Happy Valley, Clairwood and Sea Cow Lake. Suicide rates increased as many considered death the more attractive alternative.[5]

For Africans, the most exploited, the government used the unemployment crisis as a means of endorsing out thousands to the rural areas and reserves. Even in the rural areas, Africans had to 'compete' with convicts amassed for slave labour on the farms. The Bantu Affairs Department (BAD) made no attempt to establish statistics on the number of Africans unemployed during this period, although SACTU and other bodies made a conservative estimate of 100,000 Africans out of work. On one occasion in late 1961, the Johannesburg office of the BAD admitted that there were at least 25,000 permanently unemployed in that area alone, and no new work-seeker permits were being issued. An African who lost his/her job in the urban area had only fourteen days in which to locate alternative employment before being removed to the reserves and left there to starve.

As in all capitalist countries, a system of unemployment insurance designed to appease working class militancy exists in South Africa. The Unemployment Insurance Act of 1937, re-enacted in amended form in 1946, provided for a UI Fund to which certain classes of workers falling within defined wage limits were obliged to contribute. The employers and the state also 'contributed' to this Fund, investing the millions of pounds in profits and monies previously stolen from the workers themselves. The 1946 amendments included urban African workers as contributors as part of the Smuts Government's 'reforms' following the Mine Workers Strike. Important exclusions, however, were African mine and farm labourers, whose slave-driving bosses objected to such welfare-oriented schemes as obstacles to the efficient exploitation of cheap labour. Also excluded were domestic servants, public servants, casual workers and certain categories of seasonal labour.

When the Nationalists came to power in 1948, they excluded virtually 90 per cent of African workers from eligibility under the UI Act by restricting benefits to those making more than £182 per year. In 1957, this was changed again to exclude all Africans making less than £5 3s. 3d. per week. Furthermore, African workers eligible under these conditions were obliged to take any job available, and failure to do so resulted in a forfeiture of benefits. Nationalist changes in the legislation from 1948 onwards meant that African workers who had paid into the Fund in previous years were robbed of an estimated £9 million in contributions and denied all benefits.

The UI Fund grew in size to an estimated R140 million (£70 million) by 1962, but the exclusion of the majority of unemployed from benefits meant that the Fund did little to alleviate suffering. In fact, the Minister of Labour used a portion of the workers' money to subsidize companies forced to lay off staff in 1959. Three years later, the Minister made a tour of Europe as part of the government's scheme to promote White immigration to South Africa. Rather than allowing Black workers to assume skilled positions, the racist regime went out of its way to ensure that the 'civilized labour' policy was maintained while the African masses starved.

Against these intolerable conditions, SACTU Local Committees throughout the country took the initiative to organize the unemployed. As Stephen Dlamini recalls, it was 'SACTU's role to explain the capitalist system to the people so that individual workers did not become depressed but rather collectively organized to fulfil the working class role of changing society'. Not surprisingly, the momentum for the SACTU campaign came from Durban, where Indian workers were starving and Africans were 'sleeping in water drains'.[6] Port Elizabeth, Johannesburg and Cape Town followed the Durban lead by organizing mass meetings of the unemployed throughout the early 1960s.

In April 1959, the Durban LC enrolled 150 members into an Unemployed Workers Union (UWU), and from this base called on the other four Congresses to get involved in a 'Jobs for All' campaign. SACTU Head Office and LCs demanded: that the UI Fund be used to increase the size and length of UI benefits; an end to White immigration and equal opportunity for *all* workers to take on skilled jobs; amendments to the UI Act to cover all workers; and a national minimum wage of £1-a-Day which, if granted, would make a large proportion of African workers eligible for benefits under the Act.

In September 1961, as conditions worsened in Natal, a SACTU delegation from Durban decided to present these and other demands in the form of a memorandum to the Minister of Labour in Pretoria. The Minister agreed to meet the delegation and five SACTU activists left by car for the 400-mile trip to the Transvaal. In Pietermaritzburg, they were intercepted by the Special Branch and told that the meeting had been cancelled, but they proceeded in any case. Stopping in Johannesburg, the delegation went to SACTU offices where the SB again harassed and interrogated everyone present. The following day, upon arriving at Compensation House in Pretoria, they were met by armed police and told that the delegation must turn back. The group, which consisted of Stephen Dlamini, Mate Mfusi and three Indian trade unionists, resisted this intimidation and eventually talked officials into at least accepting the memorandum. Upon their return to Durban, Dlamini and others were arrested. It was later reported that the Minister cancelled the meeting because Africans were part of the delegation; that is, he would discuss unemployment only with regard to those workers covered by the IC Act. For the African workers, *Workers Unity* described the alternatives: '. . . a whole population is either forced to starve or sell its labour on the slave market'.

The Wits LC followed the example set by Durban. Numerous rallies were held on the Johannesburg City Hall steps, and an Action Committee of Unemployed Workers was formed. Initial signs of cooperation with the White workers' Council of Unemployed Workers disappeared quickly as the latter were intimidated by the authorities into severing all relations with SACTU. The Council did, however, call for an end to Job Reservation, White immigration, and a national minimum wage of £1-a-Day as well as equal coverage for African workers under the UI Act. In Cape Town and Port Elizabeth, more rallies were held. Alven Bennie recalls that in PE sympathetic liberal organizations tried to organize a soup kitchen, but the Local Committee rejected this approach because 'our approach was to seize power and we could not achieve that by becoming a charity organization'.[7]

As with Workmen's Compensation, SACTU was left with few options except to lobby wherever possible for changes in the UI Act. In September 1962, Head Office sent a memorandum to the Minister of Labour requesting representation on the UI Board. Listing its numerous objections to provisions in the Act, SACTU argued that other coordinating bodies represented on the Board could not speak for – and did not care about – the interests of African workers. These other bodies either had few African trade unions affiliated (as was the case with TUCSA) or, more commonly, they refused Africans affiliation. Only SACTU, representing 40,000 African workers, could speak for the most exploited section of the working class. For precisely this reason, the Minister of Labour refused to even acknowledge receipt of the memorandum. To the Nationalist government and the capitalist class, unemployed Africans do not constitute a human dilemma worthy of attention; they are only a force to be disciplined and controlled and cast out of sight to the barren reserves.

Housing and Rent Arrears

The fantastic situation then arises where the (Johannesburg) City Council as an employer pays its employees starvation wages and then jails and fines those employees for not being able to pay the rents which the Council itself has fixed.[8]

After starvation wages and unemployment, the third side of this triangle of exploitation and suffering was the housing and rents crisis. Under the Native (Urban Areas) Act, Africans in urban areas were required to live in designated, racially segregated areas – hostels, villages or townships. Only African domestics who stood at the beck and call of their White oppressors in the suburbs were exempt from these restrictions. Using cheap African labour in the construction trade, 'model' townships sprang up on the perimeters of the industrial centres in the 1950s.

Associated with the forced removals to 'African areas' was a significant increase in the total cost of subsistence living: rents payable to local authorities sky-rocketed and transport costs to travel the average 10–12 miles to work now became a matter of daily necessity. Only wages failed to increase. For the many workers averaging around £8 per month income, payment for transport, rent and food purchased at work would normally cost £7 10s. leaving only 10s. (shillings) for the month to cover all other expenditures. In essence, the 'slum clearance' programme meant greater suffering and starvation in only slightly better accommodation.

Until the end of 1954, the state housing policy focused on what was termed 'sub-economic' units. Residents of these units who earned less than £15 per month had average rents of £2 5s. or about 15 per cent of total monthly income. From 1955 onwards, the government policy shifted to the 'economic' housing scheme, whereby tenants earning £15 per month paid a rent equivalent to 20 per cent of their income; the Johannesburg City Council raised the income level to £20 as the base rate for 'economic' rentals. These flat percentage rates became a tremendous burden on African families living on poverty wages, a burden that for most could not be met.

The assessed rentals bore no relationship to the tenants' ability to pay. SAIRR concluded that a *minimum* monthly subsistence budget, *excluding rent*, for the Johannesburg African family in 1958–59 was as follows:

Food	£13 12s. 8d.
Clothing	£4 13s. 0d.
Fuel and light	£1 9s. 8d.
Cleaning materials	16s. 6d.
Transport	£1 3s. 5d.
Tax	2s. 11d.
Total Minimum Expenditure	£21 18s. 2d. (excluding rent)

If, for example, a tenant made £16 per month, the 20 per cent reduction for rent (£3 2s. would leave only £12 18s. for all other expenses. As the SAIRR study excludes rental payments from the budget, this means that the *minimal* shortfall between income and expenditure would be around £9 per month. Thus, payment of 'economic' *and* 'sub-economic' rents was a virtual impossibility for the vast majority of African tenant families.

The inferior quality of these tiny, rapidly-constructed township houses added to the difficulties of African workers. Inadequately heated during the winter months, and unbearably hot in the summer, the majority of the homes had no electricity, no running water, no inside toilet facilities, no ceilings, no room partitions and only earthen floors. Harry Loots, a SACTU leader in the Transvaal FCWU who had worked as a surveyor for the City Council during the construction of the Soweto township, recalls that the houses were 'just four walls with no internal divisions and no concern for the comfort of the occupants. Living conditions were appalling.'[9] In Kwa Mashu, the African township built 14 miles from Durban in the late 1950s, houses were within a short period of time in bad repair, roads and drainage systems were poor, lighting was inadequate and recreational areas were nonexistent. The same conditions obtained in Merebank, an area where poor Indian families resided. These realities led SACTU to warn the government in 1962 that it was 'sitting on a time bomb which will explode if this situation continues'. Indeed, the 'time bomb' exploded into violence on many occasions throughout the 1960s and 1970s, particularly during the Durban strikes of 1973-74 and the Soweto uprisings of 1976.

Returning to the rent issue, thousands of African tenants throughout the country had no alternative but to default on these exorbitant rents. In Kwa Mashu, for example, over £45,000 in rent arrears was owed by Africans (over 80 per cent of the township population), and 53 per cent of Indian families in Merebank were behind in their payments. Instead of adjusting rents to reasonable levels based on the ability to pay, the local authorities resorted to the brutal practice of invoking Section 38 (3) (p) of the Native Urban Areas Act which allowed for criminal prosecution of rent defaulters.

The Johannesburg City Council became the most notorious local administration to make criminals out of poverty-stricken African tenants. In early morning raids, police would enter the townships and after a sufficient number of defaulters were rounded up, they would be put in jail, held there for 1 to 2 days and then taken before the local Magistrate's Court for trial. Sentences ranged from 5s. for an admission of guilt to £2 or two weeks in jail. For the thousands who were forced to choose jail, jobs were lost making rent arrears even higher, workers were re-imprisoned, families evicted and personal possessions sold by the City Council to cover the cost of rents owed. The families would then, in most cases, be 'endorsed out' of the urban areas, either to starve in the reserves or become slave labour on the farms.[10]

Many of those prosecuted by the City Council were among township residents who refused to pay rent increases when the transition to 'economic' rents was made; over 2,000 also refused to fill out Council questionnaires regarding family incomes. The Council then merely assumed incomes of £20 per month, charged 'economic' rents and prosecuted with abandon all defaulters. Most nonsensical of all was the practice of making defaulters pay fines that did not apply towards the rent arrears, thus having the effect of increasing indebtedness. Or, on other occasions, defaulters would be given a six-month period in which to pay, and if payments were late or missed, the tenant would be put in jail for six months for contempt of court. Also, persons found innocent in rent arrears cases were still forced to pay the cost of the summons. As a *Workers Unity* article put it in 1961, 'for city councils to persist in this attitude is sheer economic exploitation'.[11]

Although the Johannesburg City Council defended its victimization in narrow legalistic and economic terms, the fact was that low wages paid to its 20,000 Council workers created the very poverty that made rents impossible to pay. Approximately 10,000 of these workers received less than £13 per month, and 87 per cent received less than enough to meet the SAIRR minimum subsistence budget. In some jobs, City employees were paid only 50 per cent the average wage given by private employers. With this high basic rental rate, plus court fines for arrears, many tenants were spending up to one-third of their incomes on rent-related costs. For the Council, however, prosecution was lucrative as an estimated £38,000 came from rent arrear payments not credited

Johannesburg dustmen spend their working lives chasing the White lorry-drivers who never stop. Their life expectancy is 37 years

against the original unpaid rents. If one considers that in at least one month in every year, the mandatory lump-sum deduction of £2 for the African poll tax is taken out of wages by employers, it is no surprise that almost all township residents would be in rent arrears at one time or another. Understandably, parasitic money-lenders lost no opportunity in further exploiting African workers as they waited outside the factory gates. As Phyllis Altman, SACTU Assistant General Secretary, concluded in 1962:

The African workers live in a nightmare of debt, fines and imprisonment. They walk a tight-rope where one unanticipated event (such as the death of a parent in a rural area, involving travelling or funeral expenses) throws their budget out and they are immediately in arrears with their rent.[12]

In response to these deplorable situations in Johannesburg, the Wits LC and SACTU Head Office took the initiative on behalf of township residents. A high profile publicity campaign exposing the Council's practices, coupled with mass meetings and demonstrations and the formation of Residents' Associations forced the City Council to curb the most excessive examples of victimization and criminal prosecution. For example, the Council was forced to stop sending tenants 'final warnings' where no previous warnings had been issued; often the 'final warnings' reached the tenants after the date designated for payment and subsequent eviction.

The SACTU campaign operated at two levels. The most difficult but also most successful part entailed intervention on behalf of individual tenants. An estimated 90 per cent of rent defaulters earned between £3–4 per week. Desperate for assistance, these persons would be lined up at the SACTU office each morning, waiting to speak to Phyllis Altman and others about their respective situations. In almost every case where either SACTU or Residents' Associations challenged the Council, the summons against the individual was either withdrawn or satisfactory alternative arrangements made. In fact, Altman discovered later that the Council files of individuals assisted by SACTU were marked 'Don't arrest' or 'Don't jail'.

At a more general level, SACTU and other supportive groups campaigned for an end to criminal prosecutions, a reduction in rents and rents based on the type of accommodation rather than as a percentage of income. All of these demands were related to the demand for a general increase in the wages of African workers. A SACTU delegation met with the Johannesburg City Council, pointing out the crucial relationship between low wages and rent arrears. Other specific objections were made – for example, SACTU called for an end to the 'lodger's fee', whereby the Municipality could charge for children sixteen years or over living at home with their parents. The 1962 SACTU Annual Conference added new demands, which included the waiving of all arrears, a lowering of house rentals to 75 cents per room and a 50 per cent reduction in public transport costs.

Mounting pressure initiated by SACTU on the City Council led it in 1962 to agree to end criminal prosecutions, but only with the added counter-threat of increased evictions. The Council also proposed that employers automatically deduct 25 per cent of the wages for those workers in rent arrears, but SACTU and others vehemently objected to a scheme which would maintain high rents and in effect make the capitalist bosses 'rent collectors' for the City. As SACTU said in a press release:

The scheme will ensure that the City Council gets its rent and then the Africans will be free to starve on the rest of their salaries. There would of course be no problem with rent collections if the Africans were paid a living wage.

Yet the City Council resisted wage increases and voiced the old argument that increased 'efficiency, production and supervision of the African workforce' must precede wage hikes.

Other Local Committees in Durban, Kimberley, the Cape Western Province and Port Elizabeth took up the campaign in their respective areas. In Cape Town, the major focus was on the forced removal of Africans from the Western Cape; in Port Elizabeth, the LC presented a memorandum to the City Council opposing rent increases and high unemployment. Although Councils pretended to make special allowances for 'hardship' cases, unemployment was consistently rejected as the basis for 'hardship' exemptions. In Durban, the LC monitored the Kwa Mashu situation closely, as Kwa Mashu had been the new township where most Africans were forced to live after the violence in Cato Manor in 1959 (see Chapter 9). The high incidence of kwashiorkor, a malnutrition disease resulting from poverty, was linked to the low wage-high rent issue by SACTU activitists in Durban.

In conclusion, SACTU leaders considered the housing-rents campaign as one of the most effective ever waged. As with the £1-a-Day campaign, the demand for lower rents and better housing emerged from the objective needs of the people. Both were clearly the consequences of class exploitation under Apartheid. It must also be kept in mind that these non-wage campaigns discussed in this chapter were conducted most enthusiastically during the early 1960s when state repression reached its peak. Even in the final moments of above-ground activity, SACTU never failed to base its campaigns and goals on the needs and aspirations of the South African working class.

NOTES

1. Quoted in *Workers Unity*, February–October 1962.
2. *Workers Unity*, October–November 1957.
3. *Workers Unity*, February–October 1962.
4. *Workers Unity*, November 1961–January 1962.
5. *New Age*, various issues, 1961; interview, Stephen Dlamini.
6. Interview, Stephen Dlamini.
7. Interview, Alven Bennie.
8. SACTU Memorandum on Rents and Criminal Prosecutions for Rent Arrears, presented to Johannesburg City Council, 8 December 1961.
9. Interview, Harry Loots.
10. P. Altman, 'The Rents Scandal', *Workers Unity*, November 1961–January 1962.
11. *Workers Unity, 1961.*
12. P. Altman, op. cit.

8 STRIKES AND INDUSTRIAL ACTIONS

... A strike teaches workers to understand what the strength of the employers and what the strength of the workers consist in: it teaches them not to think of their own employers alone and not of their own immediate workmates alone, but of all the employers, the whole class of capitalists and the whole class of workers. . . .

A strike, moreover, opens the eyes of the workers to the nature, not only of the capitalists, but of government and the laws as well. . . . Strikes, therefore, teach the workers to unite; they show them that they can struggle against the capitalist only when they are united; strikes teach the workers to think of the whole working-class against the whole class of factory owners and against the arbitrary police and government. This is the reason that socialists call strikes 'a school of war', a school in which the workers learn to make war on their enemies for the liberation of the whole people, of all who labour, from the yoke of government, officials and from the yoke of capital.

V. I. Lenin, *Collected Works*, vol. IV (1960), pp. 315–17.

Despite continuous attempts by the South African ruling class to suppress and contain the forward movement of the African working class, history has demonstrated the futility of their tactics. Since African workers were first incorporated into the economy as a cheap labour force they have waged industrial strikes and taken various forms of political action against their objective exploitation.

The 1946 African Mine Workers' strike had so threatened the structure of the total society and the profits of capital, that the state was forced to introduce further repressive measures to curb the militancy of African workers. The Suppression of Communism Act of 1950, designed in part to weaken the trade union movement, had robbed the working class of 56 dedicated trade unionists, seventeen of them Africans. However, as already shown, it was the Native Labour (Settlement of Disputes) Act of 1953, a vicious piece of anti-worker legislation, which was specifically designed to crush the rising tide of militancy among African workers and prevent the growth of African trade unions. Despite the fact that this Act rendered all strikes by African workers illegal, the workers continued to defy the legislation, never giving up their most vital weapon in the struggle against the ruling class – the right to withdraw their collective labour-power.

African workers have never been passive victims of exploitation. There is no better example of their refusal to acquiesce to the new legislation than the strikes which took place in Durban, only months after the Act became law. On 8 July 1954, 340 African workers at United Tobacco Company (UTC) took decisive strike action to achieve their demands.

Workers downed tools after management had refused to recognize the Union and the workers' demands that their wages and conditions be raised to the level of Cape Town tobacco workers. Refusing to make use of the new machinery created by the Native Labour Act, strikers were immediately harassed and intimidated. Twenty leaders were arrested and charged under the Act. As well, the Native Administration instructed all pass registration offices in Durban not to renew the permits of any African worker who had participated in the strike and lists of UTC workers were circulated to other companies. UTC dismissed the entire African workforce, some 1,360 workers, intimating that they could re-apply for their jobs. Management then expected that they would return to work and submit to the company's conditions. The strikers refused and were immediately replaced by scab labour, heavily protected by the police. The Secretary of the Union was fined £100 or 6 months hard labour (suspended for three years) and one other strike leader was fined £25 or 3 months hard labour, plus 6 months hard labour suspended for three years. All the remaining accused were fined £5 or one month hard labour.

In response to a Tobacco Workers' Union appeal, the ANC, the SAIC and the COD called for a total boycott of UTC products. This demonstration of solidarity with the victimized workers was highly successful and UTC suffered heavy losses. However, the strikers themselves were hit hard, unable to find jobs because of the blacklist. The combined forces of the state and the employers were used against these fearless workers and the provisions of the Native Labour Act were being tested on them, as a deterrent not only for them but for those African workers contemplating strike action in the future.

In another strike by African workers at Natal Cotton Spinners during this period, a similar resistance to the Native Labour Act was displayed. *New Age* reported at the time that these were 'not the usual, isolated, spontaneous outbursts of exasperated workers, but a manifestation of the African workers' realization of the need for unity, solidarity and trade union organization'. This had frightened the government, the article went on, because the initiatives had come 'straight from the factory'.[1]

In spite of the Native Labour Act, there were some 435 strikes by African workers during the period from 1954 to 1960, and only ten Works Committees set up under the Act were functioning by 1960. Thousands of workers were prosecuted and fined or imprisoned. This in itself indicates that the workers were not deterred by the punitive legislation enacted by the state and were determined to use the strike weapon as one of the means by which to challenge the basis of their exploitation.

From 1955 onwards, SACTU and its affiliated unions continued to encourage African workers to boycott the machinery of the Native Labour Act. The organization supported the use of the strike weapon by all workers, Black or White, in their attempts to gain legitimate working class demands. The industrial strike, though representing only a partial challenge to the capitalist system, was none the less recognized as an important attack on the basis of that system – the control and exploitation of labour power.

An analysis of strike activity during the SACTU year shows that between 1955 and 1957 there was a considerable upsurge in the number of strikes by African workers (see table on page 276). After 1957, there was a downturn in activity, perhaps due to the fact that many new wage determinations for unskilled workers were introduced in the years following. Increasing African unemployment, coupled with a sluggish economy, may also have had a deterrent effect on strike activity.

Because of the nature of state repression in South Africa, issues involved in any single strike can easily be connected with the struggle against the whole social order, the entire ruling class, and are not restricted to the individual employer. African workers are faced with a united front of government and employers, backed by the power of the police. State repression via racist anti-worker legislation, police and Special Branch harassment, employers' victimization and intimidation, the Pass Laws and other controls imposed on the freedom of mobility – all of these combined made it impossible for the African worker not to appreciate the whole basis of his/her exploitation and to comprehend in its entirety the social system he/she was part of.

Leon Levy, past President of SACTU, likened strikes by Black workers in South Africa to 'small scale civil wars' with 'lorry-loads of police, armed with batons, sten-guns and tear-gas bombs', where 'great

Strikes in South Africa, 1950–1961

Year	Total strikes	Strikes by White workers Number	Strikes by White workers Participants	Strikes by Black workers Number	Strikes by Black workers Participants	Number Black strikes with Prosecutions
1950	33	8	878	25	2,399	10 (40%)
1951	36	5	790	31	7,204	4 (13%)
1952	54	6	496	48	5,963	12 (25%)
1953	30	7	819	23	1,479	15 (75%)
1954	60	21	1,096	39	4,618	22 (57%)
1955	102	20	384	82	9,479	22 (25%)
1956	105	13	409	92	6,428	21 (22%)
1957	119	6	664	113	6,158	20 (17%)
1958	74	10	650	64	7,128	23 (36%)
1959	46	3	99	43	3,462	27 (63%)
1960	42	9	234	33	5,266	figures not given
1961	81	5	—	75	4,662	figures not given

Source: Department of Labour, official year-end reports.

pick-up vans arrive and all the strikers are arrested'.[2] All strikes supported by SACTU whether for higher wages and improved working conditions, union recognition or reinstatement of unjustly dismissed workers, were met with the full force of the state. Their strikes were most definitely 'schools of war'.

An analysis of some of the strikes to which SACTU gave organizational support between 1955 and 1964 follows. The purpose is not to assess the effectiveness of the organization on the basis of its quantitative strike record, but rather to examine the nature and dynamics of class struggle at the point of production, that is, to analyse the extent of class consciousness and potential for revolutionary action on the part of workers, and to study the responses of capital and the extent of state intervention in each case.

Strikes by Migrant Workers

The migrant labour system in South Africa, besides restricting the freedom of mobility of the worker and his family, creates additional difficulties within the field of trade union organizing. Migrant workers, circulating between wage-labour and the reserves, do not represent a stable and permanent labour force. However, the history of their involvement in both industrial actions and political protests over the years, has revealed that these workers, despite the disabilities forced upon them, do possess an advanced proletarian consciousness, perhaps even fostered by the system of controlled barracks and compounds. An analysis of the struggles of dockworkers in South Africa illustrates this well.

In Durban, there had been a long history of resistance by the dockers, who refer to themselves as '*oNyathi*' (meaning 'buffalo' in Zulu). In 1930, they led struggles against the poll tax, against the passes (culminating in the death of Johannes Nkosi) and against the institution of a municipal monopoly in beer-brewing. These workers continued to carry out strikes and other actions throughout the 1940s, a period of intense conflict in Durban.

In 1954, in defiance of the Native Labour Act, 1,167 stevedores struck for seven days in support of a demand for an increase in their daily wage from 10s. 3d. to 15s. They were forced to return to work after being threatened with ejection from the employer-owned compounds. The Native Labour Board granted workers a 1s. 3d. a day increase but at the same time charged workers with striking illegally. Ninety-five were found guilty and fined 10s. each.

Appalling working conditions . . .

. . . create militant African trade unions. African Milling Workers Union, Transvaal

The major issue in the struggles of Durban dockworkers in the mid-1950s was the *togt* labour system. Migrant workers were paid on a daily basis in the Durban docks; when ships were in the harbour there was work for them and they were paid by their employers. However, the system offered no security and workers could not rely on any kind of regular income. Early in 1956, dockers went out on strike, and included the elimination of the *togt* system as one of their demands. They wanted monthly contracts to ensure a regular income. In November 1956, workers struck once more. Employers had placed a small group of workers on permanent staff, with two weeks' annual leave. However, in the process they cut down the rates of pay of these permanent employees, leading to a sympathy strike by the remainder of the workers. All workers were demanding to be paid on a monthly basis but at least at the same rate of pay as they were receiving as *togt* labourers.

The elimination of the *togt* labour system of casual labour and its replacement with a contract labour system would actually enable the employers and the state to exert a more direct control over the workers. Under the old system, if labourers decided for any reason not to work on a particular day, there was little that could be done in terms of the law except deportation from the urban area. The introduction of the contract labour system meant that workers would be liable to prosecution for any breach of contract. Therefore, the workers were in a very difficult position; they had a choice between two different forms of super-exploitation.

In November 1957, the Minister of Native Affairs, Dr H. F. Verwoerd announced his intention to remove most of the stevedoring compounds in the Point Dock area, and allow only 2,000 African stevedores in the area. While the government and employers were discussing the merits of this policy, the workers themselves were preparing to take action in support of the SACTU/Congress Alliance call for a 3-day Stay-At-Home beginning 14 April 1958. For various reasons, the Stay-At-Home was not successful throughout the country (see Chapter 10). However, in Durban the dockers boldly displayed their militancy and embarked on an important struggle against stevedoring companies.

Seventy-five per cent of dockworkers went home during the Stay-At-Home and those who remained were forced out of the privately-owned compounds by the police. Nevertheless, they struck at work, demanding £1-a-Day. These workers refused to do any overtime work until their comrades returned and when they did, all workers unanimously decided to do no more overtime work until they were paid £1-a-Day. The harbour was congested and by Sunday, 27 May, over twenty-five ships lay idle in port. On that day, no workers reported for work, increasing pressure on the employers. Finally a settlement was reached which brought their wages up to 14s. per day, with other increases granted as well.

After the 1958 actions, a meeting of employers and government representatives decided to eliminate the *togt* labour system and establish a centrally-administered compound system, designed for greater control over the labour force. As part of this system, an attempt was made to incorporate *indunas* (African foremen) more effectively into the structure of authority of the stevedoring companies. These *indunas* had previously performed certain responsibilities like recruiting and marshalling workers in particular gangs, which would now be performed by the labour supply company in a centrally-run compound system. Their new tasks were those of 'sergeant-majors' of the company and they were to receive substantial wage increases of 4s. a day. This sparked off industrial action again in February 1959.

The workers had expected more from the Wage Board which sat during 1958. The SACTU Durban Local Committee had given evidence before the Board and had requested a substantial increase in wages, that the workers be put on a weekly-paid basis and urged the Board to improve their working conditions. The strike broke out on 24 February when it was clear that there would be no increase for labourers and a 4s. increase for the *indunas*. By 25 February, 1,500 labourers were out, once again crippling the harbour. Rather than negotiate with the workers, the employers, the Department of Labour and the police went ahead with the plan to force the labour supply company on the workers. All strikers were dismissed and ordered to leave the premises of the company compounds. A strong detachment of police arrived and immediately began attacking those in the vicinity with their batons. Several workers were seriously injured and 87 were arrested following this incident.

The companies took advantage of the strike to introduce the labour supply company. All workers were re-engaged on a weekly-paid basis. SACTU initially considered this an advance in their conditions of employment.

Togt labour has long been a source of friction between the workers and the employers, and the introduction of a weekly-paid permanent labour force is a definite gain by the workers.... With the establishment of a permanent labour force it will now be possible to organize the workers into a union and we hope that the employers will negotiate with this union and avoid any further trouble in the docks.[3]

However, the low wage offered (£3 per week) was rejected by the workers. Arguing that they could earn more under the previous system if work were made available throughout the week (potentially 84s.), the men demanded increased wages and refused to work overtime. The workers put their case in this way:

The employers want to kill us with overtime. In the past we used to take off a day or two whenever we felt tired, but now that we are employed on a weekly basis we could not do this. We feel that more workers should be employed by the stevedoring companies and at the same time we should be paid a decent wage for the hard work we do.[4]

The brutal response of the employers was to dismiss the entire labour force and recruit new workers from Zululand to take their place. The workers had correctly recognized and resisted the employers' attempts to increase their control over the workers' labour time. But the combined forces of the state and the employers were used to crush this resistance and the workers were defenceless.

Port Elizabeth was the scene of another fierce struggle carried out by railway and dockworkers. For a long time these workers had demanded increased wages, but their demands had been brushed aside. At the beginning of 1957, the workers embarked on a go-slow strike to draw attention to their plight. On 26 February, they decided to start work one hour later and stop one hour earlier and not to work overtime or on weekends, in support of their demands for a wage increase from 11s. 6d. per day to 25s. per day. Railway workers joined the dockworkers, demanding an increase from the present £4 10s. 0d. a month to £7.

The railway officials and shipping companies called on the state for assistance and the full range of its resources were mobilized to defeat the workers' actions. In addition to the normal representation by the Labour Bureau, the Department of Native Affairs officials, police and Special Branch, the army was called in and placed on standby orders. Stevedores were shipped in from Cape Town and East London by the companies. According to reports, these workers were told there was another bus and train boycott in progress making it impossible for Port Elizabeth stevedores to go to work. Armed police guarded the ships ensuring that there was no contact with the strikers. Govan Mbeki reported from Port Elizabeth at the time:

From March 2nd to 7th the harbour looked like a city which had recently been occupied by a foreign invading army. The armed might of a Government that regards African labour as the possession of a dominant white capitalist class strutted about in a great show of strength.[5]

The stevedores returned to work on Monday, 4 March, but the shipping companies were only prepared to allow them to resume work if they surrendered unconditionally and dropped their demands. Workers refused and were swiftly marched out of the harbour.

As they left, hundreds of barefooted convicts flooded into the harbour, driven at the point of a rifle to load manganese and to handle cargo in conditions that were not any better than those in which the slave drivers' whip cracked on the backs of slaves two centuries ago.[6]

On 5 March, railway workers were locked out and replaced by prison labour. A recruitment drive brought in workers endorsed out of major cities (with promises that their documents would be placed in order if they agreed to work in Port Elizabeth) and also large numbers from the Transkei and the Ciskei where food production had fallen. By the joint actions of the railway authorities, shipping companies, the police force, the army and the influx control measures, the essential flow of goods was not interrupted by a shortage of cheap labour.

Militant leaders like Vuyisile Mini, Caleb Mayekiso and Alven Bennie led the campaign to support the harbour workers within the SACTU Local Committee. SACTU appealed to the international working class to denounce the use of convict labour and the ICFTU took the lead in issuing a warning to the South African regime. Within hours, Minister of Labour Schoeman conceded, ordering a ban on convict labour at the docks. The workers decided that since convicts were being withdrawn they should return to work to forestall the engagement of labour recruited in the Transkei and Ciskei. The companies were clearly in a stronger bargaining position with the state ensuring them a large army of surplus labour.

Stevedores were accepted back because they were relatively skilled and would ensure greater efficiency at the docks. The unskilled railway workers however were dismissed, their work-seeker permits withdrawn, and their reference books left unsigned as a means of punishment. The re-employed stevedores were subsequently paid at the rate of railway casuals, 9s. 6d. for married men and 7s. for single men, thereby cutting the workers' wages by between 2s. and 4s. 6d. per day.

From both accounts of the struggles of dockworkers in South Africa certain conclusions can be drawn. The collective action amongst African migrant workers on the docks is an indication of their disregard for the system which attempts to control their movements and stifle their militancy. In both cases, these workers acted in complete unity against insurmountable odds. However, in such a strategic sector of the economy, it was inevitable that the full power of the state was brought in to crush their resistance. The state's role, though a secondary one to that of individual capitalist companies, nevertheless renders their action against the working class that much more effective.

In both cases the workers gained invaluable experience as to the nature of capitalism and the role of the state, experience which they were able to use in assisting workers involved in future struggles in other industries. These workers were a powerful influence within SACTU and injected local committees with the same class consciousness and militant spirit with which they had carried out their own struggles.

Non-Racial Trade Unionism

In the South African context, it was a courageous act on the part of African workers to carry out a strike in defiance of the Native Labour Act. It was an even more courageous act in many cases to come out on strike with workers of other races, whether Coloured, Indian or White. Yet there are numerous examples of strikes which embodied this kind of non-racial unity.

'I WANTED TO SUPPORT MY COLOURED BROTHERS' – SPEKENHAM AFRICAN STRIKERS SENTENCED (CAPE TOWN). That was the headline of a *New Age* article which appeared in the 10 October 1957 edition, reporting on a strike by some 200 workers at Spekenham Food Products factory, Strikland, Cape Town; the workers' demands were for increased wages and better working conditions. The solidarity between the African and Coloured workers was a key factor throughout the four-week strike. All members of the FCWU and the A-FCWU were demanding at least £1-a-Day in line with the demand put forward by SACTU throughout the country. On the first day of the strike, twenty-seven African workers were arrested for contravening the Native Labour Act and several days later four Coloured workers were arrested for allegedly interfering with scabs trying to get to work.

Since 1953, these workers had not received an increase in the cost-of-living-allowance (COLA) and were out to convince employers that they could not live on their existing wages. Their bosses responded by sacking the striking workers, claiming that they would be able to recruit sufficient scab labour to carry on production. In fact, they found it very difficult.

The non-racial unity demonstrated by strikers was followed up by the four Congresses jointly sending a deputation to see management to re-open negotiations with the workers.

We feel that the unfavourable conditions under which these employees were forced to work, the totally inadequate wages paid, left them no alternative but this action, when their employer refused to make any concessions to their demands for improvements. We wholeheartedly support the demands of these workers.

Signed by: Z. Malindi (ANC)
N. Daniels (SACPO)
D. Goldberg (COD)
L. Kellerman (SACTU)[7]

The FCWU provided strike pay and food donations to the strikers throughout.

At the trial of the twenty-seven African workers charged under the Native Labour Act, these workers told how when they first arrived at work and found Coloured workers outside the gates, they decided to stand by them. One worker said,

I didn't hope to gain anything for myself. The reason I didn't go to work was that I wanted to support my Coloured brother workers who were on strike.[8]

The Magistrate rejected these statements by African workers. They were found guilty and sentenced to a fine of £7 10s. 0d. each, or thirty days' imprisonment. Though the workers did not win immediate gains through their strike action, a Wage Determination was soon granted and their COLA increased.

This kind of unity was not uncommon between members of the FCWU and the A-FCWU who worked closely together on every issue affecting their general memberships. The same comradeship existed between the TWIU and the A-TWIU.

In March 1956, 1,200 workers staged one of the most successful strikes in the history of textile workers' struggles. The strike began on 12 March, when 900 Coloured workers walked out of Hex River Textile Mills, Western Cape. At this stage African workers remained at their jobs for fear of prosecution under the Native Labour Act and they were supported by Coloured workers in this stand. However, when a notice appeared on the factory gate advertising 900 vacancies, African workers walked out in solidarity. As predicted, these 242 African workers were rounded up by the police and taken to jail. The next day all workers were released on £3 bail, except three leaders – Joe Ndamoyi, Julius Busa and Kopie Baartman. Local Worcester residents showed their support for the workers by raising a large amount of money for the strike fund.

After four days of strike action, workers gained substantial increases in their wages as well as additional benefits. These included free overalls, the establishment of a sick benefit fund, the agreement to establish an Industrial Council for the worsted section of the industry, and the reinstatement of all workers was guaranteed. In short, by uniting as a strong force against the employers, these Coloured and African textile workers scored a victory for all workers at Hex River Textile Mills.

In another similar display of unity, 200 African male workers employed at a woolwashery in Durban went out on strike in support of twelve Indian women workers in 1959. Their employer, O. T. H. Beiers (who had been interned in South Africa during the war for pro-Nazi sympathies) owned a farm where he reared chickens, in addition to owning two factories. He slaughtered these chickens to sell to ships passing through the Durban harbour.

If Beiers failed to get rid of all of his chickens, he usually forced them upon his elderly women workers, deducting whatever price he demanded from their wages. These twelve women, all widows, were already heavily exploited by Beiers and were barely able to feed themselves and their families from the miserable wages they were paid.

Both groups of workers, the African men and the Indian women, had joined the A-TWIU in Durban only months before the strike. These twelve women, now knowing the union would support them, decided to inform their employer that they did not wish to buy his fowls. As a result Beiers dismissed the women and immediately the 200 African workers rose to support them. Assembling outside the factory gates on Monday morning in their national Zulu dress of beautiful bead and leatherwork, these men demanded that Beiers come and address them on the matter of the women's dismissal.

Melville Fletcher, the union organizer, was called in by the workers. Beiers still refused to reinstate the women and instructed Fletcher to remove all workers from the premises, in fact creating a lockout. The workers then marched to the trade union offices and Beiers informed the Labour Department that his workers were on strike. Neither the employer nor the workers were prosecuted for an illegal lockout or strike.

Strikers mingled with passers-by persuading work-seekers not to enter the factory. On weekends they explained the reasons for the strike to unemployed Africans in the Zulu 'homelands' requesting them not to accept work there. As a result of their perseverance, there were no scabs recruited. Textile workers in England sent a cable of support to the A-TWIU and Southampton dockers cabled Beiers threatening not to unload any ship carrying his wool.

After two weeks, the Municipality threatened to throw the African strikers out of the Municipal barracks and endorse them back to the homelands. The workers and the Union considered that the lesser of the two evils was to accept the employer's offer to reinstate them at a higher pay-rate. The employer refused to reinstate the women but the Union found other higher-paying work for them as well. All of the men returned to work singing their Zulu folk songs, united and strong as members of the Union.[9]

These are just a few examples of the kind of unity displayed by workers in South Africa who refused to accept the racial division of the workforce. For African workers in particular it was always a considerable risk to take. Such examples illustrate the level of working class consciousness attained by workers in SACTU-affiliated unions. True to the principles upon which SACTU was founded, they pursued a policy of unity amongst all sections of the working class and solidarity of all workers in their struggle against the South African ruling class.

A Tradition of Militancy

The strike by 3,800 African textile workers at Amato Textile Mills, Benoni (Transvaal) during February 1958, illustrates the conditions under which the state takes the lead in repression against the working class. The primary condition for such intervention is a long tradition of militancy on the part of the workers in a particular factory. A point is then reached when it becomes essential that all the power of the state be used to crush the unity and solidarity formed in the course of progressive struggles. This is exactly what happened at Amato Textile Mills, a large jute manufacturing company, in 1958.

Almost 4,400 African workers were employed at the factory and these workers provided the backbone of the A-TWIU in the Transvaal.

Wages were extremely low (£3 a week), barely enough to allow a worker and his family to survive. The workers' transport costs had also risen since they had been forcibly removed beyond the city limits to Daveyton and Watville and their rent trebled in the process. Wages had not been increased since 1951.

At Amato there was an interesting mixture of very young, militant African workers and older, more experienced trade unionists. Together they had carried out many strikes and through these had gained a Medical Benefit Fund as well as other benefits. Union dues were collected by the employer as a concession to the A-TWIU. The introduction of the Native Labour Act did not deter these workers and in December 1956, 365 workers stopped work when a foreman dismissed two fellow workers. They were all charged with striking illegally and of the 365, 202 were found guilty.

In February 1958, workers went out again to demand higher wages. Management refused to consider any increases for the workers and the Native Labour Board officials refused to allow direct talks between the A-TWIU and the employer. The militant workers were ready to take action and many of them talked of burning the factory to the ground. Union leaders Edmund Cindi (Chairman of the Benoni A-TWIU branch) and Rufus Makuru (National President of the Union) persuaded workers to go home. When they returned to work they were prevented from entering the factory by armed police. The following day when workers came to collect their pay, an unprovoked baton charge took place injuring over forty workers. Eye-witnesses described the scene as a brutal and totally unexpected attack.

All workers were dismissed and told if they required jobs to report to Influx Control and the Native Affairs Department. By a combined effort on the part of employers and the state, some 340 militants were black-listed, with their employment possibilities blocked through influx control regulations. Strike leaders were among the dismissed and many of them were endorsed out of the urban areas or banished to the reserves where in most cases they had never set foot before. Unemployed activists who avoided being endorsed out lost their township accommodation as soon as they failed to pay the rent. This was a heavy blow to the organizational strength of the A-TWIU. Although the workers' militant spirit had not been crushed by these repressive measures, the mass strike action characteristic of Amato workers ceased to exist for some time.

In this case, the intervention of the state was direct and included physical force against the workers. As a consequence, workers were defenceless after having lost the right even to sell their only possession — their labour-power. SACTU passed a resolution at its 1958 Conference demanding that the victimized workers be reinstated and all Union facilities restored; a nation-wide boycott of Amato products was threatened if these demands were not met. However, this threat failed to materialize and the solidarity of Amato workers was fragmented and destroyed.

Resistance to Super-Exploitation

Without effective trade union organization, workers are without weapons in the struggle. SACTU and its affiliated unions realized this above all else. Only by organizing workers into strong trade unions could workers prevent their bosses from reaping even greater profits from the exploitation of their labour-power.

In 1956, as reported in an earlier chapter, the head of the Central Native Labour Board publicly stated that Africans were 'too childish' to understand trade unions. Militant food workers who resisted wage cuts in their industry proved the lie to such racist and paternalistic rhetoric.

In November 1959, management at LKB in Port Elizabeth informed workers that from then on they would be paid according to the scale of wages laid down in Wage Determination No. 179, issued by the Wage Board in August of the previous year. These wage rates were lower than those already in effect under the agreement between the trade union and the employer.

LKB was the biggest canning concern in South Africa and the company's plans were to extend these wage cuts to all other branches, thus drastically affecting the lives of thousands of Black workers. Canning workers were already bitter about other recent attacks on their union by the employers and the state. During the previous session of parliament, legislation had been passed depriving workers in the food and canning industry of the right to strike. Recently too, Frances Baard, local Secretary of the Union branch, had been refused permission to collect subscriptions on factory premises and company officials had refused to cooperate with one of the Union's committees. Lastly, A-FCWU President, Elizabeth Mafekeng, was driven into exile only weeks before.

Workers refused to accept the Wage Board agreement which would mean nearly 16 per cent reduction in wages. Management told them to leave the factory and return the following day at 2.00 p.m. to collect their wages. The time cards of over 1,000 African and Coloured workers were taken and a lockout was in effect.

Liz Abrahams, Acting General Secretary of FCWU, issued a statement to the employers warning of solidarity actions: 'Food and canning workers all over the country are carefully watching the fruit as it comes into their factories and will refuse to work fruit from P.E.'[10] LKB was originally one of the firms on the Congress Alliance boycott list of the early 1950s (see Chapter 10), but after granting some concessions its name was removed. There was strong pressure from workers to request Congress to re-include LKB on the list in 1959.

African and Coloured workers remained strong and their bosses were noticeably worried about the dismal failure of their 'stay out of the factory' order. They had also failed to fill the factory with alternative labour. LKB workers were united in their opposition to starvation wages and refused all attempts to induce them to return to work.

Finally, the unity of the workers paid off. One month after the original declaration by management, the Chairman of the Board of Directors, Mr R. S. Ferreira, announced that LKB would not be introducing the new Wage Determination but would instead pay workers 'a bonus' to enable them to maintain the existing pay rates. He said this decision had been taken because LKB wanted a 'contented labour force' [sic]. The bosses' attempt to increase the rate of exploitation had been stopped.

The jubilant workers returned to the factory victorious after having won an important struggle. Their success against these savage attacks on their living standards clearly resulted from the strength of the Union and the unity of all workers.

The Verwoerd plan for the establishment of 'border industries' to make better use of readily-available cheap, Black labour from the reserves, led to the setting up of the Hammarsdale Clothing Factory in Hammarsdale, twenty-seven miles from Durban. It was one of the first examples of the border industry developments discussed in Chapter 4.

Employers at Hammarsdale did not expect the resistance that they encountered from the African workforce who refused to accept the conditions of exploitation imposed on them. In February 1959, 388 African workers walked out of the factory in support of a demand for increased wages. The workers were angered when they were told that the present owners had shut down their factories in Fordsburg and Durban to come to Hammarsdale where labour-power had been promised at a lower rate. After an agreement was concluded between employers and workers' representatives, the labour force returned to the factory. Agreement was also reached on other outstanding issues: (a) full recognition of the African Clothing Workers Union (Hammarsdale); (b) negotiations to be held before April 1960 for improvements in wages and working conditions; and (c) officials to be allowed to use the factory cloakroom for all trade union meetings.

However, due to the disruptive tactics of J. C. Bolton, Secretary of the Garment Workers Union (Natal), in his effort to smash the ACWU (a SACTU affiliate) workers were forced to resort to strike action again in February 1960. Chairman of the ACWU, Johannes Hlongwana, had approached management with a proposal to meet the Union's executive to discuss the question of wage increases as set down in the previous agreement. Management refused to deal with Hlongwana, instead labelling him an 'agitator', and then said that the only people they would negotiate with were 'Jimmy Bolton's union' from Durban and the Industrial Council for the Garment Workers.

When this was reported to the workers, the whole factory of over 500 workers walked out. They demanded that both Billy Nair (their Secretary) and Moses Mabhida (Chairman, SACTU-Natal) be present at all negotiations on their behalf. The employer eventually agreed to this but only on the condition that Bolton also be present; he further charged that the present committee of the Union did not represent the workers and that a new ballot to be conducted by Bolton had to be arranged. Apparently Bolton and the Industrial Council had agreed to certain wage increases which would bring wages of beginning workers up to £1 7s. 9d. per week. SACTU stated that Bolton had no right to interfere with the African workers at Hammarsdale, workers who were demanding £3 5s. 0d. per week.

The strike continued and 137 African workers were arrested under the Native Labour Act, including members of the Union committee. SACTU appealed to all workers to assist the Hammarsdale strikers, and people living in the surrounding area rallied a great deal of support. As a result of the strike the clothing factory was closed down and the proprietor decided to move back to Durban. The workers stood firm against the threats and intimidation of the bosses and the White trade union leaders who collaborated with them in an attempt to break the Union. Eventually this solidarity led to a resounding victory as the employer subsequently reopened the factory on terms acceptable to the ACWU and its members. Workers won their demands for the recognition of their trade union and the guarantee of increased wages from the 1st of April. The only unsatisfactory outcome was that the employers refused to reinstate the Chairman of the Union, Hlongwana. After several meetings with the workers, Union officials agreed to accept this condition of the settlement; immediately afterwards at a general meeting of workers Hlongwana was appointed full-time organizer of the Union.

The agreement concluded was also a defeat for Bolton and the Natal GWU, a Union notorious for betraying the interests of the workers and making 'sweetheart deals' with the employers. It was, however, a solid victory for the African workers at Hammarsdale in their struggle against below-subsistence wages. Even in the border industry areas, the ruling class could be defeated.

Strikes Initiated by New SACTU Unions

Most of the above examples involved established unions like the TWIU and the FCWU, strong and militant unions which had a history of strike actions by their members. In the course of SACTU's organizing campaigns, several new African unions were organized, in many cases by workers who had immediate grievances which they wanted settled. Some of the examples of strikes carried out by these newly-formed unions demonstrate a fresh spontaneity and surprising willingness to carry out sustained opposition to conditions imposed on them by the bosses.

The strike by Bay Transport Company workers of Port Elizabeth was one of the major disputes of 1961, and is of significance in that the Native Labour Act officials were by-passed by both the employers and the workers. It is also significant because four years after the strike, in December 1965, ten African workers were sentenced to four and a half years' imprisonment for having 'furthered the aims of the banned African National Congress' by taking part in the 1961 strike.

Alven Bennie and other members of the Port Elizabeth Local Committee had been actively organizing these workers into a union during 1960. The union was still very small when the workers themselves decided to take action. African bus drivers were dissatisfied with the one-man operation (which they had agreed to try for a trial period) and they claimed the Company had not honoured certain promises with regard to wages and other matters. The registered trade union had negotiated an agreement with the Port Elizabeth transport company to cover White and Coloured bus drivers, but it could not

Striking Amato textile workers brutally attacked by police, 1958

Port Elizabeth bus workers give their sign of solidarity during 1961 strike

represent the African workers at the bargaining table. The African drivers demanded that the agreement be extended to them and that they be guaranteed a minimum wage of £1 per day. (The banned ANC had supported the SACTU demand for minimum wage legislation.)

On 10 January 1961, the 194 workers informed management that if their demands were not met, the single-decker buses would remain at the depot and the double-deckers would 'go slow'. When demands were not subsequently met, the union members carried out their threat and the workers of New Brighton walked to work. The African drivers were arrested but were allowed out on bail. Although the Company operated a skeleton service during the strike, the Black population of Port Elizabeth boycotted the Bay Transport buses for 40 days, often walking twelve to twenty-eight miles to and from work – an outstanding demonstration of solidarity.

The Port Elizabeth SACTU Local Committee, actively involved in the strike throughout, protested against the recruitment of scab labour by the Company. At one mass meeting chaired by SACTU activist Vuyisile Mini, the workers adopted three significant resolutions, pledging:

(a) to use all available recognized means employed by workers throughout the democratic world to protect workers' rights;
(b) to wage an uncompromising struggle against the Native Labour Act; and
(c) to register the appreciation of the untiring efforts of the bus workers to resolve the bus dispute amicably in spite of the hostile attitude adopted by the representatives of capital.

Finally, because of the economic disruption caused by the boycott, the Mayor of Port Elizabeth, together with representatives of the local Chambers of Commerce and Industry, called both parties to a meeting. At no time during this historic meeting was there any indication that those present regarded the matter as anything other than an industrial dispute; the Mayor and his followers did not consider themselves to be involved in a discussion of 'subversive' activity. They were merely anxious to break the deadlock that had almost brought the city to a standstill.

An independent tribunal was set up after negotiations between the Company and the African drivers failed. The SACTU LC as well as Head Office assisted the workers in the nomination of their legal representative (progressive lawyer, Joe Slovo) and spokesperson (banned trade unionist, Ray Alexander). Ex-Chief Justice Centilivres chaired the tribunal and the case was given a fair hearing.

As a result of the tribunal's findings, the Company raised wages. The starting rate for African drivers was to be £7 13s. 2d. per week, rising to £9 18s. 6d. and those drivers who did the work of conductors on one-man buses were to be paid an additional 10s. per week. Like their White and Coloured fellow workers, they were to receive an annual bonus representing 3 per cent of their annual pay, they were to be issued with free protective clothing, and they were to be given the right to become members of the Sick Benefit Society. A new SACTU Union, the Bay Transport Company Workers Union was formed on a much stronger basis than its predecessor.

The workers had scored a significant victory, but one which they had to pay for three years later. By 1963, the state had launched a vicious attack on the progressive elements in the Eastern Cape, a traditional stronghold of the banned ANC. Over 1,000 people were arrested in the Port Elizabeth area, the majority forced to serve long prison sentences for having furthered the aims of the ANC after its banning.

Ten of the PE busmen, whose 1961 strike became 'subversive' in 1964, were also among the victims of Apartheid justice. During their trial, the defence brought three leading members of the ANC from Robben Island prison, where they were serving life sentences, to give evidence on behalf of the accused to the effect that their strike was in no way connected with the ANC. But the Magistrate ignored this evidence, concluding that the workers had 'danced to the tune of the ANC' and that by taking part in the strike they had furthered the aims of the banned organization.

The trial received little publicity and the ten workers were herded into prison quietly. Though their sentences were later reduced from the original four and a half years, this case represents a glaring example of the response of the South African ruling class to African workers who dare to challenge the system by demanding improved wages and working conditions through strike action. Upon release from prison, these men were further victimized by being sent out to the bantustans to rot.

In March 1961, 360 workers, members of a new SACTU affiliate, the Match Workers Union (Durban) staged a successful demonstration at the Lion Match Company, demanding higher wages. The police and the Labour Department tried to intervene but workers refused to speak to them. They won increased wages, a non-contributory pension scheme and a medical benefit fund.

In August of the same year, one of the trade union leaders was dismissed and the factory workers tried to send a deputation to the Manager in regard to his reinstatement. When this failed they held a lunch-hour demonstration with placards stating: 'NO DISMISSALS'; 'RECOGNIZE OUR UNION'; 'DEMAND £1 A DAY'; 'LOW WAGES BREED CRIME'; 'KWASHIORKOR IS KILLING US'. Police were called in and a convoy armed with sten guns arrived. Workers were told to stop demonstrating and their claims would be considered later, but they were not satisfied with this assurance. They were then given five minutes to disperse and 140 were arrested and later released on £5 bail. Of those 140, 136 were charged with an 'illegal strike' and fined £5 or ten days' hard labour. The Durban SACTU Local Committee spared no effort in attempting to negotiate with the management of the firm, but this was refused. Once again the full force of the state was used against the strikers. Though only recently organized into a union, they demonstrated their willingness to stand up to the bosses and government in pressing for trade union rights and a living wage.

In each of these examples of strike action taken by SACTU unions, one thing is common. Despite the restrictions imposed upon African workers even before contemplating strike action, each case has demonstrated the courage and commitment of those workers in their struggle against exploitation. Restrictions like the Native Labour Act and other punitive legislation, the operation of the Labour Bureaux established under this Act, and the threat of the industrial reserve army of unemployed labour being used by the state – all of these obstacles and more did not deter these workers from carrying out their collective strike actions.

Through these various actions these SACTU affiliated unions managed to gain some important concessions from the ruling class; consequently, they prevented an even greater rate of exploitation of themselves and their brothers and sisters in other industries and areas. They also gained for themselves and for other workers a stronger sense of class solidarity and heightened class consciousness. By conceiving of strike action as one method of attack on the whole exploitative system under South African capitalism, workers demonstrated that there is no power greater than the combined force of a united working class.

If, as Lenin said, each strike was a 'school of war' where workers learned more effective ways of carrying forward the struggle against their common enemy, then SACTU was one of the 'classrooms' in which they were taught. As a trade union coordinating body, its role in strike actions was a supportive and educative one. However, because of SACTU's belief in the importance, indeed the necessity, of linking economic with political struggle, the 'lessons' delivered to workers always centred on ways in which one individual strike could be connected to a whole network of broader issues central to the nature of the total society. Again, to quote Lenin:

> The struggle of factory workers against the employers inevitably turns into the struggle against the entire capitalist class, against the whole social order based on the exploitation of labour by capital.[11]

Learning, however, is a dialectical process. What the workers learned from SACTU was at every step along the path of struggle equally matched by the militant inspiration provided by the Black rank-and-file workers themselves.

NOTES

1. *New Age,* 9 September 1954.
2. Leon Levy, 'African Trade Unionism in South Africa', *Africa South in Exile*, London, vol. 5, no. 3, pp. 32–43.
3. *New Age,* 5 March 1959.
4. *New Age,* 9 April 1959.
5. *New Age,* 14 March 1957.
6. Ibid.
7. *New Age,* 5 September 1957.
8. *New Age,* 10 October 1957.
9. Information on this strike was taken from B. du Toit, op. cit.
10. *New Age,* 17 December 1959.
11. V. I. Lenin, *Collected Works*, vol. 2, Lawrence & Wishart, London, 1960, p. 107.

9 WOMEN PLAY A LEADING ROLE

When women massively become political the revolution has moved to a new stage.
Vietnamese Women, December 1970

'Wathin't a bafazi, way ithint' imbolodo uzo kufa'
(Now you have touched the women (Strydom), you have struck a rock, you have dislodged a boulder; you will be crushed).
a Freedom Song sung by South African
women protesting against the extension
of Pass Laws to African women, 1956

The Historical Roots of Oppression

The unprecedented militancy demonstrated by South African women during the 1950s advanced the liberation struggle significantly. However, to speak generally of South African women is to obscure the real importance of these bitter struggles. It is the African women in particular — those who suffer from both national and sexual oppression — who sacrificed most in the struggle against the South African state's definition of them as 'superfluous appendages' of African male workers.

African women workers have had a specific role to play. Exploited as workers, oppressed as Africans, they bear the additional burden of sexual inequalities. In South Africa, women provide another source of readily available cheap Black labour so necessary for the system to survive. Yet these women, whose consciousness has spanned several dimensions of oppression, played a crucial role in the advancement of the working class struggle spearheaded by SACTU.

Similarly, African women played a leading role in the general political struggle of the 1950s and 1960s. Specific campaigns led by the women were those which attacked the basis of their particular oppression. In their campaigns against the extension of pass laws to African women, against the government-sponsored beer halls and their attacks on the dipping tanks in the rural areas, the women represented a strong, united force to be reckoned with. Their strength and determination inspired the men who fought alongside them and they advanced the liberation struggle considerably during this period.

The origins of the oppression of African women in South Africa are similar to those which characterized all colonized nations during the plunder of previous centuries. Expropriation of tribal lands, slavery, forced labour, destruction of indigenous culture – these were the effects of the onslaught of colonialism on the people of Africa and elsewhere. Two aspects combined to define the particular form of oppression suffered by women in these societies: the destruction of traditional social structures which had given status to both sexes, and the sexual exploitation of African women by the White colonizers. They became a 'colony within a colony'.

In South Africa, the Apartheid state has ensured the continuation of a system in which African women are oppressed on the basis of their skin colour and their sex. Through the system of migrant labour, the pass laws and other special laws affecting African women, the regime has created a particularly unique form of oppression, distinguishing it from other forms of female oppression within capitalist societies. In South Africa women are stripped of all those rights considered basic human rights throughout the world – the right to choose where to live and work, the right to live with their partners and husbands, the right to bring up and care for their own children.

Apartheid Laws and African Women

The most devastating laws affecting African women are those which ensure the maintenance of the migrant labour system. Robbed of their productive lands, burdened with numerous taxes, African men have been forced to sell their labour-power on the farms, in the mines and in the factories of 'White' South Africa. Their wives and children are 'superfluous appendages' left to live in the barren and desolate bantustans, termed 'homelands' by the Apartheid regime.

The men and women who work in the cities are illegal immigrants in their own country – 'labour units' to be defined as productive or nonproductive. Even those who have spent all of their working lives in the townships surrounding the White cities are treated as 'temporary sojourners'. More and more people are being forcibly removed from their dwelling places in the towns and cast out to the barren reserves as all African workers are being turned into migrant labourers.

Women serving no purpose for the White economy are discarded, unable to live with their husbands except perhaps during the annual two-week holiday allowed migrant workers. They fight for survival in the barren reserves, eking out a miserable existence from what little land is available, supplemented only by the meagre earnings sent by their husbands. Kwashiorkor and other diseases associated with malnutrition are widespread and death from starvation, particularly among children, is common in the reserves.

Insofar as capitalism always seeks the highest rate of profit, it is in the interests of the South African ruling class to keep the Apartheid system intact and refine the migrant labour policy accordingly. By shifting the burden of the maintenance of the workers' families onto the backs of African women in the reserves, the reaping of super-profits is guaranteed. Employers can then justify the below-subsistence wages paid to African workers by arguing that they are partially supported from subsistence farming in the 'homelands'. In reality, poverty and disease are rampant in the reserves and a stable family unit is an impossibility.

The pass laws have been described as the 'African worker's handcuffs'.[1] By controlling the movement of the African labour force, they prevent Africans from selling their labour freely. All Africans over the age of sixteen are forced to carry these 'passes' which prove they are employed, that they have a permit to live in the city where they work and that they have permits to seek work. Failure to produce these on demand renders the African workers liable to summary arrest and conviction.

Passes for women were not introduced until the mid-1950s. When the announcement was made, South African women launched a massive campaign against passes, realizing what the consequences would be. They had seen their men harassed and arrested, fined, imprisoned and deported to White farms as forced labour – all as a result of their failure to produce passes on demand. They had suffered through the pass raids and the disappearance of their husbands and sons and knew what this would mean if they too had to carry passes. The women's resistance campaign is documented in a later section of this chapter.

What has been described so far are the effects on African women of laws which apply to both men and women. But what of those laws which oppress women solely on the basis of their sex? To maintain its subjugation of women in the bantustans, the Apartheid regime has devised a special interpretation of the customary life and laws of traditional African society, an interpretation which is an insult to the heritage of the African people. These laws have been distorted and applied by alien White courts and do not reflect the true position of women in traditional, pre-colonial society.

Under what is now termed African customary law, unless an African woman has been 'emancipated', she is deemed a perpetual minor, always under the guardianship of a man (firstly her father and when she marries, her husband). Only unmarried women, widows or divorcees can apply for 'emancipation' to a Native Commissioner's Court, which takes into account the woman's 'character', education, other abilities and whether she owns immovable property. If granted emancipation, the woman becomes free of her guardian's control. As it stands, however, women cannot own property in their own right, claim inheritance, or act as guardians of their children. They cannot enter into contracts, sue or be sued without the aid of their male guardians.

Regardless of their age and marital status, African women are always subject to the authority of men. The government dares not make significant changes in these laws for fear of greater independence and militancy of African women. The system is designed to ensure a largely docile, subservient reserve army of labour to be brought into capitalist production when it is needed, discarded when not.[2]

Indian and Coloured women also suffer oppression based on skin colour and sex. The position of White women corresponds with that of women in most other male-dominated societies. They endure inequalities in employment, wages and in law but at the same time enjoy other advantages merely because they are White in South Africa; for example, White women have the vote. Coloured and Indian women on the other hand, are discriminated against in the sphere of education, housing, employment, wages and health. Laws which have had detrimental effects on their family lives are those such as the Group Areas Act which has legislated the forced removal of Black families to townships based on racial grouping, leaving the inner-city areas as 'White areas'.

Black South African women suffer oppression at the hands of the Apartheid state which differs in degree and in kind from that of their male counterparts. In spite of this and in spite of the attempts to divide women by racial categories, South African women have consistently stood up and confronted the state in unity. No better example can be provided than the women's campaigns of the 1950s. Their struggles illustrate the spontaneous militancy which emerged and once directed, proved to be a significant threat to both employers and the state.

Women Rise Up Against the State

Women's resistance campaigns are not a recent phenomenon in South

Africa. As far back as 1913 in the Orange Free State, African women in urban locations organized demonstrations against being forced to buy new residence permits each month. Demonstrations spread throughout the province and the campaign continued for years, eventually leading to the withdrawal of these permits. Similarly in 1918, the newly-formed Bantu Women's League of South Africa launched a series of anti-pass campaigns which raised the political consciousness of African women.

In later years, Indian women organized mass campaigns and strikes against the taxes they had to pay. These women, brought to South Africa as indentured labourers, recognized that they were a source of cheap labour on the colonial plantations and fought against these slave conditions. Coloured women too, continually resisted attempts by the successive racist regimes to use them as pawns in the implementation of segregation policies.

The African National Congress Women's League had for many years been organizing women for the national liberation struggle. These women also performed a more traditional function, that of providing food and accommodation for ANC conferences and meetings.

It was not until April 1954, when the Federation of South African Women (FSAW) was born, that women of all races united to carry on the struggle against racial and sexual discrimination. At the founding conference, 146 women delegates representing 230,500 women from all over South Africa gathered in Johannesburg, 'to discuss how to win social, economic and political rights, and how to make a greater contribution in the struggle to win freedom for all of the people of South Africa'.[3] Many women who were later to become SACTU leaders attended this historic conference. Veteran trade unionist Ray Alexander praised the past efforts of women in her speech:

We are here because we want to find solutions to the problems which mean so much to us and to those we represent. Our women have shown their worth in building the A.N.C., trade unions, in strikes and demonstrations. They have played an important part in the Defiance Campaign – our women defied the unjust laws and went to jail. Many were expectant mothers, while others had babies on their backs.[4]

In 1955, the Minister of Native Affairs announced that African women were to be issued with passes beginning in January 1956. This was the impetus for the major women's campaign of the 1950s – the Anti-Pass Campaign. The first major protest against the pass laws occurred in October 1955, when 2,000 women, mostly Africans, converged in

Pretoria to voice their opposition and to present their signed protests. Lilian Ngoyi, garment worker and President of FSAW, explained the militancy of the women to their men, who were in most cases shocked by this well-coordinated and bold stand: 'Men are born into the system and it is as if it has become a life tradition that they carry passes. We as women have seen the treatment our men have – when they leave home in the morning you are not sure if they will come back. If the husband is to be arrested, *and* the mother, what about the child?'[5]

The campaign intensified in 1956 when the government began issuing passes to sections of women least likely to protest – women farm workers in particular. Protests grew throughout the country and in many towns women gathered together to burn their passes, their 'badges of slavery'. The campaign, spearheaded by the FSAW with assistance from the ANC Women's League and SACTU, steadily gained momentum during 1956 and culminated in a mass demonstration in Pretoria on 9 August 1956, the date now designated as South African Women's Day. On that day in 1956, women poured into Pretoria and Johannesburg from all over South Africa by train, bus and car. Port Elizabeth women had raised £700, enough for 70 women to attend. On this day some 20,000 women assembled in Pretoria, all heading for the Union Buildings to present their protest to the Prime Minister himself, Johannes Strydom. The women sang, 'Strydom you have struck a rock, you have touched the women' as the four leaders (Lilian Ngoyi, Rahima Moosa, Sophie Williams and Helen Joseph) representing each 'racial' group, marched up to the Office of the Prime Minister where they left thousands of petition forms at the door. After 30 minutes of complete silence, the women sang freedom songs and then dispersed, walking away from one of the most incredibly organized and fantastic demonstrations in the history of women's struggles in South Africa.

Despite this tremendous opposition, passes for women were introduced and as predicted brought increased suffering to Africans. However, this did not mean an end to women's protests as they continued to organize against the pass laws throughout the country.

Thousands of women took part in massive rallies, processions and demonstrations in Johannesburg during 1958. Zeerust, in the Western Transvaal, was the centre of the most bitter struggle. In one village, only 76 out of 4,000 women accepted pass books, many burning them as an expression of defiance. The women's anger was directed not only against the state, but also against any chiefs who collaborated with the

South African regime. Some bloody incidents occurred during these acts of resistance and many women were beaten, shot, their houses burned and some forced into banishment.

Elsewhere throughout the country groups of women continued to resist the pass system by refusing to accept reference books. In every centre, women members of SACTU actively campaigned against passes, calling on women workers to defy these oppressive laws. Throughout this period countless women were arrested, detained and beaten, but this repression did not stop the women.

Natal Erupts: Protests Against Beer-Halls and Dipping Tanks

Uprisings led by the women spread throughout Natal during 1959 and 1960. The major protests emanated from the Cato Manor shack settlement, where African residents lived in extreme poverty. Their homes had no lighting or sewerage provided and families were subjected to constant raids by police. The women's resentment focused on the system of municipal beer-halls.

The law prevented Africans from brewing their own liquor at home and yet allowed men to go to municipal beer-halls to drink the 'Bantu Beer' provided there. These beer-halls were a source of tax revenue to assist in the administration of Apartheid machinery. African women continued to defy the law, brewing liquor at home to sell in order to earn a few pennies more and retain a traditional form of hospitality. Because of the already meagre wages their men brought home, the women deeply resented the money they drank away in the beer-halls. They argued that the beer-halls should be closed and that they should be allowed to brew at home. Police raids intensified as the women's anger built up.

On 18 June 1959, some 2,000 Cato Manor women gathered to tell their grievances to a local official. The response they received was vicious: hundreds of women and children struck down by police wielding batons. The township erupted and violence spread. Municipal buildings were burned down and vehicles were destroyed. Three Africans were shot and killed as they tried to burn down a beer-hall. ANC leaders called on the people to be non-violent and appealed for peace, but the disturbances spread. This incident provided the impetus for an unprecedented movement which spread throughout the city and countryside.

The militant women of Natal called for a total boycott of the beer-halls. Leaders like Dorothy Nyembe, Florence Mkize and Gladys

Manzi inspired the women who carried out an intensive campaign of picketing the beer-halls in a number of municipalities. There were huge demonstrations and women marched right into the beer-halls, attacking the men who dared to come and drink there, and destroying the object of their oppression – the beer-hall itself. Stephen Dlamini recalls how effective their campaign was: 'In the evenings when beer-halls were normally 100 per cent full, only a handful were there and it was suspected that even some of these may have been police spies. But the ordinary rank and file workers never went in.'[6]

When men in the beer-halls saw the women coming, they fled immediately. The police were always there. They tried to prevent the women from entering, but they were usually outsmarted. Mate Mfusi observed one such incident:

These women were very powerful. Some came half dressed (in traditional dress) with their breasts exposed, and when they got near this place the Blackjacks (police) tried to block the women. But when they saw this, the women turned and pulled up their skirts. The police closed their eyes and the women passed by and went in![7]

Elias Mbele recalls a time 'when the women took off their panties, filled them with beer and said, "Look, this is what happens," as they squeezed them out'.[8]

At first the men were shocked by the actions of the women; chauvinist attitudes were revealed as they witnessed their women attacking a symbol of their domain. However, they did not retaliate or fight back and once they saw police attacking the women viciously, they fully supported the women in their struggle. ANC and SACTU men gave their support to the women and the youth in particular backed them up, often coming back to the beer-halls the following week to finish off the job. Many beer-halls were closed but police action intensified against illegal brewing. As a result, many leaders were jailed and women severely beaten.

In all of the various acts of resistance, the unifying current was the women's hatred of the dreaded pass laws and influx control and their effect on family life, both in the urban townships and in the rural areas. When the uprising spread to the rural areas, women attacked yet another edifice of their particular oppression – the dipping tanks. Women were forced to fill and maintain these dipping tanks for cattle without payment. They reacted against this form of exploitation by burning and destroying the dipping tanks. The protests spread throughout Natal and three-quarters of the tanks were destroyed. In one village, police arrested the entire crowd of demonstrators, nearly 400 women, and they were given the option of a fine of £35 or four months' imprisonment. They all chose prison, many taking their babies with them to the jails.

Despite police beatings, arrests and imprisonments, the spirits of the women in Natal remained high. At the December 1959 Conference of the ANC in Durban, as Govan Mbeki spoke from the chair, the women were rushing at the door and yelling, 'We must go out and defy . . . !' Mbeki said, 'Bavulele Mabangeni!' (Open the doors for them).[9] That year also, the men made a special bright red banner for the Conference which read, 'Makabongwe Amakosikazi' (We Thank the Women).

Violence erupted again in Cato Manor early in 1960. The people still lived in appalling slum conditions and police raids had intensified. One African policeman, Dludla, was notorious for his treatment of residents. Determined never to walk away from a house-raid without an arrest, Dludla would always carry a spare bottle of illicit spirits in his pocket and conveniently place it under a pillow or elsewhere in order to ensure his quota of victims. He often said, 'I'll ask for your passes here and in heaven too!'

A series of events occurred which further added to the build-up of hatred for police actions in Cato Manor, by now a nest of seething uneasiness. At one weekend demonstration police shot a baby on the mother's back and this proved too much for the people to take. Shortly thereafter the masses retaliated, killing nine police (including Dludla) and the ANC declared that this kind of occurrence was a result of the degrading conditions and vicious police harassment of residents.

The upsurge of women's protests in 1959 posed some vital questions for the ANC leadership at the time. Firstly, the women's actions – especially in the rural areas – were unexpected even by their male counterparts in the organization. Moses Mabhida has made some interesting comments on the situation at the time. For instance, the fact that women had to take the stand they did, without their men knowing, indicated to him that perhaps the leadership of the ANC did not understand very well the problems of the people. 'The fact also may be that because of African attitudes, the society didn't expect women to participate in the way that they did.'[10]

Another interesting question which emerged from this campaign was the apparent readiness of the people to take up arms against the Apartheid state. Certainly many of the women, and many rank and file members of the ANC, thought that the time had come for an armed uprising. Among the leadership though, there were those who feared that the situation would become uncontrollable. Reflecting on this situation, Mabhida had this to say:

> When the women demonstrated, I think it was one of the most powerful demonstrations. Unfortunately for our people, we didn't realize the extent of the organization of the people, which was at that time very high, and the women formed a very strong nucleus for a powerful organization. If I may say, if our people had taken it further, it might have taken the same trend as it did in Iran — maybe not exactly the same, but the extent of organization and the militancy of the people was almost the same.[11]

A prominent woman member on the Natal ANC Executive kept asking the others, 'How long shall we go on with these demonstrations which are one-sided in the sense that the police assault our people, and in all ways we ask them not to retaliate?' It was a question which was to be posed over and over again in the next few years and one which was resolved to some extent by the decision of the ANC in 1961 to turn to armed struggle.

SACTU and Women's Struggles

Throughout the years, SACTU has consistently recognized that women, and particularly African women, suffer an additional form of oppression and therefore have a distinct role to play in the political and trade union struggles in South Africa. Their support for the struggle of women was part of the commitment to the general struggle for complete emancipation of the people of South Africa and a commitment to build a South Africa free from oppression on the basis of race, class or sex.

As SACTU stated in a letter of fraternal greetings to the Transvaal Provincial Conference of the Women's Federation in November 1956,

> It is the women of South Africa who have demonstrated to all progressive forces the true meaning of militancy and organization and we in the trade union movement are determined to follow your courageous example.
>
> The campaign against Pass Laws is 'basic to the struggle for freedom'. As you fight laws for women, we fight them for workers.
>
> Let us not rest until the absolute value of every individual is recognized and all oppressive legislation defeated.

Year after year SACTU joined with all other progressive forces to condemn the pass laws, and particularly their extension to African women. At its first Annual National Conference in March 1956, held in

Cape Town, Frances Baard led a lengthy discussion on the effect on women of the pass laws. 'Once women accept the passes,' she said, 'they will be jailed every day.' Resolutions condemning the pass laws were approved at every conference and May Day pledges always included a call to continue the fight against them. Local committees in each area were called upon to unite with the women in their struggle and take action relevant to the local situation.

During 1958 and 1959, when employers were making the possession of passes a condition of women's employment, SACTU considered it necessary to take effective counter-action.[12] In this case, SACTU was defending their rights both as workers and as women. The SACTU 1959 Conference Report stated that SACTU had contacted the Chamber of Industry and Commerce requesting they intervene because African women opposed pass laws and in the interests of harmonious labour relations the Chambers should bring pressure on the government. Their request was refused. SACTU later wired the Associated Chambers of Commerce meeting in Margate, asking them to oppose the issuance of reference books to African women. The reply: 'Your telegram acknowledged. Questions of this nature entirely outside scope of our Industry and no comment can be made.'[13] This response was then strongly attacked by SACTU in a press release and SACTU decided to approach employers directly.

In October 1958 a circular went out to 400 employers of African women. In it, SACTU stated that there was no legal compulsion for employers to register African women, nor for them to take out reference books. 'The Pass system,' the circular pointed out, 'is the greatest cause of unrest and dissatisfaction among African men. With the extension of this system to African women, this unrest and dissatisfaction will be increased 1,000-fold.'

Within the trade union movement, SACTU alone campaigned against passes for women. In November 1958 they appealed to the SATUC to join SACTU in a deputation to the Johannesburg Chamber of Commerce and the Federated Chambers of Industry, stating that the issue of passes to women was a violation of their rights as workers for freedom of movement and association, and of their right to sell their labour freely. Once again, the TUC betrayed the interests of the majority of African workers and sent no reply to SACTU.

The 1958 SACTU Conference labelled the whole Pass System as basically anti-worker and anti-trade union. Referring specifically to the case of African women, Conference recognized that the women's struggle against passes was the concern of all workers and called on all affiliated unions, local committees and the trade union movement as a whole to support the women's campaign without qualification. Though as we know the campaign did not result in the abolition of passes, it contributed greatly to the politicization of the African working class and to the mobilization of the masses throughout the country in the late 1950s. At the 1960 SACTU Conference, congratulations were extended to the African population in their fight against the pass laws, *'the very basis of cheap labour in South Africa, and the instrument of the capitalist class to preserve wage slavery'*.[14]

The Effect of the Natal Uprisings

The militancy demonstrated by the women in Natal in 1959 had a profound impact on SACTU as well as activists in the political movement. One delegate at the 1960 SACTU Conference stressed the importance of SACTU linking up with the struggles of peasants and in particular the women. He felt that SACTU had 'missed the boat in this recent situation, that old methods had to be discarded and that it was important to know and feel the pulse of the people'.[15]

In Natal itself, the SACTU Local Committeee was already active in tapping this upsurge of militancy in its campaign to double the SACTU Natal membership and build up 100 new factory committees. Billy Nair, Secretary, explained:

The 1959 demonstrations in Natal and the tremendous advances in the trade union field must be exploited to the full. SACTU is aware that it has a decisive role to play in advancing the struggle not only for higher wages and better working conditions but also for freedom for all in South Africa.

Over 10,000 members joined SACTU during the great political upsurge in Natal last year. Our task in the coming months is to consolidate this force and to increase our membership and influence amongst the working people of Natal.[16]

The 1959 campaigns by peasant women and the women's campaigns in general, did influence SACTU to devote greater attention to organizing workers and peasants in the rural areas and to promote greater unity among the oppressed people of Natal generally. This became even more crucial after the banning of the ANC in April 1960. A Natal Rural Areas Committee was formed and together with SACTU called several 'Workers and Peasants' Conferences'. Women played a leading part in these and other conferences. At one meeting in December 1962, attended by 1,500 people, the women's leaders Gladys Manzi and Dorothy Nyembe (Secretary and Chairman of the FSAW, Natal, respectively) were the principal speakers. On other occasions, speakers included Vera Ponnen, President of the Federation in Natal, and member of the SACOD before her banning in April 1962, and Fatima Meer of the Natal Indian Congress. Natal thus became a vital area of SACTU organizing in the early 1960s before the period of heavy repression directed against its leaders and members.

Other SACTU campaigns which focused on women's issues specifically included one against the introduction of taxes for African women, and another calling for equal compensation for African and White widows following the death of 435 miners at Clydesdale Colliery in January 1960.

At the 1959 Conference, a FCWU delegate described the introduction of taxes for women as a 'terrible blow' and appealed for unity, stressing that the 'men must help the women; it is their struggle too!' African women earning between £15 and £20 per month now had to pay £1 per year tax and an extra £1 per year for every £5 above a wage of £20 a month. The poll tax for African men earning between £15 and £20 a month was raised to £2. These represented large amounts to Black workers and their families, barely existing on their starvation wages.

The discrepancy between compensation offered African and White widows of the Clydesdale victims was outrageous. A White widow would receive a lump sum of £75 for immediate expenses and £40 for medical expenses, a pension of £13 11s. 4d. a month with an extra £6 15s. 8d. a month for each child (up to three children), and on remarriage, two years pension in a lump sum with children's allowances up to the age of seventeen. African dependants were to receive one lump sum payment of approximately £180, nothing more.[17] The inhumanity displayed by the mining company, which more than a month after the disaster could still not provide a full list of African miners killed, shocked the world. SACTU took on the responsibility of arranging for a memorial service and launching a fund to assist the African dependants. The campaign for equal compensation fell on deaf ears, and African miners' widows were left destitute.

In sum, SACTU welcomed the campaigns undertaken by women in the late 1950s and pledged political and material support for their militant actions. The organization recognized the oppression of women as being of a specific kind distinct from that based on class and race alone. But it is the women within SACTU, women who experienced this particular form of oppression directly, who had the least to lose and who contributed a great deal to the struggle for non-racial trade unionism.

Women Workers and SACTU

Because of the practical issues of our society, the differences between men and women died a natural death . . . a worker is a worker whether Black, White, man or woman.[18]

Certainly the 'practical issues' confronting both men and women workers demanded a special kind of unity in their fight against employers and the state. Under Apartheid, class and racial divisions are fostered to a much greater extent than divisions between the sexes. However, the fact remains that African women workers are at the bottom of the scale in terms of wages, rights of residence in the towns, working conditions and other basic rights.

From the beginning, SACTU recognized the vulnerability of African women workers to super-exploitation by the bosses:

It must be the task of the entire trade union movement to lend a helping hand to organize all women in the industry, especially African women, so they can take their rightful place in the trade union movement of South Africa and make an end of the system which uses women as the source of cheap labour. . . . The key is *organization*. Only when women in the trade union movement are well-organized with men, can it be a truly representative trade union movement. We call upon all trade unionists to encourage women workers in their place of work to become active members of their unions and play a part in strengthening the trade union movement in this country and taking up the great issues of an end to the inferior position of women in the industries and trades, and for equal pay for equal work.[19]

In one sense, however, African women workers had one less obstacle compared with African men at the time SACTU was formed. The IC Act of 1924 included in the definition of 'employees' all those who were not 'pass-bearing natives' (Africans). This meant that African women workers were not excluded from forming trade unions and being part of registered unions (until passes for women were introduced). The state was perhaps unaware of the potential militancy of African women when the first IC Act was passed. Hence, until women were forced to carry passes, they were able to take an active role in the formation of trade unions and participate in strikes. Many African women rejected any tendencies toward passivity in the labour movement and gained invaluable experience during this period.

The standard occupation for African women who came to the city for work was in domestic service in the homes of White South Africans. The work itself was largely an extension of the traditional concept of a 'woman's role' – cooking, cleaning, laundering and child-care. Housed in tiny servants' quarters behind the White homes, these women were constantly at the beck and call of their employers and consequently endured severe restrictions on their own personal lives and freedom of movement. They worked long hours for poverty wages and were separated from their families and children except for brief vacation periods. It was common for employers to deduct a certain portion from their already dismal wages if any breakages or damages occurred. This form of employment remains a glaring example of the super-exploitation of cheap Black labour in South Africa.

With the tremendous upsurge in industrialization during and after the Second World War, more and more African workers, including women, were drawn into the labour force. Women workers were increasingly employed in food processing and canning, textile and garment manufacturing and laundering, with a smaller number entering teaching and nursing. Even up to the present time, however, the majority of women workers are still employed in either domestic service or farm labour. African women have been excluded from a large range of jobs and are thus subject to double discrimination on the basis of skin colour and sex.

Throughout the years of SACTU's open activity women played a major part in the struggle for a better quality of life for South African workers, and in particular for the oppressed African workers. Side by side with the SACTU men, African, Coloured, Indian and to a lesser extent White women actively participated in the organizing campaigns, the local committees, Head Office work and of course the numerous strikes by workers – especially in the textile and food processing industries. African women, again like their male co-workers, continued to defy the legislation which prohibited them from taking part in strikes. Nothing could deter these women from playing an active part in the progressive trade union movement. By taking the stand they did, they were rejecting the role normally extended to them and instead standing up to the employers and the state in their struggle against oppression as Africans, as workers and as women.

Militant Women Workers Play Their Part
At one time I was invited to attend an international conference for women

trade unionists on behalf of SACTU. But when I began to talk of the militancy of African women trade unionists in South Africa, I was not believed! . . . It is a story which must be told.[20]

In August 1961 twelve African nurses were severely caned by the matron of the nurses' home at King George Tuberculosis Hospital in Durban. This incident sparked off a historic strike which demonstrated very clearly the kinds of issues facing African women workers and the steps they were prepared to take in order to achieve their demands.

SACTU had assisted in forming a Hospital Workers Union in Durban in 1959, a Union for all hospital workers whether doing skilled or unskilled work, whether men or women. Before this incident however, the Union could not operate openly at the hospital for fear of victimization.

The matron who had caned the twelve women, allegedly for arriving to classes a few minutes late, had a past history of cruel treatment and contemptuous attitudes towards the African women working in the hospital. Her previous employment had been in the penal system, a fact which might partially explain her actions. Immediately following the caning incident, all of the African nurses marched to the Superintendent's Office demanding that this matron, Mrs Malan, be fired for her actions. Informed that the Superintendent was not available, they spread the word that all work must stop and the workers must take a united stand against this tyrannical administration. Within minutes, sweepers, staff nurses, clerks and technical assistants – Indians, Africans, men and women – joined the striking nurses.

After the initial walk-out, women leaders such as Mate Mfusi, Queeneth Dladla and Doris Mnyandu, assisted by SACTU-Durban Local Committee members, drew up a memorandum to present to the hospital authorities. The list of grievances was extensive. African nurses were forced to eat apart from Coloured and Indian nurses and were fed lower quality meals; African staff nurses were forced to pay more for board and lodging; Africans had to supply their own eating utensils. The workers were demanding changes in all of these areas. Their demands also included free uniforms, a minimum wage of R3 a day (for seniors), R2 for nurse aids, maids and labourers, and the establishment of an Unemployment Insurance Fund.

One of the most crucial demands for the African nurses was that the right to maternity leave be extended to unmarried pregnant women. The nurses had seen too many of their friends buried after submitting themselves to 'backyard abortions' in order to preserve their jobs; these women had considered expulsion from work a worse fate and did not have the choice of a legal abortion.

Another degrading practice which the nurses were determined to put an end to, was that which required African employees to make a cross when collecting their pay envelopes, rather than sign for them. The hospital administration clearly worked on the assumption that all Africans were illiterate but the workers were not prepared to submit to these insults any longer. African nurses, previously offered no protection from TB were also demanding some form of protection from the disease. These and all other demands reflected the workers' anger and bitterness over the inhuman conditions of work and residence in the hospital.

The next day there was another work stoppage by 300 workers at the hospital, while six nurses presented the demands to the Superintendent. After he refused to dismiss the matron or to discuss their demands, the furious nurses began their strike in earnest. The strike continued for two weeks during which time the hospital was cordoned off by police who harassed supportive demonstrators. SACTU leaders Stephen Dlamini, Bill Nair, Curnick Ndlovu and Memory Vakalisa assisted the women throughout this period. The nurses had instigated a boycott of the hospital food and so SACTU comrades were active in organizing an alternative food programme for the striking women. They approached Indian merchants for donations of sugar, tea and other basic commodities, cooked food at Memory Vakalisa's house and brought in additional tinned foodstuffs for them. SACTU Local Committee Chairman Dlamini was arrested outside the hospital for failing to produce his pass (which he never carried with him), but was later released on bail.

In the end, the women did receive some improvements as a result of the strike. The diet was improved and eating was no longer segregated, unmarried nurses were given maternity leave, Africans could sign for their pay package, uniforms were provided and masks as well. Tablets to guard against TB were distributed and some small wage increases granted. Along with these, however, came reprisals against the Union and twenty-one leaders were dismissed. All nurses were threatened with dismissal if they belonged to the Union.

Not content to let the hospital administration break the Union, some of the nurses thought that they should do something to retaliate. One of them slipped out to get some petrol . . . a short time later, a linen room in

Striking nurses at King George TB Hospital shout 'Amandla Ngawethu' (Power is Ours), 1961

Victimized nurses become SACTU organizers
Left to right: Doris Mnyandu, Mate Mfusi, Queeneth Dladla

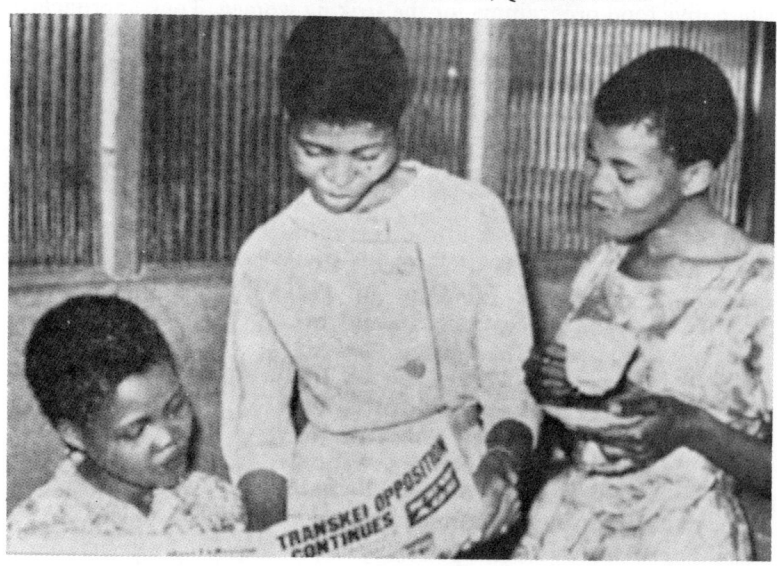

the nurses' hostel was on fire. Queeneth Dladla and Doris Mnyandu were arrested along with another young woman who later was forced under interrogation to give evidence against the other two. Each received a two-month prison sentence as a result.

A major achievement during the strike was the display of unity amongst workers, inspired by the leadership of these militant young African nurses undeterred by the intimidation from the police and hospital authorities. Though they did not succeed in getting the matron dismissed, they did gain some worthwhile improvements for African hospital workers and raised the consciousness of workers in general through their actions.[21]

Once again, SACTU received assistance from the international working class after publicizing the threat of the wholesale dismissal of these women workers. Telegrams and letters of protest poured into the Superintendent's Office from the WFTU, the ICFTU, and workers in Canada, England, the USA, Europe, Latin America, Australia and other countries. This tremendous display of solidarity saved the nurses from massive retrenchments and only the original twenty-one leaders were dismissed. Dr Dorner, the Superintendent at the hospital, was later refused a visa by the Nigerian government to attend a conference of scientists in January 1962.

Some of the nurses involved in the strike later became part of a contingent which was sent by the ANC to assist in the hospitals of newly-independent Tanzania as a gesture of solidarity. The three leaders of the strike all went to work for SACTU as full-time organizers after their dismissal. Mate Mfusi in particular played a major role in SACTU-Natal work from that time until she left South Africa in 1962. She was instrumental in organizing unorganized workers in the Ladysmith area until forced to leave because she didn't have a permit to remain in the area. Remembered as 'a dynamic young SACTU organizer', Mate spoke on many platforms at SACTU meetings in Natal, inspiring all workers to take up the struggle for higher wages and better working conditions.[22] Like many other SACTU leaders, she was harassed by the police and Special Branch until she left South Africa.

Profiles of other SACTU Women

It is our purpose in this section to document the contributions made by some of the women who became working class leaders in South Africa. In doing so, the intention is not to elevate the individual above the collective group of workers, nor is it to illustrate the importance of women leaders *vis-à-vis* their male comrades. Rather, it is to examine the class origins of these women and to determine how it was that these women rose up out of the confines imposed upon their sex in South Africa to become highly respected, strong leaders of all workers and fighters in the cause of liberation.

Any tribute to women workers who strengthened SACTU through these years would be incomplete without a special mention of the women who belonged to the Food and Canning Workers Union and the African-FCWU. We have already examined some of the strikes in the food and canning industry and the role played by women workers in Chapter 8 above. What follows is a series of sketches of some of the leaders of these women workers as well as other SACTU women who played a crucial part in the development of non-racial trade unionism.

Ray Alexander

Discussion of the food and canning workers of South Africa immediately brings to mind the name of Ray Alexander, the woman largely responsible for the formation of the Union and for its strength over the years. Ray Alexander was already banned from trade union activity by the time SACTU came into existence. However, even with the restrictions on her open activity, she continued to work behind the scenes, advising, writing, researching and doing whatever possible to assist the workers and leaders of the FCWU and A-FCWU and SACTU.

Born in Latvia of a progressive Jewish family, Ray was active in an illegal Socialist group at the age of fourteen. It was this activity which led her mother to make hasty arrangements to get Ray out of the country on a ship bound for South Africa. Though she considered it the correct tactic politically to try to do political work in a capitalist country like South Africa rather than go to the Soviet Union as many others did (the 'easiest way'), Ray was apprehensive on arrival. Two days after she arrived, as she was out buying vegetables, Ray saw African workers coming out of a factory. She asked, 'Are you members of a union?' They said, 'No'. As she passed by a furniture factory she asked a mixed group of workers the same question. Some answered 'Yes', others 'No'. She thought to herself, 'There's a lot of work to be done here!'

From the early 1930s onwards, Ray Alexander began organizing workers into trade unions throughout the Cape. She played a leading role in the formation of the Commercial Employees Union (forerunner in Cape Town of the National Union of Distributive Workers) and later assisted in organizing Black workers into unions in the transport, chemical, sweet, laundry, tin and footwear industries.

In late 1940, Ray began organizing the Food and Canning Workers Union. By the end of November 1941, the FCWU was well-organized with branches in Cape Town, Paarl, Daljosophat, Wellington, Worcester, Groot Drakenstein and Stellenbosch. The Union represented all workers in the industry until 1947, when the Department of Labour threatened the Union with deregistration if African workers were not removed. A decision was then taken by the members to set up the African-FCWU which would continue to work closely as an equal partner with the FCWU.

African workers made up about 15 to 20 per cent of the labour force in the industry at this time, Coloured workers 80 per cent and White workers less than 5 per cent. Of the Coloured workers, 55 per cent were women. With the exception of the White workers who occupied skilled positions, the food and canning workers represented some of the most exploited in the country; their wages were extremely low and they worked long hours, without protective clothing and other benefits.

Ray Alexander, along with other leaders in both unions, fought hard for better wages and working conditions for these workers throughout the 1940s and 1950s. They also succeeded in mobilizing workers around broader issues; the food and canning workers were in the forefront of political campaigns initiated by the ANC and other groups in the Congress Alliance.

During this time, Ray was part of the minority in the SAT & LC continually struggling to keep Apartheid out of the trade union movement. In September 1953 she was ordered to resign from her position as General Secretary of the FCWU and prohibited from attending any gatherings of any nature for two years. At the bottom of her banning orders a special sentence, handwritten by the Minister of Justice Swart, added that she must not assist in any way whatsoever any group of workers to improve their wages and working conditions.[23]

Frank Marquard, President of the FCWU at the time spoke out against the banning:

We and our members fully understand that Ray Alexander has been expelled for this life-long devotion to the cause of the oppressed. The men who have done this are the representatives of the rich and employing class. They have for long shown deep-seated hatred and fear of the workers and the oppressed people. Their whole political life has been directed towards maintaining privileges and power for a small class of exploiters.

Nothing that they do – the Swarts, the Schoemans and other enemies of the workers will destroy what Ray Alexander has built up, or uproot her from our hearts. She is ours, and will remain so long after the fascists who are now in power have disappeared from the scene of South African history.[24]

The workers, however, were not satisfied with mere words attacking the ruling class; they carried out spontaneous protest strikes throughout the entire Cape Province. Thousands of workers from factories in Paarl, Groot Drakenstein, Worcester, Wellington and Port Elizabeth staged strikes varying from three hours to one day in length, and vowed to continue to fight against these banning orders on their General Secretary. One hundred African women migrants from the Transkei went on strike in an East London factory. They wrote a tribute to Ray, which said, 'By encouraging African workers to organize, you have brought new hope and dignity to thousands of workers. *Sobuye Sibonan* (We will meet again).'[25]

The regime had robbed the workers of one of their most respected leaders. The sense of outrage expressed by the workers at the time of Ray's banning is in itself an indication of the tremendous work carried out by her during the years. Undaunted by the ban on her open activities associated with trade unions, Ray continued to actively assist the workers 'behind the scenes' right up until she was forced to leave South Africa in 1965. Many Black trade unionists owe their training to her and will never forget this disciplined young White woman who delivered lectures and generally assisted them in their work, always exuding tremendous warmth and amazing energy. A further tribute was paid to Ray by the food and canning workers who elected her Life General Secretary of the FCWU in 1957.

Elizabeth Mafekeng

One of the most outstanding women trade unionists, who has given her services to the Canning Union since she was a girl of fourteen, has been arbitrarily ordered to abandon her eleven children, her husband, her work and her home, for no other reason than that she has demanded higher wages for her members, the right to skilled jobs and human dignity for all.[26]

The news of Elizabeth Mafekeng's banishment order was received with shock throughout progressive circles in South Africa and other parts of the world.

Ray Alexander (*centre*) discussing Union issues with Bettie du Toit (*far left*), Oscar Mpetha, General Secretary, A-FCWU (*second left*), Maria Williams (*second right*) and David Jaantjies (*far right*), c. 1952

Elizabeth Mafekeng, President, African Food and Canning Workers Union

Born in Lesotho (then Basutoland), Elizabeth came to Paarl in 1927 and began working at H. Jones and Co. canning factory in 1939. At that time – before the Union was formed – the workers' wages were 7s. 6d. per week, they worked long hours without overtime pay, they had no sick-leave, no workmen's compensation, no confinement allowance and no protective clothing. Active in the Union from its beginnings in 1941, Elizabeth was later elected President of the A-FCWU. She became a highly respected leader, able to combine her trade union work with the struggle for women's rights in the Federation of South African Women and for the political rights of oppressed Africans in the ANC. She participated in the Defiance Campaign of 1952 and went to jail carrying her child on her back.

In 1955, Elizabeth was elected to represent South African food workers at an international conference in Sofia, Bulgaria, organized by the WFTU. Possessing no passport and disguised as a servant, she boarded a ship bound for Europe on 24 June 1955, and as soon as she left South Africa 'tasted for the first time real human treatment with no discrimination whatsoever'. She first attended the International Youth Festival in Warsaw where she was impressed with the rapid reconstruction which had taken place in Poland since the war.

In Sofia, she represented African workers at the Second International Conference of the Food, Tobacco, Hotel, Cafe and Restaurant Workers, attended by 122 delegates from 66 countries. The only Black delegate there, Elizabeth spoke on the conditions of African workers in South Africa, the history of the FCWU and A-FCWU and detailed the attempts by the ruling class to divide workers along racial lines, all the time infusing examples from her own experience. The response was overwhelming, 'a great uproar ... which lasted for over half an hour ... delegates crowded round me, some shaking hands, some kissing me, assuring us of their hearty support'.[27] She was crowned 'Queen Elizabeth', President of the A-FCWU.

From Bulgaria she travelled to China and was surprised to learn that conditions there previous to the Revolution had been worse than in South Africa. The remarkable changes, won through the struggles of the people, were an inspiration for her as she made her way back to South Africa. Of special interest to her were the improved conditions of work for women, particularly child-care facilities for working mothers.

On her return, Elizabeth addressed many meetings of workers, all eager to learn of her experiences overseas. Between 1955 and 1959, she continued to organize African workers into trade unions and represent them as President of the Union. By 1959, she was also National Vice-President of the ANC Women's League, member of the Cape ANC Executive and active in the FSAW.

In October of that year, Elizabeth and Liz Abrahams (Acting General Secretary of the FCWU) went out to Port Elizabeth to assist workers in organizing the campaign against proposed wage cuts by Langeberg Kooperasie management. Within weeks, Elizabeth received her banishment orders. She was to be sent to Southey, a Bantu Affairs Department trust farm, 50 miles from the nearest large town and 15 miles from the nearest clinic, with no transport available. No legitimate reason was given for her banishment, only a statement that her presence was 'injurious to the peace, order and good administration [sic] of the people of the Paarl district'.

SACTU, the FCWU and the A-FCWU launched a tremendous publicity campaign. Letters and telegrams poured in from everywhere and thousands demonstrated in protest.[28] Elizabeth delivered a farewell message on Sunday, 8 November 1959:

I think everybody is upset today in this country. But I personally am not upset about my going, because I think that we mothers feel what the pass laws and other oppressive laws mean to us.

We mothers are the people who gave birth to children and we are the people who suffer most from the laws of the Nationalist Government.

We must stand together and unite to fight for freedom.[29]

SACTU demanded the repeal of the banishment order and announced:

From the workers of Paarl, whose parents and grandparents built the canneries into one of the largest industries of its kind in the world, the truth cannot be hidden. The workers know that it is the great farming interests who back the Verwoerd rule who demand Mrs Mafekeng's banishment. It is these same interests which recently secured a ban on canning workers which prevents them from striking for higher wages and has silenced ten Food and Canning Workers' officials.[30]

With the comradely assistance of her fellow workers, Elizabeth Mafekeng was saved from the fate of banishment and smuggled into Basutoland (Lesotho) a week later, taking only the youngest of her eleven children with her. Though physically isolated from her comrades in South Africa, she kept in touch with the plight of South African workers. SACTU continually made appeals to South African workers for funds to assist her and her family. In May 1961, she sent this message to her fellow-workers regarding the proposed Stay-At-Home on 29 May:

Today the Power is in your hands. Through the use of the weapon of your labour power, you will find that nothing can prevent freedom in our lifetime.[31]

She also reminded workers of the Freedom Charter preamble and especially the section dealing with the restoration of the national wealth to the people.

Even in Basutoland, Elizabeth was not free from persecution by the authorities. There were continual threats issued to her by some officials of the Basutoland Congress Party for her involvement in the Basutoland Congress of Trade Unions.

Despite these hardships and the loneliness of life away from her family and fellow workers, Elizabeth remained strong in her belief in the ultimate victory of the workers and people of South Africa in their struggle for freedom and dignity. She stands as a bold example of an African woman worker who defied the subordinate role assigned to her under South African capitalism and Apartheid. Carrying out the struggle on behalf of women workers and the African people, Elizabeth posed a threat to the Apartheid state and therefore had to be silenced. However, just as she herself predicted, other leaders rose to take her place. She remains today in exile in Lesotho, never forgotten by the workers of South Africa whose cause she championed.

Frances Baard

'Hier is n'groot agitator' (Here is a great agitator), an Afrikaner policeman once described Frances Baard as he shoved her into a police van during the Anti-Pass Campaign in Port Elizabeth.

One of the Eastern Cape's many dynamic leaders, Frances played a leading role in the women's movement, the trade union movement and the political struggle. She was a former domestic servant, then a teacher and later became Secretary of the FCWU, Port Elizabeth branch. Until she became Secretary, she was constantly victimized by the canning employers and dismissed from work for her fearless stand in demanding just treatment for the workers.

Frances joined the ANC in 1948, and by 1950 was Secretary of the ANC Women's League in PE. She participated in the Defiance Campaign and played a major role in the Boycott of Bantu Education in 1955. After her arrest in the Treason Trial, Frances sent a message from the dock: 'No matter where you work, unite against low wages ... unite into an unbreakable solidarity and organization which is the only protection we can possess against low wages, injustice and oppression.'[32]

It was in this militant spirit that Frances Baard carried out her trade union work throughout the 1950s and 1960s. She represented food and canning workers on the PE-SACTU Local Committee and regularly attended SACTU Annual Conferences as their delegate. As well, she was one of the few women members of the SACTU National Executive.

Frances is perhaps best remembered as a women's leader in the Port Elizabeth area. In 1954, she was an inspiring speaker at the founding conference of the FSAW and played a major role in the organization in the ensuing years. In August 1956, she went to Pretoria with other PE women. But it was in the Eastern Cape itself that the Anti-Pass Campaign took on great importance under her guidance and leadership. Hundreds of African women in the canning industry and woolwasheries were affected by the introduction of passes for women. With the assistance of other women trade unionists such as Sophie Williams of the TWIU, the women of Port Elizabeth launched a massive Anti-Pass Campaign. They organized pickets next to a Reference Books Unit set up by the authorities, dissuading other women who came to get their passes. They staged a demonstration and marched to the Mayor's garden with placards and leaflets. Whatever they could do to resist the imposition of passes, these women attempted it.

Because of her militant stand on behalf of African women and in particular women workers, Frances was persecuted by the Apartheid state, ably assisted by the bosses. In 1962, she was prohibited by the management of Langeberg Kooperasie Besperk from entering their premises, in her view 'an attempt by the bosses to sabotage the activities of the Union'. Detained in 1962 and banned in January of the following year, this was just the beginning of the state's attack on her. On being arrested in 1963, she was kept in solitary confinement for one year before her trial. She then served a five-year prison sentence for contravening the Suppression of Communism Act and was released in 1969. Banishment orders were served soon after, forcing her to leave her family and friends to go and live in an old two-roomed corrugated iron shack in Mabopane in the northern Transvaal, a thousand miles away from her home. Though her banishment order has been lifted, she is over sixty now and finds it difficult to move around. Hence, she remains in Mabopane, unable to pick up the threads of her life in Port Elizabeth again.

Mabel Balfour

Another courageous fighter from amongst the ranks of the food and canning workers, Mabel Balfour gained valuable trade union experience, first as an organizer, then from 1962 as General Secretary of the A-FCWU (Transvaal). She is remembered as an exemplary leader of both African and Coloured workers in the factories.

Because of her experience in the trade union movement, Mabel contributed greatly to SACTU work in the Transvaal. After the loss of many leaders in the Treason Trial arrests, she was co-opted (along with Uriah Maleka, Edmund Cindi, John Gaetsewe and Viola Hashe) onto the Management Committee of SACTU in January 1957. She was also an active member of the Witwatersrand Local Committee.

In 1958, she was arrested in connection with the April Stay-At-Home (see Chapter 10). Several other trade unionists, including Christina Matthews – another militant SACTU and FCWU leader – were among the twenty arrested and convicted for 'inciting non-white workers on the Rand' in the weeks leading up to the general strike. Her sentence, £20 or thirty days' hard labour, was later suspended.

Mabel continued to fight for higher wages and better working conditions within SACTU and the A-FCWU until she too was the victim of state repression. In 1963, she was banned and confined to a small house in the Roodepoort area.

Liz Abrahams

After the successive bannings of Ray Alexander and Becky Lan, Elizabeth ('Liz') Abrahams was elected Acting General Secretary of the FCWU. She continued in this position throughout the SACTU years and ably represented all workers in the industry during that time.

Mary Moodley

Throughout her life, 'Auntie Mary' of Benoni was one of South Africa's most valiant fighters and a constant menace to the Apartheid regime. Active in the South African Women's Federation and the Coloured People's Congress, Mary also organized workers into the Food and Canning Workers Union in the East Rand in the 1950s. She served on the Witwatersrand Local Committee of SACTU during these years and was responsible for training many younger trade unionists in the tradition of militant opposition to oppression and exploitation.

Mary Moodley's home in the 'Coloured' area of Wattville Township housed not only her own large family and grandchildren but also anyone else who suffered homelessness under the Apartheid system. For example, she adopted a blind and paralysed African man whom she had found lying in the street and for whom no hospital or state institution existed. During the heavy repression of the early 1960s, Mary was instrumental in assisting many Congress Alliance members to flee the country.

Although she suffered from a weak heart, the state unrelentlessly pursued its attack on Mary. She was subjected to the 'statue torture' for 90 days in 1963, the same year in which she was banned from trade union and political activity, from attending meetings, and was confined to the magisterial district in which she lived. For the next sixteen years, she had only *three days* in which she was 'free' from Apartheid restrictions. Despite the regime's attempt to turn Mary Moodley into a 'non-person', her determination and spirit of struggle remained with her until her death in October 1979. For those who knew 'Auntie Mary', that spirit will remain forever.

These six women – Ray Alexander, Elizabeth Mafekeng, Frances Baard, Mabel Balfour, Liz Abrahams and Mary Moodley – typify the militant spirit of the food and canning workers during the 1940s, '50s and '60s. Deeply committed women, they sacrificed a great deal to devote their lives to the struggle of the workers and people of South Africa as a whole. Yet they were by no means alone in this struggle. They always had the strength of the workers behind them, and many other leaders came to the fore to assist them or replace them when they were banned. We must not overlook the contributions made by other women like Christina Matthews, Dolores Telling (FCWU, PE) and Stella Damons (FCWU, PE), all of whom played an equally important role in the struggle.

Viola Hashe

When Viola Hashe was elected Secretary General of the South African Clothing Workers Union (SACWU) in March 1956 she became the first women leader of an all male union in South Africa.

This union is one of the oldest African trade unions in the country, founded in 1928 by Gana Makabeni. When large numbers of African women began to enter the garment industry, 'Solly' Sachs of the Garment Workers Union organized them into a separate union for African women only, the GWU of African Women. This was done because in terms of the IC Act, 'pass-bearing natives' could not be registered as 'employees' and African women were not yet obliged to carry passes.

Born in 1926, in Gabashane, Viola Hashe was a teacher by profession. At one time she was Assistant Secretary of the Chemical Workers Union and the Dairy Workers Union, but from 1956 on, she worked with SACWU. She began as a typist in the office, then became private secretary to the late Gana Makabeni, and after his death in 1955 she succeeded him as Secretary General.

In 1953 and 1954, Viola Hashe served on the Transvaal Provincial Executive of the ANC, and became the first woman regional chairperson of the West Rand region of Congress. In 1956, she was the first woman to be threatened with deportation under Section 29 of the Urban Areas Act. As in the case of Elizabeth Mafekeng a few years later, no reasons were given for the notice except a vague reference to Viola 'not being good' for the township in which she lived. However, with the help of expert counsel in Mrs Shulamith Muller, the Town Council was forced to back down barely seven hours before the order was to take effect.

This was a fortunate turn of events for the people of South Africa who would otherwise have been robbed of a distinguished and fearless leader. In her capacity as Secretary General of the SACWU, 'she displayed exceptional qualities as a leader and served the union very well'.[33] An equally well-respected leader in SACTU, she was a member of the Management Committee from 1956 onwards, and in 1960 became Vice-President of SACTU.

An interesting sideline to the story of Viola's election to the Vice-Presidency is relevant to this chapter. It was actually Lucy Mvubelo who made history in the South African trade union movement as the first woman Vice-President of SACTU. She was elected at the Inaugural Conference of March 1955 but by 1959 had been seduced into the SATUC–FOFATUSA camp and betrayed the principles of non-racial trade unionism on which SACTU was founded (see Chapter 11). Viola Hashe, on the other hand, resisted co-optation by the reformist elements and became one of SACTU's most dynamic leaders.

Viola was elected to represent SACTU at various Wage Board Hearings, public meetings and in 1959 to the ILO Conference in

Geneva. At SACTU's important 1959 Conference in Durban, she was a main speaker on 'Passes for Women'.[34]

Presiding over the SACTU Annual Conference in October 1960 after the State of Emergency had been lifted, Viola summed up SACTU's attitude to the increasing attacks on the organization and its members. 'We will not budge an inch. We will not be divided. The interests of the workers are one.' Viola Hashe continued to carry out her work in the interests of all workers until the inevitable retribution of the state was directed against her. In 1963, she was banned and restricted to Roodepoort where she lived until her recent and untimely death in 1977.

Rita Ndzanga

Secretary of the Toy Workers Union and an active leader of the SAR & HWU alongside her husband, Lawrence, Rita was banned from trade union activity in 1964. In 1969, she was charged under the Terrorism Act, acquitted and re-arrested along with 21 others. Rita is one of the countless detainees who has given evidence of torture while under interrogation. Police worked in shifts, questioning her day and night, in the course of which a White policeman picked her up by the hair and dropped her on to a gas pipe. When she screamed in pain the police merely closed the windows. In 1976, Rita was once again detained and it was during this time that Lawrence was murdered in detention. The state continued its brutal attack on these courageous trade unionists by barring Rita from attending her own husband's funeral.

Phyllis Altman

From 1956 to 1963, Phyllis Altman was the only full-time paid employee of SACTU. As Assistant General Secretary, she played a valuable and indispensable role in the organization during those years. Phyllis' childhood and education were similar to that of many White South Africans. At high school the only time students were given a chance to contemplate the plight of Africans was on Thursdays, when the girls were required to 'sew for the poor Blacks'. After completing university, Phyllis became a primary school teacher and then later worked for the Springbok Legion, an anti-fascist organization for ex-servicemen formed during the Second World War. In this work she came face to face with the disastrous effects of the Apartheid system on African men, bitter from their treatment on release from the armed forces.

She joined SACTU in 1956, initially to do part-time office work. Soon, however, she became very much involved in every part of SACTU work emanating from Head Office. In her own words, she became the 'International Department', always sending out information to other trade union bodies throughout the world, fostering international working class solidarity. In 1957, Phyllis represented SACTU at the Fourth Congress of the WFTU and made first-hand contact with representatives from other trade union bodies. It is largely due to the efforts of Phyllis in sending SACTU publications and primary materials to libraries and trade unions overseas that it is possible to write this book today. In order to prevent the Special Branch from confiscating all copies of SACTU materials, she would periodically send them out of the country to be kept on record elsewhere. Much of the material used in writing this book has been gathered from these sources safely kept outside the borders of Apartheid.

Phyllis contributed to SACTU in yet another way. A novelist herself, she always appreciated the cultural aspect of the struggle for liberation and injected her enthusiasm into SACTU activities, whether by organizing a '£1-a-Day play' for one of the conferences or merely encouraging African workers to sing freedom songs at social gatherings.

Phyllis and other comrades working out of Head Office did a commendable job in coordinating the various strands of SACTU work in Johannesburg until she too was banned from trade union activity in September 1963. Though she continued to assist the organization, it became virtually impossible and Phyllis Altman left South Africa in 1964 believing she could contribute more from abroad.

Though her origins were not working class, Phyllis joined the struggle of African workers and always felt privileged that as a White woman she was accepted into SACTU so completely. Like Ray Alexander, this was because Phyllis always elevated the emancipation of Black workers in South Africa above all else.

At this point, mention should be made of other progressive White women trade unionists who contributed much to the South African trade union movement, and who, like Ray Alexander, were banned either before SACTU was formed or shortly after. Nancy Dick had been Secretary of the Cape Town TWIU branch when she was banned in 1954. Bettie du Toit was elected to the National Executive Committee of the SAT & LC in 1949, and had been active in

Frances Baard, Secretary, A-FCWU
Port Elizabeth

Liz Abrahams, Acting General Secretary,
FCWU (*lower left*)

Phyllis Altman, Assistant General
Secretary, SACTU

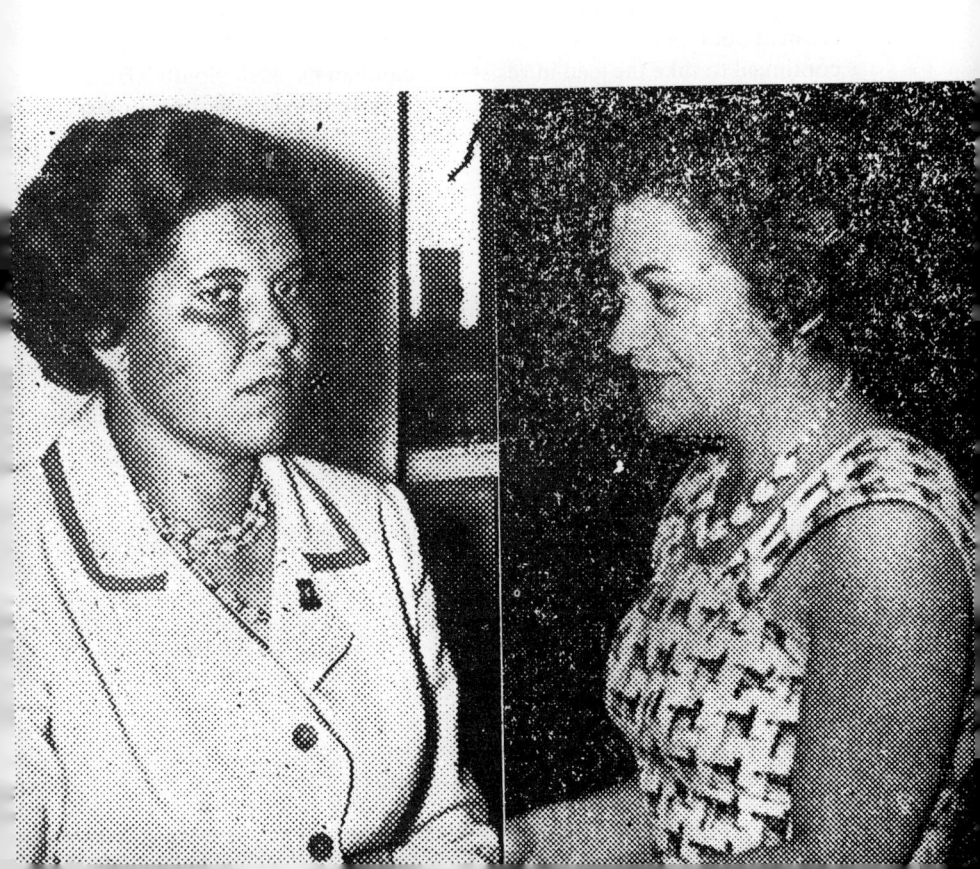

organizing sweet workers, textile workers and was Secretary of the Laundry Workers Union in the Cape before her banning in 1953. Becky Lan was elected to replace Ray Alexander and although banned in 1954 herself, she was not ordered to resign from her Union until 1956. In her letter of farewell to the Union, Becky said,

(The Minister of Justice) can remove leader after leader, but for every leader removed, new leaders will arise! He will still have to face the mass of the workers in the factories and homes. Men and women who will speak with one voice, who will be victorious in their struggle for their aspirations expressed in the Freedom Charter.[35]

As we have illustrated, new leaders did arise and many of these had their origins in the African working class. The militancy of these women in the South African context is unique in comparison with women's struggles elsewhere. Their oppression spans race, class and sex and hence their struggle is against a greater menace than women face elsewhere, that is, the Apartheid system of exploitation.

Like the men who struggle alongside them, they were silenced in various ways by the ruthless policies of the regime. This did not, however, prevent the women from contributing to the struggle for the emancipation of the workers and the people of South Africa. They have continued to take the lead in resistance campaigns inside South Africa, for example, organizing the women of Crossroads squatter camp most recently, and in exile many women have joined the ANC military wing to carry the struggle forward.

NOTES

1. *Workers Unity*, no. 3, May 1977.
2. For more information on laws affecting African women in South Africa, see H. Bernstein, op. cit., and SAIRR, *Laws Affecting . . .*, op. cit.
3. Quoted in a speech by Ray Alexander on the occasion of the commemoration of twenty years of the FSAW.
4. ibid.
5. Mary Benson, *Struggle for a Birthright*, Penguin, Harmondsworth, 1966.
6. Interview, Stephen Dlamini.
7. Interview, Mate Mfusi.
8. Interview, Elias Mbele.
9. Interview, John Gaetsewe.
10. Interview, Moses Mabhida.

11. ibid.
12. At this time women were not yet compelled to possess passes. In 1959, revised Labour Regulations specified that no one might engage an African (including women) who was not registered with a local Labour Bureau. However, it was not until 1963 that it became compulsory for African women to possess reference books. See *Laws Affecting* . . ., op. cit.
13. General Secretary Report, SACTU Fourth Annual National Conference, 28–29 March 1959.
14. Minutes, Fifth Annual National Conference, 8–10 October, 1960.
15. ibid.
16. *New Age*, 21 January and 18 February 1960.
17. *New Age*, 14 February 1960.
18. Interview, Stephen Dlamini.
19. *Workers Unity*, August 1955.
20. Interview, Phyllis Altman.
21. An interesting sideline to this story is that after consulting a witch doctor, some nurses threw a spear at the matron's mirror. 'Unfortunately or fortunately one of the matrons did die during this time.' Interview, Mate Mfusi.
22. *New Age*, 10 May 1962.
23. Gladstone Tshume of the A-TWIU in the Eastern Cape was the only other person whose banning orders included this sentence. Tshume died of a stroke in 1957.
24. *New Age*, 24 September 1953.
25. *New Age*, 8 October 1953.
26. *Workers Unity*, November 1959.
27. *Morning Star/Ikwezi Lomso*, January 1956.
28. In particular, Australian trade unions and workers responded to this campaign with telegrams and letters of protest. Later, the Australian Meat Employees Society sent a letter and donation of £12 for Elizabeth Mafekeng.
29. *New Age*, 12 November 1959.
30. *Workers Unity*, November 1959.
31. *New Age*, 25 May 1961.
32. *Workers Unity*, March 1957.
33. Interview, George Monare, former Assistant General Secretary, SACWU, 1960.
34. Minutes, SACTU Fourth Annual National Conference, 28–29 March 1959.
35. *Morning Star/Workers Unity*, vol. 3, no. 16, September 1956.

10 SACTU AND THE CONGRESS ALLIANCE

I am glad that SACTU has not listened to the ill advice that they should not be interested in politics. There is a Zulu saying that if you are pricked by a thorn you also have to use a thorn to get it out. Workers are oppressed by political action; they must take political action in reply.[1]

Chief Lutuli

Chief Lutuli's central message at the historic 1959 SACTU Conference was on the importance of the dialectical relationship between the trade union struggle and the political struggle. He emphasized the necessity for a stronger link between the two organizations which embodied these, SACTU and the ANC. This conference was to have a profound effect on the working relationship between the two organizations in the ensuing years.

As we have seen in Chapter 3, from its inception SACTU committed itself to an alliance with all other progressive forces fighting for the total liberation of their country. In turn, the ANC expressed their solidarity with the new organization:

... we welcome warmly the formation of the South African Congress of Trade Unions, a federal Trade Union body which will coordinate the activities of all workers, without consideration of their race or colour. This bold step ushers in a new era in the development of our Trade Union movement.

In the same speech, Oliver Tambo, Acting Secretary-General of the ANC, called for ANC members to become organizers in factories, farms, mines, vineyards and sugar plantations. Recalling the role of the ANC in the African Mine Workers Union he stressed that 'this must come to life again'.

A strong Trade Union movement will mean a strong Congress movement and the message of both the Trade Unions and the ANC must be carried into every factory and every workshop in the land.[2]

At SACTU's First Annual National Conference in March 1956, the President in his address to the delegates reiterated the position of the new body:

While the South African Congress of Trade Unions must thus pursue an independent policy in the interests of the workers, it must also participate unreservedly in the struggle to mobilize the people behind their demands as embodied in the Freedom Charter and must cooperate with all other organizations engaged in this struggle.[3]

Even before SACTU was formed, however, the CNETU had also recognized that its role was 'not only to ask for daily bread, but to widen our interests and our activity in the political sphere. . . . We were a great intrument in supporting anything which related to all spheres.'[4] This understanding of the inextricable link between economic and political power strengthened the political movements and added force to the campaigns initiated jointly by the movements in the 1940s and early 1950s.

From 1912 to 1949, the African National Congress had pursued all constitutional and peaceful means possible to try to win basic changes in South African society which would benefit the African masses. During the 1940s, however, the newly-formed Youth League of the ANC injected a fresh radicalism into the organization and the result was a significant change in leadership and a new blueprint for methods of resistance. A Programme of Action drawn up by Youth Leaguers such as Nelson Mandela, Walter Sisulu, O. R. Tambo and Anton Lembede was passed at the 1949 ANC Conference and outlined methods which included boycotts, strikes, civil disobedience and non-cooperation. The first step in the implementation of this Programme was a call for a 'national stoppage of work for one day as a mark of protest against the reactionary policy of the Government'.[5] 1 May 1950 was chosen as the date for this first demonstration of protest. The issue was the impending Suppression of Communism Act and the restrictions placed on J. B. Marks, Moses Kotane and Yusuf Dadoo and others under the Riotous Assemblies Act. It also called for support of workers' wage demands and the CNETU played a crucial role in the organizational work leading up to the day of protest.

The Nationalist Government prepared their response by placing a ban on demonstrations and meetings during this period. Despite this show of force, more than half of the African workforce in the Johannesburg area stayed at home on May Day and in several areas workers and residents defied the ban on meetings. The South African police reacted brutally, brandishing guns and bayonets against defenceless African protestors and at the end of the day 19 had been killed and 38 wounded. The police had demonstrated how effectively they could carry out the policies of the Apartheid state in crushing the people's resistance. Victimization and harassment continued after the day of protest but in spite of this, the political leadership planned a new national strike for 26 June, to protest against the May Day police killings and raise the same issues as before.

'If ever there was a time when the African people were required to put their eight-million force behind the principles of democracy, in alliance with other freedom-loving members of the South African community, that time has come,' said ANC President Dr Moroka. Leaders of the other nationally-oppressed groups like the Indian Congress, the African People's Organization (representing Coloured People) and the Communist Party joined in. Dr Dadoo of the Indian Congress commented: 'Never before in the history of South Africa have the national leaders acted so swiftly and with complete oneness of purpose to beat back the fascist attack of the Government on the lives and liberties of the people.'[6] Unmistakable steps towards non-racial unity were clearly being taken.

The response on 26 June was widespread but uneven throughout the country. Port Elizabeth witnessed the most effective mass response from Africans, Indians and Coloureds affecting all industries in the area. Emergency preparations were required to ensure a steady supply of coal to the furnaces of the municipal power stations. In Durban, the Indian community responded to the call but amongst African workers the protest was not well-observed. In the Witwatersrand area also, the response was disappointing except in Alexandra and Evaton townships. The pattern of response seemed to reflect the strengths of the political movements in each area. Workers on the Rand were probably exhausted after the long build-up to the May Day action and the repression which followed. The Port Elizabeth response stands out as an example of a close working relationship between ANC and the Black labour movement typical of the area. In Natal, the Indian Congress leadership had recognized the need for a grass-roots base amongst Indian workers.

The strike itself highlighted an important lesson for the political movement, the need to carefully gauge the mood of the working class before embarking on political mass action. It also pointed to the need for a national trade union coordinating body to appeal to workers throughout the country to respond to the political campaigns, a void which SACTU later filled. During this period the CNETU successfully organized Black workers in the Transvaal for the first protest strike, and in Port Elizabeth a high degree of class consciousness amongst Black workers existed largely as a result of the efforts of the FCWU, the A-FCWU and on the political front, the ANC. Similarly, in Durban there was a tradition of militancy on the part of the Indian trade unionists. The time was ripe for a truly representative trade union movement which could unite all of these various strands into one entity.

In 1952, the ANC launched a Defiance Campaign against selected racial laws. During the course of the campaign, 8,000 volunteers in every corner of the country were jailed for deliberately defying Apartheid restrictions. Workers throughout the country responded to this call in large numbers and it was the first time that Africans, Indians, Coloured and Whites had participated together in such a massive display of resistance. As a result of this campaign membership in the ANC dramatically increased from 7,000 to 100,000 and it was an indication of the preparedness of the people for the unprecedented mass struggles carried out throughout the decade. As one ANC veteran recalls: 'Even those just out of jail were ready to go back. It looked like Freedom was very near. I thought that it would come by 1963 or 1964.'[7]

The Congress of the People

Following this successful campaign, a nation-wide movement was launched to convene a 'Congress of the People' bringing together South Africans of all races to put forward their demands for a free South Africa. The ANC formed an alliance with the SAIC, SACPO, SACOD and SACTU to prepare for the most representative assembly ever held in the country. The actual Congress took place on 26 June 1955 in Kliptown, a town near Johannesburg, though the COP Committees were active for 16 months beforehand. Circulars went out asking people in the cities and the villages throughout the country: 'IF YOU COULD MAKE THE LAWS ... WHAT WOULD YOU DO? HOW WOULD YOU SET ABOUT MAKING SOUTH AFRICA A HAPPY PLACE FOR ALL THE PEOPLE WHO LIVE IN IT?'[8]

SACTU had been formed only months before the COP took place, but many of its working class leaders were fully involved in the organizing committees, actively collecting demands from workers in the factories and townships, especially in Natal and the Eastern Cape. At its Inaugural Conference SACTU had welcomed the COP and endorsed the submission of workers' demands for inclusion in the Freedom Charter.

Archie Sibeko (*right*), Secretary, Cape Western Province, Local Committee, collecting workers' demands for Freedom Charter, 1955

Newclare Township delegates to the Congress of the People, 1955

Alven Bennie describes how the Port Elizabeth SACTU Local Committee mobilized workers around the campaign:

The workers responded with enthusiasm and we were working day and night preparing for the Congress of the People. . . . That campaign helped us a lot. . . . The workers would bring their demands to the offices after work. We worked till late and they would come in with their papers from different industries. We set up small committees, not only for the Congress, but we would organize a committee of workers so that they could continue with the work of organizing for the trade unions – in the dairies, laundries, road construction, with building workers, railway workers, etc.

The real organizing of the workers was boosted by the campaign. . . . You see, they had something to keep them together to discuss common problems. Some of their problems were those of higher wages, better working conditions, and then with the set up in South Africa this can only be solved by having a union. We explained that workers must unite, have a union to represent them. So, this gave us a chance to organize workers and explain to them that some of these problems would not be solved by the Congress of the People. Some workers were under the impression that by taking these demands to the Congress, when we came back these demands would be accepted by the bosses. So this also brought us nearer to the workers.[9]

On Saturday, 25 June 1955, on a large field in Kliptown, 3,000 delegates elected in COP Committees all over South Africa came together to coordinate their demands. The people arrived dressed in their colourful traditional dress or wearing the new Congress uniforms, people of all races and representing various class positions – doctors, ministers, shopkeepers, labourers, domestic servants, peasants, students and teachers. Throughout Saturday and on Sunday morning the Freedom Charter, drafted by the National Action Council representing the Congress Alliance, was read in English, Sotho and Xhosa. The important part of the economic demands in the Freedom Charter reads:

The national wealth of our country, the heritage of all South Africans, shall be restored to the people; the mineral wealth beneath the soil, the banks and monopoly industry shall be transferred to the ownership of the people as a whole.[10]

The speaker who moved this section of the Charter explained it to the Congress delegates in these words:

It says ownership of the mines will be transferred to the ownership of the people. It says wherever there is a Gold Mine there will no longer be a compound boss. There will be a committee of the workers to run the Gold

Mines. Friends, we also say that wherever there is a factory and where there are workers who are exploited, we say that the workers will take over and run the factories. In other words, the ownership of the factories will come into the hands of the people.

Friends, there is one more thing. . . . Let the banks come back to the people, let us have a people's committee to run the banks.

The next speaker at the COP was Billy Nair of Durban, one of SACTU's most militant leaders. He stated:

Now, comrades, the biggest difficulty we are facing in South Africa is that one of capitalism in all its oppressive measures versus the ordinary people – the ordinary workers in the country. We find in this country . . . the means of production, the factories, the lands, the industries, and everything possible is owned by a small group of people who are the capitalists in this country. They skin the people, as a matter of fact in exploitation. They oppress in order to keep them as slaves in the land of their birth.

Now friends, this is a very important demand in the Freedom Charter. Now we would like to see a South Africa where the industries, the lands, the big businesses and the mines, and everything that is owned by a small group of people in this country, must be owned by all the people in this country. That is what we demand, and that is what we fight for and until we have achieved that we must not rest. I appeal to you all to fight and struggle towards this end until we have achieved it.[11]

In this speech, Billy Nair articulated clearly the conditions of exploitation of the South African working class, particularly African workers. SACTU represented these workers and as a class-based organization, differed from the other members of the Congress Alliance representing the various national groups. Nevertheless, the formation of the Congress Alliance was as important to the political struggle as SACTU's formation was to the trade union struggle. In both cases, tremendous advances were made in the struggle for non-racial unity and the fight for liberation. This was the first of many campaigns carried out jointly by SACTU and the Congress Alliance throughout the 1950s and early 1960s, campaigns which focused on both national and class oppression. SACTU held true to the belief that the struggle for immediate economic demands was inherently bound up with the struggle for political rights for all South Africans. However, SACTU also recognized the workers as the driving force in the liberation struggle, those who owned no property and had nothing to sell but their labour-power – and consequently, nothing to lose.

Out of the COP, a National Consultative Committee (NCC) was

formed, incorporating representatives from each of the five Congresses. The stated aims of the NCC were firstly to popularize the aims and objectives of the Freedom Charter, and secondly, to coordinate the activities of the Congress Alliance on matters of common interest.

During the Sunday afternoon session of the COP, the police, armed with sten guns, marched into the midst of the gathering and proceeded to confiscate all papers, documents, camera film, posters and banners. The meeting continued as Special Branch policemen harassed speakers and members of the audience. People finally drifted away from the field at dusk on Sunday evening, away from a historic conference which gave birth to the Freedom Charter, encompassing the demands of the South African masses in their search for a new society based on equal rights for all its members.

The real essence of the Freedom Charter reflects the attitude or consciousness of the working class as a proletariat and reflects the immediate objectives of the working class. . . . The only way out, to eliminate all the problems in South Africa is through the ideas enshrined in the Freedom Charter. But the real instrument to bring this about should be the working class . . . the Freedom Charter . . . is not in itself a socialist document but it is the basis, the foundation stone for socialism because of the objective conditions in South Africa.[12]

SACTU pledged its wholehearted support to the demands incorporated in the Freedom Charter, stating that:

While the South African Congress of Trade Unions must pursue an independent policy in the interests of the workers, it must participate fully and unreservedly in their struggle to mobilize the people behind their demands as embodied in the 'Freedom Charter' and for the realisation of its aims and objectives, and must towards this end, cooperate with all other organizations engaged in the struggle.[13]

The Boycott Strategy – A 'Silent Weapon'

In keeping with the aims set out by the ANC Youth League in the 1940s and incorporated into the Programme of Action in 1949, the boycott strategy became an important weapon in the struggle waged by the Congress Alliance during the 1950s. The consumer boycotts in particular proved to be very successful counter-attacks against the suffering inflicted by the Apartheid regime on the African people who were beginning to realize the might that lay in their purchasing power alone.

The first boycotts called for by the ANC in the 1940s were directed against various Apartheid institutions like the Native Representative Council, the Native Advisory Boards and White representation in Parliament. Abolition of these institutions was what the Youth League demanded as well as direct representation for the African masses. It was in 1954, however, that the boycott strategy was fully embarked upon and implemented in various ways.

Early in 1954, the New Brighton branch of the ANC in Port Elizabeth led a boycott of local shops where African customers were maltreated or where Africans were refused employment. A picket was organized and when anyone moved towards the door Africans would yell, 'Akungenwa' (Don't Enter). The boycott, although small in comparison with the major boycotts of the decade, was successful; several shopkeepers met the Congress requests and the boycott was withdrawn. In Chapter 8 we have already documented the struggles of the workers at United Tobacco Company and the boycott of their products initiated by the ANC, the SAIC and the SACOD in 1954. The tobacco workers themselves called for such an action and were successful in affecting the profits of the Company which was exploiting them, despite the retribution they suffered as a result of the strike.

With clear intentions of controlling the African people and ensuring the continuation of its cheap labour policy, the Nationalist Government passed the Bantu Education Act in 1953. According to the Nationalists, there was to be 'no place for him (the "Bantu") in the European community above the level of certain forms of labour'.[14] It was a system of inferior education designed to keep the African masses in a subservient and subjugated role and signalled the ending of traditional missionary education. April 1955, the month chosen for the transfer of control of Bantu Education to the Department of Native Affairs, saw the beginning of a campaign to boycott this racist education system.

More than 7,000 children stayed away from school in various parts of the country, and the ANC organized alternative education in the form of 'cultural clubs' particularly in the Eastern Cape and the Transvaal. The leaders of these 'clubs' were teachers who opposed Bantu Education and provided the students with a political content that they never would receive elsewhere. In the Port Elizabeth area, SACTU took the lead in the boycott, even though it was initiated by the powerful ANC Branch there. Labour leaders and workers were strongly opposed to Bantu Education and assisted in the setting up of the 'cultural clubs', some of which survived for two to three years.[15] Police repression, however, forced the closure of most of these throughout the country. The government introduced legislation making the running of independent schools a criminal offence, unless they were registered under and accepted the inferior syllabus of the Bantu Education Act. Such a campaign is difficult to sustain unless carried out on a mass scale and only if sufficient resources are available to provide alternative means of acquiring an education which can prepare for liberation. As a strategy this boycott could never have been as successful as the economic boycotts carried out by the Congress Alliance.

Before detailing the economic, or consumer boycotts called by the progressive movement in South Africa it is helpful to briefly review other campaigns which were limited to certain localities but were nevertheless an attack on the total system of Apartheid and contributed towards the general struggle for liberation. Bus boycotts were carried out by the African people as early as 1945 in Alexandra township and 1949 in New Brighton; both were successful in preventing the imposition of increased transportation costs. In Chapter 5 we have described in detail the historic Alexandra bus boycott of 1957 where the combined might of the masses succeeded in halting the state in its attempt to place the burden of increased transportation costs on the backs of the poorly-paid African workers. Other campaigns include the boycott of beer-halls and dipping tanks, initiated by the militant women of Natal and documented in Chapter 9.

Govan Mbeki, ANC national leader from the Eastern Cape, once described the advantage of the boycott as follows:

An economic boycott is one of those weapons which may be silently used by all without fear of victimization. Not all the police nor all the military are sufficiently powerful to compel one individual to spend one penny on a commodity he does not want.[16]

This is obviously one reason for the success of the Congress Alliance-sponsored boycotts during the 1950s; the people could actively participate in the collective withdrawal of their purchasing power to cripple the ruling class without any fear of harassment or victimization. Furthermore, there was no legislation to prevent them from boycotting. Such actions are effective not only for their educational value but because they represent a direct attack on the basis of exploitation, the cheap labour policy under Apartheid. This is particularly the case for the potato boycott of 1959.

Before that, however, a mass boycott of the products of

Nationalist-controlled business concerns was initiated. In 1957, the Congress organizations jointly announced a boycott of a number of brands of cigarettes, tea, coffee and clothing.

'You attack me and degrade me in a thousand ways,' he says in effect, to the Government. 'You force my wages down and then increase my taxes. You throw me out of my job and my home. You deny my children education and force my wife to carry a pass. Why should I buy Nationalist cigarettes and jams? Why should I do business with Nationalist firms?'[17]

Among the products listed in the boycott were Rembrandt cigarette products, Senator Coffee, Braganza Tea, Glenryck Canned Fish, Neptune Canned Fish, Laaiplek Farm Feeds and Protea Canned Fish. In the case of Rembrandt products, there was a long-standing tradition of close ties between the company executives and the Afrikaner Broederbond. At the time the company attempted through an expensive newspaper and film-advertising campaign, to appear as 'British' (with its Rothmans of 'Pall Mall' brand) or as 'American' (Peter Stuyvesant, 'founder of New York') as possible. These attempts have continued to the present as Anton Rupert (head of Rembrandt and still a member of the Broederbond) and his cohorts try to ward off an international boycott of their products. Despite this, boycott campaigns have been initiated by anti-Apartheid groups in Britain, Canada, Australia and New Zealand, directed against a variety of Rembrandt/Rothmans-controlled tobacco and other products.[18]

The Congress Alliance called for a national boycott of all these Nationalist products to begin on 26 June 1959. The announcement followed a victory over attempts by several of these companies to prevent the Congress from calling for such a boycott; a nine-month-long court interdict against them for distribution of literature on the economic boycott was withdrawn. The Nationalist employers feared such a campaign, recognizing the power of mass action directed against them. The mere announcement of the boycott had induced one large company to reinstate its African workers who were victimized following the previous year's Stay-At-Home.

At the 1958 SACTU Annual National Conference, the Management Committee expressed support for this kind of boycott, 'especially because of the anti-Trade Union policy of this Company' (Rembrandt). As an educational tool, this boycott was an important weapon in the struggle against Nationalist domination and exploitation. Though the potato boycott was launched during that same year, the boycott of

Nationalist products continued into the early 1960s with renewed emphasis by the Congress Alliance from time to time. In general, it was considered an effective campaign.

The potato boycott stands out as one of the most successful of all the joint Congress campaigns conducted during these years.

The effectiveness of this boycott was such that it paralysed the potato farming industry because this boycott was directed against a single product, the potato and was easy to carry out, unlike a boycott aimed at selected products of Nationalist firms which workers did not know.[19]

Back in the late 1930s and early 1940s, Gert Sibande was active in organizing farmworkers in Bethal, Transvaal, where conditions on the farms were intolerable. Sibande, who came from a family of farm labourers, tried every avenue to plead for the lives of these exploited workers. He joined the ANC, formed a Bethal branch and became its Chairman in 1942.

In 1947, Sibande decided to try to publicize the conditions of workers there and called on a journalist and a priest to investigate conditions at Bethal. Ruth First and Michael Scott subsequently exposed the inhuman conditions on the Transvaal farms and their disclosures were taken up in *New Age* and by various groups including a succession of magistrates, one of whom described the conditions as 'tantamount to slavery'.[20] Following an inquiry, only a few foremen and 'boss-boys' (Black foremen) were charged with assault.

Twelve years later at the 1959 ANC Conference, reports presented there indicated that conditions on maize and potato farms remained the same. In fact, the situation had become even worse since unemployed Africans and petty offenders of the pass laws were now forced to accept these slave conditions and labour on the farms. Under a so-called volunteer scheme, 'petty offenders' were given the option of prosecution or six to twelve months of farm labour.[21] In practice, however, the alleged offenders were given no choice and were simply lined up and sent out to the farms.

Whilst his relatives hunt high and low for him, he may be groaning under the vicious clutches of a 'slave driver' in Bethal. He might return one day to present to his family the fruits of his labour – a network of weals all over his body, blistered hands and a broken man. Many workers disappear and never return.[22]

Over 3,000 labourers were supplied to farmers in 1947–48, and by

1953, the number had risen to 32,582. Other methods of recruitment including the use of convict labour subsequently replaced this scheme. A typical account of conditions for farm labourers stated:

> (I was) taken to a brick building with only one entrance, consisting of a door constructed from iron bars, and all the windows were barred with iron. That first evening all my clothes except my trousers were taken back by one of the bossboys, who gave me a sack and told me to wear it. I soon found that the living conditions were of the most primitive kind and worse than anything I have ever heard of. We were only allowed water to drink on our return from the fields in the evenings and before we started work in the morning. . . . During the whole time that I was on the farm I was not able to wash or shower, and I never saw any other worker wash or bath himself. . . . The building in which we slept was in a filthy condition. There were two half drums provided as a lavatory, and those two half drums remained inside the building where we slept. This was the only sanitary arrangement for approximately 60 workers employed on this farm. During the whole period I was there, the dilapidated blankets and sacks given to us were never washed or aired. There were bloodstains and they were infested with insects and smelled; the walls crawled with bugs and other insects, and they were never cleaned when I was there. . . . During the day, whilst we worked in the fields, we were continuously guarded by bossboys who carried knobkerries (clubs). They were 9 in number to guard 60 workers. The bossboys continuously assaulted the workers, more especially when they wanted the workers to do their work more hurriedly. On some occasions there appeared to be no reason whatsoever for the assaults other than to initiate newly arrived workers into a general pattern.[23]

Conditions on the potato farms were particularly horrific. Young children and adults were forced to dig the potatoes with their bare hands and there are many accounts of workers being beaten to death and left to die and be buried in the fields. These accounts prompted the delegates at the ANC conference to unanimously support the call by Robert Resha to place a ban on the purchase of potatoes. This was the start of the potato boycott; the campaign itself was launched on 31 May in Johannesburg at a national Anti-Pass Conference and mass meetings were then held in various parts of the country.

SACTU took a leading role, recognizing that the plight of these workers was the responsibility of all South African workers and that farm workers must be organized to resist low wages and the degrading living standards being forced upon them. Calls went out across South Africa: 'If you eat a potato, you are eating the blood of a fellow worker who has been killed and buried on these farms.' SACTU and the

Congress Alliance saw the struggle as one which was directed against both the state and agricultural capital. In actively encouraging the continuation of the forced labour system, the state assisted the White, racist farmers in their exploitation of Black workers and their families.

The boycott was a resounding success and demonstrated that African workers and consumers were prepared to sacrifice their cheap source of a staple food to fight together to end the exploitation of their brothers and sisters in the rural areas. Potatoes piled up in markets all over the country and rotted in the fields. Sympathetic merchants refused to stock their shelves. Fish and chip shops sold only fish as African workers stood strong in their refusal to eat potatoes. Many shopkeepers who continued to stock potatoes were forced to close down as the local people created angry scenes outside their stores. Despite government attempts to confuse the people with leaflets (for example, suggesting they should boycott mealie-meal (maize)), they could not break the solidarity and strength of the people in their commitment to the boycott.

POTATO BOYCOTT LIFTED. A VICTORY FOR THE PEOPLE. A WARNING FOR THE FARMERS.

This was the message on posters issued by the Congress Alliance in August 1959, explaining that the campaign which was planned as a short-term one, had been successful in calling attention to the conditions of farm labourers. Subsequently the government was forced to introduces changes in the farm labour system, even though limited, and White farmers could no longer get away with the same treatment of their workers. The boycott victory coincided with the close of the Transvaal potato season.

A similar campaign, although on a smaller scale, took place in the Eastern Cape during this period. The ANC called for a boycott of oranges, highlighting the miserable wages paid by the local farmers. Due to the strength and perseverance of this consumer boycott wages were raised slightly.

An extremely important outcome of the use of the boycott weapon by the Congress Alliance in the 1950s was its transferral to the international scene. By 1960, anti-Apartheid groupings in Britain called for a boycott of imported South African goods, encouraged to do so by the Congress Alliance. In January of the same year, the Second All-African People's Conference resolved to boycott South African products. The WFTU had always supported the struggle of Black workers and this support included a commitment to the international boycott.

When the call for an international boycott of South African products was issued, the fruit and wine corporations reacted with instant panic. The state also sensed the potential threat to exports and profits and within one year passed the Liquor Amendment Act, No. 72 of 1961. This Act reversed the previous restriction on the purchase of alcohol by Africans and subsequently permitted the purchase of hard liquor in licensed bottle stores in the 'White' parts of towns. As well, there was an immediate end to the degrading practice of liquor raids in African areas, where police would force their way into homes and terrorize the residents in the middle of the night.

As the international boycott campaign developed, it provided encouragement to the people of South Africa to continue their struggle against the exploitation of those who produced the wealth of their country. The African Food and Canning Workers Union and the FCWU, representing the heavily exploited food workers, realized the crucial importance of boycotts undertaken by the international community. It was these workers who themselves initiated the boycott of the goods which they produced – the tinned fruit, vegetables and fish, all commodities which embodied their very exploitation – and their plea was repeated each year at their national conferences.

Here then is the answer to the oft-repeated question: 'Won't a boycott of South African goods hurt the African workers?' As SACTU articulated in a resolution passed at its Eighth Annual National Conference in 1963:

It is sometimes argued even by well-meaning people abroad, that if the world boycotts South Africa, we, the working people, will suffer most. Even if this were true – and we do not believe it – let us assure our well-wishers abroad that we do not shrink from any hardship in the cause of freedom. As it is, we are starving and our children are dying of hunger.

The working people of our country do not eat imported food or wear foreign made clothes; nor do we benefit from the export of South African mealies, wool, wine and gold.

To our friends and well-wishers abroad we say that trafficking in the fruits of Apartheid can never be in the interests of the workers who suffer under Apartheid.[24]

The consumer boycott strategy pursued by the Congress Alliance inside South Africa indicates to what lengths the masses will go to ensure that improvements in their objective conditions are realized. It is a powerful weapon against the ruling class attempts to increase the rate of exploitation of Black workers and extract greater profits at their expense. The boycott is an effective educational tool as well, as Walter Sisulu points out:

> In these boycotts our experience is that each time they have roused the political consciousness of the people, brought about a greater solidarity and unity among the masses. In this way they have raised the peoples' organizations to a higher level, demonstrating the correctness of the action.[25]

The Political Strike or 'Stay-At-Home'

Cold skies and drizzle. The closed shops in Market Street. The closed stalls at the Indian Market. The solitary watchman at the closed factory gate. An air of desolation hangs over the city. Not the bustling morning crowds leaving the city stations and the bus stops. Not the coffee drinkers at the coffee carts. But empty trains, and empty buses. The workers have stayed at home.[26]

Inspired by the upsurge of militancy generated by the Alexandra Bus Boycott in January and February 1957, the NCC called for a day of 'protest, prayer and dedication' for 26 June, South Africa Freedom Day. There was renewed optimism regarding the power of mass action as an effective weapon against ruling class domination and so the preparations for a country-wide demonstration began.

Pamphlets were issued listing the demands of the people:

Asinamali! We want £1 0s. 0d. a day.
Asinamali! No increase in taxation.
Stand by our leaders.
No passes for women.
Stop the police raids.
Away with Group Areas.
No Bantu Education.
Withdraw the Native Laws Amendment Bill.
No interference with the freedom of worship.
Stop deportations, bannings, censorship.
Open universities for all.
No Apartheid in nursing.
Verwoerd must go.
Down with Apartheid.
Forward to a multi-racial conference.

These reflect both direct working class demands for 'Asinamali' and those which are less directly relevant to workers like open universities and freedom of worship. In the Johannesburg area, preparations were thorough with pamphlets and posters distributed throughout the townships on the Rand, urging workers to strike for £1 0s. 0d. a day and rejection of passes and permits. The only other area where a strike call was issued was in Port Elizabeth.

In Port Elizabeth and Uitenhage, thousands of workers walked to and from work and stood for one minute to pledge themselves to fight against Nationalist tyranny. In Durban and Pietermaritzburg mass demonstrations and torchlight processions were held in support of the call. Mass meetings, prayers and speeches in the evening were called by the Cape Town and Bloemfontein leadership and in Worcester meetings of workers in all the industrial sites were held between 11.00 a.m. and 12 noon with a mass demonstration that evening. Despite police intimidation, baton charges on peaceful demonstrators and a threat by the Transvaal Chamber of Industries that workers who stayed away would be summarily dismissed and banished, most of the industries in the city of Johannesburg came to a standstill and the strike was estimated to be 70–80 per cent effective. In Port Elizabeth, too, although the dockworkers failed to strike due to threats of repression, many other factories came to a halt.

The most radical response to the Congress Alliance call came from the Rand and Port Elizabeth where the workers had recently participated in the Bus Boycott, suggesting that involvement in mass action has a cumulative effect. Workers gain strength from previous victories and their collective class-consciousness is raised by each action taken along the way.

The national strike, though not widespread in its effectiveness, did gain results in the form of some government concessions. From 1957 there was an increase in Wage Board activity which was more than likely a response to both the Bus Boycott and the 26th June strike. The government recommended the re-investigation of the position of unskilled workers on the Rand, in Cape Town, Durban, Pretoria, Bloemfontein, East London, Port Elizabeth, Pietermaritzburg and Kimberley who fell under Wage Determination No. 105. This Determination had not been revised since November 1952, when the minimum wages payable were set at £1 7s. 0d. per week. New determinations were to be drafted for the laundry, cleaning and dyeing trade in all principal towns; the bread and confectionery industry on the Witwatersrand and Pietermaritzburg; stevedoring in the four main ports; the clothing industry in the Transvaal and uncontrolled areas;

and for the meat trade in the principal centres. These determinations reversed the trend of declining real wages after 1957.[27]

The 26 June actions were regarded as an overall success by the Congress Alliance, and it was on the basis of this assessment that the movement went ahead with the planning of an extended political strike to continue for three days in April 1958.

Organizing support for a political strike or 'Stay-At-Home' (SAH) in South Africa is a much more difficult task than organizing workers to respond to a strike call which focuses on specific issues and concrete demands at the workplace. For workers to withdraw their labour power *en masse* they have to be well-organized, issues have to be extremely clear and relevant to the lives of the workers and they must be prepared for large scale intimidation and repression carried out by the state. The relationship between the trade union movement and the political movement is also a crucial factor in the dynamics of a call requiring mass response. All of these factors came into play during the 1958 SAH which subsequently provided many lessons for the Congress Alliance in its bid for mass support against the state.

In November 1957, in Congress Alliance discussions on how Blacks could influence the national elections to be held on 14 April 1958, Chief Lutuli called for the formation of a united front amongst all anti-Nationalist organizations, including the United Party. He suggested that the disenfranchised masses would influence the electorate through mass gatherings of prayer and dedication to freedom on election day. Pressure from SACTU pre-empted this form of action, however.

SACTU called a National Workers Conference for 15 and 16 March, where worker delegates could, as Lutuli said, 'get together to speak their hearts about what steps they will take to win their demands from the employers and from the Government.... The steps to be taken by the workers to implement their demands will be decided by them, not us.'[28] At the same time, Chief Lutuli expressed the concerns of some ANC members regarding the National Workers Conference:

Because of the name of the Conference, some people in our Congress organization are treating it as though it is to be a trade union affair, primarily concerning the active trade unionists and confined exclusively to delegations elected from the factories. Such conceptions are mistaken.[29]

He went on to stress the necessity of avoiding two errors: firstly, of assuming that a 'Workers Conference' is the same thing as a trade union conference, something that it could not be with the overwhelming majority of workers not organized into trade unions. Secondly, he warned of the error of forgetting that Congress is not exclusively a workers' organization in that it has in its ranks businessmen, professionals, housewives, etc. Lutuli urged *all* elements to go out amongst the workers in factories, shops, farms and mines, taking care to work in the townships as well, 'where we are strong'.

In February, SACTU organized Regional Workers Conferences in the Transvaal, Natal, Eastern and Western Cape as a prelude to the National Conference; these were to mobilize workers around the £1-a-Day slogan. Out of all the conferences came the message that workers wanted a national strike to coincide with the elections. As reported in *New Age*, 'the resentment and indignation of the workers was simmering to the boiling point'.

The National Workers Conference was held at 'Congress Square' Newclare township, Johannesburg, attracting 1,673 delegates from Ladysmith, Middleburg, the Eastern and Western Cape, Bloemfontein, Durban and all the Johannesburg townships, as well as an estimated 3,000 observers. Conference resolved to organize a 'week of National stay at home, protest and demonstration in support of the people's demands'. The twin slogans which came out of the discussions were 'Forward to a £1-a-Day Victory' and 'The Nationalists Must Go'. It was the £1-a-Day demand which was crucial for the Black workers and the final Conference resolution reflects the heightened awareness of their naked exploitation:

We the workers of South Africa, whose labour creates the country's wealth, we do not share in that wealth. Our wages are so little that we cannot live. Our children are naked and starving. The pass laws are killing us. Day and night the police are raiding, arresting us from home and wife.

A list of demands, signifying a call for an end to the cheap labour system and for participation in the parliamentary process came out of the Conference:

- We want higher wages for all workers, in factories and offices, on mines and on the farms, and in domestic service. We want a legal minimum of £1 0s. 0d. a day.
- We want an immediate end to all pass laws, for women and for men.
- We want Apartheid to be scrapped, including Group Areas and Job Reservation.
- We want an end to the Nationalist Party Government.
- We want a voice in the governing of the country.[30]

Four weeks of preparation preceded the national strike called for 14–16 April, this time with a different focus from the 1957 SAH because of the impending elections. 30,000 pamphlets were printed for distribution to a representative section of the voters, describing the Nationalist Government as the worst ever imposed on South Africa and calling for it to be ousted as well as for the United Party to break with its past policies. The Congress Alliance publicized that the stoppage was not to be directed against commerce and industry but against the government in a bid to force it to make political concessions and to legislate a minimum wage of £1 0s. 0d. a day.

Black workers soon realized what forces were aligned against them as the state and the employers began their onslaught, fearing a repeat of the 1957 strike but on a national scale. Employers called their workers in, either appealing to their loyalty and good sense or threatening them with pay cuts, demotions and dismissals if they withdrew their labour for the 3-day strike. City Councils undertook compound visits to persuade workers not to participate in this 'illegal' action and not to destroy the 'growing goodwill' that was developing between employers and employees. An appeal by the Zulu Paramount Chief, Cyprian ka Dinizulu – who had been used against strikers before – went out to Natal workers.

Threats followed the appeals. The Minister of Labour promised a 'counter-demonstration' which would show the 'non-White what was meant by White supremacy'; the Chief of Police, Major-General Rademeyer, promised stern action by the country's 23,000 police as he cancelled their leave and alerted them for election-week duty. It was also announced that the Union Defence Force would be on hand if needed. Lastly, a top-secret special committee was appointed by the Cabinet consisting of the Secretaries of Labour and Native Affairs and the Director of Prisons. They placed on standby a prison labour force of several thousand, within a short distance of all the major industrial centres to maintain essential services.

Next came the police raids throughout the townships and many workers were endorsed out of the urban areas. The Port Elizabeth leadership distributed leaflets in the reserves before the strike calling upon the people not to make themselves available for recruitment to industrial areas, a farsighted measure. Three weeks before the strike, the government placed a ban on meetings of more than ten Africans creating a further stranglehold on the preparations for the national demonstrations.

A final factor inhibiting the struggle at this stage was the position taken by the Africanist elements within the ANC. Though constituting a small anti-White force in African politics at this time, these men attempted to thwart the strike and were actively dissuading the people from responding to the Congress Alliance call.

On the actual morning of 14 April, squads of police in riot vans and armed with sten guns entered the townships at 2.00 a.m. and UDF troop carriers were placed on alert. Many workers were assaulted and beaten by the police even before the protest began.

All of these factors contributed to the disappointing overall response to the call for the SAH. In Port Elizabeth (New Brighton township), workers came out in large numbers but repression against strikers was fierce. 150 striking workers, including the entire executive of the FCWU from H. Jones Canning factory, were fired. Fifty-four women workers from the factory were arrested for constituting a crowd as they walked to New Brighton station. Melville Fletcher, Caleb Mayekiso and seven other Congress leaders were also arrested. In the city of Port Elizabeth itself, police charged striking workers who went to trade union offices with holding an illegal gathering. Despite this extensive harassment, it was estimated that the strike was 50 per cent effective in the Eastern Cape on the first day.

In Durban, major successes occurred in the textile, milling and public transport sectors and approximately 40 per cent of the workers (some 31,000 workers) responded, according to various reports. The most significant aspect of the strike in Durban was the support it received from the dockworkers where an estimated 75 per cent of the workforce went home to the reserves and on their return refused to work overtime until paid £1 0s. 0d. a day. These workers had forged the link between the political and economic demands voiced during the Stay-At-Home.

In Johannesburg, the main response came from Sophiatown and Newclare townships. Laundry, milling and clothing workers came out in large numbers and most unions affiliated to SACTU showed a good response. Additional responses in areas outside the major cities were sporadic. Some examples were quoted in *New Age*: workers at two Ermelo farms stayed away, and large demonstrations in Pietersburg were crushed by police.

On the evening of Monday, 14 April, the ANC leadership called off the SAH, urging workers to return to work. They announced that the one-day stoppage had ensured that the grievances and aspirations of the people were considered while the country was engaged in the serious

The state mobilizes its forces to victimize strikers during 1958 Stay-at-Home

question of choosing a government. Whether or not the leadership should have taken the decision to end the protest after the first day became a much-debated issue within the Congress Alliance. Certainly the workers' leaders in Port Elizabeth, where momentum for the strike seemed to be picking up at the end of day one, were upset with the decision – especially as it had been made without their consultation. A similar response came from Durban, as Moses Mabhida recalls:

In Durban we thought that it was most successful. Dockers were out. . . . Billy Nair, M. P. Naicker and myself toured the city and we felt that it was a success. The Whites in the suburbs even supported us. The ANC leadership had not been involved enough in the organization of the campaign.[31]

A more crucial factor in the ANC decision to call off the strike was the fact that the SACTU leadership had not been consulted. The Management Committee of SACTU reacted very strongly to this and the relationship between the ANC and SACTU suffered a temporary but serious strain. The question of SACTU's equality with its partners in the Alliance came to the fore, and SACTU leaders realized that many ANC members did not regard SACTU as an important force in the struggle. The decision also pointed to the need for SACTU to take a more independent stand on matters directly affecting the working class; since February, when the organization had called the Workers Conference, the strike call had become less and less a SACTU-oriented campaign and more and more one focusing on the White elections.

In Sophiatown and Newclare townships, the workers stayed at home for the entire three days, ignoring the call to end the SAH after the first day. Riots had erupted in both of these townships on the first day and police actions resulted in injuries to several residents. Throughout the second day tension mounted and violence continued. 'In this atmosphere of brooding trouble, Sophiatown and Newclare spent the three days of the Stay-At-Home, a solitary pocket of resistance.'[32]

We must not underestimate the effect of the mass media in influencing workers to disregard the call to stay away from work. The SA Broadcasting Corporation and newspapers falsely reported that large numbers of workers were turning up for work. Workers who heard this on radio before they left for work were confused and leaders too were influenced to some degree. This is yet another reason for the failure of the strike.

In its own analysis of the failure, the National Executive Committee of the ANC gave the following reasons: firstly, inadequate preparation.

Criticisms were mainly that there was a lack of tight organization and specifically a failure to implement the 'M-Plan'; also little attention had been given to political education. Secondly, the NEC pointed to the disunity within the Transvaal ANC and the non-participation of sections of the ANC because they regarded it as purely a SACTU trade union affair.

Banned trade union and ANC leader, Dan Tloome, in an article on the 'Lessons of the Stay-Away', pointed to additional factors that would explain the failure. One important lesson, he stressed, was that for mass industrial action to succeed it was vital that trade union and factory organization should be strong. (The relative strength of the Durban and Port Elizabeth SACTU Committees and their attention to organizing the unorganized was most probably a factor in the greater participation in their areas.) Tloome suggested that ANC branches still did not fully understand the importance of trade unions and factory committees as vitally necessary for the freedom struggle.

Yet another weakness which Tloome and others recognized was the confusion of issues on which the political strike was based:

Why did the Stay-At-Home fail, when the bus boycott and the June 26 protest strike were spectacularly successful? Apparently there was confusion in the average African's mind over the nature of the demonstration he was being called upon to make. He had been told that the intention was to dissuade White voters from electing another Nationalist Government; he had been told that the struggle was for £1 a day; he had been told that the demonstration was an anti-Apartheid one. No doubt he supported each specific issue, but the trilogy of pleas was too complex.[33]

Tloome was more specific in his analysis of the issues:

It must be conceded that the slogan: 'DEFEAT THE NATS' was wrong and misleading. It is highly probable that, taken on its face value, the slogan led a considerable section of the people to believe that the Congresses were in favour of the United Party coming into power, as a party capable of solving our problems in South Africa. Yet, taken more profoundly, it is clear that the use of the slogan was intended to place emphasis on the ruthlessness of the present ruling party, and to focus attention of the country to the impoverishment and the relentless and incessant persecution imposed upon the vast majority of South Africans in the name of Apartheid.[34]

Although there was no comparative analysis of the involvement of organized and unorganized workers in the strike, the Communist Party's post-mortem on the SAH failure concluded that mass action depended on the level of working class organization. Participation by the Black proletariat in the national strikes was seen as an index of maturing political consciousness which recognized the need for concrete action against the state, but SACTU began to realize that organizing and agitating around specific demands at the point of production as a transition stage was vital, providing a firm basis for undertaking national strike action.

In general, the reasons for the failure of the 1958 SAH can be divided into two areas: firstly, the ruling class attack on the organizers and participants; and secondly, the weaknesses within the Congress Alliance itself. However, no such demonstration of protest on the part of the exploited masses, even if participation was less than expected, can ever be termed a complete failure. Those who heeded the call displayed their refusal to be ignored while the Whites went to the polls, and instead put forward the demands of the voteless and voiceless masses for an end to class exploitation and Apartheid, a legislated minimum wage of £1-a-Day and an equal say in the future of their country.

The effect on the Congress movement itself was very encouraging. A great deal of internal discussion and analysis of the campaign followed the SAH. Though the SACTU–ANC relationship at one level had suffered a setback, the strike was to be the impetus for building a much stronger relationship based on the recognition of the importance of organizing the working class in the struggle for liberation. The emphasis changed to more basic methods of mobilizing the people with the important areas of concentration being the organization of workers at the factory level and in particular in the basic industries and organizing people in the townships under the M-Plan. The most positive outcome was the joint campaign by ANC and SACTU to organize the African working class, given added impetus by a call from Chief Lutuli to this effect at the 1959 SACTU Conference.

Another effect of the SAH was less positive in nature. Arrests of workers' leaders followed in each area, and victimization by employers was common. Twenty-five leaders in the Johannesburg area alone, many of them SACTU activists like Mabel Balfour, John Tsele and Christina Matthews, were charged with incitement to strike and given sentences varying from 10 or 15 days to 12 months' imprisonment with hard labour (later reduced to 6 months). In Cape Town too, workers and their leaders suffered heavy penalties, and in certain areas trials continued for a year after the Stay-At-Home. Despite these setbacks, South African workers gained valuable experience in carrying out advanced political action against the ruling class and went on to participate in more successful political strikes in 1960 and 1961. Before analysing those SAHs, however, it is necessary to discuss the SACTU Conference that provided a turning point for both SACTU itself and for SACTU–ANC relations in many industrial areas.

The 1959 SACTU Conference

SACTU is the spear, ANC the shield. – Chief Lutuli, Guest speaker

This was the message delivered by ANC President Chief Lutuli to the workers' delegates at the 1959 SACTU Conference, a message which had far-reaching implications for the relationship between SACTU and the ANC.

Walter Sisulu, ANC leader, wrote the following in the August 1955 issue of SACTU's *Workers Unity*:

> ... The victory can only be won and imperialism uprooted by forging strong ties of alliance between the liberation movements and the trade union movements, by correcting any misconceptions that the trade unions had nothing to do with politics. *Similarly, political leaders must know that the struggle of the people depends on the workers, and therefore it must be their duty to organize workers into trade union movements.*[35]

Chief Lutuli echoed this in his speech to the delegates and emphasized that, 'No worker is a good member of Congress unless he is also a Trade Unionist. No Trade Unionist is a good Trade Unionist unless he is also a member of Congress.' Veteran trade unionists recall Chief Lutuli insisting that workers must have two membership cards, one from the ANC and one from SACTU. At the same time, he stressed the importance of the working class as a major force in the struggle; in this context, he coined the expression 'SACTU is the spear and ANC the shield!'

It was fitting that Chief Lutuli was the one to bring this message to the SACTU delegates on 29 March 1959. Since the 1930s when tribal elders urged him to accept the Groutville chieftainship, Chief Albert Lutuli, formerly a teacher at Adams College, had served the people as a conscientious chief and was highly respected in the rural area in the heartland of Natal's sugar plantations. After he joined the ANC he was quickly promoted to President of the Natal ANC in 1951, and participated actively in the 1952 Defiance Campaign. This involvement led to his dismissal from the chieftainship by the government. Still regarded by the African masses as their 'Chief', however, he was elected President-General of the ANC by a large majority in 1952. Throughout the 1950s, he was shackled with one banning order after another, and in 1956 was arrested for High Treason along with 155 other Congress members. At the time of the SACTU Conference in March 1959, the Chief's latest ban had expired. Moses Mabhida, strongly influenced by Chief Lutuli's exceptional leadership, recalled the changes that took place in the Chief's attitude to working class people:

> The ANC was no longer the organization of chiefs and nobles. It was now an organization of ordinary people (and) the Chief himself had participated in reconstructing this part of the ANC. Therefore, he had a high regard for workers in a practical sense and for their participation in the struggle and I think he had made the proper assessment. The very fact that they are the spear, the fighting side, indicated that he understood their role in the struggle.[36]

Banned for five years again in May 1959, Lutuli was confined to the Groutville reserve. His powerful influence, considered a danger by the Apartheid regime, continued to be felt from then until his accidental death in 1967. His messages to go forward in the struggle were relayed to the people as the repression mounted in the early 1960s. In October 1961, he was awarded the Nobel Peace Prize at the time when the ANC realized that lasting peace and freedom could be achieved only through armed struggle against the state.

The Chief's address to SACTU members had far-reaching consequences. Armed with his mandate, and determined to prevent another failure like the 1958 SAH, SACTU and the ANC went forward to organize the African masses into stronger organizations which would more directly challenge the regime. For SACTU, the emphasis was to be on organizing new trade unions in the basic industries of metals, mining, transport and agriculture, in all cases around the £1-a-Day campaign. Organizing the unorganized achieved great victories, especially in Natal, as new unions emerged at the turn of the decade.

The ANC turned its attention to strengthening mass organizations through implementation of the M (Mandela)-Plan in the townships; the goal was to build up membership and to prepare the people for the conditions of underground organizing and illegality. In each township a network of cells would exist, each cell incorporating the residents of perhaps ten houses on one street. The township itself was zoned into blocks of ten streets, with four zones forming a ward. Each ward then elected leaders who formed the ANC branch committee with authority

"Workers Are The Spearhead Of Struggle!"
—Chief Lutuli Tells Conference

Chief Albert Lutuli, President-General, African National Congress, 1952–1967

flowing downwards from the branch. The person who was the overall leader became 'like a helicopter hovering over the whole township'.[37]

This organizational strategy was very effective in mobilizing workers for meetings on short notice. Within an hour a meeting with everyone in attendance could be convened. For example, in one Cape Town township, Thomas Nkobi arrived once on his way to Port Elizabeth and asked to see a 'few volunteers'. Within thirty minutes he was surrounded by over two hundred people and understandably surprised by this impressive accomplishment. The Plan worked very well in the Western and Eastern Cape regions, and although leaders from these regions went to Natal and Transvaal to implement the Plan there the same degree of organization was never achieved. The banning of the ANC in 1960 made this kind of organizational base even more important in the transition to underground work.

Together, the Congress organizations planned to implement industrial area committees to assist SACTU in strengthening its organizing campaign. In the Port Elizabeth, Durban and Pietermaritzburg areas, the plan had already been effectively carried out. William Khanyile, SACTU organizer for the region, explained:

SACTU organizers trained these area committee workers to move as a team. They were responsible for an area encompassing a certain number of streets. They moved as a team to factories and places of employment, including shops, to meet the workers of the area during lunch hour. In this way SACTU's influence would spread well beyond the area because workers in shops and factories would be drawn from many different residential areas.[38]

At NCC meetings in 1961, the Plan was discussed extensively and taken up at SACTU-MC meetings as well, emphasizing the need to tackle the various industrial areas in Johannesburg. A special Action sub-committee was appointed to implement the plan which was scheduled to begin with a 'Trade Union Week'. During this week there would be placard demonstrations at bus stops and at other locations exhorting workers to join unions, house-to-house campaigns and preparations for a Workers' Conference in each province. In Johannesburg, the plan was to tackle each industrial area on a given day – Industria one day, then Jeppe, etc. Workers would be addressed during lunch hours and they could then either elect or nominate members of the area committee.

Although the plan had been adopted within the NCC, there were some SACTU MC members who objected to it on the grounds that this kind of campaign should definitely be controlled by SACTU. At SACTU–NEC meetings held in November 1961, one speaker emphasized that the people appointed should be trade unionists and that the Action Committee should be solely responsible to the SACTU NEC or MC, not the NCC of the Congress Alliance. His main point, a valid one in the wake of the confusion during the 1958 SAH, was that at all costs SACTU's identity had to be preserved. These fears were largely placated after the whole issue of the relationship between Congress Alliance groups was discussed in an Action Committee meeting. At subsequent meetings of the NCC it became clear that the campaign would be led by SACTU.

Uriah Maleka, SACTU–NEC member in Johannesburg, has commented on this concern of preserving SACTU's identity:

SACTU was very much conscious of itself being a labour organization and didn't want to lose its identity. We thought we should work together but we must know the demarcation. We are a labour body with our own constitution and with affiliated unions, whereas if we say the directives come from somewhere else to the Trade Union movement, SACTU would lose its identity.[39]

The Congress Alliance regarded this industrial area campaign as well as the campaign to boycott all 'dummy institutions' of Apartheid as part of the second phase of the campaign for a National Convention which would draft a Constitution representing the interests of *all* South Africans. Within the campaign, SACTU's role was clarified:

It is SACTU's function to play a leading role in both these sections of the campaign, but its main emphasis will be to take the lead in realizing the plan to organize thousands of workers into the Trade Union movement (NCC Document, 1961).

The Action Committee made four recommendations. Firstly, since the campaign was designed to strengthen the trade union movement, it was felt that SACTU machinery should be used to further this campaign and that additional machinery would be created where none existed. Secondly, the four National Organizing Committees (in metals, mines, transport and agriculture) already established by the SACTU-MC would be directed by the Action Committee to increase the number of members so as to include Congress Alliance persons. Thirdly, the Action Committee would ensure that each SACTU Local Committee established an industrial area committee for the purpose of recruiting workers from other industries into the movement. The Action

Committee was also suggesting to Local Committees, NOCs and industrial area committees that Workers' Conferences be held on specific days on a national scale to highlight the need for organization and action in respect of workers' grievances and demands. The fourth recommendation was that the Action Committee supply guide notes to all activists on how to organize workers into trade unions, factory or area committees. The slogans for the campaign were: ORGANIZE OR STARVE; EVERY FACTORY A FORTRESS; FORWARD TO £1-A-DAY; TRADE UNIONS MAKE US STRONG; and JOBS FOR ALL.

We need not stress here the fact that the workers' demands for the slightest improvements in their conditions and to organize freely are political demands too, and those rights must be fought for and linked to the demand for a National Convention where workers' rights can be written into a Constitution.[40]

The campaign began in earnest on 7 February 1962, the Day of International Solidarity with the Workers of South Africa (see Chapter 11). At the 1962 SACTU Conference, a resolution was passed which expressed the organization's gratitude for the Congress Alliance assistance:

This Seventh Annual National Conference . . . welcomes the campaign of the Congresses to strengthen existing trade unions, to establish new trade unions, to recruit new members and to organize the unorganized workers. It fully realizes that only the united efforts of the Congresses can enable us to achieve the liberation of the workers and oppressed peoples of South Africa from White domination and capitalist exploitation.[41]

The successful implementation of this joint campaign on the trade union front was pre-empted by the various forms of repression directed against the Congress Alliance organizations and members in the early 1960s. As well, there was still a certain degree of reluctance on the part of some Congress Alliance members to participate fully in a specifically working class campaign. However, it had been implemented on an initial basis in several areas throughout the country where the campaign reportedly contributed to a greater degree of participation in the Stay-At-Homes of 1960 and 1961. Most importantly, it represented a commitment to the role of the working class by the Congress Alliance and a realization of the workers' strategic role in any mass actions planned.

A brief examination of the response of workers to the Congress calls for political strike action in the early 1960s is now in order. The mass response to the call for a National Day of Mourning after the Sharpeville Massacre on 21 March 1960, constituted an unexpected display of militancy on the part of workers who were angered by the vicious response of the state. In Cape Town, strikes spread from one factory to the next, beginning on 21 March and continuing for a week. In Vereeniging and Vanderbilj Park a similar reaction occurred.

On Monday, 28 March, the day of mourning called by Chief Lutuli, African workers throughout South Africa stayed away from work to protest the massacres at Sharpeville and Langa. In many cases they extended the one day SAH into a prolonged strike and organized marches through the townships and into the cities. Tension was high and violence flared up in several areas. The workers were demonstrating that they were prepared to act collectively and extend their opposition beyond the original call. It was a bold and militant stand.

On Wednesday, 30 March, the ANC and PAC were banned and nation-wide arrests of leaders and supporters of the campaign took place. In Cape Town, police entered Langa and Nyanga townships, rounding up ANC and PAC leaders and beating up striking workers. The workers responded to a PAC call by gathering in Langa township and moving in a broad column of 15,000 people along the ten-mile route to the city centre, swelling to some 30,000 as they entered the city. On their arrival, they demanded an interview with the Minister of Justice and eventually dispersed only when they were assured of such a meeting.

Strikes continued in Cape Town until 4 April, with 60,000 workers out on strike on the peak days of 30 March and 1 April. A significant aspect was the solidarity of Coloured workers, resulting in a disruption of industry, commerce, shipping and supplies of fresh foodstuffs. In Durban, about 5,000 people marched from Cato Manor to the Bantu Affairs offices in the city and demanded the release of arrested leaders. Cato Manor workers, representing approximately 20 per cent of the workforce, stayed on strike for ten days causing major difficulties in industry and commerce. Lamontville workers clashed with police who fired shots killing one person and wounding two others. All of these actions reveal the readiness of the Black working class to move spontaneously beyond the Congress Alliance leadership into further resistance in the form of political strike action.

By 1961, the Congress Alliance had come to the realization that armed force was necessary against the state; no longer could the people merely stand by helplessly and watch their comrades being shot down in the streets by the police and the military. However, before embarking on any campaigns of armed resistance, the Congress Alliance was trying in the early months of 1961 to pressure the government into calling a National Convention of all political leaders to work out an alternative to a 'White's only' Republic. Another protest strike was called for 29–31 May, on the eve of the celebrations surrounding South African Republic Day. Meticulous preparations ensued and efforts were made to reach out to all, including rural and urban workers, peasants on the reserves and compound workers. SACTU played a crucial role in organizing workers in various areas, preparing them for collective strike action. As the workers came out on strike, the state reacted with greater force than ever before and 10,000 Blacks were arrested in raids (supposedly for pass and tax defaulters). A new law was passed entitling the government to detain a person for 12 days without bail; this was but the prelude to the massive repression of the months that followed.

Despite predictable state repression, the 1961 strike was considered an important and successful demonstration of the people's attitude towards White South Africa's new Republic status and their demand for freedom and self-determination in their own country. One report sums this up:

The Nationalists huddled in the rain in Pretoria to install their new President in a South Africa where all gatherings but their own were banned; where martial law had been proclaimed in all but name; where for three days past a large proportion of the country's industry had slowed to a trickle; where empty lecture theatres and classrooms were an eloquent testimony to the contemptuous rejection by the youth to the 'Republic' from which every vestige of the noble principles of republicanism had been deleted by the Verwoerdites . . .

By passing from words to action (the African people) dramatically exposed, as nothing else could have done, the people's rejection of state forms decided on by a minority in its own interests; their unequivocal claim for government of the people, by the people and for the people.[42]

Painstaking organizing efforts by SACTU and the Congress Alliance paid off as workers responded in all the major centres. A survey based on organizers' reports indicated the strong areas and industries affected; this is reproduced in the table on pages 366–7. The report drew the following conclusion which pointed to the importance of SACTU's role in mass campaigns:

Workers who are organized into trade unions are more responsive to a political call than unorganized workers. Their trade union activity has given them heightened political consciousness and they also respond more readily when the appeal is made on a factory as opposed to a residential basis as they feel that there is less chance of dismissal if the whole factory is involved.[43]

Once again, the response of Coloured and Indian workers was encouraging and can be credited to the efforts of the Congress Alliance in its relentless pursuit of unity between national groups throughout the 1950s. Edward Ramsdale recalls a particular incident in Cape Town where armed police converged on factories in the industrial areas, attempting to intimidate workers and prevent them from striking:

I recall the police outside one factory, Robinson's Paper factory, urging Coloured women workers not to come out because they would be raped by the African men. I'll never forget how those women came out![44]

It was a national general strike to remember and the NCC had realized that 'the advantage of organizing people at their places of work is that it enables us to mobilize them at short notice and to effectively bring a halt to the industrial life of the country at any appropriate time'.[45]

This was the last general strike called by the Congress Alliance before it was fragmented by the Apartheid regime and driven underground. The political movement embarked on a sabotage campaign shortly after the strike. By the early 1960s, the full force of the state, protecting the interests of White capital, was mobilized and used against the oppressed peoples of South Africa (see Chapter 12). However, the non-racial unity achieved by the members of the Congress Alliance could never be shattered entirely and the welding of the trade union movement with the general political struggle for liberation forged a permanent bond which remains unbroken to this day.

After the ANC had been banned it became important for SACTU to expand its role and to extend the message of Congress further afield, embracing other sections of the exploited African masses. It is for this reason that SACTU, especially in Natal, was instrumental in organizing several very successful Workers and Peasants Conferences. These focused on more general issues affecting the oppressed, issues such as housing, rent, pass laws, unemployment as well as poverty wages and poor working conditions. In this way SACTU mobilized more people for greater participation in the political campaigns until its own leaders were silenced by the regime.

Survey of Responses to the Strike Call

Industry/Service	Sample response of individual factories	General
	Johannesburg	
Textile	100% strike out of 250	First four factories
	45 workers out of 50	closed for all 3 days.
	495 workers out of 500	No response at Amato
	495 workers out of 500	where Union suffered
	16 workers out of 17	after the 1957 strike.
Laundry	100% all 3 days	In addition to the 3
	6 of 40 drivers attended work	surveyed here, 9 factories employing 1,000 workers
	100% strike out of 300	closed down for the
	76 workers out of 80	period
Food and canning	325 workers out of 500	No response at LKB in
	100% strike out of 80	Benoni
	100% strike out of 50	
Furniture	100% strike out of 60	
	100% strike out of 100	
	300 workers out of 400	
	154 workers out of 160	
Clothing	100% response	In all provinces. One factor: clothing industries, hit by border industries. Many on short time. Many manufacturers did not mind closing down
Municipality	10% response	
	Vereeniging/Van der Bijl/Pretoria	
	No response	*Except Lady Selbourne* township, Pretoria, 80% on Monday. All beer halls closed. Alexandra township (between Johannesburg and Pretoria) *85% response* Monday; 65% Tuesday ⅔ of *PUTCO drivers from township strike*
	Cape Town	
Building	At standstill	70% of Malays respond 40% of Coloureds respond

Industry/Service	Sample response of individual factories	General
	Port Elizabeth	
Textile	75% participation	Both African and Coloured workers. Strike gained momentum on 2nd and 3rd days
Clothing		
Docks		
Dairies		
Bakeries		
	Durban	
Clothing	80% for 3 days	
Textile	70–80% 1st and 2nd days	
Distributive	50% 1st day only	
Timber	70–80% 1st and 2nd days	
Sheet metal	70–80%; 50% 1st and 2nd days	
Metal	50–60% 1st day only	
Twine and bag	80%; 40% 1st and 2nd days	
Milling	60% 1st day only	
Sweet	100% for 3 days	
Leather	60–70% Bata Shoe Co; closed 3 days	
Match	50%	
Municipal	–	Warnings of dismissal
Docks and railways	–	Police and army cordoned off compounds and workers were forced to work
Indian traders	Total response on 1st day	
	Pietermaritzburg	
Howick rubber	All 1,500 workers on strike	

Throughout the mass campaigns of the 1950s and early 1960s, SACTU remained clear on its specific tasks in the struggle against South African capitalism. An article in the August 1955 issue of *Workers Unity* sums up this dialectical relationship between the trade union and political movements:

Why then do we find trade unionists discussing larger political questions? We are workers and we have our own points of view – the industrial workers' point of view – and it is not always the view of shopkeepers or teachers – it is the view of those who have no property stake in the country, of those whose only property is their hands and their ability to put these hands to work. Others may differ because they have property – a shop, a farm or a taxi of their own. This often makes them think differently.

So, sometimes it happens that where we are ready to act, bold, ready to sacrifice for what we want, others amongst us hesitate, hold back and retreat. That is why it is necessary always for us to discuss our point of view, the point of view of the working class. And therefore we must put it forward strongly and determinedly in the broad political field in which Congress works.

That is why it is necessary for every trade unionist to be a Congress member and an active Congress worker. This is so that the working class point of view is not ours alone, but is accepted by the whole Congress Movement and all classes can go forward under our working class slogans.[46]

The close working relationship between the ANC and SACTU was best expressed in Port Elizabeth and Natal. In both cases, an overlapping membership amongst the leadership, coupled with a solid working class perspective, not only minimized any potential conflict but, more importantly, resulted in a model of militancy necessary for the South African struggle. Here is how Sampson Mbatha, a young SACTU–ANC activist in Durban in the early 1960s, described this relationship:

ANC is a mass political organization. SACTU is an organization for the whole working class in South Africa. Workers themselves are a force. The workers are the people who know what they are doing. They work, they go to the factories and sell their labour-power. They know they are being exploited and have nothing to lose, only the chains they'll cut off their hands.

We have seen this in other countries . . . that the working class are the decisive factor in any liberation movement because they are the people who are clear, conscious, know what they are doing . . . they form alliances with other groups but they are the spearhead because they control the industries, the towns, the whole economy. Without the working class there will be no successful revolution.[47]

NOTES

1. Chief Lutuli, *Workers Unity*, May 1959.
2. Karis and Carter, *From Protest to Challenge*, vol. III, Hoover Institute, Stanford University, 1977, p. 236.

3. Report, SACTU First Annual National Conference, 1–3 March 1956.
4. Interview, James Phillips. Quoted in R. Lambert, 'Black Working Class Consciousness and Resistance in South Africa, 1950–1961: A Historical Materialist Analysis'. Unpublished M.A. thesis, University of Warwick, September 1978.
5. Draft Report of the ANC–NEC submitted to the ANC Annual Conference, 15–17 December 1950. Quoted in Karis and Carter, vol. II, op. cit., p. 452.
6. *Guardian*, 15 June 1950.
7. Interview, Graham Morodi.
8. Quoted in M. Benson, op. cit., p. 212.
9. Interview, Alven Bennie.
10. See Appendix II.
11. Karis and Carter, vol. III, op. cit., pp. 195–6.
12. Interview, Stephen Dlamini.
13. SACTU Statement of Policy, adopted at the First Annual National Conference, 1956.
14. Dr H. F. Verwoerd, Minister of Native Affairs, speaking in the Senate, 7 June 1954.
15. Interview, Alven Bennie. In the Germiston ANC School (Transvaal), one of the teachers was SACTU member Bennett Molewa.
16. *Fighting Talk*, March 1958.
17. M. Harmel, *Fighting Talk*, May 1959.
18. These brands include: Rothmans, Peter Stuyvesant, Pall Mall, Number 7, Dunhill, among others.
19. Interview, George Monare.
20. M. Benson, op. cit., p. 145.
21. The scheme was agreed to in 1949 by the Department of Native Affairs, the Secretary of Justice and the Commissioner of Police but was never officially published after a public outcry at the scandal.
22. Zola Gambu, *Workers Unity*, July 1957.
23. *Unit on Apartheid*, United Nations, No. 41/71.
24. *Forward*, vol. 1, no. 11, June 1963.
25. W. Sisulu, 'Boycott as a Political Weapon', *Liberation*, no. 23, February 1957.
26. A. Hutchinson, 'June 26', *Fighting Talk*, vol. 11, no. 6 (July), 1957.
27. R. Lambert, op. cit., pp. 99–100.
28. Chief Lutuli's comment on the National Workers' Conference, quoted in *New Age*, 13 February 1958.
29. ibid.
30. *New Age*, 20 March 1958.
31. Interview, Moses Mabhida.
32. S. Uys, 'The Strike that Failed', *Africa South*, vol. 2, no. 4 (July/September), 1958.
33. Dan Tloome, 'Lessons of the "Stay-Away"', *Liberation*, no. 32, 14 August 1958.
34. ibid.
35. W. Sisulu, 'The Alliance of the Trade Union and Liberatory Movements in Africa', *Workers Unity*, August 1955. Emphasis added.
36. Interview, Moses Mabhida.
37. Interview, Archie Sibeko.
38. Interview, William Khanyile, quoted in Lambert, op. cit., p. 122.
39. Interview, Uriah Maleka.

40. NCC meeting, 1961.
41. SACTU, Seventh Annual National Conference Resolutions, 21–22 April 1962.
42. Alan Doyle, 'Striking Out Under the Republic', *Fighting Talk*, July 1961.
43. Organizer's Report. 1961 Stay-At-Home.
44. Interview, Edward Ramsdale, Coloured trade unionist, Cape Town.
45. 'Discussion Notes for a Proposed Plan', NCC Document, May 1961. Quoted in Lambert, op. cit., p. 149.
46. B. Giles, 'Trade Unions – Yes, and Congress Too', *Workers Unity*, August 1955.
47. Interview, Sampson Mbatha.

11 SACTU ON THE INTERNATIONAL FRONT

Of the different types of solidarity with the oppressed peoples of Southern Africa, international working class solidarity is the most important and potentially the most effective because it emanates not from charity or humanitarian motives but rather out of a recognition of common class interests and shared conditions of life under capitalism. The purpose of this chapter is to document the strengths and weaknesses of trade union solidarity work in support of SACTU's non-racial trade unionism from 1955 to 1964.

Before doing so, it is essential to point out that effective international working class solidarity is never a one-way process whereby initiatives and actions flow in only one direction. Nor is such solidarity meaningful if restricted to rhetoric rather than proletarian action. It would be politically incorrect for SACTU to have called for international solidarity against Apartheid if it were not also willing to educate and commit its membership to support workers' struggles elsewhere.

Although confronted daily by the extreme conditions of economic exploitation typical of Apartheid society, SACTU's record clearly demonstrates that the organization never fell victim to the narrow nationalism so characteristic of many trade union centres. Travel restrictions and geographical isolation notwithstanding, SACTU leaders persisted in acquainting themselves and their organized workers with the major world processes of the day – de-colonization, anti-imperialism and working class struggles throughout the world.

Between 1955 and 1963, SACTU Head Office in Johannesburg established regular contact with both major international trade union federations (the International Confederation of Free Trade Unions (ICFTU) and the World Federation of Trade Unions (WFTU)), twenty national trade union centres in Africa and at least fifty such bodies in North America, Europe, Asia, Latin America, Australia and New Zealand. Most of this work was handled by Phyllis Altman, Assistant General Secretary, between 1956 and September 1963, when she was banned from all trade union activity.

Workers Unity, the official organ of SACTU, and newspapers of affiliated unions[1] devoted considerable space to workers' struggles on both the economic and political fronts in other parts of the world. International working conditions in given industries were analysed and always compared with the super-exploited conditions of the African workers in South Africa. The inferior education system for Black people in South Africa, reinforced by the rigid censorship of news, made these trade union papers among the few sources of information on the international political situation available to the oppressed masses. The revolutionary content on both domestic and international issues was undoubtedly the major reason for their being banned in the 1960s.

In the era of imperialist-inspired cold war hysteria (1950s), SACTU never failed to voice its unqualified support for revolutionary and progressive struggles. *Workers Unity* and related union papers condemned the intervention of imperialist powers in Egypt and endorsed the nationalization of the Suez Canal in 1956. Similarly, the organization never failed to oppose repression and undemocratic actions. Also in 1956, a protest meeting was called against the closure of the Soviet Consulate and the severing of diplomatic relations with the USSR. SACTU leaflets stated: 'The South African people have no quarrel with the Soviet people. We want peace and friendship.'

This commitment to international peace and disarmament was annually confirmed at national conferences. Calling for an end to the nuclear arms race, the cessation of atomic tests in the Sahara, and the removal of all rocket and military bases in Africa, the 1960 Conference resolved that, 'We affirm that peace will not come to workers as a gift but must be won through their own efforts.' SACTU opposition to militarism was inextricably linked to the fact that South African defence spending had risen greatly in comparison with expenditures for social amenities for Blacks. Every Black person in South Africa identifies an armed Apartheid state as a direct obstacle to the liberation of the oppressed people from White supremacy in Southern Africa.

The Chinese revolution also inspired SACTU activists. Solidarity visits by Elizabeth Mafekeng (President, A-FCWU) and Phyllis Altman brought first-hand observations of the social benefits resulting from a radical restructuring of society. Mafekeng's comments on China reflected the concerns of an African woman and working class leader:

Today (1956) there are big factories and no unemployment. There are hospitals for the sick, creches for the children and a doctor attending each factory. Mothers have special time off for feeding their babies. Children do not suffer because their mothers are at work. These remarkable changes in China have been won through the struggles of the people and the sincerity of the leaders.[2]

Throughout the 1950s, SACTU's paper featured stories on the new society being created by the Chinese people, in obvious contrast to the appalling conditions of life for Black people in South Africa.

Elsewhere in Asia, SACTU took consistently progressive stands in support of workers' rights. Each year SACTU would campaign on behalf of the famous twenty Matsukawa railway workers on trial for twelve years in Japan and sentenced to death. Their 1961 acquittal was followed by this statement from Acting General Secretary Mark Shope:

... Above all, please convey our admiration to our twenty fellow-workers who remained steadfast throughout the twelve long years they were on trial with the constant threat of death hanging over them. They are the real heroes of the working class. ... We know that this victory was only made possible through the solidarity of the workers of Japan and the workers throughout the world. It represents a great defeat for imperialists.[3]

Long before Vietnam became an international issue, SACTU in 1959 condemned the death of political detainees near Saigon and called for the independence of the South Vietnamese people from imperialism. On 23 March 1962 SACTU wrote directly to US President Kennedy, accusing the United States of conducting a full-scale war in South Vietnam. The letter concluded: 'We join with workers throughout the world in demanding the withdrawal of all American aid in terms of advisers, troops and arms from South Vietnam, the release of imprisoned workers and the restoration of democratic and trade union rights.'

In the late 1950s, relations were established between SACTU and progressive trade unions in Australia and New Zealand. The historical parallel of white settler colonialism and its subjugation of aboriginal peoples in both South Africa and the South Pacific made the latter a fertile area for anti-Apartheid working class solidarity. This was made clear when the reactionary Menzies government revealed its pro-Apartheid stance by threatening legislation making it an offence for Australian workers to carry out solidarity actions with workers of South Africa or other countries — for example, the Australian trade union boycott of South African products called for by SACTU and the

Congress Alliance in 1959. In the spirit of proletarian internationalism, the 1960 SACTU National Conference passed a resolution stating,

> South African workers for their part will always defend the right of Australian workers and trade unions to stand together with their brothers in other countries. We warn the Australian government that it is embarking on the same undemocratic path as the Nationalist Government in South Africa. This demonstrates that the Menzies Government and the Verwoerd Government, as partners in the British Commonwealth, are acting to intensify exploitation of workers of our two countries. These designs will be met with the united and firm resistance of the workers of South Africa and Australia, and like all attempts to divide the workers will, in the long run, end in failure.

In the Americas, the Cuban revolution was a tremendous inspiration to the SACTU struggle in South Africa. Special tribute was paid to the Cuban victory against the imperialist-supported Batista regime and, most importantly, against racism. In turn, the Cuban trade union movement expressed its support for the principled lead SACTU had taken against racism by requesting a copy of the SACTU Constitution in 1959. In the early 1960s, the real lessons of the Cuban revolution were spelled out in the pages of *Workers Unity*: the campaign to eliminate illiteracy was contrasted with the 65 per cent illiteracy of the Black population in South Africa (which was even higher than in Cuba before the revolution).

American imperialism's determination to reverse Cuban independence was also quickly challenged by SACTU. During the missile crisis of 1962, SACTU-NEC member John Gaetsewe hand-delivered a protest letter to the office of the American consul in Johannesburg. The letter accused the US of using the excuse of a missile crisis to smash Cuba and re-impose the conditions of starvation, imprisonment without trial, and exploitation characteristic of the defeated Batista regime. SACTU went on to point out that the US had 360 military bases in Western Europe and the Far East and charged that the American government was 'holding the whole world to ransom under the threat of nuclear annihilation'. This SACTU and Transvaal Indian Youth Congress deputation was turned away with: 'No Comment now.'

On the African continent, SACTU consistently promoted rank-and-file trade unionism as an integral component to de-colonization and national liberation struggles. Afro-Asian Solidarity Conferences and All-African People's Conferences were regarded as strategic continental efforts to unite African peoples with their brothers and sisters in the 'Third World' against divisions created by neo-colonialist interests. Although SACTU and the Congress Alliance leaders were frequently prohibited from travelling to these Conferences, SACTU regularly prepared memoranda documenting the workers' struggle and presenting the case for workers' unity throughout Africa.

Numerous resolutions of support were passed on behalf of workers in the Sudan, Nigeria, Cameroons, Tunisia, Somalia, Nyasaland (Malawi), Morocco, Ghana and the French Congo. The Congolese independence from Belgium was warmly welcomed, but SACTU warned against further intrigues by Belgian, British and American imperialists. The murder of Patrice Lumumba a few months later saw SACTU-sponsored protest meetings throughout South Africa. In Algeria, SACTU was more confident that the progressive forces were in firm control following the revolution, and a close relationship developed between SACTU and the Union Generale des Travailleurs Algerians (UGTA) following Algerian liberation. The General Secretary of the UGTA wrote, 'We are particularly touched to receive such an expression of solidarity from the workers of South Africa who themselves have such a hard struggle for liberty and independence.'

In Southern Africa, SACTU internationalism focused on the issue of White minority regimes and the exploitation of Black workers who suffered alongside their brothers and sisters in South Africa itself. In October 1956 SACTU and the Congress Alliance issued a press statement in support of striking African miners on the Copperbelt in Northern Rhodesia (now Zambia) and condemned the State of Emergency which threatened attempts to organize legitimate African trade unions. A subsequent issue of *Workers Unity* presented a historical analysis of the collusion between the government and the mining corporations, the same exploiters of African labour in the South African mines. In May 1962, 28,000 African mine workers struck again on the Copperbelt to increase their miserably low wages and improve working conditions. Of importance to SACTU in this strike was the position of the White miners' union which agreed not to scab on African workers; although White miners in South Africa to this day have refused to unite on class lines with their African co-workers, SACTU heralded the Northern Rhodesian situation as a symbol of the theory and practice of SACTU struggles.

Solidarity with the oppressed peoples living under Portuguese colonialism also featured prominently in SACTU campaigns. The 1962

Conference endorsed a letter to the Secretary-General of the United Nations expressing 'outrage and indignation' at the war of extermination being carried out in Angola. The letter read:

The workers of South Africa know that the workers of Angola do not possess the most elementary human rights and that they are subject to forced labour on a scale unknown in any part of the world. Their living conditions beggar description and death from starvation is common.

We appeal to the United Nations to take immediate action to call a halt to the mass murder of the people of Angola and to demand that democratic rights are granted not only to Angola, but to Portugal itself and other Portuguese-held territories.

It follows that SACTU fully supported the turn to armed struggle by the MPLA in Angola, the PAIGC in Guinea-Bissau and FRELIMO in Mozambique as the only means available to ensure emancipation of the working people in those countries.

In the British protectorates bordering South Africa, SACTU fulfilled its obligation to come to the assistance of workers' movements whenever possible. In 1961, three SACTU Executive members travelled to Basutoland (now Lesotho) to advise on trade union problems and to help draft a bill for trade union rights and protection of workers. In June 1963 in a letter to the High Commissioner for UK Protectorates, SACTU condemned the use of British troops to smash a general workers' strike at Mbabane in Swaziland. In these cases and others, SACTU circulated information on strikes in the neighbouring countries to affiliated unions and urged them, if possible, to contribute financial assistance.

Finally, within South Africa itself, SACTU persisted in the face of Government hostility to organize all workers around May Day campaigns. The tradition of May Day celebrations has a long history in South Africa, dating back in this century to the progressive trade unions of the 1930s and carried on in the 1940s by the CNETU and its affiliates.

In the late 1940s, the move to the right by the SAT & LC leadership, as reflected in the Executive's willingness to promote Apartheid trade unionism, made the perennial United May Day Committee more difficult to sustain. Furthermore, the Nationalist Government was beginning to interfere in Industrial Council agreements between employers and unions by preventing May Day as a public workers' holiday, a right gained as far back as 1926. In 1961, the Minister of Labour wrote to SACTU: 'I have to advise you that it is not government policy to approve of wage determinations and industrial council agreements which provide for May Day as a public holiday.'

Yet it was the 1950 May Day demonstrations above all else that stand out as a factor rendering May Day activities difficult to organize during the late 1950s. The impending Suppression of Communism Act (which allowed the state to declare as unlawful any organization it considered to be 'furthering the aims of Communism') led the Transvaal ANC, the CNETU, the Johannesburg District Communist Party and the Transvaal Indian Congress to call a one-day general strike on 1 May 1950. The strike led to violence in many African townships; nineteen Black workers were killed and thirty-eight injured as a result of police attacks.[4]

Against this background of intimidation and repression, SACTU attempted to revive May Day to its rightful place in the political calendar of the South African working class. Workers were encouraged by Frances Baard, militant leader of the Food and Canning Workers Union in the Eastern Cape, to hold demonstrations and celebrations in homes, halls, factories and the streets. 'It is the duty of every trade unionist to organize functions vigorously to ensure that every worker can celebrate May Day in one way or another together with his comrades in all parts of the world' (*Morning Star*, April 1957). Throughout the years, the pages of *Workers Unity* were filled with May Day messages to the workers from SACTU affiliates and international trade unions.

By the late 1950s, May Day had ceased to be an important day of international working class solidarity within the White-dominated trade unions and coordinating bodies in South Africa. The May Day message from SACTU President Leon Levy and General Secretary Leslie Massina, both banned following the Treason Trial arrests of December 1956, commented: 'We believe this is a surrender to the capitalist class, who for so long have hated May Day and have tried to take it away from those who have won it.' In the early 1960s, with no support from the South African trade union movement generally, SACTU and particularly the South African Clothing Workers Union organized May Day meetings and demonstrations to further promote SACTU campaigns for the recognition of African trade unions, a national minimum wage of £1-a-Day, and an end to Job Reservation in industry.

Again, outside of the South African context, the promotion of May Day may be an activity taken for granted and not worthy of the attention given it here, except for one point: every mention of May Day in

SACTU documents was used as evidence by the Crown in its assertion that the twenty-three SACTU Treason Trial defendants (as part of the total 156 defendants) had committed treason against the state. Such is the state of freedom for workers in South Africa.

This review of SACTU's internationalism clearly demonstrates the principled solidarity that marked SACTU struggles during its first decade. Veteran trade unionists around the world will recall that engraved at the bottom of SACTU stationery was the motto: 'An Injury to One is an Injury to All'. The remainder of this chapter will assess the response of the international trade union movement to SACTU non-racial trade unionism in South Africa.

International Affiliation to the WFTU

Shortly after the Inaugural Conference, the issue of international affiliation was raised at the second Management Committee meeting held on 13 April 1955. A motion was proposed by Lucy Mvubelo (SACTU Vice-President and representative of the GWU-AW), and seconded by Cleopas Sibande (A-TWIU) 'that the South African Congress of Trade Unions should affiliate to the World Federation of Trade Unions, and that the Secretary should enquire about the affiliation fees.' The motion was passed and then referred to the first NEC meeting held in Johannesburg on 27 June 1955.

At the June meeting, with representation present from all SACTU Local Committees (Cape Town, Port Elizabeth, Durban and the Witwatersrand), the issue of international affiliation was tabled for discussion. Following comments made by President Beyleveld and General Secretary Massina regarding the benefits of WFTU affiliation, Stella Damons (FCWU, Port Elizabeth) and John Nkadimeng (SACTU National Organizer) moved and seconded that 'SACTU affiliate to the WFTU'. The motion was passed unanimously. Minutes from this meeting add that '. . . with regard to the payment of affiliation fees it was agreed that the full amount be paid after which an exemption would be sought until such time as our financial position improved'. This decision to affiliate to the WFTU was included in the General Secretary's report to the first Annual National Conference held on 1–4 March 1956 in Cape Town. For reasons of political security, the WFTU never regarded its association with SACTU as that of an official affiliation, and SACTU never actually paid affiliation fees.

The SACTU policy of attempting to have cordial and productive relations with both of the international trade union federations (the

WFTU and the break-away ICFTU) might suggest that the political decision to openly affiliate to the WFTU so early was unwise, or at least ill-timed. Such a view would, however, be incorrect for two reasons, the first historical and the second political.

Historically, it is important to recognize that the predecessor to SACTU, the Transvaal CNETU, had been affiliated to the WFTU since the latter's formation in 1945. The WFTU, in the early post-war years, included the CIO unions from the United States, British trade unions and trade union bodies from the socialist world; it was a truly international body that was recognized at the founding conference of the United Nations as the world spokesman for labour. Black trade unions in South Africa, struggling to organize the exploited masses in the post-war era of South African industrialization, naturally looked to the WFTU for assistance, and support was always forthcoming. There was never an attempt to create reformist trade unions that would accept the line 'no politics in the trade union movement', a slogan that was later to become the rule-of-thumb for the ICFTU in its relationship to African trade unions inside South Africa.

Thus, throughout the late 1940s and early 1950s, Executive members of the CNETU corresponded with the WFTU and attempted — in most cases unsuccessfully — to attend WFTU conferences. Prominent African and Coloured trade unionists who were prevented from freely travelling to WFTU and other trade union meetings in Europe included Dan Tloome, J. B. Marks, James Phillips and Gana Makabeni.[5] It is perhaps worth quoting the Minister of Labour Schoeman who attempted to articulate the 'logic' of Apartheid reasoning on this question:

I think it is unfair to the Non-European himself to allow him to go overseas, especially in a country where there is no colour bar and no discrimination, to attend a conference there and then have him come back to our conditions here. . . . While there is a Nationalist Government, I don't think that will be permitted.

As detailed in Chapter 2, heavy bans against trade unionists under the Suppression of Communism Act took their toll on CNETU leaders in the early 1950s. In October 1953 Dan Tloome, James Phillips and Arnold Selby (a progressive White trade unionist serving as Secretary of the A-TWIU) were forced to send the following telegram of apology to the WFTU meetings in Vienna:

We who were elected as delegates of the Transvaal CNETU deeply regret we are unable to attend your great conference because of the undemocratic travel restrictions imposed by the Union government. Following our election as delegates, all three of us were ordered . . . to resign from our trade unions and desist from our trade union activity under pain of imprisonment. Thirty-three other prominent trade unionists have also received similar orders recently.

Only Leslie Massina of the CNETU Executive (and subsequently first General Secretary of SACTU) escaped these early banning orders and managed to attend international trade union meetings. In February 1955 Massina went to the International Miners' Conference and also represented the CNETU at WFTU meetings. On his return to South Africa, Massina spoke favourably of his visit to Czechoslovakia, Poland, Hungary and Rumania, concluding, 'South Africa has the iron curtain. We restrict entry and declare individuals prohibited immigrants.' Two years later, Massina was to be among the first SACTU-NEC members to be banned from trade union activity.

Therefore, for reasons of historical continuity and overlapping membership between the CNETU and SACTU, the latter's affiliation to the WFTU in mid-1955 can be easily understood.

Yet an equally important reason for this affiliation rests at the level of international politics. Instead of asking the question 'Why affiliation to the WFTU?', the more compelling question was 'What would be the price to SACTU of affiliating to the ICFTU?' Space prevents a complete review of the factors leading to the break-up of the WFTU into rival and antagonistic bodies, but in hindsight few could honestly deny that the ICFTU was a creation of cold war politics and an institutional means through which labour aristocrats could manipulate Third World labour movements in the interests of British and American imperialism.[6]

Having had almost six years to assess the ICFTU, those who came together to form SACTU in 1955 realized that affiliation to the ICFTU would be in complete violation of the principles laid down in SACTU's Constitution. As the next section will document, such an international affiliation would have rendered SACTU and the Black workers it represented helpless in the face of South African capitalism and Apartheid.

Before telling that part of the story, there is a certain irony regarding SACTU affiliation to the WFTU that deserves mention here. Lucy Mvubelo, the person who initially moved this affiliation in April 1955, was the only SACTU Executive member to break from SACTU and the Congress Alliance to join the reformist camp of the SATUC-FOFATUSA. She has subsequently become the symbol of anti-SACTU and anti-progressive forces for the past two decades. Interviews with SACTU comrades reveal that few were surprised at her opportunism and willingness to sell-out to the workers' struggle for total liberation. Perhaps it was the lure of a privileged position, or the knowledge that she was not capable of enduring the wrath of the regime's inevitable repression against SACTU[7] — whatever the reason, only a short time passed before Lucy Mvubelo was exempted from the Minister of Labour's prohibition on African trade unionists travelling abroad to international conferences.

SACTU–ICFTU Relations and the Creation of FOFATUSA

Notwithstanding the SACTU affiliation to the WFTU, it is important to stress that SACTU always sought support from all international trade unions and federations. The 1960 General Secretary's report makes this point emphatically: 'We believe that we must obtain support from every possible source, otherwise we risk isolation.' The partisanship and political manoeuvring came solely from *outside* South Africa and SACTU–ICFTU relations throughout this period must be understood accordingly.

The strongest measure of ICFTU solidarity for the Black workers of South Africa has been its principled call over a period of many years for a total boycott of South African products, leading to a complete isolation of the South African regime in the international community. It is to the credit of the ICFTU that this stand has been consistently advanced in trade union circles throughout the world.

What is contradictory, however, is the fact that those coordinating bodies supported by the ICFTU inside South Africa — the SATUC (TUCSA) and the Federation of Free African Trade Unions of South Africa (FOFATUSA) — did *not* support the boycott campaign in words or in actions. Instead, it was SACTU and the Congress Alliance that had developed the boycott strategy, first within South Africa through the campaigns initiated in the mid-1950s, and in 1959 as an international appeal for solidarity. This contradiction between ICFTU theory and practice begs the question of the overall ICFTU position towards the workers' struggle in South Africa in the 1950s and 1960s.

The dissolution of the T & LC in October 1954 and the simultaneous creation of the SATUC on the fundamental premise of exclusion of African trade unions from its ranks, created the situation whereby international trade union bodies were forced to clearly define their political allegiances regarding the struggle of the oppressed Black workers and their organizations. The British TUC in 1954 agreed to 'temporize on basic principles' and support this exclusion of African trade unions, whereas, in contrast, the Australian trade union movement took a progressive stand and threatened to intensify blockades against South African products unless African trade unions were recognized in law.

The ICFTU did not become directly involved in South African trade union affairs until 1957; by this time many of the SACTU militants had been hindered in their day-to-day trade union work by the Treason Trial. M. Becu, then President of the ICFTU, made the first official visit to Johannesburg in 1957. He met with the SATUC Executive and scheduled the first ICFTU team of Sir Thomas O'Brien and P. H. de Jonge to tour South Africa in June of that year. During this tour, SACTU presented the ICFTU with a memorandum stating its desire to cooperate with both international federations in creating united action against Apartheid. A second tour followed in 1959 and another in 1960. On the basis of these ICFTU visits and subsequent events it is possible to piece together a picture of ICFTU politics in relation to the aspirations of the African working class.

In general, the ICFTU was willing to recognize and support SACTU if the former would be allowed to set the conditions. Short of this, the ICFTU was willing to slander SACTU as a 'Communist front' and commit its energies and resources towards the creation of an anti-SACTU organization. They took that course of action from 1959 onwards. Although unsuccessful, the ICFTU nevertheless greatly disrupted the real workers' voice, SACTU, in the fulfilment of its policies and objectives.

In addition to official ICFTU visits, members of international trade union federations affiliated to the ICFTU made periodic tours of South Africa to investigate certain industries. Phyllis Altman recalls an International Metalworkers Federation (IMF) representative, a Mr Carron, entering the SACTU office one day in 1962, fully steeped in SATUC prejudice against SACTU. He was rude, paternalistic (not an uncommon trait amongst White trade unionists in the South African situation) and fully convinced in advance that SACTU unions existed in name only. SACTU President Leon Levy, although involved with the Treason Trial at the time, asked SACTU organizers to be at Head Office during the lunch hour to meet with the IMF representative.

Though at first he (Carron) said, 'I only have thirty minutes', the meeting lasted until 6.00 p.m. His initial anti-Communist polemics were ignored by SACTU comrades, who in turn took the opportunity to educate Mr Carron on the *real* problems facing African workers. Such incidents did not change the basic ICFTU position but they do point to the arrogance and basic ignorance of South African realities imported by many trade union leaders from abroad.

The most important visit from the ICFTU was in 1959, when P. de Jonge and H. Millard scheduled a number of meetings with both SATUC and SACTU. SACTU leaders in Johannesburg and Durban clearly recall the tactics of intimidation. The ICFTU offered its support for SACTU – politically and financially – on two conditions: first, that SACTU agree to sever all ties with the Congress Alliance; and second, that SACTU divorce the economic and political struggle, that is, reject the goal of liberation and embrace reformist ends. SACTU's answer was unequivocal and consistent with its founding principles and Constitution: to accept economic concessions without struggling for the political emancipation of Black workers and citizens would be a betrayal of the masses and their aspirations.

Again, arrogance and ignorance by the ICFTU stand out boldly. The visit came shortly after SACTU's most successful National Conference in Durban in March 1959.[8] Chief Lutuli of the ANC had further cemented the solidarity of groups within the Congress Alliance by calling on all ANC members to hold trade union cards and SACTU members to join the ANC. Phyllis Altman remembers the ICFTU team being very upset when Lutuli's statement was repeated to them in meetings with SACTU; they totally misread the situation and furthermore failed to appreciate the suspicions Black workers held for trade union chauvinists of their kind. They came with 'inbuilt superiority complexes'.[9]

Stephen Dlamini, Durban SACTU Local Committee Chairman at the time, recalls being treated to dinner in an expensive Durban hotel by the ICFTU team. Not the usual fare for an African worker, the meal was gratefully accepted but not the intimidation and unconcealed bribery that accompanied it. After being promised trade union training in Uganda and given the 'no politics in the trade unions' line, Dlamini responded, 'Can I ask one question; Are you through?' He politely excused himself, 'with a full stomach'.[10]

In Johannesburg, an evening meeting between the ICFTU and SACTU was arranged. Viola Hashe (Secretary, SACWU), who resided in Roodeport fourteen miles from the city, was present in violation of the regulations against the freedom of movement for Africans. At this time, too, security concerns were of great importance due to the atmosphere created by the Treason Trial. Phyllis Altman recalls driving Viola Hashe home late at night and fearing that she was being followed by the Special Branch. The ICFTU representatives, also in the car, later told the progressive politician Alex Hepple that Altman was just 'playing games' for their benefit. Anyone who fully appreciated the realities of repression in South Africa, which apparently did not include the ICFTU, would know that the dangers were indeed real.

Failure to sway SACTU from its position forced the ICFTU to look elsewhere in establishing roots in African trade unionism. The truly amazing developments that followed this 1959 visit point to the fact that the ICFTU and certainly the SATUC were becoming very anxious about the viability and increasing strength of SACTU. The only strategy remaining was to disrupt SACTU by creating an anti-SACTU African trade union coordinating body – FOFATUSA – that would be propped up locally by the SATUC. As Leslie Massina put it at the time, 'The ICFTU came to disorganize the organized.'

FOFATUSA emerged on the scene in October 1959, a few months after the completion of the ICFTU tour. A coincidence? Hardly. Although shortlived, FOFATUSA began as a result of many political forces: (a) the SATUC anti-SACTU position; (b) in all probability money provided by the ICFTU; and (c) a Pan-Africanist Congress (PAC) leadership looking for a base amongst African workers. As such, FOFATUSA combined national and international currents prevailing at the time. On the national front, the PAC Black nationalism had come to the fore following the confusion of the 1958 Stay-At-Home; on the international front, it was an abortive attempt to give the SATUC greater international credibility in the eyes of world trade union centres.[11]

One cannot really speak of FOFATUSA as a legitimate trade union coordinating body for African trade unions and workers. More correctly, it was a collection of individuals who for various reasons had broken from the Congress Movement in the previous decade. Jacob Nyaose, FOFATUSA Chairman, had in the 1940s and early 1950s been with the CNETU but on many important issues deserted the progressive line of the Council. For example, in 1953, he and Gana Makabeni attempted to split the CNETU by refusing to boycott the Native Labour (Settlement of Disputes) Act – a piece of vicious legislation which African workers completely rejected. The splitters sent a memorandum to Cape Town to plead with the Minister of Labour not to implement the Act; they also promised not to defy the Act if their memo was ignored (which it obviously was). Nyaose's union, the African Bakers Industrial Union, was regarded by SACTU workers as nothing more than a mutual aid society. The importance of Nyaose was that he served as Minister of Labour in the PAC – beyond that, he had no mass following in the African proletariat.[12]

Lucy Mvubelo and Sarah Chitja were the other key figures in the FOFATUSA Executive. Both had been with SACTU in the early years but had broken with the progressive movement in 1957. The strength of their union, the Garment Workers Union of African Women, was the only legitimate base among workers that FOFATUSA could claim. Both Mvubelo and Chitja were also greatly influenced by Dulcie Hartwell, Executive member of the registered Garment Workers Union, SATUC Secretary and staunch anti-SACTU trade unionist.

The crucial question is whether this anti-SACTU organization commanded the respect of the African working class. Only in a few townships near Johannesburg, where these three leaders could be assured of personal followings, did FOFATUSA have any substantial support. Whenever the body tried to extend its influence elsewhere it met with resistance from the workers.

In Durban, a SACTU-Congress Alliance stronghold, FOFATUSA meetings attracted more SACTU supporters who came to pose the real issues and Special Branch personnel than pro-FOFATUSA workers. In January 1961 Curnick Ndlovu (SARHWU, SACTU) interrupted a FOFATUSA meeting and warned the ten persons in the hall that FOFATUSA was a splitter organization designed to create disunity within SACTU and the African working class; he also accused the South African Liberal Party of assisting in these efforts. In a later attempt also in Durban, Stephen Dlamini and twenty SACTU supporters walked out of a FOFATUSA meeting to the cry of 'Amandla Ngawethu' (Power to the People), leaving only three persons in the hall with Nyaose. When the PAC tried to hold a meeting in Durban, their leaders fled because of ANC-SACTU opposition. In Port Elizabeth and Cape Town, FOFATUSA had no following whatsoever.

These examples add weight to the major objection raised by SACTU to the formation of FOFATUSA. The 1960 Conference stated,

The tragedy of the South African Trade Union movement is that it is so racially divided and weak – a new racial body serves no purpose other than to divide and weaken the workers and can only confuse them. We have no knowledge of any campaign carved out by this body on behalf of the workers, particularly during the (State of) Emergency.

There is little doubt, therefore, that the SATUC and the ICFTU were largely responsible for creating FOFATUSA. De Jonge and Millard had made it clear during their 1959 tour that a large amount of money (estimates ranged up to £30,000) could be made available for organizing African trade unions within the reformist confines of ICFTU policy. FOFATUSA had no independent financial base with such a small membership, so it was more than idle speculation to suggest that the short-lived FOFATUSA was underwritten with ICFTU funds channelled through SATUC politics. The entire history of African trade unionism in South Africa shows clearly that such an organization as FOFATUSA was not indigenous but rather an artificial transplant, alien to Black working class soil. FOFATUSA did not succeed in holding one national conference, and in January 1966, after six years of inept existence, dissolved itself and called upon African trade unions to affiliate to TUCSA.

The South African Liberal Party (SALP) is also implicated in this fiasco. Following the banning of Phyllis Altman in 1963, she received in the mail a set of photostated documents revealing that the SALP was at one time considering a 'takeover' of SACTU. Written on official Liberal Party stationery, the documents spoke of 'wanting to get the "Commies" out of SACTU', and what is even more disgusting, '... with a little guile and some money it should be possible to crush SACTU'. The strategy was apparently to organize a conference on the Swaziland border to cordinate these nefarious plans, but the ICFTU refused to fund the conference as there was no trade union recipient to justify the expenditure.

Instead, and according to the documents, the ICFTU agreed to fund an organizer to work in the food and canning industry in the Cape province. Workers in this industry, however, remained totally committed to SACTU and the African-FCWU. Yet, from the point of view of the disrupters, it was an obvious place to start after the heavy repression against SACTU organizers in the early 1960s.[13]

One final incident bears upon the ICFTU manipulations in these years. In the early 1960s, another ICFTU visitor came to SACTU Offices and in the course of discussion admitted that FOFATUSA had been a total failure. Instead of learning from this mistake, however, he

£30,000 AID FOR AFRICAN UNIONS—BUT NOT SACTU

ICFTU Continues Splitting Campaign

JOHANNESBURG.

THE visit of two International Confederation of Trade Union delegates to this country and their scheme to set up a new African trade union body rival to the S.A. Congress of Trade Unions, the only non-colour-bar trade union co-ordinating council, had echoes in London recently when the Africa Bureau held a two-day conference to discuss help for South African trade unions, the economic boycott campaign and the campaign against the sport colour bar.

Star of the discussion on the trade union topic was Mr. Millard, one of the two ICFTU representatives who was involved in negotiations when he was in the Union to get the Trade Union Council to set up a new African trade union committee and who told SACTU that if it wanted help in organising African workers it should keep out of the Congress alliance.

The ICFTU has undertaken to spend £30,000 in the Union on helping organise African unions—as long as they organise through the trade union committee TUC officials are trying to help get going and on which the Pan-Africanist 'Minister of Labour' Mr. J. D. Nyaose is working.

Mr. Millard did not change his stand when he spoke to the Africa Bureau in London. He made it plain that unions that work through SACTU and do not link up with the new committee will not get ICFTU financial assistance.

Meantime SACTU has had no reply from ICFTU headquarters, to whom it wrote protesting at the splitting tactics of the two spokesmen who represented that body in the Union earlier this year.

OPPOSITION

The suggestion that SACTU trade unions with the Congresses, notably the African National Congress, has greatly strengthened the trade unions, they say. The ANC helped put the national demand for a minimum wage of £1 a day on the map in South Africa by vigorous campaigning up and down the country for this demand.

The ANC has helped recruit new members into unions and to explain trade unionism to the workers.

Trade unionists further cite the example of SACTU association with the Congress bringing direct results in the negotiations with the Langeberg Canning company which made big concessions to the Food and Canning Workers' Union just before the launching of the economic boycott this year.

The strange position now exists that the ICFTU refuses to recognise SACTU as the most representative trade union body in South Africa in the same year that the ILO tells

An Old Socialist Passes

JOHANNESBURG.

Arthur Harmel, who died on August 4 at the age of 75, will be missed by the labour and progressive movement. During his youth, in Dublin, Ireland, he was an ardent labour man and republican, and in his capacity as secretary of the local Socialist Society he shared the platform with many famous

asked SACTU to allow him to organize the unorganized motor workers in the Johannesburg area. His purpose was to 'show FOFATUSA and SATUC how to organize African workers. I beg you (SACTU) to leave these workers alone'.[14]

These episodes combine to present a vivid picture of the role that the ICFTU played during SACTU's first decade. Their call for 'no politics in the trade union movement' was a disguise for a certain and limited type of political trade unionism that agreed not to fundamentally challenge the *status quo*. Trade unions are inevitably political organizations given the nature of social relations under the capitalist mode of production. This much is obvious. SACTU's politics have always been committed to liberation, not concession. Any African trade union in South Africa that fails to rest its policies and practice on the principle of self-determination and emancipation of the African proletariat from national oppression and class exploitation will never command the allegiance of the workers. This point above all others explains the failure of the ICFTU–SATUC–PAC–FOFATUSA initiative.

This should also go a long way towards explaining SACTU's decision in 1955 to choose affiliation to the WFTU, an international federation that has placed no conditions and forced no compromises on the workers' struggle.

The International Labour Organization (ILO) and SACTU

Like the CNETU before it, SACTU always took advantage of the opportunity to present the case of the oppressed Black workers before international forums. The ILO, a creation of the United Nations representing governments, employers and employee organizations, was never regarded by SACTU as a body that could effectively initiate the necessary changes being called for, but it could and did serve as an arena within which the truth about conditions under Apartheid could be brought to the attention of the world community. The South African government treated ILO sessions and resolutions with the same contempt it showed to all international bodies. Nevertheless, it is important to briefly summarize the SACTU initiatives which contributed towards the eventual expulsion of South Africa from the ILO in 1963.

SACTU's primary goal between 1955 and 1963 was to object to the total exclusion of African trade unions (and coordinating bodies) from representation on South African delegations to ILO conferences.

Because the selection of delegates is left to the government, successive Apartheid regimes refused to even consider the selection of a SACTU representative. In other words, the majority of the South African working class could never present its case directly to the ILO. Instead, reactionary Whites-only unions, representing a small minority of privileged workers, annually mis-represented the true working class of South Africa. As Moses Mabhida points out, 'the White trade unionists make the world believe that an African is a bit of an imbecile, and as such, not capable of representing the opinions of his people or the African working class. This had to be proven wrong, and South Africa exposed for what she was.'[15]

SACTU each year called for the ILO Credentials Committee to unseat the South African delegation and instead force the government to consult with SACTU prior to the selection of ILO delegates. But SACTU placed equal emphasis on the preparation and presentation of detailed memoranda documenting the slave labour conditions inside the country, always tailoring the memoranda to fit the agenda items of respective ILO conferences. Until 1962, it was never the position of SACTU that South Africa should be excluded or expelled from the ILO; rather, the government should be pressured by that body to become a signatory to ILO resolutions and to make its workers' delegations representative of the working class at home. Because South Africa refused to allow SACTU personnel to attend the ILO conferences, the permanent WFTU delegate to the ILO was given the responsibility of presenting the SACTU case each year.

In 1959, SACTU's argument to the 43rd Session of the ILO struck a responsive chord with the Credentials Committee and resulted in a limited victory. Previously SACTU had always argued its right to be consulted on numerical strength alone. This argument failed in that the four coordinating bodies consulted by the South African regime (the SATUC, the SA Federation of Trade Unions (SAFTU), the Co-ordinating Council of South African Trade Unions, and the Federal Consultative Council of SA Railways and Harbours Staff Associations – *all colour-bar bodies*) had a combined membership far in excess of SACTU. The 1959 memorandum pleaded the case differently, correctly asserting that SACTU was the 'most representative organization' in that its membership was open to *all* workers, regardless of race and hence consistent with Paragraph No. 5 of Article 3 of the ILO Constitution.

With this new information, the Credentials Committee ruled that

SACTU was indeed the 'most representative organization' and in its final report stated, 'The Committee can see no reason why the objecting organization (SACTU) was not consulted. This is particularly so, since it would appear that the Congress is the only truly multi-racial body of all the trade union organizations concerned.'

The South African delegate to the ILO was forced to change his line of defence, admitting that SACTU was not consulted because SACTU 'consists partly of bodies which are not registered trade unions in terms of the relevant (South African) legislation', that is, African unions are not recognized under Apartheid laws. Mr Berlinson, Chairman of the Credentials Committee, recorded this admission in his final summary which recommended government consultation with SACTU in future ILO proceedings.

Berlinson's report, however, also reflected the powerlessness of the ILO by admitting that despite this decision, at the national level 'the Union of South Africa is entirely free to pursue its own policy and to frame its laws in the way it deems fit'. Assuming that this decision would be carried out subsequently, the Credentials Committee refused to unseat the South African workers' delegate, H. Liebenberg, at the 43rd Session.[16]

Whether the ILO took this position regarding SACTU consultation because of the logic of SACTU's argument or because of increasing international pressure to do something constructive against Apartheid, the decision was predictably ignored by the South African government in 1960. The 44th Session of the ILO took place during the State of Emergency when many SACTU activists were in detention. During the Emergency and prior to the Geneva meetings, SACTU sent an objection to the appointment of a SATUC delegate as the South African workers' representative, referring of course to the 1959 ILO decision mentioned above. The government responded with its usual slander of SACTU, claiming that the latter was closely associated with organizations (e.g. the African National Congress) declared illegal 'by reason of their subversive activities'.

At the ILO Conference in 1960, the SATUC delegate made the truly remarkable claim that his organization, despite an official colour-bar against African trade union affiliation, had a liaison relationship with six African trade unions. This obviously referred to the bogus FOFATUSA and its largely paper unions discussed above. Mr Hannah, the South African government delegate, corroborated this TUC distortion and went so far as to say that 'non-White' unions are

'... entitled to take part in collective bargaining and do so.' This statement was totally untrue under the terms of the Industrial Conciliation Act (1956) and the Native Labour (Settlement of Disputes) Act of 1953.

With SACTU comrades in jail, and no doubt with the manoeuvring by the Western powers, the ILO Credentials Committee reversed its decision of 1959 and accepted the argument that the SATUC was a 'multi-racial' centre; it concluded, '... if there were no legal obstacle concerning registration, the SATUC would freely open its doors to African workers with whom it has established positive trade unions.' This is tantamount to saying that if things were different, they wouldn't be the same.

Furthermore, the 1960 ILO Session ignored its 1959 ruling by failing to call on the South African government to consult with SACTU in the future. The ILO also agreed not to send any additional protests to South Africa regarding its policy of forced labour (a major agenda item at the 44th Session) because it would simply continue to ignore these protests. Despite this total compromise to Apartheid, SACTU continued during and after the Emergency to submit detailed information on oppression under Apartheid, especially information on the increasing victimization of SACTU organizers arrested and prevented from fulfilling their legitimate trade union tasks.

In December 1960 the ILO held its first African Regional Conference in Lagos, Nigeria. SACTU elected three delegates to attend, but again they were refused exit and re-entry permits. South Africa itself refused to participate and thus no one represented the toiling masses of South Africa at the inaugural conference called to discuss continental labour conditions. Only through Brother K. Descan, President of the Printing Workers Union, Mauritius, were SACTU's views made known to the Conference.

SACTU's 13-page memorandum to the 45th ILO session in 1961, was a strongly-worded document which, in addition to briefing the international community on housing conditions, employment practices and a lack of vocational training opportunities for Black workers in South Africa, took exception to the SATUC 1960 claim of 'multi-racial' status. SACTU pointed out that the SATUC practised 'self-imposed' racial discrimination and that no legal obstacle prevented equal affiliation of African trade unions. The TUC was also chastised for rejecting all SACTU efforts at unity on the trade union front inside the country. Despite the fact that the ILO submission was necessarily incomplete due to the seizure of SACTU documents during the Emergency at home, the Credentials Committee returned to its 1959 position and called for government consultation with SACTU in the appointment of the 1962 ILO delegation.

Most significant at the 1961 meetings was a Nigerian government resolution calling for the expulsion of the South African delegation from the ILO proceedings. The South African government and workers' delegates spoke against the resolution but to no avail as it passed by a vote of 163 to 0, with 89 abstentions. A SACTU memorandum circulated to delegates at the Conference supported the resolution:

> For too long have the interests of South African workers been represented by sectional trade union bodies, which themselves practise racial discrimination and are not qualified to speak on behalf of all workers. SACTU has lodged objections against this practice. The resolution asking South Africa to withdraw is an indication of the support which South African workers have among member states.... The resolution ... is the first step. It should be followed by the imposition of diplomatic, economic and political sanctions on South Africa.

The State of Emergency of 1960 and the three-month (April–June) ban on SACTU meetings in 1961 had obviously angered certain member states into demanding international action against Apartheid.

South Africa refused to voluntarily withdraw from the ILO following this 1961 vote and in 1962 again chose a delegation without consulting or including SACTU. At SACTU's 1962 Annual National Conference, it was agreed to follow the Nigerian initiative and call for the total expulsion of South Africa from the ILO instead of the usual appeal for the un-seating of the racist delegates.

One month before the ILO's 46th Session that year, SACTU again filed a detailed memorandum documenting: (a) the continued violations of ILO conventions by the government; (b) prohibitions against African workers' right to strike; (c) anti-trade union propaganda by government departments; (d) entrenchment of Apartheid in trade unions and related statutory Job Reservation in industry; and (e) the persecution of individual SACTU leaders under the notorious Sabotage Act of 1962 (see Chapter 12). A summary of this memorandum was sent to ILO member states calling on their delegations to vote in favour of South African expulsion at the June meetings. Not by coincidence the registered memorandum never reached the ILO office in Geneva, and the SACTU Management Committee was forced to launch an investigation with the Post Office in South Africa in August of that year. As well, Moses Mabhida, then residing in London, England, was refused a visa by the British government to attend the Geneva conference.

In 1963, SACTU updated the 1962 memorandum with additional data on the repression against its leaders and again called for the expulsion of South Africa. Under pressure, Senator Trollip, the South African Minister of Labour, ordered the Apartheid delegation to remain seated at the meetings, adding, 'The Government will not be forced to recognize SACTU for future nominations of workers' representatives.' But the African states in particular had had enough. They withdrew completely from the ILO proceedings and workers' representatives from all over the world staged a walk-out when H. Liebenburg, the South African workers' delegate, rose to speak. The remaining government and employers' delegates voted unanimously for South African expulsion. There were 57 abstentions as compared with the 89 two years before. In March 1964 South Africa withdrew its membership from the ILO.

Expulsion of South Africa by ILO member states expressed their collective disgust at Apartheid and the contempt South Africa showed to international bodies in general. By 1958, South Africa had ratified only eleven out of the one hundred and two ILO conventions. In 1964, when it left the ILO, the government had still not ratified Convention No. 87, concerning Freedom of Association and Protection of the Right to Strike, or Convention No. 97, regarding the Application of the Principles of the Right to Organize and to Bargain Collectively.[17] Expulsion of South Africa was an important act of international solidarity with the voteless and voiceless workers of that country, but it could not be expected to change the nature and degree of class exploitation under Apartheid.

The Emergence of the AATUF and Continental Trade Unionism

A Trade Union movement in a colonial territory cannot divorce itself from the national struggle for political independence.

With these words, the then Prime Minister of Ghana, Kwame Nkrumah, opened the Accra conference in November 1959, where it was decided to form the All-African Trade Union Federation (AATUF). This Preparatory Conference had been convened by a steering committee struck at the All-Africa People's Conference also held in Accra the previous year. At the 1959 meetings, national trade union centres from seventeen African nations and representing over 55 per cent of African trade unionists resolved to work for African trade union unity by remaining independent of both the ICFTU and WFTU. In the face of neo-colonial and imperialist ventures throughout the continent, the Conference set itself no small task:

... to banish every form of sterile partnership ... in order to achieve national unity, strengthen the All African Trade Union Federation and make an effective contribution to the struggle for African independence and unity, the development of the wealth of Africa in the interest of the African peoples, the economic improvement of the masses and the raising of their standard of living, and the establishment of true democracy, guaranteeing to everyone liberty, justice, social well-being and peace.

SACTU was selected as one of the nineteen bodies that would plan and convene the Inaugural Conference of AATUF in May 1960 in Casablanca, Morocco. The fifth SACTU National Conference pledged to support AATUF, and expressed the view that divisions amongst African workers could only be eliminated with the defeat of imperialism in Africa. SACTU also agreed with the decision that the new body should not be affiliated to any international federation, but later held to the position that AATUF affiliates should be free to maintain or establish such affiliations.

Rivalries between the ICFTU and the WFTU on the African continent provided the dynamics against which the success of AATUF would be assessed. As well, the American AFL–CIO was rapidly extending its influence into the African labour movement, challenging both the ICFTU and the British TUC (which was described as an arm of British imperialism by the American interventionists). Using money and, where necessary, the CIA, the US labour aristocracy began to carve out a sphere of influence on African soil that would later be embodied in the African-American Labour Centre (AALC), administered by the notorious Irving Brown from his office in New York City.[18]

The decision to form AATUF coincided with the period of sharp decline in ICFTU influence in Africa. Its continental trade union membership had dropped from 25 to 7 per cent according to *Workers Unity* (February 1960). This can be partially attributed to the splitting tactics of the ICFTU in Nigeria and South Africa, for example, the ICFTU complicity in the creation of FOFATUSA as outlined above.

Trade union journals in Africa and even in Asia featured articles exposing the ICFTU–FOFATUSA connection, ever aware of similar dangers posed to the independence of their own trade union movements. The Egyptian Confederation of Labour stated in 1959: 'African workers must unite more closely to strengthen brotherhood between workers and to the colonialists we say: "Hands Off Africa – Africa Must Be Free".'

The imminent formation of the AATUF led the ICFTU to call a rival conference in Lagos, Nigeria to coincide with the AATUF Preparatory Conference in Accra. This pattern of meeting and counter-meeting was to be repeated many times over the next few years.[19]

1960 passed without the AATUF Inaugural Conference being convened. Organizers attributed this delay to 'imperialist sabotage', although the details of this charge were not specified. Another ICFTU African Regional Conference was held in October of that year in Tunisia. SACTU had been invited by Jack Purvis, ICFTU Regional Officer, during his 1960 tour of South Africa, but, as usual, SACTU representatives were unable to leave the country. After consulting with John Tettagah, head of the Ghana TUC and key figure in AATUF, SACTU circulated a letter to the Conference accusing the ICFTU of disruptive tactics in South Africa and objecting to the issuance of invitations to the SATUC and FOFATUSA.

Two months later, the Preparatory Committee of AATUF held its second meeting and claimed that more African trade union centres were abandoning their previous allegiances to the ICFTU and joining the AATUF. SACTU had token representation at these meetings in the person of Tennyson Makiwane, a South African journalist who later broke with the ANC.

The Inaugural Conference of AATUF was finally held in May 1961 in Casablanca. Delegates from thirty-three trade union centres in twenty-eight African countries attended; seven additional African states sent observers. SACTU was represented at the Conference by its two international representatives – Moses Mabhida and Wilton Mkwayi. The Credentials Committee's recognition of SACTU was challenged by Nana Mahomo, self-proclaimed PAC-FOFATUSA representative who also demanded the right to speak for South African workers. Mahomo's appeal was rejected following an address by Wilton Mkwayi who explained the position of the PAC and FOFATUSA; Mahomo then joined the delegation from the Rhodesian TUC as an observer.[20]

In the spirit of constructive criticism, the SACTU Management Committee had prepared a detailed analysis of the AATUF draft Constitution in advance of the Conference.

Firstly, SACTU objected to the use of the terms 'African Personality' and 'African Race' in the wording of the draft. The former was considered dangerous and misleading in that repeated nationalistic provisions of this kind 'can be disastrous to the workers of Africa, leading to an African chauvinism which misleads the workers . . . from their basic interests of working class struggle and unity'. Similarly, the term 'African Race' should not be used where it might detract attention from the ultimate goal of total working class unity, regardless of race or colour.

Secondly, on the issue of international affiliation, SACTU encouraged AATUF independence from the ICFTU and the WFTU as a pre-condition for maximum unity. This would ensure that the ICFTU would not be able to use the AATUF to promote its interests throughout the African continent. SACTU strongly disagreed, however, with the proposed clause which disallowed international affiliation of AATUF members. The Management Committee explained that the net effect of this would be to drive ICFTU affiliates away from the AATUF, leaving the latter as a minority of progressive union centres from Ghana, Guinea and Mali. As SACTU stated,

By purposely excluding affiliates in this way, we are giving them just the excuse they want to stay out of any Federation. On the other hand, by ensuring that there is no obstacle of this kind to their entry into a Federation we shall be utilising the contradictions which exist between the ICFTU African affiliates and the rest of the ICFTU and the imperialists, because these ICFTU African affiliates are forced to take up a determined stand – with all other African trade unions – against imperialism.

The AATUF Conference reflected the many contradictions existing within the African trade union and political spheres. Notwithstanding SACTU's criticisms and suggestions, the AATUF Charter read as follows on the international affiliation issue:

The Federation of All-African Trade Unions is an independent organization which rejects all foreign interference in African trade union affairs. It is composed of independent trade union organizations. Nevertheless, as a temporary measure, national trade union organizations belonging to central international trade unions at the time of the Congress are given a term of ten months in which to achieve disaffiliation.

This section of the Charter and the heated debate which surrounded it led to a walk-out by twelve pro-ICFTU delegations on the final day of the Conference, thus confirming SACTU's charge of sectarianism.

With certain important exceptions, colonialism in Africa meant that many national trade union centres did not have the long history of working class struggle and industrial unionism as SACTU did. Emergent leaders were in many cases from petty-bourgeois backgrounds, suddenly appointed to trade union positions following independence. Understandable as this is within the context of colonial history and underdevelopment, the new AATUF could not escape the consequences that flowed from these realities.[21]

Six months after the formation of AATUF, SACTU–NEC members began to articulate these weaknesses and adjust their expectations of AATUF accordingly. Over the next two years SACTU encouraged the establishment of an AATUF Regional Office in Johannesburg and the calling of special conferences to grapple with the problems faced by African agricultural workers and mine workers. All of these proposals were beyond the resources or organizational capability of AATUF, and SACTU was in no position to offer tangible assistance to the fledgling organization.

Nor were the ICFTU and its African affiliates willing to struggle within the AATUF to overcome these initial difficulties. Instead, no sooner had the ink dried on the AATUF Charter than the ICFTU called a series of conferences in 1961 in Kenya and Dakar. Their intention was to form a rival continental body. Ahmed Tlili, Tunisian member of the ICFTU Executive Bureau, was the leading figure in these divisive tactics which resulted in the formation of the anti-Communist Pan African Federation of Trade Unions in January 1962. Delegations attended from Kenya, French Congo, Senegal, Gambia and a splinter group from Nigeria, and British and American labour attaches were very much involved in the background. John Tettagah, AATUF General Secretary from Ghana, correctly identified the impetus behind this move when he said, 'Western imperialism has decided to show its naked form to the African workers'.[22]

Finally, the June 1964 AATUF Conference in Bamako found SACTU's two representatives – Mark Shope and Mate Mfusi – challenged by FOFATUSA's President Nyaose. Each group was required to present its case to the Credentials Committee. SACTU spoke first and took a trade union line, not bothering to go into a discussion of its relationship to the ANC and the Congress Alliance.

Nyaose, on the other hand, took the opportunity to avoid trade unionism completely and launched into a pro-PAC speech, complete with photos of himself and Robert Sobukwe (PAC leader) heading demonstrations at Sharpeville. Swayed initially by this presentation, and ignorant of many internal South African issues, the AATUF Secretariat ruled that South Africa was a 'special case' and gave both SACTU and FOFATUSA the right to be seated.

Shope and Mfusi then talked Nyaose into challenging this 'special case' ruling and each group was given the right to address the entire AATUF delegation the following day. Shope changed his tactics and delivered a powerful speech analysing the political shortcomings of the PAC and exposing Nyaose (and FOFATUSA) in the process. The response was positive and SACTU emerged victorious; they were even offered invitations to visit African countries in attendance and mention was made by the Ghanaian and Tanzanian/Zanzibarian delegates of possible SACTU external offices in each country.

This SACTU success did not, of course, alter the nature of AATUF itself. In Shope's report to Head Office, he observed that many of the delegates were not representing legitimate trade unions. Furthermore, the level of discussion was considered very low as crucial policy documents were often passed without comment. This complements opinions expressed by Moses Mabhida about the problems with AATUF:

AATUF never really took off. It was in many respects a paper organization, but it was also a body torn between the Arab world and African trade unionism elsewhere on the continent. Where there was practical work to be done, AATUF simply had no financial strength and thus could not provide assistance to organize African trade unions properly.

Yet despite these weaknesses, SACTU consistently supported the principles and objectives of AATUF. It is no doubt fair to conclude that SACTU's participation greatly assisted trade union brothers and sisters in Africa to better appreciate the disruptive and manipulative role played by the ICFTU, the British and American trade union bodies in their imperialist designs for the entire continent.

The WFTU 7 February Campaign

The 1960 Sharpeville and Langa massacres in South Africa, coupled with the five-month State of Emergency, brought to the world's attention more clearly than ever before the nature of repression under

Apartheid. The general session of the WFTU met that year and resolved: 'The fight of the workers and people of the Union of South Africa against the worst type of repression and exploitation built on Apartheid and racial discrimination has come to a point where individual support is no longer effective.' With this resolution, and in consultation with the SACTU Management Committee, the WFTU further resolved to form an International Trade Union Committee for Solidarity with the Workers and People of South Africa (Solidarity Committee).

SACTU's *Workers Unity* (April 1961) issued a Special Supplement endorsing the idea of the Solidarity Committee and encouraging support from national and international bodies on a non-partisan basis, independent of international affiliation. To the credit of the WFTU, a special conference was called at Accra on 24–26 July 1961 where the WFTU, the Ghana TUC, the Central Council of Soviet Trade Unions, the All-China Federation of Trade Unions, the General Confederation of Labour (France) (CGT), the All-India TUC, the General Union of Workers of Mali, the Nigerian TUC and SACTU (in the person of Moses Mabhida) combined to form the Solidarity Committee. An appeal was distributed to trade unions throughout the world, calling for a united front against Apartheid and in support of SACTU and the workers of South Africa. The conference and follow-up work was totally sponsored by the WFTU, and Mabhida, Wilton Mkwayi and Arnold Selby were the SACTU overseas representatives who worked tirelessly on the coordination of the campaign abroad.

Inside South Africa, the Management Committee and the NEC decided that the Solidarity Committee would be most effective if a given day were selected to launch the campaign. After considerable debate within the NEC, 7 January 1962 was selected to commemorate the beginning of the Alexandra Bus Boycott in 1957. Because of difficulties in coordinating the internal and external work, the date was set back one month to 7 February.

Local Committees in Durban, the Transvaal, Port Elizabeth and Cape Town began the work of organizing locally for the February campaign, which was to be the beginning of a new thrust to organize the unorganized and to push harder for the demand for £1-a-Day. Funds from Head Office were made available to employ two full-time organizers for the campaign.

The 1962 National Conference minutes report that on 7 February 1962 100,000 leaflets were distributed on the Reef and placard demonstrations took place at all railway stations, bus stops and termini in Johannesburg. Slogans read: 'Join Your Unions Now'; 'Fight for a Pound a Day'; 'Abolition of the Industrial Colour Bar'. Another 5,000 leaflets were distributed in Kimberley and a mass rally in Port Elizabeth was regarded as a success. Durban held factory meetings, mass meetings and deputations were sent to employers' organizations demanding a national minimum wage; additional rallies were held on 8 February and 17 March. Most importantly, the Cape Town Local Committee, in addition to calling mass meetings and issuing 25,000 leaflets, presented SACTU's draft legislation for a National Minimum Wage Bill. The Minister of Labour described the proposed legislation as 'unfeasible, impracticable' and '(it) would fail to achieve its objects'. This was the first occasion that a Minister of Labour had ever been obliged to publicly respond to a campaign that began back in 1957.

Solidarity telegrams and letters poured into SACTU offices and protest letters from all over the world landed on the desks of MPs and Cabinet Members in Cape Town. SACTU singled out the letter from the Angolan workers of the Union Nationale des Travailleurs Angolais (UNTA) in exile in Leopoldville for special mention: 'We salute the heroes, the fighters and we bow our heads in memory of those who have died and those who will die for this noble cause.'

SACTU's emphasis following the launching of the campaign on 7 February was to concentrate on the primary industries where hundreds of thousands of African workers remained unorganized. Realistically, as past efforts had shown, not all industries could be tackled simultaneously, so it was the iron and steel and metallurgical industry with 200,000 workers of all races that received immediate attention by all local committees. As was so often the case, heavy repression under the Sabotage Bill prevented the realization of this objective.[23]

In assessing the Solidarity Committee and the 7 February campaign, it must be said that within the constraints of South African conditions the campaign was a limited success. In addition to bringing together SACTU internal work – organizing the unorganized, demanding a national minimum wage and mobilizing other constituent groups of the Congress Alliance – the campaign marked the first time in modern history that such a large part of the international trade union community responded in unity with the oppressed workers in South Africa. The principled support of the campaign by the WFTU also showed that the struggles of African workers need not be approached as an arena for cold-war politics but as struggles that stand on their own merit.

NOTES

1. *Morning Star*, of the Food and Canning Workers Union; *Textile Unity*, of the Textile Workers Industrial Union; and *Truth*, of the National Union of Laundry, Cleaning and Dyeing Workers. These papers represented both registered and African unions of each industry.
2. *Morning Star*, February 1956.
3. General Secretary's Report, SACTU 7th Annual National Conference, 1962.
4. For greater detail, see R. Lambert, op. cit.
5. Occasionally, progressive White trade unionists like Issy Wolfson and Vic Syvret were able to attend international trade union conferences, but even these persons were soon to fall victim to banning orders.
6. For an excellent exposé of these issues, see D. Thompson and R. Larson, *Where were you Brother? An Account of Trade Union Imperialism*, War on Want Publication, London, 1978.
7. Lucy Mvubelo's husband was the victim of an attack by thugs (perhaps hired by the employers) as a result of his organizing work among Africans in the transport industry. It was at about this time that she broke with SACTU.
8. The ICFTU team had been invited to attend the 1959 SACTU Conference but refused because the WFTU had also been invited. Tom Mboya, the Kenyan ICFTU spokesman in Africa, had been invited to give the opening address at the Conference, but the South African authorities refused him an entry visa. These examples show that SACTU was far from being dogmatic on the international front.
9. Interview, Phyllis Altman.
10. Interview, Stephen Dlamini.
11. The SATUC's exclusion of African trade unions was beginning to be an embarrassment internationally. Lacking even the façade of liberalism, the TUC regarded FOFATUSA as its 'official liaison' with African trade unions. It was this pressure from abroad, more so than a serious commitment to African workers, that led the TUC to drop its 'colour-bar' in the early 1960s. The name of the body changed at that time to the Trade Union Council of South Africa (TUCSA).
12. Is this an example of the ICFTU policy of 'no politics in the trade union movement'?
13. In all likelihood, these documents were sent to SACTU by a sympathetic worker employed in the duplicating office of the Liberal Party. His/her identity remains unknown.
14. Interview, Phyllis Altman.
15. Wilton Mkwayi and Moses Mabhida were SACTU's overseas representatives following their escape from South Africa during the State of Emergency in 1960. Mkwayi re-entered South Africa at a later date and is now serving a life sentence on Robben Island.
16. SACTU elected Moses Mabhida and Viola Hashe to present the case to the Geneva meetings in 1959, but they were both prevented from leaving South Africa. In the same year, Lucy Mvubelo (FOFATUSA) was allowed to attend the ILO meetings with a passport valid for two months.
17. The 1964 ILO Session passed a resolution calling on South Africa to repeal all legislation prohibiting the Freedoms covered by ILO Conventions Nos. 87 and 97.

18. See Thompson and Larson, op. cit.
19. Once again, the South African government allowed Lucy Mvubelo to leave the country to attend the Lagos meetings.
20. Before leaving South Africa, Nana Mahomo had never been a trade unionist. Yet Moses Mabhida recalls Mahomo working closely with the American Irving Brown, the man most closely associated with AFL-CIO/ICFTU intrigues in the African labour movement.
21. Interview, Moses Mabhida.
22. The Nigerian TUC even wrote to US President Kennedy to lodge complaints against Irving Brown and ask that he be removed as US Ambassador to Nigeria.
23. Interview, Moses Mabhida.

12 STATE REPRESSION

In all capitalist countries, the state maintains and promotes 'order' through whatever means necessary to protect the interests of the capitalist class and its ability to extract maximum profits from the collective labour-power of the proletariat. The 'means necessary' vary historically, depending on the specific conditions of national oppression and class conflict and the organized strength of opposition forces. Except in revolutionary situations, we know that the state has the monopoly of organized force at its disposal; the legal system and the police-military apparatus are the institutional weapons employed under 'normal' conditions of capitalist society.

South Africa is certainly no exception to this general rule. Its uniqueness rests with the extraordinary 'means necessary' to impose order on the majority of the people who are virtual prisoners in their own country. Insofar as Apartheid is an extreme variant of capitalist society, it is not difficult to appreciate why the ruling class requires special forms of repression to attempt to destroy the revolutionary organizations of the oppressed masses within.

The exaggerated conditions of exploitation characteristic of Apartheid mean that the 'rule of law' in itself is often insufficient. The entire system of Apartheid — forced labour, poverty wages, pass laws, bantustans, destruction of family life — is geared towards the production of wealth upon which South African capitalism depends. Non-racial and political trade unionism obviously threatens this system insofar as the effective organization of Black workers challenges the social basis of exploitation, that is, the capitalist-worker relationship.

Yet, as we have seen, there is no law in South Africa to prevent the formation of African trade unions and coordinating bodies representing the interests of organized and unorganized Black workers. SACTU, and its affiliated unions, have always been perfectly legal in the strict sense of the term.[1] Legislation preventing this does not exist for one simple reason — it would not be effective. No law, no matter how comprehensive or carefully formulated, could prevent African, Coloured and Indian workers from organizing to protect their common class interests.

Rather, the repression conducted by the South African state against workers' organizations has been more refined and subtle in its operations. In sum, SACTU is legal, but its activities and objectives are illegal. Therefore, SACTU activists are subject to the 'rule of law' relevant to political offences against the state and the rule of physical force employed by the massive machinery of administrative repression consisting of labour bureaux, police and the military. And, although never codified in writing, the rule of capital accumulation under capitalism is the motive force behind all these social institutions.

As with other groups in the Congress Alliance, repression against SACTU was cumulative and increasingly severe between the years 1955 to 1964. Instead of banning the organization, as was done in the case of the African National Congress and the South African Congress of Democrats, the strategy with SACTU was that of systematic victimization and the elimination of individuals. As we shall see, the organization was virtually forced to go underground and into exile as a result of the heavy repression carried out between 1962 and 1964.

Banning of individual trade union leaders, followed by house arrests, banishment to remote areas, detention without trial, torture and execution — these were the 'means necessary' to the state in curbing the revolutionary activities of SACTU and the workers' movement. The purpose of this chapter is to outline this chronology of repression, a story which is largely unknown to the international community.

Such an account cannot possibly pay tribute to the countless individuals who sacrificed so much during these years. Emphasis on victimization of individuals, especially in the early 1960s, is not intended to elevate any person(s) above the workers' movement as a whole. Biographical information is considered important, however, to show the degree of dedication and commitment made by SACTU activists as their contribution to the heritage of struggle for freedom in South Africa.

In many cases, it is difficult and unnecessary to separate repression on strict political (ANC) and trade union (SACTU) lines. Indeed, this underscores the close working relationship within the Congress Alliance before and after the banning of the ANC in 1960. After the State of Emergency, SACTU's limited 'legality' allowed it to play a greater political role as an organizational cover for ex-ANC persons as well as continue its historical role in the class struggle.

The Treason Trial (1956–1961)

4.00 a.m., 5 December 1956: Nazi-like raids throughout South Africa signalled the beginning of the infamous Treason Trial which interfered with the political and personal lives of many Congressites throughout the next four years. One hundred and fifty-six persons were rounded up, flown to Johannesburg in military aircraft and taken to the Fort for imprisonment. The charge was High Treason and the goal of the state was to smash the Congress Alliance and the nationwide political movement that had emerged since the Congress of the People and the signing of the Freedom Charter in June of the previous year.[2]

After periodic releases of groups of defendants over the first two years, a final group of thirty, consisting of the most easily identified leaders of the Congresses, remained on trial until 29 March 1961. On that day, Justice Rumpff interrupted the proceedings and stated, 'You are found not guilty and discharged. You may go.' Among this final group were Leon Levy and Leslie Massina, banned President and General Secretary of SACTU respectively.

The charge of treason against the original 156 defendants – many of whom had not been directly involved in the political struggle since the 1940s and many who were rank-and-file workers – was essentially based on the state's zealous desire to prove that the ANC and the Congress Alliance called for a violent overthrow of South Africa in order to establish a 'Communist' society based on the principles laid down in the Freedom Charter. Within a few months, it had become clear to all that the trial was a farce from the point of view of the Crown's evidence and its willingness to lie, distort documents and generally resort to any means necessary to prove the charge. Skilful defence attorneys (including some of the defendants themselves) destroyed the credibility of the Crown's arguments and on numerous occasions reduced the state witnesses to the appearance of the imbeciles that they were.

Massive raids had been carried out during the fifteen months between the Congress of the People and the December 1956 arrests. Local and national offices of the Congresses as well as the private homes of individual defendants had been raided; thousands of documents were seized and subsequently used as 'evidence' of High Treason. Among these documents were many official minutes of SACTU–NEC and MC meetings, the 1955 and 1956 Conference reports, leaflets, trade union lectures and correspondence. The Crown attempted to make the most of this documentation to prove that SACTU as part of the Alliance was involved in an internationally-orchestrated conspiracy to establish a 'Communist' South Africa.

If the state's real intent was to remove Congress leaders from the streets and thus divide the leaders from the masses, this strategy, with certain important exceptions, also failed. Never in the history of the movement had there been such an excellent opportunity for progressive South Africans of all races and walks of life to assemble together in one location for such a protracted period. Even the courtroom itself became the venue for political meetings and strategy sessions; it also allowed many of the defendants to fully appreciate for the first time the courtroom procedures associated with political trials.[3]

The Trial did, however, create certain serious problems for the day-to-day work of the Congress Movement and SACTU in particular. Leaders were in large part prevented from maintaining constant contact with the workers they represented. This put tremendous strains on the new organization, but it also served to heighten political awareness and create stronger structures through the co-option of new cadre taken from their respective unions to become full-time functionaries for SACTU Local Committee and Head Office routines. For example, Uriah Maleka, Viola Hashe, Edmund Cindi and John Gaetsewe became full-time SACTU workers in Johannesburg during this period and all four were soon nationally recognized trade union leaders. Phyllis Altman, a SACTU typist beforehand, became Assistant General Secretary during the early months of the Trial and remained in this position until her banning in September 1963. In most cases, co-optation involved giving up regular employment and poverty wages in the factories for SACTU work and no income at all. Yet there was never a lack of volunteers in these critical months of 1957.

This recruitment process was essential if SACTU was to become a viable trade union coordinating body. The Treason Trial arrests hit the eighteen-month-old organization hard; the following twenty-three national and local leaders were tied up in courtroom procedures for many months and years.

Johannesburg: Leon Levy (Pres.); Leslie Massina (Gen. Sec.);
P. Beyleveld (TWIU); A. Mahlangu (A-FCWU);
C. Sibande (Vice-Pres.); R. Press (TWIU);
M. W. Shope (A-LCDWU); J. Nkadimeng (National Organizer);
N. Sejake (I & SWU)

Cape Town: A. Sibeko (SAR & HWU); B. Turok (MWU);
J. Busa (A-TWIU)
Port Elizabeth: W. Mkwayi (A-TWIU); C. Mayekiso (A-TWIU);
S. Damons (FCWU); F. Baard (FCWU); C. Jasson (TWIU)
Durban: K. Moonsamy (DWU); B.Nair (SATWU); M. P. Naicker
(Natal AWU); S. Dlamini (A-TWIU); P. Mei (A-TWU);
V. S. M. Pillay (SACTU–NEC).

Six of these persons sat on the National Executive Committee at the time of the arrests and many more were on executives of local committees and key organizers in industries strategic to SACTU organizing campaigns.

At the local committee level, SACTU detainees from Durban and Cape Town have commented on the shortage of full-time personnel during this period; on the other hand, Archie Sibeko and Stephen Dlamini both recall an increase in political consciousness among workers with the arrest of their leaders. As Dlamini says, '. . . we were all convinced that we were on the right track'.

The heaviest blow came during the early weeks of the Trial in January 1967. Leon Levy and Leslie Massina were banned (a) under the Riotous Assemblies Act from leaving the magisterial district of Johannesburg for allegedly 'promoting hostility between Europeans and Non-Europeans', and (b) under the Suppression of Communism Act from attending gatherings that could be defined as 'furthering the aims of Communism'. These five-year bans were issued against SACTU's highest ranking officers one day prior to a change in their bail conditions which would have allowed them to attend meetings essential to trade union work. SACTU and other progressive organizations protested against this obvious attempt to cripple the work by confining the national officials to Johannesburg. The charge of promoting inter-racial 'hostility' was especially disgusting given SACTU's commitment to non-racial workers' unity. African laundry workers carried out work stoppages but with no effect.[4]

During the Trial years, the Head Office routine consisted of SACTU defendants spending their free time (usually afternoons) at the factories talking to workers and attending to correspondence in the evenings. Aside from keeping very long hours, there were times when the Treason Trialists could not contribute properly to strike situations. As Ronnie Press has described this period, 'nothing could be done in a logical way'.

This points again to the importance of the co-optations of new SACTU leaders.

Ronnie Press (TWIU) was himself the next victim of banning orders. A progressive White South African, he had become Secretary of the registered textile union in 1956, after finding it impossible for political reasons to gain employment in his chosen profession of chemistry. His Congress involvement and the Treason Trial arrest led the Government to issue the first ban in January 1957 preventing attendance at social gatherings. As Secretary of a registered union he was not initially banned from trade union work. This more severe restriction came in June 1957 when Press was flying back and forth between the Johannesburg courtroom and Durban to assist in a strike of Indian workers against the Philip Frame textile magnate. The second banning order restricting his movement to Johannesburg was personally presented at the Drill Hall courtroom on 24 June 1957.

Returning to the Trial itself, a good portion of the contents of SACTU documents confiscated during heavy raids on 27 September 1955 was produced as evidence in support of the charge of treason. This material consisted of the following types of information: SACTU lectures headed, 'Teaching that the workers are Oppressed by the Bourgeois or Capitalist Class'; discussions and leaflets on May Day; affiliation to the WFTU; opposition to the Nationalist Party's Apartheid labour legislation, endorsements of the Freedom Charter and support for the Congress Alliance. In addition, many excerpts from lectures and speeches which condemned the capitalist mode of production in general and the South African system of racial capitalism in particular were included among the materials presented by the Crown. An example is the SACTU statement, 'We have often heard that the African people are not ripe enough for trade unions. They are, however, ripe enough to be used as labour power and to be exploited,' and '... all workers have a right to share in the wealth of this country of ours ...'.[5]

With this type of material, the Crown argued the case for treason. Obviously SACTU documents, with emphasis on working class emancipation and proletarian internationalism, were highpoints in the state's grandiose design to prove its claim of 'Communist' conspiracy and social change through violent revolution. The state failed miserably in this respect, and the Judge in dismissing the remaining group of defendants pointed out that the ANC had proven the reverse – that its entire history had been committed to non-violent action against Apartheid.

The masses protest against Treason Trial arrests, 1957

SACTU as an organization had little direct involvement in the Trial. Annual national conferences regularly passed resolutions condemning the continuation of the Trial and the personal hardship it brought to many defendants and their families.[6] The masses were encouraged to strengthen and continue the 'We Stand By Our Leaders' campaign and to contribute financially to the Defence Fund. Letters were sent by Leslie Massina to international trade union federations asking for financial assistance for court costs; the British TUC contributed £500, the WFTU, £400, and the ICFTU, £250.

In sum, the overall outcome of the Treason Trial was positive for SACTU and the movement in general. Despite difficulties in maintaining the trade union work in some centres owing to the loss of key organizers, SACTU was able to bring in new functionaries and utilize the heightened political consciousness of the people to advantage in its organizing drives. Although the Trial dragged on for over fifty months, it was soon overshadowed by the more militant mass campaigns of the late 1950s. The state had realized by this time that more repressive measures would be necessary to defeat the people. Regarding the original charge of treason and Communist conspiracy, the state was forced to concede that the Freedom Charter was nothing more than a basic document of democratic rights.

The State of Emergency (1960)

Faced with the increased militancy of the people, the state abandoned all pretence of the 'rule of law' and instead chose to deal with the Congress Movement outside the courtroom. Under the Unlawful Organizations Act introduced in 1960, the government banned the ANC and the Pan-Africanist Congress (PAC) on 8 April of that year. One week earlier, on 30 March, the government had declared a State of Emergency which gave it broad and sweeping powers to act against alleged subversion. The Emergency lasted for a period of five months and was officially lifted at the end of August. On the first day following the Emergency declaration, all original Treason Trialists were re-arrested and many were detained for the entire five months.

The most immediate 'cause' of these actions was the outrage, at home and abroad, associated with the massacres of Africans at Sharpeville and Langa townships on 21 March 1960. An ANC campaign against the pass laws scheduled for the end of March had been pre-empted by the PAC who called for demonstrations on that date. It was only in the areas of the Southern Transvaal (Sharpeville) and the Western Cape

(Langa) that the people responded in large numbers. Following the PAC leaders' directives, people congregated in front of police stations to carry out non-violent pass-destroying protests and then volunteer themselves for arrest.

In Sharpeville, a contingent of young, trigger-happy White policemen opened fire, and in a short space of time, 69 Africans had been killed and another 180 wounded, many shot in the back. At Langa, a thousand miles away, a crowd of 10,000 people was ordered to disperse in three minutes. Failing to hear and heed this demand, the crowd was first baton charged and then came the 'order to fire'. Two Africans were killed and 49 injured. That evening violence spread throughout the township, which was essentially a 'bachelor's quarters' for African male workers whose families had been forcibly removed under Influx Control regulations. More deaths were recorded by the following morning.

These are the events usually associated with the banning of the political movements and the declaration of the Emergency. Yet it is important to point out that the preceding year had witnessed the emergence of mass militancy at the rank-and-file level beyond previous experience. Women's campaigns against passes, beer-halls and other forms of oppression, particularly in Durban and Natal, had reached revolutionary proportions.

The important role SACTU assumed in this period has not been properly appreciated in the literature dealing with the pre-Emergency period. As part of the Congress campaign against passes, SACTU called for National Workers Conferences to be held in all major centres on 28 February 1959. The response throughout the country was one of the greatest ever to a SACTU campaign for an end to poverty wages and political oppression.

In Durban, a record attendance of 4,000 people gathered for two days, demanding general strike action, boycotts and political defiance. In Pietermaritzburg, meetings drew 3,000. The Port Elizabeth Local Committee reported 'one of the most successful meetings ever held in our area', and Pretoria drew 600 workers 'which is outstanding for this area'. Two equally successful meetings in the Transvaal attracted 2,000 workers, and in Cape Town, at a well attended and emotionally-charged rally, SACTU militant Archie Sibeko personally escorted the Special Branch from the hall. Such an act was not uncommon at SACTU and Congress meetings, but it could only be carried out with mass support from the people rising up against police harassment. As

SACTU reported, the Workers Conferences 'gave a jolt to the Government and capitalists of South Africa'.[7]

From the end of March, hundreds of SACTU leaders and rank-and-file workers were among the thousands of people detained without trial during the Emergency. Many full-time functionaries were kept in prison for the entire five month period. Those militants who escaped detention were forced to go underground (as was the case for Archie Sibeko and Stephen Dlamini) or leave the country to continue the work in exile. Moses Mabhida and Wilton Mkwayi left South Africa at this time to become SACTU's overseas representatives responsible for promoting and coordinating international solidarity work. Thus, the crisis was to test once more the strength of the organization between the months of April and August.

In Johannesburg, Head Office was largely depleted of full-time personnel with the re-arrest of Levy and Massina and the departure of Phyllis Altman to Swaziland during the Emergency. Anticipating such a crisis, the Management Committee had previously agreed to follow the model used earlier by the Indian Congress in India; that is, the appointment of one person to be solely responsible for managing the affairs of the organization. Bob Hepple, son of Labour Party politician and SACTU supporter Alex Hepple, assumed this gigantic task and was ably assisted by Don Mateman (TWIU) who became Acting General Secretary. Another volunteer, Shanti Naidoo, became a full-time office worker during this period; from a historically political Indian family in South Africa, Shanti had also worked for the SAIC and the COD on a regular basis prior to the Emergency.[8] Another trade union leader to assist Head Office was Rita Ndzanga.

As was the case in the early months of the Treason Trial, leaders were co-opted from affiliated unions and the factories. In addition to Mateman, Mark Shope (A-LCDWU) became a full-time functionary and NEC member during this period. Within a matter of days a new Management Committee formed and met daily to monitor the national situation and attempt to maintain the on-going work of a trade union coordinating body. This new Committee was itself reduced to only three members with a new wave of arrests on the day the ANC was outlawed. Six more members had been recruited by June.

The determination of SACTU comrades was equal to the challenge, and during the Emergency the organization not only survived but scored some of its most 'crowning achievements'. In May 1960 largely through the initiative of Billy Nair (Durban), the £1-a-Day campaign was given greater momentum with the preparation and presentation of wage-demand memoranda to the employers' organizations. Leaflets were also issued by the Wits and Durban Local Committees to tell workers that their unions were still legal and to encourage them to renew wage demands on the bosses and campaign for an end to the Emergency.[9]

Local committees struggled to keep their offices open. In Pietermaritzburg, SACTU leader Harry Gwala reported in September that 'every single functionary and a large number of our leading members were detained'. Similarly, the ANC–SACTU stronghold of Port Elizabeth was largely decimated by the arrests. In both cases, new unions organized before the Emergency ceased to function properly throughout most of 1960. In the Western Cape, workers took to the streets in strike action following the Langa massacre and trade union leaders were arrested as elsewhere.[10] The strength of the Food and Canning Workers Union stood out again, however, as a threatened strike by these workers forced the release of their General Secretary, Liz Abrahams. In Durban, veteran ANC–SACTU militant, Memory Vakalisa, terminated his employment to work full-time as a SACTU organizer but was then arrested for the duration of the Emergency. Eric Mtshali joined the Local Committee in July, and later became a SACTU organizer in Pinetown, Natal. A woman worker from the local tea factory left her job to do secretarial work in the Durban office.

The SACTU Fifth Annual National Conference, postponed from April to October, praised these valiant efforts of SACTU volunteers during the Emergency period:

We announce with the greatest possible pride that the period April 1959 to October 1960 has been the period of our greatest achievement. We have grown in stature both nationally and internationally. Through our consistent £1-a-Day Campaign, we have forced the entire country to recognize the need for wage increases. . . . Our membership figure is the highest it has been in the five years of our existence . . .

The courageous way in which our comrades in jail have carried on and the manner in which our Congress has continued its work despite the State of Emergency shows that the Government cannot succeed in its deperate attempt to suppress the people. It is not the Government which is 'teaching the people a lesson'; but increasingly it is the workers and the people who are demonstrating that the just cause for which they fight is invincible.

The official lifting of the Emergency did not bring an end to the harassment of SACTU leaders, however. Raids of offices continued in the weeks that followed and workers were intimidated with police searches as they entered trade union offices. Three more trade unionists were banned from trade union work, and four SACTU activists from Port Elizabeth (Alven Bennie, Melville Fletcher, Eddie Heynes and William Kupe) where charged with 'incitement to strike' speeches dating back to the 1958 national Stay-At-Home. Also, many workers detained without trial during the Emergency faced victimization by their bosses after release from jail in August.

The mention above of SACTU's international support refers in part to the massive letter-writing campaign conducted during the Emergency. Solidarity messages and protests to the South African regime poured into South Africa as the international community had been outraged by the news of the Sharpeville and Langa massacres in March. In fact, the Secretariat's Report to the 1960 Conference made the following claim:

> We know . . . that it was this campaign of ours, together with the pressure exerted by all democrats both inside and outside South Africa which forced the Government to end the State of Emergency.

SACTU 'Beats The Ban' (1961)

The acquittal and release of Treason Trialists on Wednesday, 29 March 1961, after over four years of harassment, was a victory for not only the defendants but the oppressed people of South Africa as a whole. Outside the Pretoria courtroom, crowds sang and danced in the streets, amidst a furious contingent of South African police. The 'Treason Trial bus' was about to make its final trip to Johannesburg, marking the end of one phase of repression . . . and, for some, the beginning of another.

When Leon Levy and Leslie Massina walked into the Johannesburg SACTU office, they were met with jubilant victory cries from rank-and-file workers who had packed the premises. Brandy was consumed from ordinary coffee cups in case the Special Branch decided to make one of their frequent, unannounced visits. Everyone talked about the acquittals and there was a general enthusiasm in the air as SACTU's Sixth Annual Conference would convene in Durban in two days time. The Conference in Durban would highlight SACTU's increased support and influence, reflected by a membership strength of 53,000 workers in fifty-one affiliated unions. The militancy and vitality of the Durban Local Committee made Natal an excellent venue for the meetings, especially as the local organizers had promised that for the first time representatives from farm workers would attend the SACTU proceedings. Also planned was a mass rally to commemorate the Sharpeville and Langa shootings of March 1960.

Back at Head Office, the phone rang. An ally at the office of the *Johannesburg Star* asked to speak to Phyllis Altman: 'Have you heard that the government has banned all SACTU meetings for three months, effective midnight on March 30th?' The celebration ended abruptly as the Management Committee went elsewhere to convene an emergency meeting to deal with this crisis and to protect the banned persons in attendance. Never a willing subject to such intimidation, the SACTU leadership decided to proceed with the Conference and to begin one day earlier than planned to 'beat the ban'. Durban was contacted by phone and the Local Committee immediately began to organize transport for workers throughout Natal, particularly from Pietermaritzburg.

Phyllis Altman caught the 6.00 a.m. Thursday plane to Durban, carrying with her the bundles of correspondence and documents rapidly put together the night before. Transvaal delegates, travelling for 15 hours in private cars and by train, arrived at 11.00 p.m. after the evening proceedings had almost ended; a few of the Cape Town delegates, making the longest journey on the least expensive transport, did not arrive until after the ban had gone into effect.

The Conference agenda and normal business procedures were scrapped, and instead the pre-midnight session consisted mostly of angry speeches made by SACTU activists. Speeches were translated from 'Cape Dutch' to English to Zulu. Liz Abrahams (FCWU), who spoke with a combined English-Afrikaans dialect shouted, 'Tell the filthy Boers that we stand on our rights.' The Special Branch had ringed the Textile Workers' Hall and at times were told to 'shut up' by angry Natal workers. At five minutes to midnight, the Conference ended abruptly. Rowley Arenstein, Durban Congressite lawyer, had been called to ensure that no victimization occurred. At midnight, the SB raided the Conference. To avoid the arrest of out-of-town delegates who were planning to sleep on the floor of the hall, taxis were summoned, and ironically, Arenstein managed to arrange a loan from the SB detectives to cover the expense. Needless to say, the Conference reconvened at a different setting within a few hours.

Such was the defiant response of SACTU delegates to the state's direct reprisal against SACTU for the Treason Trial verdict. The 1961 Conference, although 'chaotic, like a mad country dance', defeated yet another attempt by the Apartheid regime to silence the workers' movement. All delegates agreed that the 'Beat the Ban' Conference had been 'a great success'.[11]

The three-month ban issued by the Minister of Justice Vorster under the Suppression of Communism Act definitely affected SACTU's ability to organize mass public rallies, which had become very effective in the previous two years. But the ban in no way forced SACTU to forgo its major responsibilities to the workers. In fact, it served as a reinforcement of the 1959 Conference decision to organize factory committees *at the point of production* and to establish a solid corps of shop stewards within the workplace to carry out SACTU programmes.

Nor did the ban prevent SACTU from continuing to mobilize workers for Congress campaigns. An All-In Conference in Pietermaritzburg earlier in March, organized primarily by ex-ANC members and fellow Congressites, called for a multi-racial convention to challenge the South African Republic proclaimed early in 1961 and speak for all the oppressed people and progressive groups within Apartheid society. The Conference called for a nation-wide Stay-At-Home on 29–31 May, and SACTU played its part in assuring workers' participation in this protest. Despite massive intimidation in a state of siege atmosphere, and the passage of special legislation allowing for 12-day detentions without trial,[12] the Stay-At-Home was considered a general success throughout the country.

As during the Emergency, SACTU devoted much of its energies towards informing the international community on the state of affairs at home and calling on trade unions in particular to step up the boycott and embargo of all things South African. A letter to the WFTU dated 13 May 1961 reviewed the internal conditions: an increase in the mass arrests of persons for pass-law violations (1,300 arrests in a two-day period); the mobilization of Army reserves in preparation for the end of May Stay-At-Home; a ban on meetings of all political groups until 26 June; and raids on the private residences of Africans, Coloureds and Indians. The SACTU letter concluded, 'It is obvious ... that the Government is preparing for a show-down, and now more than ever before we need the concrete support of our fellow trade unionists throughout the world.' This situation in all likelihood prompted the WFTU decision to sponsor the formation of the International Solidarity Committee discussed in the previous chapter.

The international community answered SACTU's requests with a seriousness never before experienced. Trade unions in Commonwealth countries in particular, aware of South Africa's withdrawal from that body, sent strongly-worded letters of protest against the arbitrary and fascist-like banning of SACTU meetings. Australian, Canadian and British unions never previously in contact with SACTU responded in large numbers. For the first time, the British TUC openly stood with SACTU brothers and sisters in the struggle. Additional workers' bodies from Trinidad and Tobago, India, Burma, Ireland, France, the United States, Ghana, Hungary, Japan, Scotland, Northern Ireland, the German Democratic Republic, Czechoslovakia, Gambia and many other countries expressed similar solidarity. Inside South Africa, the Congress of Democrats, the National Union of Distributive Workers (NUDW) and even the Liberal Party attacked the Government for its blatant repression.[13]

Exiled SACTU activists to this day strongly believe that this 1961 expression of international solidarity was the decisive factor that prevented the regime from extending the ban on meetings beyond the end of June and banning the organization altogether. There is also the possibility that the state feared that a simultaneous banning of all Congress Alliance groups would create an uncontrollable underground movement. Stephen Dlamini, for example, believes the strategy was 'to let us surface again after three months and then trace our people back to the nest of the movement'.[14] In any event, trade unionists throughout the world, then and especially now, should realize that their collective actions do have the intended effect and are greatly respected by the oppressed workers of South Africa.

However, in hindsight, this three-month ban was but the prelude to the period of the most brutal repression against SACTU. The strategy of the state was vicious in its simplicity; by victimizing SACTU individuals through 'security' legislation and physical force the organization could be broken without being legally banned. Indications of this strategy date back to the mid-1950s, but by late 1961 the methods became more refined and effective.

Before, during and after the meetings-ban, arrests and bannings of SACTU organizers increased. The entire year of 1961 was, in essence, an 'undeclared State of Emergency'. In February, Melville Fletcher was banned in Durban at precisely the time he was gaining workers' support in a bid to oust the reactionary leadership in the registered Garment Workers Union. In May, Vuyisile Mini and Alven Bennie were arrested for their involvement in an important Bay Transport Co. bus strike in Port Elizabeth. Billy Nair was arrested in June and charged with

NEW AGE, THURSDAY, APRIL 6, 1961

In Protest Against 3-Month Ban

SACTU CALLS FOR WORLD BOYCOTT

JOHANNESBURG.

THE South African Congress of Trade Unions has called on trade unions throughout the world to boycott South African goods, declare South African ships 'black' and take any other solidarity action in protest against the Government's three month ban on all SACTU meetings.

The ban was slapped on SACTU by the Minister of Justice under the Suppression of Communism Act. It was intended amongst other things to block SACTU's sixth annual conference last week-end (see below).

SACTU immediately sent off cables to the All African Trade Union Federation, the WFTU and the ICFTU urging vigorous protests.

The call to trade unions to declare South African ships 'black' is a call to dockers not to load or offload South African vessels. It is an extension of the economic boycott movement and could be the start of a demand for countries to declare economic sanctions against the Union.

Millions have already endorsed the call for the boycott of South African goods and SACTU commented the day after the ban: "This action by the Government will only strengthen this endorsement and should make the boycott a complete success."

Two principal lines of action appear possible. First, such a committee may consider issuing an international financial appeal to assist South African trade unions as well as workers who have been imprisoned or were in the treason trial. Next, the Committee will consider organising an international trade boycott by calling the workers all over the world not to handle South African goods.

Mr. John Tettegah, President of the Ghana TUC, is said to be committed to an active policy on South Africa and may call for similar action from African trade unionists at the inaugural conference of the All-African Trade Union Federation due to take place in Casablanca in May.

'incitement to strike' during the May Stay-At-Home;[15] three hours after the arrest he was given a five-year banning order preventing movement outside Durban magisterial district and not allowing him to enter any factory, African location, hostel or village. Trade union work under these restrictions was virtually impossible. The progressive Durban lawyer. Rowley Arenstein, also banned, was not allowed to handle Nair's defence.

After the meetings-ban expired on 30 June, it was re-imposed on the Kimberley Domestic Workers Union in September, when the Union attempted to get a wage determination for grossly underpaid African domestic servants. The official reason given by the Kimberley magistrate was that 'poor lighting (in the hall) might lead to riots'. In Cape Town, Zollie Malindi (Garage Workers Union), Tofie Bardien (Executive member of the CPC and leader of the Taxi Drivers and Owners Association) and Archie Sibeko received five-year banning orders under the Suppression of Communism Act.

Nor were SACTU affiliated unions exempt from Security police harassment. In December 1961 a raid on the SAR & HWU office resulted in the seizure of individual membership cards and subsequent intimidation of workers for their union membership through threats of dismissal and actual transfers to lower paying jobs. Here again, the attack was directed against SACTU in that the transport workers were one of the strategic sectors being organized by SACTU's National Organizing Committees. Among many international trade union protests, the General Secretary of the Australian Railways Union, a Mr O'Brien, reacted as follows:

This Union, together with others, views with concern the intimidation practiced by your Government through the Security Police. An elementary knowledge of history should demonstrate . . . that the workers will continue to organize and unions will continue to prosper. You should realize in some countries prior to World War II those trade unions were forced underground. Despite this, they continued to function actively and in World War II those trade unionists who had been denied their citizenship rights under the Nazi regime played a memorable role in the success of Democracy over Fascism. We are surprised to think that this most recent lesson of history has been lost on your Government. While you may obtain some immediate advantage by the persecution of the railway workers concerned, you can be assured that the ultimate advantage will be for the organized working class movement.[16]

The absurdity of life under Apartheid society never ceases to create comical as well as tragic situations. One such comical incident occurred during the tension of 1961, when SACTU leaders prepared for the worst by disguising their personal identities, moving the office to different locations and avoiding sleeping at home whenever possible. Phyllis Altman, Mark Shope, Don Mateman and Leon Levy, all assuming disguises, planned to meet one morning at the Johannesburg watertower to discuss the current state of affairs. Afterwards, they walked together down a Johannesburg street, only to confront four equally disguised Special Branch detectives walking in the opposite direction. Each group immediately recognized the other, and all eight broke into hilarious laughter before proceeding along their respective paths. Life histories are full of such fortuitous events, but a few months later such an incident might have produced a more tragic ending.

Massive Repression (1962–1964)

The banning of the ANC forced a reassessment of the viability of a non-violent programme against the Apartheid system. On 16 December 1961 the first acts of sabotage were conducted by *Umkhonto we Sizwe* (MK) – 'The Spear of the Nation' – the military wing of the ANC formed one month earlier. For the next eighteen months, at least 150 incidents of sabotage were carried out throughout South Africa. After nearly fifty years of non-violence and passive resistance to oppression, the historical inevitability of this new stage of struggle was described in an MK proclamation: 'The people's patience is not endless. The time comes in the life of any nation when there remain only two choices – submit or fight. That time has now come in South Africa.'

The massive counter-action mounted by the regime effectively weakened the leadership of the Congress Movement and smashed the organizational structures of the groups within it. The repression against the political organizations – the ANC, the SAIC, the SACOD (banned in 1962) and the CPC – is a story well covered in the existing literature.

The story of repression against SACTU, strangely enough, is one of the most important yet least known aspects of this period. Why this is the case is a matter of speculation to a large extent. Perhaps a tendency for outside observers to romanticize guerrilla warfare, coupled with a tendency to regard the trade union struggle as subordinate to the political struggle (and thus to see SACTU as a branch of the ANC rather than an equal partner in the Congress Alliance) partially explains this gap in our total knowledge of the struggle. Whatever the reason(s), the repression directed against SACTU and the oppressed Black working class is essential to our understanding of the South African system. It is equally vital in the international anti-imperialist struggle against that system.

The close relationship between groups in the Congress Alliance meant that with the banning of the ANC in 1960, there would necessarily be a greater merging of actors and organizations over a broader range of activity. Many SACTU militants became active members of MK units engaged in sabotage against property, not people. On the other hand, SACTU as an organization functioned as a 'legal' political platform for ex-ANC members. In Natal, for example, SACTU organized Workers and Peasants Conferences and a Natal Rural Areas Committee emerged in the early 1960s to mobilize rural and urban masses; inevitably the speakers would be ex-ANC and SACTU activists. Stephen Dlamini recalls these meetings attracting more enthusiasm than earlier ANC Branch meetings and rallies.

The explanation for this popularity is simple: SACTU continued to represent the workers' interests and aspirations. The greater open involvement in the political arena was not a change in policy, as the SACTU Constitution testifies, but merely reflected a change in the real conditions that obtained in the country. In sum, SACTU pressed on with its broad and numerous campaigns to increase wages, improve working conditions and struggle against all forms of political oppression. This is why the Government could not relax after the banning of the political movements: new and more effective means of systematic repression directed simultaneously against individuals and organizations had to be found.

Between 1962 and 1964, the South African regime enacted some of the most vicious legislation known to modern world history. The 'rule of law' became the 'rule of punishment'. A proper appreciation of the degree of repression in these years requires a summary of the new legislation – the General Law Amendment Act (GLAA), No. 76, 1962 (Sabotage Act); the GLAA, No. 37, 1963; and the GLAA, No. 96, 1965.

The Sabotage Act stands out as the most important piece of legislation in that it modifies, covers loopholes and supplements the Suppression of Communism Act (1950), the Public Safety Act (1953), the Criminal Procedure Act (1955, and as amended) and the Unlawful Organizations Act (1960). In addition to being comprehensive, Section 21 of the Act introduces, defines (albeit vaguely) and prohibits 'sabotage'. The sweeping definition is worth quoting in full:

A person commits sabotage if he injures, damages, destroys, renders useless or unserviceable, puts out of action, obstructs or tampers with, pollutes, contaminates or endangers any of the following:
  (a) the health or safety of the public;
  (b) the maintenance of law and order;
  (c) any water supply;
  (d) the supply or distribution at any place of light, power, fuel, foodstuffs or water, or of sanitary, medical or fire extinguishing services;
  (e) any postal, telephone or telegraph services or installations, or radio transmitting, broadcasting or receiving services or installations;
  (f) the free movements of any traffic on land, at sea or in the air; and
  (g) any property, whether movable or immovable, of any person or of the state.

The penalty for sabotage, as for treason, is death by hanging, and if the court decides against the death penalty it must impose a minimum sentence of no less than five years' imprisonment.

Contrary to conventional procedure, a person charged with sabotage is not assumed innocent, but rather must prove that innocence. To be more specific, the defendant must show that what he/she did 'objectively regarded was not calculated and that such an offence was not committed with intent:

  (a) to cause or promote general dislocation, disturbance or disorder;
  (b) to cripple or seriously prejudice any industry or undertaking – or industries or undertakings generally or the production or distribution of commodities or foodstuffs at any place;
  (c) to seriously hamper or to deter any person from assisting in the maintenance of order;
  (d) to cause, encourage or further an insurrection or forcible resistance to the Government;
  (e) to further or encourage the achievement of any political aim, including the bringing about of any social or economic change in the Republic;
  (f) to cause serious bodily injury to or seriously endanger the safety of any person;
  (g) to cause substantial financial loss to any person or to the state;
  (h) to cause, encourage or further feelings of hostility between different sections of the population of the Republic;
  (i) to seriously interrupt the supply or distribution at any place of light, power, fuel or water, or of sanitary, medical or fire extinguishing services; or
  (j) to embarrass the administration of the affairs of the state.

Other inroads on traditional legal procedures included the denial of a preparatory examination, a South African procedure whereby the accused is made fully aware of the charges against him/her. Also, a person acquitted on a charge of sabotage might be tried again on any other charge arising out of the acts alleged in respect of the charge of sabotage, another reversal of traditional procedure. Juveniles (under the age of 18) could be charged with sabotage unlike the case of other criminal offences. Finally, the Attorney-General was given total power to determine whether or not a person is to be so charged.

Before continuing with the other equally draconian measures of the Sabotage Act, let us pause to consider the implications of the above. Normal trade union activity obviously becomes a potential criminal offence. The right to strike is effectively denied as such action would 'cause financial loss' to employers, 'encourage hostility' between employers and workers and would 'bring about social or economic change'. Could any trade union organizer or worker effectively discharge these onuses? Of course not. Even to write a slogan on a wall could lead to a charge of sabotage, whereas outside this Act it would be a minor offence.

SACTU, representing primarily African workers, had long been accustomed to the prohibition of strikes against Africans under the Native Labour (Settlement of Disputes) Act of 1953. The penalty under that Act was R1,000 (£500) and a maximum of three years' imprisonment. African workers, however, had always boycotted this legislation and strikes continued to occur regardless of the penalties. Now with the Sabotage Act the stakes would be higher: hanging was to be the punishment for struggling to end poverty wages and anti-Black worker legislation.

In May 1962 SACTU promptly wrote a letter to TUCSA asking the latter to unite in opposition to the Sabotage Act, pointing out that only broad opposition could prevent its enactment. Instead, a TUCSA delegation consisting of the President, General Secretary and four Executive members went, cap in hand, to the Minister of Justice to plead its case for exemption for registered unions. The TUC managed to get a promise of a 'safeguard' in the legislation and left the meeting without voicing any opposition to the Act in principle. The TUC later stated that another meeting was to be arranged to discuss the Act in respect of 'African unions which were acceptable to the TUC'. SACTU correctly charged that TUCSA opportunistically 'sold the trade union movement down the river', by 'allying itself with the fascist regime to break the militant African trade unions and win over a few tame African "welfare societies" into its ranks'.[17] One might also note the extreme paternalism made explicit in TUCSA's belief that it had a right to decide on the 'acceptability' of an African trade union.

But, as many political observers pointed out at the time, TUCSA's 'safeguard' was completely worthless. Aside from the TUC ignoring the interests of the majority of South African workers — the Africans — the charge of sabotage could still be brought against any registered union or group of workers within such a union which failed to comply with the complicated machinery laid down in the IC Act (1956) regarding strike action. Furthermore, by implication, all industries could be defined as 'essential industries' according to the vague working of the Act. In any case, no legal protection would exist for any worker or trade unionist going on to company property or on a picket line. Thus, Section 21 effectively denied all trade union, political and civil rights of South African workers. And of the many coordinating bodies *only SACTU objected*.

The Sabotage Act also filled loopholes in earlier legislation passed in previous decades. Since 1950, under the Suppression Act, the Minister of Justice had the power to suppress newspapers; this power was used to ban *The Guardian*, *Advance* and the *Clarion*. There was no law, however, to prevent these papers of the Congress Alliance from reappearing under new titles, which in fact they did successfully. The new Act made this virtually impossible by requiring the banned newspaper to forfeit a sum of R20,000 (£10,000) whenever the banning order was issued. This meant that economic strangulation would silence progressive papers as they could not come up with this amount of money to cover each potential banning. A Publications and Entertainments Bill, passed in 1963, complemented this provision by broadening the scope of 'undesirable' publications.

Section 2 of the Sabotage Act also widened the powers of the State President to ban organizations. Specifically, he can ban 'any organization that carries on directly or indirectly any of the activities of an unlawful organization'. The primary purpose of this was to legally equate the MK with the ANC, and Poqo (the PAC military wing) with the PAC. But it also raised a number of related questions. Is it legal, for example, for the second organization to carry out activities of the banned organization, even if those activities in themselves were perfectly legal? In other words, could SACTU be banned for opposing the pass laws, a campaign historically associated with the ANC?

We shall see below how this dilemma worked itself out in practice.

The Sabotage Act also gave sweeping powers to the Minister of Justice regarding the treatment of individuals over a broad range of behaviour. First, since 1950, the Minister had been able to ban trade unionists who were 'Communists' by statutory definition (although not necessarily so in fact) from all trade union activity. As we have seen, at least fifty progressive trade unionists of all races were banned as 'statutory Communists' by 1954.

The new Act further allowed the Minister to order any person 'in respect of whom any prohibition' has been served under the Suppression Act, not to become an office-bearer, officer or member of *any* organization without the Minister's consent. In other words, a person prevented from gatherings in, say, 1956, could automatically be prevented from being a member, etc., of any organization in 1962. Even those never convicted of 'statutory communism' could now be victimized.

The meaning of this provision was made clear on 28 December 1962 with the issuance of Government Gazette Extraordinary Proclamation No. 408. Thirty-six organizations, including SACTU, were listed and the following groups of persons prevented from being officers, office-bearers or members of these organizations:

(a) 432 persons previously 'listed' under the Suppression of Communism Act;
(b) any person who, whether in (a) or not, has been banned by the Minister of Justice from attending meetings; and
(c) any person, whether in (a) or (b) or not, who was a member of the banned South African Congress of Democrats.

In addition to the fact that these three groups of persons could not belong to the thirty-six named organizations, they also could *not* belong to *any* organization which:

(a) is in any manner affiliated to or a subsidiary of any of the thirty-six organizations which promotes or furthers any activity which promotes the objects of these organizations; and
(b) which in any manner propagates, defends, attacks, criticizes or discusses any form of State of any principle or policy of the Government of the State or which in any manner undermines the authority of the Government of the State.[18]

In short, all members and officers of all remaining Congress Alliance groups were effectively silenced with this proclamation issued under the

Sabotage Act of 1962 (hereafter, this is referred to as the 'Blanket Bans').

A second and similar extraordinary proclamation in 1963 prohibited all persons in these categories from 'becoming or continuing to be office-bearers, officers, members or active supporters of any organization which in any manner compiled, published or disseminated any newspaper, magazine, pamphlet, book, handbill, or poster, or which assisted in doing so'.[19] On the basis of this order, *Spark*, the successor to *New Age* (banned in November 1962) was forced to suspend publication on 28 March 1963.

Returning to the Sabotage Act, the Minister of Justice was empowered to place any 'statutory Communist' or person engaging in activities 'furthering communism' under up to 24-hour house arrest. Restrictions on movement from a designated place and on intercourse with other persons could be as severe as dictated by the Minister. This internment without trial gave the Nationalist Government absolute power over every South African citizen.

The definition of 'gatherings' was also made more specific. In the past, courts had ruled that gatherings had to have a 'common purpose', for example, a trade union meeting. This necessity was eliminated in the 1962 Act making, in theory, a visit to the theatre a possible gathering if the Minister so determined. Furthermore, anyone previously dealt with under the Suppression Act could be ordered to report to the police at specified times and provide information on changes of address or employment. Failure to fulfil these obligations could lead to imprisonment from one to ten years.

Another provision of the Act made it an offence, punishable by up to three years' imprisonment, to reproduce, in any way, a statement or speech of a person banned from gatherings. In this way, banned SACTU executive officers could no longer prepare statements to be read at conferences or other meetings.

Previous to this, it had been common practice at Congress meetings to play tape recorded messages from banned leaders. One such meeting held in one of the lecture rooms at the Johannesburg Public Library produced yet another farcicial situation that could only occur in South Africa. While playing the second of four speeches prepared by banned Communist Party members, a 'posse' of about fifteen Special Branch detectives broke into the hall, rushed to the front of the room and promptly arrested the tape recorder. One perspiring policeman, flanked on all sides by his cohorts, carried the old-fashioned heavy recorder towards the back door amidst the jeers and catcalls of those in attendance. One Congress woman shouted, "twenty thousand voices will rise in their place".'[20]

Another provision prohibited the possession of any banned publication, and again violation carried with it a possible three-year sentence. Finally, an amendment to the Criminal Code, introduced by this Act, made it easier to convict a person for leaving South Africa without a passport. Previous difficulties in proving that the person actually left the country were overcome by allowing any document which suggested departure to serve as *prima facie* evidence if it was certified by the Secretary of Foreign Affairs as of foreign origin.

The next Act directly affecting SACTU leaders and other progressives was the GLAA No. 37 of 1963. A commissioned officer of the police might, without warrant, arrest or cause to be arrested anyone suspected of committing or intending to commit sabotage or any offence under the Suppression Act, or who might have information regarding same. Such a person could be detained for interrogation until he/she satisfactorily answered all questions. At the end of 90 days, the order would lapse, but the person could be re-arrested and re-detained and this process could be repeated indefinitely. Except for a weekly visit from a magistrate, no visitors would be allowed and only the Minister of Justice could authorize the person's release. Detainees lost all normal privileges of witnesses and accused; that is, the police were given absolute power to demand answers to their questions. An amendment to the Criminal Procedure Act in 1964 allowed confessions to the police to be admissable as evidence in the courts. This sanctioned the common practice of solitary confinement and police brutality being used to force a confession, with no possibility of challenge in the courtroom as the victim would not be personally present. In other cases, confessions were simply invented.

Finally, the GLAA No. 96, of 1965, extended the 90-day detention period to 180 days, with the same general conditions as stated above in effect.

SACTU correctly identified all of this repressive legislation as directed in general and in particular against non-racial trade unionism. *Workers Unity* (February–October 1962) stated,

(the Sabotage Act) . . . closes every avenue of legal expression for the people of South Africa. The Act also constitutes a grave threat to the trade union movement. It renders nearly all trade union activity illegal and will strip the militant trade unions of practically all their remaining officials and leaders. Trade Union publications will become virtually impossible. Strike action and other universally accepted procedures of workers' action may be visited by the death penalty. Such is the price of apartheid.

Various SACTU leaders spoke at rallies pointing out to workers that all power had been given over to the Minister of Justice and the police. Don Mateman (General Secretary, TWIU) spelled out the implications of the Act for registered textile workers: 'If we were to go on strike for higher wages while the employers were busy filling a government order for army blankets, it would be called sabotage. The vagueness of the clause that refers to "embarrassing the administration of the Government" will inhibit all legal collective action on the part of trade unions.'

Aside from the protests of international trade union centres, the only non-SACTU trade union to openly oppose the Sabotage Act was the National Union of Distributive Workers (NUDW). Speaking as much against TUCSA opportunism as the legislation itself, the NUDW commented:

... when democracy is threatened, the trade unions cannot stand by idly and concern themselves only with those aspects of legislation which affect them directly. The trade unions also have a duty to make their voices heard on the subject of civil liberties and the rule of law, and when a Government invests a Minister of Justice with powers which will enable him to stifle all opposition to it, then assurances to registered trade unions are insufficient to preserve democracy.

The statement went on to point that the TUCSA-negotiated 'safeguard' for registered unions had no effect on the Government's main intention of intimidating African workers with 'statutory sabotage' – a flagrant disregard of the ILO Convention on Freedom of Association. The NUDW concluded, 'The General Law Amendment Bill ... should be rejected in toto by the democratic trade union movement.'

Also to protest against the Sabotage Act were the unions represented at the Job Reservation Conference held in Cape Town in June 1962. Again, TUCSA had no official delegation at this important Conference and FOFATUSA never issued a public statement or took any action against the Sabotage Act.

SACTU predictions of massive victimization and persecution with the implementation of these laws were soon proven correct. The Blanket Bans Proclamation came into effect on 1 February 1963. By 28–29

March 1964, at the time of the Ninth Annual National Conference, no less than forty-five SACTU officials and members had been banned, removed from office and in most cases confined to magisterial districts. Many more were detained without charge under the 90-day detentions for various lengths of time. The following tables provide the names of these SACTU victims; behind each name is a story of individual sacrifice and suffering in the cause of the workers' struggle.

SACTU Leaders Banned After 1 February 1963

Name	Union/Position
Leon Levy	SACTU, President
	NULCDW, Secretary
Mark Williams-Shope	SACTU, General Secretary
	A-LCDWU, Chairman
John Gaetsewe	SACTU, Acting General Secretary
Lawrence Ndzanga	SACTU–NEC
	SAR & HWU, Secretary (Tvl.)
Marks Rammitloa	S & OWU, Secretary (Tvl.)
Mary Moodley	FCWU, Organizer (Tvl.)
Melville Fletcher	TWIU, Organizer (Durban)
Aaron Mosata	A-GWU (Kimberley)
Frances Baard	FCWU, Secretary (PE)
Alven Bennie	GWU, Secretary (PE)
Eddie Heynes	TWIU, National Treasurer (PE)
L. Kukulela	HWU, Secretary (Cape Town)
Lily Diedrichs	FCWU, Secretary, Sick Benefit Fund (PE)
Viola Hashe	SACTU, Vice-President
Phyllis Altman	SACTU, Assistant General Secretary
Piet Vogel	SACTU LC, Chairman (PE)
M. Lekoto	GWU
S. Ntunja	Port Elizabeth LC
E. Mahoko	SACTU typist (Tvl.)
H. Gwala	SACTU LC, Chairman (Pietermaritzburg)
D. Mekgoe	A-LCDWU
R. Takalo	A-MWU, Secretary (Tvl.)
F. Manemela	A-MWU (Tvl.)

Name	Union/Position
Mabel Balfour	A-FCWU, Secretary (Tvl.)
Edmund Cindi	PWU, Secretary (Tvl.)
	Secretary, Wits LC
S. Khunyeli	TWU (Tvl.)
	SACTU–NEC
L. Seloro	S & OWU (Tvl.)
	SACTU–NEC
S. Naidoo	SACTU typist (Tvl.)
Graham Morodi	GWU (Tvl.)
C. Ntuli	A-MWU
Curnick Ndlovu	SAR & HWU (Durban)
Christmas Tinto	SAR & HWU, Secretary (Cape Town)
J. Molefe	A-FMBWU (Tvl.)
Rose Schlacter	NULCDW
Eddie Davoren (UK)	SACTU, Assistant General Secretary (Tvl.)
Mr Makaringe	A-LCDWU
Mary Turok	TWIU (Tvl.)
J. Mampies	GWU, Organizer (Kimberley)
A. Zondi	Domestic WU (Tvl.)
E. Sibisi	Domestic WU, Acting Secretary (Tvl.)
J. C. Tsele	A-LCDWU (Tvl.)
D. Thambiran	SATWU (Durban)
D. Mateman	TWIU, Secretary (Tvl.)
G. Ngqunge	SAR & HWU (Cape Town)
S. Tobias	AP & BWU (PE)
G. Monare	SACWU (Tvl.)
R. Ndzanga	TWU, Secretary (Tvl.)
Mr Tshabangu	African Coal and Cement WU

STATE REPRESSION

Ninety Day Detentions of SACTU Activists
Note: Numbers in brackets indicate the time spent in detention beyond 90 days up to 29 March 1964

Name	Union/Position	Date of detention
Stephen Dlamini	SACTU, President A-TWIU, General Secretary (Durban)	10–5–63 (150 . . .)
C. Mayekiso	SACTU LC, Secretary (PE)	10–5–63 'Died' in detention
Vuyisile Mini	SACTU LC (PE) MWU, Secretary	10–5–63 Executed
L. Mancoko	GWU, Secretary (PE)	11–5–63 (149 . . .)
Elijah Loza	A-C & DWU (Cape Town) SACTU LC, Chairman (CWP)	10–5–63 (150 . . .) Released and re-arrested on 8–8–63; habeas corpus application denied; later under 24-hour house arrest
S. Mbanjwa	A-M & TWU, Secretary (Durban)	22–6–63 (100 . . .)
Letty Sibeko	AWU, Secretary (Cape Town)	22–6–63 (100 . . .); banished
Lydia Kazi	A-FCWU, Secretary	28–6–63; 5 months pregnant when released after 2 months
Mildred Lesier	BQ & CWU, Secretary (Cape Town)	25–6–63 (100 . . .)
Bernard Huna	AWU, Secretary (Cape Town)	25–6–63 (100 . . .)
Jerry Khumalo	SAR & HWU, Secretary	7–7–63 (93 . . .)
Billy Nair	CWU, Secretary (Durban)	7–7–63 (93 . . .) 20-year sentence
Mannie Isaacs	TWIU, Secretary (Durban)	6–8–63 to 8–10–63
Uriah Maleka	SACTU–NEC A-FMBWU, Secretary (Tvl.)	4–9–63
Cardiff Marney	(Union not SACTU affiliate)	3–7–63
John Nkadimeng	SACTU, National Organizer	24–6–63
Zollie Malindi	Garage WU (Cape Town)	24–6–63
M. Qumbela	Municipal WU (Cape Town)	24–6–63
J. Ndabezitha	A-C & DWU (Cape Town)	25–6–63
B. Nkosi	?	18–7–63

Name	Union/Position	Date of detention
'Looksmart' Ngudle	A-C & DWU (Cape Town)	19–8–63 'Died' in detention by 'hanging'
Leon Levy	SACTU, President NULCDW, Secretary (Tvl.)	15–5–63 to 3–7–63 Released on exit permit
John Gaetsewe	SACTU, Acting General Secretary	2-year sentence for leaving South Africa illegally; reduced to 9 months on appeal. 24-hour house arrest in 1964
S. Khunyeli	TWU (Tvl.)	24–6–63 (86 days)
L. Seloro	S & OWU SACTU–NEC	(90 days)
G. Ngqunge	SAR & HWU (Cape Town)	?
Graham Morodi	GWU (Tvl.)	4–7–63
Curnick Ndlovu	SAR & HWU (Durban)	25–6–63 20-year sentence
Christmas Tinto	SAR & HWU, Secretary (Cape Town)	8–10–63
J. Molefe	A-FMBWU (Tvl.)	25–5–63 to 8–8–63
Eddie Davoren (UK)	SACTU, Assistant General Secretary (Tvl.)	Detained and deported

These lists are not exhaustive but reflect the documentation available at this time.

These tables show that the majority of victimized trade union leaders were Africans; some were veterans, such as J. C. Tsele (25 years) and V. Hashe (17 years), and many others were young recruits to the work of SACTU. It is important to keep in mind that the banned persons were never charged or convicted of any crime against the state, and the detainees were swept off the streets simply because it was believed that they might have had information concerning the commission of unspecified acts. They were all democratically-elected trade union leaders prevented from carrying out the interests of their members.

Including SACTU leaders, at least 102 persons were banned under the Sabotage Act of 1962. In December 1963 the progressive monthly, *Forward*, gave comprehensive statistics on the 90-day detentions. Over 500 persons had been detained and confined to their cells for twenty-three hours a day. Many had been detained for their second 90-day period, and at least two had been detained for over 180 days.

Additional arrests and harassment of SACTU Local Committees and affiliated unions occurred regularly throughout these years. In 1962, the entire executive of the Kimberley African General Workers Union was arrested for 'holding a meeting without permission'. In Cape Town, Archie Sibeko (although banned) and other comrades were continuously in and out of jail as a result of underground ANC and SACTU organizing. In Johannesburg, SACTU organizers were frequently arrested for trespassing on mine company property and for distributing 'illegal' leaflets to railway workers. In Durban, the Local Committee maintained its high level of activity through the recruitment of young workers trained by veterans Billy Nair, Stephen Dlamini and Memory Vakalisa. Workers continued to pour into SACTU offices despite the fact that the SB detectives made daily visits to take the names and addresses of everyone involved with SACTU. A January 1963 raid on the Durban office was conducted with no warrant and documents were seized at will.

The October 1962 conference of the Metal Workers Union (SACTU) in Johannesburg lost all of its documents to a police raid. Eight months later in Cape Town, the Food and Canning Workers Union office was raided and correspondence searched for names of Management Committee and Branch officials. In Parliament, the Minister of Labour justified the raid as in the interests of anti-subversive activities, yet in actual fact only legitimate trade union correspondence was found. These raids were obviously being conducted in association with the 90-day detentions sweeping the country. For example, Lily Diedrichs (FCWU, Port Elizabeth) was banned shortly after the raid in Cape Town. The SACTU 1963 Conference was attended by no less than sixteen SB detectives, armed with a search warrant authorizing the confiscation of any and all papers. Organizing meetings with farm and mine workers were surrounded by lorry-loads of police armed with sten guns.

The heaviest repression, however, occurred in the ANC–SACTU stronghold of Port Elizabeth. In November 1962 fifty-two persons were arrested and detained for lengthy questioning regarding sabotage activities in the area. Alven Bennie was later re-arrested for failing to report to the local police (as per his banning order) on the same morning he was arrested by the Special Branch. Brutality and intimidation were the order of the day in the Eastern Cape: Caleb Mayekiso, one of SACTU's most outstanding organizers, was told by the policeman: 'I am an outstanding expert at thrashing a dog if it offends me.' Four months later, while interrogating Sampson Ntunja, police threatened to 'fix up' Mayekiso, Vuyisile Mini and Mountain Ngyungwana, and proudly boasted of their desire that SACTU would soon be outlawed.

On 2 February 1963, the day following the Blanket Bans order, the Port Elizabeth magistrate banned under the Riotous Assemblies Act a SACTU meeting called to agitate for the forty-hour week, R2-a-day wages, and the repeal of the colour-bar and Job Reservation on the grounds that such a meeting would 'endanger the public peace'. By October of that year, workers entering the Local Committee office were threatened with 90-day detentions simply because of their interest in SACTU.

All of these specific cases, taken together, prove that SACTU was a major target of government repression due to its persistence in advancing the struggle of oppressed Black workers. SACTU's press releases ranged from moods of militant optimism to cautious concern through these tense months. One of its most bitter attacks on these 'Nuremburg measures' deserves lengthy quotation:

Does he (Minister Vorster) believe that by sealing off these (house arrested) people in their homes or flats he will make Apartheid workable and just? Does he think that the non-White workers will now abandon their struggle for living wages and their opposition to Job Reservations and all discriminatory laws?

Does he think that if these few courageous voices are no longer heard, the people will abandon their struggle for a truly democratic South Africa with equal rights for all? Does he think that Bantustans will come into existence with no voice to say 'NO'?

And when he has turned South African life into one vast unfunny game of rugby with every non-Nationalist citizen 'marked' by a member of the Special Branch, what then? Apartheid will be as unworkable and as unjust . . .

Mr Vorster has yet to learn that not even gas chambers or concentration camps can kill ideas. Nor can they defeat the will of an oppressed people to freedom.[21]

This statement and others like it were dispatched to trade unions throughout the world, with the result that international solidarity with SACTU was expressed from all corners of the globe. Trade unions in the capitalist world increasingly responded with principled criticism of the Sabotage Act, the Blanket Bans and the 90-day detentions. British TUC and ICFTU statements correctly accused the Apartheid regime of destroying all forms of legitimate trade union activities, and specific communiques were sent to the government calling for the withdrawal of banning orders against SACTU leaders.[22]

British, Australian and Canadian trade unions distinguished themselves in supporting SACTU. The Waterside Workers Federation (Australia) took action by 'blacking' cargoes of fish, carbide and asbestos from South Africa; this union also pushed for the Australian Council of Trade Unions (ACTU) to endorse a general ban against the handling of all South African imports and the provision of financial assistance to SACTU whenever possible.

In Canada, the United Electrical and Machine Tool Workers of America (UE) branches contributed money to assist SACTU and its paper, *Workers Unity*. A statement regarding the Sabotage Act said, '... (the Act) violates every concept of human justice, substituting savagery for civilization and fascist concentration camps for human rights.' Other Canadian unions to offer support were the International Union of Mine, Mill and Smelter Workers of Canada, the United Fishermen and Allied Workers Union, the Oil, Chemical and Atomic Workers and the Vancouver Civic Employees Union.

In England, Scotland and Ireland, unions responded either individually or through their association with the Movement for Colonial Freedom (mentioned in Chapter 11). The MCF publication, *Solidarity*, regularly reported the details of victimization against SACTU and Congress leaders to its nineteen union contacts representing three and one half million workers. And in Europe, dockers in Denmark and Sweden sent telegrams and letters to SACTU Head Office reporting their decision to refuse the off-loading of South African ships. These are but a few of the examples of international solidarity that testify to the respect SACTU had developed amongst the workers of the world by 1964.

A major reason for this respect rests on the fact that SACTU never failed to focus its energies and concerns on the needs of the workers it represented. Despite bannings, detentions, torture, and ideological attacks on SACTU by Radio South Africa, the African workers in particular continued to turn to SACTU for assistance. SACTU had proven to these workers that it had none of the paternalism and opportunism characteristic of other coordinating bodies in South

Africa. SACTU also stood with the African workers in the most severe periods of repression.

In 1962, the total number of Africans convicted under the pass laws and influx control regulations increased to more than 384,500. Africans were being forcibly removed from the Western Cape area as the regime was attempting to perfect its system of migrant labour and bantustan 'homelands'. SACTU regarded the victimization of its leaders as merely a part of the overall and systematic attack on the entire Black population. Even in the darkest hour of victimization against SACTU leaders in 1963, the organization devoted its energies to mobilizing opposition to the Bantu Law Amendment Bill that would soon become law.

There can be no greater tribute to SACTU's total dedication to the emancipation of Black workers from White supremacy and class exploitation than its ability to proclaim at the 1964 Annual National Conference:

The trade union movement lives in the hearts of the workers. In February 1964, within days of the 24-hour house arrest of our General Secretary (John Gaetsewe), the deportation of our Assistant General Secretary (Eddie Davoren) and the banning of another five officials, three new unions affiliated to SACTU. What greater expression of confidence could the workers have given us?[23]

Yet, the objective realities of oppression and the necessity to convert to new methods of underground activity were now apparent to all. The final paragraphs of the 1964 Conference Report capture the mood of the day and the shape of the future:

The future for SACTU is grim. Our loyal and devoted officials are suffering privations in every city in South Africa, unable to find employment anywhere since their bans, hounded and watched by the police, confined and restricted — punished with such severity because they dared to organize their fellow workers. Official after official is banned and we are carrying on in the face of such difficulties that it is like trying to swim against a tidal wave.

But SACTU is not doomed and can never be. Let this be absolutely clear. A trade union is not the Secretary in the office, but the workers in the factory; in the workshop; on the mines and on the farms. A trade union lives for as long as there are workers in it, and it is because of this that SACTU and its affiliated unions can never die. To those many thousands of workers who support SACTU we say:

Make very factory, every workshop, every mine, every farm a trade union fortress.

You are the trade union. See that your factory committee meets and that your boss knows that you represent the workers.

If your Secretary is banned and you cannot go to the office with your complaints and those of your fellow workers, take them up yourself – speak to the boss. He knows that for good relationships in the factory he must listen to the complaints and difficulties of his workers and he will listen to you.

Your unions are legal. Do not be intimidated or frightened. There is nothing to stop you from getting together with your fellow workers.

NOTES

1. The exception was registered, 'mixed' unions that were forced under the IC Act of 1956 to separate into 'racial branches', which they did.
2. The story of the Treason Trial has been told by many authorities and will not be repeated here in any detail. See Lionel Forman and E. S. Sachs, *The South African Treason Trial*, John Calder, London, 1957, and M. Benson, op. cit.
3. Mary Benson summarizes some of the ludicrous incidents occurring during the Trial: 'There was the day that the prosecution solemnly pushed a motorcycle into the front of the Court to prove that it was possible for him (a policeman) to have sat on it at an outdoor meeting and taken verbatim notes, that he had not just gone home and written up only what he could remember. But he failed miserably, and the motorcycle was taken away. There were the two placards, "Soup without Meat" and "Soup with Meat" seized by the police in their raid on the Congress of the People and handed in as exhibits for a charge of High Treason,' op. cit., p. 99. Other defendants tell of the state's expert witness on 'communism' being tricked by the defence counsel, V. Berrange, into identifying his own writings as an example of the 'communism' he proposed to know so well.

    An example of the role that banned people continued to play was that of Eli Weinberg, celebrated political photographer. During the Trial, he arranged a location, complete with tiered seating, to photograph all 156 Treason Trialists. A few moments before the photo was to be taken, Weinberg was told that the park that had been chosen could not be used because: 'You're not going to bring all those "Kaffirs" in this park.' Alternatively, four photos of smaller groupings of defendants were taken and then made into a montage, resulting in the famous Treason Trial photograph published throughout the world. Over 1,000 copies were sold in South Africa alone.
4. The lengthy bans on SACTU's highest ranking officers led some SACTU leaders in other centres to feel that new officers should be elected at subsequent annual conferences. Rightly or wrongly, this was never done.
5. Chairman's Address, Inaugural Conference, March 1955. During the Trial SACTU denied affiliation to the WFTU, arguing that while the organization had applied for affiliation it was never able to afford the fees. This position was taken

with full knowledge of how such an affiliation might have been used in the context of the state's attempt to prove treason and destroy the Congress Movement. Despite subsequent confusion created by this purely 'paper argument', the close relationship between SACTU and the WFTU never changed, at that time or in later years.
6. Veteran activist, E. P. Moretsele, died as a defendant during the Trial, and Lawrence Nkosi was dismissed from the Trial due to poor health. He later died of tuberculosis in 1962 at the age of 43. During the last five years of his life, he was frequently interrogated by Special Branch detectives, and the poverty of his family prevented them from travelling from the Transvaal to Natal to visit him during these years.
7. SACTU, Fifth Annual Conference Report, October 1960.
8. Shanti Naidoo returned to assist SACTU during the heavier repression of 1963.
9. During these months, one Government Minister – Paul Sauer – was quickly brought back into line by his Nationalist peers when he publicly stated that wage increases to African workers might be necessary as a 'concession'. SACTU expressed its awareness of the dangers of accepting concessions: 'We must constantly guard against the danger of getting small reforms for the price of our freedom. And, on the other hand, we now have the opportunity of taking advantage of the fight among the bosses to drive home our demands.'
10. Edward Ramsdale says that the Langa massacres shocked many Coloureds and Indians into the realization that they must stand together with their African brothers and sisters. A Relief Committee, organized by Coloureds and Indians, countered attempts to starve African workers in Langa into submission. Organizers, assisted in many cases by Indian shopkeepers, would manage to purchase all the bread from delivery trucks before they entered the 'White areas', and this food would then be distributed amongst the Africans. Interview, Edward Ramsdale.
11. Interviews, Phyllis Altman and Stephen Dlamini.
12. The General Law Amendment Act, No. 39, of 1961; this Act was a predecessor to the 90- and 180-day detention Acts described below.
13. The NUDW leadership had for many years supported the principles and objects of SACTU, although its membership could never be swayed to affiliate to SACTU. Throughout most of the decade under investigation, the NUDW opposed the SATUC's 'colour bar' policy and remained unaffiliated to any coordinating body.
14. Interview, Stephen Dlamini.
15. The GLAA, No. 39 (1961) had amended the Riotous Assemblies Act to make it an offence to encourage or promote the assembly or attendance of a prohibited meeting, in this case the Stay-At-Home.
16. Quoted in *Workers Unity*, February–October 1962, p. 14.
17. SACTU President's Statement, 1 June 1962.
18. Among the thirty-six organizations, in addition to SACTU, were the Federation of South African Women, the Natal and Transvaal Indian Congresses, the South African Indian Congress, the Coloured People's Congress and the South African Peace Council.
19. Quoted in *Laws Affecting* . . . , op. cit. These two proclamations relieved the state of listing individuals as such in separate orders.
20. Interview, Phyllis Altman.

21. *New Age*, 22 November 1962.
22. Despite their previous difficulty in supporting SACTU's political trade unionism, it had apparently become clear that of all the coordinating bodies in South Africa, *only SACTU* had stood up to confront the regime and represent the interests of *all* workers.
23. Report, Ninth Annual National Conference, 23–24 March 1964. Eddie Davoren had been brought in to replace Phyllis Altman following her banning in late 1963.

13 LOOKING BACK

Until now, the only other book which has been written about SACTU is Edward Feit's *Workers Without Weapons: The South African Congress of Trade Unions and the Organization of African Workers* (Archon Books, 1975). Feit has consistently and intentionally distorted the historical material in order to defend his basic argument that SACTU was a 'failure'. The present effort is in no way a response to Feit as the latter's contribution is so deliberately malicious as to fail to deserve serious rebuttal. It should be pointed out, however, that Feit made no effort to establish direct contact with SACTU members in exile to corroborate his essential position, but rather relied on information provided by organizations (e.g. the ICFTU) and individuals (in TUCSA) openly hostile to SACTU during the years 1955–64. Beyond this, his research, even by bourgeois academic standards, is simply shoddy: dates are incorrect in many places, documentation is often lacking, and clearly disreputable sources such as Bruno Mtolo (see Chapter 6) who turned State's evidence against the liberation movement are used extensively for information. Motivated by outright hostility to the South African working class, Feit's analysis is scarcely more than a mixture of cold war anti-communism and a call for exploited African workers to cease all involvement in the political struggle to seize state power.

The assessment of SACTU during its first decade hinges on a clear perception of the struggle itself. To discuss the organization within the framework of bourgeois criteria of trade unionism or social change generally is to fail to grasp the historical significance of not only SACTU but more importantly, the class consciousness and aspirations of the African proletariat. The struggle was first and foremost, and at all times, for *total* liberation from the institutions of Apartheid and class rule. Quantitative gains in the form of higher wages, lower taxes, greater workmen's compensation and other benefits were not ignored in the process; in fact, they constituted the basis for rank-and-file support and a realization that SACTU alone among trade union coordinating bodies mobilized workers according to their real, objective conditions of exploitation. Although SACTU campaigns around these demands generally exposed the ruling class, such demands alone could always be channelled into reformist solutions. The classic example was that of African wage increases being accompanied by even larger increases for the privileged White workers. This was in fact the entire basis of TUCSA's 'concern' for African workers, that is, as a means of protecting its White workers. In sum, reformist demands never threatened the fundamental *status quo* of racial oppression and class domination, but merely served to reinforce a divided working class along racial lines. SACTU's strength was in its refusal to accommodate to these pressures of reformism advanced by a reactionary and self-serving registered trade union movement. *Planting the roots of non-racial trade unionism in the soil of Apartheid South Africa was one of SACTU's lasting achievements, a success that cannot be measured by membership figures, financial statements or number of paid organizers.*

Of even greater importance to the oppressed Black population as a whole was SACTU's unequivocal commitment from the outset to the revolutionary struggle for political emancipation. Continuing in the tradition established by the progressive trade unions of previous generations, particularly the African Mine Workers Union and the Transvaal Council of Non-European Trade Unions, SACTU never refrained from defining the workers' struggle in both economic and political terms. Working closely with the radical nationalist organizations that made up the Congress Alliance, SACTU concerned itself with workers as citizens deprived of basic rights as well as producers of wealth. As we have seen, in certain regions SACTU comrades provided the crucial and most militant leadership in Congress campaigns. It is this dedication to the political struggle above all else that awakened the wrath of the coordinating bodies of registered unions, the capitalists as a class and the state. To Feit, this was the basis of SACTU's 'failure'; to the Black workers of South Africa, this was the strength of SACTU.

Commemorative histories need not exaggerate strengths without mentioning the weaknesses, as only through an examination of the latter can advances be made in the present and future. On the trade union front, the lack of financial resources, resulting from the employers' hostility to SACTU at the workplace and the inability to collect regularly the subscriptions of workers, made full-time organizers difficult to sustain. Regional variations and unevenness also characterized SACTU work throughout the years, making the goal of establishing national, industrial unions only partially realized. All of these problems were made more difficult by a coordinated hostility of TUCSA (and its anti-SACTU creation, FOFATUSA), the employers and Industrial Councils, City Councils and the Apartheid regime. With each SACTU success, the victimization of individuals and repression of the organization intensified. Yet it would be incorrect to lay the blame for all of the difficulties encountered by SACTU on state repression alone; to do so would only serve to encourage greater pessimism today as the state machinery for repression is certainly more sophisticated now than in the 1950s and early 1960s.

And it is to the present workers' struggle that this book is dedicated and directed. The lessons of past struggles must be utilized in the struggles of today and tomorrow. Heavy repression in 1964, as documented, forced SACTU and other Congress Alliance groupings to adjust their work to the conditions of underground activity and operation in exile. The regime has conceived new strategies on both the trade union and political fronts to attempt to solve the old problems: that of dividing people and breaking down working-class consciousness and political resistance.

While correct strategy and tactics must flow from the objective conditions that exist in any given era, the past decisions cannot be ignored except at the expense of repeating mistakes. Of particular importance in this regard is the complementary nature of the struggle that shaped the Congress movement in the 1950s. While the national and class struggles could then, as now, be distinguished as qualitatively different aspects of the same liberation process, the strength of the Congress Alliance was always in the *equality* of SACTU as a class-based organization and the other four organizations mobilized around national oppression. The interdependence of the struggle against both class exploitation and national oppression has always meant that neither can be subordinated to the other. As we turn our attention to the post-1964 period, it is essential to remember that the process of liberation consists not only of eliminating the oppressive structures of Apartheid but also that of emancipating the South African working class from capitalist exploitation.

14 THE HISTORY UPDATED

When the Ninth Annual Conference of SACTU opened in Johannesburg on 28 March 1964 it had to note that:

- its General Secretary, John Gaetsewe, was under 24-hour house arrest;
- its Assistant General Secretary, Phyllis Altman, was banned from trade union work, and severely restricted;
- its President, Stephen Dlamini, was detained under the 90-day detention law;
- its Vice-President, Viola Hashe, was banned;
- its Assistant General Secretary, Eddie Davoren, appointed to replace Phyllis Altman, was detained and then deported;
- twenty-six other SACTU activists and trade union officials were banned from the trade union movement;
- at least forty-one trade union secretaries and officials were detained under the 90-day law.

Yet the report to the 1964 Conference records page after page of continued SACTU activity in every part of South Africa and in every important field affecting the workers. It reports three new affiliations. It notes new successes in the R2-a-Day campaign. It reports on organizing activities amongst farm workers and notes that demands for the inclusion of these workers under the Workmen's Compensation Act had been acceded to. It reports further action against the use of convict labour in industry and representations made on that point by SACTU to the ILO. The report details activities on behalf of Black railway and harbour workers and efforts to reorganize the dockworkers in Cape Town, Port Elizabeth and Durban. It records the 'most striking successes' in the metal and engineering industry, despite the detention, banning and removal from office during the preceding year of 'every single metal workers' organizer from every province'.

It documents numerous cases where SACTU used the press to expose the Johannesburg City Council's continued practice of jailing workers for failure to pay rent arrears. That same Council paid its workers wages of R14 to R20, far below its own admitted minimum cost of living of R48 per month. The report also refers to the high standard of SACTU memoranda submitted to Wage Board investigations. Ironically, it mentions that Professor Steenkamp, Chairman of the Wage Board, congratulated Marks Rammitloa, of the Shop & Office Workers Union (a SACTU affiliate), on his outstanding presentation of the workers' case; Rammitloa, however, had been banned from trade union work by this time and was compelled to accept employment as a night-watchman.

The report goes on to point out that almost all of SACTU's work had been done on a voluntary basis and that for most of the time SACTU only had *one* paid employee.

We write this with pride for we have been supported by the workers and we have used their subscriptions for organizers, leaflets and pamphlets and not for staff and magnificent offices. SACTU has been built on the pennies of the workers who support us because we have earned their confidence and their loyalty.[1]

Yet, despite this impressive record the organization was unable to sustain its efforts in this form in the next few years. The removal from their elected positions of so many dedicated, experienced organizers and officials of SACTU trade unions as a result of bannings, detentions, imprisonment and murder, had taken its toll. The years 1965 to 1970 found the African trade union movement in South Africa fighting for its very survival against tremendous odds. Nevertheless, SACTU continued to organize, adopting new forms of struggle necessary to face the new situation.

One major aspect of SACTU's post-repression strategy was the systematic development of an *External mission*. The National Executive Committee's decision in 1960, during the State of Emergency, to send certain of its members abroad had been a carefully considered step. As our history has shown, the Apartheid regime made it impossible for progressive trade unionists to travel freely from South Africa to attend international trade union conferences and to present the case of the exploited majority of South African workers abroad. By the early 1960s, most SACTU officials had been banned and imprisoned, and those still 'free' were refused passports and travel papers.

On the other hand, TUCSA and other trade union coordinating bodies which accepted Apartheid were freely travelling all over the world with the connivance of the racist regime. They clearly acted as emissaries of the government, as reflected in a statement made by J. A. Grobbelaar, Secretary of TUCSA, in a July 1968 newsletter:

The South African trade union and labour movements are urged to support the new 'outward looking' policy initiated by the Prime Minister in a bid to better the country's image abroad, and give aid and advice to workers' organizations in other African states. They are asked to be mindful of the fact that the government of South Africa recently announced a programme of giving economic assistance to African neighbour states. . . .

While TUCSA travelled around the world as defenders of Apartheid policy, SACTU was restricted to presenting the case of the exploited African working class in written memoranda from within the borders of Apartheid. For these reasons, it became a vital necessity for SACTU to establish its own external machinery from which to mobilize international support for the struggle at home.

SACTU NEC members abroad subsequently formed committees in England, Zambia and Tanzania and meetings of the NEC are held annually. The work of these offices and their links with the international trade union movement are discussed in Chapter 15.

The major priority of all SACTU's work remains – as it has been for the past 25 years – the organization of the workers of South Africa into powerful trade unions. For obvious reasons our work inside South Africa since 1964 cannot be documented in detail. As mentioned at the outset, SACTU's complete history can only be told after the day of liberation. However, the various trials of trade unionists and activists throughout the country are indicative of our continued work. The purpose of this chapter is to review the recent upsurge and struggles of the Black working class against Apartheid and to explain SACTU's assessment of these crucial developments.

The past fifteen years have witnessed great advances in the liberation struggle against an increasingly hostile and dangerous Apartheid regime. Popular, anti-imperialist movements in Angola and Mozambique have defeated the Portuguese colonial rule that ruthlessly exploited the peoples of those countries for 500 years. These victories also had the important effect of depriving South Africa, the bastion of White supremacy in Southern Africa, of buffer states to the north that shielded Apartheid from the progressive forces in Africa, including the liberation movements based in the frontline states. In effect, the decade of the 1970s has been a period of greater polarization of the forces of progress and the forces of reaction, with the international community being forced to declare its support for either continued racism and oppression or liberation.

The South African regime has intensified its repression against the people, as it has had to confront both political and economic crises at home and greater isolation abroad. Despite the heavily financed propaganda campaign to sell Apartheid to the world, the reality is that South Africa has become one of the most hated regimes in the world and constitutes a danger to world peace. For the Black masses at home, the mobilization of the people for a final onslaught against Apartheid has developed dramatically as a response to the regime's efforts to divide and rule through Bantustanization and to create a Black middle class to administer oppression and exploitation in its place.

The period from 1965 to the early 1970s were years of re-building and reorganizing after the heavy repression directed against the Congress Alliance in the early 1960s. The African working class had lost some of its most dedicated leaders as many were forced to flee South Africa and others were forced to languish in the prisons of Apartheid. SACTU as a trade union federation was forced to convert its operations to that of underground organizing, and unions affiliated to SACTU were similarly forced by the objective conditions of repression to carry forward the SACTU principles and programme without daring to raise the name of SACTU openly. Yet there can be no doubt that SACTU comrades of preceding years, and many new trade union recruits who recognized the necessity of carrying on the SACTU tradition, worked laboriously amidst great dangers and tremendous difficulties to maintain underground contact with each other and with SACTU leaders outside the country.

As the entire history of African trade unionism has shown, the elimination of the workers' leaders through bannings, detentions, and even murder, never resolves the problems faced by the exploiting class. Black, and particularly African workers, had no alternative but to reorganize their collective strength to do battle with the employers and the Apartheid state. New, *independent* trade unions of African workers had to be created to struggle for higher wages and improved working conditions, while, simultaneously, underground networks of working class resistance carried forward the struggle at a different level.

It was very clear to the vast majority of African workers that reformist and collaborationist trade union federations such as TUCSA offered nothing but compromise and concession to the ruling class. Its policy of parallelism, i.e. subordination, of African trade unions failed completely to respond to the needs of the African workers.

In contrast, SACTU continued to promote the development of strong, independent unions of Black workers. On the occasion of SACTU's sixteenth birthday in 1971, General Secretary Mark Shope sent a special radio broadcast to the exploited workers at home. After reiterating the fundamental principles upon which SACTU had been created, he called for intensified efforts to organize African, Indian and Coloured workers and 'work for strong, powerful and united trade unions'. Shope went on to address himself directly to the experience of the Black working class, calling for a revision of the outdated R2-a-Day demand to R4-a-Day as the national minimum wage demand; he concluded by urging workers to demand the release of all political prisoners and detained trade unionists. Again, Mark Shope reflected SACTU's determination to lead the workers' struggle when he addressed the 57th Session of the ILO in June 1972:

> Let me put it categorically that we, the Black workers and the people of South Africa, the suppressed silent majority of the country, know that the main burden of liberating ourselves from this fascist terror and violence which has gripped the Black people of South Africa is the historic task of the Black workers and the people of South Africa *themselves . . . we accept this binding responsibility.*

Mass Strikes in the Early 1970s

Regardless of state legislation and repression, African workers throughout this century have demonstrated a consistent determination to organize against their conditions of exploitation. In the late 1960s there was a lull in industrial strife, but by 1973 the Apartheid regime was challenged by the greatest strike wave in the country's history as an estimated 100,000 workers downed tools in factories and workplaces throughout the country.

Before discussing these strikes inside South Africa, we must first pay tribute to the Black workers of Namibia who, beginning in 1971, carried out a massive general strike against the conditions of exploitation imposed upon them by an illegal Apartheid regime. Between 13 December 1971 and 20 January 1972 approximately 20,000 migrant workers brought the mining industry to a halt and seriously interrupted the communications and transport systems, commercial operations and rural production. The strikes were a direct attack on the system of migrant-contract labour and influx control. While they are generally referred to as the 'Ovambo strikes' (because of the involvement of large numbers of Ovambo workers from the north), the strike wave received the full support of the Kavango and Herero as well.

The Namibian strikes were an attack on not only intolerable conditions of work at the point of production but also the entire system of slavery that is characterized by Apartheid rule. The South African authorities immediately sensed the fundamental challenge to the *status quo* posed by the Namibian workers and sent in South African Defence Force contingents to reinforce armed policemen in late January 1972. Mass arrests of striking workers took place and detainees were kept in 'cages' or concentration camps during the insurrection. On 30 January South African troops opened fire on Ovambo people as they left the Anglican Church mass at Epinga; four were shot dead and four wounded, two of whom later died in what has become known as the 'Bloody Sunday' massacre. Although the strikes were eventually quelled by force, workers did receive small gains in wages and working conditions; they also forced the elimination of the South West Africa Native Labour Association (SWANLA), which had been responsible for administering the contract labour system. The most important effect of the strikes, however, was on the workers themselves. Their collective resistance to Apartheid demonstrated their determination to advance the struggle for national liberation. This mass strike wave also inspired the Black workers in South Africa itself in the early 1970s.[2]

Returning to the South African situation, poverty wages were the major catalyst for this expression of advanced class consciousness. Inflation, a product of the general crisis of international capitalism and specifically South Africa's inability to sell its manufactured commodities in international markets, hit Black workers particularly hard. Essential expenditures on food, clothing and transport rose by some 30 per cent between 1972 and 1973 alone. Closely associated with this crisis of South African capitalism was the rapidly increasing rate of Black unemployment and greater disparities in the racially-determined wage system characteristic of Apartheid. While academics and government bureaucrats were frantically trying to adjust the official Poverty Datum Line to these economic realities, the exploited workers themselves asserted their collective role as producers of wealth and took to the streets in what became the first great explosion of the 1970s. It was clearly a time to 'Organize or Starve'.

While it is true that the largest strike actions in 1973 centred around Durban, it is important to mention that strikes in the transport industry, the vital nerve centre of the economy, signalled the beginning of mass action as early as 1970. 10,000 Coloured workers at Gelvandale, Port Elizabeth, staged a peaceful demonstration against fare increases, and the state's reponse, as at Sharpeville in 1960, was to open fire on the people. Ten persons were wounded in this incident, and at Hammarsdale, Natal, police killed one and injured many more protesters against transport increases.

In the Transvaal, hundreds of PUTCO bus drivers responsible for transporting workers from African townships to the centre of Johannesburg struck for wage increases in June 1972. Massive arrests of over 300 workers and a management threat to dismiss all the drivers only reinforced the workers' militancy. Township residents rushed to the police station following the arrests, and the authorities were soon forced to release the strikers although many were later charged under the Riotous Assemblies Act. PUTCO received an annual government subsidy of R2·5 million but still claimed an inability to pay an increase and an unwillingness to eliminate the system whereby drivers were penalized R5 per week for 28 weeks if an Inspector found a passenger on board without a ticket. As a result of this strike, a transport union was formed in 1972. Working class militancy also exploded on the mines in the early 1970s (see below), and this revival of mine workers' activity must also be seen as a major factor in the entire strike wave that shook the country in these years.

In 1973, Durban textile and metal workers led the mass strikes which swept from one industrial area to another. Factory after factory shut down; as workers returned to work in one plant, another group of workers would walk out elsewhere. At one time between January and the end of March, an estimated 50,000 strikers were directly confronting their bosses *at the point of production*. In this three month period, more than 160 strikes involved a minimum of 61,410 workers.

David Hemson, at the time Research Officer for the Textile Workers Industrial Union (TWIU) and later banned for his participation in the 1973 strikes, has recorded the following crucial information concerning the strikes:

The mass strikes in the Natal province demonstrated the unity of the black working class across the divisions between migrant and urban workers, between different industries, and even between industrial and agricultural workers. . . . The 'negotiations' took the form of workers shouting demands for between R20–30 and refusing to elect leaders or return to work. Employers and the police responded by threatening mass dismissals and prosecutions and eventually offering some minor wage increases. The workers then shouted down the offer but were forced through necessity eventually to return to work. The momentum of the strike was ultimately broken through the growing presence of the police in army uniforms flown in from other centres, and the lack of strike funds. Despite the relatively small wage increases (between R1 and R2.50 per week) the consciousness of the workers had advanced considerably beyond the relative caution of the period of repression before the strikes. The overwhelming number of strikes had been successful (in the sense that wage increases had been won and strikers not dismissed) because the strikes were able to take on a mass form.[3]

The state was obviously shaken by the mass nature of this strike wave. Compared with the 1959 strikes, when 24 per cent of the strikers were prosecuted, only 0·2 per cent of the 98,029 Black strikers were prosecuted in 1973.

Of greater importance, the Black working class eruption brought forward both political and economic demands. Following closely the spirit and principles of SACTU, strikers advanced economic demands that could not be accommodated without a total transformation of Apartheid society itself. Also, striking Black workers demanded the fundamental right to organize independent unions and to receive recognition by employers on the workers' terms. Such rights were obviously a threat to the power of capital; in the British Leyland subsidiary operation, for example, the Chairman of the Metal and Allied Workers Union (MAWU) and other members of the Union were subsequently 'retrenched'.

The state responded with legislative efforts to lessen the independence of and tighten its control over independent African trade unions. The Bantu Labour Relations Regulation Act, No. 70 of 1973,[4] gave African workers the same status as all other workers with regard to the legality of strike action. As we have pointed out in Chapter 4, the complicated procedures for conducting a 'legal' strike are designed to lesson the spontaneous militancy of the entire South African working class. In the case of the 1973 Act, African workers were still subject to greater penalties for striking 'illegally', not to mention the wide range of security legislation which renders strikes by African workers illegal. The Act also provided for a greater emphasis on industrial relations gimmicks, such as liaison and works committees, designed by *status-quo* ideologists to reduce class conflict.

SACTU immediately exposed the Bantu Labour Relations Regulation Act as a fraud. John Gaetsewe, then SACTU

Representative in Western Europe, issued a memorandum which correctly argued:

In an attempt to prevent a repetition of these industrial actions (the strikes of 1973), the government has now taken measures to make strike action more difficult, while at the same time appearing to permit in theory lawful strikes by Africans. . . . Thus, the industrial action by African workers which took place earlier this year would still have been outside the law. The net effect of the new measures, therefore, is not to strengthen the hands of African workers, but to strengthen the power of government bureaucrats. Furthermore, the works committees will serve merely to expose African leaders to repression and victimization without giving them the protection of belonging to industry-wide unions. The new measures do more to expose the harshness of the present laws than to remedy them.

SACTU also immediately rose in defence of the bannings imposed on David Hemson, Halton Cheadle (Acting Secretary, A-TWIU) and David Davis (Administrative Secretary, General Factory Workers Benefit Fund) on 1 February 1974. As the TWIU and the A-TWIU were former affiliates to SACTU, the regime clearly singled out workers' leaders carrying forward the SACTU banner. The SACTU statement deserves quotation here:

These three men, like the former militant leaders of this Union (Stephen Dlamini, President of SACTU, who after serving a prison sentence of six and a half years for calling a joint mass meeting of industrial and farm workers in 1959, was banned and banished from Durban; Arnold Selby, former General Secretary of the Union; Don Mateman, former General Secretary of the registered Union; Edmund Cindi, Transvaal Secretary; and many others before them), have now been removed from their trade union activity in South Africa for five years – for no crime but to help organize African workers into unions. One such leader, Caleb Mayekiso, Secretary of the African TWIU in the Eastern Cape province, was permanently silenced. He died only three days after being taken into detention. . . .

By banning these men, the racist regime hopes to suppress the upsurge of the militant African trade union movement in the country, and force the workers to accept the so-called 'Liaison Committees' and 'Works Committees' created by the government. They are stooge committees – replicas of the Bantu Labour Boards set up by the notorious Bantu Labour (Settlement of Disputes) Act of 1953. As recently as January 13, 1974, 6,000 African workers assembled at Claremont Football Stadium, reiterated their rejection of these aims and demanded full trade union rights and democratic liberties.

The South African Congress of Trade Unions condemns the banning of the three men, and calls for the immediate lifting of the bans on them. We call on all Black workers of South Africa not to accept this blatant intimidation of the workers, but to press forward the demand for trade union rights and democratic liberties.

The statement concluded with an appeal to international trade union organizations to send protests to the Apartheid regime.

The strike wave that hit Durban in early 1973 continued throughout that year and also into 1974. The Minister of Labour reported in August 1974 that in Natal alone a total of 22 work stoppages occurred between June 1972 and June 1974. In the second half of 1974, a total of 135 strikes involving Africans took place throughout the country. All but ten of these strikes resulted from wage demands, testifying to the increased economic suffering by the African proletariat. In 69 of these strikes, police had intervened and 841 strikers had been charged.

The Apartheid regime and its defenders tried desperately in these years to conceal the realities of suffering by juggling statistics that would mystify the international community. The following table shows clearly the meaningless nature of the government's argument that

Myths of the Apartheid Economy Exposed

Racial Group	Claimed monthly Household income 1962	1973	% Increase	Increase in Rand/month
Whites	R258	R519	101	261
Indians	91	195	114	104
Coloureds	60	143	138	83
Africans	25	55	120	30

By 1976, even the relative advantage for African workers had been reversed. As *Workers Unity* (March 1978) demonstrated:

Average Monthly Income

	1972	1976
White wages	R324	R489
African wages	48	106
Wage gap	R276	R383

African wages had risen at a higher rate (120 per cent) than those of White workers (101 per cent' since 1962. (See table opposite.)

In assessing the 1973–74 strikes, it is important to point out that while the strikes were undoubtedly spontaneous, they were not unorganized. Such a large scale interruption of production could occur only if workers had their own underground organization that made decisions and refused to expose individual leaders to a hostile regime. In the context of Apartheid repression, open and legal trade unions cannot act as the vanguard of proletarian action; rather, the underground must play that role, while that underground machinery itself emerges from the close comradeship and class consciousness that emanates from the daily routines of social production.

The strike wave also gave impetus to the formation of new, independent African trade unions in a wide range of industries. These unions have subsequently led the struggle for economic gains and trade union recognition. It is the very existence of and mass support given to these unions by African workers that forced the regime to make changes in the industrial relations legislation (see discussion on the Wiehahn Commission below).

Resurgence of African Mine Workers

The early 1970s also marked the revival of militant workers' struggles in the South African mining industry. Reminiscent of the great 1946 African Mine Workers Strike, these migrant labourers, the overwhelming majority of whom have been recruited from the 'hostage' territories surrounding South Africa, were engaged in some of the most important confrontations between capital and labour in this decade.

Despite the highly publicized wage increases paid to African mine workers, the situation in 1972 was one of Africans holding 70 per cent of the jobs but receiving less than one-third of the industry's wage bill. In aggregate figures, White miners received R370 million (a *per capita* average of R4,300 per year) whereas African miners received R155 million (a *per capita* average of only R246 per year). Even the government collected more in taxes from the mining companies (R210 million) than did the African workers whose sweat and blood creates the wealth that is the backbone of the Apartheid economy.

Such gross exploitation can only be maintained through a system of military discipline on the job and physical separation in compound residences. The high wages of White workers often depend on their ability to realize certain levels of production from African 'gangs' whom they supervise. Physical brutality against African miners is a direct consequence of this system, and under these rules of production a high accident rate is inevitable. SACTU reported to the 63rd ILO meetings in 1977, that 'between 1973 and 1975, approximately 3,000 workers lost their lives and 110,169 were injured on the gold, diamond, coal and other mines'.

The strike wave that began in September 1973 at Anglo-American's Western Deep Levels Mine in Carletonville, met with violent retaliation by the state. By 1976, an estimated 178 Black miners had been killed and another 1,043 injured in clashes on the mines. The struggles took the form of mass action that demonstrated the capacity of the most exploited workers to engage in insurrection. Mine administration property was directly attacked, documents destroyed and open pitched battles were carried out against the police. By September 1975 some 60,000 Black mine workers had broken contract with the mining monopolies with full knowledge that such action constituted a 'crime' under the penal code.

The Carletonville massacre resulted from a strike by Black workers following the granting of wage increases to White workers that more than doubled the increases given to Black workers five months earlier. The wage differential under the new rates would be 16:1. On 11 September, a squad of 22 policemen entered the Number Two shaft of the Western Deep Levels mine and proceeded to baton charge the workers who had assembled there. Volleys of tear gas followed and soon the order to open fire was given: 12 workers were killed, another 26 injured and 37 arrested. A magistrate who conducted an 'inquiry' on the massacre ruled that, 'The Africans died of gunshot inflicted by police in the execution of their duty, and their deaths were not due to any act or omission by any person amounting to an offence.'

The dislocations to production suffered by the mining companies as a result of the strikes led the government to appoint an 'Inter-Departmental Committee of Inquiry into Riots on the Mines' in March 1975. One year later, the Minister of Labour refused to table the Report of the Committee because of the 'sensitive nature' of its contents. This secrecy became understandable when SACTU's organ, *Workers Unity*, obtained a copy and was the first source to disclose the Inquiry's findings. The Committee concluded that the *migrant labour system* itself was the *single most important cause* of the 'riots' on the mines. Furthermore, the mining industry was considered to be 'very vulnerable' in the face of a politically conscious labour force that 'will cooperate to an increasing degree to realize their political ambitions'.

Riddled with racism, the Report develops a 'theory' that 'Southern Bantu tribes' have an 'inclination to become violent'. But, more importantly, the Report ignores its findings and instead calls for an intensification of repression in order to ensure the viability of the migrant labour system. In this respect, both 'soft' and 'hard' measures are advocated as solutions to mine violence. The former pertain to minor changes such as reducing the number of workers per compound, providing certain 'key mine workers' with the privilege of living with their families, *encouraging religion* and allowing workers to elect their own *indunas* (boss-boys). There is not even a single mention of trade unions as the Apartheid policy is that African workers are not 'ripe' for their own workers' organizations.

The 'hard' measures reveal the major thrust of the Report's recommendations. Stronger security units equipped with patrol dogs, teargas, batons, and 'where practicable, an armoured vehicle', all of these devices to be used in coordination with the SA police force. Better lighting facilities which cannot be disrupted by the workers are to be installed, electricity instead of coal (because coal has been used as ammunition), special television equipment for identifying 'agitators', and special cells are to be constructed to hold workers until police can be called to the scene – these are but a few of the proposals made to protect the profits of the mining capitalists.[5] Finally, the Report assumes that the Bureau of State Security, subsequently renamed Department of National Security, and the Security Division of the South African police will actively infiltrate the mines to discover the 'agitators' before violence erupts. As *Workers Unity* concluded this important exposé:

> For the slave-owners in time past there certainly seemed to be no 'practical alternative' to slavery. So it is for capitalists and their political representatives in South Africa. They can offer no alternative to the continuation of their own crimes.[6]

And, as John Gaetsewe, General Secretary, concluded in the SACTU 1978 ILO memorandum, 'it (the secret report) shows unequivocally that for capitalist exploitation in South Africa to be preserved, *Apartheid cannot in any fundamental way be changed'*.

The Soweto Uprisings, 1976

What began as a peaceful demonstration by African students against the forced imposition of Afrikaans, the language of the oppressor, as a medium of instruction, soon became a national uprising against the entire structure of Apartheid society. The regime, faced with the loss of its peripheral strongholds of Mozambique and Angola within the previous two years and saddled with all the economic contradictions of capitalist crisis, responded in typical reactionary fashion. Within the first few days of the initial demonstrations, the South African police had massacred at least 500 unarmed students. By September, the death toll surpassed 1,000 victims, and the repression continued to intensify. The volleys of Apartheid guns and equipment, much of it produced by Western corporations, echoed around the world. Protests, boycotts, disinvestment campaigns and all other forms of anti-Apartheid activity gained momentum as the international community expressed its solidarity with the struggling masses of South Africa.

The rise of the Black Consciousness Movement, of which the student demonstrations were an expression, represented a new and positive force in African politics. Its leader, Steve Biko, clearly represented and articulated the demands of millions of Africans, particularly the youth, who had come to the same realization as past generations that Apartheid and White domination must be destroyed forever.

To some people both inside but mainly outside South Africa, Biko and Black Consciousness became a potential alternative to the banned ANC and PAC, a 'third force' in the South African revolution. When the Apartheid state ruthlessly murdered Biko in detention and subsequently banned nineteen organizations, including the Christian Institute, in October 1977, the path of non-violence that Biko symbolized was quickly blocked, as it had been to the ANC many years before. Subsequent events have confirmed the simple truth that only through the violent seizure of state power can the liberation of the people from exploitation and oppression be guaranteed. It is also essential to point out that a movement as powerful as Black Consciousness could not emerge in a political vacuum. Many young people who led the Soweto uprising were the sons and daughters of ANC and SACTU veterans; after being forced into exile during and after 1976, large numbers of young comrades have joined the ANC as the only legitimate liberation movement of South Africa. Indeed, even during the uprisings in 1976, it is significant that the traditional demand of the ANC became more and more prominent as the revolt spread throughout the country. AMANDLA! POWER TO THE PEOPLE!

The general outline of the Soweto uprising is by now well known and need not be repeated here. What is of importance is the massive response of the Black working class to the call by the students, in many cases their children, to carry out political strikes during 1976. In August and September, over half a million workers staged successful three-day Stay-at-Homes throughout the country. The Stay-At-Home weapon, initiated by the Congress Alliance in the 1950s, developed far beyond previous experience. The first general strike involved an estimated 100,000 Black workers; the second, 132,000; and the third in September mobilized some 500,000 African and Coloured workers in Johannesburg and Cape Town. There is also evidence to show that organized workers gave more support to the political strikes than other workers. This again confirms the interrelationship between economic and political struggle as advanced by SACTU since the mid-1950s. The question of the relationship between politically conscious, organized workers and mass struggle is obviously one of the many issues that comes to the fore when SACTU analyses the 1976 workers' response.

Immediately before and during the Soweto uprisings, important and bitter struggles for union recognition were being waged by Black workers. A 12-day strike at Natal Cotton and Woollen Mills in Durban recorded a loss of some 7,200 striker-days, almost 40 per cent of the total striker-days in 1975. Eventually the striking workers were dismissed. In the Transvaal, workers at Heinemann Electric, a US subsidiary, were baton charged in March 1976, after they submitted a petition calling for recognition of MAWU, the Metal and Allied Workers Union. Union organizers were later victimized and found guilty in the courts for inciting the strike.[7] Finally, at Pilkington's Armourplate Safety Glass Company, a legal strike was broken by police interference and arbitration through the Department of Labour was rejected. Strike funds were raised by workers on the Rand, and 205 workers held out for an exceptionally long period of ten weeks: In all three cases, workers were relearning the lessons of militant resistance that were a part of the everyday experience of SACTU affiliates in the 1950s and early 1960s.

During the peak of the Soweto uprisings, the SACTU–NEC was meeting in Lusaka, Zambia. From this meeting and from SACTU's office in London, communiques were issued expressing solidarity with the workers and students at home. SACTU memoranda and speeches not only transmitted information about the struggles at home but also pointed the blame in the direction of Western imperialism. As John Gaetsewe stated at an anti-Apartheid rally in London on 27 June 1976:

Let if be known that the children of Soweto carry with them to their graves, bullets on which was written: Made or Produced with the licence from the United States of America, France, Italy or here in England. The police who did the shooting were licenced to kill by foreign investors. This evidence of complicity will be there for future generations to remember.

Lest we forget! It took a world war and the loss of 30 million lives to dispose of the Nazi menace, simply because those who had the power refused to use it in time to stop Nazism from over-running Europe. Let us hope, friends, that the cost of ending Apartheid will not be so great.

Following the workers' Stay-At-Homes in August–September 1976 the regime banned twenty-four trade unionists active in organizing African workers. Other veteran SACTU militants were detained in November, and two – Lawrence Ndzanga and Luke Mazwembe – were killed in detention. Nine working class leaders were tried under the Terrorism Act for reviving SACTU in Natal; they were subjected to torture and electric shocks and humiliated by the Security Police. Five of these persons – Harry Gwala, Anthony Xaba, John Nene, Mathews Meyiwa and Zakhele Mdlalose – were imprisoned for life. The other four defendants – Vuzimuzi Magubane, Cleopas Ndhlovu, Azaria Ndebele and Joseph Nduli – received sentences ranging from 7 to 18 years' imprisonment.[8] In the case of Gwala, who had previously spent 8 years on Robben Island, the defence council demonstrated that after being released Gwala had been organizing workers into trade unions. During the trial, Mathews Meyiwa, speaking of South African trade unionism said, 'SACTU still lives on in the hearts of Black workers'.

SACTU immediately issued a call to the international labour movement, informing organizations throughout the world of these bannings and detentions and requesting workers from all corners of the globe to step up their solidarity actions against Apartheid. SACTU stated at that time:

Why is it necessary to make special mention of those banning orders when so many hundreds have been killed, so many thousands badly wounded, and when South Africa's jails are filled with political prisoners? Because they reveal the systematic attack which is being conducted by the South African racist regime against the growing Black labour movement.

A similar statement was issued jointly by SACTU and the Secretary General of the Organization of African Trade Union Unity (OATUU), J. D. Akumu, on 9 December 1976.

The South African ruling class learned many decades ago that repression against trade union leaders is insufficient in itself. Repression has always been combined with anti-worker legislation designed to further divide the working class not only along racial lines but also as a means of intimidating those workers and unions that fall short of being willing to confront the state. From events of the early and mid-1970s, the regime fully recognized the inherent danger in allowing independent trade unions of Black, particularly African, workers to develop strong roots in the exploited masses. Consequently, the government set up two Commissions of Inquiry to investigate firstly, the industrial relations system and secondly, influx control and pass laws. The former became commonly known as the Wiehahn Commission and the latter the Riekert Commission. It is to these two Commissions that we now turn.

Wiehahn and Riekert: Ruling Class Strategies

The most important point to keep in mind when considering these Commissions is that they were established in response to a crisis. On the economic front, South African capitalism has been facing its deepest recession since the Second World War; consequently, the imperative for the regime is to find ways of increasing productivity and profitability for South African industry. This dilemma obviously brings us to the second aspect of the crisis — the increasing political resistance by the masses, particularly the Black working class, and the regime's inability to contain this resistance throughout the 1970s. Both the economic and political components of the crisis are magnified by the increasing international opposition to Apartheid.

In order to assure the capitalist class greater productivity and higher profit margins, the government hopes to further develop the process of breaking down skilled jobs and, correspondingly, introducing cheap African labour in semi-skilled operative categories. The accomplishment of this goal necessitates the strict control of African workers and their trade unions, the breaking down of Job Reservation (which has historically protected Whites in privileged jobs) and the tightening up of the pass laws.

The most widely publicized recommendation of the Wiehahn Commission Report is that which calls for the recognition, i.e. registration, of African trade unions. While the propagandists of Apartheid have spent countless millions in promoting this as an end to racial discrimination in the industrial relations field, the facts of the matter speak otherwise. The purpose of encouraging the registration of presently unregistered African unions is simply to be able to *control* them and to bring them under the dictates of the repressive industrial relations system first introduced in 1924, and significantly amended in 1956 (see Chapter 4). By incorporating these unions of African workers, *the government hopes to eliminate their independence and reduce their militancy.*

Under the new set-up, only registered unions will be allowed to conclude agreements with employers and to have subscriptions automatically deducted. Yet, the sole decision of eligibility for registered status rests with the Industrial Registrar and its criteria of 'stability' and 'suitability'. In fact, under the legislation, registered unions are prohibited from engaging in political activity. The registration of African unions under the Wiehahn proposals would also serve to reduce the likelihood of presently registered unions de-registering and uniting with unregistered African unions. Finally, the state gives presently registered unions the right to veto applications by African unions to join Industrial Councils; this is another sinister method of preventing these unions from gaining strength in relation to the employers or the White labour aristocracy.

Thus, under these conditions, the legal right of African trade unions to register is a sham designed to weaken and smash the strength, unity and independence of these unions. As SACTU stated in its condemnation of the Wiehahn Commission at the ILO Conference in June 1979:

SACTU has always maintained that recognition must come through the struggle and the strength of the workers *vis-à-vis* the exploiters – it can never be a concession granted by the oppressors themselves. Legality must not be confused with emancipation.

Secondly, the Wiehahn Recommendations call for the abolition of statutory Job Reservation, except in five specific cases. Again, the historical struggle against JR, led by SACTU since 1956, would appear on first glance to have been won. Such is not the case.

The Mines and Works Act and the Black Building Workers Act, two separate statutes legislating JR fall outside the scope of the Commission and thus will remain in effect. The abolition of statutory JR, while having great propaganda appeal, is largely irrelevant as only some 2 per cent of jobs are covered by such determinations. The majority of JR clauses are to be found in agreements between employers and registered unions, and it is certain that the latter will maintain JR classifications by race presently in effect. Future struggles between the capitalist class and the registered unions on this question will be adjudicated by an Industrial Council. For the African workforce, the elimination of statutory colour bars will have no real effect – except perhaps to increase their rate of exploitation.

In line with Wiehahn, the Riekert Commission recommends the tightening up of pass laws, thus further restricting the mobility of African migrant labour. Under Section 10 of the Urban Areas Act, no African can be present in an urban area for more than 72 hours unless he/she has fulfilled certain obligations. Those exempted from these restrictions are generally referred to as 'Section 10 dwellers'. Under the Riekert proposals, these persons will be given the right to move between different urban areas in search of work without registering with the labour bureaus; in addition, they will be given job preference over migrants. There will also be an easing of restrictions on Black businessmen in urban areas.

For the majority without Section 10 rights, however, the pass laws will be more rigorously applied. The goal of the state is to have greater control over the movement of the Black working class. This, in turn, complements the recommendations outlined in Wiehahn.

Therefore, both Wiehahn and Riekert aim at the intensification of state control over African workers and the development of a more streamlined divide-and-rule policy for the entire Black population. To assess these Commissions, and changes in legislation resulting from them, in isolation from the structure and history of Apartheid is to fall into the trap created by the regime itself. Both Commissions presuppose the entire Apartheid system, and only attempt to make that system of oppression and exploitation more efficient. They are bodies set up by the Apartheid regime, staffed by its own supporters, to deal with its own crisis and recommend 'solutions' to crises for which the African working class has no responsibility. Every single piece of industrial relations legislation introduced in South Africa since 1924 has attempted to deal with previous crises by restricting the freedom of the South African working class. These recent examples only reinforce the lessons of history. They also serve to strengthen SACTU's position that the basis of the trade union movement will have to be built underground.

SACTU has called upon the African trade unions to reject the Wiehahn Commission and the proposed Conciliation Amendment Bill. African workers have been told: 'THIS IS NO NEW DEAL! THERE IS NO NEW ERA FOR BLACK LABOUR!' SACTU further calls upon the workers to make the proposed legislation ineffective by:

1. FORMING TRADE UNIONS OF YOUR CHOICE
2. ELECTING YOUR OWN LEADERSHIP
3. DEMANDING RECOGNITION OF YOUR UNION
4. DEMANDING THAT THE EMPLOYERS NEGOTIATE WITH YOUR ELECTED UNION REPRESENTATIVES
5. NOT ALLOWING ANYONE TO FORCE INDUSTRIAL COMMITTEES OR UNION UPON YOU.

FOR THE PROTECTION OF THE WORKERS AGAINST CRUEL HUMILIATION, VICIOUS EXPLOITATION AND BRUTAL NATIONAL OPPRESSION, MAKE SURE THAT THE PROPOSED LEGISLATION IS INEFFECTIVE.

DO NOT APPLY FOR REGISTRATION

From early indications there is every reason to believe that independent African trade unions will boycott this new Act in the same militant spirit as they boycotted the Native Labour (Settlement of Disputes) Act in 1953. Both were designed to 'bleed the African unions to death', but neither will succeed in doing so.

The Emergence of FOSATU

Since the early 1960s, when SACTU was forced underground, there has been no coordinating body representing the interests of the majority of Black workers. Although TUCSA has continued to have a small number of African trade unions as affiliates, the most significant being Lucy Mvubelo's National Union of Clothing Workers (NUCW), it has always been evident that independent African trade unions do not consider TUCSA to have the real interests of the most exploited workers as its priority.

In the late 1970s, the Federation of South African Trade Unions (FOSATU) appeared upon the scene as yet another coordinating body. It is important to briefly put on record SACTU's position with regard to the many new, independent African trade unions that have emerged in the past decade and also its position on the formation of FOSATU. In general, it is part of the work of SACTU to

> guide and influence, firmly but carefully, the work of the open trade unions, etc., to which the workers belong, so that the errors of the union leaders and officials may be corrected by the rank and file, and the organizations kept on the right course and strengthened. . . . Our policy is to fight for independent unions and to give these new organizations our support – in as far as they advance the workers' struggle.[9]

With regard to FOSATU's emergence as a new trade union co-ordinating body, the SACTU General Secretary's Annual Report of 1977 argued that it was wrong to create a proliferation of umbrella bodies at a time when the workers of South Africa should be striving for maximum unity. He went on to say:

> There are already several coordinating bodies, but only one of these is firmly based on the basic principle of fullest unity of *all* workers, irrespective of race or colour. This is the South African Congress of Trade Unions, whose members and adherents are very much alive and active despite the terror tactics of the government. There have also been disturbing racial overtones in these attempts to form new bodies. We have nevertheless advised our comrades to maintain friendly contacts with people who are behind these moves, until their motives have become clear.

Subsequent discussion and assessment of the situation has led SACTU to maintain its commitment to be identified as the symbol and organization of solid working class principles. However, it has also been agreed that the expansion of the trade union movement has necessitated the establishment of a legally functioning co-ordinating body. In this respect, SACTU has issued the following statement:

> It (FOSATU) is severely limited in its area of operation, but it can and will act as a focus of opposition to Apartheid in spite of the actions which will inevitably be taken against it and its leaders by the Apartheid state. Trade unions, trade unionists and trade union federations which do not support the liberation struggle will try to make FOSATU a safety valve with which to turn the workers away from the struggle for national liberation. If they succeed in this the Federation will fail.

The statement goes on to mention that 'FOFATUSA' – the ICFTU and TUCSA creation in the late 1950s – failed to break the strength of SACTU precisely because it tried to turn workers away from the political struggle. SACTU concludes: 'There is no reason why SACTU and FOSATU should not complement each other in their opposition to Apartheid.'

Obviously an important indication of FOSATU's political position will be whether or not its affiliated unions register under the new industrial relations machinery being established by the regime. Already, however, it is interesting to note that FOSATU has had to do battle with the TUCSA-initiated 'parallel' (subordinate) trade unions of African workers. In late 1979, FOSATU charged that management favoured the 'tame' parallel unions because they 'will not cause employers difficulties'. FOSATU goes further to correctly argue that TUCSA's effort to organize more parallel unions of African workers is motivated by the fear that if Job Reservation is eliminated the White workers will be undercut in their privileged positions. Arthur Grobbelaar, TUCSA General Secretary, lends support to the accusation when he says,

> I don't know if our unions have formed an alliance with management – but if they have, good luck to them. Cooperation with management is the crux of industrial relations. I hope TUCSA unions are co-operating with management. This falls within the ambit of partnership in industry.[10]

TUCSA

This chapter would not be complete without a brief statement regarding TUCSA's role in the decade of the 1970s. The very fact that FOSATU has emerged is evidence that many African workers in South Africa regard TUCSA as largely irrelevant to their interests and needs. In view of TUCSA's history, as summarized throughout this book, such a conclusion seems most correct.

The 1975 Report of the TUCSA–NEC begins with a gross distortion. The claim that the founding Conference back in 1954 was 'representative of all races' is totally untrue; in fact, as we have seen, the body was specifically formed to exclude African workers following the dissolution of the SAT & LC in October 1954. By 1977, the total African membership of TUCSA-affiliated (unregistered) unions amounted to 26,982 workers; of this number, 23,000 belonged to Mvubelo's NUCW, leaving only 3,982 workers in a body with 155,153 registered union members.

Other aspects of the 1975 Report include information worthy of consideration. It mentions an Amendment to the Constitution providing that affiliation must be on the basis of membership returns submitted to the Registrar of Trade Unions under the IC Act. As African unions are excluded under the terms of that Act, this provision is clearly an act of racial discrimination. On the question of pensions, TUCSA correctly 'appealed' to the government to increase pensions in relation to the rise in the Consumer Price Index, but failed to protest against the inequalities in pensions between Africans, Coloured and Whites. Another TUCSA resolution 'emphasizes (the) belief that banning without trial is an undemocratic and repugnant principle' and instead demands that banned people be 'charged and tried in court'. Implicit in this formulation is TUCSA's acceptance that the Apartheid regime has the right to persecute and harass trade union leaders in the first place.

TUCSA also gave evidence before the Commission of Inquiry into the Mine Disturbances discussed above. No mention was made of the miners' demands for higher wages nor the terrible working conditions they must endure. As for the miners' mass uprising, TUCSA alleges that 'there was apparently no common cause or discernible pattern'. No demand was made by TUCSA for the right of African miners, the most exploited workers, to organize trade unions. This body which wishes to present itself to the outside world as representative of all workers under Apartheid actually had the impudence to suggest that the insurrection was nothing more than 'inter-nation clashes' and to actually recommend ethnic segregation of miners in the compounds. Yet, the Report also admits that 'the growth of black nationalism' cannot be ignored and that 'at times the various national groups amongst the blacks ... submerged their identities to form a common front against either the White management or the South African police'. Truly, none so blind as those who do not wish to see.

Most amazing is reference to a meeting in Geneva between TUCSA Secretary Grobbelaar and a discredited former official of 'FOFATUSA'. The Report comments: 'The degree of co-operation which was achieved between TUCSA and FOFATUSA will still prove to be of great benefit to the members of both organizations.' Are we to expect yet another attempt by the bogus 'FOFATUSA' to create further divisions amongst South African workers? The record of TUCSA has not altered significantly since the period between 1955 and 1964; it is a tale of vacillation, lack of working class principles and outright betrayal of workers' unity. Although formed in the same year, the contrast between SACTU's and TUCSA's twenty-five-year history is a contrast between struggle and opportunism.

SACTU Advances New Fighting Demands

SACTU's principled determination to lead the workers' struggle against class exploitation and Apartheid was again evidenced in May 1977. A well-researched memorandum was submitted at that time to all employers' organizations in South Africa, calling on them to respond to the fundamental grievances and immediate demands of the Black working class. Predictably, the South African regime declared this memorandum a banned document.

In the memorandum, SACTU focused specific attention on the

economic crisis of South African capitalism and its drastic effect on the most exploited African workers. An official inflation rate of 12 per cent had not only led to a decline in the real income of African workers, but had also produced intolerable levels of unemployment. By the end of 1976, at least *two million* African workers were unable to find work; in early 1978, this figure was rising at the alarming rate of 27,000 per month. The Apartheid regime responded by passing legislation under the Urban Areas Act which made unemployment amongst urban Africans a crime under the law. Any African unemployed for a total of 122 days in any one year is now liable to arrest as an 'idle and undesirable Bantu'. Once arrested, Africans will be 'endorsed out' to the bantustans and may be sentenced to (a) detention in a 'rehabilitation centre', farm colony, or similar institution under the Prisons Act; or (b) 'prescribed labour' at any rural village, settlement or 'rehabilitation scheme' within a 'Bantu area'. This is the way Apartheid chooses to deal with the victims of its own capitalist crisis.

In the face of these realities, SACTU's memorandum to the employers' organizations outlined *fifteen minimum and essential demands* on behalf of the South African workers.[11] They are as follows:

SOUTH AFRICAN WORKERS DEMAND:

1. WE DEMAND THE IMMEDIATE RECOGNITION OF THE RIGHT OF ALL WORKERS TO FORM AND JOIN TRADE UNIONS OF THEIR CHOICE.
2. WE DEMAND THE ABOLITION OF THE PASS LAWS AND OF THE MIGRATORY LABOUR SYSTEM.
3. WE DEMAND THE UNCONDITIONAL RIGHT TO STRIKE FOR ALL WORKERS IN SUPPORT OF THEIR DEMANDS.
4. WE DEMAND A NATIONAL MINIMUM WAGE FOR ALL WORKERS, REGARDLESS OF RACE OR SEX, OF R50 PER WEEK, INDEXED TO INFLATION.
5. WE DEMAND THE ABOLITION OF ALL DISCRIMINATION IN THE WORKPLACE ON THE GROUNDS OF SEX OR RACE, AND AN END TO JOB RESERVATION.
6. WE DEMAND FREE AND COMPULSORY EDUCATION FOR ALL CHILDREN, REGARDLESS OF COLOUR OR CREED, AND EXTENDED TRAINING FACILITIES FOR ALL WORKERS. WE DEMAND THE ABOLITION OF DISCRIMINATION IN EDUCATION AND TRAINING, INCLUDING APPRENTICESHIPS.

7. WE DEMAND AN EIGHT-HOUR WORKING DAY FOR ALL WORKERS, WITH A TOTAL OF 40 HOURS BASIC WORK (EXCLUDING OVERTIME) PER WEEK.
8. WE DEMAND THAT WORKERS SHOULD NOT BE COMPELLED TO WORK OVERTIME, AND WHEN OVERTIME IS WORKED, THE TOTAL NUMBER OF HOURS WORKED PER WEEK, INCLUDING OVERTIME, SHOULD NOT EXCEED 50 HOURS. WORKERS SHOULD BE PAID DOUBLE THEIR NORMAL RATE FOR OVERTIME WORKED DURING THE WEEK, AND TWO-AND-A-HALF TIMES THE NORMAL RATE ON WEEKENDS AND PUBLIC HOLIDAYS.
9. WE DEMAND FOUR WEEKS LEAVE PER YEAR FOR EVERY WORKER.
10. WE DEMAND THAT EVERY WORKER BE ENTITLED TO TWENTY-ONE DAYS SICK LEAVE PER YEAR WITH FULL PAY, TO BE EXTENDED IN CASES OF SERIOUS ILLNESS.
11. WE DEMAND THAT ALL WORKERS SHOULD ENJOY FULL MEDICAL BENEFITS.
12. WE DEMAND UNEMPLOYMENT PAY AND INJURY COMPENSATION FOR ALL WORKERS, WITHOUT EXCEPTION OR TIME LIMIT, AND FIXED AT 100 PER CENT OF CURRENT SALARY.
13. WE DEMAND THAT ALL WORKERS SHOULD BE ELIGIBLE FOR RETIREMENT AT 60 YEARS OF AGE, ON FULL PENSION.
14. WE DEMAND THAT WOMEN WORKERS BE ABLE TO PARTICIPATE FULLY IN ALL ASPECTS OF PRODUCTION, WITHOUT DISCRIMINATION IN WAGES, TRAINING, JOB ALLOCATION OR PENSION BENEFITS.
15. WE DEMAND FULL POLITICAL RIGHTS FOR ALL SOUTH AFRICANS.

Black Workers on the Move Again

During 1978 the attention of the world community was alerted to the courageous struggle of 22,000 African people living in Crossroads 'squatter camp' near Cape Town. 'SIYAHLALA' (WE WILL NOT MOVE) became their cry of resistance against the Apartheid policy of forced removals.

Only male migrant workers are permitted to remain in the towns, living in all-male hostels and separated from their families for forty-nine weeks of every year. Women, old people, children and the unemployed are forced out into the barren reserves which offer no viable means of subsistence. The struggle of the people at Crossroads represents the struggle of the oppressed to live and work where they choose without restriction and to live together as families. A viable community had been created at Crossroads – with schools, literary classes, craft groups, sports clubs and self-help projects – and the people were united in their determination to defy the inhuman Apartheid laws.

The regime has used all sorts of tactics to break this unity and force the people out. Despite demolitions, pass raids, police harassment and arrests, the people have stood strong. The women took the lead in mobilizing the residents who collectively challenged the whole system of injustice and oppression. Even after a brutal attack on the morning of 14 September 1978, when one person was shot dead and over 500 persons arrested, the people continued to resist. For twenty-five years, SACTU has campaigned against the forced removals of African workers and their families from the urban areas in the Western Cape, and SACTU once again salutes the people of Crossroads in their determined stand.

Another important strike in the late 1970s continues the militant spirit of Black working class resistance established throughout the decade. Again in the Western Cape, the Food and Canning Workers Union and the African-FCWU have been waging a valiant struggle for a minimum wage of R40 per week and an 8-hour day. For over a year, Coloured and African members of both unions have stood firm against the Fatti's and Moni's management and the state's attempt to divide the workers' unity characteristic of these traditional SACTU unions.

After management broke off negotiations with the unions, claiming that the latters' demands were 'inconsistent with government policy', the registered union prepared to apply for a conciliation board hearing. When five workers who signed the application were sacked, their fellow workers protested; another five workers were dismissed in April 1979. The entire workforce went on strike, demanding the reinstatement of their comrades and the right of their trade unions to represent them in negotiations. When Department of Labour officials tried to split the united workers along racial lines, the workers resisted, saying, 'We are all workers for the same firm.'

One of the strikers, Mzami Maxanti, was arrested because he could not show permission to remain in the Western Cape – this notwithstanding the fact that he had been employed continuously for ten years by the company. Once again the true meaning of the pass laws is made clear. These laws not only provide the bosses with their cheap labour, but also serve as a political weapon to bludgeon the workers into submission, whenever they stand up for their rights.

The self-sacrifice and determination of these workers knows no bounds. At one point in the strike, a striker's child lay ill. The parents, holding to their working class principles, refused to accept alternative employment, although without the income from that employment their child was unable to receive medical attention. The child has since died. At the funeral the parents, together with the other strikers, pledged their support for the struggle, re-dedicating themselves to the cause of the workers. Fatti's and Moni's crime now extends beyond the field of industrial relations; this super-exploiter of Black labour stands guilty of murder.

The Black community in Cape Town came out strongly in support of the workers' demands. Students at local colleges and the University of the Western Cape and the University of Cape Town initiated a boycott of Fatti's and Moni's products. This action received the support of Mr Hassan Howa, President of the South African Council of Sport (SACOS); Howa, in turn, urged all schools affiliated to SACOS to join the boycott. Mrs Helen Joseph, veteran of the women's campaigns in the 1950s and Secretary of the Federation of South African Women, also gave her support to the boycott. Further pledges of assistance came from the National African Federated Chamber of Commerce and the Western Cape Traders' Association.

The entire community of the Western Cape and also the international community have responded to the unions' and SACTU's appeal for financial assistance for the 88 workers dismissed by management. Recent developments suggest that the company is trying to bypass the unions and take back workers on a selective basis. Many groups within South Africa have pledged to intensify the boycott activities.

As this and other strikes by increasingly militant African workers occur, as they inevitably will, it is perhaps appropriate to end this brief summary of the post-1964 workers' struggles by stressing that SACTU has designated 1980 as the 'YEAR OF THE WORKERS' and the 'YEAR OF THE TRADE UNIONS'. The determination of the FCWU and the A-FCWU in the Western Cape also testifies to the strength of SACTU over the past twenty-five years. At no point has SACTU turned away from the real needs of the workers — both at the workplace and in the society generally. SACTU has at all times, and will continue, to keep in close touch with the rising tide of the Black working class. Through SACTU's external mission that contact and knowledge of the conditions of the workers has been communicated in every part of the world. The following chapter will discuss SACTU's role in building international solidarity with the exploited workers under Apartheid.

NOTES

1. SACTU, Report presented to the Ninth Annual National Conference, 28–29 March 1964.
2. For a detailed account of the Namibian strikes and the general conditions of Namibian workers, see *The Workers of Namibia*, International Defence and Aid Fund, London, 1979.
3. David Hemson, 'Trade Unionism and the Struggle for Liberation in South Africa', *Capital and Class*, no. 6 (Autumn 1978), pp. 20–1.
4. This Act replaced the Native Labour (Settlement of Disputes) of 1953.
5. Another example of the para-military nature of corporate capital was revealed in 1978, when it became known that General Motors Corporation has 'contingency plans' in the 'event of civil unrest'. GM plants will be designated as 'key points' and 'will be accorded protection in emergencies by the Citizen Force Commando system made up of plant personnel with military training'.
6. *Workers Unity*, no. 9, May 1978.
7. In October 1979 the state agreed to pay R21,359 to nineteen Black workers and a banned White trade unionist injured during the baton charge at Heinemann Electric; legal costs of more than R10,000 will also be borne by the state, although there was no admission of liability in the settlement.
8. Joseph Mdluli did not appear at this trial because he was tortured to death by the Security Police.
9. *Workers Unity*, no. 5, September 1977.
10. *Financial Mail*, 16 November 1979.
11. The SACTU Memorandum of Demands was also submitted to the Director-General of the ILO.

15 INTERNATIONAL LINKS ARE FORGED

Our action alone will not of itself bring freedom and trade union rights to the working people of South Africa. We are nevertheless convinced that our actions are assisting the people of South Africa to achieve their political and economic independence from the fascist regime of Vorster/Botha and their multinational partners in crime.

You may be assured of our continuing support as a cog in the giant wheel of international unity and friendship. . . .

> Don Henderson, Secretary Firemen & Deckhands Union of New South Wales, Australia, in a letter to SACTU

At present, SACTU and the workers of South Africa can depend on the support and solidarity of trade unionists throughout the entire world; it is indeed a 'giant wheel' of international working class solidarity in the struggle against Apartheid and capitalist exploitation. Ironically, it is largely due to the fact that some of SACTU's leaders were forced into exile following the spate of bannings, imprisonment and deaths in detention in the early 1960s, that the organization has been able to bring the struggle of the South African working class to the attention of the world. Throughout the past twenty years, SACTU representatives have effectively laid bare the harsh conditions of exploitation and oppression of the African majority in South Africa; these workers in turn have been greatly encouraged in their struggle by all of the actions directed against the regime on their behalf.

After escaping from South Africa during the State of Emergency in 1960, Wilton Mkwayi and Moses Mabhida became SACTU's first respresentatives in exile. Immediately, they set about their task of winning more allies in the struggle and were ably assisted from the outset by the WFTU and its affiliates. In that first year they made important contact with trade union federations all over Africa and received valuable assistance from various Trade Union Internationals. From this beginning, SACTU's external representatives have been able to openly expose the realities of Apartheid exploitation to people throughout the world and appeal directly to them for political and material support.

As early as 1961, before a properly constituted SACTU office was set up, expressions of support came from various trade unions in Britain and elsewhere. These were channelled directly to SACTU Head Office inside South Africa. A fine example is the assistance given by Dagenham Ford workers to their brothers and sisters involved in the strike at Lion Match Company, Durban (described in Chapter 8). Even after SACTU was forced to close down its office and convert to the conditions of underground work inside South Africa, there was a clear understanding of its role in exile. SACTU realizes that it will only win international solidarity provided that it retains direct links with the workers at home. This has remained the guiding principle for SACTU's external representatives throughout the 1960s and 1970s.

After 1964, several other SACTU stalwarts were forced to leave South Africa and subsequently assisted in the external work, among them Ray Simons, Mark Shope and Phyllis Altman. In London, a small committee existed throughout the 1960s, with its members attempting to build more effective links with the trade unions in Europe. However it was not until the appointment of John Gaetsewe as a full-time SACTU functionary to co-ordinate this valuable work, that the London office became a viable centre for establishing solid links with the labour movements of various countries. Gaetsewe has worked tirelessly to bring the message of SACTU to trade unions and organizations not only in Europe, but throughout the world, and as a result has elicited a great deal of support for the workers' struggle at home.

Similarly, the offices in Dar es Salaam, Tanzania and Lusaka, Zambia have spread the word of SACTU far afield and have also maintained close and important contacts with the Arab and African trade union movements, especially of Tanzania and Zambia. Aaron Pemba has been largely responsible for furthering these contacts from the Dar es Salaam office. In recent years the overall SACTU work has been enhanced since Stephen Dlamini, SACTU's last elected President, and Eli Weinberg escaped from South Africa in 1976 and 1977, and immediately threw themselves into the SACTU work abroad.

The International Trade Union Conference Against Apartheid

SACTU has played a major role in the achievement of some very important breakthroughs in international actions directed against the Apartheid regime since the external machinery was established. For example, the ILO decision in the mid-1960s that the Director General is to prepare an annual report on the activities of racist South Africa in relation to labour, came about after representations by SACTU and the affiliates of the WFTU. In June 1970 SACTU sent its first delegation to the ILO, with Mark Shope and Ray Simons representing the interests of South African workers.

The International Trade Union Conference Against Apartheid in 1973 was an extremely significant development in the building of opposition to the Apartheid regime. Some background information is helpful before reviewing the outcome of this Conference.

When SACTU representatives gave evidence to the United Nations Ad Hoc Working Group of Experts on Human Rights on 13 August 1970 they took the opportunity to call for greater involvement by the world trade union movement in the struggle against Apartheid. Global interest in the problems of South African workers and outrage at their conditions of exploitation was increasing, despite the regime's claims that Apartheid was being modified or even dismantled. Ray Simon's attendance at the ILO Conference in June 1971, on behalf of SACTU, was of decisive importance. During the Conference, Simons carried out a frantic round of discussions with workers' delegations from every part of the world, assisted by Tandau, General Secretary of the National Union of Tanzanian Workers (NUTA) and Kabwe and Zimba of the Zambian Congress of Trade Unions.

While the WFTU was cooperating with the World Confederation of Labour (WCL) in an attempt to organize a united conference of the trade union movement against Apartheid, it appeared that the ICFTU had reservations about attending a joint conference with the WFTU.[1] However, these misgivings were removed and the International Trade Union Conference eventually became a reality, due in large measure to the relentless efforts of Ray Simons.

During the 1971 ILO sessions she had met the delegates of many ICFTU affiliates as well as ICFTU top level officials and had impressed them with vivid descriptions of the conditions of oppression suffered by Black, and particularly African, workers at home. Simon's task was facilitated by the appearance of Arthur Grobbelaar (TUCSA), whose clumsy attempts at defending the Apartheid regime aroused the indignation of workers' delegates.

Finally, after years of persistent campaigning and mobilization by SACTU outside South Africa, the International Conference was convened in Geneva, 15–16 June 1973. For the first time since the

Second World War, an international trade union conference embracing all trends the world over took a unanimous stand to condemn the inhuman practices of Apartheid and work out a common programme and plan of action against the regime. The WFTU and the ICFTU, backed by the WCL, the Organization of African Unity (OAU), the UN and the Governing Body of the ILO, convened this historic conference attended by 380 delegates, representing more than 200 trade union organizations. As well as the three world bodies, included were trade unions from socialist countries, the International Confederation of Arab Trade Unions (ICATU) and numerous unaffiliated organizations, altogether perhaps speaking for some 200 million workers of the world.

It is significant that at this Conference, Lucy Mvubelo, Johanna Cornelius and Arthur Grobbelaar were sent by the South African regime to represent its interests. SACTU, however, had a tremendous following at the Conference, particularly from trade union federations on the African continent. When Mvubelo tried to deliver her pro-Apartheid stand against the international boycott and isolation of South Africa, the African trade unions theatened a walk-out and she was forced to withdraw. Workers of the world had demonstrated their collective solidarity with the cause of the oppressed majority in South Africa and their true representatives at this Conference.

The discussions and resolutions adopted reflected the support for the Black workers' struggle for trade union rights and national liberation. Conference exposed and condemned almost every aspect of the reactionary Apartheid system and called for more militant action against it. Among other things, Conference declared that it:

STRONGLY URGES all workers and their trade union organizations, irrespective of international, continental, political or religious affiliations, to give full support to the oppressed workers in South Africa engaged in a legitimate struggle against the racist minority regime of South Africa, by:

— condemning South Africa's continued suppression of fundamental human rights and democratic liberties;

— campaigning for the recognition of African trade unions with full rights to collective bargaining and to strike, the right to organize and freedom of expression and association;

— campaigning for an immediate and unconditional release of all trade union and political prisoners and a stop to the rule of police terror and oppression;

— campaigning for a general amnesty for opponents of Apartheid and the lifting of all bans on African and progressive political organizations and trade union and political leaders and militants, both in South Africa and in exile;

— calling for an end to the notorious system of contract or migrant labour in South Africa, which is a disguised form of modern slavery;

— giving financial, moral and material support to the workers and people of South Africa through their authentic trade union and political organizations.

Trade union organizations throught the world were finally called upon to continue and intensify their actions and to bring pressure on their governments to isolate South Africa by various methods. Specific actions to be taken by workers throughout the world were also urged. The resolution called on workers to:

— strongly oppose emigration of skilled labour to South Africa;

— bring pressure on economic and financial groups which collaborate with South Africa to cease such collaboration;

— boycott the loading and unloading of goods to and from South Africa and/or Namibia, and South African ships and planes;

— organize, in co-operation with consumers' associations, a boycott of goods imported from South America;

— bring pressure, through workers employed in companies with branches in South Africa, on such companies to abolish wage discrimination against African workers in these branches;

— boycott all sporting and cultural activities in which representatives of South Africa take part;

— keep their members and public opinion regularly informed of the situation in South Africa through all information media;

— insist on the effective implementation of the resolution concerning Apartheid and the contribution of the ILO to the International Year of Action to Combat Racism and Racial Discrimination, adopted by the International Labour Conference in 1971, which provides for a long-term ILO programme to eliminate discrimination in employment and restore fundamental human and trade union rights in South Africa;

— take an active part in the Decade of Action to Combat Racism and Racial Discrimination which, in accordance with the decision of the UN General Assembly, is to begin on 10 December 1973, on the occasion of the 25th Anniversary of the Universal Declaration of Human Rights.

This united front against Apartheid has been maintained in successive years. The International Trade Union Conference Against Apartheid has become a permanent feature of the ILO and its resolutions have been the stimulus for countless actions taken in support of the struggle of Black workers in South Africa. The call for a Week of Action in January 1977 initiated by the ICFTU and supported by the WCL and the WFTU, is but one example. Also numerous individual campaigns by workers in every part of the world have expressed firm working class solidarity.

SACTU's decision in 1960 to establish an external mission had therefore proven to be an important contribution to the development of international solidarity. The decision also assisted the furthering of *unity* in the struggle against Apartheid amongst trade unions throughout the world.

The Broadening of Solidarity Work

By the mid-1970s, the work of SACTU's external mission had expanded tremendously, and many important steps were taken in making direct contact with workers in various countries.

Trade unions in the socialist world have consistently supported SACTU throughout its existence by means of moral, political and material assistance. In the true spirit of internationalism, the trade union centres in these countries have provided facilities for long and short term training of trade union functionaries and also medical treatment and rest facilities for many South African trade unionists. As well, they have contributed materially to our struggle by conducting large scale solidarity campaigns amongst their members, resulting in ship-loads of material aid being sent to assist SACTU and ANC refugees. These include foodstuffs, medical supplies, clothing and technical equipment.

A recent tour of several socialist countries by SACTU representatives did much to solidify the firm relationship that exists between the workers of these countries and our organization. In 1978, the SACTU delegation was hosted by the trade union centres in Hungary, Romania, Bulgaria, Czechoslovakia, the German Democratic Republic, Poland and the Soviet Union. Also in that year, the Yugoslav trade union federation generously hosted SACTU's annual 1977–78 NEC meeting.

Equally important have been SACTU's external links with the trade union movements in the Middle East and on the African continent. In this regard, we have received a great deal of support from the Iraqi

Trade Unions. SACTU retains close links with the International Confederation of Arab Trade Unions and our attendance at the Afro–Arab Trade Union Conference held in Algiers in October 1977 resulted in renewed ties of friendship with Arab trade union organizations. This Conference helped to cement the community of interests of African and Arab workers. The role played by SACTU in the consolidation of unity within the African labour movement in the early 1960s has been documented in Chapter 11. Its role in the AATUF carried over when the AATUF's successor, the OATUU, was formed as the trade union wing of the OAU. SACTU now maintains a very close relationship with the OATUU and its affiliated trade union centres throughout Africa.

Some major breakthroughs have been achieved by SACTU in the capitalist world as well, and the organization views the extension of these contacts as an extremely crucial step. Each time we receive assistance and solidarity from workers and trade unions or other groups in these countries, it signifies an important *political victory* for the working class majority in South Africa. No less important is the fact that such support demonstrates an advanced proletarian consciousness on the part of those extending the assistance.

SACTU is now known throughout the world-wide trade union movement, and there is hardly a single trade union which has not at some time in the past two decades heard SACTU's plea on behalf of the Black workers in South Africa. Every action taken is a further encouragement to the exploited majority, the African workers, to advance their struggle against the Apartheid state and employers to greater heights. It is impossible to document all of these various acts of solidarity over the past twenty years, but at the same time it is necessary to highlight in particular some of the actions taken in the capitalist world.

The Development of Solidarity Work in Europe

From initial contacts made in the early 1970s by John Gaetsewe, there has been continued support and solidarity extended by the Scottish Trade Union Congress (STUC). Various Trades Councils and some Trade Union branches in Scotland have also demonstrated their willingness to see the struggle as a common one. As early as 1973, for example, the Edinburgh and District Trades Council passed the following resolution:

This Trades Council condemns, without qualification, the murder of 12 African miners by the Vorster regime at the Transvaal Western Deep Levels gold mine on Tuesday, 11 September 1973. This blatant act of mass murder against the black miners employed at this mine indicates the inhumanity of the policy of Apartheid applied by the Vorster regime. We reiterate our support for the policy of the South African Congress of Trade Unions and call upon all affiliated branches to press through District levels and at National level the condemnation of these industrial atrocities and to further pledge all forms of support for the defeat of fascism in South Africa and to meet the just demands and aspirations of the South African Congress of Trade Unions (passed at the Statutory Meeting of the Trades Council held on Tuesday, September 18, 1973).

It is a credit to the spirit of proletarian internationalism fostered by the STUC that its members have not only consistently invited SACTU to speak at their Annual Congresses, but have at various times sent their own representatives to speak on behalf of Scottish workers at SACTU meetings. One example was the occasion of the 23rd Anniversary of SACTU in March 1978. At its most recent 82nd Annual Congress (1979), the STUC reiterated its support for the South African workers in the following resolution, unanimously adopted:

That this Congress asks the General Council to give practical support for the plea of the South African Congress of Trade Unions (SACTU) in their call for the severance of all financial, industrial and cultural relations with the South African government and institutions while the policy of apartheid continues to exist within that country.

The support extended has never remained at the level of resolutions, however, and the STUC and the workers it represents, continue to engage in concrete actions directed against Apartheid. SACTU's educational tours have been well received and conversely, SACTU speakers have learned a great deal from Scottish rank-and-file workers in the shipyards and factories where common struggles are discussed.

Similarly, the Irish Congress of Trade Unions has expressed its solidarity with SACTU and has worked in close association with the Irish Anti-Apartheid Movement throughout the 1970s to educate trade unionists as to the threat to world peace Apartheid represents. It has consistently called on its 700,000 members to do everything possible to carry out actions against the regime and to provide material and political support for the struggle.

In England, early contacts were made with sympathetic national trade unions like DATA (Draughtsmen and Technical Association), later to be known as TASS (Technical, Administrative and Supervisory Section), of the Amalgamated Union of Engineering Workers, the National Union of Mineworkers, and also various Trade Union Branches and Trades Councils. SACTU received assistance from the Anti-Apartheid Movement in developing the work among British trade unions and in turn the AAM was strengthened by SACTU's presence. As with anti-Apartheid organizations elsewhere, there has in recent years been a greater emphasis on mobilizing trade unionists to develop specific strategies to fight Apartheid.

SACTU representatives consistently made efforts to establish greater contact with the Executive of the British TUC, but any developments on this front were severely set back in 1973 with the TUC decision to send a delegation to South Africa. In 1971 and again in 1972, the TUC had adopted firm resolutions condemning Apartheid and proposing concrete measures to combat it. However, in March 1973, following wide publicity regarding poverty wages paid by British subsidiaries to their Black employees in South Africa, and after correspondence with TUCSA, the TUC General Council declared its intention to send a fact-finding mission to South Africa. Even after TUC representatives attended the International Trade Union Conference Against Apartheid in Geneva in June 1973 the Congress went ahead with its plans for the visit which took place on 6–10 October.

SACTU presented an extremely impressive 'Memorandum to the British workers and their TUC', which had been prepared by Mark Shope. We outlined the reasons for our total opposition to the visit, but to no avail. After the visit, SACTU voiced its criticisms of the tour in a letter which went out to British workers. This letter read in part:

The Conference (International . . .) at which the British TUC was represented, adopted unanimously a long resolution setting out a comprehensive programme of action to isolate the apartheid regime politically, economically and militarily, and to support the struggle for democratic rights, including workers' rights.

These developments had clarified as never before the question 'What can trade unions and workers do to combat apartheid'? We were therefore puzzled by the TUC's decision to visit South Africa. And we were even more puzzled, studying the delegation's report, that no mention was made of the only South African trade union centre which has steadily, since its inception in 1955, pursued a policy of organizing all workers, regardless of race, and linking that to the overall struggle of the black majority for freedom and equality, that is, the South African Congress of Trade Unions (SACTU).[2]

Only one year before the TUC visit, the International Metalworkers Federation had sent a delegation to South Africa. In their report they declared that SACTU was 'the only trade union organization with a relatively high proportion of African members'.

SACTU went on to point out that not only did the TUC delegation avoid saying anything about SACTU, but its report omitted any account of the past efforts of African workers to organize themselves. Also, it seemed that the delegation spent most of its time talking to White trade unionists, employers and the government, and spent little time talking to Black workers and trade unionists. Therefore, they did not report on the long history of persecution of Black trade unionists – and White trade unionists as well – who were associated with SACTU. Most of the proposals suggested by the TUC after the visit were very weak and did not represent any real attack on the structural basis of exploitation of South African workers.

Despite this temporary strain in relations between SACTU and the TUC Executive, in recent years there has been a marked improvement in the relationship. By 1975, the TUC had passed an important resolution which had positive repercussions throughout the British trade union movement. The resolution read as follows:

Congress reaffirms its opposition to Apartheid and pledges its support for policies to produce majority rule in South Africa and Rhodesia and which will end the illegal occupation of Namibia by South Africa.

In particular, Congress recognizes that the British Trade Union movement can best assist these objectives by working closely with the South African Congress of Trade Unions and pressing the British Government to take all steps to withdraw investments by British companies in South Africa.

An important consequence of this resolution was the formation of the British Trade Union–SACTU Liaison Group, a body which continues to carry out valuable work amongst British workers. After the original resolution was passed at the TUC Congress a few trade union Executive Council members and officials met to consider how best they could, at the trade union level, assist the Black workers of South Africa in their struggle for trade union rights.

The following aims were stated by the Liaison Group:

1. To disseminate information on the role and policy of SACTU and on the conditions of Black workers in the Republic (of South Africa), with special reference to the labour relations and the conditions under which they are employed by British companies operating in South Africa.

2. To campaign for the promotion of meaningful trade unionism for all workers in the Republic, and in particular to campaign for the recognition of *all* trade unions by British companies, especially multinationals. Where no trade unions for Black workers exist or are allowed, to campaign for the setting up of such unions in full consultation with SACTU.

Thirteen major unions had indicated their support by July 1976 and the Group began its campaign by contacting large British companies regarding labour relations and employment practices in their South African subsidiaries. The Group has now expanded to include representation from twenty unions.

A further resolution on the winning of trade union rights in South Africa was passed by the TUC in 1977. Congress also urged the General Council to 'work closely with SACTU' in the implementation of this resolution. It has been left largely to the Liaison Group to carry this out. In its work the Group has been greatly assisted by Edward Ramsdale, presently working with SACTU in its London office. SACTU now has direct access to TUC affiliates and their response to the South African workers' struggle has been encouraging in recent years. Between April and November 1979 more than ninety invitations have been extended to SACTU to address meetings of workers from all areas of the country.

A fine expression of rank and file solidarity occurred in Britain in 1978. The shop stewards at British Leyland's Rover plant at Solihull, England, published a broadsheet demanding an end to Leyland's involvement in South Africa. In it they state: 'Over the past five years British Leyland has made five times as much profit from each of its workers in South Africa as it has from its workers in Britain. The question is: How is this possible?'

The broadsheet explained in detail how Black workers are exploited under Apartheid, and how this enables corporations like British Leyland to squeeze high profits out of their labour. Demonstrating how Leyland actively perpetuated the intolerable conditions in South Africa, they pointed out that firstly, Leyland has consistently refused to recognize the African Metal and Allied Workers Union (MAWU), and secondly, that the Company had decided – despite international opposition to Apartheid – to expand its South African operations, and thirdly, that it continued to supply the South African Defence Force and Police with military vehicles, including Land-Rovers, armoured personnel carriers and trucks.

It just shows what sort of wages and conditions Leyland workers in this country would suffer, if it were not for the strength of our trade union organization which we have built up over the years. . . .

Trade Unionists have realized that their strength in one factory can be undermined by the bosses playing on the weaknesses of workers in another factory and dividing them against each other. That is why we work hand in hand with other Leyland workers throughout Britain. Now that we can see how the bosses play us off against workers in other countries – threatening to close down plants here and shift investment abroad – we must unite internationally for our mutual benefit.

The broadsheet called for an end to all investment in South Africa and other demands which included an end to all arms sales to Apartheid and 'the establishment of increased contact with Black workers and fellow trade unionists through direct links with shop stewards in Britain and South Africa, in conjunction with SACTU'. A final call was issued:

Leyland workers, do not allow the products of your labour to be used against your brothers and sisters in South Africa to maim and kill them!

Support the struggle waged by your brothers and sisters in South Africa against Apartheid, oppression and exploitation. SANCTIONS AGAINST CAPITAL! SOLIDARITY WITH LABOUR! NO MORE LEYLAND VEHICLES FOR APARTHEID!

Leyland workers also included a poem written by a young student in a Mozambique school:

> 'We Are Decolonizing the Land Rover!'
>
> No more is it the car of the collector of taxes –
> We have decolonized it!
> Now there is no terror when it enters a village
> For the Land Rover no longer belongs to the colonial
>   policeman or soldier . . .
> Once it was the sure ally of the exploiter's whip –
> But now we have decolonized it!
> Through the mud and the sand
> Its power and its four wheels
> Will guarantee a safe arrival at the most distant
>   machambas,
> And the Peasants' co-operatives.
>
> With our products
> We buy the fuel it consumes,
> With our intelligence
> We mend any breakdowns that happen,

With our struggle
We make a friend of this enemy –
We are the decolonizers!
We are liberating the Land Rover
And now it is independent at last! . . .

The hands of the workers who made you
Are equal to the hands of the workers of our land –
Those English hands which forged you
Know that one day they will help to make their own
    Revolution,
And raise the clenched fist of their solidarity! . . .

We are decolonizing a weapon of the enemy!
We are decolonizing the Land Rover!
Those four wheels and the powerful motor,
That cab with its control dials
That shape of the chassis that was once linked with fear
Now doesn't make the people run away!
Men, women and children of the countryside
Make signals to the driver,
Ask for lifts –
We are decolonizing the Land Rover!
And the people don't run away any more.

The Rover shop stewards ended their broadsheet: 'In Mozambique the Land Rover is now a vehicle used for its proper purpose – to assist in the development of production, agriculture and to improve the working and living conditions of the Mozambique workers.'

Before leaving the issue of British solidarity, it is important to point out that over the years there have been several British trade unionists who emigrated to South Africa and who subsequently became involved in promoting the principles of SACTU. Eddie Davoren, who replaced Phyllis Altman as Assistant General Secretary of SACTU after her banning in 1963, was eventually deported. David Kitson, however, was less fortunate and is at present serving a 20-year sentence for his trade union activity. SACTU salutes the courageous actions of these and other British workers who committed themselves to the struggle of the African workers for trade union rights and liberation.

In France, SACTU has established friendly relations with the Confédération Générale de France (CGT) and the Confédération Française Democratique du Travail (CFDT). As early as 1971, after a successful tour by SACTU representatives John Gaetsewe and James

Phillips, a Joint Declaration of SACTU and CGT was issued, a part of which is reproduced here:

The SACTU delegation notes the struggles in pursuance of claims led by the CGT for the improvement of living and working conditions of French workers; it wishes new successes for the CGT in its actions in defence of the interests of the working class of France...

SACTU, which has always appreciated and saluted the anti-imperialist and anti-colonialist struggle of the CGT, considers that the solidarity which it shows with the workers and people of South Africa for its liberation contributes to strengthening of the anti-imperialist struggle of the workers in the world.

The CGT and SACTU denounce the actions of the majority of governments of capitalist countries and certain African governments which, in violation of the UN and of various specialized international bodies, such as the ILO, give assistance to the racist Pretoria government. The two organizations consider that the whole world community must build up its pressure through multiple initiatives on the racist South African government in order that the Africans and people of all races may enjoy freedom and basic human rights in that part of the African continent...

In September 1979, at the port of Le Havre, 200 mine workers, members of the CGT union, occupied a French-owned ship carrying coal from South Africa. Their opposition challenged exploitation on two fronts. At home, it was directed against the closing down of French mines, where the struggles of French workers had forced the mine owners to pay higher wages. As an act of international solidarity, the occupation of the ship was an expression of support for the grossly exploited mine workers under Apartheid. SACTU commends this principled stand by the French working class.

Similarly, SACTU has developed relations with the Nordic Federation, the FNV (Holland) and the Swedish Labour Organization (LO). The LO has recently expressed its solidarity with financial assistance to enable SACTU, the National Union of Namibian Workers (NUNW) and the Zimbabwe African Congress of Unions (ZACU) to hold a Joint Solidarity Conference in 1980 (see below). In Holland, the Anti-Apartheid Movement has also played an important supportive role in organizing trade union conferences, coordinating SACTU visits, conducting educational work with European workers and mobilizing material support.

Australia and New Zealand

In 1972 John Gaetsewe travelled to New Zealand at the invitation of the Wellington Trades Council and the May Day Committee. This was the first time that a SACTU representative had ever set foot on the tiny islands that make up this country. The reception was tremendous as he travelled to numerous centres in New Zealand, addressing not only national unions but their members in various factories. During a 5-day visit to Christchurch, Gaetsewe addressed approximately 300,000 workers. In a speech to the Federation of Labour Conference, he called upon the New Zealand workers to do everything possible to stop the proposed rugby tour of New Zealand and to isolate South Africa in the areas of economic relations, culture and immigration. Through united actions by the workers and people of New Zealand, the rugby tour was eventually cancelled. Several unions have consistently offered material and political support since these early contacts were forged, including the Seamens' Union and the Wellington Waterside Workers.

It was the Seamens' Union of Australia which extended an invitation to SACTU to address the Australian workers after the completion of a very successful tour of New Zealand. During his brief stay, Gaetsewe met a number of trade union officials and executives of various trade unions in the Sydney area. While he was there, a major victory was scored by the Waterside Workers' Federation in support of their fellow workers in South Africa. Ship-owners using flags of convenience on ships belonging to South Africa, were forced to pay African seamen wages agreed upon by the International Transport Federation. The ship-owners at first refused to listen to the Waterside officials and the Seamens' Union, who threatened that if the agreement on wages was not accepted, the ships would not move from Australia. The Director was called from South Africa to negotiate with the workers and after long discussions it was agreed that the African workers' wages would be increased from R60 to R220 per month. This was the first time that such a success had been achieved outside South Africa.

As a result of these and subsequent visits to both Australia and New Zealand, SACTU has forged close ties with various trade unions in both countries. The New Zealand unions have been steadfast in their financial and political support for SACTU and the workers' struggle throughout the 1970s. In Australia, largely as a result of initiatives by SACTU and the progressive unions there, significant concrete actions have been directed against the South African regime. From 1 July to 31 July 1976 the Australian Council of Trade Unions (ACTU) called on its affiliated unions to instigate a month of action against the Apartheid regime, immediately following the senseless murder of unarmed children in Soweto. Subsequent actions were taken in other countries as a result of this nation-wide call.

In a letter to SACTU in 1977, the Acting Secretary of the Firemen and Deckhands' Union of New South Wales, Australia, reported:

> In line with the policy of WFTU and the above Union, I have to advise that the South African Flag Vessel 'Safocean Auckland' was refused tug crews and linesmen in the port of Sydney from 16 to 30 September, 1977.

The Union took this action to support the just struggle of the people of South Africa 'against the terror and oppression of Apartheid'. A meeting of the Linesmen and Tug crews at Sydney harbour decided to withhold their services from the ship until such time as the following questions were answered by the South African government:

> What was the official cause of the death of Lawrence Ndzanga (SACTU) who died in the notorious cells of the Security Police at John Vorster Square?
>
> Why was his wife Rita Ndzanga (SACTU) refused permission to attend her husband's funeral?
>
> What is she guilty of under the fascist law known as the Terrorism Act?
>
> What was the cause of the death of Steve Biko who also died whilst being held in detention cells?

A deputation from the Union, together with the Seamen's Union of Australia and the Sydney Waterside Workers put these questions to South African diplomats, but received unsatisfactory answers. The Unions eventually allowed the ship to sail 'on condition that the next port of call would be Melbourne, where another ban was placed on her'. Similar actions have been repeated in 1978 and 1979; the General Secretary of the Seaman's Union of Australia explained in a letter to SACTU:

> Seamen in Australia believe the Government of South Africa is guilty of a crime against humanity when it treats the original inhabitants of Africa as second class human beings and therefore Australian seamen have waged a guerilla campaign against shipping trade with South Africa. South African ships trading to Australia are subject to harassing tactics by seamen and dockers resulting in indeterminate delays by immobilization of the ships.
>
> The dilemma of the South African ship-owner is that he does not know where, when or how a ship is going to be delayed . . .

In the present international political and industrial climate, we believe our tactics and actions are an effective demonstration of our solidarity and support of the struggle of the African people . . .

North America

In 1971 and 1972, John Gaetsewe made contact with some Canadian trade unions, particularly in the Vancouver area. One of these, the Canadian Union of Public Employees (CUPE) not only gave a direct donation to SACTU but also issued circulars of appeal to approximately 80 branches affiliated to it. Subsequent tours by Gaetsewe in 1975 and Stephen Dlamini in 1977, have established further links with the Canadian labour movement, especially the unions in Quebec — the Council of National Trade Unions (CSN) and Corporation of Quebec Teachers (CEQ). In 1977 also, James Stuart represented SACTU at a nation-wide anti-Apartheid conference in Vancouver and subsequently toured other centres mobilizing support. In Toronto, Ontario, SACTU now has a Canadian representative, Enver Domingo, who is assisted in the development of solidarity work by veteran Natal trade unionist, George Ponnen. Through their consistent efforts substantial aid has been given to SACTU by the United Auto Workers (UAW) and United Electrical (UE) local branches, among others.

At its annual convention in November 1978 the Ontario Federation of Labour passed a significant resolution which will provide a basis for increased action by Canadian workers in support of the workers' struggle led by SACTU.

Whereas the United Nations declared 1978 International Year Against Apartheid, calling on peoples and governments everywhere to support the struggle of the the Black majority of South Africa to gain unconditional independence in their own country,
Therefore be it resolved that the Ontario Federation of Labour declare full solidarity with . . . (the) 'South African Congress of Trade Unions' and (the) 'African National Congress'.

In 1977, Zola Zembe, SACTU NEC member based in London, was invited to the USA to address the National Convention of the United Electrical, Radio and Machine Workers of America (UE). This invitation then served as the basis for an extended tour of major cities from coast to coast. This visit was the first of its kind in the United States, and it represented a significant breakthrough for SACTU, laying the foundation for the growth of solidarity between workers there and in South Africa.

There have been two additional tours of the United States since the initial visit and solid links have been built between SACTU and American workers represented by UE, the International Longshoremen's Union, and the Coalition of Black Trade Unionists in particular. In this latter respect, SACTU comrades have been able to express solidarity with the struggles of their Black brothers and sisters exploited under American capitalism.

It is significant to note that while Zola Zembe was addressing trade unions on the West Coast of the USA during his most recent tour in September–October 1979 Lucy Mvubelo was completing a speaking tour in the East, a tour sponsored by the pro-Apartheid South Africa Foundation. SACTU views with constant concern the way proponents of Apartheid like Mvubelo are paraded around the world as if they have the support of the African working class, while legitimate trade unionists are denied passports to leave South Africa. It is a measure of the effective educational work done by solidarity groups in the USA and the impact of SACTU amongst American workers and progressive people that Mvubelo encountered a great deal of opposition to her stand against disinvestment campaigns.

SACTU's appeal for working class solidarity with the struggle of South African workers has extended as far afield as Japan and India, where concrete support has been achieved from trade unions who adhere to the principles on which SACTU was founded. We reiterate that it is impossible to document all the tremendous assistance and support our friends around the world have given us. It is not overstating the case to say that when the total liberation of the workers and people of South Africa has been achieved, that victory will be due in large measure to the actions taken by the workers and progressive people from every corner of the globe.

Developments in Recent Years

Following the vicious state repression directed against students and workers' leaders in 1976, the world community responded with horror and outrage and there were renewed efforts to build up the strength of anti-Apartheid forces and activities. Beginning in January 1977, with a call from the ICFTU for a Week of Action directed against Apartheid, the international trade union movement stepped up its activities. The WFTU and WCL joined with the ICFTU to strike a blow at the South

African regime in unity. Many successes were recorded. Norwegian trade unionists had persuaded their government, which holds a state wine monopoly, to cease buying from South Africa and, as well, to institute a permanent freeze on new investments. In Australia, New Zealand, Canada, Belgium and West Germany, boycott actions took place at the docks; in France, postal workers blacked South African mail, and in Italy three unions jointly organized a boycott of South African aircraft. In Britain, John Gaetsewe paid tribute to the 'bold stand taken by the Union of Post Office Workers and the Post Office Engineering Union, supported by TGWU, the NUS, ASTMS, GMWU and others'.

SACTU has welcomed this call from the ICFTU and all other demonstrations of its consistent opposition to Apartheid, including its participation in the 2nd International Trade Union Conference Against Apartheid in 1977. In particular, the ICFTU must be congratulated for its continued campaign against investments in South Africa. It is at times disturbing, however, to notice that in reports on South Africa, ICFTU publications studiously avoid the mention of SACTU, the only truly multi-racial trade union coordinating body. As well, the ICFTU at times supports all kinds of unrepresentative bodies and individuals and passes them off as 'representatives of the South African workers', in many cases undermining important work being done by SACTU. Despite all this, SACTU has had good relations with many affiliates of the ICFTU who have demonstrated their unprejudiced adherence to the sacred principle of working class solidarity by giving direct and massive help to SACTU. As far as the ICFTU leadership is concerned, SACTU is determined to continue its firm policy of friendship and cooperation with all genuine trade union bodies of the world.

It is very significant that the presence of SACTU at the ILO has now become a constitutional fact. Because of a precedent set in affording the Palestine Liberation Organization (PLO) status as a liberation movement, SACTU is required to attend ILO Conferences as part of an African National Congress delegation. This does not alter the fact that it was SACTU which all along fought for its status and has thus achieved a victory for the oppressed majority in South Africa whose voice can now be heard throughout the world trade union movement. SACTU's annual memoranda to the ILO have consistently been praised for containing reasoned and extremely well-researched arguments.

In the last few years SACTU has been represented at some very important conferences dealing with specific aspects of the Apartheid attack on the working class. A conference on Migrant Labour organized by the Economic Commission for Africa and the ILO, was convened in Lusaka, Zambia, 4–7 April 1978. SACTU submitted a statement of policy which had a marked influence on the outcome of the conference. Included was *SACTU's stand on migrant labour.*

Ever since its formation, SACTU has steadfastly opposed the system of migrant labour on which the apartheid economy is based. But in fighting for the rights of South African workers, SACTU fights at the same time for the rights of *all* workers. In the same way as SACTU rejects the concept of 'foreign worker' when applied to black South Africans, so too does it reject that concept when applied to other workers, regardless of their country of origin.

SACTU stands firmly by the Freedom Charter which says that South Africa belongs to all who live in it, and that the wealth of South Africa shall be restored to the people. To live is to work – every worker knows this. Accordingly, we say that those who have contributed to the wealth of South Africa, regardless of their country of origin, will be free to live and work in South Africa if they so choose. They and their families will enjoy the same citizenship rights enjoyed by their South African brothers and sisters, sharing in the wealth they have collectively created. SACTU fights for the rights of *all* workers, including those who, at the end of their contract, are made to return to their country of origin, leaving behind the wealth they have produced. They too have put their lives into building South Africa's industrial might, and they have a just claim to the fruits of their labour.

Although SACTU does not distinguish between one worker and another, we nevertheless recognize the need for an extension of our programme of action in order to fight for the immediate rights of workers who are drawn from neighbouring countries. These workers are cruelly and callously exploited, and are hired and fired at the whim of the capitalist.

SACTU presented workers' demands to the conference, based on the organization's general fighting demands put forward in the interests of *all* workers in South Africa.

In recognition of a common struggle against Apartheid regimes in Southern Africa, SACTU has in recent years, joined together with the National Union of Namibian Workers (NUNW) and Zimbabwe African Congress of Trade Unions (ZACU) to form a Joint Consultative Committee (JCC). The three organizations agreed to consult and work together on all matters of mutual interest, to inform each other on all developments in their own territories, and to protect each other's interests. In 1980, the JCC will convene a Solidarity Conference to further these aims and to invite trade union organizations throughout the world to join them in their common struggle for freedom and justice for the working class of Southern Africa.

In 1976, a decision was taken to begin printing again the SACTU organ of the 1950s and 1960s, *Workers Unity*. It has enjoyed wide circulation and there is a constantly growing demand for copies from all over the world. Inside South Africa, each issue has been banned, but that does not deter us. SACTU recognizes the need for strengthening its educational and propaganda work amongst South African workers and will continue to concentrate its energies on meeting their needs in the future. On this question of future tasks, it is fitting to quote our President, Stephen Dlamini. In addressing a large gathering in Dar es Salaam on SACTU's 23rd Anniversary, 5 March 1978, Dlamini reviewed our achievements over the years and pointed the way forward:

> We must counter the treachery and trickiness of the enemy, by being more clever than he, by developing new forms of organization, new ideas of struggle. We must think deeply and long, how to outwit the enemy, how to frustrate his plans, how to advance the interests of the workers with a minimum of losses and sacrifice.
>
> But we must not think that we can achieve this without struggle or sacrifices. We must be ready, literally, to face the utmost dangers without fear and without hesitation, when the situation demands it. This we can learn from our young people, from the new generation of fighters which has grown up in recent years. This fearless generation have realized that they have nothing to lose but their chains. Their courage must be directed and organized, so that it is not lost in wild spontaneous outbursts, but in well-planned and sustained actions, designed to shake the very foundations of the racist structure and to bring it tumbling down.
>
> Above all, we must learn that slogan shouting is not enough. What we need is hard, painstaking, slogging and methodical work; organizing trade unions means careful planning, checking up on decisions, following up every advantage gained and keeping our eyes open for opportunities and loopholes which the struggle presents.

This is our task and we call on the international community to play its role alongside SACTU and the South African working class in our struggle against Apartheid oppression and class exploitation.

NOTES

1. The early 1970s witnessed further attempts by the ICFTU to circumvent SACTU. During visits to South Africa they found it difficult, however, to convince the workers that SACTU was dead, proof of the valuable work being done by the SACTU underground inside the country.
2. SACTU letter to the British TUC, 22 April 1974.

16 'AN INJURY TO ONE IS AN INJURY TO ALL'

Apartheid owes its continued existence to the many forms of direct and indirect assistance received from international capitalism. In return, multinational corporations which invest in Apartheid South Africa extract huge profits from the sweat and blood of the Black working class. The equation is simple: Apartheid and international monopoly capitalism need each other.

But the workers – the toilers, the producers of all wealth – in South Africa and in every capitalist country need neither Apartheid nor multinational corporations. The case of British Leyland cited in the previous chapter can be multiplied thousands of times. In every foreign corporation that invests in Apartheid there is a group of workers who must ask themselves one fundamental question: 'can our interests, no matter how strong our trade union, be protected as long as cheap, Black labour is exploited in South Africa?' The answer is clearly NO! From this essential starting point, it then becomes imperative that workers throughout the capitalist world make the struggle against Apartheid *their struggle* as well. SACTU's motto is not a slogan devised in South Africa for only South African conditions. It is a fighting weapon to which every worker who sells labour power to another must attach himself/herself. AN INJURY TO ONE IS AN INJURY TO ALL.

The militant struggles waged by the oppressed people of South Africa in the 1970s have alerted the multinational corporations, and the Western governments that do their bidding, to realize that some initiative must be made to protect the massive investments – past, present and future – in Apartheid. Governments and corporations, therefore, have begun to devise 'Codes of Conduct' for regulating capitalist behaviour in Apartheid.

These Codes of Conduct, while they vary in detail from one country to the next, share certain fundamental premises. Firstly, they were devised completely independent of consultation with the Black working class of South Africa. Secondly, they intentionally confuse the entire issue by suggesting that Apartheid can be reformed without the necessity of it being completely overthrown. This, of course, is done so as to protect capitalism's long term interest in exploiting the human and natural resources of not only South Africa but also the entire subcontinent. Thirdly, they fail in every respect to respond to the real needs of the people of South Africa, as outlined in the Freedom Charter (see Appendix II).

The oppressed people of South Africa, through their trade union movement (SACTU) and through their liberation movement (ANC) and its allies, have clearly told the multinational corporations and Western governments that the only acceptable 'code of conduct' is to GET OUT NOW!

We, the South African Congress of Trade Unions, have now told you our story of a quarter of a century of struggle and sacrifice. Our victory is certain! That victory, however, requires the principled solidarity from everyone who shares our goals and aspirations to create a free and democratic South Africa. On behalf of the exploited workers of South Africa, we call upon you to commit yourself to the following tasks which are necessary for the realization of our struggle against Apartheid. Join hands with the workers of South Africa and DEMAND:

- AN END TO ALL FOREIGN INVESTMENT IN SOUTH AFRICA
- AN END TO ALL FOREIGN LOANS TO THE APARTHEID REGIME AND COMPANIES OPERATING IN SOUTH AFRICA
- THE NATIONALIZATION OF SOUTH AFRICAN MULTINATIONALS OPERATING IN YOUR COUNTRY
- AN END TO ALL TRADE WITH SOUTH AFRICA
- A COMPLETE ISOLATION OF SOUTH AFRICA IN EVERY SPHERE – CULTURALLY, POLITICALLY, ECONOMICALLY, MILITARILY AND THROUGH SPORTING LINKS
- A COMPLETE ARMS EMBARGO AGAINST THE REGIME
- AN INTERNATIONAL OIL EMBARGO AGAINST APARTHEID
- AN END TO EMIGRATION OF SKILLED WORKERS TO SOUTH AFRICA
- A CONSUMER BOYCOTT OF PRODUCTS OF APARTHEID
- AN END TO THE PROMOTION OF BUSINESS WITH SOUTH AFRICA AND TO THE ADVERTISEMENT OF SOUTH AFRICAN GOODS AND SERVICES
- THE PROHIBITION OF AIRLINES AND SHIPPING LINES REGISTERED IN YOUR COUNTRY FROM PROVIDING SERVICES TO AND FROM SOUTH AFRICA

WORKERS, CEMENT YOUR SOLIDARITY BY TAKING THESE ACTIONS NOW:

- IMPLEMENT A BAN ON THE HANDLING OF ALL SOUTH AFRICAN GOODS COMING IN BY SEA, AIR, ROAD OR RAIL
- CONTINUE TO DEMAND THE RIGHT OF ALL SOUTH AFRICAN WORKERS TO ORGANIZE AND FORM INDEPENDENT TRADE UNIONS, AND DEMAND THAT EMPLOYERS RECOGNIZE AND NEGOTIATE WITH THE WORKERS' ELECTED REPRESENTATIVES
- FORGE DIRECT LINKS WITH YOUR FELLOW WORKERS IN THE SAME INDUSTRY IN SOUTH AFRICA IN CONSULTATION WITH SACTU
- DEVELOP AND PROMOTE THE EFFECTIVE USE OF EDUCATIONAL MATERIALS ON APARTHEID WITH YOUR FELLOW WORKERS
- ORGANIZE FINANCIAL SUPPORT FOR THE SOUTH AFRICAN CONGRESS OF TRADE UNIONS
- INVITE SACTU TO ADDRESS YOUR WORKERS COLLECTIVELY

BY CARRYING OUT THESE ACTIONS, YOU WILL BE ADVANCING THE STRUGGLE WAGED BY YOUR BROTHERS AND SISTERS IN SOUTH AFRICA AGAINST APARTHEID, OPPRESSION AND EXPLOITATION!

APPENDIX I

DECLARATION OF PRINCIPLES ADOPTED AT THE FOUNDATION CONFERENCE OF THE SOUTH AFRICAN CONGRESS OF TRADE UNIONS, ON 5 MARCH 1955, AND INCLUDED AS A PREAMBLE TO ITS CONSTITUTION

History has shown that unorganised workers are unable to improve their wages and conditions of work *on a lasting basis*. Only where workers have organised in effective trade unions have they been able to improve their lot, raise their standard of living and generally protect themselves and their families against the insecurities of life.

The whole experience of the Trade Union Movement the world over has furthermore established the fact that the Movement can only progress on the basis of unity and in the spirit of brotherhood and solidarity of all workers. Trade Unions must unreservedly reject any attempts to sow disunity among the workers, on the basis of colour or nationality or any other basis.

Just as the individual worker, or any group of workers, are unable to improve their lot without organisation into Trade Unions, so is the individual trade union powerless unless there is in existence a coordinating body of trade unions which unites the efforts of all workers. For such a trade union federation to be successful, it must be able to speak on behalf of all workers, irrespective of race or colour, nationality or sex.

The future of the people of South Africa is in the hands of its workers. Only the working class, in alliance with other progressive minded sections of the community, can build a happy life for all South Africans, a life free from unemployment, insecurity and poverty, free from racial hatred and oppression, a life of vast opportunities for all people.

But the working class can only succeed in this great and noble endeavour if it itself is united and strong, if it is conscious of its inspiring responsibility. The workers of South Africa need a united trade union movement in which all sections of the working class can play their part unhindered by prejudice or racial discrimination. Only such a truly united movement can serve effectively the interests of the workers, both the immediate interests of higher wages and better conditions of life and work as well as the ultimate objective of complete emancipation, for which our forefathers have fought.

We firmly declare that the interests of all workers are alike, whether they be European, African, Coloured, Indian, English, Afrikaans or Jewish. We resolve that this coordinating body of trade unions shall strive to unite all workers in its ranks, without discrimination, and without prejudice. We resolve that this body shall determinedly seek to further and protect the interests of all workers, and that its guiding motto shall be the universal slogan of working class solidarity: –

'AN INJURY TO ONE IS AN INJURY TO ALL!'

APPENDIX II

The Freedom Charter

We, the People of South Africa, declare for all our country and the world to know:

that South Africa belongs to all who live in it, black and white, and that no government can justly claim authority unless it is based on the will of all the people;

that our people have been robbed of their birthright to land, liberty and peace by a form of government founded on injustice and inequality;

that our country will never be prosperous or free until all our people live in brotherhood, enjoying equal rights and opportunities;

that only a democratic state, based on the will of all the people, can secure to all their birthright without distinction of colour, race, sex or belief;

And therefore, we, the people of South Africa, black and white together—equals, countrymen and brothers—adopt this Freedom Charter. And we pledge ourselves to strive together, sparing neither strength nor courage, until the democratic changes here set out have been won.

THE PEOPLE SHALL GOVERN!

Every man and woman shall have the right to vote for and to stand as a candidate for all bodies which make laws;

All people shall be entitled to take part in the administration of the country;

The rights of the people shall be the same, regardless of race, colour or sex;

All bodies of minority rule, advisory boards, councils and authorities shall be replaced by democratic organs of self-government.

ALL NATIONAL GROUPS SHALL HAVE EQUAL RIGHTS!

There shall be equal status in the bodies of state, in the courts and in the schools for all national groups and races;

All people shall have equal right to use their own languages, and to develop their own folk culture and customs;

All national groups shall be protected by law against insults to their race and national pride;

The preaching and practice of national, race or colour discrimination and contempt shall be a punishable crime;

All apartheid laws and practices shall be set aside.

THE PEOPLE SHALL SHARE IN THE COUNTRY'S WEALTH!

The national wealth of our country, the heritage of all South Africans, shall be restored to the people;

The mineral wealth beneath the soil, the Banks and monopoly industry shall be transferred to the ownership of the people as a whole;

All other industry and trade shall be controlled to assist the well-being of the people;

All people shall have equal rights to trade where they choose, to manufacture and to enter all trades, crafts and professions.

THE LAND SHALL BE SHARED AMONG THOSE WHO WORK IT!

Restrictions of land ownership on a racial basis shall be ended, and all the land redivided amongst those who work it, to banish famine and land hunger;

The state shall help the peasants with implements, seed, tractors and dams to save the soil and assist the tillers;

Freedom of movement shall be guaranteed to all who work on the land;

All shall have the right to occupy land wherever they choose;

People shall not be robbed of their cattle, and forced labour and farm prisons shall be abolished.

ALL SHALL BE EQUAL BEFORE THE LAW!

No one shall be imprisoned, deported or restricted without a fair trial;

No one shall be condemned by the order of any Government official;

The courts shall be representative of all the people;

Imprisonment shall be only for serious crimes against the people, and shall aim at re-education, not vengeance;

The police force and army shall be open to all on an equal basis and shall be the helpers and protectors of the people;

All laws which discriminate on grounds of race, colour or belief shall be repealed.

ALL SHALL ENJOY EQUAL HUMAN RIGHTS!

The law shall guarantee to all their right to speak, to organise, to meet together, to publish, to preach, to worship and to educate their children;

The privacy of the house from police raids shall be protected by law;

All shall be free to travel without restriction from countryside to town, from province to province, and from South Africa abroad;

Pass Laws, permits and all other laws restricting these freedoms shall be abolished.

THERE SHALL BE WORK AND SECURITY!

All who work shall be free to form trade unions, to elect their officers and to make wage agreements with their employers;

The state shall recognise the right and duty of all to work, and to draw full unemployment benefits;

Men and women of all races shall receive equal pay for equal work;

There shall be a forty-hour working week, a national minimum wage, paid annual leave, and sick leave for all workers, and maternity leave on full pay for all working mothers;

Miners, domestic workers, farm workers and civil servants shall have the same rights as all others who work;

Child labour, compound labour, the tot system and contract labour shall be abolished.

THE DOORS OF LEARNING AND OF CULTURE SHALL BE OPENED!

The government shall discover, develop and encourage national talent for the enhancement of our cultural life;

All the cultural treasures of mankind shall be open to all, by free exchange of books, ideas and contact with other lands;

The aim of education shall be to teach the youth to love their people and their culture, to honour human brotherhood, liberty and peace;

Education shall be free, compulsory, universal and equal for all children;

Higher education and technical training shall be opened to all by means of state allowances and scholarships awarded on the basis of merit;

Adult illiteracy shall be ended by a mass state education plan;

Teachers shall have all the rights of other citizens;

The colour bar in cultural life, in sport and in education shall be abolished.

THERE SHALL BE HOUSES, SECURITY AND COMFORT!

All people shall have the right to live where they choose, to be decently housed, and to bring up their families in comfort and security;

Unused housing space to be made available to the people;

Rent and prices shall be lowered, food plentiful and no one shall go hungry;

A preventive health scheme shall be run by the state;

Free medical care and hospitalisation shall be provided for all, with special care for mothers and young children;

Slums shall be demolished, and new suburbs built where all have transport, roads, lighting, playing fields, creches and social centres;

The aged, the orphans, the disabled and the sick shall be cared for by the state;

Rest, leisure and recreation shall be the right of all;

Fenced locations and ghettoes shall be abolished, and laws which break up families shall be repealed.

THERE SHALL BE PEACE AND FRIENDSHIP!

South Africa shall be a fully independent state, which respects the rights and sovereignty of all nations;

South Africa shall strive to maintain world peace and the settlement of all international disputes by negotiation—not war;

Peace and friendship amongst all our people shall be secured by upholding the equal rights, opportunities and status of all;

The people of the protectorates—Basutoland, Bechuanaland and Swaziland shall be free to decide for themselves their own future;

The right of all the peoples of Africa to independence and self-government shall be recognised, and shall be the basis of close co-operation.

Let all who love their people and their country now say, as we say here: "THESE FREEDOMS WE WILL FIGHT FOR, SIDE BY SIDE, THROUGHOUT OUR LIVES, UNTIL WE HAVE WON OUR LIBERTY."

Adopted at the Congress of the People, Kliptown, South Africa, on 26th June, 1955.

INDEXES

SELECTED NAME INDEX

Abrahams, 'Liz', 128, 235, 243, 289, 321, 324, 325, 329, 413, 415
Africa, D., 236
Ainslie, Rosalynde, 258
Akumu, J. D., 458
Albai, M., 245
Alexander (Simons), Ray, 52, 53, 63, 75, 77, 87, 99, 113, 121, 124, 125, 126, 140–1, 142–3, 150, 226, 227, 235, 240, 294, 301, 316–18, 319, 324, 325, 328, 330, 472, 473
Altman, J. R., 143, 144
Altman, Phyllis, 9, 192, 225, 257, 258, 270, 272, 327–9, 331, 371, 372, 382, 383, 384, 386, 401, 406, 412, 415, 420, 429, 438, 439, 443, 472, 483
Andrews, William ('Bill'), 44, 50, 52
Arenstein, Rowley, 250, 415, 419

Baard, Frances, 228, 229, 230, 288, 322–4, 325, 329, 377, 407, 429
Baartman, Ben (Kopie), 236, 238, 285
Balfour, Mabel, 160, 218, 324, 325, 356, 430
Balli, R. S., 246
Bardien, Tofie, 419
Batty, A. F., 40
Becu, M., 382
Beiers, O. T. H., 285–6
Bennie, Alven, 172, 177, 210–12, 228, 231, 232, 258, 265, 272, 282, 337, 369, 414, 417, 429, 434
Bennum, Tollie, 228
Benson, Mary, 330, 369, 437
Berlinson, Mr, 390
Bernstein, Hilda, 26, 27, 330
Berrange, V., 437
Beyleveld, Piet, 85, 96–7, 119, 149, 378, 406

Biko, Steve, 456
Bolton, J. C., 54, 252, 256, 290–1
Botha, P. W., 471
Braverman, E. R. (Ray Alexander), 121, 150
Brown, Irving, 394, 402
Bunting, Brian, 75, 149, 240
Busa, Julius, 236, 239, 285, 407

Caddy, B. J., 86
Calder, J., 82
Calmeyer, Alex, 235
Carlson, Joel, 197
Carneson, Fred, 240
Carron, Mr, 382–3
Cele, Wilson, 64
Centilivres, Ex-Chief Justice, 294
Champion, A. W. G., 41, 42, 43, 44, 45, 53, 55
Cheadle, Halton, 451
Chitja, Sarah, 385
Chiya, O., 209
Cindi, Edmund, 217, 287, 324, 406, 430, 451
Coe, Gus, 228, 235
Cooper, P. T., 64
Cornelius, Johanna, 76, 144, 474
Curran, P. B. H., 237
Cyprian Ka Dinizulu (Zulu Paramount Chief), 351

Dadoo, Yusuf, 333, 334
Damons, Stella, 95, 96, 228, 325, 378, 407
Daniels, Norman, 126, 284
Davies, R., 149
Davis, David, 451
Davoren, Eddie, 430, 432, 436, 439, 443, 483

INDEXES 501

de Jonge, P. H., 382, 383, 386
de Klerk, Minister, 114, 149, 157
Desai, Arvind, 252
Descan, K., 391
Diamond, Mike, 64
Dick, Nancy, 87, 235, 328
Diedrichs, Lily, 229, 231, 429, 433
Dladla, John, 229
Dladla, Queeneth, 256, 312, 314, 315
Dlamini, 192, 257
Dlamini, Stephen, 11–13, 146, 150, 205, 209, 245, 246, 250, 253, 254, 257, 264, 265, 272, 304, 313, 330, 331, 369, 383, 385, 401, 407, 412, 417, 421, 431, 433, 438, 443, 451, 472, 491
Domingo, Enver, 487
Dorner, Dr, 315
Doyle, Alan, 370
Driver, W., 53
du Toit, Bettie, 79, 83, 89, 150, 296, 319, 328, 330

Eaglehoff, Mrs, 236
Ensor, Linda, 99

Feit, Edward, 440, 441
Ferreira, R. S., 289
Fillies, J., 96
First, Ruth, 139, 199, 343
Fletcher, Melville, 227, 285, 352, 414, 417, 429
Flusk, B., 162
Forman, L., and E. S. Sachs, 437
Fourie, Joey, 87
Friedman, L., 226
Froneman, Minister, 136

Gaetsewe, John, 9, 15, 122, 124, 150, 161, 166, 168, 192, 217, 324, 330, 374, 406, 429, 432, 436, 443, 450–1, 455, 457–8, 472, 477, 483–4, 485, 487
Gambu, Zola, 369
Gelb, Arthur, 149
Giles, Ben, 370
Goldberg, D., 285
Gomas, Johnny, 43, 52
Gordon, Max, 51
Gosani, David, 51, 60

Grobbelaar, J. A., 445, 464, 465, 473, 474
Gwala, Esther, 256
Gwala, Harry T., 77, 254, 255, 257, 413, 429, 458

Hannah, Mr, 390
Harmel, Michael, 369
Harry, P. M., 55, 56, 64
Hartwell, Dulcie, 142, 385
Hashe, Viola, 20, 22, 222, 324, 325–7, 383, 384, 401, 406, 429, 432, 443
Hemson, David, 449, 451, 470
Henderson, Don, 471, 486
Hepple, Alex, 59, 76, 89, 126, 135–6, 150, 167, 384, 412
Hepple, Bob, 227, 412
Heynes, Eddie, 414, 429
Hlalukwana, Gilbert, 185
Hlongwana, Johannes, 290–1
Horrell, Muriel, 89, 99
Howa, Hassan, 469
Huna, Bernard, 240, 244, 431
Hutchinson, Alfred, 167, 369
Huyser, Piet, 76

Isaacs, 'Mannie', 246, 431

Jaantjies, David, 319
January, Ben, 96, 121, 236, 237, 239, 241
Jasson, Chrissie, 96, 407
Johns, Sheridan W., III, 88
Joseph, Helen, 302, 469

Kabwe, Mr, 473
Kadalie, Clements, 40, 41, 42, 44, 45, 46, 49, 88
Kahn, Sam, 75, 242
Kalk, Willie, 49
Karis, T., and G. Carter, 368, 369
Kasrils, Ronnie, 252
Kazi, Lydia, 431
Kellerman, Louise, 236, 284
Kennedy, President John, 373, 402
Ketani, Chris, 228
Khaile, Edward, 43
Khanyile, William, 254, 360, 369
Khayinga, Wilson, 20, 177

Khumalo, Jerry, 431
Khunyeli, S., 430, 432
Kika, George, 85
Kitson, David, 483
Klenerman, Fanny, 49
Kotane, Moses, 49, 60, 72, 333
Kukulela, L., 240, 244, 429
Kumalo, Mrs, 257
Kunene, Joel, 254
Kupe, William, 414
Kuzwayo, Mr, 245

La Guma, James (Jimmie), 43, 49, 52
Lambert, R. V., 369, 370, 401
Lan, Becky, 77, 85, 149, 235, 240, 324, 330
Lati, Arnold, 228
Lekoto, M., 429
Lembede, Anton, 333
Lenin, V. I., 273, 295, 296
Lesier, Mildred, 244, 431
Levy, Leon, 85, 91, 96, 99, 120, 123, 143, 146, 174, 192, 202, 214, 217, 222, 226–7, 246, 257, 258, 275, 296, 377, 382, 405, 406, 407, 412, 414, 420, 429, 432
Liebenberg, H., 390, 393
Loots, Harry, 218, 267, 272
Loza, Elijah, 20, 22, 240, 244, 431
Lumumba, Patrice, 375
Lutuli, (Chief) Albert, 332, 349–50, 356, 357–9, 363, 368, 369, 383

Mabhida, Moses, 9, 150, 163, 168, 174, 209, 245, 246, 248, 254, 255, 257, 258, 290, 305–6, 330, 354, 358, 369, 389, 393, 395, 398, 399, 401, 402, 412, 471
Madeley, W. B., 62
Maeka, George, 78, 84, 112
Mafekeng, Elizabeth, 235, 288, 318–22, 325, 326, 331, 372
Mahlangu, Aaron, 96, 167, 223, 406
Mahoko, E., 429
Mahomo, Nana, 395, 402
Majoro, James, 66, 67
Majozi, Fanyana, 255
Makabeni, Gana, 49, 51, 53, 60, 63, 70, 109, 325–6, 379, 384

Makanya, Raymond, 253, 254
Makaringe, Mr, 430
Makheta, Simon, 177, 244
Makiwane, Tennyson, 395
Makuru, Rufus, 217, 287
Malan, Mrs, 312
Maleka, Uriah, 67, 121, 122, 147, 168, 192, 200, 201, 219, 225, 324, 361, 369, 406, 431
Malindi, Zollie, 240, 244, 284, 419, 431
Mamfanya, Mr, 240
Mampies, J., 207, 430
Mampuru, Elijah, 201–3, 258
Mancoko, L., 431
Mandela, Nelson, 333
Manemela, F., 429
Manzi, Gladys, 303–4, 309
Marks, J. B., 63, 66, 67, 70, 71, 75, 77, 82, 181, 191–2, 333, 379
Marney, Cardiff, 126, 431
Marquard, Frank, 235, 317–18
Mase, Mr, 237
Masomela, Morris, 225
Massina, Leslie, 20, 23, 85, 91, 96, 120, 142, 159, 179, 211, 217, 221, 377, 378, 380, 384, 405, 406, 407, 414
Mateman, Don, 91, 120, 122, 146, 412, 420, 428, 430, 451
Mati, A. P., 78, 81, 228
Matomela, Florence, 229
Matthews, Christina, 218, 324, 325, 356
Maxanti, Mzami, 468
Mayekiso, Caleb, 20, 22, 96, 172, 176, 210, 212, 228, 229, 230, 234, 282, 352, 407, 431, 434, 451
Mazwembe, Luke, 458
Mbanjwa, Solomon, 209, 431
Mbatha, Sampson, 368, 370
Mbeki, Govan, 228, 282, 305, 341
Mbele, Elias, 210, 304, 330
Mboya, Tom, 401
McCormick, George, 82
Mdlalose, Zakhele, 458
Mdluli, Joseph, 470
Meer, Fatima, 309
Mei, Pious (P. G.), 95, 96, 245, 407
Mekgoe, D., 429
Mentz, S. D., 112

Menzies, R. G. (Prime Minister, Australia), 373, 374
Meyiwa, Mathews, 458
Mfusi, Mate, 210, 256, 265, 304, 312–15, 330, 331, 398
Mgoma, Amos, 252
Mhlaba, Raymond, 228
Millard, H., 383, 386
Mini, Vuyisile, 20, 22, 177–8, 210–12, 228, 232–3, 234, 282, 293, 417, 431, 434
Mkaba, Zinakile, 20, 177
Mkize, Florence, 303
Mkize, Louis, 171, 210, 253–4
Mkwanazi, Johannes, 245, 246, 257
Mkwanazi, Marie, 219
Mkwayi, Wilton, 85, 182, 184, 228, 229, 230, 231, 234, 395, 399, 401, 407, 412, 471
Mlamla, Mr, 237
Mnyandu, Doris, 312, 314, 315
Modise, Johannes, 256
Mofutsanyana, Edwin, 66
Mokanya, Raymond, 253–4
Molefe, J., 430, 432
Molewa, Bennett, 369
Monare, George, 146, 185, 192, 222, 331, 369, 430
Monare, Miriam, 219
Moodley, Mary, 20, 23, 324–5, 429
Moonsamy, Kesval, 245–6, 407
Moosa, Rahima, 302
Moretsele, E. P., 438
Morodi, Graham, 181, 192, 200, 212, 213, 214, 222, 257, 258, 369, 430, 432
Moroka, Dr, 334
Morolong, Joe, 20–1, 23, 244
Mosata, Aaron, 208, 429
Mosiane, J., 240
Mosupyi, John, 225
Motsabi, John, 67, 78, 88
Motsoaledi, Elias, 78
Moumakoe, Isaac, 78, 87
Mpetha, Oscar, 85, 121, 122, 235, 240, 241, 319
Mphahlele, Aaron, 85, 91
Mphemba, J., 240
Mpoza, S., 236

Msimang, Selby, 40, 41
Mtalane, Ignatia, 257
Mtambo, S., 256
Mtolo, Bruno, 252–3, 440
Mtshali, Eric, 99, 205, 210, 245, 255–6, 413
Muller, Mike, 78
Muller, Shulamith, 326
Murray, T. P., 148
Mvubelo, Lucy, 96, 125, 126, 142, 178, 219, 326, 378, 380–1, 385, 401, 402, 462, 464, 474, 488
Mvubelo, McKenzie, 178, 401

Naicker, M. P., 57, 64, 199, 204, 246, 354, 407
Naidoo, H. A., 54, 55, 56, 57, 64, 204
Naidoo, Shanti, 214, 412, 430, 438
Nair, Billy, 96, 184, 208, 227, 245, 246, 247, 256, 290, 308, 313, 338, 354, 407, 412, 417, 419, 431, 433
Nangu, Don, 210, 212, 228
Ndabezitha, J., 431
Ndamoyi, Joe, 85, 236, 285
Ndavemavota, Brown, 192–3
Ndebele, Azaria, 458
Ndhlovu, Cleopas, 458
Ndlovu, Curnick, 174, 176, 245, 247, 256–7, 313, 385, 430, 432
Nduli, Joseph, 458
Ndzanga, Lawrence, 21, 23, 172–3, 174, 176, 257, 327, 429, 458, 486
Ndzanga, Rita (More), 21, 160, 172, 327, 412, 430
Ndziba, Mr, 240
Nene, John, 458
Ngcobo, Dora, 257
Ngedlane, J., 52
Ngotyana, Greenwood, 172, 238, 244
Ngoyi, Lilian, 302
Ngqunge, G., 430, 432
Ngudle, 'Looksmart', 21, 23, 240, 244, 432
Ngulube, J., 177
Ngwenya, Mr, 254
Ngyungwana, Mountain, 434
Nkadimeng, John, 96, 182, 200, 222, 226, 378, 406, 431, and cover photo

Nkobi, Thomas, 360
Nkosi, B., 431
Nkosi, Johannes, 49, 53–4, 277
Nkosi, Lawrence, 438
Nkrumah, Kwame, 393
Nqose, Z., 244
Ntlatlane, Tibe, 225
Ntuli, C., 430
Ntunja, Sampson, 228, 429, 434
Nyaose, Jacob, 84, 384–5, 397, 398
Nyembe, Dorothy, 303, 309

O'Brien, Mr, 419
O'Brien, Sir Thomas, 382
October, H., 53
O'Donoghue, Mr, 147
Olsson, O. A., 96, 99
O'Meara, Dan, 88–9
Oppenheimer, Harry, 193–4

Parker, John, 178, 257
Pemba, Aaron, 472
Phillips, James, 60, 61, 70, 71, 76, 369, 379, 483–4
Pillay, M., 245
Pillay, R. G., 257
Pillay, R. R., 64
Pillay, V. S. M., 96, 245, 407
Plaatjes, Sol, 89
Ponnen, George, 54, 55, 56, 57, 64, 78, 89, 204, 210, 258, 487
Ponnen, Vera, 78, 309
Porto, V. (Paramount Chief of Pondoland), 69
Press, Ronnie, 168, 214, 220, 246, 258, 406, 407–8
Purvis, Jack, 395

Qgabi, Joe, 224
Qumbela, M., 431

Rademeyer, Major-General, 351
Rammitloa, Marks, 169, 225, 429, 444
Ramothebe, Joel, 155
Ramsdale, Edward, 365, 370, 438, 481
Ramsunder, L., 64
Rapolai, Gabriel, 224–5, 258
Reddy, S. V., 246
Redebe, Gaur, 66

Resha, Robert, 344
Ross, W. H., 96
Rotberg, R. I., and A. A. Mazrui, 88
Roux, Eddie, 54, 88
Rumpff, Justice, 405
Rupert, Anton, 342
Rutherford, T. C., 141, 142

Sachs, E. S. ('Solly'), 49, 50, 52, 58, 75, 76, 88, 113, 326
Sauer, Paul, 438
Scheepers, L. C., 144, 148
Schlacter, Rose, 430
Schoeman, B. J., 103, 108, 110, 282, 318, 379
Scott, Reverend Michael, 343
Segwale, Mr, 192
Sejake, Nimrod, 181–2, 184, 406, and cover photo
Selby, Arnold, 79, 87, 379, 399, 451
Seloro, L., 430, 432
September, Reg, 240
Shabane, Mr, 253
Shangase, Mr, 254
Shanley, Errol, 54, 56, 64, 204
Shope, Mark, 38, 95, 96, 145, 148, 211, 217, 221, 257, 373, 397, 398, 406, 412, 420, 429, 447, 472, 473, 479
Shuba, J., 52
Sibande, Cleopas, 85, 91, 96, 227, 378, 406
Sibande, Gert, 197–8, 200, 202, 343
Sibeko, Archie, 120, 171–2, 174, 182–3, 234, 236, 237, 238, 240, 241, 242, 243–4, 257, 258, 336, 369, 407, 411–12, 419, 433
Sibeko, Letty, 431
Sibisi, E., 430
Simelane, P. J., 192
Simons, H. J. (Jack), 125, 140–1, 150
Simons, H. J., and R. E. Simons, 44, 88–9
Sisulu, Walter, 333, 347, 357, 369
Slovo, Joe, 36, 38, 218, 294
Smuts, Prime Minister, 69
Sobukwe, Robert, 398
Somana, Brian, 224
Stadler, Mr, 245
Steenkamp, Professor, 165, 444

Stein, M., 89
Strydom, Johannes, 297, 302
Stuart, Bob, 44, 48
Stuart, James, 487
Swart, Minister of Justice, 317, 318
Syvret, Vic, 180–2, 401

Takalo, Richard, 185, 187, 192, 429
Tambo, Oliver, 332, 333
Tandau, Mr, 473
Taylor, M., 245
Telling, Dolores, 228–9, 232, 325
Temba, Paulos, 210–11, 228, 230, 258
Tettagah, John, 395, 397
Thambiran, D., 430
Thompson, D., and R. Larson, 401
Tinto, Christmas, 244, 430, 432
Tlili, Ahmed, 397
Tloome, Dan, 60, 79, 81, 98, 355, 369, 379
Tobias, Frances, 230
Tobias, Stephen, 228, 232, 258, 430
Topley, I., 96
Trollip, Senator, 393
Tsele, John, 220, 356, 430, 432
Tsele, Philemon, 174
Tshabangu, Mr, 430
Tshume, Gladstone, 79, 81, 228, 331
Turok, Ben, 174, 182–4, 237, 241, 242, 407
Turok, Mary, 183, 430

Uys, S., 369

Vakalisa, Memory, 205, 209, 249, 250, 251, 252, 257, 258, 313, 413, 433
Van den Berg, L. J., 82
Verwoerd, Dr H. F., 130, 134, 279, 289, 321, 347, 369, 374
Viljoen, M. M., 167
Vogel, Piet, 429
Vorster, J., 416, 471, 478

Walker, Ivan, 88
Walton, 'Liz', 230
Wanless, A. T. (Alec), 54, 246
Weinberg, Eli, 9, 52, 79–80, 81, 83, 87, 89, 99, 120, 121, 192, 226, 437, 472
Weinbren, Ben, 49, 50, 88
Welcher, L., 149
Wentzel, Sarah, 235
Williams, Maria, 319
Williams, Sophie, 228, 231, 302, 323
Wolfson, 'Issy', 75, 401
Wolpe, Harold, 117, 149

Xaba, Anthony, 254, 458
Xuma, Dr A. B., 69

Zembe, Zola, 487–8
Zimba, Mr, 473
Zondi, A., 430

INDEX OF TRADE UNIONS AND ORGANIZATIONS

African Bakers and Confectioners Union, 84
African Bakers Industrial Union, 385
African Building Workers Union, 67, 78, 223
African Chemical Workers Union (Durban), 86, 172, 253–4
African Clothing Workers Union, 49, 50, 51
African Clothing Workers Union (Hammarsdale, Natal), 249, 290–1
African Coal and Cement Workers Union, 430
African Commercial and Distributive Workers Union:
  Cape Town, 20, 21, 431, 432
  Port Elizabeth, 78, 232
African Federation of Trade Unions, 31, 50
African Food and Canning Workers Union (A-FCWU), 31, 84, 86, 99, 217, 235, 284, 288, 316, 319, 320–1, 346, 372, 401, 406, 431
  Cape Western Province, 121, 234, 235, 283, 317, 386, 468–9
  Port Elizabeth, 228–9, 288–9, 329, 335
  Transvaal, 324, 430
African Furniture, Mattress and Bedding Workers Union (A-FMBWU), 31, 78, 121, 147, 219, 430, 431, 432
African Garment Workers Union, 52
African Gas and Power Workers Union, 67
African Iron, Steel and Metal Workers Union (Port Elizabeth), 182, 232
African Laundry, Cleaning and Dyeing Workers Union (A-LCDWU), 20, 91, 95, 99, 122, 216, 217, 401, 406, 412, 429, 430
  Cape Town, 235
  Transvaal, 220, 430
African Laundry Workers Union, 49, 50, 51, 78

African Milling Workers Union (Tvl), 87, 167, 223, 278
  Natal, 245, 256
African Mine Workers Union (AMWU), 28, 31, 63, 66–70, 71, 75, 77, 89, 107, 108, 191–2, 332, 441
African Mine Workers Strike (1946), 28, 63, 65–73, 80, 107, 109, 189, 191, 263, 273, 453
African Motor Industry Workers Union, 179–80
African Municipal Workers Union:
  Cape Town, 431
  Durban, 165, 249–52
African National Congress (ANC) of South Africa, 20, 28–9, 31, 37, 60, 65–6, 69, 70, 72, 77, 78, 79, 89, 97–8, 130, 152, 155, 163, 167, 177, 192, 197, 198, 200, 202, 203, 211, 217, 218, 228, 230, 232, 233, 240, 242, 255, 285, 293–4, 303, 304, 305, 306, 308, 315, 317, 320, 322, 326, 330, 332–5, 339–41, 343–4, 345, 352, 354–7, 358, 360, 363, 365, 368, 369, 377, 390, 395, 397, 404, 405, 406, 410, 412, 413, 416, 420–1, 424, 426, 433, 456, 476, 487, 494
  Programme of Action (1949), 333, 339
  Umkhonto We Sizwe (MK)/The Spear of the Nation, 420, 421, 424
  Women's League, 301–2, 321, 322
  Youth League, 72, 252, 333, 339–40
African Painting and Building Workers Union (Port Elizabeth), 232–3, 430
African Peoples Organization, 334
African Publisher, Newspaper and Distributor Workers Union, 223
African Tea and Coffee Workers Union (Durban), 249
African Textile Workers Industrial Union (A-TWIU), 31, 79, 86, 91, 96, 99, 123, 217, 236, 245, 284, 378, 379, 401, 407, 451

INDEXES 507

African Textile Workers Industrial Union
   (A-TWIU)—*cont.*
   Cape Town, 234–5, 236
   Durban, 245, 246, 285–6, 431
   Port Elizabeth, 229–30, 331, 451
   Transvaal, 286–8
African Tobacco Workers Union, 95,
   213
   Natal, 245
Amalgamated Building Workers Union
   (Port Elizabeth), 232
Amalgamated Engineering Union, 181
Amalgamated Union of Building Trade
   Workers of South Africa, 76
Amalgamated Workers Union (Cape
   Town), 235, 244, 431
Anti-Fascist League, 54
Associated Chambers of Commerce
   (ASSCOM), 164, 307

Bag Workers Union (Cape Town), 235,
   242
Baking Workers Union (Durban), 249
Bantu Womens League (1918), 301
Bay Transport Workers Union (PE), 232,
   292, 294
Biscuit Workers Union (Durban), 249
Black Consciousness Movement, 456
Blanke Tekstielwerkers Nywerheidsunie
   van Suid Afrika, 150
Blankewerkersbeskermingsbond, die
   (The White Workers Protection
   Society), 58, 149
Brick, Quarry and Cement Workers
   Union (Cape Town), 244, 431

Cape Federation of Labour Unions, 48,
   52
Cape Town Stevedoring and
   Dockworkers Union, 177, 236
Cement, Quarry and Lime Workers
   Union (Pietermaritzburg), 255
Chemical and Allied Workers Union
   (Natal), 245, 431
Chemical Workers Union, 86, 326
'Christian-Nationalist' Trade Unionism,
   47, 52–3, 57–9, 75
Christian Institute, 456
Commercial Workers Union, 52, 316–17

Committee of United Metal Workers
   Unions, 184
Communist Party of South Africa
   (CPSA), 31, 42, 43, 48, 49, 50, 51,
   53, 54, 60, 64, 65, 66, 70, 72, 73, 75,
   77, 79, 90, 107, 236, 334, 355–6,
   377, 426
Congress Alliance, 31, 37, 57, 72, 98,
   101, 102, 126, 128, 130, 148, 193,
   197, 208, 210, 211, 214, 216, 218,
   226, 227, 228, 230, 236, 240, 250,
   253, 257, 259, 279, 284, 289, 317,
   325, 332–70, 374, 375, 381, 383,
   384, 385, 397, 400, 404, 405, 408,
   411, 417, 420–1, 424, 425, 438,
   441–2, 446, 457
   Industrial Areas Committees, 360–2
   National Action Council, of (1955), 337
   National Consultative Committee, of,
      32, 338–9, 347, 360–1, 365, 370
   National Convention, 361, 362, 364
Congress of the People (1955), 28, 31,
   98, 211, 232, 335–9, 405, 437
   Freedom Charter, 98, 322, 330, 333,
      335, 336, 337–9, 405, 408, 410,
      490, 494, 499
Coordinating Committee of African
   Trade Unions, 51
Coordinating Council of South African
   Trade Unions (CCSATU), 31,
   82–4, 389
Council of African Trade Unions, 63
Council of Non-European Trade Unions
   (Transvaal) (CNETU), 28, 31, 52,
   59–65, 66, 67, 69, 70, 71, 76, 77, 78,
   79, 82–4, 87–8, 90, 91, 96, 100,
   109, 110, 111, 112, 179, 332, 334,
   377, 379, 380, 384, 388, 441

Die Afrikanerbond van Mynwerkers, 58
Distributive and Allied Workers Union
   (Pietermaritzburg), 255
Domestic Workers Union:
   Kimberley, 419
   Natal, 245
   Transvaal, 223, 224–5, 430
Durban Indian Municipal Employees
   Society (DIMES), 249

Durban Rubber Industrial Union, 245

Engine Drivers and Firemens Union, 82

Farm, Plantation and Allied Workers Union (FPAWU), 31, 165, 197, 201–5, 223

Federal Consultative Committee of Railway Unions, 84

Federation of Free African Trade Unions of South Africa (FOFATUSA), 28, 31, 124, 126, 140, 142, 150, 213, 222, 326, 381–8, 390, 394, 395, 397, 398, 401, 428, 442, 463, 465

Federation of South African Trade Unions (FOSATU), 462–4

Federation of South African Women (FSAW), 31, 301–2, 306, 309, 320–1, 323, 324, 330, 438, 469

Food and Canning Workers Union (FCWU), 31, 63, 77, 84, 86, 87, 99, 114, 119, 122–3, 124, 125, 128, 165, 203, 215, 235, 284, 289, 291, 309, 316, 318, 320–1, 324, 329, 330, 346, 401
  Natal, 246
  Port Elizabeth, 228–9, 322–3, 325, 335, 352, 377, 378, 429, 433
  Transvaal, 20, 217, 218, 220, 267, 324, 429
  Western Cape Province, 234, 235–6, 243, 244, 283, 317, 413, 433, 468–9

Food, Canning and Allied Workers Union, 86

Garage and Motor Industry Workers Union (Cape Town), 244, 419, 431

Garment Workers Union (Transvaal), 31, 52, 58, 76, 113, 117, 149, 162, 201, 326, 385
  Natal, 252, 290, 417

Garment Workers Union of African Women (GWU-AW), 31, 96, 125, 126, 150, 178, 219, 222, 326, 378, 385

General Workers Union, 170, 205–14
  Durban, 206–10, 249, 256
  Kimberley, 193, 206, 207, 208, 210–11, 429, 430, 433
  Ladysmith, 210, 256
  Orange Free State, 214
  Pietermaritzburg, 255
  Pinetown, 209–10
  Port Elizabeth, 207, 208, 210–12, 232, 429, 431
  Transvaal (Wits), 206–7, 212–14, 223, 430, 432
  Western Cape Province, 207, 212, 244

'Grey Shirts' Fascists, 54

Hairdresser Employees Union (Cape Town), 87

Hospital Workers Union:
  Cape Town, 244, 429
  Durban, 249, 312, 313–14, 315

Howick Rubber Workers Union (Natal), 245, 367

Indian Passive Resistance Council, 70

Industrial and Commercial Workers Union (ICWU), 41

Industrial and Commercial Workers Union of Africa (ICU), 28, 31, 39–46, 47, 49, 51, 53, 55, 88, 205–6

Iron and Steel Workers Union (Natal), 55

Jewellers and Goldsmiths (Jhb), 86

Johannesburg Council of Unemployed Workers, 262, 265

Joint Committee for African Trade Unions, 51

Laundry, Cleaning and Dyeing Workers Union, 150, 215

Laundry Workers Union (Pietermaritzburg), 255

Match Workers Union (Durban), 165, 294–5

Metal and Allied Workers Union (MAWU), 450, 457, 481

Metal Workers Union, 32, 184–6
  Cape Town, 182–3, 187, 235, 407
  Natal, 187, 249
  Port Elizabeth, 431
  Transvaal, 187, 429, 433

INDEXES 509

Mineral Water Workers Union (PE), 232
Motor Industry Employers Association, 108
Municipal Workers Union (PE), 232
Musgrave Ratepayers Association (Natal), 252

National African Federated Chamber of Commerce, 469
Natal Aluminium Workers Union, 245, 246, 407
Natal Box, Broom and Brush Workers Union, 245, 246
Natal Dairy Workers Union, 245–6, 407
Natal Indian Congress (NIC), 32, 55, 57, 132, 246, 250, 309, 438
Natal Indian Youth Council, 252
Natal Rural Areas Committee, 308, 421
Natal Sugar Field Workers Union, 64
Natal Sugar Industry Employees Union (NSIEU), 32, 63–4
National Baking Industrial Union, 86
National Union of Clothing Workers (NUCW), 32, 150, 222, 462, 464
National Union of Commercial Travellers (NUCT), 32, 80, 87
National Union of Distributive Workers (NUDW), 32, 86, 123, 143, 161, 225, 317, 417, 428, 438
National Union of Laundry, Cleaning and Dyeing Workers Union (NULCDW), 91, 95, 99, 119, 121, 150, 216, 218, 401, 429, 430, 432 Cape Town, 234, 236
National Union of Metal Workers, 187
National Union of Railway and Harbour Servants, 58
Native Mine Clerks Association, 45, 67
Native Representative Council, 70, 340
Non-European Metal Workers Joint Committee, 179–80, 182, 184
Non-European United Front, 57

Pan-Africanist Congress (PAC), 28, 32, 167, 363, 384, 385, 388, 395, 398, 410–11, 424, 456
Pietermaritzburg All-In Conference, 416
Poqo, 424

Port Elizabeth Stevedoring and Dockworkers Union, 177, 232
Printing Workers Factory Committee, 165
Printing Workers Union (Transvaal), 223, 430

Rubber and Cable Workers Union (Pietermaritzburg), 255
Rural and Industrial Workers Conference, 204

Sebatakgomo, 202
Sheet Metal Workers Union, 187
Shop and Office Workers Union (SOWU) (Transvaal), 32, 223, 225, 429, 430, 432, 444
South African Canvas and Rope Workers Union (Cape Town), 86, 235, 236, 243
South African Clothing Workers Union (SACWU), 20, 32, 150, 219, 221–2, 325–6, 331, 377, 383, 430
South African Coloured Peoples Congress (SACPC/SACPO/CPC), 32, 37, 98, 227, 229, 284, 324, 335, 419, 420, 438
South African Confederation of Labour (SACOL), 32, 143
South African Congress of Democrats (SACOD), 32, 37, 64–5, 98, 250, 252, 284, 309, 335, 340, 404, 412, 417, 420, 425
South African Congress of Trade Unions (SACTU):
    Ban on meetings (April–June, 1961), 392, 414–20
    Conferences:
        (1956), 97, 119, 149, 227–8, 230, 232, 234, 237, 254, 258, 306–7, 332, 369, 370, 378, 405
        (1957), 121, 168
    Special Conference (1957), 123, 142
    National Workers Conference (1957), 158, 159
        (1958), 143, 288, 307, 342
    National Workers Conference:
        (1958), 168, 207, 237, 240, 349–50, 369

South African Congress of Trade Unions (SACTU)—*cont.*
(1959), 163, 200, 201, 211, 249, 307, 309, 327, 331, 332, 356, 357–8, 383, 416
(1960), 126, 168, 205, 210, 233, 258, 261, 308, 327, 331, 372, 374, 385, 394, 413–14, 438
(1961), 254, 370, 414–16
(1962), 145, 148, 150, 167–8, 201, 203, 206, 271, 362, 375–6, 392, 399
(1963), 128–9, 166, 214, 235, 346, 433
(1964), 168, 187, 429, 436–7, 439, 443, 470
External Mission, 444, 445, 447, 476
Formation and Inaugural Conference, 25, 37, 80, 88, 90–9, 177, 215, 236, 245, 326, 335, 378, 405, 437, 497–8
Local Committees:
  Cape Western Province (Cape Town), 20, 31, 126, 149, 165, 181, 206, 212, 215, 234–44, 271, 336, 378, 399, 400, 411
  Durban (Natal), 165, 174, 193, 204–5, 208–10, 215, 244–57, 264–5, 271, 280, 295, 308, 312, 313, 355, 378, 383, 399, 411, 412, 414–25, 433
  East Rand (Benoni), 226
  Kimberley, 193, 271
  Ladysmith, 254, 256
  Paarl, 235
  Pietermaritzburg, 77, 254–5
  Pinetown, 254, 255–6
  Port Elizabeth, 20, 165, 177, 181, 182, 203, 206, 211, 215, 227–34, 271, 282, 293, 323, 337, 355, 378, 399, 411, 434
  Pretoria, 226, 411
  West Rand, 226
  Witwatersrand, 165, 203, 206, 212, 215–27, 265, 270, 324, 378, 399, 411, 413, 433
  Worcester, 236
National Organizing Committees (NOCs), 32, 170, 214, 361–2, 419

Agriculture, 170, 194–205
Metals, 170, 179–87
Mines, 170, 187–94
Transport, 170–9, 186, 207
£1-a-Day (R2-a-Day) Campaign, 28, 111, 128, 155, 158–68, 175, 185, 192, 194, 195, 201, 209, 213, 219, 222, 224, 229, 232, 237, 246, 250, 264, 265, 271, 279–80, 283, 293, 328, 350, 355, 356, 358, 362, 377, 399, 400, 412, 413, 434, 443, 447
Principles and Policy, 37, 91, 94–5, 97, 101, 383, 441, 463, 466–7, 494, 497–8
Workers Unity, 64, 77, 121, 123, 124, 142, 167, 172, 184–5, 194, 226–7, 243, 257, 258, 261, 265, 268, 272, 330, 331, 357, 367, 368–70, 372, 374, 375, 377, 394, 399, 427, 435, 438, 452, 454, 455, 470, 491
South African Council of Sport (SACOS), 469
South African Diamond Workers Union, 194
South African Federation of Non-European Trade Unions (SAFNETU), 49–50
South African Federation of Trade Unions (SAFTU), 32, 83–4, 389
South African Glass Workers Union, 223
South African Indian Congress (SAIC), 32, 37, 98, 334, 335, 340, 412, 420, 438
South African Institute of Race Relations (SAIRR), 33, 51, 66, 109, 116, 150, 266–7, 268
South African Labour Party, 43, 54, 126, 412
South African Liberal Party, 252, 385, 386, 401, 417
South African (White) Mine Workers Union (SAMWU), 58, 65, 104
  White Mine Workers Strike (Rand Revolt) (1922), 72, 104–5
South African Native National Congress, 41
South African Peace Council, 438

INDEXES

South African Railway and Harbour
  Administration, 170–2, 174, 175
South African Railway and Harbour
  Workers Union (SAR & HWU), 32,
  53, 78, 170, 172, 175, 407, 419
  Cape Town, 120, 172, 174, 235, 244,
    430, 432
  Durban, 172, 174, 176, 249, 385, 430,
    432
  Port Elizabeth, 20, 172, 176, 232
  Transvaal, 21, 172, 173, 174, 327, 429
South African Tin Workers Union
  (Natal) (SATWU), 245, 407, 430
South African Tin Workers Union (Cape
  Town), 235
South African Trade Union Congress
  (SATUC), 1926, 43, 44, 48
South African Trade Union Council
  (SATUC) 1954 Trade Union
  Council of South Africa (TUCSA)
  (1962), 33, 86, 91, 103, 111, 118,
  119, 121, 123, 124, 125, 126,
  140–8, 150, 165, 187, 213, 219,
  221–2, 243, 265, 307, 326, 381,
  382, 383, 384, 385, 386, 388, 389,
  390, 391, 401, 423–4, 428, 440–2,
  444–5, 446, 463–5, 473, 479
South African Trades and Labour
  Council (SAT & LC), 28, 33, 48, 59,
  60, 61, 75–6, 77, 79, 80, 90, 92, 94,
  95, 109, 122, 140, 144, 179, 236,
  317, 328, 376, 381, 464
  1954 Dissolution, events leading to,
    80–8
  'Unity Committee', 82–4, 86
Springbok Legion, 327
Spoorbond, 53, 58, 59

Taxi Drivers and Owners Association,
  419
Tea and Coffee Workers Union (Durban),
  249
Textile Workers Industrial Union
  (TWIU), 33, 78, 86, 87, 91, 96, 99,
  120, 122, 123, 124, 125, 146, 165,
  168, 210, 211, 215, 284, 291, 328,
  401, 406–7, 408, 412, 428, 449, 451
  Cape Town, 234, 235, 236

Natal, 246, 429, 431
Port Elizabeth, 229–30, 323, 429
Transvaal, 220, 430
Timber Workers Union (Cape Town),
  242
Tin Workers Union (Durban), 165
Tobacco Workers Factory Committee
  (Transvaal), 165, 212–13
Tobacco Workers Union (Durban), 78,
  274
Toy and Plastic Workers Union (Toy
  Workers Union), 187, 223, 327,
  430, 432
Trade Union Coordinating Committee
  (TUCC), 91–2, 94
Transport Workers Union:
  Port Elizabeth, 165
  Transvaal, 178–9, 223
Transvaal Agricultural Union, 200–1
Transvaal Brewery and Distillery
  Workers Union, 223
Transvaal Broom and Brush Workers
  Union, 223
Transvaal Dairy Workers Union, 223,
  326
Transvaal Hospital Workers Union, 223
Transvaal Indian Congress, 203, 377,
  438
Transvaal Indian Youth Congress, 374
Transvaal Iron, Steel and Metal Workers
  Union (Tvl. IS & MWU), 33, 179,
  181–2, 406
Transvaal Municipal Workers Union
  (City and Town Council Workers
  Union), 223, 224
Twine and Bag Workers Union (Durban),
  86, 165, 249

Unemployed Workers Union (Durban),
  264
United May Day Committee, 376
United Party, 349, 351, 355

Western Cape Traders Association, 469
Western Province Federation of Trade
  Unions, 84
Workers and Peasants Conferences
  (Natal), 308–9, 365, 421
Workers Councils of Action, 84, 85

INDEX OF APARTHEID LEGISLATION AND ADMINISTRATION

Apprenticeship Act, 1922 (and, as amended, 1944), 116, 149

Bantu Affairs Commission, 136
Bantu Labour Relations Regulation Act, No. 70 (1973), 450–1
Bantu (Native) Laws Amendment Act, 31
  (1937), 129
  (1952), 110, 129–32
  (1957), 129–30
  (1963), 130–2, 150, 436
Border Industries (Border Industrial Areas), 103, 133–6, 256, 366
  Proclamation No. 74 (1968), 136
  Permanent Committee for Location of Industry (Decentralization Board, 1971), 134
Broederbond (Brotherhood), 57–8, 342
Bureau of State Security/Department of National Security, 455

Cape Provincial Council, 174, 237
Colour Bar, 50, 244, 434, 438
Criminal Procedure Act, 1955 (and, as amended), 421, 427

Department of Bantu Affairs (Administration) and Development, 131, 150, 213, 260, 261, 263, 281, 287, 301, 321, 340, 363, 369

Extraordinary Proclamation No. 408 (1962), 425, 426

Factories, Machinery and Building Works Act, 1941 (and, as amended, 1960), 64
Fagan Commission (1948), 66
Federal Consultative Council of South African Railways and Harbours Staff Associations, 389
Federasie van Afrikaanse Kultuurverenigings (Federation of Afrikaans Cultural Society) (FAK), 58

General Law Amendment Acts:
  No. 39 (1961), 438
  No. 76 (1962)/Sabotage Act, 29, 131, 147, 392, 400, 421–7, 428, 433, 435
    'Sabotage' defined, 422
  No. 37 (1963), 421, 427, 428–32, 434, 435
  No. 96 (1965), 421, 427
Group Areas Act (1950), 73, 126, 212, 213, 229, 300, 347, 350

Immorality Act (1950), 73
Industrial Conciliation Act (1924), 28, 55, 61, 75, 88, 104–6, 108, 118, 127, 219, 310, 460
Industrial Conciliation Act (1956), 28, 92, 104, 109, 112–26, 140–1, 143, 147, 149–50, 212, 227, 237, 265, 326, 391, 424, 437, 464
  SACTU opposition to, 118–26
  1959 Amendment, 128
Industrial Conciliation (Natives) Bill/Smuts' Bill (1947), 107, 108
Industrial Legislation Commission of Enquiry, 103, 108–9
Influx Control measures, 26, 66, 110, 129–32, 287, 411, 436, 459
Inter-Departmental Committee of Inquiry into Riots on the Mines (1975), 454–5, 465
Internal Security Amendment Act (1976), 73
Iron and Steel Corporation of South Africa (ISCOR), 32, 184–6

Job Reservation (Industrial Conciliation Act, 1956), 114–18, 121, 124–6, 131, 133, 136, 141, 143, 149, 224, 244, 265, 350, 377, 392, 434, 459, 460, 464

INDEXES

Job Reservation – *cont.*
  1959 Amendment, 118
  All-In Conference (1962), 126, 147, 428

Liquor Amendment Act, No. 72 (1961), 346

Masters and Servants Acts, 63, 146, 149, 195
Mines and Works Act, 1911 (and, as amended, 1926), 116, 138, 149, 460
Motor Carrier Transportation Act, 1930 (and, as amended, 1955, 1959 and 1976), 155

Nationalist Party and Government, 28, 37, 43, 57, 58, 59, 70, 72, 73, 82, 83, 100, 103, 104, 107–9, 111, 112, 114, 116, 119, 121, 122, 125, 126, 128, 132, 134, 136, 140, 141, 142, 189, 227, 229, 237, 262–4, 265, 321, 333, 340, 348, 350, 351, 355, 364, 374, 376, 379, 408, 426, 438
Native Building Workers Act (1951), 116–17, 460
Native Labour Regulation Acts, 70
  No. 15 (1911), 149
Native Labour (Settlement of Disputes) Act (1953), 28, 32, 84, 104, 107, 108, 109–12, 113, 122, 123, 130, 146, 149, 179–80, 217, 218, 228, 243, 250, 252, 273–4, 275, 277, 283, 284, 287, 290, 295, 384, 391, 423, 451, 462, 470
  Bantu Labour Officers/Committees, 110–11, 131–2
  Central Native Labour Board, 31, 110, 112, 288
  SACTU opposition to, 111–12
  Works Committees, 110, 112, 149, 275, 451
Native Services Levy Act, 155
Non-European Affairs Department, 112, 154

Pass Laws, 26, 41, 276, 298–9, 304, 310, 323, 326, 327, 331, 403, 410, 459

Pneumoconiosis Act (1956), 260
Prisons Act, 1959 (and, as amended, 1965), 466
Prohibition of Mixed Marriages Act (1949), 73
Public Safety Act, 421
Public Utility Transport Corporation (PUTCO), 32, 151–5, 178, 366, 449
  strike (1972), 449
Publications and Entertainment Act (1963), 424

Railways and Harbours Amendment Act (1949), 73
Reddingsdaadbond (an Afrikaner financial society), 58
Riekert Commission, 459–62
Riotous Assemblies Act, 70, 333, 407, 434, 449
Robben Island prison, 77, 257, 294

South African Broadcasting Corporation (SABC), 354, 435
South African Bureau of Census and Statistics, 156
South African (Union) Defence Force, 351–2, 448, 481
South West Africa Native Labour Association (SWANLA), 448
Suppression of Communism Act (1950), 28, 33, 59, 73–80, 81, 83, 88, 109, 273, 323, 333, 377, 379, 407, 416, 419, 421, 424, 425, 426, 427
  1954 Amendment, 74–5

Terrorism Act (1967), 21, 327
Tomlinson Commission (1956), 134

Unemployment Insurance Act (1949), 73
  (1937), 263
Unlawful Organizations Act (1960), 28, 131, 410, 421
Urban Areas Act (1950), 84
  (1945), 131, 266, 268, 326, 461, 466

Wage Act, 1918 (and, as amended, 1924, 1925, 1937 and 1957), 127, 128

Wage Boards, 51, 60, 62, 63, 68, 69, 127–9, 157, 165, 166, 201, 222–3, 228–9, 280, 288, 326, 348, 444
War Measures Acts, 109
  No. 145 (1942), 62, 107
  No. 9 (1942), 107
  No. 1425 (1944), 69, 107
Wiehahn Commission, 453, 459–62
Witwatersrand Mine Natives' Wage Commission (Lansdowne Commission), 66–70
Witwatersrand Native Labour Association, 190, 192
Workmens Compensation, 17, 176, 259–62, 265, 443
  1941 Act, 260, 261

INDEX OF INTERNATIONAL ORGANIZATIONS AND SOLIDARITY ACTIONS

African-American Labour Centre, 31, 394
Afro-Arab Trade Union Conference (Algiers, 1977), 477
Afro-Asian Solidarity Conferences, 374–5
All-African Peoples Conferences (1958/1960), 345, 374–5, 393
All-African Trade Union Federation (AATUF), 28, 31, 393–8, 477
All-China Federation of Trade Unions, 399
All-India Trade Union Congress, 399
American Federation of Labour-Congress of Industrial Organizations (AFL-CIO), 31, 394, 402
CIO, 379
Anti-Apartheid Movement (UK), 479

Basutoland Congress Party, 322

Central Intelligence Agency (CIA), 394
'Codes of Conduct', 493–4

FRELIMO (Mozambique), 376

Indian Congress, India, 412
International Conference of the Food, Tobacco, Hotel, Café and Restaurant Workers (1955), 320
International Metal Workers Federation, 32, 382, 480
International Miners Conference (1955), 380
International Confederation of Free Trade Unions (ICFTU), 32, 144, 145, 282, 315, 371, 379, 380, 381–8, 394, 395, 396, 397, 398, 401, 402, 410, 435, 440, 463, 473, 474, 476, 489, 492
Week of Action Against Apartheid (1977), 488

International Labour Organization (ILO), 29, 32, 44, 144, 175, 194, 200, 326–7, 388–93, 401, 428, 443, 455, 470, 473, 474, 476, 484, 489
(1959), 389, 391, 392
(1960), 390, 391, 392
African Regional Conference (1960), 391
(1961), 391, 392
(1962), 392, 393
(1963/Expulsion of South Africa), 388, 393
(1964/Withdrawal of South Africa), 393, 401
(1971), 473
(1972), 447
(1977), 454
Migrant Labour Conference (1978), 490
(1979), 460
International Trade Union Conference Against Apartheid (1973), 473–6, 479
Second Conference (1977), 489
International Transport Federation, 485
Irish Anti-Apartheid Movement, 478

MPLA (Angola), 376
Matsukawa Railway Workers, Japan, 373
Movement for Colonial Freedom (UK), 435

Organization of African Unity (OAU), 474, 477

PAIGC (Guinea-Bissau), 376
Palestine Liberation Organization (PLO), 489
Pan-African Federation of Trade Unions, 397

Red International of Labour Unions, 49

Trade Union Movement, Africa:
  Basutoland Congress of Trade Unions, 322
  Joint Consultative Committee (SACTU, NUNW, ZACU), 490–1
  Joint Solidarity Conference (1980), 484
  General Union of Workers of Mali, 399
  Ghana Trade Union Congress, 395, 399
  National Union of Namibian Workers (NUNW), 484, 490–1
  National Union of Tanzanian Workers, 473
  Nigerian Trade Union Congress, 399, 402
  Organization of African Trade Union Unity (OATUU), 458, 477
  Printing Workers Union, Mauritius, 391
  Rhodesian Trade Union Congress, 395
  Union Generale des Travailleurs Algerians (UGTA), 375
  Union Nationale de Travailleurs Angolais (UNTA), 400
  Zambian Congress of Trade Unions, 473
  Zimbabwe African Congress of Trade Unions (ZACU), 484, 490–1
Trade Union Movement, Arab:
  Egyptian Confederation of Labour, 395
  International Confederation of Arab Trade Unions, 474, 477
  Iraqi Trade Unions, 476–7
Trade Union Movement, Australia, 373–4, 382, 417, 435, 485–7, 489
  Australian Meat Employees Society, 331
  Australian Railways Union, 419
  Firemen and Deckhands Union of New South Wales, 471, 476
  Seamens Union, 485, 486
  Waterside Workers Federation, 435, 485, 486
Trade Union Movement, Britain, 379, 398, 417, 435, 471, 480–3, 489
  Amalgamated Union of Engineering Workers (Technical, Administrative and Supervisory Section) (AUEW–TASS), 479
  Association of Scientific, Technical and Managerial Staffs (ASTMS), 489
  British Trade Union-SACTU Liaison Group, 480–1
  Dagenham Ford workers, 472
  General and Municipal Workers Union, 489
  Leyland workers, 481–3, 493
  National Union of Agricultural Workers, 201
  National Union of Mineworkers, 194, 479
  National Union of Students, 489
  Post Office Engineering Union, 489
  Trades Union Congress, 33, 43, 382, 394, 410, 417, 435, 479–80, 492
  Transport and General Workers Union, 489
  Union of Post Office Workers, 489
Trade Union Movement, Canada, 417, 435, 487
  Canadian Union of Public Employees, 487
  Centrale de l'Enseignement du Quebec (CEQ), 487
  Confederation des Syndicats Nationaux (CSN), 487
  International Union of Mine, Mill and Smelter Workers of Canada, 435
  Oil, Chemical and Atomic Workers, 435
  Ontario Federation of Labour, 487
  United Auto Workers, Canada, 487
  United Electrical and Machine Tool Workers of America (Canadian Branches), 435, 487
  United Fishermen and Allied Workers Union, 435
  Vancouver Civic Employees Union, 435
Trade Union Movement, Europe:
  Belgium, 489
  Federal Republic of Germany, 489

Trade Union Movement, Europe—*cont.*
  France, 483–4, 489
    Confederation Generale des
      Travailleurs, 399, 483–4
    Confederation Française
      Democratique du Travail, 483
  Holland FNV, 484
  Italy, 489
  Scandinavia, 435, 489
    Nordic Federation, 484
    Swedish Labour Organization, 484
Trade Union Movement, Ireland, 435
  Irish Congress of Trade Unions, 478
Trade Union Movement, New Zealand, 485–7, 489
  New Zealand Federation of Labour, 485
  Seamens Union, 485
  Wellington Trades Council, 485
  Wellington Waterside Workers, 485
Trade Union Movement, Scotland, 435
  Edinburgh and District Trades Council, 477–8
  Scottish Trade Union Congress, 477–8
Trade Union Movement, Socialist, 476
  Central Council of Soviet Trade Unions, 399

Cuba, 374
Trade Union Movement, United States of America, 398, 487–8
  Coalition of Black Trade Unionists, 488
  International Longshoremens Union, 488
  United Electrical and Machine Tool Workers of America, 487–8

United Nations Ad Hoc Working Group of Experts, 473
United Nations International Year Against Apartheid (1978), 487

World Confederation of Labour (WCL), 473, 474, 476, 488–9
World Federation of Trade Unions (WFTU), 33, 80, 180, 315, 320, 328, 345, 371, 378–81, 388, 389, 394, 396, 399, 400, 408, 410, 416, 437–8, 471, 473, 474, 476, 488
  International Solidarity Campaign (7 February 1962), 29, 186, 362, 398–400

GENERAL INDEX

Adams College (Natal), 357
Advance, 89, 424
Advance Laundries, 216
Africa South in Exile, 296, 369
African Mine Workers strikes, early 1970s, 449, 453
Alexandra Bus Boycott (1957), 28, 128, 151–9, 236, 347–8, 399
    Alexandra Peoples Transport Committee (PTC), 152, 155
    1945 Boycott, 167, 341
Amato Textile Co., 217, 286, 366
    Amato Strike (1958), 217, 286–8, 292, 366
Anglo-American Corporation, 137, 454
Anti-Pass Laws Campaigns, 28, 50, 53, 163, 297, 299, 301–3, 306–8, 322, 323, 344, 411

Bantu Education, 97, 340–1
Bantustans, 103, 446
Bay Transport Company (PE) and Strike (1961), 178, 291–4, 417
Boston Bag Company and Strike (Cape Town), 183, 241, 242
Boycotts and Protests, 333, 339, 369
    Bantu Education, 322, 340–1, 347
    Beer-halls, 154, 163, 297, 303–4, 341, 411
    Dipping tanks, 297, 303–5, 341
    Fatti's and Moni's, 469
    International, 345–7, 381, 416, 418, 474–5, 494–5
    Nationalist Products (1959), 341–3
    New Brighton Bus Boycott (1949), 340
    Port Elizabeth Bus Boycott (1961), 29, 293
    Potato (1959), 28, 197, 204, 341, 343–5
    United Tobacco Company (1954), 274, 340
British Leyland subsidiary, 450

Cape Times, 149

Cato Manor township (Durban), 271, 303–6, 363
Chambers of Commerce and Industry, 154–5
Chamber of Mines, 58, 65–70, 89, 157, 162, 189–90, 194
Clarion, 424
Clydesdale Mine Disaster (1960), 137–40, 144, 192, 309
Commercial Opinion, 157
Consolidated Gold Fields, 137
Consolidated Textile Mills (CTM) Ltd. (Jacobs, Natal), 246
Crossroads resistance campaign (Western Cape), 330, 467–8

De Beers, 137, 193
Defiance Campaign Against Unjust Laws, 28, 79, 301, 320, 322, 335, 357
Die Bouwerker, 76
Dorman Long (Africa) Ltd., 185
Dunswart, 185
Durban Corporation (Municipality), 249–52, 286
Durban Strikes (1973–4), 267, 448–53

Falkirk Iron and Steel Strike (Natal) (1937), 55, 57
Fatti's and Moni's Strike (1979), 468–9
Fighting Talk, 167, 369–70
Fine Wool Products (Uitenhage) Strike, 229–30
Ford Motor Company (S.A.), 186
Forward, 369, 433

General Box Co. (Retreat, Cape) Strike, 242–3
General Motors (S.A.), 186, 470
George Weston conglomerate (Canadian), 213
Good Hope Textile Mills (Kingwilliamstown), 229–30
Guardian, The, 9, 53, 89, 113, 369, 424

INDEXES

H. Jones & Co., 218, 220, 320, 352
Hammarsdale clothing factory and Strike, 289–91
Hebox Textile Co., 246
Heinemann Electric Strike (1976), 457, 470
Hex River Textile Mills (Worcester) Strike, 236, 284–5
Housing and Rent, Conditions, 266–72
Howick Rubber Company, 255
Huletts Corporation, 204

Industrial Development Corporation, 134
International Defence and Aid Fund for Southern Africa (IDAF), 27, 150, 470
Iron and Steel Trades Association, 82

Job Reservation and the Trade Unions, 125–6, 150
Johannesburg Chamber of Commerce, 162–3, 307
Johannesburg City Council, 62, 224, 266, 268, 270–2, 443
Johannesburg Star, 415

Kimberley City Council, 207
King George Tuberculosis Hospital (Durban) Strike (1961), 312–15
Klipfontein Organic Products, 213
Kwa Mashu township (Durban), 250, 252, 267–8, 271

Langa township, 174, 240
  Massacre (1960), 126, 243, 363, 398, 410–11, 413, 414, 438
Langeberg Ko-Operasie Besperk (LKB), 32, 218, 288–9, 321, 323, 366
Liberation, 79, 369
Lion Match Company (Durban), 294–5, 472
Lystra zip factory (Cape Town) Strike (1956), 182–3

M (Mandela)-Plan, 230, 355, 356, 358, 360
Maitland district (Cape Town), 241

May Day demonstrations, celebrations, 376–7
  1950 Protests, 333–4
Meadowland Housing Scheme (Jhb), 224
Merebank township (Durban), 267–8
Mooderfontein East Mine Protest, 69
Morning Star/Ikwezi Lomso, 150, 331, 377, 401

Nambian mass strikes (1971–2), 447–8
Natal Cotton Spinners, 274–5
Natal Cotton and Woollen Mills (Durban) Strike (1976), 457
National Food Storage, 218
National Stay-At-Homes:
  (1950), 334
  (1957), 28, 347–9, 351
  (1958), 28, 207, 279, 324, 342, 349, 351–6, 358, 384, 414
  (1960), 167, 362, 363
  (1961), 29, 167, 175, 226, 243, 255, 256, 322, 362, 364–7, 370, 416, 419
Nationalist-Labour Pact (Hertzog) Government, 43, 88, 116
Native Republic Thesis (CPSA), 50, 89
New Age, 9, 149, 150, 160, 167, 168, 178, 199, 202, 209, 212, 223, 227, 252, 258, 272, 274, 283, 296, 331, 343, 350, 369, 387, 426

Odendaalsrus Mine Disaster (1962), 193

Paarden Eiland (Cape Town), 183, 241
Philip Frame textile conglomerate, 246, 408
Pilkington Armourplate Safety Glass Co. Strike (1976), 457
Port Elizabeth City Council, 165
Poverty Datum Line, 32, 159, 164, 448

Rand Mines, 137
Rand Steam Laundries, 216
Rembrandt Tobacco Company (Rothmans), 165, 342, 369

Saamtrek, 89
Sharpeville Massacre, 28, 126, 164, 243, 363, 398, 410–11, 414, 449

Smuts United Party Government, 66, 67, 68, 72, 88, 104–5, 107, 263
Solidarity, 435
South African Federated Chamber of Industries (SAFCI), 32, 162–4, 307
South Africa Freedom Day (June 26), 347
South African Republic Day (1961), Protest against, 364
South African Titanium Products (Natal) Strike (1962), 253
South African Womens Day (9 August 1956), 302
Soweto Uprisings (1976), 267, 455–9, 486
  Workers Stay-At-Home (1976), 457, 458
Spark, 168, 169, 426
Spekenham Food Products Strike (1957), 283–4
State of Emergency (1960), 79, 164, 207, 211, 216, 226, 233, 327, 386, 390, 392, 398, 401, 404, 410–14, 416, 444, 471
Steel and Engineering Industries Federation of South Africa (SEIFSA), 185
Stewart and Lloyds, 183

Textile Unity, 401
Thomas Barlow and Sons, Ltd., 184

Togt labour system, 279–81
Treason Trial (1956–61), 20, 183, 216, 233, 240, 246, 322, 324, 358, 377, 378, 382, 384, 405–10, 412, 414, 415, 437, 438
Truth, 120, 401

Ukubamba Amadolo: Workers Struggles in the South African Textile Industry, 79
Umteteli wa Bantu, 157
Unemployment, conditions, 262–6, 275, 312, 448
Union Steel Corporation, 184
United Tobacco Co. (UTC) Strike (1954), 212–13, 274, 340
University of Cape Town, 469
University of Natal (Durban), 252
University of Western Cape, 469
University of Witwatersrand, 212, 213, 214

Van Zyl Bus Co. (Transvaal), 179
Victoria Falls Power Company, 67
Village Main Reef Disaster (1960), 137

Western Deep Levels Mine (Carltonville) Strike (1973), 454, 478
Workers and Trade Unions Against Apartheid, 257
Workers Herald (ICU), 46